INSIDERS' GUIDE® TO
COLORADO'S MOUNTAINS

THIRD EDITION

LINDA CASTRONE AND JIM CASTRONE

INSIDERS' GUIDE®

GUILFORD, CONNECTICUT
AN IMPRINT OF THE GLOBE PEQUOT PRESS

The prices and rates in this guidebook were confirmed at press time. We recommend, however, that you call establishments before traveling to obtain current information.

INSIDERS' GUIDE®

Text design by LeAnna Weller Smith
Maps by XNR Productions Inc. © Morris Book Publishing, LLC

ISBN-13: 978-0-7627-4181-6
ISBN-10: 0-7627-4181-3

Manufactured in the United States of America
Third Edition/First Printing

CONTENTS

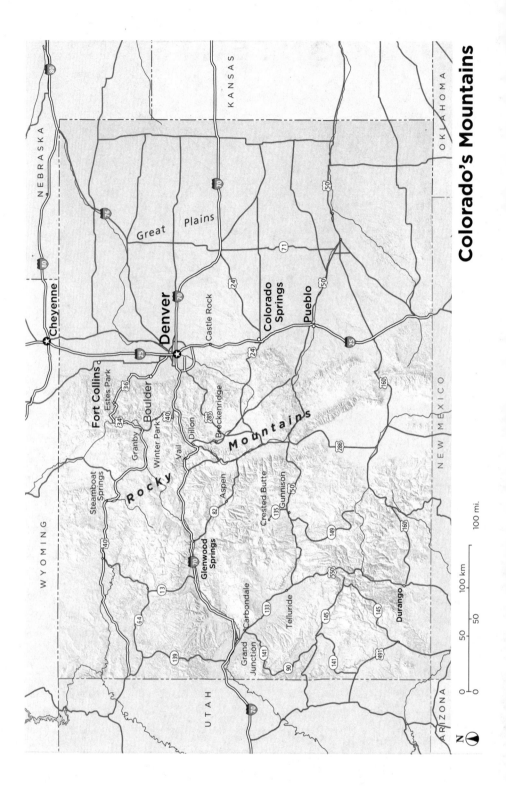

Colorado's Mountains

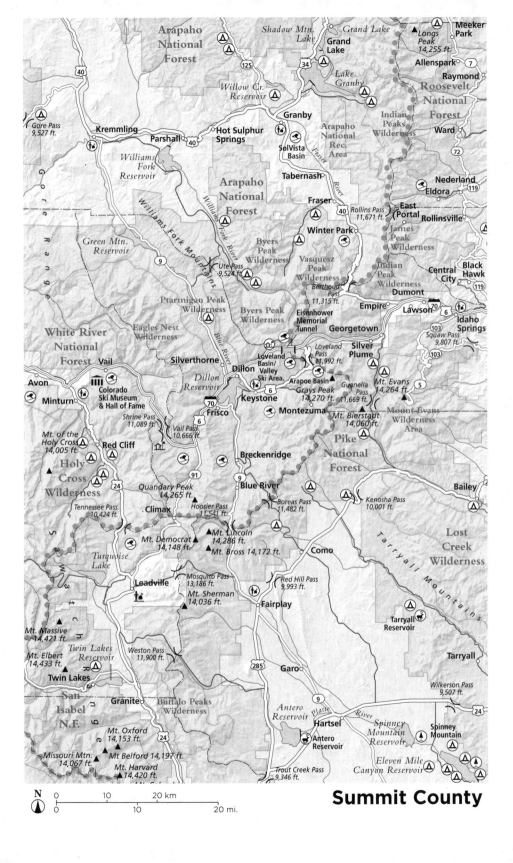

Summit County

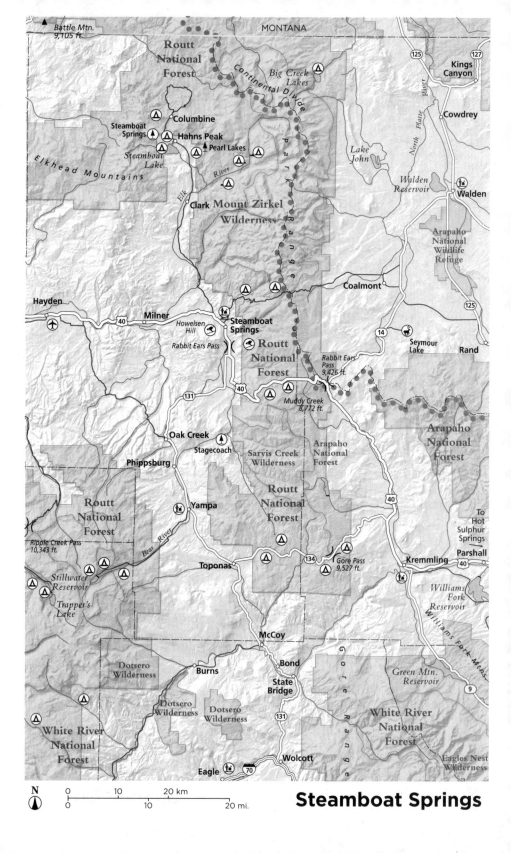

Steamboat Springs

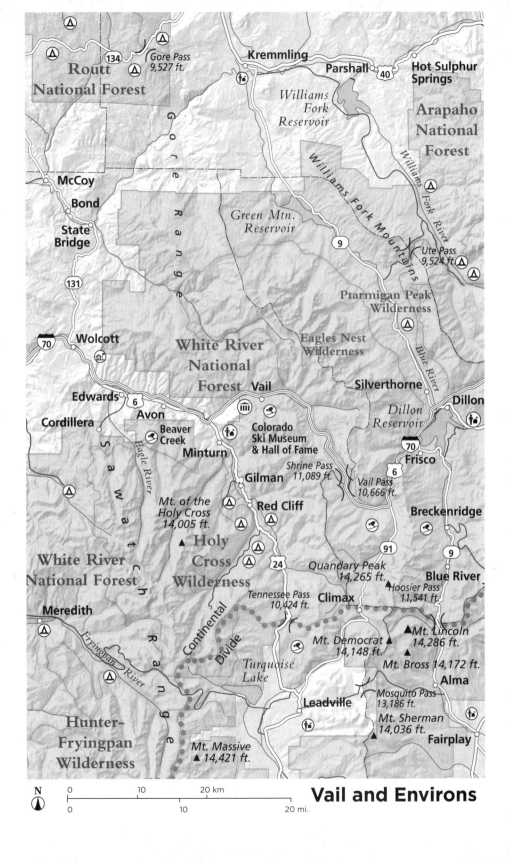

Vail and Environs

Routt National Forest

Gore Pass 9,527 ft.

134

Kremmling

Parshall

40

Hot Sulphur Springs

Williams Fork Reservoir

Arapaho National Forest

Williams Fork Mountains

McCoy

Bond

State Bridge

131

Green Mtn. Reservoir

9

Williams Fork River

Ute Pass 9,524 ft.

Ptarmigan Peak Wilderness

70

Wolcott

White River National Forest

Eagles Nest Wilderness

Vail

Silverthorne

Blue River

Dillon

Edwards

6

Avon

Cordillera

Beaver Creek

Minturn

Colorado Ski Museum & Hall of Fame

Dillon Reservoir

70

Frisco

Eagle River

Gilman

Shrine Pass 11,089 ft.

Vail Pass 10,666 ft.

6

Mt. of the Holy Cross 14,005 ft.

Red Cliff

Breckenridge

White River National Forest

Holy Cross Wilderness

24

91

9

Quandary Peak 14,265 ft.

Blue River

Hoosier Pass 11,541 ft.

Meredith

Tennessee Pass 10,424 ft.

Climax

Continental Divide

Fryingpan River

Mt. Democrat 14,148 ft.

Mt. Lincoln 14,286 ft.

Mt. Bross 14,172 ft.

Alma

Turquoise Lake

Leadville

Mosquito Pass 13,186 ft.

Mt. Sherman 14,036 ft.

Fairplay

Hunter-Fryingpan Wilderness

Mt. Massive ▲ 14,421 ft.

Sawatch Range

N

0   10   20 km

0   10   20 mi.

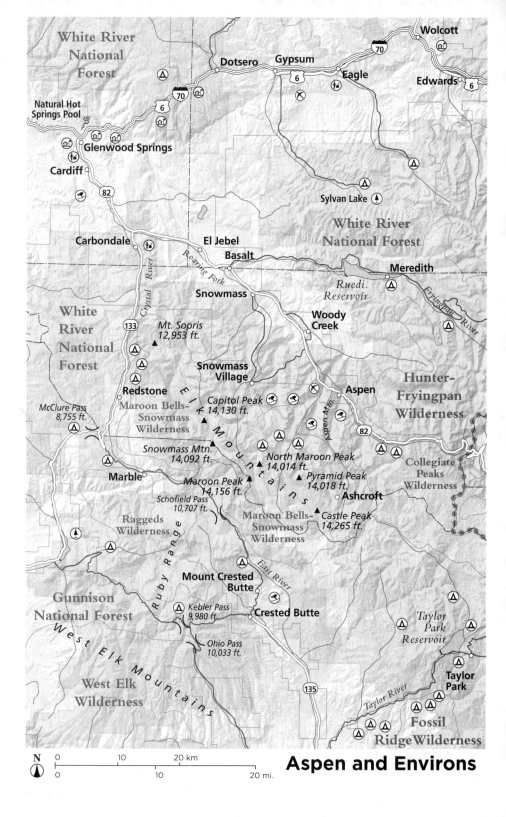

Aspen and Environs

PREFACE

Most ancient indigenous cultures of the world view their highest peaks as the home of the gods, very spiritual sacred places: Mount Fuji in Japan, Mount Agung in Bali, the Andes in South America, Mount Sinai in Israel, Mauna Loa in Hawaii, Mount Everest in Tibet. Mountains tend to give perspective to the rest of our lives and put us in our proper place with respect to nature and the Earth. We are forced to acknowledge a power and eternal rhythm of life that's greater than ourselves.

For this reason—and with its sheer beauty and magnificence—Colorado attracts people like a magnet. The "Rocky Mountain High" is a real thing, as many of us discovered years ago when we packed up our lives on the East or West coasts or the Midwest and moved here—overwhelmed and drawn by the splendor and majesty of the Rockies. The mountains make people forget their troubles and the rest of their lives and surrender to the beauty. Even Colorado natives find they are always drawn back to their mountain homeland.

Not counting Alaska, Colorado claims 79 percent of our nation's peaks higher than 14,000 feet. Of the "14ers" in the contiguous United States, 54 are in Colorado. California claims 13, while Washington boasts Mount Rainier. More than 1,500 Colorado peaks rise above 12,000 feet, and 637 separate summits reach more than 13,000 feet. Colorado's mean elevation is 6,800 feet, making it truly "the crest of the continent." Five major rivers are born in the Colorado Rockies, among them the Rio Grande and the Colorado.

So many people who spend time in Colorado for recreation, college, work, or vacation eventually decide to move here. It's the siren call. When you find something you love, you must go to it. Those of us who live here visit the mountains on a regular basis for renewal—kind of like going to church but more fun and with better scenery. In our busy work lives, we need only to gaze toward the mountains to connect with that feeling.

Thirty-some years ago when the late John Denver sang about the Colorado Rocky Mountain High, it changed many lives—and continues to do so. A Boulder-based Japanese businessman once confided that he was drawn to Colorado because he liked John Denver, who apparently had a large following in Japan.

Colorado has seen many changes in the 150 or so years since gold was discovered in "them thar hills"—some good, some extremely destructive. In *Colorado*, David Lavender writes, "It's a vast land and it has been a hard-used one. The Anasazi overstrained their part of it. So did the miners who recklessly slashed down the forest around their workings and who spewed such great quantities of waste into the streams that they became rivers of gray sludge. Stockmen overgrazed the mesas. Dam builders drowned the canyons and are still drowning them." Happily, though, many have come to realize that one of Colorado's greatest natural resources is its beauty. Though it's no longer the frontier state it once was, it's still a state that holds much of the heart and soul of America—the pristine wilderness, our primordial home as human beings.

As we enjoy the many recreational opportunities provided by Colorado's mountains, we must also remember their vulnerability. There used to be a saying, "Can man survive in the wilderness?" Now the question is, "Can the wilderness survive man?" As huge ski corporations project seemingly endless growth plans, what will happen to the mountains? As the forests are cut for more condos and ski

The Breckenridge Whitewater Park, located north of town along Colorado Highway 9, provides kayakers a picturesque place to paddle. THE DENVER POST/CYRUS MCCRIMMON

runs, where will the elk graze? How will they follow their ancient migration routes? We do not want to destroy the very thing that has drawn us here—the magic and beauty of the wilderness.

So come to Colorado, feel the exhilaration of its beauty, ski and play in its mountains, inhale the fragrance of its wildflowers, soothe your spirits in its clear rushing waters—and join us in treasuring and protecting it.

ACKNOWLEDGMENTS

As one of those rare creatures, a Colorado native, I thought I knew a lot about my state until I began to research this book. Over the course of six months I spent more time skiing, golfing, snowshoeing, fishing, riding horseback, dining, swimming, and generally exploring the mountains than in the past 20 years combined. What I've learned is that hundreds—maybe even thousands—of people have been busy developing the mountains I've been so content to admire from down below.

Granted, the crowds are thicker than when I first started skiing at Winter Park in the 1960s, when I first vacationed in Glenwood Springs in the 1970s, or when I got my first close looks at Beaver Creek and Telluride in the 1980s. Along with the crowds have come pollution, traffic congestion, long lift lines at ski resorts, and NO VACANCY signs at popular hotels. What I also discovered, however, is that people flock to Colorado's mountains because there's a lot to be done in them. Uncomfortable T-bar lifts have been replaced with heated gondola cars. Once-muddy lots now hold gourmet restaurants and lively nightclubs. Off-limits forests have been leased and developed into challenging cross-country skiing courses, sophisticated mountain biking trail systems, and world-class resorts.

Once thing has remained constant throughout the growth spurt. Mountain people are still as friendly as those I remember from my early days in Durango (where I was born), Cortez, and Dove Creek. Most are still happy to answer questions, give directions, and even tell a few semi-true stories over a cup of morning coffee.

As with any project of this magnitude, public relations managers and experts in each field of interest are indispensable. Darcy Morse, Kate Osborn, Beth Buehler,

John Buckley, Lisa Weiss, Loryn Kasten, Linda Lichtendahl, Stephanie Keister, Heidi Thomsen, Scott McQuade, Matt Sugar, Katie Coakley, and Heather Latvala provided all the help I requested and more. A special thanks goes to Larry Price and Steve Nehf for providing me with photos from *The Denver Post*'s archives. But most of all I am indebted to my husband, Jim, without whom none of this would have been possible.

—Linda Castrone

The first people I want to acknowledge are all the friends and family who didn't have me put away when I told them I was going to coauthor a book with my wife, Linda. Everyone knows the horror stories about working with one's spouse, and this venture seemed fraught with even more danger since we are both strong-willed and editor-averse writers. Nevertheless, this has turned out as one of the great learning experiences of my writerly life, and there are several other people to acknowledge for the pleasure of this journey.

First, of course, would be my wife, Linda, whose consummate professionalism not only allowed us to successfully navigate the land mines, but taught me the meaning of living with a deadline. While some might finish a project like this and say "never again," I say "when's the next one?" I confess to having a favorable bias toward my coauthor, wrought from 30-plus years of marriage. But the truth is that she is a fine journalist, editor, and writer, and working at her side has been a pleasure, an honor, and an education.

I would also like to acknowledge Liz Taylor at Insiders' Guides and thank her for her generous and thoughtful patience with us through a difficult period during the revision of this book.

—Jim Castrone

HOW TO USE THIS BOOK ?

Two-thirds of Colorado is covered by mountains, so information about all the state's high-altitude areas was more than we could publish in one book. We focused on the central mountain region for three reasons. First, it's the most accessible. Interstate 70 slices the central mountains roughly in half and carries travelers on four to six well-maintained lanes past the state's busiest ski resorts. Second, it's the most popular area with instate and out-of-state visitors. Ski resorts in Summit County alone account for more than two-thirds of the state's annual ski visits. Third, the area is fairly self-contained. Visitors to Vail, for example, aren't all that far away from Dillon, Breckenridge, or even Glenwood Springs.

In this book we've provided readers with (almost) everything they've ever wanted to know about skiing in Aspen and Vail, as well as their lesser-known siblings Keystone, Breckenridge, Copper Mountain, Arapahoe Basin, Winter Park, Sunlight Mountain Resort, Steamboat Springs, SolVista Basin, Loveland, and Ski Cooper. For those who don't ski, we've included information about other winter sports, as well as complete listings of sightseeing attractions, shopping, arts, and other summer activities. Because Colorado's mountains are so popular with active, sports-oriented people, we've also added sections about golfing, fishing, camping, backpacking, and health spas. For those of you who want to know what else the state has to offer, the final chapter provides a shorter—but still meaty—look at Rocky Mountain National Park in the northern mountains, Crested Butte in one remote corner of the central mountains, and Durango, Telluride, and Mesa Verde National Park in the southern mountains.

Authors Linda and Jim have spent more than 40 years exploring the state they call home. Both are active outdoors enthusiasts who have skied, hiked, biked, or golfed their way through all the areas they write about. In this book they've shared details you can't get by phone, tips designed to make your visit more enjoyable.

The central mountains are a little like a 12-course banquet table. The region is so large you probably won't want to read the book in one sitting. It's meant to be consumed in little bites and is arranged to make that simple. If you've decided to set up your vacation base in Vail, for example, you can turn right to the Vail chapter, which is divided into sections that deal with everything from where to stay and where to eat once you've arrived to how to occupy yourself once you've settled in.

Because portions of eight different counties fall within the central mountain region, we've chosen to organize our chapters to flow from east to west, following visitors from their arrival in Denver through all the towns they will pass as they work their way west into the mountains. They begin with Winter Park and SolVista to the north; work across Loveland Pass from Loveland Ski Area to Arapahoe Basin and Keystone; jut north to Steamboat Springs; then contine west through Frisco, Breckenridge, Leadville, and Copper Mountain. Vail follows, as do Beaver Creek, Avon, and Edwards. Just beyond is Glenwood Springs, where our path hooks south through Carbondale, El Jebel, Basalt, and Snowmass to Aspen.

Unless otherwise mentioned, all phone numbers listed are in the 970 area code, but calls between counties are long distance. Leadville uses the 719 area code, and Loveland Ski Area (not to be confused with Loveland the city, near Fort Collins) uses the 303 code.

We suggest that all readers spend time with the first six chapters, however, before jumping throughout the rest of the menu. The Area Overview chapter explains the region and introduces the many towns we'll be covering. It may help you decide between a trip to family-friendly Loveland, let's say, or to glitzy Aspen. The Getting Here, Getting Around chapter explains the ways to fly, drive, or ride the train into Denver and travel to the high country. The History chapter outlines our colorful past. The Mountain Safety and Environment chapter points out the hazards inherent in any trip to this high-altitude playground. Reading it carefully can mean the difference between a vacation that's memorable and one that's a painful memory.

That said, mix and match to your heart's content. And throughout the chapters, don't forget to check out the tidbits of insiders' knowledge (look for the **i**). And if you find places you think should have been included but weren't, we'd like to know about them. Please send your additions and comments to: The Globe Pequot Reader Response, Editorial Department, P.O. Box 480, Guilford, CT 06437. You can also send us e-mail at editorial@GlobePequot.com.

AREA OVERVIEW

Colorado's first white settlers came to mine the treasure hidden deep beneath our imposing mountains. Today the state mines those same mountains for their recreational resources. Colorado has more high-altitude terrain than any other state, averaging about 6,800 feet of altitude, or more than a mile high. Generally speaking, the mountains dominate two-thirds of Colorado, and the highest peaks are concentrated in the middle of the state. More than 50 peaks are taller than 14,000 feet, and many get an annual snowfall of as much as 350 inches, creating the perfect setup for a winter playground.

Like the rest of the state, Colorado's mountain communities have swollen with population growth over recent years. Surviving and managing the rampant expansion are the major issues from Winter Park to Aspen. Old-timers in each mountain town shake their heads at bumper-to-bumper traffic, air pollution, and burgeoning property values—things many think diminish the quality of life. Eagle County, home of Vail, Beaver Creek, and a slew of former ranching communities, may have been hit the hardest. It has grown 625 percent since 1970 and now has a cost of living 25 percent above the national average.

Interstate 70 splits the state horizontally and is the access point for Colorado's major ski areas, carrying more than 10.7 million vehicles annually. At times, it's an eight-lane superhighway. At others it becomes a four-lane snake winding its way through deep canyons and lofty mountain passes. It is heavily traveled, especially between Vail and Denver. If you're driving in, prepare for a long and sometimes harrowing trip. You'll be rewarded with spectacular alpine scenery and vistas that seem to stretch to Kansas.

In this chapter we'll survey the territory and give you a feel for each of our special mountain communities. We'll also give you an overview of what's in store in each chapter. We've saved the details and recommendations for the chapters that follow.

A GEOGRAPHICAL OVERVIEW

Just outside Denver on the way west, I-70 begins to climb Mount Vernon Canyon. Going eastbound into Denver, the hill is a truckers' nightmare, falling so quickly and with so many curves that too frequently a truck driver loses control and causes a multi-car pile-up. It may be the only stretch of interstate with signs that say TRUCKERS BEWARE: YOU ARE NOT DOWN YET and MILES OF STEEP, WINDING ROAD ARE AHEAD.

Heading west, however, the canyon is a nice climb that whets the appetite for the Rockies ahead. The tiny towns that line the road were founded in the 1800s as mining towns and survived after the bust primarily because of their proximity to Denver. The landscape between Idaho Springs and Silver Plume is still littered with mining debris and mountainside scàrs. Along both sides of the road, look for dilapidated mining machinery, abandoned sheds, and yellowish pyramids that look like piles of salt poured from a shaker. They're called tailings and are what was left over when gold and silver were extracted from the mines.

WINTER PARK AND GRANBY

The first ski exit for Winter Park and SolVista Basin via U.S. Highway 40 (exit 232) is about an hour west of Denver.

Say "Colorado" and the first thing that comes to mind is skiing. Yet skiing is just one way to enjoy the state's snowy mountains. Here, sledders take advantage of high-altitude fun atop Loveland Pass. THE DENVER POST/GLENN ASAKAWA

Berthoud Pass stands between you and the ski areas of Route 40, however, and at 11,315 feet it can be a bear in winter. The pass is a narrow, steep shelf of a road that, at times, seems to have nothing to keep you and your car from sliding into the valley below. The road is well maintained, but can be unnerving to those not used to mountain driving. At the top of the pass is the defunct Berthoud Pass Ski Area.

Your reward for braving the pass is the Fraser Valley, a broad, fertile farming and ranching valley (population about 1,700) that in the 1940s was the site of Denver's first mountain park, Winter Park.

The ski area by that name, still owned by the city, is now one of the most popular among local day skiers. Just 90 minutes from Denver, it gets an average of 350 inches of snow each year and provides varied skiing for all ability levels. The towns of Winter Park and Fraser are popular with tourists year-round, although Fraser has the dubious distinction of holding the nation's coldest temperature records, for which it has earned the nickname "the nation's icebox."

About 20 miles beyond is SolVista Basin, a smaller ski resort designed to provide families with cheap, easy skiing terrain. If you continue driving north, you'll reach Granby and then Grand Lake, known as the gateway to Rocky Mountain National Park and also as home to the headwaters of the Colorado River.

LOVELAND SKI AREA

Back on I-70 and just beyond the Winter Park exit sits Downieville, a wide spot in the road that is known among locals as the last chance to fuel up, rent skis or snowboards, or grab a quick bite to eat before entering the Eisenhower Tunnel. The tunnel, the symbolic entrance to Colorado's ski country, was built in the early 1970s to streamline traffic on the nation's busiest east-west interstate highway and was named for U.S. President Dwight D. Eisenhower. (His wife, Mamie Doud, was raised in Denver, and they vacationed annually in the state.) In the past two decades, however, traffic has gotten so heavy that the tunnel's four lanes are no longer adequate. Once you've been stalled in one of the tunnel's famous traffic jams—with stop-and-go driving for several hours at a time—you'll do everything possible to avoid it during peak hours (Friday evenings if you're westbound, Sunday afternoons going east).

Maybe that's why Loveland Ski Area is so popular with locals. Skiers can drive there from Denver and exit I-70 just before the tunnel. Loveland was built on the east side of the Continental Divide decades before its peaks were blasted to make room for the tunnel below. The ski runs now straddle the tunnel and collect enough snow to provide good skiing well into spring.

Destination skiers usually drive on into Summit County, home of four of the state's most popular ski areas: Keystone, Arapahoe Basin, Copper Mountain, and Breckenridge. Each year those ski areas attract more than three million skiers. That's more than visit the entire state of Utah.

KEYSTONE/DILLON/ SILVERTHORNE

Quaint mountain towns provide the hotel rooms, restaurants, nightclubs, and gas stations that keep tourists occupied before and after they ski. The first stops west of the tunnel are Silverthorne and Dillon, twin towns on either side of the interstate (exit 205) with a combined permanent population of 4,600. These towns sit in a wide valley that served as a stage stop and ranch land at the turn of the century. In the 1960s residents voted to dam the Blue River, burying the old city of Dillon beneath the Dillon Reservoir. The lake is vast enough to support boating, camping, and fishing in the summer, but the water is cold, fed by snowmelt from the peaks and glaciers above.

Keystone, located to the southeast of Dillon, is a built-for-skiing resort. A dozen miles beyond is Arapahoe Basin, nicknamed "The Legend" because its slopes are so snowy and rugged that the ski season often stretches to the Fourth of July.

STEAMBOAT SPRINGS

Steamboat Springs, population 9,800, is a ranching community that coexists with an expanding ski resort owned by the giant ski conglomerate American Skiing Company. Still, visitors find themselves in a bustling resort community surrounded by the picturesque landscape of the broad and beautiful Yampa River Valley. Horses, cattle, buffalo, and cowboys still dominate that landscape, although ranch land is slowly being usurped by housing developments and business growth. Clark, an as-yet untouched piece of the nostalgic West, sits just 20 miles north, at the end of a very scenic ride along the sparkling Elk River. Don't be surprised to sidle up to the counter of the Clark Store, a general store and ice cream parlor, and find yourself shoulder-to-shoulder with a rugged, chaps-wearing cowboy. Clark is known for its guest ranches and the many trails that lead into the Mount Zirkel Wilderness Area.

French trappers arrived in the Steamboat Springs area in 1865 and heard what sounded like a steamboat rounding the bend of the river. They were actually hearing a pulsing geyser that shot hot mineral

water out of the ground, but the name Steamboat Springs stuck. Long before their arrival, however, Native Americans used the Yampa Valley for hunting and fishing, and the mineral springs for medicinal and social purposes. Cattle drovers who passed through the area on long cattle drives from Texas during the late 1800s were the first settlers and gave the town its homespun complexion. A legendary Norse skier named Carl Howelsen added his imprint in the early 1900s, building a ski jump on a hill overlooking town and introducing locals to his sport of choice.

Today people are drawn by the beauty of the nearby areas. Routt National Forest covers 1.2 million acres, and the Mount Zirkel Wilderness spans 50 miles along the Continental Divide. Three state parks also are near: Steamboat and Pearl Lake state parks are close to the historic gold-mining towns of Hahns Peak and Columbine, and Stagecoach Reservoir State Park is 20 minutes south of Steamboat Springs. Visitors flock to the area for the great fishing, boating, camping, picnicking, wildlife and bird watching, or just plain relaxation.

During the winter, the Steamboat ski resort dominates the area's economy, but summer brings many tourists looking for an authentic western experience and a friendly atmosphere not quite as prevalent at many of Colorado's other ski resort towns. As the most western (in style, not geography) of Colorado's mountain resorts, Steamboat is popular because of its unique take on the skiing and summer recreation experiences.

BRECKENRIDGE/FRISCO

Frisco, population 2,400, sits on the west bank of the Dillon Reservoir, bisected by the Tenmile and Miner's Creeks. It serves as a bedroom community for ski employees and a gateway to Breckenridge. In 1859 gold was found in Breckenridge, and the town has been occupied ever since; today there are 2,600 year-round residents. It may be the state's cutest ski

town, with 254 of its downtown buildings preserved as part of Colorado's largest National Historic District. You'll find burro barns now serving as gift shops and gingerbread-trimmed Victorian houses now used by ski-rental companies. Because it's about 10 miles off the interstate, Breckenridge also has a cozier feel than some ski towns.

COPPER MOUNTAIN

Seven miles west on I-70 (exit 195), Copper Mountain sits at a "Y" in the road. Looking south into one canyon, visitors get an alpine view that's right out of *Heidi*. The surrounding mountains are so tall and craggy that their volcanic rocks look burnt, like they were tortured for eons before being thrust upward to form the Rockies. They're hard, cold granite with trees that can take root only halfway up the slope before reaching inhospitable terrain. Those same hard peaks provide great skiing at Copper Mountain, a self-contained resort nestled in the valley below.

LEADVILLE

If you follow Highway 91 south, you'll continue climbing to Leadville, Colorado's highest mountain town at 10,152 feet. The mining legacy of this town (home to 3,000 hardy year-round residents) has been preserved, with much of the downtown area still resembling the silver boomtown it was in the 1880s. Ski Cooper, the ski area developed for U.S. Army troops to train on during World War II and donated to the town once the war was over, is just outside town. It's a favorite among locals but is small and remote enough that tourists rarely visit it.

VAIL

Back on I-70, the next stop is Vail, the internationally known playground for mul-

Copper Mountain's base village is being rebuilt to include village-style restaurants, clubs, retail, and hotel/condo units. *THE DENVER POST*/JERRY CLEVELAND

timillionaires and jet setters. Vail is separated from Copper Mountain by 21 miles and 10,000-foot Vail Pass. The pass is treacherous enough to have chain-up lanes at its base, and during bad winter storms, snow chains are required on any vehicle that travels it. During the worst storms the pass is closed altogether. The town of Vail is a 10-mile straight shot that is aligned east to west, with just a few streets to the north of I–70 and a dozen more south of the freeway. A sheep pasture until it was founded in the 1960s by a veteran of the Army's mountain camp near Leadville, the town was built to resemble a Tyrolean village. Critics call its architecture "shake and bake Bavaria" because of the kitschy white-walled buildings with dark roofs and flower boxes.

More recent growth has turned Vail into a real alpine village with 4,500 full-time residents. And although the ski mountain that frames the town seems small, most of the terrain is hidden behind that first ridge. Covering 5,289 acres, Vail is North America's largest single ski mountain. Vail Resorts, Inc., the corporation that owns the mountain, also owns Breckenridge, Beaver Creek, and Keystone ski areas. It is Colorado's largest ski company, with a little more than 30 percent of all ski terrain.

The town of Vail also is known for the golf course that follows the river through the middle of town. Former president Gerald Ford, a part-time Breaver Creek resident and ardent golfer, made it famous when he was still in the White House. The town also is known for its pricey four- and five-story

Colorado Vital Statistics

Gained statehood: Aug. 1, 1876 (38th state)

Nickname: Centennial State

Motto: *Nil Sine Numine* (Nothing without Providence)

Governor: Bill Owens (R)

Population: 4,601,403

Capital: Denver

Area: 102,730 sq. miles

Highest point: Mt. Elbert, Lake County (14,443 ft.)

Lowest point: Arkansas River (3,350 ft.)

Average Denver temperature: January: 29.5
July: 73.4

Average Denver snowfall: 59.8 inches per year

Major attractions: Rocky Mountain National Park, Mesa Verde National Park, Black Canyon of the Gunnison National Park, Dinosaur National Monument, Great Sand Dunes National Monument

Major universities: University of Colorado at Boulder, Colorado State University (Fort Collins), University of Denver, United States Air Force Academy (Colorado Springs)

Famous Coloradans: Tim Allen, Scott Carpenter, Lon Chaney, Jack Dempsey, Douglas Fairbanks, Horace Tabor, Byron White, Don Cheadle

lodges, the only practical way to pack 20,000 visitors into a long, narrow valley.

The town of Vail is divided into four villages built around ski bases. Golden Peak is at the eastern edge of town; Vail Village is at the town's core; Lionshead is farther west; and Cascade Village is on the western edge of town. Vail Village is the oldest and most exclusive part of town, with a pedestrian mall and some of the town's best restaurants, nightclubs, shops, and art galleries.

Real estate gets cheaper in either direction until you reach West Vail. Interstate travelers often pull off in West Vail to grab a bite at McDonald's or visit the Safeway store before continuing on. Vail may be the jewel in this valley's crown, but it's just the start of the development.

BEAVER CREEK/AVON

Tiny Minturn is tucked into a side canyon a few miles west of Vail. This former railroad switching station is at the base of a scenic canyon that leads to Camp Hale, the former base camp for the Army's mountain troops. It has become a popular stopping-off point for mountain bikers, backcountry skiers, and visitors looking for an alternative to fast-paced Vail.

The next stops on I-70 are Eagle-Vail (exit 147), a bedroom community for Vail proper and home to its own mountain golf course, and Avon (exit 167), the gateway to exclusive Beaver Creek ski resort. Visitors to this tony resort must exit at Avon and then pass through a guard station before they work their way up the mountain to the million-dollar homes, golf course, resort hotels, and slopes of Beaver Creek. The less affluent often stay in Avon's chain hotels and eat at Denny's before buying a day ticket to ski at Beaver Creek.

EDWARDS

Next stop is Edwards (exit 163), another former ranching community that is now being consumed by the sprawl of growing Vail Valley, with a year-round population of 50,000. It's home to two excellent golf courses—Sonnenalp and Cordillera's Valley Course—and is the exit for the Cordillera Spa and Lodge, perhaps the valley's most exclusive resort. Cordillera has 56 guest rooms and is located, like a castle, on the top of a remote peak above Edwards. Trailer parks below house the people who keep the Vail Valley running, as do the trailers in Eagle and Gypsum, 16 and 33 miles farther west, respectively, along I-70.

GLENWOOD SPRINGS

By this point, the Colorado River has joined I-70 and is a constant companion as travelers wend their way first through scrubby high-altitude desert land and then through the spectacular Glenwood Canyon. The stretch of interstate that bisects this canyon took nearly 30 years to build in order to preserve the area's pristine beauty. The canyon is a deep cut made by a fast river that left behind cliffs so high and steep they resemble the Grand Canyon. The cliffs are made of hard, old rock that was forced into striated masses by volcanic pressures that left them covered with horizontal cracks. They've been weathered into odd shapes resembling fortress towers, chimneys, and water spouts. The cliffs stay with you until Glenwood Springs (population 8,500) appears almost magically around the corner. Then the rocks disappear almost as quickly as they appeared.

Visitors once flocked to Glenwood Springs' hot springs for their health. In the 1880s the town was incorporated around the natural hot springs the Ute Indians named Yampah, or "Big Medicine," because of their healing powers. In its early days, the town hosted such celebrities as U.S. President Teddy Roosevelt, who used the town as a base for his notorious hunting trips, and gunslinger Doc Holliday, who came to battle the tuberculosis that killed him anyway within a year.

Today the two-block-long hot springs

In the 1960s the Blue River was dammed to create Dillon Reservoir. The lake is vast enough to support boating, camping, and fishing in the summer, but because it is fed by snowmelt from the peaks and glaciers above, the water is always chilly. THE DENVER POST/RJ SANGOSTI

pool, the world's largest outdoor natural spa, still packs in the tourists. Kept at 90 degrees F., it feels like a bathtub. A smaller hot pool at 104 degrees is recommended for 15-minute soaks. In the winter, the town cashes in on nearby Sunlight Mountain Resort, a small local ski area known for its long intermediate runs and low lift prices. Visitors often base a winter vacation in Glenwood, then take day trips to Vail, an hour to the east, or Aspen, an hour to the south. Two excellent mountain golf courses—Snowmass and the River Valley Ranch in Carbondale—are within 28 and 12 miles, respectively, and the Roaring Fork River between Glenwood and Aspen is known for its Gold Medal trout fishing waters.

SNOWMASS/ASPEN

Aspen sits like a smug celebrity at the base of Independence Pass. Although it's remote and off the beaten path, it still enjoys the reputation as Colorado's most interesting ski town. Unlike Vail, the ski area was built around an existing mining town so it maintains some of the wonderful Victorian architecture that also makes Breckenridge so pleasant. Unlike Vail, Aspen sits in a valley so broad it allows the town to spread out until it feels like a real community, not a roadside attraction.

Aspen was first founded by miners intent on removing the natural treasure buried inside the mountains that surround it. They made fortunes from the silver they extracted and had a high old time until the market for silver crashed in the early 1890s. While Aspen never officially became a ghost town, its glorious buildings fell into ruin until another group of Army mountain vets returned to revitalize it in the 1950s. The town, named after its thick natural aspen groves, proved a natural skiing spot, and three more ski areas were developed to provide a mix of beginner, intermediate, family, and expert skiing to the region.

Before too long, wealthy movie stars and celebrities discovered the town. Jet setters also fly into Aspen airport, often in their own Learjets, to play in the snow. Visiting Aspen is expensive; living there is almost impossible, unless your pockets are deep enough to fork over several million for a fixer-upper. Still, about 5,800 people live in Aspen year round, and another 1,800 live in Smowmass Village, 14 miles up Route 82. Most people just choose to visit and enjoy, then drive back to their affordable lifestyles in whatever town or city they came from.

Now that you're familiar with the cities, towns, and resorts we'll be covering in this guide, here's a rundown of what you can expect to find in each to make your stay more enjoyable. Again, we've arranged the book from east to west, with chapters about each resort you'll pass between Georgetown and Glenwood Springs. Within each chapter, we've included a vast amount of information about the town and its attractions, everything from where to hang your hat and find a good restaurant to how to keep yourself occupied while you're visiting. Whether you're prone to sitting in one place while fishing cold mountain streams or rocketing on skis down vast acres of white powder, this chapter will help you find ways to fill your time. For those toying with the idea of staying longer, we've added facts about the real estate market, health care, and community services that can make our resort towns feel like home.

ACCOMMODATIONS

From the rustic log cabins and historic hotels to modern motels, luxury resorts, and skier home stays, Colorado has a range of lodging options to suit almost every taste and price range. Some of the most charming are restored Victorian homes that have been turned into bed-and-breakfast inns. A number of Colorado hotels also belong to the Association of Historic Hotels of the Rocky Mountain West, a group formed in 1983 by independent owners of properties on the National Register of Historic Places. The owners' goals were to protect, preserve, and restore these local and national landmarks and to emphasize their history while treasuring their diverse architecture, character, and cultures.

Families looking for an economical vacation option may want to consider renting a condo, most of which come with kitchen, washer/dryer, and such on-site amenities as swimming pools, tennis courts, and exercise rooms. These often can be rented on a nightly basis, but it varies by season; it's always a good idea to call ahead for information.

A number of Colorado hotels also belong to the Historic Hotels of America, a program of the National Trust for Historic Preservation that "identifies quality hotels that have faithfully maintained their historic integrity, architecture, and ambience." To be accepted, hotels must be located in a building that is at least 50 years old and be listed in, or be eligible for listing in, the National Register of Historic Places.

In Colorado, the Hotel Boulderado (Boulder), Hotel Jerome (Aspen), the Strater Hotel (Durango), The Brown Palace Hotel (Denver), The Cliff House at Pikes Peak (Manitou Springs), The Oxford Hotel (Denver), The Redstone Inn (Redstone), and The Stanley Hotel (Estes Park) are designated Historic Hotels.

These hotels—along with others such as the Delaware in Leadville and the Hotel Colorado in Glenwood Springs—are wonderful choices for those who enjoy turn-of-the-20th-century charm and history. Often these historic treasures are less expensive than their modern counterparts and offer the same amenities with a lot more ambiance.

Because the towns covered by this book are resort towns, the prices for accommodations vary according to the time of year and the day of the week—weekend prices can be more expensive than during the week, for example. For the sake of comparison, we've listed summer prices. Our mountain resorts have two low seasons—spring and fall—with high and higher seasons on either side, summer and winter. Within those categories, however, there are many variations that make pricing hotel rooms tricky. Just remember that the best bargains for anything will be in April and May—sometimes called the "mud season" since it's too muddy to ski or hike—and again in October and early November, before ski season starts up again. Summer high season begins mid June and lasts through Labor Day. Winter high season begins with Thanksgiving and extends through Spring Break. Christmas is the highest (and most expensive) of the high seasons, followed closely by March because of the popularity of Spring Break trips for high school and college students. Summer months may be the best time for condominium rental bargains, since the investment rule of thumb is that condo owners will make most of their money from winter rentals; any summer income then becomes "gravy."

All the accommodations listed in our chapters accept children and are at least partly wheelchair accessible unless otherwise noted. Pets are generally *not* allowed in most of the accommodations. Some cabins permit pets, but most hotels and condos don't. Note that as communities throughout the state have adopted no-smoking ordinances, many hotels and motels no longer offer smoking rooms. Smaller historic wooden inns, cabins, and bed-and-breakfasts generally do not allow smoking. Assume that major credit cards are accepted at any accommodation listed unless otherwise specified.

All the larger resort towns have central reservations numbers for booking hotels, motels, inns, bed-and-breakfasts, condos, and vacation rentals in private homes. Central reservations offices also provide other services; some handle car rentals and airport transfers and even sell discounted lift tickets.

In most destination chapters, accommodations are broken down into three categories: Resorts (including ranches and hotels offering all-inclusive packages or such amenities as athletic clubs, tennis camps, horseback riding, restaurants), Hotels and Motels (including some ranches and lodges), and Condo and Vacation Rentals (including private homes and skier home·stays). Some smaller areas, such as Leadville, do not have resorts; other areas, such as Copper Mountain, are self-contained resorts themselves and have only condos and hotel rooms.

Most ski resorts provide food service at or near their summits. During summer months, those restaurants serve scenic views that are often more dramatic than the food. KEN MCGRAW

PRICE CODE

Each accommodation entry includes a price range, indicating the approximate cost for a double-occupancy, one-night stay during the summer season. Taxes, gratuities, and extras such as premium TV channels are not included. Our three price ranges:

$.	**less than $100**
$$	**$101 to $150**
$$$	**more than $150**

Many of the accommodations listed have a wide range of rooms, suites, or condos with corresponding prices that reflect differences in room size, views, type of decor, and amenities such as hot tubs, pools, tennis courts, and other guest services.

RESTAURANTS

Rocky Mountain cuisine ranges from the sublime to the ridiculous: from the most chic Asian fusion cuisine—combining French style and technique with Asian ingredients—to Rocky Mountain oysters (a part of the bull you'd probably prefer not to think about too much). Prime rib and steaks figure large in the cattle-rearing Rockies, but portobello mushrooms seem to be stampeding for a close second. Like these large, beefy fungi, brewpubs have been springing up all over the Rockies, making tasty local microbrews and creative pub dishes on-site.

Perhaps because southern Colorado used to belong to Mexico, Mexican food and its Southwestern and New Mexican variations are standard fare in the Rocky Mountain region. The larger resort towns—

especially Aspen, Vail, and Beaver Creek—cater to an international crowd and offer cuisine to please a vast range of palates. Along with numerous chic bistros, you'll find such ethnic choices as Thai, Chinese, German, Greek, Japanese, and French.

Aspen is really the apex of fine dining in Colorado's Mountain areas (and probably all of Colorado as well) with Vail a close second. But for those seeking the real Rocky Mountain down-home dining experience, the 19th-century saloons, inns, and log cabin restaurants around Leadville and Dillon have no equal. A great burger or bowl of chili can sometimes be more satisfying than a filet mignon.

PRICE CODE

As with accommodations, restaurants are listed with price ranges to indicate the average cost of two entrees, excluding appetizer, alcoholic beverages, dessert, tax, and tip. All the restaurants listed accept major credit cards unless otherwise noted. Our four price ranges:

$	less than $16
$$	$17 to $26
$$$	$27 to $34
$$$$	$35 and over

NIGHTLIFE

Although Colorado's mountain towns know how to host a party, visitors who come here for nightlife may be sorely disappointed. They'll find nothing to match the bright lights of the big city. Most people visit Colorado's high country to enjoy the environment, either skiing or sledding, mountain biking, or hiking around the mountains. Once the sun sets, many don't have the energy—or the desire—for carousing or late night drinking.

That's why après ski is such an institution. The French term literally means "after ski," but in Colorado the meaning is much more complex. Après ski can refer to the time of day, as in, "We'll spend the après ski with Bob and Ethel." It also can mean the afternoon parties staged by ski town

bars and restaurants, as in, "Visit us for good après-ski specials." Those who follow the strict guideline about no imbibing before 5:00 P.M. will miss a lot in the high country, since après ski traditionally begins about 3:30 P.M. or earlier when bad weather drives skiers from the slopes prematurely. That's another reason why early nights are so common in the high country. Just try starting your party at 3:30 in the afternoon and continuing it until the bars close at 2:00 A.M.!

As bar owners and locals will undoubtedly add, not all merrymakers are home in bed by 9:00 P.M. Nightclubs—especially those in Vail and Aspen—attract their share of business in the wee hours of the morning, but they're special cases. On an average winter night, the streets of Keystone, Dillon, Frisco, Winter Park, or Glenwood Springs are empty before the 10:00 P.M. news comes on. Summer months have a slightly different feel, with bars staying open longer and pedestrians lingering in town until well past dark. The crowds aren't as consistent as they are in winter however, and some clubs close for the summer.

Depending on what's happening in town, things can go from dead to lively in the span of a week. When the mountain bike races come to Vail, for example, Vail Village bars burst at the seams as losers drown their sorrows, winners celebrate their victories, and groupies cozy up to their favorite superstars. Aspen thrives when visiting artists take up residence for the summer. The bars do a booming business, as always, but concerts and artist receptions and recitals crop up in every performance hall around. During the so-called shoulder seasons (the slower times on either side of the busy summer and winter tourist seasons), mountain towns can be worse than boring. That's when bar and restaurant owners close for vacation, renovation, or just plain lack of business. The deadest of all dead times are May, when snowmelt and spring rains leave the mountains too muddy for most kinds of activity, and October, when the weather has turned nippy enough to drive outdoor enthusiasts inside but before it's cold enough for winter sports.

Visitors will do well to rely on hotel concierges for advice about how best to spend the evening. Most hotels also have racks filled with brochures and weekly calendars of events, and all mountain towns have visitor information booths brimming with suggestions.

In each chapter, we include the major nightspots, what they're known for, and what kind of people frequent them. Some of the information was collected firsthand; some was provided by locals whose job it is to keep track of the entertainment scene.

A few tips about Colorado: The legal drinking age for any kind of alcohol is 21 years old, so the vast majority of the nightclubs are closed to anyone younger. Liquor stores are closed on Sunday.

It should be no surprise that drunk driving laws are strictly enforced here. Navigating our steep, winding mountain roads is tricky enough under normal conditions. Don't endanger your life—and ours— by getting behind the wheel after you've had a few drinks. Designate a driver before you go out, or find a bar to lean on that's within walking distance of your lodging.

ATTRACTIONS

It's tacitly understood that Colorado's main attractions are the mountains, with everything else human-made playing second fiddle. Peaks higher than 14,000 feet dominate Colorado's skyline, and 11,000- and 12,000-foot passes between them make for spectacular scenic drives. Beautiful lakes, wildflowers, creeks, and slopes of evergreens and golden aspen trees are among Colorado's finest attractions.

But Colorado's recent human history has left many colorful marks upon its lush landscape. Old gold and silver mines; historic towns that have gone boom and bust; elegant Victorian hotels, opera houses, and homes; and rustic miner's cabins make wonderful points of interest and

destinations themselves. It's the places like these that the Attractions section of each chapter will focus on.

Towns like Aspen, Breckenridge, Leadville, and Vail are tourist attractions in themselves. Many county historical societies offer fine, inexpensive tours of the top historical attractions, from mines to early settlers' homes. Some historic opera houses have been preserved and restored and still offer entertainment. Nature and environmental centers, such as the Vail Nature Center and Aspen Center for Environmental Studies, educate everyone from local schoolchildren to visiting adults with tours, seminars, and nature programs year-round. Many ski areas operate lifts and gondolas in the summer months for a scenic ride to the top of the mountain.

KIDSTUFF

Colorado's mountain resorts were developed with adults in mind, but that doesn't mean children aren't welcome, too. It just takes a little effort to translate grown-up activities such as skiing (not to mention après-ski partying), skating, hiking, biking, and sightseeing into pint-size pleasures. The major ski resorts help, knowing that many parents want to vacation with their kids. They provide everything from day care to ski lessons to summer camps that keep kids occupied while Mom and Dad have time to themselves. Winter Park, for example, turns the summertime slopes into a playground, running an alpine slide, a human maze, minigolf, climbing walls, bungee jumping, mountaintop disc golf course, and a full-day adventure camp for kids. Nearly every ski resort has designated portions of its ski mountain as a kids-only zone. The best resort programs offer a nice blend of family and adult-only activities, allowing families to have fun together during the evening, for example, but ski at their own individual paces during the day. Some resorts also offer night-time activities for kids whose parents would like a leisurely dinner or an evening of dancing. Choosing the right resort to fit

your needs can make all the difference between a good vacation and a bust.

If you're planning to ski, look carefully at what kinds of slopes each area has. SolVista Basin and Snowmass are known as family-friendly resorts with reasonable prices, gentle slopes, and lots of patient instructions. Arapahoe Basin, on the other hand, is a rustic area favored by expert skiers who like to ski hard and then party even harder. Only you can decide which best suits your family's tastes. Also check to see what else is nearby. If your resort is self-contained and remotely situated, you'll find yourself driving to the nearest town (sometimes 30 minutes away) for anything you'd like to do that isn't on the resort agenda for that day. Obviously, resorts with full-fledged towns surrounding them offer a wider range of spare-time activities. We've listed a variety of ways to entertain the children, with everything from rodeos to natural wonders. If you find yourself shor of something essential during your stay, Baby's Away will deliver rental cribs, high chairs, strollers, packs, toys, and other child needs to any hotel or condo. You can reach them in the Aspen/Snowmass area at (970) 920-1699 or merle@sopris.net; in Summit County at (970) 668-5408 or rvirostek@juno.com; in Steamboat Springs at (970) 879-2354 or Doman@cmn.net; and in the Vail Valley at (970) 328-1285 or babysawayofvail@aol.com.

SHOPPING

Tourists who come to the Colorado mountains to shop may be in for a shock—with a few exceptions, these resorts are not known for their mega-malls or full-service boutiques. Starstudded Aspen and Vail boast designer boutiques that appeal to the Rodeo Drive crowd, but Granby's best clothing buys come from the western wear store that outfits local ranchers. Each resort town has its own flavor and shops that match its unique ambiance. Glenwood Springs has the state's largest hot springs pool and excels at selling beach toys, sun

lotion, and souvenirs. Frisco and Breckenridge have what look to be ski and bike stores on every corner, but those stores also stock sailing supplies for people who come to navigate Lake Dillon. Twin cities Dillon and Silverthorne, split in two by I-70, also support marina stores, but they're better known as home to one of Colorado's largest outlet malls. People from around the state swarm in to do their shopping, among them locals from Aspen and Vail who don't have boutique budgets.

The trick to shopping the Colorado mountains is to relax and enjoy the process. Just when you think there's nothing to buy, you'll stumble onto a craft store, a store that sells Christmas items year-round, or an antiques store that carries rusty spurs. And watch for sales. Prices aren't cheap in these remote parts, but you'll get the best buys in March and October, when tourist crowds thin and merchants are eager to move on to the

Hunting for bargains at the many unique boutiques is a sport in itself. VAIL IMAGE/JACK AFFLECK

next season's merchandise. If you arrive in the thick of things, consider stopping at one of Denver's mega-sporting goods stores for ski clothing, accessories, or sporting goods needs. Once you enter the resort zone, prices will begin to climb.

ARTS

Culture in the mountains? An oxymoron? Nature is really considered Colorado's highest form of art. But such beauty has inspired humans to imitate it in all media and has drawn many notable artists from around the world to perform, work, live, and find their inspiration in Colorado's mountains. Aspen's Anderson Ranch attracts well-known visual artists from around the country and world, just as the Breckenridge Music Festival attracts classical musicians throughout the summer. Much of the art and culture found in Colorado derives from the surroundings—the mountains, landscape, wildlife, history, and western underpinnings.

Most of the mountain communities have galleries, museums, theaters, theater companies, and musical performances that operate, if at times in name only, year-round. But summer is the time for the great bloom of art and culture. The larger mountain communities host festivals of all types, many of which revolve around the arts. The Aspen and Breckenridge summer music festivals are practically institutions. Aspen's annual music festival is an extension of the Aspen Music School. The ongoing programs at the Anderson Ranch make way for special summer workshops and programs. Vail's summer music festival attracts nationally known performers. Breckenridge is the focal point for the arts in Summit County, with the area's largest concentration of galleries, museums, and arts events, although other communities stage their own events.

Within each destination chapter we've included information about arts of all kinds, organized by category and followed by an exhaustive listing of festivals and events (see below). All galleries in the list, unless otherwise noted, are free and operate during normal business hours.

EVENTS AND FESTIVALS

Colorado's mountains have become a year-round playground, with something going on every month of the year. During the winter months, events focus on paying homage to the snow, the commodity dearer than gold to towns that make their living off winter sports. Snow festivals are as unique as the towns that sponsor them. Aspen residents throw a costume ball during Winterskol, for example. Breckenridge residents put on horned hats and display their swordsmanship during Ullr Fest, which honors Ullr, the Norse god of winter. Come spring, people's thoughts turn to fun, with wacky Spring Massive and Spring Splash carnivals making the most of slushy slopes and bright sunny days.

During the summer, visitors are treated to an almost endless array of choices, from wildflower festivals to cooking and wine-tasting events, from bike races to rodeos, from golf tournaments to arts and crafts shows. Summer is also the time when mountain institutes of all kinds act as talent magnets, attracting nationally known musicians, dancers, artists, and writers to summer workshops in Vail and Aspen. Visitors and residents also benefit from these confabs—when the maestros meet, they also schedule public performances of their works in progress. In Vail, internationally famous ballet dancers demonstrate their *pas de deux*. In Aspen and Snowmass, jazz and classical stars fill the towns with music.

As summer winds down, fall weather is celebrated with a host of citywide sales and festivals that celebrate the turning of the aspen leaves. By November, all attention is focused on measuring the snow-pack and opening the ski areas. In December, early season guests are treated to Colorado's famous white Christmases and celebrate the holiday season by joining skiers who form torchlight parades down the mountainsides. Within each

chapter, we've organized the events chronologically by month. Because specific dates, features, and prices change each year, you'll want to call ahead for specifics before you attend.

SKIING AND SNOWBOARDING

Say "Colorado," and the first thing that comes to most people's minds is skiing. The word and state are synonymous, and it's no wonder. The U.S. Continental Divide—spine of the Rocky Mountains— slices through Colorado, creating some of the world's best skiing terrain and scenery. Fourteen-thousand-foot peaks blanketed in pure, white powder give way to endless bowls, open slopes, and meadows sparkling in the sunlight against cobalt blue skies. Expert skiers find challenges dropping from high rugged ridges and steep slopes, while beginners and inter- mediates enjoy the broad open meadows and gentler hills.

In 1915 Colorado's first ski resort, How- elsen Ski Hill, opened at Steamboat Springs. Snowgrooming equipment fist came into use in Colorado nearly 40 years later. Today 20 percent of all U.S. skier days occur in Colorado, even though only 5 percent of the nation's ski areas are here. Colorado boasted more than 12.53 million skiers and snowboarders during the 2005–2006 season. The state has 37,000 acres of skiable terrain, more than any- place else in North America, and at least 5 of its 27 ski resorts are regularly named as among the nation's most popular destina- tions. A kind of musical chairs of regroup- ing occurred in 1997 with Vail and Beaver Creek merging with Keystone and Breck- enridge to make America's largest ski- resort company, and Intrawest buying Copper Mountain here and Whistler in British Columbia. Dundee Realty Corpora- tion, based in Avon, Colorado, bought Ara- pahoe Basin.

Statistics aside, Colorado offers a range of skiing terrain and resorts to fit every abil- ity and pocketbook—from snazzy, jet-set Aspen and Vail to homey, "the-way-it-used-

to-be" Ski Cooper and Sunlight Mountain Resort. Skiers can choose from enormous ski areas with so many runs and lifts that they can't possibly be done in a day to small areas that take only a few hours to figure out. Some areas are complete resort villages or historic towns unto themselves; others are for day visits only.

Snowboarding has elbowed its way onto the slopes during the past decade and now accounts for about 20 percent of the business at many resorts. Snowboard- ing is easier to learn than skiing, if you can survive the first few days of falling. Snow- board falls tend to be more dramatic and injurious since the whole body crashes down at once like a falling tree and because both feet are rooted to the board. All Colorado ski areas permit snow- boarding.

Most ski areas offer nursery care, chil- dren's ski schools, instruction for disabled skiers, and seniors programs. Special cen- ters for skiers with mental and physical disabilities have been established at Breck- enridge, Aspen, Winter Park, Vail, and Beaver Creek. See those chapters for more detailed information.

Ski areas designate the difficulty of their different slopes by using the colors green (easiest), blue (intermediate), and black (advanced). All ski areas listed here rent equipment and offer instruction for all ages. A seemingly unlimited supply of ski boots, poles, and snowboards is available for rent at all the ski areas. Rental prices vary according to the equipment, area, and length of rental time. You will pay more for high performance racing skis than for basic beginners' skis. Reservations are not necessary for rental equipment, but during holiday weekends and peak season, they may be advisable. A ballpark figure for rental cost is $25 to $30 per day for skis, boots, and poles at the one-day rate.

In each chapter, we present informa- tion about downhill (Alpine) skiing first; then cross-country (Nordic). Nordic skiing is further divided into "track skiing," or ski- ing at a Nordic center, where ski tracks are machine set and there is generally a trail

The National Brotherhood of Skiers, a group of African-American skiers from throughout the U.S., visits one Colorado resort each year for a week of fun. Here, two participants enjoy a sunny day at Copper Mountain. *THE DENVER POST*/HELEN H. RICHARDSON

fee charged; and backcountry skiing, where skiers make their own tracks on national forest trails. Those venturing into the backcountry should have wilderness experience, maps, compass, and survival gear. Every year, avalanches claim many lives in Colorado. Downhill skiing in out-of-bounds areas (outside ski resort boundaries) also poses this extreme hazard, and skiers should obey trail-closure signs or take the risk that one great run could be their last. Backcountry, or wilderness, skiers heading out for a day or more should always let someone know where they are going and when they plan to return. (Please refer to our Mountain Safety and Environment chapter for more information about what to wear, how to avoid problems, and a detailed explanation of backcountry hazards.)

We strongly recommend that readers interested in wandering outside the confines of organized ski resorts supplement this book with detailed maps available from the U.S. Forest Service and sporting goods stores. Several specialized ski books that offer more detailed information on downhill skiing are *Rocky Mountain Skiing* and *Skiing on a Budget,* both by Claire Walter (Fulcrum, 1997).

Lift rates have been updated to reflect 2005–2006 prices. Lift tickets listed here reflect the price of one full-day adult lift ticket, although less than half of all tickets are sold at face value. Discounted tickets are widely available at area grocery stores, in coupon books, and though on-site resort package deals. Before you pay face value, ask about other potential deals currently available. Kids' lift tickets cost less. Special packages, including the beginners' lift-lesson-rental package, can be great moneysavers. Many areas also offer early- or late-season packages. Winter Park, for example, offers two nights' lodging and two days of lift tickets for about $230 per person, double occupancy, available mid-November to mid-December and again in April. Expect to pay as much as three times more during the high season.

Colorado is known for its light, fluffy "Champagne Powder" snow. Those who learned to ski on icy slopes in the East will find it much easier in Colorado's soft snow—except for thigh-high powder, which requires a whole different technique. Those who take a lesson should ask for tips on deep-powder skiing. Otherwise, just have fun and enjoy it. It's very forgiving.

OTHER WINTER RECREATION

Aren't interested in skiing? Tried it but didn't like the sensation of sliding down a chilly slope? Relax. Colorado's snow country has lots more to offer than dodging moguls. Choose from traipsing through the woods on snowshoes, zipping along in a snowcat or snowmobile, relaxing while horses or dog teams pull your sleigh, careening downhill in an inner tube, or gliding across an icy lake on skates.

Noticing that the number of skier visits was flattening out—up just 6 percent in the last decade—resort analysts began to ask why. They found out that even the most ardent skier likes variety, preferring not to ski every day of a winter vacation. They also found that skiers brought non-skiers when they vacationed, people who often were plopped in the lodge all day with a Thermos of hot chocolate and a good book. Not anymore. Vail added a sizable new complex of non-ski activities atop its Lionshead gondola, enticing first-timers to join their friends for ice skating, ski biking, snowmobile racing, snowshoeing, mountaineering, tubing, and sledding. Other resorts have followed suit, adding snowmobile rental, snowcat tours, and even snow-biking to their list of winter activities. (Snowcats are enclosed two-track vehicles that maneuver over snow the way

Humvees maneuver over the desert. Snowbikes are bikes with runners where the tires should be.)

Snowshoe rentals and tours have been the hands-down favorite, however. The appeal may be the sport's laid-back nature. Anyone who can walk can walk in snowshoes, often with no more than a 10-minute introduction to the mechanics. And once they're buckled in, snowshoers can go almost anywhere there's snow. By speeding up or slowing down, they can control the intensity of the workout, and runners eager to get in their miles have been known to strap on a pair and run some trails. Most resorts welcome snowshoers, with one caveat: Hiking the ski hills is fine as long as you go before the lifts open or after they close and keep to the side of the trails.

Renting equipment is simple in most ski towns. If you can't find what you want at the ski area, look in the Yellow Pages under Sporting Goods or Ski Rental listings. Hospitality desks or information centers at most major ski resorts can connect you with guides, tours, and other non-skiing services. Most innkeepers also can make recommendations. Keep in mind that prices quoted in our destination chapters are for the 2005–2006 season and most likely will increase a few dollars in subsequent seasons.

Colorado's winter season generally lasts from Thanksgiving to Easter. But, depending on how much snow falls during the year and when it falls, the season can begin earlier and last longer. It's a safe bet that all these recreational activities will be offered in December, January, February, March, and the first half of April. Colorado winters are sunny but cold. Temperatures span a wide range over the course of the season—from 60s in the sunshine to well below zero. Winds can be anywhere from calm to gale-force, even stronger on the higher mountains. Remember to dress warmly and in layers for anything you do during the winter. Wear sunglasses or goggles and sunscreen on your face, and drink plenty of water to guard against sunburn, windburn, and altitude sickness. Since body heat escapes through your head, wearing a hat can help keep your body warm. Colorado is known for its fickle weather, and what starts out as a clear, bright day can turn nasty within an hour. Never wander into uncharted territory or head for the hills without telling someone where you're headed. It's easy to get disoriented on mountain trails or to wander into avalanche territory (see our Mountain Safety and Environment chapter). That said, get out there and enjoy the snow!

HIKING, BACKBACKING, AND CAMPING

Once Colorado's high-altitude snowpack melts, those same peaks that thrill winter skiers provide hikers and backpackers with nearly infinite summertime trails. Thousands of square miles of national forest and wilderness lands have been preserved in the central mountains, and most of them are open to all kinds of foot-powered wanderers.

The casual hiker can take just about any foot trail that isn't someone's driveway, but the concierges at most resort hotels have maps of more ambitious trips. Day hikers often find themselves walking along old logging roads or dirt-packed Forest Service trails. More serious overnight hikers must put more thought into their trips, since permits may be required to camp in some areas (the Indian Peaks Wilderness Area, for example) and often must be done in designated campgrounds or backcountry campsites. To minimize the damage of human impact on our wilderness areas, we also recommend following the standard rules of low-impact camping, especially those that recommend camping at least 100 feet from trails and streams, and carrying out all trash.

Colorado is a huge state, and entire books have been devoted just to hiking trails, but in each of our chapters we have included a sampling of our favorites. Also refer to the Skiing and Snowboarding sections, because many of the cross-country ski trails make good hiking trails once

they've thawed. Serious hikers and backpackers will want to purchase additional guidebooks and maps with enough detail to get them where they want to go—and back again—safely. And for those who would rather camp in recreation vehicles than on the ground, we've also included a selection of car/tent and RV campsites in each chapter.

We recommend the following books to get you started, although many more are published every year: *Hiking Colorado: A Guide to Colorado's Greatest Hiking Adventures* by Maryann Gaug (Falcon), *Hiking Colorado's Summit County Area: A Guide to the Best Hikes In and Around Summit County* (Falcon), *100 Classic Hikes in Colorado* by Scott S. Warren (The Mountaineers Books), *Colorado Summit Hikes For Everyone* by Dave Muller (Colorado Mountain Club Press), *Exploring Colorado's Wild Areas: A Guide for Hikers, Backpackers, Climbers, XC Skiers + Paddlers* by Scott S. Warren (The Mountaineers Books).

GOLF

There's nothing quite like golfing at 9,000 feet, surrounded by alpine scenery and sharing the course with elk, red foxes, and sometimes even bears. Sure, the courses still have tee boxes and fairways. They still require that players hit the ball into a tiny hole on the green, and they still provide plenty of obstacles to make that task difficult. But anyone who has ever golfed in Colorado's mountains will attest to the fact that the game is somehow different up here.

First of all, there's the matter of gravity. Balls travel as much as 15 percent farther at 9,000 feet than they do at sea level, and they often go straighter. The more poetic explain the phenomenon by saying golfers are nearly 2 miles closer to heaven when they're in the Rockies. Scientists explain it this way: The atmosphere gets thinner—and exerts less drag on a golf ball—as it gains altitude. And because spinning causes balls to curve, when there's less air to spin against, there's less chance for them to hook.

Then there's the terrain. Golf courses designed on flat land can take any shape they want, but mountain golf courses must follow the twists and turns of stream-cut valleys, climb mountain-goat paths up hillsides, and leap across inconvenient arroyos. Many mountain courses also play across rivers, plunge deep into wooded valleys, gain as much elevation as a hiking trail, and are surrounded by rough so dense it swallows poorly hit balls.

To top it all off, many of the golfers on Colorado's mountain courses are on vacation, which means they're relaxed, enjoying the scenery, and reveling in the cool summer air. While August temperatures can top 100 degrees in some parts of the nation, high-country temperatures usually hover in the 80s with very little humidity. Greens fees can be steep at mountain golf courses, partly because the season is so short—usually June through September, with snow possible any time—and partly because guests are willing to pay $150 or more a round for access to the state's most exclusive courses. The weather can also get dicey. That's why every mountain course has at least one lightning shed and rain shelter. The best rules of thumb are to play in the mornings when possible and to wait out any afternoon squall. Most rainstorms blow through in the afternoon and last no longer than 10 or 15 minutes. Have patience, and never foolishly try to play through any storm with lightning.

One more piece of advice: Reserve your tee times early. Golf has become such a summertime draw in ski resorts that the courses often sell out days, sometimes weeks in advance. Some clubs require that golfers be registered guests at neighboring resorts, but most will accept walk-ons whenever they have room for them. Remember that prices listed in our chapters are for the 2005 season and most likely will rise in following years.

FISHING AND HUNTING

President Dwight D. Eisenhower spent many of his off-duty hours dangling a line in the swift rivers of Colorado's high country. His favorite fishing spots were between Granby and Winter Park, but the cold waters of many Rocky Mountain lakes and streams are the perfect habitat for rainbow, brown, cutthroat, and brook trout so large they qualify as trophies. In fact, many world-record trout have been pulled from Colorado waters. The best part is that you don't have to be a world-class angler to enjoy world-class success here. A little planning, patience, and the willingness to ask the local pros for advice are really all it takes.

True anglers can fish year-round in Colorado, although some say the best high-country fishing is from March through October. Some high mountain lakes are frozen until early July and again after mid-September. Enjoy them for 10 to 11 weeks a year during the midsummer. Angling in Colorado's high country comes in two styles—recreational and sportfishing—the primary difference being the

With a backdrop like this, it's amazing anyone can concentrate on putting. VAIL IMAGE/ JACK AFFLECK

Colorado has some of the nation's best fly-fishing streams, but because most are fed by melting snowpack, the waters can be chilly except during hot summer months.
VAIL IMAGE/JACK AFFLECK

amount of time, effort, and skill you are willing to put in. Each has unique requirements regarding equipment, location, technique, and regulations, and each offers the opportunity to experience the excitement of hooking and landing trout that, pound-for-pound, are among the greatest fighters in the world.

Recreational fishing is abundant in Colorado, with more than 6,000 miles of streams and more than 2,000 lakes and reservoirs. In the area we're covering, the best recreational fishing is found at the numerous high-country lakes and reservoirs that are typically accessed from either National Park Service camping areas (Dillon and Green Mountain reservoirs) or from well-signed National Forest service roads.

As with all fishing in Colorado, a license is required to fish in all public areas, and catch limits do apply. Anglers 16 and older must have licenses, but they're easy to get. Most major sports and outdoor stores carry annual licenses for $20.25 if you're a Colorado resident, or $40.25 if you're not. One-day and five-day passes are less, as are special licenses issued to senior citizens and people with disabilities. Free unlicensed fishing is offered the first full weekend of June. Unless otherwise posted, all waters also are open to ice fishing with a few restrictions about fires and size of fishing holes (they must be no bigger than 10 inches in diameter, for example). Daily bag and possession limits vary by type of fish and often by fishing location. Be sure to read the Colorado Division of Wildlife Fishing Regulations before venturing out. The brochure is available online at http://wildlife.state.co.us/fishing/hotspots.asp.

Recreational fishing is usually done from the shoreline of a lake, occasionally from a small boat or canoe (where permitted and/or available). Most often these shorelines are reached after a brief hike from your car and are (unfortunately) heavily populated by other recreational anglers. Not to worry, though. The advantage of fishing from the shoreline is that all of it is available, and you can almost always find a little privacy if you are willing to walk a little ways. Live bait, in the form of worms or minnows, is legal at most lakes and reservoirs (always check local regulations first), and within a few minutes after setting up your lawn chair you can be offering these tempting morsels to the local lake inhabitants. Kids especially enjoy this type of fishing because it allows their naturally short attention spans to wander to the rocks, water, birds, chipmunks, and (once in a while) the incredible scenery, without having to spend every second watching their fishing poles.

For those who prefer a little more activity in their fishing, trout are very susceptible to a well-placed artificial lure or fly. A popular technique around lakes is to tie a swivel onto the end of your line, then tie a loop at one end of several 3- to 5-foot pieces of leader line (ordinary fishing line will work just fine). You can then tie various lures to the other end of the leader lines, and changing from lure to lure becomes quick and simple. Remember, trout are smart, and offering them what they want when they want it is the whole key to a successful outing. To improve your odds, swallow your pride, go into one of the local angler shops, and ask for advice on what the fish are biting. You will be absolutely amazed at how helpful and eager the proprietors and employees of these places will be. After all, fishing is their business; the more they help you catch 'em, the more likely you'll be to return the favor by purchasing the tackle you need right from them. And nobody knows the local conditions better than the locals!

Some rules of thumb for fishing from the shoreline:

• Trout feed most actively in the early morning and late afternoon, when temper-

atures are coolest. During the midday heat, trout tend to head for deeper, colder water and become sedentary.

• You don't need to cast your bait/lure/fly a hundred yards out into the lake. Remember, trout are smart; they typical feed in shallower waters where the amount of food per volume of water is greater.

• Practice good fishing courtesy around the shoreline. Give a wide berth, and stay quiet when walking past another angler's spot, and whenever possible keep 75 to 100 yards between yourself and other anglers. Sometimes crowding can be a problem, but even then it's possible to give everyone enough room. If not, it's probably time to go home or go fish someplace else.

• Practice good sportsmanship and fishing ethics. Many of Colorado's lakes and reservoirs are stocked with young, legally catchable trout. Catching, keeping, and eating a "mess" of frying pan sized rainbow trout can be the highlight of a fishing trip. But if you aren't going to eat them, then fish with barbless hooks and release them to grow bigger; they just might be there next year when you return. To release a fish with minimal harm requires a little work on your part. First, don't pull the fish from the water onto the shore. Second, handle the fish as little and as delicately as possible and never touch the fish's gills or the flaps around them. Finally, while gently holding the fish submerged, carefully remove the hook by pushing down and back to release the hook.

For those interested in world-class sportfishing for trout, Colorado boasts more than 168 miles of Gold Medal, catch-and-release waters, so designated because they have a high-quality aquatic habitat, a high percentage of trout 14 inches or longer, and a high potential for trophy fish. This is the quintessential trout-fishing experience. Accordingly, your equipment, skill level, and willingness to seek advice must match the prowess and intelligence of your quarry. Above all else, remember that the fish inhabiting these waters have been caught and released several times over the years. They are both smart and wary, and can easily spot the offerings and efforts of the inexperienced and unadvised. The rewards for your efforts, however, can be rainbow or brown trout well more than 20 inches in length and often weighing in at several pounds.

Parts of the Blue River, the Colorado River, the Fryingpan River, Gore Creek, and Roaring Fork River are Gold Medal waters. The Colorado Division of Wildlife Web site also provides complete information—including interactive maps—about the state's 11 Gold Medal waters. Go to http://wildlife.state.co.us/fishing/hotspots.asp. General information about fishing seasons and dates is available 24 hours a day from the Division of Wildlife at (303) 291-7533. For information about fishing conditions, call (303) 291-7534.

There are several basic guidelines to follow, some of which are legal requirements. We'll cover the regulations first. All fishing in Gold Medal waters is catch-and-release; you may not keep any fish you catch. Accordingly, use good fishing ethics, and fish only with barbless hooks. All fishing in Gold Medal waters is with artificial flies and lures only; you should check for other or special restrictions that apply to the section of water you intend to fish, as regulations are frequently changed in order to most effectively manage the fish population. All fishing in Gold Medal waters is from public access areas only; fishing Gold Medal waters that flow through private property is illegal without permission from the property owner. It is very important that you check locally to understand where public access ends and private property begins. In Colorado, as elsewhere, it is always the angler's responsibility to respect private property, whether marked or not.

The practical guidelines for a successful fishing trip all revolve around using local knowledge. Seek out local angler shops or outfitters, and ask questions about fishing conditions, including:

• How high is the runoff, or how fast is the water? Rocky Mountain streams and rivers are fed by melting snow from the mountains (that's why the water's so cold), and the speed and flow of the water can not only mean poor fishing conditions, but can also be dangerous to wading anglers.

• Are there any hatches going on, where are they, and what are they? A "hatch" refers to the hatching of aquatic insects in streams and rivers. These insects are the main food source for trout, and if you can match the timing, location, and type of insect in the hatch, your chances for extraordinary success go up dramatically. Your best chance for success is to hire an experienced local outfitter. As with any sporting endeavor, the home field advantage—local knowledge—is invaluable.

An outfitter should be able to answer any questions and should know several good alternate fishing spots. Indeed, some outfitters have access, through prior arrangements, to private property unavailable to others and can provide the always-welcome addition of companionship.

Colorado is also famous for its big game, including elk, mountain lion, black bear, mule deer, bighorn sheep, mountain goats, and pronghorn antelope. However, it is important to note here that hunting in Colorado is not, and should not be considered, a tourist activity. Even though 30 percent of the big-game hunters annually in Colorado are from out-of-state, and even though the dollars generated by these hunters are considered "tourist" revenues, hunting in the mountains of Colorado is serious business requiring extensive planning and preparation. Each year the mountains of Colorado claim the lives of those who ignore this requirement.

Elk season begins in mid-August with an archery season, followed by muzzle-loaders in September and four rifle seasons from mid-October through mid-November. The deer season starts mid-October and runs through mid-December. In some areas, you may do a combined hunt for deer and elk. If you plan to hunt in Colorado, contact the Colorado Division of Wildlife for information on hunting regulations, costs, and for books and brochures that you can use to plan a safe and enjoyable trip. The Division of Wildlife Web site provides complete information, including hunting seasons for all game species, regulations, and licenses, at http://wildlife.state.co.us/hunt/.

All hunters are required to have hunter safety cards as well as licenses for each species they are hunting. Prices for hunting licenses vary widely and favor the resident hunter. Elk licenses, for example, are available to residents for $30.25. Nonresidents pay $250.25 for a cow elk license and $485.25 for a bull elk license. Moose licenses are the most expensive at $203.25 for residents and $1,633.25 for nonresidents. Elk and deer are the most popular big-game animals. The Colorado Division of Wildlife's main number for information and publications on hunting, fishing, wildlife watching, and other outdoor opportunities, including forecasts and possibilities for hunting success in each Game Management Unit, is (303) 297-1192.

OTHER RECREATION

Although Colorado is nationally known for its summer fishing, hiking, golfing, and camping, those activities just begin to scratch the surface of our smorgasbord of fair-weather fun. The central mountains are a sportsperson's paradise, offering everything from ballooning to climbing, bicycling to horseback riding, trail running to boating, tennis to whitewater rafting.

Some resorts are best known for their boating, usually because they're located near a high mountain lake (Dillon Lake, Grand Lake, Lake Granby, and Shadow Mountain Lake are among the biggest). Others have intentionally carved out niches for themselves to attract summer visitors. Winter Park and Fraser, for example, cater to mountain bikers. Steamboat Springs is known for its dude ranches and horseback riding, while Keystone has a thriving summer tennis program. Glenwood Springs is a favorite of river rats who

raft down the Colorado River, and Snowmass Village has one of the state's most colorful hot-air balloon festivals.

Many rock jocks and mountaineers are drawn to the sheer canyon walls and 14,000-foot peaks scattered throughout the region. Both are highly specialized and potentially dangerous sports that require training, equipment, and skill. They also require detailed route guides and descriptions not possible in a generalized guidebook of this nature. Some general rock-climbing areas are offered, but serious rock climbers will want to obtain specialized local guidebooks available at sporting goods and climbing/mountaineering shops, or go one step further and hire a guide.

Most whitewater rafting in Colorado is done on the Arkansas, Colorado, Blue, South Platte, and Eagle Rivers and on Clear Creek. Other rivers throughout the state are also navigable but not near the areas covered by this book. The Colorado River Outfitters Association publishes a brochure listing members and guidelines for choosing the right rafting company to meet your needs. Its members must meet experience and training qualifications that often exceed state licensing requirements as well as adhere to a strict code of ethics. The brochure is available online at http://croa.org/brochure.htm, or by contacting CROA, 10281 U.S. Highway 50, Howard, CO 81233.

The same companies that offer rafting usually offer kayaking, too. The popular departure spot for raft trips along the Arkansas River is Buena Vista, a town located about 45 minutes south of Leadville. Those who prefer the Eagle River often depart from Eagle, 30 miles west of Vail. The Colorado River departure area is near State Bridge, about 70 miles east of Steamboat Springs. Rafting also is done on the Colorado at Glenwood Springs and on the Blue River and Clear Creek near Dillon, but resort guests may have to travel quite a ways to reach the actual rafting sites. The river rafting/kayaking season is from May through August, depending upon how much snowpack accumulates during the winter and how quickly it thaws during the spring. Heavy summer rains may also swell the rivers, providing more exciting rapids that last well into September.

Mountain biking is gaining popularity at most resorts, since many ski runs can also be used as bike trails once they have thawed. Just be forewarned—pedaling up steep mountain grades at high altitudes is difficult for those not in excellent physical condition and well acclimated to the elevation. Many ski areas offer an easier alternative, providing uphill transportation on ski lifts and letting riders power themselves back down the mountainside. Private outfitters often do the same type of shuttle service for downhill riders with Jeeps and vans.

Running and walking can, of course, be done anywhere, but ultrarunners seem drawn to Colorado's steepest trails on even the 14,000-foot mountains. They may be training for such races as the Leadville Trail 100—a 100-mile run through the mountains—or the Pikes Peak Marathon, which climbs that 14,000-foot mountain. A number of paved and unpaved riverside bike trails make for excellent running as well as bicycling. Such flat places are rare in Colorado's mountain areas, but trails have been carved along the Blue River in Silverthorne and Breckenridge, along the Fraser River between Winter Park and Fraser and, perhaps the best known and most challenging, between Copper Mountain and Vail on a paved trail that climbs the 10,000-foot-high Vail Pass. A less steep but still breathtakingly scenic paved bike trail snakes alongside the Colorado River through Glenwood Canyon, ending in Glenwood Springs. Winter Park offers some 50 miles of lift-accessible, single-track mountain bike trails and has an excellent free trail map available to cyclists. Go online to www.skiwinterpark.com/biking/mountainbiking.htm.

Sports such as racquetball and tennis are offered at private clubs, hotels, resorts, and condominiums to their members/guests. Some public tennis courts exist in mountain communities as part of the city/town recreation districts/centers. Most of the ski resorts offer summer clinics and camps for tennis, golf, and other activities. In-line skating is best done on flat, paved bike paths in Aspen, Breckenridge, Glenwood Springs, and Vail, but skates often can be rented from bike shops. Some resorts also offer peeks back into Colorado's history, with gold panning, hayrides, and all-terrain-vehicle rides to ghost towns and abandoned mines.

HOT SPRING AND SPAS

For at least 400 years, Colorado has been known as a great place to spa. In the early days it was a magnet for Native Americans who came to soak in the healing waters of natural hot springs. The springs still attract visitors today, but they have been joined by a new class of mountain spa, the lavish place for one-stop healthy shopping. Many of the fancier mountain resorts now include among their amenities spas that offer massages, facials, body wraps, wellness counseling, and such holistic treatments as reflexology and acupressure.

The hot springs came first, of course. Due to geological coincidence, Colorado has hundreds of hot springs, if you count all the small caches of geothermal water that sprinkle the state, but most are too small to enjoy. As counted by the Colorado Geological Survey, 93 are large enough to crawl into. Of those, 60 are on private land and are used to heat everything from personal pools to private fish ponds. The other three dozen, strewn across the western half of the state, welcome guests. Seven are within the boundaries defined by this book and will be covered in detail in the appropriate chapter. For more details on hot springs in our state, check out *Touring Colorado Hot Springs* by Carl Wambach (Falcon Publishing, $15.95).

"Hot springs are the earth's warm, sweet breath," as author Deborah Frazier explains in her book, *Colorado's Hot Springs* (Pruett Publishing, 2002). Steam

The Hot Springs Pool complex includes three separate hot water pools, a fitness center, a gift shop, and a restaurant. Children enjoy the enclosed slide in the upper right-hand corner of the photo. THE DENVER POST/SHAUN STANLEY

and hot water from subterranean reservoirs escape from cracks in the earth's surface in springs as hot as nearly 200 degrees F. and sometimes with enough pressure to cause geysers (Old Faithful in Yellowstone National Park is a good example). To qualify as a hot spring, water must be at least 90 degrees F. Colorado's hottest is Mount Princeton in Buena Vista, at 182. The springs are formed when snow and rain water trickle into the earth and fill deep reservoirs that are heated by the Earth's molten core, which has burned for billions of years. When the water boils, it swells and sends off steam, shooting to the surface through faults and rock fractures. On the way up it collects minerals from the rock layers it passes through. Colorado's mountains are ideal for hot springs because the turbulent bending and buck-

ling that formed the Rockies left hundreds of fractures through which the springs can escape.

Since before the Greeks and Romans, humans have believed that soaking in hot springs clears the mind, cleanses the body, and recharges the spirit. Ponce de Leon searched in vain for the spring of eternal youth, but Colorado's earliest settlers—the Ute Indians—could have given him directions. For 150 years before Europeans arrived here, the Utes had been using the springs for rituals and religious ceremonies. They parted with the springs reluctantly, clinging to them long after homesteaders had stripped them of most other parcels of their land. In 1881, the Utes were escorted by the U.S. Army to two reservations in southwest Colorado and one in Utah, leaving the springs behind to be purchased by city governments and private businesspeople.

Since many springs were near the gold strikes, miners were some of the earliest Europeans to soak in them. Leadville miner Isaac Cooper founded Glenwood Springs when he gave up the dirty work to harness the curative powers of Yampah Springs. In the early 1900s, Colorado hot springs took their place on the international spa circuit. After the Depression, many languished until they were rediscovered by hippies in the 1960s. Spiritual seekers and baby boomers with aching joints and playful children now keep them busy.

Although developed hot springs are regularly inspected by county health departments, there are a few things to beware of. The minerals in the water do collect and cause algae to grow. If you see green growths in the springs, think twice about lounging in them. Don't drink the water, especially in primitive springs, because it can be filled with bacteria that

will play havoc with your digestive system. Feel free to drink water provided for that purpose at some hot springs, either in bottled form or from spigots labeled for drinking. People with high blood pressure and heart problems, pregnant women, and young children may also want to think twice about immersing themselves in the hot water.

A few hot springs also offer spa treatments, although mountain spas and hot springs are distinctly different animals. Spas are often attached to hotels and provide everything from weight workouts to personal training, holistic evaluations, and beauty treatments. Hot springs are often just places to soak and swim. (Yampah Vapor Caves in Glenwood Springs and the Lodge and Spa in Hot Sulphur Springs are exceptions.) Mountain spas have become favorite destinations of visitors interested in some healthy pampering, with many of the most exclusive clustered in the Vail and Aspen areas. Details about them will follow in the appropriate chapters as well.

GETTING HERE, GETTING AROUND

Getting to and around in the central Colorado mountains is fairly simple—barring winter blizzards and avalanches—since most areas are accessed by Interstate 70. (Durango, Telluride, and Crested Butte are the exceptions.) Driving I-70 is also quite scenic with great views of 13,000- and 14,000-foot peaks and such points of interest as 10,000-foot Vail Pass and the Eisenhower Tunnel, an engineering marvel that burrows beneath the U.S. Continental Divide, just west of the Loveland Ski Area.

Ground transportation from Denver International Airport (DIA) and Colorado Springs Airport is plentiful. Those on their own can choose between shuttles, limousines, and buses; those staying at the larger resorts should ask about the availability of special resort shuttles. It's always best to call ahead for reservations and schedules to avoid unpleasant surprises. Since tourism is big business in Colorado, the infrastructure between airports and ski resorts is excellent and well-maintained.

Generally people drive or take a bus, train, shuttle, or limousine service to Summit County, which is just less than a two-hour drive from Denver and Denver International Airport. Breckenridge, for example, is 85 miles from Denver and 100 miles from DIA. Some people prefer to fly directly to Vail and Aspen, since these areas are farther away. Vail is 100 miles from Denver and 115 miles from DIA. Aspen is 162 miles from Denver and 177 miles from DIA. The Vail/Eagle County Regional Airport serves Vail, and the Aspen/Pitkin County airport serves Aspen. A number of airlines fly to Vail and Aspen from DIA and the Colorado Springs Airport (please refer to the "Airports" section of this chapter).

For private planes, Colorado has many small airports scattered around the state. Mountain flying can be hazardous with canyons, currents, and extreme weather and topography, and non-instrument pilots should consider having mountain checkouts, which are offered at various airports. Landing in some Colorado airports can be demanding, so official FAA-approved, up-to-date landing information is a must. The FAA reissues the official flight guide every 63 days. For instance, at the Glenwood Springs airport, there is only one specific canyon through which pilots can fly to approach the airport. Other canyons are one-way and have oncoming planes! Check official flight guides and FAA sources for details about mountain flying.

For automobile drivers, all the destinations along I-70 have their own well-marked exits. Beware of shortcuts over dirt roads or Jeep roads if you don't have a true off-road vehicle (and refer to "Mountain Driving" in our chapter on Mountain Safety and Environment). Otherwise you may find yourself stranded in the wilderness with your car's transmission high-centered on a large rock.

I-70's passage through Glenwood Canyon, which leads to Glenwood Springs, is one of the nation's most scenic drives—something those who fly to Aspen will miss. Vast red stone cliffs tower above the curving highway alongside the Colorado River. Rafters, kayakers, and anglers dot the riverway. There are good rest stops in Glenwood Canyon and even a short, but rigorous, hike at Hanging Lake (10 miles east into Glenwood Canyon—see our Glenwood Springs chapter for details) for those who want to stretch their legs. In summer, late spring, or early fall—before the snow flies—driving over such high passes as Independence and Loveland can be a memorable and exhilarating experience, offering spectacular vistas of the mountain ranges and close-up views of alpine wildflowers and wildlife. Some of these passes are closed during winter or close frequently due to weather and road conditions, which are announced on radio and TV.

Greyhound Bus Lines provides service to many mountain communities, and Amtrak trains from Chicago (via Denver) or San Francisco make various stops in Colorado—a relaxing way to enjoy the mountain scenery.

ROADWAYS

Leaving Denver International Airport, the route west to I-70 is well-marked. From Colorado Springs Airport, which is located just off Interstate 25 on the far southeast end of town, the fastest and easiest way to the central mountain region is to drive north on I-25 to Denver, then follow the signs for I-70 west.

From Colorado Springs, a scenic route to the mountains is also possible via U.S. Highway 24, which goes through Woodland Park and intersects (temporarily becomes) the north-south U.S. Highway 285. At US 285 drivers headed to Breckenridge will turn north and continue to Fairplay (gas and good food and lodging are available). At Fairplay drivers need to take Highway 9 over Hoosier Pass (11,541 feet and well-maintained year-round), which drops down to Breckenridge.

For Leadville, drivers from Colorado Springs following US 24 continue on US 24 past US 285. At Johnson Village, US 24 turns north to Buena Vista and Leadville and ultimately intersects I-70 past Vail at Minturn. The scenery makes this an enjoyable and interesting mountain ride, but it is recommended only for those headed to Buena Vista or Leadville and during summer or early fall when roads are dry and clear of snow. The twisting mountain roads can be treacherous when covered with snow and ice—especially from Leadville over Tennessee Pass down to Redcliff and Minturn.

Visitors bound for Crested Butte from Denver should take I-25 south to the Santa Fe Drive exit, follow Santa Fe Drive south to US 285, and US 285 south to Poncha Springs. Once there, they will follow U.S. Highway 50 west to Gunnison, and then turn north on Highway 133 to Crested Butte.

Drivers traveling to Telluride may follow I-70 west to Glenwood Springs or Grand Junction before cutting south on either Highways 82, 133, and 92 (from Glenwood Springs) or US 50 (from Grand Junction). Either way, they will find themselves heading south on US 50 to Ridgway, where they will take Highway 62 southwest to Placerville and then Highway 145 southeast into Telluride. Airplane service to Telluride depends on good weather, which means airplanes are frequently diverted to nearby Montrose. Shuttle vans then carry passengers the rest of the way to the remote box canyon in which Telluride hides.

Reaching Durango is more direct, if not faster. Although there are other scenic mountain routes, the easiest all-weather route takes visitors from DIA or Colorado Springs south on I-25 to Walsenburg, picking up U.S. Highway 160 west to Durango.

Although Colorado's speed limits are 65 to 75 mph on interstate highways, mountain roads range from 10 to 55 mph, depending on the terrain and the weather.

SKI AREAS AND OTHER DESTINATIONS

As visitors will discover, I-70 is the main artery through Colorado's central mountain region, leading directly to Summit County, Vail, and Glenwood Springs and from which drivers will exit to the other areas below.

Grand County: To reach Winter Park, Fraser, and Silver Creek from I-70, take U.S. Highway 40 across Berthoud Pass (11,315 feet, but very well-maintained during winter). This exit is clearly marked and is also the exit for the picturesque town of

Interstate 70 is the main route from Denver through the mountains, tunneling beneath the Continental Divide via the Eisenhower Tunnel. Loveland Ski Area is visible to the left.
THE DENVER POST/BARRY STAVES

Empire, where you might spot some bighorn sheep grazing on the roadside. Winter Park, Fraser, and SolVista Basin are all located along US 40.

Summit County: Dillon, Silverthorne, Frisco, and Copper Mountain are all right on (or visible from) I-70. For Keystone Resort, take the Dillon/Silverthorne exit and backtrack 6 miles on U.S. Highway 6 to the resort. For Breckenridge, take the Frisco exit, then go south on Highway 9 for 9 miles. A more scenic but much slower route to Keystone Resort is to exit I-70 at Loveland Pass and take US 6, a hairpin-turn pass road, past Arapahoe Basin, to the Keystone Resort. Loveland Pass is often closed during winter due to heavy snow and avalanches.

To Steamboat Springs: Located 157 miles northwest of Denver, Steamboat Springs is most easily accessed by taking

I-70 to Dillon/Silverthorne (exit 205) and following Highway 9 to Kremmling. When it intersects with US 40, take US 40 west. It will become Lincoln Avenue, the north-south street through downtown Steamboat Springs.

To reach Leadville, follow I-70 to the Highway 91 turnoff at Copper Mountain. The highway crosses Fremont Pass (11,318 feet), but the road is excellent—four lanes in some areas for passing—and is well-maintained year round. This is the shortest and best route to Leadville and is also very scenic, passing the huge (and now closed) Climax Molybdenum Mine—the world's largest—near Fremont Pass.

Vail, Beaver Creek, and Avon are on I-70 on the western side of Vail Pass.

Glenwood Springs is directly on I-70.

For Aspen take Highway 82 south at Glenwood Springs. Carbondale is about halfway between the two. A shortcut to Aspen, which can shave about a half-hour off the 162-mile ride from Denver, can be made only in summer when Independence Pass is open. Take I-70 west to Copper Mountain (79 miles from Denver), then take Highway 91 south past Leadville to the junction with Highway 82. Go west of Highway 82, driving over Independence Pass to Aspen, which can be a bit hair-raising for those not used to mountain driving but is safe if you observe speed limits and signs. The road is extremely narrow and curving with precipitous dropoffs on the side, but it's a spectacular, above-timberline mountain ride.

AIRPORTS
Major Commercial

Colorado Springs Airport
7770 Drennan Road
(719) 550-1972
www.springsgov.com/airportindex.asp
Six miles southeast of Colorado Springs and 70 miles south of Denver, this pleasant municipal airport has become increasingly popular nationwide because fares to it are often lower than to Denver International Airport, which levies a sizable tax on every ticket sold. Colorado Springs Airport handles more than 110 arrivals and departures daily and is served by Allegiant Air, American West, American, Continental, Delta, Mesa, Northwest, and United Airlines. The airport offers a variety of bus, shuttle, and limo services, including: Ramblin Express (719) 590-8687; Peak Transit (719) 687-3456 or (877) 587-3456; Allendac Limousine Service (719) 393-0013; and Yellow Cab (719) 634-5000. Rental car companies are Alamo, Avis, Budget, Hertz, and National.

Parking is a better deal at the Colorado Springs Airport than at DIA. Short-term parking is $1.00 per half-hour with a maximum daily rate of $8.00. Long-term parking is $5.00 a day and valet parking is also available for $10.00 per day. Major credit cards and local checks are accepted.

In 1994, the Colorado Springs Airport went through a major overhaul with $140 million worth of improvements. The city financed it hoping to bring in more bookings and nonstop flights—and it worked. A 13,500-foot runway was added; the old runway—still in use—is 11,000 feet but couldn't accommodate certain aircraft. Baggage handling capacity increased, and yearly passenger capacity went from 900,000 to more than 2.5 million. The airport's interior space was more than doubled from 110,000 square feet to 280,000. The original number of gates more than doubled from 6 to 16.

Architectural improvements included the Great Hall at the airport's entrance. This three-story atrium with windows and skylights provides a broad view of the mountains and is adorned with a giant mobile by Boston artist Michio Ihara. Comfortable seats were another improvement, and the airport's old slogan of "Easy come, easy go," still fits the new, beautifully updated airport.

Denver International Airport
8400 Peña Boulevard, Denver
(303) 342-2200, (800) 247-2336
www.flydenver.com
DIA celebrated its 10th anniversary in 2005, and is now ranked the 5th busiest airport in the nation. United Airlines utilizes DIA as one of its operations hubs, but other major airlines include Air Canada, American, America West, British Airways, Continental, Delta, Frontier, Jet-Blue, Mexicana, Northwest, US Airways, and Southwest Airlines. DIA extends over an area of 53 square miles, twice the size of New York's Manhattan Island and larger than the city limits of Boston, Miami, or San Francisco. Its six runways can land three aircraft at once using state-of-the-art radar.

The 34 distinctive peaks of DIA's roof are made of Teflon-coated woven fiberglass and are supported by a steel cable system similar to that of the Brooklyn Bridge. The peaks symbolize the Rocky

Mountains, but also resemble an encampment of tepees, an appropriate image since the site was once migratory land for Native Americans. Inside the airport, gleaming granite floors usher the visitor through the various sections of the airport, and white marble quarried from Marble (a tiny town just up the road from Carbondale) lines the terminal walls. The airport's centerpiece is the main lobby under the translucent "peaks," filled with foliage, shops, sidewalk cafes, and artwork. DIA has a variety of gift and novelty shops for last-minute gifts, reading material, and food. With the advent of stricter airport security measures, shops and restaurants located on the concourses are available only to ticketed passengers. Once you have passed through security, however, you are free to roam all three concourses. Among the venues to choose from are Chef Jimmy's Bistro & Spirits, KFC/Pizza Hut, Lefty's Colorado Trails Bar & Grille, McDonald's, Quizno's, Wolfgang Puck Express, Colorado Sports Bar & Deli, and Cozzoli's Italian Specialties. Everyone has access to concessions in the main terminal. Look for Brew Mountain ExpressO, Burger King, Creative Croissant, Red Rocks Bar, Taco Bell, and Stephany's Chocolates. Concessions with shops in the main terminal and also on the concourses include TCBY Yogurt, Seattle's Best Coffee, Pour La France, Panda Express, Domino's Pizza, Cantina Grill Express, and Auntie Anne's

Pretzels. Most of the cafes are open from 7:00 A.M. to 11:00 P.M. DIA spent $7.5 million on commissioned artwork, some of it replaced periodically with new exhibits. Don't miss the twirling pinwheels on the walls inside the train tunnels that shuttle passengers between the concourses, baggage claim, and main terminal.

Despite its intimidating 5 million-square-foot interior, DIA's ticket counters are conveniently located near the passenger drop-offs for both the East and West terminals. There are three concourses, and it's possible to walk to Concourse A (rather than taking the train) via an air bridge. Doing so provides some of the best views of the site, and allows you to watch planes taxiing into and out of the gates along Concourse A. The subway trains arrive and leave about every 60 seconds and whisk passengers quickly to all parts of the airport.

DIA is northeast of Denver and is reached via Peña Boulevard, which is at exit 284 off I-70. Travelers from the north can take 104th Avenue or 120th Avenue to Tower Road and then drive south to Peña Boulevard. These aren't great routes, however, because they have many traffic lights.

All the major car rental agencies service DIA including Alamo, Avis, Budget, Hertz, and National, as do numerous shuttle, limousine, taxi services and public buses. (See the "Airport Shuttles/Limousines" section in this chapter.)

DIA offers a variety of parking options, from remote shuttle-serviced lots to up-close valet parking. The remote lots charge $5.00 a day and are serviced by regular shuttle buses. Uncovered close-in, long-term parking is $9.00 a day, or $1.00 per hour, and also is serviced by shuttle buses. Covered close-in parking is $18.00 a day, or $2.00 per hour; valet parking is $27.00 a day, or $11.00 for the first hour and $2.00 per hour thereafter. Short-term, close-in parking charges $3.00 per hour, but overnight parking is not allowed. In addition, several privately owned parking lots offer economy-priced parking and

---

i *Post 9/11 security measures have made it necessary to drop off and pick up passengers quickly. Follow the DEPARTURES signs into Terminal Level 6 for drop-offs, and ARRIVALS signs into Terminal Level 4 for pickups. Cars are not allowed to park and wait at curbside, however, and unattended cars will be immediately towed. If you find yourself with a fair amount of time to kill before meeting a plane, you can pull your car into a 45-minute waiting area located alongside inbound Peña Boulevard just past the E-470 overpass.*

---

free shuttle service to DIA. USA Parking charges $8.00 to $12.00 a day and offers various automotive services—oil changes, car washes, windshield replacement—while your car is parked. Additional charges apply for these services.

DIA phone numbers: general information (303) 342-2000 or (800) AIR2DEN; airport police (303) 342-4212; ground transportation (303) 342-4059; lost & found (303) 342-4062; paging (303) 342-2300; parking information (303) 342-7275; security wait times (303) 342-8477. Online links to most of these services can be found at www.flydenver.com/search/contact.asp.

Regional Airports

Aspen/Pitkin County Airport-Sardy Field
69 East Airport Road
(off Highway 82)
(970) 920-5384

Located 3 miles northwest of Aspen, and 8 miles southeast of Snowmass Village, Sardy Field offers nonstop service to Los Angeles, Minneapolis/St. Paul, Phoenix, and Denver. It is served by United Express (operated by Air Wisconsin), Northwest Airlink (operated by Mesaba Airlines), and America West (operated by Mesa Airlines). With a 7,006-foot asphalt runway, the airport is nearly as busy serving the private planes and jets flown in by the celebrities and big-spenders who prefer to provide their own transportation. A free public bus system ferries visitors into town. Courtesy cars, limousines, van services, taxis and Avis, Budget, Eagle, Hertz, and Thrifty rental cars also are available on-site.

Vail/Eagle County Airport
Cooley Mesa Road, Eagle
(970) 524-9490
www.eaglecounty.us/airport

Located 25 miles west of Beaver Creek, 35 miles west of Vail, and 70 miles west of Keystone and Breckenridge, the Vail/Eagle County Airport provides daily nonstop service from 13 major cities (Dallas/Ft. Worth, Chicago, New York, Newark, Los Angeles, Miami, Houston, Atlanta, Cincinnati, Minneapolis/St. Paul, San Francisco, Philadelphia, and Charlotte), plus commuter service from Denver. It is serviced by United, American, Continental, Delta, Northwest, and US Airways. Rental cars and shuttles to Eagle and Summit County resorts are available on-site.

Yampa Valley Regional Airport
Hayden (near Steamboat Springs)
(970) 276-3669
www.co.routt.co.us

Located 22 miles west of Steamboat Springs, the Yampa Valley airport offers nonstop flights from eight major cities (Minneapolis/St. Paul, New York/Newark, Chicago, St. Louis, Atlanta, Dallas/Ft. Worth, Houston, and Salt Lake City) as well as commuter flights from Denver International Airport. Airlines that service the airport include American, Continental, Northwest, Delta, and United Airlines. For complete schedules, go online to www.steamboat.com/air. Rental cars are available from Avis and Hertz.

County and Municipal Airports

Centennial Airport and
Denver JetCenter
7625 South Peoria, Englewood
(303) 790-0598
www.centennial-airport.com

Fifteen miles southeast of Denver and open 24 hours daily, Centennial is a large and busy airport for private and charter flights. It has three asphalt runways measuring 10,001 feet, 7,003 feet, and 4,903 feet; an on-field Holiday Inn; and the Denver JetCenter (303) 790-4321 or (800) 343-3413, which provides limousine and taxi service, rental cars, a full-service restaurant overlooking the runway, hanger, and fuel service.

Front Range Airport
5200 Front Range Parkway, Watkins
(303) 261-9100
www.ftg-airport.com
Front Range is 9 miles east of Denver and has two 8,000-foot asphalt runways. Shuttle bus, limousine service, and taxis are available, as are fuel and hangars.

Glenwood Springs Municipal Airport
1172 Airport Center, Glenwood Springs
(970) 618-0778
www.glenwoodspringsairport.com
The Glenwood Springs Municipal Airport is 3 miles south of the city and has a 3,305-foot asphalt runway and a tiedown fee. Shuttle bus, courtesy car, limousine, and vans take riders to town, and rental cars are also available. Airport hours are daylight only.

Jeffco
11755 Airport Way, Broomfield
(303) 271-4850
www.co.jefferson.co.us/airport
Located near U.S. Highway 36—also known as the Boulder-Denver Turnpike—Jeffco is home to the weather-monitoring aircraft of the National Center for Atmospheric Research in Boulder. Amenities include an on-site cafe, and shuttle bus, courtesy car, limousine, rental cars, and public transportation to the surrounding areas. Jeffco has three runways with lights—9,000, 7,000, and 3,601 feet long.

Lake County Airport
915 County Road 23, Leadville
(719) 486-2627
www.leadvilleairport.com
Leadville claims the highest airport in North America at 9,927 feet elevation. It's 2 miels southwest of the city and has a 6,400-foot asphalt runway. Fees charged for parking, tiedown, and hangar. Courtesy car, limousine, and taxi service are available along with rental cars. Hours are 8:00 A.M. to 5:00 P.M.

Meadow Lake (Colorado Springs area)
Judge Orr Road and US 24
(719) 683-3062
www.meadowlakeairport.com
Three miles east of Colorado Springs, this small airport has no designated airport office and no national airline service. For private pilots, it has a 6,000-foot asphalt runway and 2,084-foot dirt runway.

Steamboat Springs Airport
Steamboat Springs
(970) 879-1204
www.yampavalleyinfo/transport0028.asp
With just one runway, this tiny municipal airport is open sunrise to sunset for private planes only. It is located just west of downtown Steamboat Springs.

BUSES

Avon/Beaver Creek Transit
(970) 748-4120
www.avon.org/avonshuttlewinter.cfm
Beaver Creek Transit (BCT) and the Town of Avon run regular shuttles between Beaver Creek, Avon, and Vail. The cost for these destinations is $3.00 per person. The BCT also makes stops in Minturn, Leadville, and Edwards. The fare for these destinations is $2.00 per person.

Greyhound Bus Lines
1055 19th Street, Denver
(303) 293-6555, (800) 231-2222
www.greyhound.com
Greyhound stops in Silverthorne, Frisco, Breckenridge, Glenwood Springs, Aspen, Winter Park, and most other major destinations around the state. Call for a complete schedule and "Go Greyhound."

Roaring Fork Transit Authority (RFTA)
51 Service Center Drive, Aspen
(970) 925-8484, (800) 854-5588
www.rfta.com
This local Aspen bus line serves Snowmass, Aspen, Glenwood, El Jebel, Carbondale, Woody Creek, and Basalt. Depending on how far you plan to travel, one-way

fares range anywhere from $2.00 to $6.00 per person. Pick up a fare and route schedule for more details. Special para-transit services within Aspen and services to the airport for persons with disabilities are also available.

Steamboat Springs Transit
Steamboat Springs
(970) 879-3717
www.ci.steamboat.co.us/transit/
The Steamboat Springs Transit bus line runs throughout the ski area and down-town Steamboat Springs. Bus stops are well-marked with white metal signs and black lettering. To travel downtown from a ski mountain condo or lodge, take any bus marked Condos or Downtown from the many stops in the ski area. All buses in town are free for rides anywhere in the local transit system, and the bus stops at least once every 20 minutes at all the stops on the line. Ask the driver for a complete bus schedule on your first ride.

TNM&O Coaches
Nevada and Arvada Avenues
Colorado Springs
(719) 635-1505
www.tnmo.com
From Colorado Springs, this line serves Colorado Springs with frequent runs to Denver.

TRAINS

Amtrak
Union Station, 1700 Wynkoop, Denver
(800) USA-RAIL
www.amtrak.com
Amtrak runs from Chicago (via Denver) or from San Francisco. The train stops at depots in Glenwood Springs twice a day and also Fraser. In Glenwood Springs, the train stops in front of the Hotel Denver. In Fraser, it stops in the middle of town.

Rio Grande Ski Train
Union Station, 1700 Wynkoop, Denver
(303) 296-4754
www.skitrain.com
More of an event than a form of trans-portation, the Ski Train passes through dozens of tunnels on its journey from Den-ver to Winter Park, including the 6²/₁₀-mile historic Moffat Tunnel (elevation 9,239 feet), which runs beneath the Continental Divide. Operating since 1940 and Amer-ica's longest-operating train in a ski area, the Ski Train has an on-board guide who describes the historic route as you go along. The 60-mile trip takes about two hours and winds through scenic South Boulder Creek Canyon, taking you through beautiful countryside you can't see from a car. The train stops at the base of Winter Park ski area. Free and frequent shuttle buses leave from there for the town of Winter Park and nearby cross-country ski-ing and tubing centers. Even people who don't ski enjoy the historic ride.

The Ski Train has 17 rail cars stretching more than a quarter-mile long. The round-trip price for coach class is $49 for adults, $39 for kids ages 3 to 13 and seniors (over 62); Club car prices are $74 for everyone. The Club car includes continental breakfast buffet and complimentary après-ski snacks. Train/lift-tickets are sold on the train. All fares are for same-day rides and are nonrefundable.

FREE TRANSPORTATION

Breckenridge Free Shuttle and Town Trolley
Breckenridge Ski Area
(970) 547-3140
http://breckenridge.snow.com/info/summer/pb.trp.asp
This free shuttle is provided by Brecken-ridge to provide transportation from the ski resort's base areas to parking lots and along the perimeter of town. During the ski season, it begins at 8:00 A.M. and runs about every 20 minutes. The free town trolley operates during the summer, travel-

ing up and down Main Street and to the area's condo and hotel areas. It runs about every 30 minutes and begins service at 9:00 A.M.

Dial-A-Ride
Beaver Creek
(970) 949-1938
This complimentary intraresort service is provided only for Beaver Creek Resort lodging guests. Call an hour or so before you need a ride in the Vail-Beaver Creek areas.

RFTA (Roaring Fork
Transportation Authority)
51 Service Center Drive, Aspen
(970) 925-8484, (800) 854-5588
Free City Shuttles follow specific routes

Since 1940 the Ski Train has ferried passengers between Denver and the base of Winter Park's ski mountain. Here, a crew member prepares the lead locomotive for its first trip of the season. THE DENVER POST/ANDY CROSS

within the City of Aspen, including the Ruby Park Transit Center, Hunter Creek, Aspen Highlands, and a special Festival Shuttle for the annual Aspen Music Festival each summer. Pick up a schedule for Free & Special Services of RFTA at the Ruby Park Transit Center on Durant Street in Aspen. All service in Aspen is free, and buses run from 6:00 A.M. to 2:30 A.M. daily throughout the Aspen area. Free shuttles provide transportation from the Aspen airport every 10 minutes during peak commuting periods (6:15 to 10:00 A.M. and 3:00 to 6:30 P.M.), and every half-hour during off-peak periods until 8:00 P.M. There is no service on Saturday or Sunday.

Summit Stage
Third Street, Silverthorne
(970) 668-0999
www.co.summit.co.us/summitstage
Each resort in Summit County has its own internal shuttle system, but the Summit Stage is a free transportation service that goes to Copper Mountain, Keystone, Breckenridge, the Frisco Transfer Center, Dillon, and Silverthorne.

Vail Bus System
Vail Village Center, Vail Transportation
Center, South Frontage Road
(970) 479-2358
The town of Vail bus system has the largest free bus system in the country and offers complimentary bus shuttles daily. Buses run regularly between the eastern end of Vail Village and western end of Lionshead. Frequently scheduled buses run to outlying properties, such as in East and West Vail.

AIRPORT SHUTTLES/ LIMOUSINES

Colorado Mountain Express/ Resort Express
0331 Metcalf Road, Avon
(800) 525-6363
www.ridecme.com
Colorado Mountain Express provides shut-

tle service to Vail, Beaver Creek, Brecken-ridge, Copper Mountain, Keystone, Glen-wood Springs, Aspen, and Snowmass Village from DIA and Vail/Eagle County Airport, as well as between those towns. To make reservations or check rates, visit the Web site.

Home James
Denver International Airport
Denver/Winter Park Airport Shuttle
Winter Park
(800) 359-7528
www.homejamestransportation.com
From Denver International Airport, this shuttle makes 22 trips daily with door-to-door service to Winter Park, YMCA Snow Mountain Ranch, Granby, Silver Creek, and Grand Lake. Rates are $46–$62 per person one way, depending upon the destination.

HummersOfVail, Inc.
2121 North Frontage Road
Suite #212, Vail
(970) 977-0028
http://hummersofvail.com/index.html
Serving Vail, Beaver Creek, and Aspen, HummersofVail provides service from Vail/Eagle County, Aspen, and Denver International Airport in H2 Hummer limou-sines. Prices range from $119 for a trip between Vail and the Vail/Eagle County Airport, to $295 for a trip between Vail and DAI.

Resort Express
Denver International Airport
(800) 334-7433
From DAI, this company offers frequent shuttle service to Keystone, Breckenridge, and Copper Mountain. Rates are $44 per person one-way and $88 round-trip to all three destinations. Reservations are required 24 hours in advance.

Smiddy Limousine
410 Silverload, Aspen
(970) 925-7505, (888) 925-7505
www.lightninglimoaspen.com
This service offers local and long-distance transportation that serves airports

throughout the state. Rates vary with des-tination. Call to discuss your needs.

Storm Mountain Express
Steamboat Springs
(970) 879-1963, (877) 844-8787
www.stormmountainespress.com
Storm Mountain Express provides private shuttle van service between Steamboat Springs and Yampa Valley Regional Air-port, Vail/Eagle County Airport and Den-ver International Airport.

TAXIS

Alpine Taxi and Limo
Steamboat Springs
(970) 879-2800
www.alpinetaxi.com
Alpine Taxi provides shuttle service between the Yampa County Regional Air-port and Steamboat Springs.

High Mountain Taxi
111 Aspen Airport Business
Center, Aspen
(970) 925-8294, (800) 528-8294
www.hmtaxi.com
In Aspen this service offers bike shuttles, trailhead rendezvous, and group charters of any size. Four-wheel-drive vehicles are available.

Vail Taxi Service
(970) 476-8294
www.vailtaxi.com
In Vail, taxis are available 24 hours a day. Rates vary according to destination but are generally about $5.00 to $10.00 for short in-town rides.

HISTORY 🏛

O beautiful for spacious skies
For amber waves of grain
For purple mountain majesties
Above the fruited plain!

—written in 1893 by Wellesley College English professor Katharine Lee Bates, inspired by standing on the 14,110-foot summit of Pikes Peak.

GEOLOGY

It's odd to think that the majestic Rocky Mountains we see today all began as mud, sand, and lime at the bottom of an ancient sea. But that's the primordial stuff of which mountains are made. The oldest rocks in Colorado are the gneisses and schists of what geologists call the Idaho Springs Formation—and are at least 1.8 billion years old. "These rocks appear to be the remains of ancient sediments, folded and metamorphosed into vast mountain areas long before recognizable life inhabited the earth," write Colorado geologists John and Halka Chronic.

The Idaho Springs Formation is visible near the town of the same name, west of Denver along Interstate 70. These accumulated layers of ancient mud, sand, and lime were eventually metamorphosed by volcanic activity, which is still evident today in the thermal hot springs after which the town was named.

The Rocky Mountains we see today have formed, eroded, and reformed several

i

Geology buffs who plan to drive around the state should purchase a copy of **Roadside Geology of Colorado** *by Halka Chronic. Much of Colorado's geology is easily visible from your car window as you are driving along Interstate 70.*

times by a complex series of events. These events include repeated uplifting, crumpling, folding, faulting, erosion, and various degrees of re-melting and re-crystallization. Early in the Pleistocene Epoch (from 3 million years ago to the present), the great continental glaciers covered much of the northern United States. Although the continental ice sheets did not extend as far south as Colorado, large glaciers formed in the valleys of many of Colorado's mountain ranges and created the contours, formations, deposits, and lakes that are visible now.

Great glaciers formed along the crests of the Front Range (the eastern side of the Rockies) and around the state in the Sawatch Range (near Leadville); the Elk Mountains and West Elk Mountains (south of Aspen); the Sangre de Cristo Range (near Crestone); Mosquito Range (Leadville area); the San Juan Mountains (Durango-Silverton area); and the Park and Gore Ranges (south of Steamboat Springs). By the time humans arrived on the scene about 15,000 years ago, the glaciers were melting. Several small glaciers measuring several football fields in size still exist in Colorado, among them St. Mary's Glacier west of Denver, Arapaho Glacier west of Boulder, and Tyndall Glacier in Rocky Mountain National Park.

HUMANITY

The search for game and good hunting rounds probably drew the first humans to Colorado some 15,000 years ago. About 14,500 years later it was the search for gold that drew a second big influx of humanity with the exploration and exploitation of the New World by Europeans. Mining, cattle ranching, agriculture—and more recently, tourism—have shaped Colorado's modern history. Native American, Hispanic, and Anglo cultures have blended to shape Colorado's character and flavor.

Colorado's first human inhabitants are believed to have descended from Asians who migrated over the Bering Land Bridge about 20,000 years ago. Scientists have found evidence of early humans near the Colorado border in northeastern New Mexico near the town of Folsom. Animal bones were found along with spear points from hunting weapons, known as "Folsom points." In 1924, scientists discovered "Folsom Man," the name given to Ice-Age human remains unearthed in the area. Folsom Man is believed to have hunted bison, mastodons, woolly mammoths, and giant sloths in a very different ecosystem than that found today in Colorado.

About A.D. 550, the Anasazi people created the first-known settlements in Colorado in the state's southwestern area—known today as Four Corners, because the corners of Colorado, New Mexico, Arizona, and Utah meet there. The "Ancient Ones"—until recently called the Anasazis but now known to be Ancestral Puebloans—left their distinctive signature on remnants of basketry and pottery and in the spectacular cliff dwellings of Mesa Verde, which they built and inhabited around A.D. 1150. Anthropologists don't fully understand why they abandoned Mesa Verde and disappeared in about the year 1300. Some suspect they migrated south to the Rio Grande Valley because of over-farming. Today's Acoma, Sandia, Taos, Zuni, and other Pueblo people of Arizona and New Mexico are considered to be their descendants.

By the 16th and 17th centuries, several nomadic Native American tribes had found their way to Colorado. The Utes lived in the mountains, and the Cheyenne, Comanche, Arapaho, and Kiowa lived on the plains. Other tribes found in Colorado were the Blackfoot, Crow, Navajo, Pawnee, and Sioux. Many Native Americans who lived elsewhere in the Southwest visited Colorado to collect clay for pottery, fossil seashells for their shamans, and turquoise for jewelry.

EUROPEANS

Spaniard Hernan Cortes had already conquered the Aztecs in Old Mexico by 1521 and opened up the Americas to European exploration and colonization. The search for gold enticed Spanish explorer Don Francisco Vasquez de Coronado to visit New Mexico in 1541, seeking the mythical Seven Gold Cities of Cibola, where the streets were supposedly paved with gold. Coronado is also considered to be the first European to enter Colorado. The Pueblo Indians of northern New Mexico had pointed him toward what is now Kansas (perhaps as a joke), but it's believed that Coronado passed through southeastern Colorado on his way.

Coronado never did find the Seven Gold Cities. At this time, however, the Spaniards named the area "Colorado," which means ruddy or red. By the 17th and 18th centuries, both the Spanish and French alternately claimed the territory that included the present states along the Mississippi River plus Montana, Wyoming, the Dakotas, and part of Colorado. The area was named the Louisiana Territory after King Louis the XIV of France. When the Spanish defeated the French in the French and Indian War in 1762, the territory was called New Spain. In 1800 Napoleon Bonaparte reclaimed and reinstated the name "Louisiana" in a trade with Spain—in exchange, he offered Spain an Italian kingdom.

THE COLORADO TERRITORY AND THE U.S.A.

Meanwhile, the newly independent United States was doing some expansion and exploration of its own. James Purcell of Kentucky explored the area in the early 1800s and found gold along the Platte River. Interest in the area continued, and in 1803 President Thomas Jefferson paid $15 million to France in the famous Louisiana Purchase, which doubled the size of the

United States, adding 830,000 square miles. After the purchase, the U.S. Army commissioned expeditions to explore the new territory, which included northeast Colorado.

U.S. Army Lt. Zebulon Pike led the first expedition to Colorado in 1806 by boat along the Arkansas River. He was the first to describe the mountain that bears his name, Pike's Peak. His expedition was searching for the headwaters of the Red and Arkansas Rivers, which they never found, but Pike gathered valuable information about the geography and natural resources of the Southwest and published his report in 1810. He helped define the exact boundaries of the Louisiana Purchase and the area that was still claimed by Spain (New Spain). After Pike's expedition, the two countries agreed that Spain would claim everything south of the Arkansas River and west of the Continental Divide. The United States would claim everything north and east of the same boundaries—though various portions of the land were still held by different Native American tribes.

The next significant expedition was led in 1820 by Maj. Stephen H. Long, who traveled via the South Platte River. Long didn't think too much of the area along the Front Range and called it "the Great American Desert . . . totally unfit for cultivation and, of course, uninhabitable by a people depending upon agriculture for their subsistence."

Later, in the 1840s, John Fremont, a second lieutenant with the U.S. Topographical Corps, came seeking a route across the mountains. One of Fremont's men, William Gilpin, reported that gold could probably be found in the area, and interest in Colorado's mountains started to increase. Gilpin would later become the first governor of Colorado. Meanwhile, the area's natural resources were already being rapidly exploited. In the 1820s, beaver hats were in vogue in Europe and the eastern United States, and such fur trappers and pioneers as Jim Bridger, Jebediah Smith, and Kit Carson were venturing into the unexplored wilds of Colorado.

After the beaver-hat craze died, trappers switched to hunting buffalo, completely decimating the once-numerous herds of the plains as well as the way of life of the Plains Indians. Relations with Mexico deteriorated over boundary disputes, and the United States and Mexico became engaged in a war. After two years, Mexico relinquished its holdings in present-day Colorado. The U.S. government, however, agreed to honor land grants previously given by Mexico to individuals who had agreed to settle along the Mexican frontier. Hispanic settlers founded the town of San Luis in southern Colorado in 1852, and that area became one of the state's earliest Hispanic population centers.

ℹ️ *Recreational skiing is thought to have caught on in Colorado in the 1880s, although hardy mountain residents had been doing it for decades as a way to get around once the snow was too deep for horseback travel. Scandinavian emigrant M. C. Jahran is credited with introducing the sport of skiing to winter tourists and residents of Grand Lake, a tiny town tucked into the southwest corner of Rocky Mountain National Park. In those days, participants often referred to it as "snowshoeing."*

THE GOLD RUSH

Colorado's modern history really began to take shape with the discovery of gold near present-day Denver. Colorado's first permanent white (and some black) settlers arrived in 1858, when gold was found along Dry Creek. Hundreds of prospectors arrived and worked their way north, panning Cherry Creek, Clear Creek, and Boulder Creek. Prospectors from the East, lured by newspaper reports, arrived in droves. As they exhausted these lower "placer deposits" of gold, the prospectors and miners followed the creeks up into the mountains, naming new towns after finding gold there. Idaho Springs, Central City, Breckenridge, Fairplay, and Georgetown came into being. Denver also began to grow as a supply town for the mining camps.

Colorado was beginning to have an identity of its own and, in February 1861, the Colorado Territory was officially established by the U.S. government. The following year the Civil War began, and many miners went home to fight. The Native Americans took the opportunity to raid many of the new settlements, taking revenge for the intrusion on their lands and hunting grounds. By 1964, reports of raids had stirred up the residents of Boulder, and Capt. David Nichols left with his "100 Day Volunteers" to engage in what is considered one of the most scandalous events in U.S. history. Nichols found the settlement of the peaceful Chief Niwot. The Arapaho thought the attack was a mistake and raised the American flag, but Nichols' volunteer army ruthlessly massacred the Indians, scalping women and children and murdering the gentle chief who had made peace with the first settlers in the area. The Sand Creek Massacre, as it was called, was the final blow to the fragile peace that had existed between the white settlers and the Native Americans dwelling on Colorado's eastern plains.

Gold and silver mining really began in earnest throughout the mountains by the 1870s and 1880s, and the installation of smelters in the towns and the single-gauge railway opened up the mountain areas to even greater development and exploitation. Silver became more predominant than gold, and in 1876 Colorado attained statehood and was nicknamed the "Silver State." Huge silver deposits were discovered in Leadville in 1877. Within a few months, the population went from fewer than 100 people to more than 24,000.

Just when everyone believed that nothing could surpass Leadville's silver, Walter Clark and three others discovered silver in the Roaring Fork Valley, and

In 1892 when gold was discovered in Colorado at Cripple Creek, more than $500,000 worth of the ore was dug. The following years, the total jumped to $2 million and continued to rise. By 1896, $7.4 million worth of gold came out of Cripple Creek, and by 1899 it was $16 million. Cripple Creek finally peaked in 1900 when $18 million wroth of the gleaming ore was unearthed. Still as late as 1917, more than $10 million in gold had been mined. These finds would represent the highest profits ever in Colorado history mined from a single area.

Aspen (originally called Ute City) soon became the richest silver-mining area in the United States. Aspen's glory days were from 1887 to 1893, when the town had six newspapers, telephone service, two banks, a waterworks, and—one of the few U.S. cities to have this distinction—electricity. Macy's Department store owner Jerome B. Wheeler, who had provided the town's smelter, built his famous Opera House and finished Aspen's elegant Hotel Jerome. But in 1893, it all came crashing down when the U.S. government abandoned the silver standard. Silver pieces plummeted, mines shut down in days, banks closed, and Colorado's mining glory was over.

19TH- AND 20TH-CENTURY CHANGES

After several decades of campaigning, Colorado women won the right to vote in 1893, only the second in the Union to earn that right. (Wyoming was the first state to extend the right to women.)

After the silver crash and through the 1920s, Colorado's economy shifted from mining to agriculture, ranching, and tourism. At the turn of the century, Colorado became a popular destination for people with tuberculosis, who came to be healed by the pure mountain air, dry cli-

Every day visitors came to Glenwood Springs to soak in its thermal hot springs, but those springs also created an underground fantasy world. Here, two young women pose inside Glenwood Caverns circa 1900, then known as Fairy Caves. FRONTIER HISTORICAL SOCIETY, GLENWOOD SPRINGS, COLORADO SCHUTTE COLLECTION

mate, and vigorous life. H. O. Stanley, inventor of the Stanley Steamer automobile, was one such person who came and lived for 30 more years. He opened the famous Stanley Hotel in Estes Park and helped with the establishment of Rocky Mountain National Park.

Western landscape painter Albert Bierstadt popularized the beauty of the Rocky Mountains in his paintings, as did British writer Isabella Bird in her book *A Lady's Life in the Rocky Mountains*. Bird's book circulated in Europe and the Eastern United States, and by 1882 was in its seventh edition. In 1915, President Woodrow Wilson declared Rocky Mountain National Park the nation's and world's tenth national park.

With World War I, things slowed down a bit, but during the Great Depression in the 1930s, the Civilian Conservation Corps and Works Progress Administration (WPA) built trails, bridges, and cabins in Colorado's national forests and worked on the state's highway system, increasing its attractiveness to tourists. In 1936, the WPA constructed a ski lift in Aspen out of a boat tow, two mine hoists, and a gas motor—and charged 10 cents a ride. But Aspen was not Colorado's first ski area, by a long shot.

Since 1917, Howelsen Ski Area had been operating near Steamboat Springs. Named after Norwegian skier Carl Howelsen, considered the father of Colorado ski jumping, Howelsen's was the first attempt to successfully turn a means of backcountry mountain transportation into a popular recreational sport.

With the outbreak of World War II, interest in skiing lagged, but during the war, the Aspen area was the training ground for the 10th Mountain Division. These elite ski troops were stationed at Camp Hale, where they trained for winter combat in the mountains of Europe. Members of the 10th Mountain veterans helped turn Aspen and Vail into ski resorts with the help of other financiers. Walter Paepcke, founder of Container Corporation of America, was Aspen's biggest financial investor and had initially investigated the

area as a corporate retreat. Austrian and local businessman Friedl Pfeiffer convinced Paepcke that a winter resort would be a better investment, and in 1947 the ski area at Aspen Mountain opened. In 1949, the Goethe Bicentennial Festival drew a crowd of thousands to Aspen, among them many celebrities who took notice of the area's beauty. The following winter, in 1950, the World Ski Championships were held in Aspen, placing the town and ski area firmly on the map as a world-class resort. In the continuing decades, other ski areas around the state grew, and new ones sprang up like mushrooms.

World War II also brought the creation of the Air Force Academy in Colorado Springs as a perfect training area for pilots because of Colorado's clear weather and high altitude. Ranching and agriculture continued as the state's economic backbone, while tourism continued to grow.

The late '40s were marked by a uranium rush on the Colorado plateau with Grand Junction as the base of activity. The prospectors arrived in droves, and the uranium mining continued for about a decade. The Atomic Energy Commission financed road building. Mills for processing the ore operated in Durango, Gunnison, Cañon City, Grand Junction, Rifle, and Uravan. From 1948 to 1960, Colorado produced uranium ore valued about $133 million. Production declined over the next decade, leaving scars on the land along with radioactive waste.

Manufacturing was the next boom, which continued for 40 years (from the 1950s through the '80s). The aerospace industry had a particular impact with such Eastern-based companies as Martin Marietta (now Lockheed Martin), IBM, and Ball Brothers moving to the state in the Denver-Boulder-Longmont area.

Another major economic shift came in the 1970s and '80s with Colorado's conversion to a service-based economy, keeping pace with a similar national trend. In 1987, Colorado led the mountain west in employment, with 256,000 employed in a variety of businesses including hotels,

Recommended Reading

Prairie, Peak and Plateau by John and Halka Chronic.

Roadside Geology of Colorado by Halka Chronic.

Stampede to Timberline by Muriel Sibell Wolle (stories and legends of Colorado's gold camps).

A Lady's Life in the Rocky Mountains, by Isabella Bird.

A Colorado History by Ubbelohde, Benson, and Smith.

The Coloradans by Robert Athern.

The Colorado Guide by Bruce Caughey and Dean Winstanley.

Colorado: Off the Beaten Path by Curtis Casewit, revised and updated by Alli Rainey.

Colorado Byways: A Guide Through Scenic and Historic Landscapes by Thomas P. Huber.

advertising, amusement parks, legal services, funeral parlors, and health services.

By the 1990s Colorado had the most federal employees of any mountain state with 53,000.

Among the other, smaller draws to the state include cyclical oil and gas booms near Rangely, Meeker, Julesburg, and a thriving network of educational institutions that attract students who settle in once their school days are over. The University of Colorado at Boulder is the state's largest institution with over 31,000 students; there are additional campuses in Denver and Colorado Springs. Colorado State University in Fort Collins has 25,000 students and the University of Northern Colorado in Greeley has over 11,500. The University of Denver, Metropolitan State College of Denver, and various smaller colleges and universities have turned the state into a hub of higher education. But Colorado's mountains and their beauty will always be the central force that continues to draw visitors, many of whom return year after year.

MOUNTAIN SAFETY AND ENVIRONMENT

Rugged, exposed, and untamed, the Rocky Mountains pose conditions not encountered at lower elevations around the country—or elsewhere in the world. For all of the beauty of the mountains, their power should not be underestimated. Lightning, sudden changes of weather, heavy snow, avalanches, extreme cold and high winds, dangerous driving conditions, road closures, and flash floods are a few of the hazards that can greet Colorado residents and visitors. But when adequately prepared, most of us revel in these powerful forces of nature that ultimately control our lives here, and they're much more pleasant and interesting than computers, banks, and traffic jams.

In Colorado's mountains, we're a lot closer to nature than in crowded cities or gentrified suburbs, and we need extra knowledge and respect for our environment. Otherwise, the consequences can be severe—or even fatal.

Much of Colorado's "high country" is above timberline, the level at which trees cannot grow because the weather is too harsh. Timberline ranges from 10,000 to 11,000 feet, and usually is slightly higher on southfacing slopes because of the added warmth and sunlight. The landscape above timberline is comparable in climate and conditions to the Arctic Circle.

Colorado's average elevation is 6,800 feet, giving it the highest overall elevation in the continental United States—and some of the country's most extreme climate and topography.

GENERAL SAFETY IN THE MOUNTAINS

Colorado's Rockies can take the unwary and unprepared by surprise. Remember: Traveling to timberline is much like visiting the Arctic regions of the world. Mountain weather can change from a warm, sunny day to hail, snow, thunder, and lightning in a matter of minutes. Snow above timberline can occur at any time of the year. In Rocky Mountain National Park, summer daytime temperatures at elevations of 11,000 to 12,000 feet average in the 50s (10 C). The record high temperature in the alpine tundra on Rocky Mountain National Park's Trail Ridge Road is only 63 degrees (17 C). Wind chill can make these temperatures feel much lower—and sustained winds of 30 to 90 mph at higher elevations (with even higher-velocity gusts) can quickly make summer outings quite chilly and winter ventures bitter cold.

Visiting the Colorado mountains can be a safe and extremely rewarding experience, as long as people are prepared and aware of the following dangers. As usual, knowledge and prevention are the best way to make your trip safe and enjoyable.

ALTITUDE SICKNESS

Altitude sickness can affect anyone coming from a lower altitude to a higher one—particularly the high elevations of Colorado's mountains. The air above 8,000 feet contains 40 percent less oxygen than that at sea level. Visitors often experience altitude sickness coming from sea level to Denver, which is around 5,300 feet high. Most people in good health will experience nothing more than a headache or a little light-headedness, so don't panic if you feel these symptoms. Usually, altitude sickness is not severe and goes away with a couple of aspirin and rest, or a return to lower elevations. But symptoms can also include dizziness, nausea, shortness of breath, and impaired mental abilities. Breathing into a paper or plastic bag for five minutes reduces these symptoms.

To avoid altitude sickness, refrain from strenuous activity for your first few days at high altitude. Move slowly above timberline, eat lightly, and drink fluids frequently. Alcoholic beverages may aggravate the symptoms. People with respiratory or heart problems should check with a physician before going to high elevations. Lowlanders visiting Colorado for a skiing or backpacking vacation should acclimate gradually, spending a few days at lower elevations (5,000 to 9,000 feet) before any heavy exertion higher up (9,000 to 14,000 feet). Getting off the plane from sea level in the morning and skiing an 11,000-foot mountain in the afternoon is asking for trouble. Actually, it takes a few weeks to fully acclimate, but each passing day spent at a higher elevation helps your body create the extra red blood cells it needs to capture and hold onto the limited oxygen in the mountains. Although it helps to have good cardiovascular fitness, altitude sickness can affect the fit and unfit randomly, which is still not understood by scientists. Some mountaineers in top physical condition can be stricken down by severe altitude sickness on one climb and be fine the next. So don't feel like a wimp if you become ill. It's a roll of the dice.

In severe cases, fluid can build up in the lungs, causing breathlessness, heavy coughing, and heavy phlegm. If untreated, these symptoms, called High Altitude Pulmonary Edema, can lead to seizures, hallucinations, coma, brain damage, and death. In tourist towns such as 10,000-foot Leadville, altitude sickness can be a serious threat, but the easiest remedy is simply to return to a lower elevation if symptoms persist.

SUNBURN

Even though air temperatures are lower, sunburn is much more severe at high altitudes. This is because the reduced atmosphere filters out less of the sun's harmful ultraviolet radiation. For every 1,000 feet of elevation, ultraviolet rays increase by 5 percent, meaning Colorado has more than 25 percent more damaging sunlight than Florida's beaches. Even at lower altitudes, Colorado's sun is very intense and can cause a bad sunburn on a driver's unprotected arm resting on an open car window. The most important rule is to wear sunscreen before participating in any outdoor activity. To avoid burning in summer, wear a long-sleeved shirt and a brimmed hat, and use sunscreen with at least a 15 SPF (sun protection factor) rating and apply it frequently. An SPF of 30 or higher is recommended for those with fair skin. Skiers and other winter sports enthusiasts need to be especially careful because reflection from snow can cause severe sunburn, particularly in such tender places as inside the nostrils, on the scalp, and on the ears. The worst danger comes during the spring, when the sun shines more often and reflects more off the snow. The sun also can burn your eyes if you don't wear glass lenses or sunglasses that filter UV rays.

DEHYDRATION

Colorado's dry climate, combined with exertion at high altitudes, can cause dehydration, a drop in the body's water level and often a drop in the body's level of salt. Symptoms include severe thirst, dry lips, increased heart and breathing rate, dizziness, and confusion. The skin becomes dry and stiff. There's little urination, and what is passed is dark. Salt loss causes headaches, cramps (often in the legs), lethargy, and pallor. Drink liquids— water, juice, or sports drinks—frequently in the mountains, and drink them before you feel the need. If you're feeling thirsty, your body's telling you that you're already about a quart low on liquids. Take along salty snacks such as pretzels, chips, olives, and crackers.

GIARDIA

Unfortunately, Colorado's clear rushing streams and mountain lakes are not considered safe to drink. Tempting though they might be, many mountain streams and lakes contain bacteria and a microscopic organism called Giardia lamblia, which can cause long-term intestinal problems. Symptoms include violent diarrhea, gas cramps, loss of appetite, and nausea. The organism is transmitted into water through wildlife feces and can be carried by dogs and cats. To avoid this scourge, which has ruined more than one vacation, carry your own water bottle filled with tap water. Campers and hikers should boil all stream and lake water for 10 or more minutes or use water-purification kits or the now-popular filter pumps. A microfilter must filter down to four microns to screen out Giardia.

TICKS

This small, flat, brownish-black member of the spider family is usually not a problem in the higher mountains above 9,500 feet. But at lower elevations in the warm seasons, ticks can be a concern. Wood ticks appear in the spring after vegetation begins to leaf in the Lower and Upper Montane zones, the areas below 9,500

feet. They can appear as early as February in forested and shrubby areas and remain active into late summer. They are rare in the subalpine zone and above the tree line.

Wood ticks can transmit both Colorado tick fever and the more serious but fairly uncommon Rocky Mountain spotted fever. While incurable, Colorado tick fever is not life threatening, yet it can make life miserable. It begins with flu-like symptoms, headache, body pains, and fatigue, then clears up for a few weeks and can reoccur again. Rocky Mountain spotted fever is marked by a high fever, muscular pain, and skin eruptions. It requires professional diagnosis and medical treatment and can lead to a coma or death if not treated. Lyme disease, a debilitating arthritis-like condition that can lead to heart problems (named for Lyme, Connecticut, where it was first identified), is uncommon in Colorado, but it does occur from non-native ticks that somehow hitch a ride into the state. A distinctive rash around a tick bite is an indication of possible Lyme disease infection, and a physician should be consulted. When treated early, Lyme disease is completely curable.

Ticks hang around on low-lying leaves and branches, attaching themselves to whatever unfortunate creature happens by and brushes the foliage. Applying insect repellent and wearing long pants and long-sleeved shirts helps prevent tick bites. The best precaution is to check frequently for ticks on your clothing, hair, and body, because it takes several hours for a tick to

High-altitude sun can be deceiving, even when the temperature is a moderate 30 to 50 degrees. The sun's intensity increases 4 percent for each 1,000 feet above sea level, so hiking above timberline without sunscreen can result in a ferocious burn. The sun's rays can also reflect off snow, so even a hat can't protect against them.

attach. After being outdoors, undress in a shower or tub or on a ground cloth *outside* your tent. Inspect clothing carefully before putting it back on. Destroy ticks, but do not crunch them with your fingers because if they carry disease, it can spread this way.

To remove an attached tick, disinfect the area. Grasp the tick firmly with tweezers close to its head. Gently remove it by pulling it upward and out from the skin. Never twist or jerk it—the tick's body may break off, leaving the head in your skin and increasing the chance of infection. Putting nail polish, cooking oil, or petroleum jelly on the tick can make it release its grip more easily. Consult a physician if you have localized swelling, a rash, enlarged lymph glands, or a fever in the days or weeks after a tick bite.

HYPOTHERMIA

Primarily a threat to backpackers, dayhikers, and skiers, hypothermia occurs from prolonged exposure to the cold and a resulting drop in body temperature. Hypothermia is a quiet killer and has claimed many victims in the mountains. It is most likely to occur when a person is exposed to cold for many hours, is engaged in strenuous activity (hiking, skiing, snowshoeing, bicycling) at high altitudes, is not in good physical condition, and has become overly chilled, tired, hungry, or dehydrated. Any of these factors increase the risk of hypothermia. Particularly when wet, it doesn't have to be that cold out—hypothermia can occur in 50-degree temperatures.

After shivering ceases, hypothermic people may exhibit a slowed heart rate, poor coordination, puffiness, pale skin, lethargy, and confusion. In severe cases, breathing slows, and intravenous liquids are required. Warm a person with hypothermia with warm drinks, shelter, blankets, a sleeping bag, and a warm body next to the person. Replace damp undershirts and socks with dry ones. Severe cases of hypothermia (unconsciousness, seriously lowered body temperature, such as with a person found in the snow) must be treated by professional medical personnel in a hospital or medical facility where the victim can be gradually warmed internally or intravenously with warm liquids to prevent heart failure. With hypothermia, the victim is the last to realize he or she is in danger, so keep an eye on your companions, and be particularly aware of elderly people who are more susceptible.

Proper clothing, particularly wind-resistant shells, greatly reduces the chance of hypothermia. Staying well-hydrated by drinking water frequently also helps. Keep a hat on if it's chilly because most body heat is lost from the head. Generally a person who is downhill skiing is not at risk because there is warmth and shelter nearby. People who are in the unpatrolled backcountry (wilderness) miles from any shelter need to be aware of the dangers of hypothermia, since help and warmth can be far away.

LIGHTNING

With frequent afternoon thunderstorms and many people interested in hiking above timberline, Colorado ranks high among the most lightning-prone states in the nation. Every year lightning strikes about a dozen people in Colorado, killing an average of three. From 1990 to 2003 in Colorado, 39 people were killed, giving the

Although beautiful, Colorado's mountains should not be taken for granted. Those interested in hiking or climbing them should prepare by getting acclimated to the altitude, bringing the right equipment, and staying in good physical condition. Here, hikers start up the trail between Grays and Torrey's Peaks near Georgetown. *THE DENVER POST*/ANDY CROSS

state the nation's third highest fatality rate.

In summer, the rule of thumb for hiking is to reach the summit or any other high-altitude goal in the morning and to be headed back down by noon. Pre-dawn starts are not uncommon among experienced mountaineers; it's best to plan on hitting the trail early to avoid danger and be back below timberline before afternoon storms roll in.

If a storm develops, stay off ridges and peaks. Keep away from trees, boulders, isolated buildings, and metal objects. If your backpack has an aluminum frame, take the pack off. The safest place to be is in your car. A tingling sensation at the base of the neck or scalp and hair standing on end with static electricity are signs that lightning is about to strike near you. Move rapidly to shelter. Do not stand still, no matter what. If you are trapped outside, squat and wrap your arms around your knees, keeping your head low. Do not lie or sit on the ground because if lightning strikes you or the ground and travels through your body, you want it to have a way out, an open circuit.

To estimate your distance from a lightning strike, count the seconds between the flash and the accompanying thunder and divide by five to get the distance in miles. It take five seconds for the sound to travel a miles.

AVALANCHES

While avalanches aren't a major concern to most visitors, Colorado leads the country in the number of people killed in snowslides. We average about six fatalities annually, according to Knox Williams, the director of the Colorado Avalanche Information Center.

Avalanches pose the greatest danger to skiers who leave marked boundaries, as well as cross-country skiers and snowmobilers traveling in the backcountry. Occasionally highways will be closed because of avalanches—either triggered as a preventa-

tive measure by the highway department or occurring naturally. Avoiding avalanches is relatively easy. Simply stay away from slopes of 30 to 45 degrees other than in groomed downhill ski areas, where the snow has been packed and any potential avalanches have been previously triggered. In the backcountry, stay out of steep-sided ravines, gullies, or obvious avalanche paths where all the trees are missing in a swath running down from the top of the mountain. Most skiers and snowmobilers caught in an avalanche have triggered it themselves. Avalanches usually start on large, open slopes, along ridge crests above timberline. If you must go into an avalanche area, do not travel alone, carry a shovel, and have every member of the party wear an avalanche beacon, a small radio device that transmits a traceable signal.

It is nearly impossible to outrun avalanches, which can travel at speeds of more than 100 mph. If you are caught in an avalanche, the most important thing to do is to get rid of your equipment—skies, poles, snowshoes—and to try to swim to the top of the snow just as you would swim in water. If an avalanche is coming from behind you, try to head out of its path into the trees. If you are buried, the most important thing is to create an air pocket around your face—keep moving. Once the snow settles, it packs like concrete. If you are being buried, try to thrust an arm up toward the sky. People have been buried and rendered completely immobile only a foot or so under, but were found and saved because a hand was sticking up out of the snow. If your car is caught in an avalanche, stay inside the car! The chances of surviving are much greater inside a car, which creates air space and protection and is easier for rescuers to find.

Since avalanches are very difficult to predict, crews from Colorado's ski areas and state highways regularly trigger them (after ensuring that all skiers and travelers are out of harm's way) to lessen public danger.

Avalanche training and awareness, while never an exact science, is very complex and requires hours in the field. Even those trained need to review and practice annually because speedy rescue is of the essence. Anyone buried in an avalanche for more than 30 minutes while probably die from suffocation.

Entire volumes have been written about avalanches, and one with good information that makes fascinating reading—including tales of survivors—is *The Avalanche Book,* by Betsy Armstrong and Knox Williams (Fulcrum, 1986). The authors are Colorado residents and experts in the field.

DANGEROUS CURRENTS AND FLOODS

Mountain streams may appear shallow and serene, but they often have strong currents, slippery rocks, and frigid temperatures that have caused many drownings. Be especially careful when fishing or when children are playing near streams. Sudden rains can raise stream levels rapidly—a foot or more in a few minutes—and even cause flash floods. If rain continues, move to higher ground. Flash floods and sudden storms are generally localized and hard to forecast. Areas with a greater danger near highways and popular areas are often marked with signs. In the event of a flash flood, don't try to drive out of it. You can't beat the water. Instead, leave your car and quickly climb as high as you can.

SAFE MOUNTAIN DRIVING

Mountain driving uses more gas than normal driving, and gas stations are often few and far between. Along Rocky Mountain National Park's 50-mile-long Trail Ridge Road, for example, there are no service stations, so begin mountain travels with a full tank of gas. The following practices will reduce your chances of car problems in the mountains, as well as heightening your enjoyment:

• Observe posted speed limits—roads are narrow, winding, and sometimes heavily used.

• Travel in early morning or late afternoon. Wildlife is more active at these times, and the light is more beautiful. During midday, traffic can be bumper to bumper at tourist attractions such as Rocky Mountain National Park.

• Be alert for wildlife such as deer and elk crossing the road. If one crosses, several more often will follow.

• Downshift to lower gears when going up or down steep grades. This will reduce engine stress and save your brakes from burning out. Manually downshift automatic transmissions. Go down hills in a lower gear than you use to go up.

• To slow down, tap brakes gently and repeatedly on downhills to reduce brake wear and possible overheating (or failure).

• At turnouts and parking areas, be sure to look first and signal. Watch for oncoming traffic. On blind corners, sound the horn to alert oncoming drivers, if necessary.

• When parking, always set the emergency brake, and park in gear (for manual transmissions).

• Lock your car when unattended, and place valuables out of sight, or take them with you.

• Stay in your own lane. Don't drive in the middle to avoid being near the edge. The roads were designed with plenty of room, and you'll only cause an accident by driving down the center.

• Don't be surprised if your car doesn't perform normally at high altitudes. Cars tuned for lower elevations may overheat or act as though they're not getting enough gas. Drive in a lower-than-usual gear to keep RPMs up and to avoid overheating. Don't pump the accelerator, as it will cause flooding and make matters worse.

• On warm days, some cars may get vapor lock in the fuel line. If this occurs, try to get the car off the road at the nearest pullout. Stop the engine, and allow it to

With its majestic curved horns, the Rocky Mountain bighorn sheep is Colorado's state animal and frequently can be viewed along Interstate 70 near Georgetown.

cool. If there is snow or cold water nearby, put it on the fuel pump and the line leading to the carburetor. Let the car cool for 15 minutes before trying to start it again.

• Never, ever leave pets in closed cars. Colorado's intense sun can heat up cars to high temperatures that will kill the animal in just a few minutes.

• For winter driving, be sure to have adequate tires—snow tires or chains are best. During bad weather, most mountain passes are closed to vehicles without good snow tires or chains.

WILDERNESS ETHICS FOR HIKING, CAMPING, AND BACKCOUNTRY TRAVEL

Various wilderness areas and national forests have their own sets of use regulations, but the following general guidelines apply to all areas. Remember: Even when we are careful, our presence and actions have an impact on the natural world. As our human population grows, negative impacts become more and more severe.

BACKCOUNTRY TRAVEL

Travel quietly and in small groups—but don't hike alone. Avoid disturbing others. Leave your pets at home to keep from bothering wildlife and other visitors. Stay on maintained trails whenever possible. Do not take shortcuts; doing so destroys vegetation and causes erosion. Tread especially lightly when trails are muddy, and minimize horse use when trails are wet. On narrow trails, walk single file rather than several abreast, and try to avoid congregating in large groups in sensitive areas.

Don't pick wildflowers or dig up plants; it's illegal in all parts, and permission is needed on private land. Be judicious in picking fruit so that you leave enough for wildlife. Comply with signs regarding vehicles and mountain bikes, which are prohibited on many trails because of erosion problems. Refrain from using bikes on muddy slopes, where deep ruts develop quickly, and yield to other trail users. If you are photographing or observing wild animals and they become nervous, you are too close. Back away. Give right of way to horses, keeping to the downhill side. The same rule applies to all large mammals, who will become stressed if you remain above them. Avoid disturbing nesting birds, and comply with closures designed to protect plants and animals. Leave gates open or closed as you find them, unless signs instruct otherwise.

CAMPSITE SELECTION

Use existing campsites in heavily visited areas to confine impact to a small area. In less-visited areas, choose a site well away from streams and lakes and out of sight of other users. Eliminate all traces of your camp. Carry out all trash. Do not bury it. If you must use soap for washing or bathing, do so at least 150 feet from any water sources, preferably with biodegradable camp soap (available at any outdoor store) and pour the water into absorbent ground.

STOVES AND FIRES

Though campfires may be romantic, they're bad for the ecology and are generally banned throughout the state after several years of drought conditions. In the past few years, carelessness in the high country—from illegal campfires to tossed cigarettes—has caused devastating wildfires. Authorities have begun cracking down hard on violators, and fines and prison terms can be imposed for those who ignore the high-country fire ban.

Colorado's mountains are well loved in all seasons because of the vast range of outdoor activities they provide. Guides on most trips offer tips about how to tread lightly on the environment. VAIL IMAGE/JACK AFFLECK

Besides, gas stoves are quicker, cleaner, and easier to cook on. Propane cooking stoves are now quite sophisticated, very portable, and easily fueled by small inexpensive propane bottles, so you don't have to worry about lugging a gas canister with you. They may not offer the glow of a campfire, but they provide the safety necessary for everyone. After dinner, instead of sitting around staring into an illegal and potentially dangerous campfire, circle your chairs and look up at the spectacular vista of a star-filled sky.

SANITATION AND TRASH

Human waste and trash are an ever-growing problem in the mountains. Treating the outdoors like "one big bathroom and trash can" is neither ethical nor courteous to those who will follow. As outdoor areas become more popular, mountain clubs have begun subscribing to the principles of zero-impact, a nonprofit organization that promotes exactly what its name implies.

Start by packing out all trash; don't bury it, don't leave it behind, and do a good deed by also packing out any other trash you come across. This includes biodegradable food. Don't just throw it on the ground thinking some local wildlife will finish it off. Human waste is trickier, because it's simply not practical to expect visitors to pack out everything. While a few products on the market offer pack-out solutions, many of them rely on plastic products, which, themselves, contribute to landfill problems. So while not the best solution, these protocols offer ideas of how to behave when nature calls, so to speak.

• Conduct bathroom stops at least 200 feet from any body of water.

• Always bury human waste in a small cat-hole. Use a garden trowel to dig a hole 6 to 8 inches deep and 4 to 6 inches in diameter. When finished, the cat-hole should be covered and disguised with natural materials.

• If you're camping in the area for more than one night, or with a larger group, cat-holes should be widely dispersed.

• Use toilet paper sparingly. Use only plain, white, non-perfumed paper and either bury it in the cat-hole or pack it out in a plastic bag.

• DO NOT burn toilet paper. It is ineffective and can start a wildfire.

WINTER PARK ❄

From ranching and railroads and resorts, Winter Park has made a seamless transition from its agricultural roots to its current status as a top-notch resort area with tons to do. Long before the first white settlers arrived in the 19th century and began ranching the land, the spacious Fraser River valley was home to bands of Ute Indians who found the abundant game and good summer weather to their liking. Winters, however, are bitter cold in the valley: Fraser frequently records the coldest temperatures in the nation. Nonetheless, archaeological digs near Granby revealed that even 1,000 years ago, the Indians had built circle habitations that would have been thermally efficient enough to withstand the minus-40 degree weather.

By the late 1800s the railroad was making its way west and the Fraser Valley was becoming settled by ranchers and farmers who raised the iceberg lettuce through World War II and periodically endured Indian attacks. One of the biggest influences on the valley was the completion of the 6-mile Moffat Tunnel in 1927, a project that allowed trains to avoid the avalanche-besieged "high route" and go beneath the Continental Divide. A staging area for construction crews, Winter Park grew into a worker's village, and some of the crews became the first to ski down the slopes at what became the ski mountain.

Winter Park ski area, one of the state's oldest, got its formal start in 1940 and actually was one of several downhill ski areas in Grand County. Known for its long runs and wide variety of slopes, the ski area was the resort of choice for Denver residents, many of whom rode the Ski Train each weekend to participate in the Eskimos ski school. In the 1970s the out-of-bounds area known for its beyond-expert terrain was incorporated into the resort. Today, the adjoining peak known as Mary Jane offers some of the state's best bump runs, open to experts only, and not much else. Beginner and intermediate skiers are better off staying to the Winter Park side. Winter Park today retains its identity as a train town, as most of the ski runs and amenities are named after train features: Gandy Dancer and Derailer, Runaway and Hobo Alley are well known; Riflesight Notch and Needle's Eye are local rail features.

Winter Park and Fraser, at the east end of the valley, are where most of the winter action is centered, and lately have become increasingly popular summer destinations offering hiking, mountain biking, camping, events, wonderful scenery, and a great climate. It now hosts Colorado's largest mountain bike race series. Unfortunately, the area has been discovered by developers in a big way. The face of the valley is changing rapidly, and condominiums and second homes are rapidly filling the open meadows that initially attracted people to the area. Housing costs, naturally, are rising quickly.

Farther west, the towns of Tabernash, Granby, and Hot Sulphur Springs have seen less impact, but more people are looking to these spots as retreats from the hustle and bustle of Winter Park. Granby Ranch, just outside Granby, is a growing ski-and-golf development after years of stagnation. The question remains whether the area will be able to retain its identity. Even further out is the cowboy town of Kremmling, which has avoided attention and still looks and feels much like the Wild West.

Up U.S. Highway 34, the summer resort town of Grand Lake also has changed little over the years and has an identity of its own. On the western boundary of Rocky Mountain National Park and nestled among three spectacular lakes, the town is a collection of summer cottages and tourist traps that remains quite charming.

ACCOMMODATIONS

Arapahoe Ski Lodge $
78594 U.S. Highway 40, Winter Park
(970) 726-8222
www.arapahoeskilodge.com

The old-fashioned ski lodge in the heart of town is cozy, functional, and family-owned. It has 11 rooms with private baths, a lounge, a rec room, an indoor pool, and an outdoor hot tub. Winter rates include dinner and breakfast, plus transportation to the ski area.

Beaver Village Condominiums $$$
50 Village Drive, Winter Park
(970) 726-8813, (800) 824-8438
www.beavercondos.com

This large project has 18 buildings with as many as 12 condos in each, ranging in size from one to four bedrooms. All have full kitchens and fireplaces. Amenities include a recreation center with an indoor pool and hot tubs, a guest laundry, free transportation to and from the Amtrak station, and a courtesy shuttle to the ski area, just 1½ miles away.

Beaver Village Lodge $$
79303 US 40, Winter Park
(970) 726-5741, (800) 666-0281
www.winter-park-colorado-lodging.com/hotels/beaver_ldg.htm

Opened on Thanksgiving Day 1940, Beaver Village Lodge is Winter Park's first lodging establishment, a perennial family-favorite, and pet friendly. All rooms in the main lodge have private baths, TV and telephone, and free Internet access. The restaurant is open only during the winter months, but room rates include the breakfast and dinner buffets. The lodge is within walking distance of most downtown destinations. Amenities include an on-site ski shop, hot tubs and sauna, laundry room, and the James Peak Saloon.

C Lazy U Guest Ranch $$$
Highway 125 northwest of Granby
(970) 887-3344
www.dude-ranch.com/clazyu.html

This award-winning, authentic dude ranch is the Cadillac of the genre, with all the amenities and ambiance of a luxury resort combined with the rustic touches of western ranch life and a price tag that would make Ralph Lauren gasp. The log walls of the two-story main lodge are covered with Indian blankets, for example, and the view from the outdoor pool and deck areas is of pine-covered mountains.

During their stay, guests lack for nothing. In summer months when rooms are rented in one-week blocks, guests are assigned horses for the duration of their stay. In winter, when rooms can be reserved for a minimum of two nights, they can ski out the doors and onto 30 miles of groomed cross-country trails, then return to hot chocolate or hot toddies served in front of the roaring fire.

Rooms are available in the main lodge or in roomy one- to three-bedroom cabins. The luxuries include top-notch service, spotless surroundings, excellent food, and niceties such as robes in each room, a sauna and hot tub, racquetball courts, a game room, a TV room, children's play areas, and a ski shop. C Lazy U also has a dining room, lounge, sledding and tubing hill, an ice skating area, and a complimentary shuttle to the Winter Park ski area 25 miles away.

Devil's Thumb Ranch $$$
3530 County Road 83, Tabernash
(970) 726-8231, (800) 933-4339
http://devilsthumbranch.com

In the 1940s, Devil's Thumb was a working ranch. In the 1970s it was an affordable, undiscovered winter haven for cross-country skiers and, in the summer, beckoned horseback riders and anglers. In 2001, new owners Bob and Suzanne Fanch decided to capitalize on this diamond in the rough, merging it with their adjacent Diamond Bar-T Ranch. They've been busy ever since, envisioning a first-class resort on the 4,000-acre parcel. They saved the original 1937 homestead and several of the original cabins that were built in the 1940s, but they've added elegant two- and four-bedroom cabins that rent for as much as $800 a night during the high season. The Broad Axe Barn was added to house an indoor pool and spa, and in 2007 a new 53-room lodge will be opened. Old friends will be relieved to hear that the Fanchs left some things well enough alone. The ranch still boasts 20 kilometers of marked snowshoe trails and more than 125 kilometers of groomed cross-country skiing trails. Guests also have private access to fly-fishing guides and lessons on nearby streams. The Ranch House Restaurant may be housed in the old homestead cabin, but there's nothing rustic about the grub. Chef Tricia Cyman keeps the menu filled with gourmet dishes, many of which are prepared with local and organic ingredients. It's tiny and so intimate Grand County residents routinely name it as the area's "most romantic restaurant." No pets are allowed in the ranch's 21 cabins, and a two-night minimum is required on weekends.

Gasthaus Eichler $
78786 US 40, Winter Park
(970) 726-5133, (800) 543-3899
www.gasthauseichler.com
An institution in Winter Park, Gasthaus Eichler is as well known for its 15 hotel rooms as for its German-American restaurant. The chalet-style inn is simple but comfortable, with a lounge, complimentary shuttle van, and adjacent ski shop. Rooms come with down comforters and whirlpool baths. Room rate includes breakfast.

Iron Horse Resort $$
257 Winter Park Drive, Winter Park
(970) 726-8851, (800) 621-8190
www.ironhorse-resort.com/index.html
If there is a prestigious address in this unpretentious resort town, Winter Park Drive is it. One of only two properties on that road, the Iron Horse is close enough to the ski area that guests can ski-in, ski-out. One caveat: Only intermediate and expert skiers can follow the trails back to the hotel, but beginners can ski to the base and shuttle back to their rooms at night. The condo-hotel has 130 rooms that include studios and two- and three-bath premium suites. All but the lodge rooms have full kitchens and sun decks. Amenities include a heated outdoor pool, four hot tubs, an exercise room, restaurant, lounge, ski shop, and free shuttle to Winter Park and Fraser.

Olympia Motor Lodge $
78572 US 40, Winter Park
(970) 726-8843, (800) 548-1992
www.olympialodge.com
If you're looking for modest rates, comfortable rooms with queen beds, and a downtown location, the Olympia Motor Lodge can't be beat. It has 15 units, some with kitchenettes.

Silverado II Resort & Conference Center $$
490 Kings Crossing Road, Winter Park
(970) 726-5753, (800) 654-7157
These two-bedroom, two-bath units sleep six. The resort provides a 24-hour manager on duty, a ski area shuttle, an indoor pool, hot tubs, saunas, a ski shop, and underground parking. All units have kitchens and fireplaces.

Snow Mountain Ranch $
1101 County Road 53, Granby
(970) 887-2152
www.ymcarockies.org
Run by the YMCA of the Rockies, this 5,000-acre retreat brings in nearly 50,000 visitors a year, many of them families. The Indian Peaks Lodge sleeps up to six in each of its 79 economy rooms, each of which has a private bathroom. Four or five can sleep in each room of the 47-room older lodges. Another 45 cabins are more expensive but range from two to seven bedrooms. Amenities include free ski shuttles, a Nordic center with lessons and rentals, an Olympic-size indoor pool, a whirlpool, an indoor roller rink, volleyball and basketball courts, a gym, a restaurant, a ski rental shop, and full-service stables.

Snowblaze Athletic Club and Condominiums $$
79114 US 40, Winter Park
(970) 726-8501

This rare condo complex comes with a full-service health club. Snowblaze is a block from town and a little more than a mile from the ski area. Units range from studios to three-bedrooms. Each unit has a kitchen. Some two- and three-bedroom units also have fireplaces and saunas. The athletic club, free to overnight guests, has a weight room, an indoor pool, a sauna, hot tubs, a racquetball court, and aerobic equipment.

Sundowner Motel $$
78869 US 40, Winter Park
(970) 726-9451, (800) 521-8279
www.thesundownermotel.com

One of the great bargains on Winter Park's main street, the Sundowner has a central downtown location, 35 large rooms with TVs, coffeepots, microwaves, and refrigerators. Shops and restaurants are a short walk away.

Super 8 Motel $
78641 US 40, Winter Park
(970) 726-8088, (800) 800-8000

This chain motel has 60 rooms, and it is centrally located in downtown Winter Park. All rooms have tables and chairs, credenzas, color televisions, and ski racks for storing your skies. A continental breakfast is served daily. Children 12 and younger stay free.

Timber House Ski Lodge $
196 County Road 716, Winter Park
(970) 726-5477, (800) 843-3502
www.timberhouseskilodge.com

No TVs, no telephones, no crowds. If you're after a traditional ski lodge experience, the Timber House may be just what you're looking for. The lodge has 35 rooms, including some in the old wing with shared baths, inexpensive dorm rooms and bunk rooms, and rooms with private baths and mountain views in the new wing. You can ski-in, ski-out of this family-run inn located just 700 yards from the Winter Park ski lifts. Full breakfast and dinner are included in the room rates.

Viking Lodge $
78966 US 40, Winter Park
(970) 726-8885
www.winter-park-colorado-lodging.com/hotels/viking.htm

Another of the businesses on Winter Park's Motel Row, the Viking is one of the most economical. It's within walking distance to downtown and on the free shuttle route to the ski area. Coffee and a continental breakfast are complimentary. Amenities include free wireless Internet, whirlpool, sauna, and ski shop. The lodge has rooms in a variety of configurations from doubles, to queens with two twins in a loft, to a double with a twin and a kitchenette. The largest has a king and a shower behind one door, two queens in a loft, a sofa bed, a full kitchen, and a bathroom below.

Vintage Hotel $$
100 Winter Park Drive, Winter Park
(970) 726-8801, (800) 472-7017
www.vintagehotel.com

One of only two properties on Winter Park Drive, just feet from the ski area, the Vintage is a condo-hotel. Guests can choose from among 118 units, some of which are traditional rooms with kitchenettes, the rest of which are studio to three-bedroom condos with full kitchens. Amenities include hot tubs, a sauna, a game room, a restaurant, a lounge, movie rentals, and a courtesy van shuttle to town and the slopes.

Winter Park Mountain Lodge $$
81699 US 40, Winter Park
(970) 726-4211, (800) 726-3340
www.winterparkhotel.com

This newly renovated hotel is located directly across the street from the Winter Park ski area. It features 162 rooms, 9,000 square feet of meeting/conference space, two hot tubs, an indoor pool, Moffat Station, and a full-service restaurant and lounge. There's also a game room for the kids, and the hotel is pet-friendly.

SolVista

Blue Spruce Motel $
170 East Agate Avenue, Granby
(970) 887-3300, (866) 512-8876
The Blue Spruce is a 14-unit mom-and-pop motel that has single rooms, one of which has three queen beds. Some rooms have kitchenettes, all have coffeepots, HBO, cable TV, and phones. Restaurants are within walking distance.

The Inn at Silver Creek $$
62927 US 40, Granby
(970) 887-2131, (800) 926-4386
www.sclodging.com/lodgning_inn.htm
You'll know you have arrived when you see this large, 342-room resort hotel appear out of the deserted countryside along US 40. The ski lifts are out of sight, 2 miles farther up the winding country road. The resort is more family-oriented and less luxurious than some, but you'll find large rooms, good mountain or meadow views from the private decks, and a restaurant and lounge. The outdoor pool is open year-round and is adjacent to an exercise room that has a few pieces of aerobic equipment and some weight machines. Tennis courts are just across the road. You'll also enjoy the guest laundry, horseback riding in the summer, and a complimentary shuttle to SolVista and Winter Park ski areas. Rooms range from the traditional hotel room to studio and master suites that sleep eight, some with kitchens and fireplaces. Children 12 and younger stay free.

Littletree Inn $
62000 US 40, Granby
(970) 887-2551
www.littletreeluxuryinn.com
On the east end of Granby, the Littletree has 48 rooms, some with kitchenettes, and an indoor hot tub that can be reserved by guests. Children 12 and younger stay free.

Mountainside at Silver Creek $$
96 County Road 8914, Silver Creek
(970) 887-2571, (800) 223-7677
www.sclodging.com/lodging_mtnside.htm
The resort's most convenient condos (they're ski-in, ski-out), Mountainside has 120 one- and two-bedroom units. Most units have fireplaces and private hot tubs; many also have lofts. The condo project maintains an outdoor pool and tennis courts. The nearest restaurants are at the base of the ski mountain and the Inn at Silver Creek.

BED-AND-BREAKFASTS

Alpen Rose $
244 Forest Trail, Winter Park
(970) 726-5039
This European-style bed-and-breakfast has five rooms, each decorated with furniture the owners collected while living in Austria and Germany. All rooms have private baths and a view of the Continental Divide, and one room has a whirlpool bath. A full breakfast and afternoon snack are included in the price. Smoking and pets are not allowed. Amenities include an outdoor hot tub.

Englemann Pines $$
1035 Cramer Avenue, Fraser
(970) 726-4632
Between Winter Park and Fraser, this seven-room bed-and-breakfast is open May through November. During the winter months it is leased to a private party. Although the home is modern, antique furnishings and family heirlooms give it a more traditional feel. Balconies off some of the rooms provide views of the mountainous countryside. Guests get a full breakfast, which also includes the Swiss Bircher Muesli, and have full access to a kitchen and TV room. A trailhead just across the street is good for hiking and mountain biking in the summer. Children are welcome, but pets and smoking are not.

Lake View Bed and Breakfast $$
164 Lake View Drive, Grand Lake
(970) 627-1200
http://lakeviewbedbreakfast.com
Built in 1998, this modern four-room inn may be best known for its unique location. It is situated just 3 miles from the west entrance to Rocky Mountain National Park and adjacent to three high-country lakes. During the summer, guests can hike, visit the Park, or indulge in water sports of all kinds. During the winter, they have free access to snowshoeing and cross-country skiing trails. Rooms come with a full breakfast and have cable TV, queen beds, and private baths. Guests also may gather around the fireplace, read in the library, or relax in the media center. Adults, no pets or smoking.

The Peck House $
US 40, Empire
(303) 569-9870
www.thepeckhouse.com
The Peck House opened in 1860 as a boarding house in the mining town of Empire and has been operating ever since. Now skiers and summer sightseers are the main customers of this charming Victorian inn. Its 11 rooms are furnished with period antiques; not all have private baths. The restaurant is known for its game-based menu and offers a continental breakfast daily. Winter Park is 40 minutes to the northwest; the gambling town of Central City is 30 minutes to the northeast.

Snowberry Bed & Breakfast $$$
1001 County Road 8, Fraser
(970) 726-5974
www.thesnowberry.com
With five guest rooms and seven acres, the Snowberry Bed & Breakfast may be the area's most secluded. It's relatively new, built in the French Country style. Amenities include a hot tub, a common room with fireplace, a terrace swing, Internet access, and massage service provided for a fee by the host. Rooms come with

private baths, and most also have private balconies. Room rates include complimentary wine and cookies, and a gourmet breakfast. Two-night minimum, children 12 and older, no pets.

Wild Horse Inn $$$
County Road 83, Fraser
(970) 726-0456
www.wildhorseinn.com
Although several miles away, The Wild Horse Inn is a sister property to the Snowberry Bed & Breakfast. It's built with 400-year-old timbers, but this log cabin is modern and very plush. The main lodge has seven rooms, all with down comforters, TV/VCRs, private baths, and private balconies. The cabins have king-size beds, tubs big enough for two, small kitchenettes, fireplaces, TV/DVD players, covered porches, and ski lockers. All guests get full gourmet breakfasts, but cabin dwellers can also request breakfast in bed. The host provides on-site massage for a fee, and all guests have access to a sauna, hot tub, and forest gardens. Two-night minimum, children 12 and older.

Woodspur Lodge $
111 Van Anderson Drive, Winter Park
(970) 726-8417
www.woodspur.com
During the summer, the Woodspur serves groups of 25 or more. During the winter, it's a 32-room bed-and-breakfast just 4 miles from the Winter Park ski area. The log cabin lodge backs up against the Arapaho National Forest and has spacious indoor common areas. Rooms are rustic, with handmade lodgepole pine furniture. The dining room has a tall ceiling and a giant stone fireplace. Prices include all-you-can-eat breakfasts and dinners, and fresh baked cookies are available après-ski. Amenities include a sauna, hot tub, game room, bar, guest laundry, and shuttle to town and the ski resort.

YMCA of the Rockies
Snow Mountain Ranch $
1101 County Road 53, 10 miles
west of Fraser
(970) 887-2152
www.ymcarockies.org
For those traveling on a budget, Snow
Mountain Ranch is a pleasant alternative
to fancier dude ranches. Nearly 50,000
visitors a year, many of them families,
absorb its 5,000 scenic mountain acres.
You'll find dozens of family-friendly activities, including biking, hayrack rides,
swimming, and hiking in the summer;
cross-country skiing and snowshoeing in
the winter.

RESTAURANTS

Caroline's Cuisine $$
9921 US 34, Grand Lake
(970) 627-9404, (800) 627-9636
Who would have thought that unassum-
ing Grand Lake would be home to a highly
praised continental restaurant the likes of
Caroline's? Diners come from miles around
for food that has been described as the
best in Grand County. Located at Soda
Springs Ranch between Granby and
Grand Lake, Caroline's offers everything
from escargot to steak Diane and a vari-
ety of fresh seafood. It also boasts a cozy
lounge, a good wine list, and live jazz on
the weekends during the summer. Reser-
vations are accepted.

Carvers Bakery & Cafe $
93 Cooper Creek Way, Winter Park
(970) 726-8202
It may be hard to find Carvers, tucked as
it is behind the Cooper Creek Square, but
locals agree it's worth the search. Its
quaint log building was there long before
the shopping center. The bakery is known
for its home-baked breads and pastries.
The cafe serves breakfast all day, and
lunch (featuring homemade soups, stews,
and sandwiches). Lest you think the food
is all fattening, Carvers also offers low-fat
treats to offset its decadent desserts.

Club Car. $
Winter Park Resort, at the base
of Mary Jane
(970) 726-8105
Skiers at "The Jane" who want a sit-down
lunch can find interesting and well-priced
food at the Club Car. The imaginative
dishes include pasta with roasted garlic,
tomatoes, and feta; burritos; sandwiches;
and soups. It is open only during ski sea-
son.

The Crooked Creek Saloon $
401 Zerex Street, Fraser
(970) 726-9250
www.crookedcreeksaloon.com
The Crooked Creek is the oldest bar in the
Fraser Valley and self-proclaimed
NASCAR headquarters for Grand County.
Breakfast, lunch, and dinner are served
here, featuring American and Mexican cui-
sine. The big, rustic bar is a local favorite,
and Winter Park employees often stop
here for a quick pick-me-up on their way
home. Monday nights feature Texas Hold
'em poker tournaments.

Deno's Mountain Bistro $$
78911 US 40, Winter Park
(970) 726-5332
Since 1973, locals have been coming
downtown to Deno's for pasta, grilled
steaks, pizzas, and daily specials. That
makes it one of the oldest restaurants in
this mountain town, serving breakfast,
lunch, dinner, and late-night meals. The
menu includes tiger shrimp and arugula
over linguine, chicken saltimbocca, baby-
back ribs, and Alaskan crab legs. Deno's
also has an award-winning wine selection
and a beer list that has more than 70
entries.

Fontenot's Fresh Seafood & Grill $
78259 US 40, Winter Park
(970) 726-4021
Comfortably settled into new digs,
Fontenot's continues to feature tangy
cajun food such as gumbo, crawfish étouffée, and blackened catfish, as well as more
standard fare such as pastas for the less

adventurous. Check for live music at the smoke-free Voodoo Lounge downstairs.

Gasthaus Eichler $$$
78786 US 40, Winter Park
(970) 726-5133

When it's time for a romantic dinner, locals and tourists alike vote for Gasthaus Eichler. The cozy Bavarian decor of this lodge with attached restaurant gets them every time. The dining room has stained-glass windows, antler chandelier, and candlelight, all the better to accent the rich Austrian and German cuisine. Featured dishes include Paprika Goulash, Kassler Rippchen, and Jagerschnitzel. The names may be hard to pronounce, but the dishes are easy to savor. Locals rave about the sauerbraten and special holiday dinners. Diners on a budget may be interested in the early-bird specials. Reservations are recommended.

Hernando's Pizza Pub $
78199 US 40, Winter Park
(970) 726-5409

When the folks in the know want pizza, many go to Hernando's for one of the widest pizza menus we've seen. Pizzas come in three styles: traditional with tomato sauce; Roma style with olive oil, basil, garlic, and sliced Roma tomatoes; and Simone garlic style, with olive oil, basil, garlic, cheese, and black pepper. If that's not enough, Hernando's also sells generous sandwiches, pasta, and stromboli (baked bread pockets stuffed with typical pizza ingredients). Food is always available for take-out.

Hungry Bear Restaurant $
5 County Road 72, Fraser
(970) 726-0069

Once a stage stop, the Hungry Bear now offers a variety of moderately priced "comfort foods" at breakfast, lunch, and dinner. Fresh fish and hand-cut rib eyes top the dinner menu, along with a variety of homemade soups and desserts. Vegetarian selections are available, as well as a Kobe burger. For those with a bear-size appetite, check out the Hungry Bear special breakfast.

The Lodge at Sunspot $$
Winter Park Resort, US 40, Winter Park
(970) 726-1446

Skiers and non-skiers alike can enjoy the scenery at this mountaintop restaurant. The upscale food court, The Provisioner, is open every day during the ski season for lunch. The dining room offers bistro-style lunches, featuring burgers, chicken, pasta, and salads. Skiers can use their lift ticket to board the Zephyr gondola, which is the only way to get to the Sunspot. Non-skiers can purchase a foot passenger lift ticket and take the ride to the top for lunch. The Lodge at Sunspot also offers elegantly romantic dinners on what are called the Seven Special Nights: December 23 to 25; New Year's Eve; Valentine's Day; Presidents' Day (a major skiing holiday in Colorado); and Thanksgiving. These are the only days the restaurant is open for dinner, and as you might imagine, the reservations fill up quickly. The gondola ride is included in the price of dinner on these special occasions, and both the service and food are top rate.

The Peck House $$$
US 40, Empire
(970) 569-9870
www.thepeckhouse.com

The Peck House, opened in 1860 as a boarding house in the mining town of Empire, now enjoys a regional reputation for its game-based meals and fresh seafood. Entrees include raspberry duck, New Zealand red deer, Mrs. Peck's beef and oyster pie, and Trout Clara Lu.

Remington's $$$
52 Fourth Street, Granby
(970) 887-3632

Settled in one of Granby's oldest restaurant locations, Remington's offers a wide-ranging menu of reasonably priced fare. Appetizers run the traditional route, including chicken tenders, onion rings, and chips and salsa. There's a wide variety of salads and hot sandwiches, and the entree portion of the menu ranges from lower priced Mexican fare all the way up to steak with all the trimmings.

Untamed Steakhouse $
78491 US 40, Winter Park
(970) 726-1111
www.untamedsteakhouse.com
Locals love the prime rib, steak, and seafood at the Untamed Steakhouse, but the menu includes lots of dishes with sizzle. Try the Ancho Crusted Buffalo Carpaccio, Martini Steamed Mussels, or Chipotle Maple Pork Ribs if you're looking for something different. Bread is fresh baked, and desserts are prepared in-house. The log-beamed dining room has high, vaulted ceilings, and the bar provides TVs and pool tables for patrons just interested in entertaining themselves with a cocktail and a game.

NIGHTLIFE

Buckets Saloon and Laundry
78415 US 40, Winter Park
(970) 726-3026
www.BucketsSaloon.com
Want to do your laundry and have a few laughs at the same time? Buckets Saloon and Laundry is the place to go. At the same time, you can watch TV, play pool on four tables, try your hand at video games, have a cocktail or two, and on special evenings hear live music or sign up for some karaoke. Since 1998, locals have kept this unique place in business, but tourists are welcome, too.

Club Car
At the base of Mary Jane, U.S. Highway 6
Winter Park
(970) 726-8105
Après-ski gets an early start here as the serious skiers and boarders who love Mary Jane take a load off before heading home. The bar has daily drink specials, four tele-

visions tuned to sports stations, live music on weekends, and a munchies menu that includes chicken tenders, artichoke dip, and smoked salmon. The action dries up for the year when the snow melts.

Deno's Mountain Bistro
78911 US 40, Winter Park
(970) 726-5332
Outside, US 40 is abuzz with tour buses bringing in new visitors, snowboarders wandering by with boards clutched under their arms, and families out in search of dinner. Inside, Deno's is filled with locals who pop in to escape the constant parade of tourists. The bar is a cozy kind of place, described as the Cheers of Winter Park, with tall bar stools parked alongside long, wooden tables. Visitors who aren't interested in catching up on who was last seen where with whom can watch sports on 10 televisions, including one as large as a theater screen.

Derailer Bar
Winter Park Resort, US 6, Winter Park
(970) 726-1564
Well positioned at the bottom of Winter Park Mountain, the Derailer gets first crack at skiers interested in après-ski libations. It's open every day from 11:00 A.M. to 6:00 P.M., with drink specials from 3:00 to 6:00 P.M. It's a loud, crowded, happy kind of place, with televised sports, music, and a great people-watching deck that collects the spillover crowd each spring.

The Silver Spur Saloon
15 East Agate Avenue, Granby
(970) 887-1411
About 5 miles north of SolVista, Granby is an authentic western town that provides entertainment for the locals. Its liveliest nightspot is the Silver Spur, which provides karaoke the first and third Saturday of each month. The saloon also serves decent steaks, but not the quality you can get at some of the posher steakhouses in Denver.

ATTRACTIONS

Cozens Ranch Museum
77849 US 40, between Winter Park
and Fraser
(970) 726-5488
www.grandcountymuseum.com/
CozensRanch.htm
In 1874 Central City Sheriff William Zane Cozens moved to the Fraser Valley for a change of pace. He and his family took up residence on a 700-acre ranch that included a home, a small hotel, a stage stop, and the valley's first post office. The house has been turned into a museum with rooms devoted to such topics as Ute Indians, Fraser's early day loggers, and Doc Susie, a frontier medicine woman. Summer hours are 10:00 A.M. to 5:00 P.M. Tuesday through Saturday and noon to 4:00 P.M. Sunday. During the winter the museum is open Thursday, Friday, and Saturday 10:00 A.M. to 4:00 P.M.

High Country Stampede Rodeo
John Work Arena, US 40 outside Fraser
(970) 726-4118, (800) 903-7275
Professional and amateur cowboys and cowgirls from throughout the Rocky Mountain region take a stab at winning prize money every Saturday between July 5 and August 30. They compete in the kind of events the West is known for—bull riding, calf roping, barrel racing, and bronc riding. Chow down before hand at a western-style barbecue.

The Moffat Tunnel
US 6 at base of Winter Park Ski Area
Winter Park
In the early 1920s banking and mining magnate David H. Moffat retired from his lucrative careers and turned his attention to shortening the arduous mountain route used by trains commuting between Denver and Salt Lake City. His solution: Bore a 6²/₁₀-mile tunnel through the mountain, eliminating a 23-mile length of track that took 2½ hours to traverse. Work began in 1923 and ended in 1927, at the cost of $18 million and 19 lives. The exit bore is visible from the base of the ski area. More information about the tunnel is available in the Caboose Museum, also at the base of the ski area.

The Peck House
US 40, Empire
(970) 569-9870
www.thepeckhouse.com
On the road to Winter Park, you may want to stop in Empire and take a peek at Colorado's oldest hotel, operating continually since the early 1860s. Although primarily an overnight venue, The Peck House also serves lunch and dinner. It was started by gold miner James Peck as a boardinghouse for travelers too tired to make the steep journey up Berthoud Pass. It has since become a favorite of locals and tourists alike who like its period antiques and game-stocked menu. It's open year-round Sunday through Thursday 3:00 to 9:00 P.M., Friday and Saturday 3:00 to 10:00 P.M.

Pioneer Village Complex
110 East Byers Avenue
Hot Sulphur Springs
(970) 725-3939
Skiing has been a part of Grand County's daily life since the late 1800s, but 1911 is a date that represents the start of something new in Hot Sulphur Springs. That year Norwegians Carl Howelson and Angell Schmidt rode the Moffat Railroad from Denver to the top of Rollins Pass and got off to ski. Nine hours later they arrived in Hot Sulphur Springs, where they demonstrated ski jumping at its Scandinavian best. The next year the town adopted the sport at its first winter carnival (it ran until 1940, when Winter Park Ski Area opened). As they say, the rest is history, and much of it has been preserved at this former schoolhouse. The skiing exhibit chronicles Colorado's first ski area, a short jumping hill on the mountainside behind the museum, and features antique wooden skis, rustic bindings, and photos of locals bundled up for snowplay. A surprising archaeological room traces man's first visits to the area 12,000 years ago, following

bison and mammoth. It includes 8,500-year-old artifacts from the nearby Windy Gap dig. The museum also houses a fascinating history of the Ute Indians, who were pushed out by white settlers in the 1800s, and photos of a German POW camp built in Fraser during World War II. Summer hours are 10:00 A.M. to 5:00 P.M. Tuesday through Saturday, and 1:00 to 5:00 P.M. Sunday. Winter hours are 10:00 A.M. to 4:00 P.M. Wednesday through Saturday. Admission is $4.00 for adults, $3.00 for seniors 62 and older, and $2.00 for students. Children 5 and under are free.

Zephyr Mountain Express
Winter Park Resort, US 40
at the base of Winter Park
(970) 726-5514
Want an aerial view of the scenery? Take the Zephyr chairlift to Winter Park's 10,700-foot summit, then choose what to do from there. You can walk back down, take a mountain bike ride, or hike along 45 miles of singletrack and jeep trails, or just have lunch at The Lodge at Sunspot. Rental bikes are available at the base of the mountain and can be transported to the top aboard the Zephyr. The chairlift is open year-round, with special "foot passenger" lift tickets available after 11:00 A.M. during the ski season.

KIDSTUFF

Alpine Slide
Winter Park Resort, US 40, at the base
of Winter Park
(970) 726-5514
The longest alpine slide in Colorado ends beneath the Arrow chairlift at the base of Winter Park Ski Area. Get to the top of the half-mile-long attraction by taking the chairlift to the top of the mountain, then ride a sled through 26 turns on your way down. Children too young to navigate their own sleds can ride with adults. It's open mid-June to September 1 daily 10:00 A.M. to 5:00 P.M. through September weather permitting. Children under 5 free.

Chairlift Ride
Winter Park Resort, US 40, at the base
of Winter Park
(970) 726-5514
Want an aerial view of the scenery? Take the Zephyr chairlift to Winter Park's 10,700-foot summit, then choose what to do from there. You can walk back down, take a mountain bike ride, or hike along 45 miles of singletrack and jeep trails, or just have lunch at The Lodge at Sunspot. Rental bikes are available at the base of the mountain and can be transported to the top aboard the Zephyr. The chairlift is open year-round, with special "foot passenger" lift tickets available after 11:00 A.M. during the ski season. Rides are free for children younger than 5.

Cozens Ranch Museum
77849 US 40, between
Winter Park and Fraser
(970) 726-5488
Some children like history; others can't be bothered. Those who do may enjoy the Cozens Ranch House Museum. This was a pioneer home, a stage stop, and a post office. Inside, rooms tell the story of early-day Ute Indians, settlers, Fraser loggers, and pioneer medicine.

Fraser Tubing Hill
455 County Road 72
½ mile behind the Safeway, Fraser
(970) 726-5954
Both the young and the young at heart enjoy sliding downhill in an inner tube at the Fraser Tubing Hill, a few miles northwest of Winter Park. The owners supply the hill, inner tubes, and a rope tow to ride up on and charge by the hour. This is a popular nighttime activity, under the lights, after a day of skiing.

High Country Sampede Rodeo
John work Arena
US 40 outside Fraser
(970) 726-4118, 9800) 903-7275
Professional and amateur cowboys and cowgirls from throughout the Rocky Mountain region make a stab at winning

Saddle Up! Colorado's Dude Ranches Wrangle Up Lots of Fun

Teddy Roosevelt once said that the best thing for the inside of a man is the outside of a horse, and that advice from nearly a century ago still applies—perhaps more now than ever.

And there's no place better for city slickers to find Trigger or Buttercup than at one of Colorado's terrific dude ranches, which offer worry-free, all-inclusive vacations at reasonable prices.

"Dude ranches provide a great escape," says Charlie Henry, director of the Colorado Dude and Guest Ranch Association. "Guests often come back again and again. And they love not having to reach for their wallets twice an hour."

Although the 34 member ranches in the statewide association vary widely by size, atmosphere, and activities, each must pass rigorous inspections guaranteeing that guests will find a great horseback program, scrumptious food, and warm Western hospitality.

While all ranches include meals in their prices, they diverge from there. Some still operate as working cattle ranches and enlist guests to help round up, drive, and feed the lowing doggies, while others cater more to the typical once-a-year rider who simply wants to enjoy some breathtaking scenery and a comfortable bed each night.

One thing dude ranches are not: public riding stables featuring head-to-tail

prize money every Saturday between July 5 and Augus 30. They compete in teh kind of events the Wesst is known for—bull riding. calf roping, barrel racing, and bronc riding. Chow down beforehand at a western-style barbecue.

Human Maze
Winter Park Resort, US 40, at the base of Winter Park
(970) 726-5514
Wooden walls form the boundaries of this popular labyrinth. Human guinea pigs enter at one end, follow the twists and turns to four check points, and finally the exit, racing the clock as they go. Friends and family can watch their progress from a deck above the maze. Prizes are given to those who maneuver their way through the fastest. The Human Maze is open mid-June to September 1 daily 10:00 A.M. to 6:00 P.M., then 10:00 A.M. to 5:00 P.M. through September, weather permitting. Children younger than 5 get in free, but getting out is where the real challenge lies.

Minigolf
Winter Park Resort, US 40
at the base of Winter Park
(970) 726-5514
This mountainside minigolf course has the usual 18 holes, but each depicts some historic aspect of Fraser Valley, such as

one-hour trail rides. Instead, most of the ranches require week-long stays during the peak summer season and offer comprehensive riding programs that turn greenhorns into top hands through hours in the saddle, lots of individual attention, and team building with a well-matched horse.

The center of Colorado dude ranching is Grand County, with its six dude ranches ranging from historic to posh that ranks the area as the "dude ranch capitol."

Drowsy Water Ranch, for example, was established in the 1930s and has been run by gracious hosts Ken and Randy Sue Fosha for more than 20 years. It offers wholesome fun for the entire family, centered on the day's horseback rides but also featuring weekly treats such as cookouts, square dances, fishing, and a terrific kids program that leaves the little cowpokes plumb tuckered out at the end of the day. The Foshas rightfully brag that most of their business comes from repeat customers and their friends from home, forming an ever-growing family.

Meanwhile, the C Lazy U ranch, located just a few miles away, offers pampering never envisioned by John Wayne. One of the few resorts of any kind to earn the Mobil Five-Star rating and the only guest ranch in the country to also receive the AAA Five-Diamond rating—repeatedly—the C Lazy U is luxurious and extravagant. In addition to miles of scenic horse trails, guests can enjoy skeet, tennis, private fishing, and massages, not to mention gourmet meals and a complimentary car wash at the end of the week.

To figure out which ranch is the best outfit for you, contact the Colorado Dude and Guest Ranch Association for a free brochure describing each of the member ranches, their amenities, and their costs by calling (970) 887-3128 or writing to the CDGRA at P.O. Box 2120, Granby, CO 80446 or visit the Web site, www .coloradoranch.com.

ranching, farming, and Native American predecessors. It is open mid-June to September 1 daily 10:00 A.M. to 6:00 P.M., then 10:00 A.M. to 5:00 P.M. through September, weather permitting. Kids younger than 5 are admitted free.

SHOPPING

Winter Park and Fraser are known more for their skiing than their shopping, but that never stopped a real shopper. Their strengths are sporting goods and gifts inspired by the alpine scenery. The top boutiques in Winter Park are concentrated downtown in Cooper Creek Square, Crestview Place, and Park Plaza malls. Fraser is just minutes away and has its own Fraser Valley Center, across the highway from a Safeway store. SolVista is an island unto itself, but visitors may enjoy strolling through the streets of Granby, a small ranching community about 10 minutes north.

Alpine Sun Ski & Sport, Ltd.
1124 Winter Park Drive, Winter Park
(970) 726-5107
www.skialpinesun.com
This store rents and repairs skis and snowboards, and sells the name-brand clothing and accessories to go with them.

Christy Sports
Cooper Creek Square, 78930 US 40
Winter Park
(970) 726-8873
Christy Sports is a full-service bike and ski shop, with rentals, sales, demo skis, and service. A boot-fitting specialist is on staff.

Elk Horn Gallery
78878 US 40, Winter Park
(970) 726-9292, (800) 285-4676
Regional and western artists are featured in this locally owned gallery. Winter Park artist Karen Vance is the most prominent of the local artists, painting ski scenes and landscapes in oils and watercolors.

Grand Mountain Trading Co.
231 East Agate Avenue, Granby
(970) 887-3776
For country-and-western gear and clothing, this place is the Real McCoy. The store serves farmers and ranchers for miles around. Any tourists who wander in get a firsthand view of the western way of life.

Rocky Mountain Roastery &
Coffee Company
543 Zerex, Fraser
(970) 726-4400
Coffee is fresh roasted here daily. Buy it by the mug or the pound. The shop also stocks exotic teas and brewing accessories.

Ski Depot Sports
Park Plaza, 78727 Winter Park Drive
Winter Park
(970) 726-8055
www.skidepot.com/index.cfm
Voted "Skiers Choice" by *Ski Country* magazine, this store specializes in ski- and snowboard-wear and accessories. You'll also be able to rent snowshoes, mountain bikes, snowboards, and telemark skis.

Trail Ridge Art Company
67 Cooper Creek Way, Winter Park
(970) 726-4959
Colorado art and crafts are featured, including contemporary paintings, prints, photographs, pottery, wood, and jewelry.

Winter Park Frame Works
78336 US 40, Winter Park
(970) 726-5656
From skiers to wildlife, this store carries limited-edition prints, posters, pottery, and gift items.

Winter Park Sports Shop
Kings Crossing, 78336 US 40
Winter Park
(970) 726-5554
www.winterparksports.com
Another favorite of locals, this store carries clothing to match the season, including a full line of adult and children's sportswear and outdoor wear.

Necessities

Fraser Valley Ace Hardware
425 Zerex, Fraser
(970) 726-5000
The valley's only real hardware store stocks all the little gizmos, including screws, lumber, tools, and whatnots, you'd normally expect from a such a place.

Hilly's Hooker Service
520 Zerex, Fraser
(970) 726-5841
No one wants to think about the possibilities, but sometimes you find yourself stuck in the snow or locked out of the car. Hilly's provides auto repair, towing, car starts, and locksmiths. In way over your head? Hilly's even provides, heaven forbid, off-road recovery and "winchouts," the industrial strength yank needed to pry your car away from snow banks and out of ravines.

Plant Orphanage & Florist
Cooper Creek Square, 78930 US 40
Winter Park
(970) 726-8494
Browse through waterfalls and listen to birds sing while shopping here for fresh flowers, silks, gifts, and greeting cards.

EVENTS
January

Mountain Dew Vertical Challenge
SolVista Basin/Granby Ranch
1000 Village Road, Granby
(888) 850–4615
www.solvista.com
Skiers and snowboarders of all ages and abilities are welcomed for a free day of recreational races, prizes and giveaways, music and entertainment. Sponsored by the Pepsi-Cola Company. Call the ski resort for dates and times, or visit their Web site.

Women's Three-Week
Progressive Ski Clinic
Winter Park Resort, US 40, Winter Park
(800) 729–7907
On three consecutive Mondays in January, women who want to improve their skiing skills are invited to enroll in supportive, six-hour classes. They must be comfortable skiing on intermediate trails. Registration is held in the Upper Balcony House at the base of Winter Park Resort.

Chef's Cup Race and
Benefit Dinner Dance
West Portal Station, base of Winter Park
Resort, US 40, Winter Park
(970) 726–1590
In early January, Fraser Valley chefs compete in two arenas to raise money for the Winter Park Competition Center. First they ski their way down a racecourse, then they prepare a fancy dinner for patrons, which is followed by a dance with live music. Spectators can watch the race for free from the base lodge. The dance and dinner costs less than $100 per couple.

February

Wells Fargo Bank Cup
Winter Park Resort, US 40, Winter Park
(303) 293–5711 (NSCD), (970) 726–5514
(Winter Park)
For over 30 years this event has brought together world-class ski racers with disabilities and Denver-area celebrities, along with amateur skiers and snowboarders of all abilities for a weekend of activities to benefit the National Sports Center for the Disabled (NSCD). The highlight of the weekend features skiers with disabilities competing head-to-head on parallel courses in the World Disabled Invitational. The Celebrity Challenge presents celebrities and former football stars doing their best to ski down the mountain racecourse. A silent auction follows after the races.

TransWorld Trans-Am
Series-Slopestyle Jam
Winter Park Resort, US 40, Winter Park
(970) 726–1590
The annual TransWorld Trans-Am is a fun-filled event for up-and-coming amateur snowboarders. Featuring never-seen-before snowboard obstacles in a relaxed and futuristic environment, the Trans-Am seeks to be a cutting-edge amateur event. For more information go to www.high cascade.com.

April

Spring Splash
Winter Park Resort, US 40, Winter Park
(970) 726–5514
When the snow melts enough that Winter Park closes for the season, they reserve the last Sunday, usually in mid-April, for a crazy celebration. Participants skid down an obstacle course wearing bikinis and funny costumes and try to ski across a 60-foot-long pool of icy water to reach the finish line. Ski area officials call it a "purely pagan ritual," and spectators crowd the deck of the Balcony House and the nearby slopes to watch the spectacle.

As spring weather brings slushy conditions, Winter Park celebrates its last day of the season with Spring Splash. Competitors ski a course that ends just beyond a pool of icy water.
THE DENVER POST/HELEN H. RICHARDSON

May

Granby Open Water Fishing Contest
Lake Granby, Grand Lake
(800) 325-1661
With the ice finally off the lake for the first time since November, anglers hit the water in search of the true trophies. There are big prizes for the winners, and a good day fishing for the others.

June

American Red Cross Fat Tire Classic
Winter Park and Fraser Valley
(970) 722-7474 ext. 197
www.redcross.org
Philanthropists willing to ride their bikes for two days to raise money for the American Red Cross are treated to up-close views of mountain scenery on the last weekend of June. Only the fit need apply, however. Even the beginners' ride is 15 miles. Experts ride Saturday and Sunday, then feast on gourmet food and dance to a live band on Saturday evening. Entry fees vary, depending on how many pledges are collected.

Pole Creek Golf Classic
Pole Creek Golf Club, Winter Park
(970) 887-9195
www.polecreekgolf.com
In early June, this 27-hole golf club north of Winter Park hosts a unique mountain golfing challenge. Players get three 18-hole rounds of top-notch golf, breakfast, parties, and live music.

July

Grand Lakes Fireworks Show
Grand Lakes
(970) 627-3372
A breathtaking fireworks display over the lake caps off a day of festivities in Grand Lake and all of the other towns in the county. Historically, Grand Lake has been the site of other fireworks on the Fourth of July, too, including a particularly bloody shootout over the location of the county seat back in the 1800s.

High Country Stampede Rodeo
John Work Arena, US 40
outside of Fraser
(970) 726-4118, (800) 903-7275
www.winterpark-info.com
Professional and amateur cowboys and cowgirls, most of them regional ranch hands, gather every Saturday night from early July through August to compete for prize money and display their skills. A western-style barbecue is served before the rodeo.

Winter Park Rock 'n Ride
Winter Park Resort, US 40, Winter Park
(800) 729-5813
In mid-July, Winter Park's base turns into a stage for classic rock bands such as ZZ Top and War. The two-day festival is supported by food, drink, clothing, jewelry, and motorcycle booths, and is sponsored by KRFX 103.5 FM and its popular drive-time jocks Lewis and Floorwax. As with any event of this type, expect free motorcycle parking.

Jazz Festival
Winter Park Resort, US 40, Winter Park
(970) 726-4221, (800) 903-7275
In mid-July the hills reverberate again a week after the Rock 'n Ride with the more mellow sounds of jazz. Past performers have included David Sanborn and Harry Connick Jr. Bring your own food, or buy it from vendors on-site. Tickets are $20 to $25.

Alpine Art Affair
Downtown Winter Park
(970) 726-4118, (800) 903-7275
One of the longest-running art festivals in Colorado is held the last weekend of the month in downtown Winter Park, with more than 80 artisans selling their work. Music, entertainment, and demonstrations accompany the show. Admission is free.

August

High Country Stampede Rodeo
John Work Arena, US 40
outside of Fraser
(970) 726-4118, (800) 903-7275
www.winterpark-info.com
Professional and amateur cowboys and cowgirls, most of them regional ranch hands, gather every Saturday night from early July through August to compete for prize money and display their skills. See our July listing for more information.

High Altitude Chili Cookoff
Winter Park Resort, US 40, Winter Park
(303) 316-1564
www.nscd.org
Some of the hottest and best chili this side of Texas is served up during this rite of summer. Participants usually are willing to share their recipes, or at least samples. But word of warning: the green often can melt a fork! Proceeds benefit the National Sports Center for the Disabled.

Rocky Mountain Wine, Beer, and Food Festival
Winter Park Resort, US 40, Winter Park
(303) 316-1543
www.nscd.org
On the first weekend in August, a Winemakers Dinner kicks off the culinary fun. Participants can attend wine and beer seminars, sample the wares, and fill up on food prepared by local chefs. The event serves as a fund-raiser for the National Sports Center for the Disabled.

**King of the Rockies
Mountain Bike Festival
Base of Winter Park Resort, US 40
(970) 726-1590**

In late August races, seminars, clinics, parties, an outdoor concert, and guided mountain-biking tours are held for bikers of all levels. If that's not enough, the Colorado Finals for offroad stage and downhill bike racing will cap the event. Entry fees vary from $32 to $42, depending on which event you enter.

October

**Annual Ski Swap Extravaganza
West Portal Station, base of Winter Park Resort, Winter Park
(970) 726-1589**

In mid-October skiers have the chance to part with gear they've outgrown or just grown tired of. Ski shops from around the region put their stuff on sale for up to 60 percent off, and locals bring their used goods to trade. Admission is $5.00 to preview the goods on Friday evening; entry to the sale on Saturday and Sunday is free.

December

**Christmas Eve Torchlight Parade
Winter Park Resort, US 40, Winter Park
(970) 726-1689**

On December 24, the town that boasts about always having a white Christmas takes advantage of the mood by staging a free torchlight parade at 5:30 P.M. In the best and oldest event of its kind, Santa Claus leads a procession of torch-bearing skiers down Lower Hughes Trail under a canopy of fireworks. Afterward, a Christmas Eve church service is held and all are welcome.

**New Year's Eve Torchlight Ski
SolVista Basin/Granby Ranch
100 Village Road, Granby
(800) 757-7669
www.solvista.com**

On December 31, resort guests and employees ski down the mountain in a torchlight parade at 6:30 P.M. A fireworks display follows.

DOWNHILL SKIING

Winter Park

**Winter Park
US 40
(970) 726-5514, (800) 729-5832
www.skiwinterpark.com
Base elevation:** *9,000 feet*
Top of highest lift: *12,060 feet*
Total vertical: *3,060 feet*
Longest run: *5⁵⁄₁₀ miles*
Average annual snowfall: *359 inches*
Ski season: *mid-November through late April*
Capacity: *33,510 skiers per hour*
Terrain: *2,762 acres, 133 trails (9 percent beginner, 21 percent intermediate, 70 percent advanced/expert)*
Lift tickets: *$72 all-day adult*
Snow reports: *(303) 572-SNOW (Denver number)*
Getting there: *Winter Park is 67 miles northwest of Denver via I-70 to US 40 west over Berthoud Pass. Amtrak provides daily service to nearby Fraser, with taxi or van service from the station to all hotels, (970) 726-5587. On winter weekends and holidays, the fabulous Ski Train carries skiers from Denver's Union Station along a spectacular route to the base of Winter Park and returns them to Denver in the evening, (303) 296-4754.*

No question about it, Winter Park deserves the self-proclaimed title of "Colorado's Favorite Resort." Winter Park has a reputation as a skier's resort (as opposed to a posh vacationer's resort). The unpretentious mountain attracts a whopping third of its million skiers from Denver and nearby cities.

The first skiers to climb Winter Park's slopes were Norwegian railroad workers hard at work building the 6²⁄₁₀-mile Moffat Tunnel beneath the Continental Divide, transforming rail service to the West. Later, the legendary ski runs at the connected Mary Jane mountain would be named after railroad terms: Gandy Dancer and Riflesight Notch, Railbender and Derailer.

Formally, the snowy playground opened in 1940 as, literally, a winter park owned by the city of Denver, and built its reputation on family skiing. Winter Park had a children's center when children at ski areas weren't cool. The tradition endures at the main ski area, where the base area is equipped with restaurants and a health clinic, trails are named for *Alice in Wonderland* characters, and nursing mothers rent beepers so they can be paged when their babies are ready for lunch. The main mountain and intermediate Vasquez Ridge area are prime terrain for most skiers, and an enclosed 30-acre beginners' area is flat and comforting to beginners taking lessons with the first-class ski instructors.

In 1975 Mary Jane mountain was opened to attract an entirely different brand of skier, one who wasn't content just to cruise groomed runs. Its average fan is 24, male, and in search of a downhill thrill satisfied by the steep chutes and endless bumps that look like Braille gone mad.

On the season's last ski day, usually in late April, Winter Park hosts Spring Splash, described by locals as a "purely pagan ritual" in which skiers in shorts and bathing suits follow crazy courses that end in a 60-foot pond of ice water.

Since 1970 Winter Park has had the world's largest and most successful ski program for the disabled. Called the National Sports Center for the Disabled, the pioneering program provides low-cost lessons and special adaptive equipment for 2,500 people a year who have all kinds of disabilities, trains serious competitors for its Disabled Ski Team, and offers snowboarding, snowshoeing, and cross-country skiing for athletes with disabilities.

Although welcome on any run in the park, snowboarders can savor three of their own terrain parks, Railyard, Dogpatch, and Discovery Park.

The nearby towns of Winter Park and Fraser provide housing, shopping, nightlife,

and leisure activities, but the social scene can be considered somewhat unfulfilling albeit improving. The nearby town of Fraser, nicknamed the Ice Box of the Nation, often has the continent's coldest temperatures—minus-20 mornings are common; minus-40 prompts locals to put on another layer and complain that it's getting a bit cool.

Granby

SolVista Basin/Granby Ranch
1000 Village Road
(800) 757-7669
www.solvista.com
Resort elevation: *8,202 feet*
Top of highest lift: *9,202 feet*
Total vertical: *1,000 feet*
Longest run: *1½ miles*
Average annual snowfall: *180 inches*
Ski season: Thanksgiving Day to mid-April
Capacity: *5,400 skiers per hour*
Terrain: *251 acres, 33 trails (30 percent beginner and novice, 50 percent intermediate, 20 percent advanced)*
Night skiing: *Three runs, open until 9:00 P.M.*
Lift tickets: *$42–$46 all-day adult*
Snow reports: *(800) 754-7458*
Getting There: *SolVista is 78 miles northwest of Denver via I-70 to US 40 west over Berthoud Pass. Amtrak stops daily in Granby (2 miles away) on its route between San Francisco and Chicago.*

In an area more gentle and rural than most Colorado ski areas, SolVista is best known as a learn-to-ski spot for budget-minded families. If loud parties and wild nightlife are an important part of your ski

---

i

Skiing doesn't always have to be expensive. Children 5 and under can ski free at both Winter Park and SolVista Basin. People of all ages can ski all day for $10 at Winter Park when they stick to Galloping Goose, a beginners' lift at the bottom of Mary Jane Mountain that runs only on weekends and holidays.

Mary Jane Mountain has been open since 1975, and is designed to attract a younger, more adventurous skier than Winter Park's more mature groomed slopes. THE DENVER POST/WILL SINGLETON

vacation, think again. In their place, you'll find a congenial resort that caters to families who want good instruction in a safe, comfortable environment.

The ski area is in a self-contained basin two miles from the sleepy utilitarian town of Granby and serviced primarily by the base lodge, several ski-in, ski-out condos, and the Inn at Silver Creek. To reach it, you'll travel 15 miles north of Winter Park.

SolVista opened in 1983 and was purchased in 1995 by Brazilian Airlines scion Marise Cipriani, who has invested bundles in the underachieving resort. Unlike most ski areas, the land beneath the ski area is not leased from the U.S. Forest Service but is privately owned. On it you will find log cabins that date back to Colorado's mining days—and the foundations of a few cabins

that weren't so durable. You'll also find skiing on two small peaks, one easy enough for beginners and the other challenging enough to satisfy intermediates. Trails on both return to the same base area.

The easy East Peak has trails so wide that navigating them has been described as ballroom skiing. The largest is called Buckhorn and is flanked by ski parks open only to kids 14 and younger. West Mountain is a little higher, with an earth-bermed half-pipe for snowboarders and a steep, bumpy run called Widowmaker. Expansion plans and development of hundreds of upper-end resort homes are in the works, with new warm-weather activities planned for summer (such as boating on Grand Lake, 20 miles away) and a broader range of cold-weather activities offered during the winter.

To attract beginners, SolVista offers a learn-to-ski promotion that costs $99 for two days of lift tickets, rentals, and full-day lessons. If you survive that you're entitled to ski free for the rest of the season. Other free tickets go to seniors 70 and over and kids 5 and under.

NORDIC/CROSS-COUNTRY

If you'd rather power yourself across gently sloping terrain, you'll find more than 200 kilometers of cross-country trails in the immediate vicinity.

Devil's Thumb Ranch
3530 County Road 83, Tabernash
(970) 726-8231, (800) 933-4339
http://devilsthumbranch.com
Devil's Thumb Ranch in nearby Tabernash has 105 kilometers of trails for all levels. It also offers lessons, rentals, and snowshoeing. Winding through the pines rimming the Fraser Valley, the groomed trails offer soul-refreshing forays.

Grand Lake Touring Center
County Road 48, Grand Lake
(970) 627-8008
About 30 miles from Winter Park, the summer resort town of Grand Lake is more widely known as the snowmobile capital of the state as soon as the snow flies. But tucked away in the trees are 30 kilometers of groomed nordic skiing trails operated by the local metropolitan recreation district, a ski shop, and pleasant fireside lodge.

YMCA of the Rockies
Snow Mountain Ranch
1101 County Road 53, Granby
(970) 887-2152
Snow Mountain Ranch maintains another 100 kilometers of groomed trails with spectacular views of the Continental Divide. Set amid a year-round resort that's open to the public, the nordic center also features a lighted 3-kilometer loop for night skiing and a biathlon shooting range.

Keeping kids warm and dry is the key to their enjoyment of the mountains. Avoid jeans and cotton, but instead clothe them in insulated ski suits and parkas. Don't forget that even children need good sunglasses or goggles to protect their eyes from the bright glare.

OTHER WINTER RECREATION
Dog Sledding

Dog Sled Rides of Winter Park
505½ Zerex, Winter Park
(970) 726-8326
www.dogsledrides.com/winterpark
Ride through the backcountry on sleds pulled by eight or ten Siberian huskies at speeds of 20 miles an hour (downhill). One-hour rides begin at 9:00 and 10:30 A.M. and 12:30, 2:00, and 3:30 P.M. Reservations are required. Prices vary.

Sleigh Rides

Hailing a sleigh in Winter Park may appear nearly as easy as hailing a cab in Manhattan. (You actually need reservations for the sleighs, though.) At least six companies offer sleigh rides through meadows, on historic ranch land, or out to lunch.

Dashing Thru the Snow Sleigh Rides
85 County Road 5101, Fraser
(970) 726-0900, (888) 384-6773
www.dashingthruthesnow.com
Bonfire and dessert rides take you through the woods snuggled under warm, woolen blankets in a sleigh pulled by a team of bell-laden draft horses. All that's missing is going over the river to grandma's house, but the hot cocoa and bonfire, or the wonderful desserts at the end of the ride make up for it. The bonfire/hot cocoa ride is $18 for adults, $15

for kids 5 to 11, and free for those under 5. For the dessert ride—a 3-mile round trip to a rustic cabin and selected desserts—the cost is $40 per person, and is generally recommended for adults.

Snow Mountain Ranch
1344 County Road 53, Granby
(970) 726-4628
Lazy U 2 Livery provides the draft horses and drives the sleighs on this YMCA-owned resort property. Catch a ride during the winter and view the snowy wonderland from beneath a warm buggy blanket. You'll stop at a bonfire to roast marshmallows midway through. During the summer months Lazy U 2 rents excellent saddle horses you can take on trail rides across the same acreage. Sleigh rides leave at 1:30, 5:00, and 7:00 P.M.

Snowcats

Winter Park Resort
US 40, at the base of Winter Park
(800) 729-7907
A more passive tour of the Winter Park mountain is conducted from inside heated Snowcats, the enclosed two-track vehicles that maneuver over snow the way Humvees maneuver over the desert. Three times a day these people movers leave the Winter Park base on their way up mountainside ski trails to the top of the mountain. Guides stop for picture taking and a lunch or snack break mid-mountain. Tours leave daily at 10:00 A.M., noon, and 2:00 P.M. from the Winter Park base area. Cost is $39 for adults and free for children younger than 3.

Snowmobiles

Grand Adventures
Beaver Village, US 40, Winter Park

304 West Portal Road, Grand Lake
(970) 726-9247
www.grandadventures.com
Grand Adventures has two locations

where you can rent snowmobiles for guided or unguided tours. Maps are provided for the 100 or so miles of trails in the area. Reservations are strongly recommended, and there is a lengthy list of rules and restrictions for rentals and unguided tours. For example, you must be at least 16 years old and have a valid driver's license with a picture ID in order to rent and drive a snowmobile, and unguided tours require at least two snowmobiles go out together. Check the Web site for complete details on rental policies and rates.

Trailblazers
22800 County Road 50, Fraser
(970) 726-8452, (800) 669-0134
With more than 100 miles of maintained trails and ridgetop tours to 12,000 feet, this guide company offers a wide array of possibilities on snowmobiles. Boots and helmets are included and snowsuits are available for a small additional fee. Call for prices and reservations.

Snowshoes

SolVista Basin
1000 Village Road, Silver Creek
(970) 887-3384
If you're staying at SolVista, rent snowshoes for $25 a day at the ski area's base lodge, and trek the trail system used by cross-country skiers. A half-mile walk will take you to a historic settler's cabin. Ignore the rumors that President Dwight D. Eisenhower stayed here on one of his many Colorado fishing trips. It's persistent, but resort owners have been unable to verify his reservation. Hours are 8:30 A.M. to 3:45 P.M.

Winter Park Resort
US 40, at the base of Winter Park
(800) 729-7907
The Winter Park ski area offers a two-hour guided trip down a wooded trail so quiet you can hear your shoes slapping against the snow. Guides introduce the basics of

snowshoeing and talk about the area's history and native wildlife. Be sure to wear warm clothing and waterproof, insulated boots. Tours are $30, which includes rentals, and leave daily at 10:30 A.M. and 1:00 P.M. from the Guest Services Desk in the Balcony House.

Tours

Grand Adventures
Beaver Village, US 40, Winter Park
(970) 726-9247
www.grandadventures.com
This outfit offers guided snowmobile tours, horse and sleigh rides, and snowmobile, ATV, and horseback rentals. For the unguided tours, maps are provided detailing over 100 miles of trails. There are age restrictions on rentals, and prices and availability vary by season.

Tubing

Tubing Hill at Fraser
Half-mile behind the Safeway, Fraser
(970) 726-5954
Both the young and the young at heart enjoy riding a tube down the Fraser Tubing Hill, a few miles northwest of Winter Park. The owners supply the hill, inner tubes, and a rope tow to ride up on. You supply the courage to plunge down the steep course, the energy required to carry the tube to the bottom of the tow, and the strength to hang on while the rope pulls you back up the mountain. Children 3 and younger are not allowed on the hill; those 4 to 7 must share an adult's tube. Be sure to bring hats, gloves, and snowpants. Hot drinks and a warming house help take the chill off any time. Tubing Hill at Fraser is open 10:00 A.M. to 10:00 P.M. weekends, 4:00 to 10:00 P.M. weekdays. The cost is $15 an hour for riders 15 and older, $13 an hour for those 7 to 15, and includes tube rental. The season begins around Thanksgiving and continues through Easter.

HIKING

It's best to pay a visit to the local forest service office for detailed maps and information about local trails. Maps are available at the Sulphur Ranger District Office, (970) 887-4100, 9 Ten Mile Drive, Granby. Grand County also publishes an excellent recreation guide, which is available from the Winter Park/Fraser Valley Chamber of Commerce, 78841 US 40, Winter Park, (970) 726-4118, or the forest service office. Another good source of information for both hiking and backpacking can be reached by calling or stopping by Never Summer Mountain Products, at 919 Grand Avenue in Grand Lake, (970) 627-3642. Be advised that in Colorado's designated wilderness areas motorized or mechanized equipment is strictly prohibited, including mountain bikes, wagons, carts, and chainsaws. Wheelchairs are permitted.

Indian Peaks Wilderness Area
Continental Divide area north and
east of Winter Park
www.fs.fed.us/r2/arnf/recreation/
wilderness/indianpeaks/index.shtml
The Indian Peaks Wilderness is a 76,486-acre area along the Continental Divide that includes parts of Arapaho and Roosevelt national forests. It shares 2,922 acres with Rocky Mountain National Park to the north and is bounded by Rollins Pass to the south. Rollins Pass is on the Continental Divide east of Winter Park. It's the only wilderness area in Colorado that requires a permit for overnight camping—probably because it's the most used wilderness area in the state due to its close proximity to Denver and other cities along the densely populated Front Range (eastern edge of the Rockies). Permits are not required for day hikers.

The western side of Indian Peaks Wilderness (the area near Winter Park, Fraser, and Silver Creek) is managed by the Sulphur Ranger District Office, (970) 887-4100, 9 Ten Mile Drive, Granby. The eastern side of Indian Peaks is managed by the Boulder District Office of the U.S. For-

---

Perhaps the most enjoyable way to get to Winter Park for a day of skiing is to take the Ski Train from Denver, which takes a spectacular route through the mountains. Call (303) 296–4754 for reservations and information.

---

est Service, (303) 541–2500. That portion of Indian Peaks is covered in the *Insiders' Guide to Boulder and Rocky Mountain National Park.*

Backpacking/overnight permits—the only type of camping allowed in Indian Peaks—are available at the Sulphur Ranger District Office (address listed previously). Permits are required only from June 1 to September 15 and cost $5 for a limit of 14 nights. Group size is limited to 12 (including dogs and pack animals). All dogs must be kept on leashes, and there is a $50 fine for those that are not. Advance reservations are required for Crater, Jasper, Diamond, and Caribou Lakes. Permits are available up to a year in advance. Indian Peaks permits are also available on the day of your backpacking trip only on the eastern side, at the Ace Hardware store in Nederland and the Estes Park Visitor Center. The money from the permits is used for trail and other maintenance in the wilderness area, so it's for a good cause.

Arapahoe Pass Trail
(Indian Peaks Wilderness)
Monarch Lake
US 34 north
This trail follows Arapaho Creek 10 miles to the top of Arapaho Pass at 11,900 feet. The first 8 miles are an easy, gradual climb; the last two are tougher and steeper. The trail begins at Monarch Lake, as does the Buchanan Creek Trail, a more difficult hike along Buchanan and Cascade Creeks to Crater Lake, a good spot for camping and fishing. For an alternative and longer trip that climbs the divide, follow the Pawnee Pass Trail east instead of turning south to Crater Lake. It's a difficult 3-mile climb to the top of the 12,451-foot pass.

All these hikes pass through the lower forested area, which is full of flowers and (in some years) mushrooms. At treeline, great glimpses of the peaks and the pass come into view. Of course, climbing to any of the passes above affords an even more spectacular view of the surrounding Indian Peaks, most of which are 12,000 and 13,000 feet high with year-round snow-fields. To reach the Monarch Lake Trailhead take Highway 34 north from Granby to the entrance of the Arapaho National Recreation Area. Travel east on Forest Road 125 for about 10 miles to the Monarch Lake Trailhead.

Caribou Pass Trail
(Indian Peaks Wilderness)
Junco Lake parking area
Caribou Pass, at 11,790 feet, offers a fine view of the Indian Peaks after a steep, uphill trudge for 4⁴⁄₁₀ miles. For those wishing to backpack and cover a greater distance, continue over Arapaho Pass to Monarch Lake. The trail to Caribou Pass begins on an old road for 1 mile then becomes a footpath at the junction with the Columbine Lake Trail. The forested trail continues for another mile until it opens to meadows and finally the timberline. From above the treeline to the pass, it's a difficult half-mile to the top. But it's worth it for the splendid views of 13,000-foot Navajo and Apache peaks. From Granby take Highway 40 south to County Road 83 at Tabernash. Shortly after turning left on 83 turn left on CR84 and left after ½ mile on Forest Road 129. Travel north for about 11 miles to Meadow Creek Reservoir. Continue around the reservoir to the Junco Lake Trailhead and the west end of the trail.

Columbine Lake Trail
(Indian Peaks Wilderness)
Junco Lake parking area
For the first 1½ miles, the route is the same as the Caribou Pass Trail (see previous write-up). Then a marked junction indicates the way to Columbine Lake. A total climb of 3 miles brings hikers to this

pretty lake at 11,060 feet and offers a great view of the Winter Park Ski Area and the whole Fraser Valley. Some anglers report cutthroat trout in the lake (see our "Fishing and Hunting" section). It's usually quite wet and marshy around the lake. From Granby take Highway 40 south to County Road 83 at Tabernash. Shortly after turning left on 83 turn left on CR84 and left after ½ mile on Forest Road 129. Travel north for about 11 miles to Meadow Creek Reservoir. Continue around the reservoir to the Junco Lake Trailhead and the west end of the trail.

Winter Park Resort
US 40, at the base of Winter Park
(970) 726-1564
Winter Park Resort offers several two-hour guided hikes for those who like to travel in groups. During summer months, hiking guides teach participants about the region's history, native plants, and animals, and offer tips about mountain safety while leading them along the Ute Trail and Fantasy Meadow paths. Routes are easy to moderate, but because they're at altitude, participants must be in good physical condition. Hikers should also wear sturdy shoes and wool or synthetic socks, and bring backpacks, rain gear, extra layers of warm clothing, sunscreen, and water. Children must be at least 9 years old; those younger than 15 must be accompanied by an adult. Hikes are $20 each and can be purchased at the main ticket window outside of the resort's Balcony House.

CAMPING

The following developed campgrounds in the Arapaho National Forest are available on a first-come, first-served basis, for tents and small trailers only. There are no RV hookups. More information is available through the Arapaho National Forest, Sulphur Ranger District Office, (970) 887-4100, 9 Ten Mile Drive, Granby. All are set in wooded areas with nice views of the surrounding valley.

Arapaho National Recreation Area
Fraser-Granby area
(877) 444-6777
There are three campgrounds on the National Reservation System in this National Recreation Area: Arapaho Bay, Stillwater, and Green Ridge campgrounds. Reservations can be made for them by calling the National Reservation Reservation Service. The campgrounds are open from Memorial Day through Labor Day with reservations, providing full services. After Labor Day campgrounds sites are available on a first-come, first-served basis.

This national recreation area nestles among Lake Granby, Shadow Mountain Lake, Willow Creek Reservoir, and Stillwater Lake, which provide beautiful vistas of mountains and forests.

About 12 miles northwest of Granby on US 34, turn right on County Road 6, and go 2 miles to Green Ridge Campground near Shadow Mountain Lake. There are 78 sites, vault toilets, drinking water, fire grates, and picnic tables. As with other forest campgrounds, there is a fee and a maximum seven-night stay.

Eight miles northwest of Granby on US 34 is Stillwater Campground on Lake Granby with 129 sites, vault toilets, fire grates, picnic tables, and drinking water. There is a fee and maximum seven-night stay. To reach Arapahoe Bay Campground (on the southeast end of Lake Granby), continue a mile south of Stillwater Lake Campground, turn left on County Road 6, and go 10 miles. There are 84 sites with the same features as above. As with other forest campgrounds, there is a fee and a maximum seven-night stay.

Denver Creek Campground
Highway 125
16 miles west of Granby
There are two loops in this campground, one on each side of the highway. Twenty-two sites include vault toilets, fire grates, picnic tables, and drinking water from Memorial Day through mid-October. As

with other forest campgrounds, there is a small fee and a maximum 14-night stay.

Fraser Experimental Forest
7 miles southwest of Fraser
(970) 726-7550
(Sulphur District Ranger Office)
New forest management techniques being tested give this lush wooded area its unusual name. Two small campgrounds offer sites for tent and trailer camping. There are drinking water, vault toilets, fire grates, and picnic tables. Try the St. Louis Creek Campground, 4 miles southwest on County Road 73 (St. Louis Creek Road) from Fraser, which has 16 sites. Byers Creek Campground is 3.5 miles farther along the road and has six sites. As with other forest campgrounds, there is a small fee and a maximum 14-night stay. The campgrounds are open from Memorial Day until late September.

Idlewild Campground
US 40, 1 miles south of Winter Park
The campground, nestled in the pines, has 24 sites, drinking water, vault toilets, fire grates, and picnic tables. The campground charges a nominal fee and has a maximum stay of 14 nights. The campground opens around Memorial Day, weather permitting, and closes September 21.

Robbers Roost Campground
US 40, 5 miles south of Winter Park
Both tents and trailers can find good sites here with a nice view of the Continental Divide. There are 11 sites with drinking water, vault toilets, fire grates, and picnic tables. This campground opens around Memorial Day and closes Labor Day. As with other forest campgrounds, there is a small fee and a maximum 14-night stay.

Sawmill Gulch Campground
Highway 125, 13 miles northwest
of Granby
There are only six sites at this small campground, but the setting is pretty and named for the old sawmill in the nearby gulch. There are vault toilets, fire grates,

drinking water, and picnic tables. The campground is open from Memorial Day until mid-October, but drinking water is not available after Labor Day. As with other forest campgrounds, there is a small fee and a maximum 14-night stay.

GOLF

Grand Elk Golf Course
1321 Ten Mile Drive, Granby
(970) 887-9122, (877) 389-9333
www.grandelk.com/golfcourse.asp
Designed by pro golfer Craig Stadler and golf course architect Tripp Davis, Grand Elk is the newest addition to the outstanding golf venues in the Fraser Valley. This par 71, 7,200-yard course is a Heathland-style track, characterized by an open, gently rolling landscape dotted with shrubs and grassland. The Continental Divide provides the requisite mountain backdrop, and the course follows the natural flow of Ten Mile Creek. This course is part of the larger Grand Elk resort development, but is open to the public.

Grand Lake Golf Course
1415 County Road 48, Grand Lake
(970) 627-8008
Another spectacular mountain golf course, the Grand Lake course is rather unforgiving, with narrow fairways and dense woods. But the 8,420-foot elevation makes those drives fly farther—just not straighter. It's probably easiest to take a penalty and drop a new ball rather than chase one into the trees with any hopes of finding it, or better yet, hitting out of it.

Pole Creek Golf Course
US 40, mile marker 220, Winter Park
(970) 887-9195, (800) 511-5076
www.polecreekgolf.com
At an elevation of 8,600 feet, Pole Creek is a classic mountain course, one of the few that have been etched into the terrain without disturbing the spectacular alpine scenery. Players have plenty of chances to savor the 13,000-foot snow-

capped peaks that form the Continental Divide and the deep glacial valley that is now covered with fairways and greens. Herds of native elk, deer, fox, and red-tailed hawks sometimes wander across the course, and recent development has started shadowing the course with exclusive homes. The 7,107-yard par 72 course, designed by Denis Griffiths and owned by the city of Winter Park, has enough climbs and descents to make it challenging. *Golf Digest* once ranked it the top public course in Colorado and among the top 75 public courses in the nation. An additional nine holes were added in late 1999. High season is mid-June to mid-September. Greens fees are $85 for non-residents during high season, $65 in low season. The best deal is a twilight special, when anyone can play for $40 to $50 (time varies depending on the season). Carts are included and reservations are accepted up to a week in advance for free.

FISHING AND HUNTING

Outfitters and Tackle Shops

Devil's Thumb Fly Fishing Center
3530 County Road 83, Tabernash
(970) 726-8231, (800) 933-4339
www.devilsthumbranch.com
Guides at this year-round resort accompany guests on half-day or full-day fishing trips. Anglers can choose from a stocked trout pond or a stretch of Ranch Creek that traverses the resort's property, or they can travel off-site to the Colorado River, the Fraser River, nearby lakes and reservoirs, or backcountry lakes in the Arapaho National Forest, Indian Peaks Wilderness Area, or Rocky Mountain National Park. The full-service fly shop sells rods, flies, and other fishing essentials. On-site classes and rentals are also offered.

Fishin' Hole Sporting Goods
310 Park Center Avenue, Kremmling
(970) 724-9407
The Fishin' Hole stocks bait, lures, camping and hunting supplies, long underwear, boots, and some sports clothing. Employees can also recommend local hunting and fishing guides for the Middle Park and Grand County regions.

Samuelson Outfitters
194 Byers Avenue, Fraser
(970) 726-8221
www.samuelsonoutfitters.com
Catering to elk and deer hunters, Dick and Cathy Samuelson maintain a full-service hunting camp on the east fork of the Troublesome River, in one of Colorado's premier elk hunting areas 25 miles northwest of Granby. Clients reach the camp by riding 5 or 6 miles on horseback, and once there, have several options. The full-service package includes guides, cooks, meals, horses, tents, and park service for any animals bagged during the hunt. The price is about $3,000 for five days. The economy package is about $1,500 for five days and includes tents, gear, food, a cook, and a packer. No horses are provided during the economy stay.

Places to Fish

Colorado River
Rocky Mountain National Park,
west and south along US 24 to Granby
and US 40 to Kremmling
The Colorado River begins in Rocky Mountain National Park before it slices its way through the United States and dumps into the Gulf of Mexico. Fishing is allowed within the park boundaries, then from Shadow Mountain Dam down to Lake Granby. It joins with the Fraser River west of Granby. The stretch from Granby Dam down to the intersection with the Fraser River is a good place to fish for brown and rainbow trout, although most of the surrounding land is privately owned and off-

The Fraser River flows down Berthoud Pass, then through Winter Park and Fraser before joining the Colorado River. It has been designated Wild Trout Water, and is Grand County's place for serious fly fishing. THE DENVER POST/AMY ELLIS

limits. Only 5 miles of the stretch between Granby and Kremmling is open to the public, with most of it flowing through cattle ranches, but it is rated Gold Medal water.

Local outfitters usually have access to more of the river, having negotiated arrangements with the ranch owners. One good 4-mile stretch begins at Hot Sulphur Springs and goes downstream through Byers Canyon. Large rainbows and browns populate this water. During the spring, outfitters recommend nymph fishing, stoneflies, mayflies, and caddis larvae. Summertime is dry fly time. When the browns spawn in the fall, streamers and nymphs are recommended.

Fraser River
Along US 40 from Berthoud Pass to Granby

Flowing down from the upper reaches of Berthoud Pass through Winter Park, Fraser, and Tabernash, the Fraser River joins the Colorado River a few miles west of Granby. This was President Eisenhower's favorite place to fish, and he visited it as regularly as he could. The upper portions near Winter Park ski resort are open to the public and are well stocked with rainbows and brooks. From 1 mile north of Tabernash to a mile above Granby, the river is designated Wild Trout Water and is the place for serious fly fishing. It has a good population of wild rainbows, browns, brooks, and an occasional cutthroat, but it can be tricky to access due to private owners along its banks. Check at local bait and tackle stores or with outfitters for suggestions on how to reach public water. Guides recommend using Royal Wulff and gray caddis imitations on top of the water, Hare's Ear and stonefly nymphs under the surface. The limit is two fish of any size.

Grand Lake
US 34 northeast of US 40

This 300-foot-deep lake holds rainbow trout (more active in the spring), kokanee salmon, and some of the state's largest mackinaw (many weighting more than 20 pounds). Boats are recommended because much of the shoreline is privately owned. Guides swear by trolling and inlet fishing from early spring through mid-July, using wet flies and lures for brown and rainbow trout, and sucker meat for mackinaw. Those who can stand the 60-degree water like to spear fish, and in the winter, Grand Lake is a popular spot for ice fishing.

Lake Granby
US 34 northeast of US 40

The largest of the Granby/Grand/Shadow Mountain Lakes, Lake Granby has 41 miles of shoreline. It is famous for its mackinaws but also has good rainbows, kokanee salmon, and browns.

Meadow Creek Reservoir
US 40 east of Tabernash to County Road 83, then left onto County Road 84 for 9 miles

At 10,000 feet, this reservoir is frozen over most of the year. Once the ice melts, however, it's a great place to fish for stocked rainbows and wild brooks. A 3-mile hike from the reservoir is Columbine Lake, a smaller and higher (11,100 feet) lake teeming with cutthroats when conditions are right. The trailhead is past the campgrounds at the end of the reservoir road.

Shadow Mountain Reservoir
US 34 northeast of US 40

Connected by boat channel to Grand Lake, this shallow reservoir is stocked with rainbow, kokanee, and some mackinaw. Through July, rainbows and browns are the catch, but you'll have a better chance with kokanee later in the summer. Ice fishing also is good here.

Williams Fork Reservoir
County Road 3, just south of US 40 near Parshall

At an elevation of 7,800 feet, this good-size reservoir is lower than some but still surrounded by the high mountain views of the Williams Fork and Vasquez mountains. Its water eventually makes its way into Denver's water system, but in the meantime, it's home to rainbow and brown trout, pike, and kokanee salmon.

Wolford Mountain Reservoir
US 40, 4½ miles north of Kremmling
Fed by Muddy Creek, Wolford Mountain Reservoir offers anglers some excellent opportunities to catch rainbows, cutthroats, brown trout, and kokanee salmon. Those who want can fish from the dam and below (park in the dam's parking lot). The boat launch and campground are another 2 miles north of US 40.

Places to Hunt

Middle Park
North and south of Kremmling
(970) 724-9004 (Ranger station)
Middle Park, 50 miles northwest of Winter Park in the Arapaho National Forest, is home to some of the state's biggest herds of deer and elk and covers terrain that can be profitably hunted. Among the favorite spots within Middle Park are the Williams Fork River area south and west of Hot Sulphur Springs (accessible by county and Forest Service roads) and the area around Chimney Rock Road, which is halfway between Kremmling and Muddy Pass off US 40. Most of the elk in Middle Park stay in the upper elevations and high timber until snow forces them to lower elevations. When calling the Division of Wildlife for hunting information, ask for publications about Game Management Unit 28 for Williams Fork River area, Unit 181 for Chimney Rock Road area, or units 18, 27, 28, 37, 181, and 371 for the entire Middle Park area.

OTHER RECREATION

Known as the Fraser River Valley, this lush area is fed by the Fraser River, which starts high up on the Continental Divide. The Fraser River Trail parallels the river as it rushes past Winter Park Resort and a renovated homestead near Fraser. The Fraser River Valley is popular for hiking and camping (please see the corresponding chapter in this book), mountain biking, rafting, and fishing (please see this chapter's fishing and hunting sections).

Cycling/Mountain Biking

The towns of Winter Park, Fraser, and Granby serve as the trailheads for many rides that offer terrain for all ability levels. On every route, you'll find spectacular views, beautiful mountain meadows and streams, pine and aspen forests, and a variety of wildlife. Look for the *Mountain Bike Trail Map* for Winter Park and the Fraser River Valley at the Chamber of Commerce in Winter Park, US 40 just south of Idlewild Road, (970) 726-4118 or (800) 903-7275.

Winter Park claims to be the premier mountain bike resort in Colorado and the country—and with good reason. With countless miles of trails, there's terrain for every ability, from flat riverside paths to challenging mountain climbs. There are also races and festivals, chairlift-accessible riding areas, free guided town rides, ladies-only excursions, full-service bike shops, comprehensive trail maps, and more. The trail system, which has developed from old Jeep and logging roads, winds through backcountry meadows and streams, along gentle paths or up steep grades, past towns, historical sites, and beautiful scenery. Trails are clearly marked and interconnected by the Frasier River Trail, a flat, paved 5-mile trail between Winter Park Resort and Fraser.

In the high country there are more than 600 miles of diverse trails, including dirt roads, Jeep trails, and double- and single-track routes. The resort's ski lifts ferry cyclists to 45 miles of lift-accessible trails and 250 miles of single-track trails. Those new to mountain biking might consider one of the many clinics offered by the resort for beginners. Organized tours with experience guides are also available through the town's many bike shops. Local outfitters can jeep cyclists to the top of the Continental Divide for a thrilling downhill bike ride back to town.

Mountain biking maps and information are also available from Sulphur Ranger District Office, 9 Ten Mile Drive, Granby, (970) 887–4100; Winter Park Resort, (970) 726–5514; and the Winter Park/Frazer Valley Chamber of Commerce, 78841 US 40, Winter Park, (970) 726–4118.

Following are a couple of recommended outfitters to get you started.

Ski Depot Sports
78727 Winter Park Drive, Winter Park
(970) 726–8055
www.skidepot.com
Rent the latest full-suspension mountain bikes or high-performance "hard tails" (with no rear suspension) and get the low down on the best riding around the area. Also offers a full line of backpacking equipment.

Viking Ski Shop
78966 US 40, Winter Park
(970) 726–8885
One of the best ski shops in the valley converts to mountain bikes in the summer. A wide variety of bikes and carriers for those too young to pedal are available at reasonable prices. Also offers in-line skating equipment for rental or sale.

YMCA Snow Mountain Ranch
1101 County Road 53, 12 miles northwest of Winter Park, near Tabernash
(970) 887–2152
Rent bikes and equipment here, or sign up for a guided tour. The ranch trails are great for mountain biking.

Horseback Riding

High Country Trails
Devil's Thumb Outfitters
Tabernash
(970) 726–1099

This outfitter provides trail rides, backcountry horseback trips, and guided hunting trips under different names, depending on the time of year and what kind of horse experience you're after. Operating out of different pasture locations, call the listed number and the wrangler-in-charge will help you make arrangements. All rides are on quality horses, and instructional rides are available.

YMCA of the Rockies
Snow Mountain Ranch
12 miles northwest of Winter Park
near Tabernash
(970) 887–2152, ext. 4146
www.sombrero.com/snowmountain ranch.asp
Sombrero Stables at Snow Mountain offers one- to four-hour rides (maximum of two hours in winter), breakfast and steak dinner rides, and inexpensive wagon-and-a-meal rides (breakfast or steak dinner). Wranglers lead the tours around the YMCA's 5,200-acre ranch, through meadows, over streams, and into the woods. Sombrero operates several stables in the Winter Park/Fraser Valley area. Check their Web site for other locations, rates, and special services.

Rafting and Kayaking

Colorado River Runs
Star Route, Box 32, Bond
(970) 653–4292, (800) 826–1081
www.coloradoriverruns.com
With licensed raft trips since 1973, this company offers trips on the Colorado, Arkansas, and Eagle Rivers. All types of trips from easy to challenging are offered. Easy trips are on the Colorado River from Rancho Del Rio near State Bridge. Moderate and more challenging trips ride the Eagle and Arkansas Rivers either on the Eagle River near Vail or the Arkansas River near Buena Vista. Reservations are required in advance for all trips.

Mad Adventures
Winter Park
(970) 726-5290, (800) 858-6808
www.madadventures.com
This company leads river trips on the Colorado and Arkansas Rivers and Clear Creek. Half- and full-day trips are available. River trips range in intensity from mild floats to wild whitewater. Mad claims to be the most popular and experienced outfitter in the area.

Raven Adventure Trips
60001 US 40, Granby
(970) 887-2141, (800) 332-3381
www.ravenraft.com
Operating since 1971, this company offers professional-quality trips on the Colorado, North Platte, and Arkansas Rivers. It has a full-service paddle shop with rafts and kayaks. Trips are run year-round in Grand County and from May through September from the Cañon City Office, (719) 275-2890, on the Arkansas River. Overnight trips are also available.

Running/Walking

Fraser River Trail
Off US 40
The 5-mile Fraser River is the ideal place to run or walk in this area. The flat, easy terrain has a few rolling hills and nice views of the mountains.

Hot Springs and Spas

Hot Sulphur Springs Resort
5609 County Road 20
Hot Sulphur Springs
(970) 725-3306, (800) 510-6235
www.hotsulphursprings.com
Hot Sulphur Springs has had only four owners in the past two centuries. The first were the Ute Indians, the original inhabitants of Grand County. They used the site as a summer hunting ground, then went south when the winter came. They called the springs Spiq-uet Pah, or Smoking Water, and used the steaming pools to heal themselves and their animals. The Utes lost their ownership of the property in 1864, when *Rocky Mountain News* owner William Byers bought the entire town of Hot Sulphur Springs from a member of the Minnesota Sioux tribe, even though a U.S. treaty recognized the Utes as rightful owners. After a lengthy court battle with the Ute tribe, Byers won and set about bringing to life his dream of creating a major health spa/resort similar to Saratoga, New York. It never thrived because travel in this remote mountain valley was so difficult, but guests did ride in on stagecoach and later by train, then waded across the Colorado River to reach a racetrack, a covered swimming pool, a hotel, and cabins.

In 1943 the resort was sold to James T. Dougherty and operated by his heirs until 1996, when they sold it to Charles Nash, a property developer from Denver. He completed $2 million renovations the next year (in 1997) and opened the resort in August with a blessing ceremony led by a Ute spiritual leader and attended by 50 tribal elders and 800 of Nash's friends and neighbors. It is now open year-round.

Children are restricted to two pools in the lower area, one of which is 75 to 80 degrees and big enough for swimming, the other a soaking pool. The upper areas include a four- or five-person pool with a waterfall called the Ute Pool that is just below the original source of the hot springs; Lupe's Pool, a small square kept at 110 degrees; an indoor solarium pool built above the old indoor pool, kept at 102 degrees; two private caves with pools built into the rock wall at 106 to 108 degrees; two indoor communal baths that are separated by sex and in which bathing suits are optional; and the Cliffhanger Pool, which is accessible by boardwalk on the hillside beyond and kept at 102 to 104 degrees. Massages, facials, and body wraps are also available. Seventeen motel rooms, ca. 1940, also are available on the property.

GEORGETOWN

Like most of its brethren, Georgetown was founded in the 1860s on the gold and silver trade and foundered in 1893 when the markets went sour. But unlike some towns that were buried deep in remote mountain valleys, Georgetown sits alongside one of the state's most heavily traveled interstates. In the early 1900s, that was its salvation, but in the latter part of the century, residents fought hard to avoid the pitfalls of other well-traveled historic sites.

A group of dedicated preservations have worked diligently to protect Georgetown's history. They have succeeded in saving and restoring such historic gems as the town's luxurious Hotel de Paris, the mammoth home of a town father, and the showiest of all, the Georgetown Loop Railroad. They are also vigilant about blocking development on mountain passes that lead to surrounding mountain peaks and pristine hiking trails.

But don't let that scare you away. Georgetown is a welcoming place to visit, with horse-drawn carriage rides, a city park that's perfect for picnicking, and shops and galleries that come together (and invite members of Historic Georgetown) to produce one heck of a Christmas celebration. Skiers at nearby Loveland Ski Areas often spend the night in Georgetown's motels, or at least stop for a hot meal on their drive back to Denver.

The Georgetown Loop Railroad provided freight and passenger service between the mining camps of Georgetown and Silver Plume and connected them with other trains to Denver. It's now a tourist attraction that gives visitors a glimpse of the 19th century. THE DENVER POST/JOHN LEYBA

ACCOMMODATIONS
Hotels and Motels

Georgetown Mountain Inn   **$**
1100 Rose Street
(303) 569-3201, (800) 884-3201
www.georgetownmountaininn.com
Pets are allowed at this 33-room motel, located next door to the Georgetown Loop Railroad's ticket office and within walking distance of historic downtown Georgetown. Also included in the price of a room at this two-story Alpine standard is a continental breakfast, the use of a heated indoor pool, and an outdoor hot tub year-round. Wheelchair-accessible rooms and guest laundry are also available.

Georgetown Super 8 Motel   **$**
1600 Argentine Street
(303) 569-3211, (800) 800-8000
www.super8.com
Look for the building that resembles a Hollywood set as you zoom by on the interstate. It's a non-traditional version of the national motel chain, designed to resemble a turn-of-the-century mining town. With 54 rooms and a conference room, game room with pool table, indoor Jacuzzi, and some business services (fax and copy machines), this motel caters to cross-country travelers (its parking lot holds large trucks and campers). It's also popular with tourists in town to ski at nearby Loveland ski areas, to host a family reunion or wedding, or to visit the historic mining town.

Bed-and-Breakfast Inns

Centennial Mill Guest House   **$-$$$**
404 Second Street
(303) 569-3067, (800) 409-1313
www.centennialmill.com
Nestled into the mountainside at the site of the Centennial Silver Mine and Mill Site, this three-bedroom vacation house sits at the base of Guinella Pass, a scenic mountain byway that leads south past ghost towns and fishing sites. It sleeps six to eight and has a full kitchen and bath with whirlpool tub. A minimum two-night stay is required. Pets and smoking are prohibited.

Silver Heels Guest Suites   **$$-$$$**
506 6th Street
(303) 569-0941, (888) 510-7628
www.silverheelsguestsuites.com
The Buckskin Trading Company occupies the ground floor of this building in Georgetown's historic downtown district. The two guest suites are tucked in above, and look as modern as any ski condo. The Merry Widow Suite has twin beds, a private bath, kitchen, and queen sofa sleeper. The Baby Doe Suite has a king bed with queen sofa sleeper, private bath, kitchen, study alcove with captain's bed, washer/dryer, and outdoor deck. A minimum two-night stay is required. Smoking and pets are prohibited.

RESTAURANTS

The Happy Cooker   **$$**
412 6th Street
(303) 569-3166
A Victorian home decorated with turn-of-the-century antiques and art work for sale, the Happy Cooker serves hearty breakfasts, quiches, pastas, and seafood specials. It serves breakfast and lunch only.

Red Ram Restaurant and Saloon   **$$**
606 6th Street
(303) 569-2300
Opened in 1953 as a ski bar to refuel those hardy enough to motor up the pre-interstate mountain roads, the name was a compromise struck by owner Bill Holmes and his wife. He had served in Britain's Royal Air Force and wanted to call it the "Bloody Ram." His wife talked him into the more genteel version. Today the place is anything but genteel, resembling a saloon more than a fine dining establishment, but it has history. Former Colorado Governor

The state's largest herd of Rocky Mountain bighorn sheep lives in the hills above George-town. In the winter, they can be spotted as they come down to lower elevations. THE DENVER POST/JOHN EPPERSON

Dick Lamm squired his wife-to-be Dottie there, and other visitors have included Robert F. Kennedy, Henry Fonda, and scores of ski champions and mountain climbers. The food is secondary to the experience, although over the years, people have driven hundreds of miles for the chance to order the prime rib dinner.

NIGHTLIFE

Red Ram Restaurant and Saloon   **$$**
606 6th Street
(303) 569-2300
A Georgetown landmark, this rollicking restaurant since the '50s is housed in a building built another 100 years before that. On historic Georgetown's main street, it's hard to miss. In sharp contrast to the staid, proper historical buildings that surround it, the Ram exudes music,

noise, and the sight of waitstaff bustling about with burgers, ribs, and fajitas. Downstairs is a small cigar bar that hosts live entertainment on the weekends.

ATTRACTIONS

Georgetown Loop Railroad
1106 Rose Street
(888) 456-8777
www.georgetownlooprr.com
The railroad arrived in Georgetown in 1877, providing freight and passenger service between mining camps in Georgetown and Silver Plume and services in Denver. Although Georgetown and Silver Plume are only 2 miles apart, the elevation climbs 600 feet, so helping the train make such a quick climb required a looping track that actually covered 4¼ miles. At one point (Devil's Gate Viaduct), the track "looped"

Georgetown may be the only turn-of-the-century mining town whose present is as bawdy as its past. In 2001 an ex-stripper named Koleen Brooks was elected mayor. One year later she had become the epicenter of a scandal that made national headlines for allegedly exposing her surgically enhanced breasts in public. This small town's politics became more run of the mill in 2002 after residents recalled the flashy young mayor.

back over itself, hence the railroad's name. The invention of the automobile and the collapse of mining killed the railroad's business, and in 1939 the tracks were dismantled. Thirty-four years later the Colorado Historical Society rebuilt the line, including the dramatic Devil's Gate Bridge, which rises 100 feet above the first set of tracks and crosses a 300-foot span.

Today visitors can take the trip from Georgetown to Silver Plume and back, starting at the historic Georgetown Depot, which also boasts a restaurant with a model-train traveling around the perimeter. Or they may start at Silver Plume for the 1 hour and 10 minute round-trip ride. An optional mine tour in Silver Plume requires another hour and 20 minutes. Bring a jacket either way, because Colorado's mountain air can turn chilly at a moment's notice, and the temperature in the mine is a constant 44 degrees. The Loop Railroad runs daily from the last weekend in May through the first week in Ocotober. Departure times from Georgetown are between 10:00 A.M. and 3:00 P.M., from Silver Plume 10:05 A.M. to 3:45 P.M. Round-trip tickets are $16.50 adults, $11.25 children 3 to 15, and those 2 and under ride free. An optional tour of the Lebanon Mine is $6.00 for adults, $4.00 for children.

Georgetown Viewing Center
Interstate 70 at Georgetown
(exit 228, left on Alvarado Road)
The state's largest herd of Rocky Moun-tain bighorn sheep lives in the hills above Georgetown, and during the winter months, the animals come down to lower elevations. It's easy to spot them from this wildlife viewing station, especially during the height of their breeding season in December. Between November and January the canyons often echo with the crack of horns as males fight to establish their position in the herd. Their lambs are born between April and June. Entrance to the center is free; the powerful viewing scopes require quarters to operate but are essential for those who want to get good views of Colorado's state mammal. Volunteers are on hand winter weekends from 10:00 A.M. to 3:00 P.M. to answer any questions.

Hamill House Museum
305 Argentine Street
(303) 569-2840
www.historicgeorgetown.org/houses/hamill.htm
Georgetown's most ambitious residence, the Hamill House was built in 1867 by Joseph Watson but was sold in 1874 to his brother-in-law, Arthur Hamill, a successful silver miner. As the profits grew, so did the house until, in 1885, it covered nearly half a town block. The last of the Hamill's five children sold the place in 1914 before moving to Denver. Historic Georgetown, Inc., bought the building in 1971 after it had served as a rooming house, a historic museum, and a restaurant/mountain lodge. It has been under renovation off and on ever since.

Twenty- and 25-minute guided tours take visitors past such treats as a solarium with indoor fountain, bay windows, walnut woodwork, a six-seat outhouse with separate sides for the family and its servants, a laundry building, and the carriage house (it still contains carriages and a sleigh). It's open during the summer daily from 10:00 A.M. to 4:00 P.M. and September to December 25 from noon to 4:00 P.M. Saturday and Sunday. Adults get in for $5.00, students and seniors 65 and over are $4.00, under 6 are free.

Hotel De Paris Museum
409 6th Street
(303) 569-2311

Frenchman Louis Dupuy worked as a miner until he was injured, then bought the Delmonico Bakery in Georgetown and began to build it into a luxury hotel that attracted guests from throughout the world. It opened in 1875 with steam heat and hot and cold running water in each room, amenities unheard of at the time. Over the years, Dupuy added two salesrooms (furnished with folding beds that served as desks used for showing samples during the day), and his own quarters, complete with a sophisticated flush toilet, bathing tub, and fold-away bed. He died in 1900 and is buried in Alvarado Cemetery in Georgetown. Restoration of the hotel started in 1954 and is still in progress.

The kitchen and the wine cellar are perhaps the highlights of the 30-minute guided tour (guests may also wander on their own). The kitchen has a wall-sized "safe" or icebox along one wall—look inside for the tiny food and wine storage areas and the gigantic area where ice was inserted. It also contains many of the gadgets required in those days to feed a large crowd—coffee and spice mill, Haviland china complete with the crate in which it was shipped, a baker's table, and washing machine and mangle. The wine cellar is in the dark basement and still contains nine barrels, a cider barrel with crystallized cider inside, and a corking machine. Nearby is a coal bin with stairs leading to delivery doors at street level.

Hours are daily 10:00 A.M. to 4:30 P.M. Memorial Day through Labor Day, weekends only noon to 4:00 P.M. in May and September through December. The museum is closed January through April. Admission is $5.00 for adults, $4.00 for seniors (60+) and AAA members, $2.00 for children 6 to 16, and free for those under 6.

John Tomay Memorial Library
605 6th Street
(303) 569-2620

Founded in 1911, this building has sometimes served as a library/city hall, and the basement was once a community center that hosted square dancing. It now has a new children's wing, offers public Internet access, holds book sales at Christmas, Labor Day, and Memorial Day, sponsors a book discussion group, and holds a preschool story hour at 11:00 A.M. Tuesday between Labor Day and Memorial Day. It is open 10:30 A.M. to 5:00 P.M. Monday, Wednesday, and Friday, 10:30 A.M. to 7:00 P.M. Tuesday and Thursday, and 10:30 A.M. to 3:30 P.M. Saturday.

Silver Plume
I-70 (exit 226)
(303) 569-2368

The area's rich silver mines gave this tiny town its name, although exactly how is still debated. Some say it's because one especially rich vein of silver was discovered that had so much ore in it that flakes broke off in feather-like patterns. Whatever the truth is, in 1875 Silver Plume had 2,000 residents. Like most others, this mining town went bust when the nation's monetary standard changed from silver to gold in the 1890s. Now 150 hardy souls live in the old Victorian town, protected by a National Historic Landmark District designation. A free, self-guided walking tour of Main Street will take visitors down the old dirt street past the George Rowe Museum, the Silver Plume Brewing Company, and the town hall. A short hike leads to a monument made of Silver Plume granite that honors Clifford Griffin, owner of the Seven-Thirty gold and silver mine.

KIDSTUFF

Georgetown Loop Railroad
1106 Rose Street
(888) 456-8777
www.georgetownlooprr.com

Kids will love the ride on this railroad,

which features an authentic steam engine (with all the requisite bells and whistles) and open-air cars that allow for excellent views of the steep trestles and hillsides.

Although Georgetown and Silver Plume are only 2 miles apart, there's a difference of 600 feet in elevation between them, so helping the train make such a quick climb required a looping track 4¼ miles in length. At one point (Devil's Gate Viaduct), the track "looped" back over itself, hence the railroad's name. The tracks in place today are a reproduction of the original line, which was dismantled in 1939.

See the "Attractions" section above for details on taking this train ride through Colorado's colorful mining past.

Skiing Lessons and Child Care

Loveland Valley and Basin
Intersection of I-70 and U.S. Highway 6
between Dillon and Georgetown
(303) 571-5580, (800) 736-3754
www.skiloveland.com
Children younger than 5 ski free at Loveland. The nursery at Loveland Basin provides day care for children 1 year and older. Reservations are recommended. Ski school for children ages 4 to 14 is headquartered at Loveland Valley and offers a sheltered beginner learning area.

EVENTS

February

Valentine's Day Wedding
Loveland Ski Area, I-70 and US 6
west of Georgetown
(303) 571-5580, (800) 736-3754
The state's only ski area with "love" in its name, Loveland makes the most of its romantic name by sponsoring a complimentary mass mountaintop wedding on Valentine's Day. Be warned: Brides should wear long johns underneath their gowns

because February temperatures can drop below zero.

April

Loveland Derby
Loveland Ski Area, I-70 and US 6
west of Georgetown
(303) 571-5580, (800) 736-3754
While other ski areas are closing due to lack of snow in mid-April, Loveland is busy sponsoring the nation's longest running amateur alpine race. National collegiate champions and members of the U.S. Ski Team also compete on this slalom course. Spectators can watch for free from the base lodge.

Silver Plume Melodrama
Town Hall, Main Street, Silver Plume
(303) 569-2023
In 1976, when the Silver Plume Historical Society planned its annual fund-raiser, George Downing suggested something different from the regular potluck suppers. He wrote a melodrama that was performed by volunteers and accompanied by a sit-down dinner. It went over so well, he's been writing a new one every year ever since. Every weekend in April, unpaid volunteers flaunt their dramatic talents for sell-out audiences. The price of a ticket and dinner is $25 for adults, $15 for children. Call for dates, details, and reservations.

July

Georgetown 4th of July
Various locations
(303) 569-2888
Each year the city fathers bring out their finest to celebrate Independence Day with a blend of modern and historical events that pull from the town's mining heritage. Expect a parade, a barbecue in City Park, bucket brigade races, and fireworks. Each year's events are slightly different, so call for details.

Loveland Ski Area makes the most of its romantic name by sponsoring a complimentary mass wedding each Valentine's Day. THE DENVER POST/GLENN ASAKAWA

SKIING/SNOWBOARDING

Loveland Valley and Basin
Intersection of I-70 and US 6, between Dillon and Georgetown
(303) 571-5580, (800) 736-3754
www.skiloveland.com
Resort elevation: *10,600 feet*
Top of highest lift: *12,700 feet*
Total vertical: *2,410 feet*
Longest run: *2 miles*
Average annual snowfall: *400 inches*
Ski season: *mid-October to mid-May*
Capacity: *12,473 skiers per hour*
Terrain: *1,365 acres, 70 trails (13 percent beginner, 41 percent intermediate, 46 percent advanced and expert)*

Lift tickets: *$50 all-day adult*
Snow report: *(303) 571-5554*
Getting there: *Loveland is 56 miles west of Denver via I-70. It's on the east side of the road at the Loveland Pass exit just before the Eisenhower Tunnel.*

In the 2002–2003 ski season, the Loveland ski trails got 36 inches of snow in one 24-hour period. Need we say more? Straddling the Eisenhower Tunnel at the entrance to Colorado's Ski Country, the natural mountain basins at Loveland catch some of the earliest snow of the year and keep it long after other resorts are reduced to mud and muck.

But that's just one reason why Colorado locals have been skiing Loveland

Trails from the top of Loveland provide some of the state's best views of the Continental Divide, the imaginary line that separates water flowing west to the Pacific Ocean from moisture flowing east to the Atlantic. THE DENVER POST/HYOUNG CHANG

since the 1930s. It's also just an hour away from Denver, sells lift tickets at roughly half the price of more glamorous resorts to the west, and is on the good end of a tight corridor that can get clogged with returning eastbound traffic on weekends and holidays. Loveland offers a one-of-a-kind lift ticket promotion popular with skiers eager to arrive after the morning traffic jams and leave before the evening rush: ski any four consecutive hours for just $40.

Because of its prime location beneath Loveland Pass, the ski area also is a gateway to extreme skiing on the craggy peaks. On days when blizzard and avalanche threats are low, Ski Patrollers open the gates above Loveland's highest ski lift

to adventurers who want to hike into the bowls above. And after the ski season is over in May, backcountry types still climb to the highest snowfields until they've melted into patches too small to ski.

Hard-core skiers have known about the snow that collects on Loveland Basin since the 1920s, when a day of skiing meant hiking to the top of a snow-covered mountain and skiing down. In the 1930s hardy skiers caught car rides to the top of Loveland Pass and skied back down, a practice still in favor among a small group of expert renegades.

In 1937 Allen Bennett leased the land from the Forest Service, incorporated as the Loveland Ski Tow Co., and installed rope tows powered by Model T engines. Every morning he started the first rope tow, strapped two 5-gallon gas cans around his neck and rode it up to the next tow, filled its motor with gas and skied off to fill the third. By that time the first engine would be running low, and it would be time to start again. The first modern chairlifts were installed in 1956. Loveland still provides skiing at its purest, with no on-site lodging or resort community. That means visiting skiers are lodged in Summit County hotels to the west or former mining town Georgetown and Silver Plume to the east. (See the "Accommodations" listings above for details.)

Named for 19th century railroad tycoon William A.H. Loveland, the ski area has nothing to do with the farming town of Loveland located on the plains north of Denver. It does make the most of its romantic name, however, sponsoring a complimentary mass mountaintop wedding each Valentine's Day.

Locals know Loveland as two areas in one: a gentle beginners' mountain called Loveland Valley and the original mountain, Loveland Basin. The two are just across the road from each other and are connected by a free shuttle and a horizontal chairlift. Most of the skiing is on broad bowls and open snowfields, and much of it is above treeline, which means your panoramic views of the powerful mountains aren't blocked by pine trees. The only drawback: Midwinter winds also can whip across the ski runs. On those cold, blustery days, the less hardy skier can retreat to Loveland Valley's tree-trimmed trails.

If you prefer skiing in forest glades, take the chairlift to the top of Loveland Basin, then ride another to adjacent Zip Basin, the mountain face under which the Eisenhower Tunnel is bored. A few acres are packed by snowcats, but the rest is left as nature intended it. When clouds have dropped recent powder, it has the best powder skiing around, but when the snow melts, freezes, or gets tracked, the basin's treacherous slopes are best left to the experts.

Snowboarders are drawn to the treeless terrain above timberline and Shredland, a snowboard park filled with a quarter-pipe, an Evel Knievel-type gap jump, and other "fun box" shapes for tricks.

CROSS-COUNTRY

Loveland has no set cross-country trails, but a bike path between Loveland and Bakerville, a town 8 miles east on I-70, is suitable for cross-country skiing and snowshoeing.

HIKING/BACKPACKING

Some of the many trails accessible from Georgetown include Saxon Mountain, which climbs 8,000 feet above the valley floor to where bristle cone pines live; Notch Trail to Silver Plume; the Union Trail stagecoach route; the Silver Creek Trail to Lawson; and the Argentine Central Trail, which follows a historic railroad grade to spectacular views from Mt. McClellan. The views include fourteeners Mt. Evans and Grays Peak.

Clifford Griffin Monument
Intersection of Main and Silver Streets
Silver Plume
Clifford Griffin owned the rich Seven-

Thirty gold and silver mine, and died near it at age 40. His father honored him with a large gravestone at the site, elevation 10,360 feet. The monument is made of hand-quarried Silver Plume granite and inscribed. Visitors interested in an easy 2.7-mile walk to the site can take a self-guided walking tour from downtown Silver Plume to the monument. The road becomes a narrow shelf trail in some spots and has occasional steep drop-offs. Remnants of the mine and others are still visible in the vicinity, but be careful how far you wander from the trail. The area has not been "sanitized," which means it's still filled with open shafts and debris.

Saxon Mountain Road
½ mile east on Main Street to the Saxon Mountain Road sign
Saxon Mountain Road is a wide, scenic shelf road that climbs 6.5 miles from the trailhead east of Georgetown to just below the high point of Saxon Mountain. Four-wheel-drives with high clearance can be driven to within 100 yards of the summit, but the road is much more enjoyable when traveled on foot. Hikers will pass the ruins of cabins and mines, and will have great views of Georgetown Lake on their way to Lamartine, another ghost town. Hikers should stay on the main road, ignoring any forks that lead downhill. After 5 miles the road will veer left at the sign that reads CASCADE CREEK AND LAMARTINE. Keep traveling the right form for another 1 4/10 miles to the sign that says OPEN LANDS, GEORGETOWN. To reach the summit, leave the road and travel to the right (north-northwest) to the northernmost of two rocky crags.

Shelf Lake
West of Guanella Pass Road, about 13 miles southwest of Georgetown
At about 11,990 feet, you'll be at least 2,000 feet lower than surrounding peaks, but don't let that fool you. Shelf Lake is tucked into a bowl at the end of one of the area's highest mining roads, northeast of the ghost town Geneva City and south-

west of the ghost town Waldorf. Don't attempt it before June 1 or after the first week in October, and prepare to be snowed on at any time in between. Early in the season, prepare for high water in the creek (you'll have to cross it several times along the trail) as snow melts and rushes to lower elevations. The 4-mile trail climbs Smelter Gulch on its way to this alpine lake, with Argentine Peak to the northwest and Decatur Mountain to the southwest. Reach the trailhead (a sturdy car is necessary) by taking Guanella Pass Road 6²⁄₁₀ miles south to a side road on the right that parallels Geneva Creek. Follow that road for 3⁴⁄₁₀ miles (don't turn off it at ³⁄₁₀ mile) and park off the road.

Square Top Mountain
Just west of Guanella Pass Road, about 12 miles southwest of Georgetown
The 13,794-foot peak is the summit of this trail, although there are a pair of lakes filled with cutthroat trout at about 12,200 feet. The mountain itself is a flatcrested peak with a gentle, grassy southern approach, and a view from the top of neighboring Mount Evans, Grays Peak, and Torrey's Peak. Its slopes are relatively untrodden, with the route from the lakes to the southeast ridge less a trail than a line of cairns. Because its flashier neighbors attract those who enjoy bagging 14ers, it's a delight for hikers who'd rather have the seclusion than the bragging rights. Park in the lot along the Guanella Pass road, past the beaver ponds but before the summit, and follow the trail signs.

CAMPING

Guanella Pass Campground
Forest Road 381, between Georgetown and Grants
(877) 444-6777
There are actually four campgrounds strung out along the scenic Guanella Pass Byway between Georgetown and Grants, all of which provide breathtaking views of alpine plant colonies, beaver ponds,

bighorn sheep, and other assorted high-mountain sights. Remember, however, that these are among the state's highest campgrounds, within miles of the Continental Divide as the crow flies, so they tend to be chilly and even snowcovered during some months considered to be spring and summer at lower elevations. Call the number listed above to make reservations.

FISHING/HUNTING
Places to Hunt

Bard Creek
About 5 miles southeast of Empire
(303) 567-2901
A popular place to hunt deer and elk is Bard Creek. Take I-70 to the US 40 exit (exit 233), follow it to Empire and turn on Bard Creek Road (in the center of town). Follow it past Republican Mountain Road until it dead ends. You'll have to hike in from that spot, but not far. Total distance from Empire is about 5 miles, most of it on a difficult, four-wheel-drive road.

Democrat Mountain
About 5 miles southwest of Empire
(303) 567-2901
The Georgetown area is known for its bighorn sheep hunting, and Democrat Mountain is one of the best places to find them (and mule deer). One caveat: Sheep licenses are awarded by lottery, and applications must be turned in by early April. To reach this site, take I-70 to the US 40 exit (exit 233), follow US 40 to Empire and turn left on Bard Creek Road (in the center of town). Follow it to Republican Mountain Road, which becomes a difficult, four-wheel-drive road soon after. It will dead end at the trailhead.

Grizzly Gulch
About 2 miles south of Bakersville
(303) 567-2901
Mountain goats are plentiful in Grizzly

Gulch, but you'll have to work to get them. Take exit 221 from I-70 (about 5 miles west of Georgetown) and follow Stevens Gulch Road south until it forks. The right-hand road will take you to Grizzly Gulch, although the road is nasty and requires a four-wheel-drive vehicle to navigate. Eventually even that won't make it, and you'll have to get out and walk about a half-mile or until all vestiges of the road disappear.

OTHER RECREATION
Mine Tours

Argo Gold Mill and Museum
I-70, Idaho Springs
(303) 567-2421
www.historicargotours.com
The sprawling Argo Gold Mill is the part that's visible from the interstate, but the mill and attached museum are warm-ups for the Double Eagle Mine. It is one of the strikes that made Idaho Springs one of the state's earliest major mining districts that stretched from Idaho Springs to Silver Plume. Visitors first get a 45-minute tour of the museum, then take a self-guided tour of the mine and the mill, where gold was extracted from the ore mined from below ground. Cost is $13.50 for adults, $8.00 for kids 7 to 12, and free for kids under age 7. The mine and museum are open from mid-April through mid-October.

Lebanon Silver Mine
Between Georgetown and Silver Plume
(888) 456-8777
www.georgetownlooprr.com
The only way to visit this mine, deep in the valley between Georgetown and Silver Plume, is as an add-on to a ticket for the Georgetown Loop Railroad. Guests take the 70-minute train ride, then get off long enough to take an 80-minute guided mine tour. The mine is not lighted, so visitors get headlamps for the 1-mile walking tour. Tours are offered only during summer

months, roughly bounded by Memorial Day and Labor Day. Cost is $6.00 for adults, $4.00 for children (in addition to the train ticket; see entry in "Attractions" category). Reservations are suggested.

Phoenix Mine
South of I-70 at Trail Creek Road (exit 239) near Idaho Springs
(303) 567-0422
www.phoenixmine.com
This gold mine opened in 1871, and was bought and reopened in 1972 by third-generation miner Alvin Mosch. Eventually he segued into the mine-tour business and now runs it with his son, David. Guides are real miners who lead 45-minute walking tours and sprinkle their presentations with lively bits of history and lore. Be sure to touch the "lucky bucket" and hear why it's lucky. (Miners who used it in the 1800s while looking for gold veins were phenomenally lucky, and visitors who touch it today report all sorts of lucky happenings.) The mine is open 10:00 A.M. to 6:00 P.M. daily. Admission is $9.00 for adults and $5.00 for children under 12. Gold panning is included in the price.

Scenic Drives

Guanella Pass
Forest Service Road 381 between Georgetown and Grant
(303) 569-2888
Driven in its entirety, this historic byway provides a half-day auto tour loop, beginning and ending in Denver. It's a 22-mile route through Pike and Arapaho National Forests, which runs between Georgetown and Grant, a small town that grew in the late 1800s as a shipping and supply point for area mines. About 10 miles of the road is paved or oil, the rest is gravel. It's not maintained from Georgetown to the summit during the winter, and it is not recommended for large RVs because of steep sections and switchback curves. Guanella Pass has an elevation of 11,669 feet above

sea level, providing spectacular views and a wide variety of recreational opportunities, including fishing, hiking, skiing, camping, biking, hunting, horseback riding, and photography.

Those content to do their viewing from the car will enjoy views of 14ers Mount Bierstadt and Mount Evans to the east, and a look at Cabin Creek Hydroelectric Plant, which has generated power to Denver during peak times since 1968. It stores water from South Clear Creek and then lets it plunge 4,300 feet through a tunnel to spin power turbines before it lands in a lower storage reservoir. It is then pumped back to the first reservoir to repeat the process.

Those interested in mountain biking or hiking can take any number of trails off the road, trekking through the Mount Evans Wilderness Area, viewing the alpine plant communities (wildflowers are in bloom only in July and August), or visiting either of two historic townsites along the way.

Waldorf Townsite rests at the base of the Argentine Mining District (served by mines in the Mount McClellen, Argentine Peak, and Otter Mountain watershed), and supported some of Colorado's earliest silver mines. The Argentine Central Railway was built in 1906 to serve that district and take tourists to the top of Mount McClellen. It was abandoned, but its railbed is a dandy road that takes visitors to Waldorf and beyond. Jeepers and mountain bikers enjoy taking the half-day excursion off the Guanella Pass Road. Parking is available at the site known as the Waldorf Cutoff. Across the creek from the parking area, look for the Marshall Tunnel, built to reroute the creek to protect a mining claim, and the 19th-century site of a silver smelter near the head of Georgetown Reservoir. It was built by a prominent black miner named Lorenzo Bowman, the first person to successfully smelt silver ore in this area.

Geneva City is at the end of a wagon route constructed in 1874 to serve the mines at the head of Geneva Creek and the smelter at Smelter Gully. Today that road is rocky for about a mile west of the Byway, then becomes quite steep and rocky for the last 3 miles to the townsite. Only high-clearance vehicles or experienced mountain bikers should continue. The townsite is nestled into a basin at the head of Geneva Creek, and historic mills and cabins dot the landscape. Those driving four-wheel vehicles are asked to park at timberline and walk to the buildings because the old roads are impassable. All visitors are asked not to touch or remove anything from the site.

To reach the Guanella Pass Byway, take Rose Street west through Georgetown. It will intersect with the Forest Service road.

HOT SPRINGS AND SPAS

Indian Springs Resort
302 Soda Creek Road, Idaho Springs
(303) 989-6666
www.indianspringsresort.com
In the 1700s and 1800s, Arapaho and Ute Indians set aside their tribal differences when enjoying the waters at Indian Springs, which was located on the boundary between their territories. In 1859 George A. Jackson "discovered" them about the same time he found Colorado's first placer gold in the surrounding hills. After that, things were never the same. The state was caught up in a major gold rush, and Indian Springs was commandeered by miners. They dug underground tunnels around the springs, looking for gold, but found nothing but water. In 1863 the first bathhouse was built on the property, making use of the tunnels for steam bathing, and in its day attracted such notables as gunslingers Frank and Jesse James, poet Walt Whitman, and actress Sarah Bernhardt.

The resort now sits alongside I-70 between Denver and Colorado's central mountain ski resorts. Its biggest draw is a dome-enclosed pool kept at 90-plus degrees year round. Admission to the pool is $12 per person Monday through Thursday; $14 Friday, Saturday, Sunday, and holidays; and children 5 and under are free. Club Mud is the only do-it-yourself mud bath in a Colorado hot spring. Guests enter the mud-filled room (swimsuits are required), cover themselves with the mineral-rich clay, let it dry, and then shower themselves off. Club Mud is $12 per person, or $10 if you combine it with any other pool or spa ticket. There are also men-only and women-only geo thermal cave baths in the underground tunnels where guests can soak in tubs kept between 104 and 122 degrees. In European tradition clothes are prohibited in the caves (that means bathing in the nude), and children under 12 are not permitted in this area. The caves cost $16.50 per person Monday through Thursday, $18.50 on the weekends and holidays. Or, you can purchase a pool/cave combo ticket for $26 and $27. Private outdoor hot tubs, kept at 108 degrees, can be rented for $20 per person per hour Monday through Thursday, $22 on weekends and holidays, or combined with a pool ticket for $29 and $33. Reservations are strongly recommended for the outdoor pools. Massage, wraps, and other spa services also are available. Indian Springs also has rustic-modern lodging available in the 135-year-old lodge, with an adjoining restaurant.

KEYSTONE, DILLON, SILVERTHORNE

KEYSTONE

When miners filled the Colorado mountains in the mid-1800s, Keystone grew into a small logging settlement founded by Swedes. By the time Max and Edna Dercum found the "town" in 1942, it was nothing more than a spectacular valley near the stage stop they bought and named Ski Tip Lodge. In 1970, the Dercums were prime movers in getting the wooded valley developed into a state-of-the-art family ski resort. It has since become the largest year-round ski and conference center in the state. In the late 1990s, ski giant Intrawest Corp. joined Keystone's owners to create the River Run Village, a quaint collection of specialty shops surrounding a pedestrian area, topped by a couple of floors of trendy condominiums—all making a pleasing architectural statement at the main ski-area base. The village has become a model for nearly every major ski-area development in the state and has set the tone for Copper Mountain and Breckenridge as well as Winter Park and Telluride.

DILLON

To visit the historic town of Dillon these days, you would need to don a wetsuit and tank. When the Dillon Reservoir was finished in 1963, providing a bulk of Denver's drinking water, the old town was, reluctantly, abandoned and inundated. Today, two prominent false-fronted structures survive from the old town, the Mint and the Old Dillon Inn restaurants, which were moved a short distance away to Silverthorne. Others are scattered throughout Summit County. Old Dillon sat in a quirky cradle of geography, a point where three major rivers—the Snake, the Ten Mile, and the Blue—all met before heading downstream toward the Colorado River. As a result, it quickly became a crossroads for the county, a place where the rails and later the highways breathed life into a ranching-turned-recreation community. Thinking ahead, the Denver Water Board began buying bargain-basement land in the area in the Depression, planning eventually to harness the water behind a dam and pipe it to the city. By the late 1950s, that dream was underway with the construction of the 23-mile Harold Roberts Tunnel and the dam. Dillon residents, however, were quite displeased with the move and some oldtimers to this day still spit every time they mention the city 67 miles away. In salvaging what they could, Dillon residents even moved the cemetery and 327 of its residents. Ironically, the reservoir has been a saving grace for Frisco, providing summer recreation long after the snow has vanished on the nearby ski slopes. The Dillon Marina was named one of the best sailing facilities in the country by *Sailing* magazine, and the assortment of bike and hiking tails, restaurants, and bars keep the condos full when the skiing doesn't.

SILVERTHORNE

Silverthorne has always been considered an underachieving little burg known more for its factory stores than for any quaint Main Street or attractive community center. But quietly the town below the dam is blooming into a tranquil residential center and embarking on the inevitable Summit County path toward growth and high prices. A few of the county's least expensive hotels—and one of its most expensive gas stations—greet travelers exiting I-70 to go to the factory stores. Unlike its recreation-oriented neighbors, Silverthorne attracts crowds for one reason: shopping, with discount stores ranging from Coach to Coldwater Creek, Pendleton to Eddie Bauer. Fortunately for hundreds of spouses dragged out for a day of shopping, the stores are adjacent to the bubbling Blue River, which offers some remarkable fly fishing. Buyers need beware of only one place, the Texaco station at the bottom of the off-ramp, which routinely charges a dime more for a gallon of gas than anywhere else, but gets away with it because of a never-ending stream of unaware tourists. Go a block north or south for cheaper fuel.

ACCOMMODATIONS

Alpen Hutte $
471 Rainbow Drive, Silverthorne
(970) 468-6336
www.alpenhutte.com
The Alpen Hutte offers bargain rooms in a friendly lodge similar to a youth hostel, but they're a hike from any ski area. Luckily, there's a free ski shuttle that runs frequently between Keystone, Breckenridge, and Arapahoe Basin. The lodge sleeps 66 people in rooms with four to eight bunks each (two bathrooms are down the hall on each floor). There is one private room with a queen bed, but it costs twice as much as the dorm rooms. The downstairs common area has a TV room and main living/dining room. Guests may cook their own meals. Rooms are closed for cleaning from 9:30 A.M. to 3:30 P.M.; the office is closed daily from noon to 3:30 P.M.

Best Western $$
Lake Dillon Lodge, 1202 North Summit Boulevard, Frisco
(970) 668-5094, (800) 727-0607
www.bestwestern.com

Best Western $$
Ptarmigan Lodge
652 Lake Dillon Drive, Dillon
(970) 468-2341
(800) 528-1234 reservations
www.bestwestern.com
The comfortable lodges have what you expect from a Best Western: comfortable, large rooms, a 24-hour front desk, room service, a bell staff, indoor pool, hot tub, game room, restaurant, lounge, and ski rental shop, all at a reasonable price. Although the Lake Dillon Lodge is not right on Lake Dillon, some of the rooms have nice views of the water. The Ptarmigan, however, is on the lakeshore. Pets are allowed in smoking rooms only; nonsmoking rooms are considered allergy-free.

Chateaux d'Mont $$$
U.S. Highway 6, Keystone
(970) 468-2316, (888) 222-9298
www.keystone.snow.com
The resort's premier units are in the Chateaux d'Mont, a small condo building at the base of Keystone's main ski mountain. The 15 units have two or three bedrooms, and each unit has a hot tub, fireplace, balcony, washer and dryer, whirlpool bath, and full kitchen. You can expect the same kind of kid-glove service you would get in a luxury hotel, including nightly turndown and daily maid service, robes, fresh flowers, free snacks and beverages, continental breakfast, après-ski hors d'oeuvres, and use of the Keystone Fitness Center. Decor ranges from Southwestern to French Provençal. You can also expect to pay top dollar.

The Inn at Keystone $$$
US 6, Keystone
(970) 468-2316, (888) 222-9298
www.keystone.snow.com
The Inn is Keystone's newest addition, a seven-story contemporary lodge built within walking distance of the Keystone Mountain base and Keystone Lake. It has 86 rooms and 17 suites, two of which have hot tubs. The decor is art deco, with colors heavy on turquoise, black, and pink.

During the winter season (November to April), two-week advance reservations are necessary for most lodging. During the "mud season" (April-May and October-November), rooms are more readily available.

All rooms have small refrigerators and coffeepots. Amenities include a restaurant known for its buffet breakfast, access to the Keystone Fitness Center, and three outdoor hot tubs that overlook Keystone Mountain.

Keystone Lodge $$$
US 6, Keystone
(970) 496-2316, (888) 222-9298
www.keystone.snow.com

The jewel in Keystone Resort's crown, Keystone Lodge has everything it takes to keep the well-heeled traveler comfortable. The lobby and downstairs lounge are of massive scale, with rock walls, roaring fireplaces, and racks of antlers to remind you that this is rugged mountain territory. All 152 rooms have either a mountain or a lakeside view, access to a half-dozen restaurants and shops that wrap around Keystone Lake, and enough recreational choices to make your head swim (see our "Winter Recreation" and "Other Recreations" sections for options). The heated outdoor swimming pool is open year-round, accessible by wading into an indoor pool and swimming out between plastic flaps. Among the luxurious touches are valet parking, a concierge, room service, ski check, turndown service, and a fitness facility.

Keystone Resort $$$
US 6, Keystone
(800) 222-9298

Keystone Resort has more than 800 condo units strewn around the base of the ski mountains, alongside the lake, and into the nearby woods. All are well decorated, although some of the older units are 20 years old. All have access to swimming pools, saunas, and/or hot tubs. The resort's centralized registration system makes it easy to make reservations and check into your condo. Units on the mountain's main and River Run base are the most expensive. Those farther away and in the woods are $50 to $70 per night cheaper.

LaQuinta Inn $
560 Silverthorne Lane, Silverthorne
(970) 468-6200, (800) 321-3509

One of the largest hotels in town, this former Hampton Inn is conveniently located at exit 205 off I-70. Prices are moderate for the recently upgraded 148 rooms. Guests will find ironing boards, irons, hair dryers, and coffeemakers in their rooms and a free continental breakfast in the lobby. Other amenities include an indoor pool, a hot tub, a ski shop, a guest laundry, and Old Chicago, a franchise of a wildly successful regional pizza and beer restaurant chain.

Lake Dillon Condominiums $$$
401 West Lodgepole, Dillon
(970) 468-2409, (800) 323-7792
www.summitresortgroup.com

Although they were the first condos built on Lake Dillon back in the '60s, most of these units have been updated, and you can't complain about the location. The one-acre lawn leads right to the lake's shoreline, and the city bike path passes in front of the development. The 30 one- and two-bedroom units, all with kitchens, share a game room, laundry, and indoor hot tub.

Spinnaker at Lake Dillon $$
317 La Bonte, Dillon
(970) 468-8001

Units in this luxury timeshare building are often available for rent, although there sometimes is a two-night minimum stay. The 28 units are each well equipped with washer, dryer, and fireplace. Guests can request daily housekeeping, but it costs extra. Amenities include an indoor pool, hot tub, and sauna.

Super 8 Motel   **$**
808 Little Beaver Trail, Dillon
(970) 468–8888, (800) 800–8000
Just off I–70 at exit 205, this well-known
national chain is a predictable oasis for
weary skiers on a budget. Rooms come
with either two double beds or one queen
bed, as well as a table with two chairs.
Free continental breakfast is served in the
lobby, and restaurants are across the
street.

Wildernest Condominiums   **$$**
200 Wildernest Road, Silverthorne
(970) 468–6291, (800) 554–2212
(outside Colorado)
Wildernest is hard to miss, a 200-unit
development clinging to the hillside north
of I–70 at the Dillon/Silverthorne exit. It is
home to housing that ranges from studio
apartments to homes, many of which are
available to rent. Guests have access to a
clubhouse that includes a pool, hot tub,
and sauna as well as free shuttle service
to nearby ski areas and towns. One
absolutely fabulous restaurant, Silverheels,
is contained in the project; others are a
short car ride away.

BED-AND-BREAKFASTS

Ski Tip Bed-and-Breakfast   **$$**
Montezuma Road, Keystone
(970) 496–4202, (888) 222–9298
Before there was Keystone, there was the
Ski Tip Lodge. This historic stage stop
served mountain mining towns until it was
turned into the county's first ski inn by
Arapahoe Basin and Keystone founders
Max and Edna Dercum. Although now
owned by Keystone Resort, it still operates as a charming country bed-and-
breakfast nestled beside the Snake River.
Growth has caught up with it, however.
The rustic log cabin that is decorated like
a Swiss chalet is being engulfed by a new
home development. Its 14 rooms are small
and cozy (the biggest ones are on the
second floor) and come with a breakfast
buffet. Be sure to make use of the com-

mon sitting rooms and grassy streamside
areas. The lodge's restaurant is well known
and requires reservations well in advance.

Western Skies B & B   **$$**
5040 Montezuma Road, Dillon
(970) 468–9945
www.westernskies-keystone-cabins.com
Just when you think the blacktop is end-
ing on Montezuma Road, you'll see a
tepee in the woods that signals Western
Skies. With 37 acres of tranquil real estate
at the head of the Peru Gulch Trail and
surrounded by Arapaho National Forest
land, the retreat is delightfully quiet. The
proprietors rent four guest rooms in their
main home and three self-contained cab-
ins that come with kitchens and sleep up
to five. Lodge guests get a generous con-
tinental breakfast and can share the living
room, sun deck, and fire-heated hot tub. If
you have trouble breathing, it's because
the lodge elevation is 10,500 feet.

RESTAURANTS

Alpenglow Stube   **$$$$**
Keystone Resort, in The Outpost
atop North Peak
(800) 354–4386
If you're looking for a new take on the
special-occasion dinner, the Alpenglow
Stube is the place to go. It claims to be
North America's highest gourmet restau-
rant, at an elevation of 11,444 feet. To get
you there, you'll ride two gondolas up to
the top of Keystone Resort's North Peak
ski mountain (fares are included in the
price of dinner). Inside the restaurant,
you'll find warm, romantic decor that
includes a rock fireplace, dark wooden
ceilings, and gigantic antler chandeliers.
The Stube's six-course meal is legendary,
with pine-cone pâté to begin with, fol-
lowed by a fresh spinach salad served
with hazelnut-encrusted Camembert,
regional game entrees that include the
likes of grilled caribou chops or rotisserie
pheasant breast, and a sweet cheese

crème brulée with berries and almonds for dessert. During the winter the Stube is open for lunch. Dinner is served year-round, except for brief closures between seasons in late spring and early winter. Dinner reservations are required.

Arapahoe Cafe $$
626 Lake Dillon Drive, Dillon
(970) 468-0873
In the early 1940s, this historic log cabin sat in downtown Dillon. Once the dam was built and old town Dillon was flooded, owners Faye and Lenore Bryant moved their little restaurant up the hill to its present site. Now within a stone's throw of the dramatic lake and marina, the Arapahoe Cafe continues to serve the same kind of down-home breakfast (served 7:00 A.M. to 2:30 P.M.), lunch, and dinner it is famous for.

Bighorn Steakhouse $$$
US 6, Keystone
(970) 496-4386
Guests of the Keystone Lodge can walk downstairs to this warm, comfortable restaurant. Of course, non-guests can join them, too, by driving through valet parking or walking through Keystone Village. The manly restaurant is ringed with deep, cushy booths; a salad and soup bar occupies the center of the room. Meals are heavy on beef—prime and choice-cut steaks, filet mignons, and prime ribs—but also include chicken, freshwater bass, and spicy pork loin steaks. It's open only for dinner.

Keystone Ranch $$$$
1437 County Road 150, Keystone
(970) 496-4386
Another of Keystone Resort's special-occasion restaurants, Keystone Ranch is located in an elegant 1930s ranch home alongside the Keystone Ranch Golf Course. Diners are treated to a prix fixe five-course meal that's heavy on Colorado cuisine. Appetizers include grilled plains pheasant breast and a foie gras trio; salad is a variety of baby lettuces with roast corn relish, baby tomatoes, pickled car-

rots, and a daikon roast pepper vinaigrette; entrees range from roast rack of Colorado lamb to filet of American buffalo to loin of high-country venison. There are also nightly seafood special entrees. Lavish desserts include the Grand Marnier soufflé with warm pistachio anglaise.

Old Dillon Inn $$
321 Blue River Parkway, Silverthorne
(970) 468-2791
A Summit County classic, this lively place defies description. Like the Arapahoe Cafe, it was ferried across the road from old town Dillon, but the similarities stop there. It dates back to 1869, when it was built in the mining town of Montezuma and moved in pieces to old Dillon. In 1962 it was loaded on a flatbed truck and moved to Silverthorne so quickly the kegs of beer didn't have time to get warm. The bar still draws big crowds on the weekends. The adjoining restaurant serves delicious Mexican food and great drinks for dinner only and in unpretentious surroundings. Reservations are not accepted.

Ski Tip Lodge $$$$
Montezuma Road, Keystone
(970) 496-4386
This 1880s stage stop turned bed-and-breakfast boasts one of the county's hottest tickets: a four-course prix fixe dinner that has people calling weeks ahead for reservations. The cozy dining room is, like the rest of the lodge, made of logs, but there's nothing rustic about the food. The menu changes daily, but appetizers can include aspargus bleu cheese veal roulade au poive, followed by an entree such as cinnamon and salt-dusted Muscovy duck. Reservations are required.

NIGHTLIFE

Keystone Lodge
US 6, Keystone
(970) 496-2316
Sometimes the best nightlife is a long, comfy couch, a roaring fire, and a nightcap

to sip with someone you love. When that's the case, Keystone Lodge has just the place. Its downstairs bar and lounge has the biggest stone fireplace this side of Hades that's kept roaring with logs so big they look like Paul Bunyan chopped them. Three couches are arranged U-shaped in front of the fire, and a gigantic antler chandelier adds a gentle glow to the nook.

Kickapoo Tavern
129 River Run Road, Keystone
(970) 496-4601

At the edge of the bustling Keystone Village, the Kickapoo is one of the resort's hot spots for après-ski, especially for the younger crowd. With a full selection of microbrews and mixed drinks, and a great feel, it's a pleasant respite from the cold night air.

The Old Dillon Inn
321 Blue River Parkway, Silverthorne
(970) 468-2791

Skiing magazine cites the Old Dillon Inn in its annual skiing awards story for having the Bluest Margaritas. The old wooden bar is long and rustic, reportedly brought in by wagon in the 1800s. Locals and live country-and-western bands keep the place jumping late into the night.

Snake River Saloon
23074 US 6, Keystone
(970) 468-2788

A real locals' hangout, the Snake often features live music and always has a lively crowd. Try not to act like a tourist (order beer—not mixed drinks—tip the bartender, and don't brag about your skiing) else you'll likely be ridiculed by the rough-and-tumble crowd.

ATTRACTIONS

Keystone Gondola
River Run Village, US 6 and
Montezuma Road, Keystone
(970) 496-4386, (800) 222-0188

Whether or not you ski, you can still ride Keystone's high-speed gondola. Inside the enclosed cars you can glide to the top of 11,444-foot North Peak, enjoy the views, and stay for dinner at The Outpost or Der Fondue Chessel (six-course meals or Swiss-style fondue). Rides are free after 4:00 P.M. or all-day passes are $15. After a brief intermission in May and June, the gondola opens again on July 4 for summer visitors. It runs daily from 8:30 A.M. to 8:00 P.M. If you'd like to transport a bike to the top for a ride down, you may do so at no additional charge.

KIDSTUFF

Dillon Reservoir
Dillon Marina, 300 Marina Drive
(970) 468-5100

Dillon Reservoir, also called Lake Dillon, is a 3,300-acre lake with 26 miles of shoreline and stunning mountain scenery. Summer boaters create a frequently photographed potpourri of color on the deep blue waters. Some visitors camp and fish, but the lake is best known for its boating. (No swimming is allowed.) At the Dillon Marina on the southeast side of the lake you can rent pontoons, fishing boats, runabouts, kayaks, and sailboats (experience is required for these). If you'd rather look at the water than float on it, you'll have an excellent view from the boat ramp. The marina also has adequate picnic grounds, restrooms, and a snack stand that opens weekends through July, then full-time on July 4. The marina is open Memorial Day to Labor Day daily 8:00 A.M. to 5:30 P.M., shorter hours through October and closed in winter.

Keystone Gondola
US 6 and Montezuma Road, Keystone
(970) 496-2316, (800) 222-0188

Kids will love this high-altitude "ride" to the top of scenic North Peak, and you don't need to be a skier to enjoy the gondola. It runs daily from 8:30 A.M. to 8:00 P.M. Ticket prices are $15 for adults and $10 for children 5 to 12. Kids under 5 are free,

Dillon Reservoir, also called Lake Dillon, is 3,300 acres of summer fun. No swimming is allowed, but visitors can camp, fish, and rent pontoon boats, kayaks, and sailboats.
THE DENVER POST/LYN ALWEIS

as is everyone after 4:00 P.M. If you'd like to transport a bike to the top, you may at no additional charge. See the listing above under "Attractions" for more information.

Keystone Lake
Keystone Resort, US 6, Keystone
(970) 468-4130

Keystone Lake in the heart of Keystone Village is an ice skating venue in the winter, but when summer comes it opens to paddleboats, canoes, kayaks, and sailboards. From mid-June to mid-September it's open 9:00 A.M. to 8:00 P.M. daily. Rental rates are as follows: paddleboats, $9.00 half hour; kayaks, $7.00 to $9.00 per half-hour; canoes, $9.00 per half-hour; sailboards, $16.00 per hour, including wet suit and life jacket.

Keystone Resort
US 6, Keystone
(970) 496-4386, (800) 222-0188

As a full-service family resort, Keystone is in the business of keeping children busy and happy. Paddleboats, kayaks, canoes, and sailboards are available for rental on the lake, and bikes and in-line skates can be rented for cruising on the excellent Snake River bike paths. Discounts are offered in the early summer and late fall. Volleyball, horseshoes, tetherball, and table tennis are free. Cyclists can pick up a creekside trail near the building or, after July 4, can take their bikes up the summit chairlift to more challenging trails.

Every winter Keystone's five-acre lake freezes solid, providing visitors with the largest maintained outdoor ice skating rink in North America. A former beaver pond, it was converted in 1970 to a skate, sled, hockey, and boating venue in the heart of Keystone Village. Throughout the winter it is decorated with lit Christmas trees, and the surface is smoothed daily with a Zamboni. The warming house is at the west end of the lake where you can rent skates and stow your gear. It's open from 10:00 A.M. to 10:00 P.M. from late November to early March. Skates, sleds, and hockey sticks can be rented at the warming house.

SHOPPING

Shopping here is dominated by the two factory outlet malls that occupy the Dillon/Silverthorne exit from I-70. Locals from as far away as Vail and Glenwood Springs regularly make the trek to the outlet malls for their good selection and great prices. Other shops are clustered along the Blue River Parkway heading north from Silverthorne, at Keystone Village surrounding Keystone Lodge, and at the bases of Keystone's ski mountains.

Christy Sports Ski & Patio
817 US 6, Dillon
(970) 468-2329
www.christysports.com
During the winter, this chain store stocks skis and related accessories. In the summer, it specializes in deck and patio furniture.

Eddie Bear's
591 Blue River Parkway, Silverthorne
(970) 468-9320
For the true sports enthusiast, Eddie Bear's carries guns and ammunition, fishing and camping gear, liquor, propane, and diesel fuel. This is perhaps the best shop in all of Silverthorne, too, with a full grocery, convenience store, and of course, full-service gasoline (when time permits). The folks there buy, sell, and trade anything.

Inxpot
195 River Run Road, Keystone
(970) 496-4627
Located in the Keystone Village, this charming coffee shop also features an eclectic selection of books and cards. Other selections by the major publishers can be ordered and shipped at no charge before your vacation is even over.

Mountain Sports Outlet
167 Meraly Way, Silverthorne
(970) 262-2836
www.mountainsportsoutlet.com
A great outlet store for the outdoors enthusiast, it's the place to rent or buy bikes or hiking boots when the weather is warm. When it turns cold, you can do the same with skis, snowboards, and snowshoes.

Mountain View Sports
22837 US 6, across from Keystone Ski slopes at Mountain View Plaza
(970) 468-0396
www.mountainviewsports.com
You can rent bikes here during the summer. During the winter the merchandise changes to skis, snowboards, and snowshoes.

Nike Factory Store
237 Blue River Parkway, Silverthorne
(970) 468-6040
Once in a while the store sets aside one whole wall and fills it with $5.00 pairs of shoes. The best times to shop it are January and February, July and August. The summer prices are slashed deeper to move merchandise quickly in Colorado's brief mountain summer season. The store also offers a full selection of Nike sportswear, for those who can't be seen without the familiar swoosh mark.

The Outlets at Silverthorne
145 Stephens Way, Silverthorne
(970) 468-9440
www.silverthornefactorystores.com
On the north and south sides of the road in Silverthorne, you'll find the original—and

much larger—outlet mall. Its tenants include Bass Apparel, Dress Barn, Great Outdoor Clothing Co., Izod, J. Crew, Jones New York, Liz Claiborne, Maidenform, Nike, Pearl Izumi, Polo Ralph Lauren, Rue 21, the Jockey Store, and Tommy Hilfiger.

Wilderness Sports
266 Summit Place, Silverthorne
(970) 468-5687

400 Main Street, Frisco
(970) 668-8804
www.wildsummit.com
Since 1976 this store has provided technical outdoor gear for the serious athlete. If you plan to participate in a sport that can be done in the mountains and requires gear, Wilderness Sports can probably outfit you. Aside from the typical bikes and skis, this store carries hiking poles, maps, and guidebooks. Tome Jones Jr. and his staff know the backcountry around Summit County like the backs of their hands, too, so they're great for advice.

Necessities

City Market
300 US 6, Dillon
(970) 468-2363
In Colorado towns too small to support a big chain grocery store like Safeway, the City Market chain steps in to provide great grocery selections, bakeries, delis, and pharmacies. Get your prescription refilled here, buy over-the-counter remedies, rent a video, or belly up to the salad bar. A source of local controversy, however, is that the new superstore was lured just across the town line from Silverthorne (it had been in the Summit Place shopping

i *Water boils slower and at lower temperatures at altitude, a fact that must be considered when baking and cooking. Many products come with high-altitude instructions.*

center, closer to I-70) with generous tax benefits. It now anchors a strip mall that has all of the suburban conveniences, including a liquor store, dry cleaner, and even a Kinko's, a Starbuck's, and a Pier 1 Imports.

Sanders True Value
160 West Sixth Street, Silverthorne
(970) 262-1338
Pop into this hardware store for housewares, keys, tire chains (you'll need them in the winter if you plan to drive on snowy mountain passes), and other incidentals. The clerks are incredibly helpful and have no problem talking you through fix-it jobs.

ARTS

Lake Dillon Foundation for the Performing Arts
176 Lake Dillon Drive, Dillon
(970) 513-9386
www.lakedillonfoundation.org
This nonprofit foundation was formed to bring quality musical and performing arts into Summit County. Its major accomplishments so far include sponsoring a 10-week free summer concert series at the Lake Dillon Amphitheatre and organizing adult and children's theater companies. The summer concerts are performed by regional musicians in a wide range of disciplines, from zydeco to steel drums. The theater company (see separate listing) does as many as 10 performances a year.

Lake Dillon Theater Company
176 Lake Dillon Drive, Dillon
(970) 513-9386
www.lakedillontheatre.org
Company instructors, under the moniker Young People's Theatre Workshop, teach children's theater classes during the summer. Classes lead to a public performance in the Lake Dillon Amphitheatre. In 2005 students performed *Wind in the Willows*. During the winter, actors perform adult plays in the Old Town Hall. Depending on time and interest, company members pro-

duce eight to ten plays a year, which always are of excellent quality. Among the performers are veterans of many prestigious acting troupes.

EVENTS

January

Mountain Dew Vertical Challenge
Keystone Resort, US 6, Keystone
(970) 468-2316, (800) 222-0188
Sponsored by Mountain Dew, this is a fun series of 50 ski and snowboard amateur races held at different resorts in Colorado, Utah, and the Northeast. Races are open to all skiers and boarders who purchase a valid lift ticket. With more than 30 available race categories, the event is open to all ages and abilities. The top three finishers in each category are awarded medals and invited to compete in the series finals.

February

Betty Fest
Keystone Resort, US 6, Keystone
(970) 468-2316, (800) 222-0188
The Keystone Betty Fest brings women together for a high-energy, weekend get-together on and off the ski slopes. The program features extensive on-hill training, video analysis, yoga, and discussions about nutrition and equipment. Snowboarders of any skill level are welcome, but the program suggests skiers should feel comfortable on the green, or beginner's, slopes. Price is $195 for the workshop; equipment rentals are extra. One-day camps are also available every Tuesday for $85.

March

Saint Patrick's Day Celebration
Copper Mountain Resort
Exit 195 off I-70, 75 miles west of Denver
(866) 841-2481, (888) 219-2441
A traditional St. Patrick's Day celebration takes place in the heart of Copper Mountain's main village on March 17. It's an Irish street fair with food and craft vendors, music, and the requisite green beer.

June

Taste of the Summit
Marina Park, off Lodgepole Street on
Dillon Reservoir, Dillon
(970) 468-3400
More than 20 Summit County chefs bring samples of their best dishes to be tasted in Dillon's Marina Park in late June. Participants can also sample wines and microbrews, browse through arts and crafts booths, and enjoy live entertainment. There's a nominal admission fee.

July

Sunset at the Summit
Lake Dillon Amphitheatre, Marina Park
on Dillon Reservoir off Lodgepole
Street, Dillon
(970) 513-9386
www.lakedillonfoundation.org
Free Saturday night concerts are sponsored throughout July and August by the

Keystone is the state's largest year-round ski and conference destination, with a 100,000-square-foot conference center across the street from the ski mountain and skating lake. It also has the state's longest ski day, from 9:00 A.M. to 9:00 P.M. After the sun sets, lights illuminate the mountains for diehard skiers and snowboarders.

Lake Dillon Foundation for the Performing Arts. These open-air concerts begin at 7:00 P.M. in the Lake Dillon Amphitheatre and include country-western, zydeco, Dixieland, Latin jazz, torch, and swing music. They've been known to attract as many as 1,200 fans.

Fourth of July Weekend
Various locations, Dillon
(970) 262-3400
www.townofdillon.com
On July 4, the Town of Dillon sponsors a morning hometown parade on Main Street, a boat parade at the Dillon Marina, a benefit barbecue, music in Marina Park, and a free concert at Lake Dillon Amphitheatre followed by fireworks over the lake. During the holiday weekend, the Dillon Yacht Club also sponsors a Regatta, details of which are available at (970) 262-5824.

Fourth of July at Keystone Resort
US 6, Keystone
(970) 468-2316, (800) 222-0188
www.keystone.snow.com
The day starts with a pancake breakfast and bike parade at Keystone Village, followed by a day of face painting, balloons, crafts, and children's entertainers. The National Repertory Orchestra performs a free patriotic concert in Decatur Field. Most events are free.

Mountain Community Fair
Blue River Park, Silverthorne
(970) 513-8081
www.mountaincommunityfair
.netfirms.com
For a real old-fashioned county fair with 4-H exhibits, contests, and a rodeo, this two-day fair is the place to be in mid-July. The small admission price includes everything but the carnival booths and rides. Two-day passes and family rates also are available.

August

Sunset at the Summit
Lake Dillon Amphitheatre, Dillon
(970) 513-9386
Free Saturday night concerts are sponsored throughout July and August by the Lake Dillon Foundation for the Performing Arts. Look for details in the July listing.

Blue Grass and Beer Festival
Keystone Resort, US 6, Keystone
(970) 496-4386, (800) 222-0188
In early August Keystone Resort clears its River Run Events Plaza for down-home cooking and blue grass music. And just in case that raises a thirst, 25 of Colorado's microbreweries are on hand with their special recipe beers. Pets are prohibited, but free parking is available at the River Run parking lot.

Dillon Open Regatta
Dillon Reservoir
(970) 262-5824
www.dillonopen.com
The Rocky Mountain's premier sailing event is hosted by the Dillon Yacht Club. The Dillon Marina was rated by *Sailing* magazine as one of the best places in the country for sailing, believe it or not, because of the spectacular scenery, great support, and unpredictable mountain weather.

Wine, Jazz & Art Festival
Keystone Resort, US 6, Keystone
(970) 496-4386, (800) 222-0188
Late August brings wine-lovers, jazz fans, and artists together for three days on Keystone's River Run Events Plaza. Live musicians share the Pavilion with experts who offer wine seminars and culinary demonstrations, and a juried art show is hung throughout the plaza. Food booths, tastings, and children's activities round out the event that benefits the Keystone Center, a nonprofit environmental group.

October

Wine in the Pines
Keystone Resort, US 6, Keystone
(303) 691-9339
www.cpco.org/wineinthepines/index.html
In mid-October Keystone hosts two days
of wine tasting, fine dining, and an auction
to benefit the United Cerebral Palsy Foundation. Tickets are $100 apiece.

November

36 Hours of Keystone
Keystone Resort, US 6, Keystone
(970) 496-4386, (800) 222-0188
Each November Keystone celebrates the
beginning of the season with 36 straight
hours of skiing and snowboarding on the
ski area's lighted slopes. The event has
become so popular that sporting goods
stores and restaurants in River Run Village
stay open throughout the event. One year
they ran out of energy drinks and coffee,
but they haven't been caught short-
handed since. One especially nice part of
the event: watching the sun rise from atop
the mountain.

December

Betty Fest
Keystone Resort, US 6, Keystone
(970) 468-2316, (800) 222-0188
The Keystone Betty Fest brings women
together for a high-energy, weekend get-
together on and off the ski slopes. The
program features extensive on-hill training,
video analysis, yoga, and discussions about
nutrition and equipment. Snowboarders of
any skill level are welcome, but the program suggests skiers should feel comfortable on the green, or beginner's, slopes.
Price is $195 for the workshop; equipment
rentals are extra. One-day camps are also
available every Tuesday for $85. The clinics
start in December and continue throughout the ski season.

DOWNHILL SKIING

Keystone

Keystone
US 6
(970) 468-2316, (800) 222-0188
www.keystone.snow.com
Resort elevation: *9,300 feet*
Top of highest lift: *11,640 feet*
Top of hike-to terrain: *12,200 feet*
Total vertical: *2,900 feet*
Longest run: *3½ miles*
Average annual snowfall: *230 inches*
Ski season: mid-October to early May
Capacity: *33,564 skiers per hour*
Terrain: *2,870 acres, 116 trails (12 percent
beginner and novice, 34 percent intermedi-
ate, 54 percent advanced and expert)*
Night skiing: *until 9:00 P.M. on 15
frontside runs*
Lift tickets: *$75 all-day adult*
Snow reports: *(970) 496-4111*
Getting there: *Keystone is 75 miles west of
Denver via I-70. You can exit at Loveland
Pass and take US 6, but the pass is filled with
hairpin turns and often closes in winter
snowstorms. Most folks follow I-70 through
the Eisenhower Tunnel to the Dillon exit, then
backtrack 6 miles on US 6 to the resort.*

The original Keystone Mountain looks
deceptively gentle, but most of it spreads
out beyond the line of sight. Out of view of
folks on the bottom is bumpy North Peak,
and behind that is The Outback, home to
wide glades and tree-free bowls. Both are
challenging areas that beginners and
novices graduate to after mastering Keystone Mountain's meandering runs. They're
accessible from the nearby Village at River
Run, a second, newer base area that serves
as the gateway to the "black-diamond" or
expert runs.

Kids are attracted by an excellent Children's Center, with extensive child care and
lesson programs (see our Kidstuff chapter
for more information), and by Gold Rush
Alley, a kids-only terrain garden with a
mining theme. Keystone offers night skiing,
a snowboarders' terrain park, and myriad
other appealing terrain features.

Kids are attracted to Keystone Resort's excellent children's program and terrain that is reserved for young boarders and skiers (and the occasional adult "chairlift"). *THE DENVER POST*/RJ SANGOSTI

Arapahoe Basin

Arapahoe Basin
US 6, between Loveland Basin and Keystone
(970) 496–7077
www.arapahoebasin.com
Resort elevation: *10,800 feet*
Top of highest lift: *13,050 feet*
Total vertical: *2,257 feet*
Longest run: *1½ miles*
Average annual snowfall: *360 inches*
Ski season: *mid-November until at least June, often later*
Capacity: *8,700 skiers per hour*
Terrain: *490 acres, 69 trails (15 percent beginner and novice, 40 percent intermediate, 45 percent advanced and expert)*
Lift tickets: *$45 all-day adult*
Snow reports: *(970) 468–4111*
Getting there: *Arapahoe Basin is 96 miles west of Denver via I-70. Exiting at Loveland Pass and taking US 6 west is a more direct route, but the pass is dangerous and often closed during snowstorms. It's safer to follow I-70 through the Eisenhower Tunnel to the Dillon exit (205), then backtrack 11 miles on US 6.*

Arapahoe Basin, or A-Basin as it is called by locals, is also nicknamed "The Legend." That may be because it is America's highest lift-served ski area, topping out at 12,450 feet above sea level. If that's not high enough for you, you can ride the highest lift and hike another 600 feet into pristine backcountry bowls.

Skiing A-Basin is like stepping back in time. The resort opened in 1947 with a war surplus truck that carried skiers from the original lodge to a rope tow at mid-mountain. The mid-mountain warming house that was built soon after from surplus timber is still home to the legendary spring outdoor barbecues.

A-Basin's skiing is in a category unto itself. Almost all of its 490 acres are in an above-timberline bowl, which means there are no trees blocking your view of the menacing snow-covered Rocky Mountains. You'll be skiing along the Continental Divide, the mountaintops that bisect the United States. Rain and snow that fall to the west flow to the Pacific Ocean; precipitation that falls to the east flows to the Atlantic. All that means for skiers is heart-stopping, peak-top views of the harsh, unforgiving gray rock faces and the deep precipices in between. Those views can be (literally) breathtaking for those who are afraid of heights or unaccustomed to the high altitude.

Long before the first skier set foot on Keystone Mountain, ski visionary Max Dercum had his sights set on opening a ski area in Arapahoe Basin. The wide, snowy bowl on the west side of Loveland Pass reminded him of the Alps but was isolated near the top of a treacherous mountain pass nicknamed "the trucker's nightmare." When skiers Larry Jump and Frederick "Sandy" Schauffler were hired by the City of Denver to survey possible ski areas in Colorado, Dercum climbed aboard. The resort you ski today is much the same as it was when Jump, Schauffler, and Dercum opened it in the 1940s.

A-Basin's high altitude preserves its snow until long after other ski areas have metamorphosed into summer retreats. Many years it closes on July 4, and then only because its regular customers are called to lower elevations for a few months of yard work and summer maintenance duties. By November, they're lured back up again by the wild, craggy peaks and legendary steep slopes. Ninety percent of the terrain is rated for strong intermediate/expert skiers, with moguls and runs that look more like ski jumps, but in spring the soft corn snow opens some of the easier slopes to all levels. A few wide, gentle boulevards along the eastern edge of the resort keep beginners challenged but happy.

Don't expect frills here. The facilities are as no-nonsense as the clientele. In the simple base lodge, you'll find cafeteria food and a simple bar with a wraparound deck, but that's just fine with the scruffy, hard-core skiers who frequent the place.

They're a young, exuberant group that skis hard and then plays hard, leaving their dogs tied to their trucks' side-view mirrors and setting up lawn chairs and hibachis to enjoy a makeshift après-ski in the parking lot.

NORDIC/CROSS-COUNTRY

Keystone Cross-Country Center
US 6, Keystone
(970) 496-4275
The Keystone Cross-Country Center offers 16 kilometers of groomed trails in the Snake River Valley and 57 kilometers of ungroomed trails in the backcountry of the Arapaho National Forest. It also sponsors guided excursions into the Montezuma Valley and Arapaho National Forest lands, monthly moonlight tours and Friday workshops for women. You can also find your own cross-country skiing areas in and around Montezuma Valley. From the Peru Creek trailhead, ski a gentle route that leads to mine remnants, or take the steeper route to mining ghost town Sts. John.

OTHER WINTER RECREATION

Gondola Rides

Keystone Gondola
River Run Village, US 6 and Montezuma Road, Keystone
(970) 468-2316, (800) 222-0188
Whether or not you ski, you can still ride Keystone's high-speed gondola. Inside the enclosed cars you can glide to the top of 11,444-foot North Peak, enjoy the views, and stay for dinner at The Outpost or Der Fondue Chessel (six-course meals or Swiss-style fondue). Rides are free after 4:00 P.M. or all-day passes are $15. Rides are free for kids 4 and younger. The gondola runs daily 8:30 A.M. to 8:00 P.M.

Ice Skating

Keystone Resort
US 6, Keystone
(800) 354-4386
Every winter Keystone's five-acre lake freezes solid, providing visitors with the largest maintained outdoor ice skating rink in North America. A former beaver pond, it was converted in 1970 to a skate, sled, and hockey venue in the heart of Keystone Village. Throughout the winter it is decorated with lit Christmas trees, and the surface is smoothed daily with a Zamboni. The warming house is a gazebo at the west end of the lake where you can rent skates and stow your gear. It's open daily from 10:00 A.M. to 10:00 P.M. from late November to early March. Skates, sleds, and hockey sticks can be rented at the warming house.

Sleigh Rides

Soda Creek Homestead
US 6, Keystone
(800) 354-4386
Belgian draft horses pull sleighs to Keystone's Soda Creek Homestead, one of the original ranches in the tree-covered valley. Following the trip, guests tour several of the rickety outbuildings, then are served a steak dinner (vegetarian meals can be requested) inside either of two cabins as a cowboy serenades them. Prices are all-inclusive except for the tip.

Snowmobiles

Keystone Resort
US 6, Keystone
(800) 354-4386
Explore the backcountry of the Arapahoe National Forest by snowmobile in tours that travel through the mountain valleys and to abandoned mining sites. Rental fees include a helmet, snowmobile suits, and boots. Half-day tours leave at 8:45 and 9:00 A.M. and 1:00 and 1:45 P.M.

Fans of Arapahoe Basin don't expect frills. The scruffy, hardcore skiers and boarders who have kept the ski area alive make their own après ski celebrations in the parking lot.
THE DENVER POST/HELEN H. RICHARDSON

Snowshoes

Keystone Resort
US 6, Keystone
(970) 496–4275, (800) 354–4386
www.keystone.snow.com/info/
snowshoe.asp

Snowshoers are welcome in the ungroomed and forested areas alongside ski runs, or may join one of the guided tours. Ecology tours, the all-day Peak to Peak tour, and the nighttime Full Moon tours charge varying fees that include the tour, trail pass, lift rides, and equipment rentals. Minimum-age restrictions apply on most tours. Check the Web site for current tour times and rates. For those who want to just wander about on their own, snowshoe rentals are $18.00 for adults, $12.00 for seniors over 65, $9.00 for chil-

dren under 12, and $4.00 for toddlers. Trail passes are $9.00 for adults, $5.00 for seniors, and children under 12 are free.

HIKING

Chihuahua Gulch
4.6 miles east of Keystone

A bracing climb levels off into a terrific half-day hike that starts at an abandoned old mining town and reaches 12,220 feet. To get there, drive 6½ miles east from Dillon on US 6 past Keystone, then turn on the Montezuma Road. At 4⁴⁄₁₀ miles, turn left on the dirt Peru Creek Road, which can be negotiated by passenger cars most of the year. After 2 bumpy miles, you'll reach the junction of the Chihuahua Gulch Road, which requires four-wheel drive. Most peo-

ple park along the road here and hike along the lightly traveled road. Look for ruins of old mines, but it's best to stay away from them: They're all still considered private property, and many of them are extremely dangerous. Looting, similarly, is considered bad form. The town of Chihuahua, which once had a post office, three restaurants, and three saloons, burned to the ground in a forest fire in 1889.

CAMPING

Dillon Reservoir
Dillon
(877) 444-6777

Owned and operated by Denver Water, Dillon Reservoir offers scenic lakeside campsites with picnic tables, fire grills, vault toilets, and plenty of drinking water from the lake. About half the sites here are available on a first-come, first-served basis; the rest can be reserved 10 or more days in advance. Among the choices available at Dillon Reservoir are Heaton Bay Campground, $14, 72 sites; Peak One, $14, 79 sites; Pine Cove Campground $12, 33 sites; and Prospector Campground $13, 108 sites. For group camping (reservations required), choose Windy Point Campground, which has 72 sites and larger parking areas at each site.

Blue River Campground, with 24 sites, is on the beautiful Blue River, 9 miles north of Silverthorne on Highway 9.

Green Mountain Reservoir
Highway 9, north of Silverthorne

At Green Mountain, another scenic reservoir, campers will find McDonald Flats Campground, with 13 sites, and Prairie Point Campground, with 31 sites. At Elliot

Creek Campground (primitive camping) there's a $5.00 fee as is there at Cataract Creek Campground, which has only four sites. To reach Green Mountain Reservoir, drive 23 miles north of Silverthorne on Highway 9. This area tends to be crowded and very noisy on virtually every summer weekend.

GOLF

Keystone Ranch Golf Club
1239 Keystone Ranch Road, Keystone
(970) 496-4250

The Keystone Ranch course, elevation 9,300 feet, is nestled into a lush valley that was a buffalo hunting ground for Ute and Arapaho Indians until it was homesteaded in the 1930s. The elegant log ranch house now serves as the clubhouse, with its dining room a well-respected restaurant. Rusted plows and tillers have been left in the rough, and dilapidated outbuildings and pole fences separate the 5th and 6th holes. The front nine holes are of the classic links design, with small landing areas carved out of the native weeds and grasses. The second nine have wide manicured fairways that follow a creek up and back through the valley and around a nine-acre lake.

The 7,090-yard, par 72 course has won its share of awards. Designed by Robert Trent Jones Jr., it is rated one of the state's top 10 courses by *Golf Digest*. Weather permitting, it's open from late May to early October, with high season between June 20 and September 21. Keystone Resort guests and homeowners have priority on the tee times, but the public is welcome. Carts are required until 4:00 P.M., but the best deal is for twilight walkers, who can play for deeply discounted rates.

The Raven Golf Club at Three Peaks
2929 North Golden Road, Silverthorne
(970) 262-3636
www.ravengolf.com

Now under the control of Canadian resort conglomerate Intrawest, The Raven Golf

Every June, residents of the Summit County community of Heeney (south of Silverthorne) host the annual Tick Festival, a celebration of the Rocky Mountains' most unpleasant arachnid.

The Blue River flows out of Dillon Reservoir and boasts fantastic rainbow and brown trout fishing. THE DENVER POST/KIRK SPEER

Club has undergone a rebirth after years of disrepair and neglect. The course has garnered significant attention and awards, including a ranking as one of the Top Ten You Can Play in the U.S. by *Golf Magazine,* and #1 Mountain Course in Colorado by *Colorado Avid Golfer* magazine. The par 71 course reaches over 7,400 yards from the tips, and greens fees range from $89 to $129 depending on the season.

HUNTING AND FISHING

Outfitters and Tackle Shops

Bar T Outfitters
Silverthorne
(970) 468-6916
www.bar-t-outfitters.com
This full-service outfitter provides one guide to every two hunters, horses, game handling, field care of any animals bagged during the hunt, meals, tent camps, and transportation to the hunt area. Clients must get their own deer and elk licenses and must find their own transportation to Silverthorne. Bar T leads hunters into the Arapaho National Forest.

Cutthroat Anglers
400 Blue River Parkway, Silverthorne
(970) 262-2878, (888) 876-8818
When Trapper Rudd, a former skier "interested in fishing the rest of my life," bought the acclaimed Arapahoe Anglers, he promised more of the great services: half- and full-day fishing trips on public and private water, on foot, or in boats. Prices range from $180 to $400 depending on the number of people. The guides also hold free casting clinics in the summer, and the pro shop stocks a full selection of fly-fishing products and rents waders and fly rods.

Summit Guides
Keystone Village
(970) 468-8945
www.summitguides.com
Summit Guides offer services that range from fly-fishing lessons along the banks of Keystone Pond to half- and full-day fishing trips on private and public waters on the Blue, Colorado, and South Platte Rivers and, after July 1, to nearby high mountain lakes. Guests can fish from boats or in waders and can bring their own equipment or rent it. They also operate a full-service tackle shop on the premises.

Places to Fish

Blue River
Adjacent to Highway 9
The crystal water of the Blue flows out of Dillon Reservoir and boasts fantastic rainbow and brown trout fishing. Below Dillon Reservoir, the Lower Blue River is designated Gold Medal water, which means catch and release only. There are plenty of places to park along Highway 9 as the river moves toward Green Mountain Reservoir. Try to fish the stretches that are as far away as possible from the road. Depending on the hatch, locals have had luck with No. 14 and No. 16 elk hair caddis imitations.

Dillon Reservoir
I-70 between Dillon and Frisco exits
Dillon Reservoir is the focal point of Summit County, and many anglers are happy to stay along its 26-mile shoreline. Casting from the shore is not as effective as fishing from a boat, but it can be worthwhile. There are boat launching ramps at Frisco Bay, Frisco Marina, Blue River Inlet, and Pine Cove Campground. Both the Frisco Marina and the Dillon Marina rent boats. Experts like fishing the lake just as the ice recedes and after it has been stocked with

small kokanee salmon and cutthroat and brook trout. A few huge trout cruise the waters in the fall, but they're wise to humans and hard to catch. The lake has been known to hold all species of Colorado trout and kokanee salmon. Dillon is also known for its night fishing, with anglers lining the shore as they pursue large brown trout.

Green Mountain Reservoir
Near Heeney, 23 miles north of
Silverthorne on Highway 9
While its waters yield many good-size trout, Green Mountain Reservoir is best known for kokanee salmon. Among the biggest in the state, the kokanee weigh 2 pounds and more; snagging is permitted from September 1 through December 31. The water level at Green Mountain Reservoir fluctuates greatly throughout the summer. Boat ramps are located at the south end of the reservoir and at the town of Heeney. Ice fishing is popular in winter.

Salmon Lake and Willow Lakes
Eagles Nest Wilderness, off Highway 9
west of Silverthorne
Although they are a bit hard to reach (6- and 7-mile hikes, respectively), these lakes are excellent places to fish. It's not uncommon to catch 10-inch cutthroats with lures and flies. The trailhead begins in Wildernest, just west of Silverthorne. Turn left off Highway 9 onto Wildernest Road, go a short distance to a fork, turn right and then immediately left onto Royal Buffalo Drive (County Road 1240). Drive less than a mile, and turn right onto Lakeview Drive (County Road 1245). Proceed to the fork with Aspen Drive and turn left, negotiating the curve to the trailhead parking area. The trailhead is marked Mesa Cortina. From there, turn right onto Gore Range Trail #60, then left at the marked intersection to the lakes.

How to Identify Your Catch

The lakes, rivers, and streams of Colorado's mountains are filled with a wide variety of beautiful, tasty, hard-fighting fish that are just waiting to gulp your bait. Here are some handy guidelines to help you identify just what it is you've reeled in. Have fun, and go fish!

Rainbow trout can best be described as having black spots on a light body with a red stripe on both sides. Mature males often have a hooked lower jaw and a brighter crimson strip on the sides. As with most trout, they predominantly eat insects.

Brown trout are similar to rainbows, except the spots include a combination of black and red-orange. Each red-orange spot is surrounded by a blue ring.

Brook trout differ from the rainbows and browns in that their bodies are darker with white and red spots. The red spots also are surrounded by blue rings. The pectoral, pelvic, and anal fins are orange and edged in a distinctive black and white.

Cutthroat (native) trout have a crimson slash on either side of the throat beneath the lower jaws. The Greenback Cutthroat subspecies was designated Colorado's official state fish in 1994.

Lake trout (also known as Mackinaw) are similar to brooks in that their bodies are dark with white spots. The spots are irregular in shape and pattern rather than round like the brook trout. No colored spots are present. Their tails also are deeply notched. Lake trout are predominately insect feeders in the high lakes but at lower elevations become almost exclusively fish eaters.

Kokanee salmon can be distinguished by the silver color of their bodies. They also have sparse patches of small black spots and then only on their backs during the fall spawning season. Males develop a deeply hooked jaw, with bodies that are brick red with green coloring on their heads.

Mountain whitefish have mouths that are smaller than those of trout. Their mouths don't extend back to below center of the eye, as they do on trout.

Northern pike are distinctly different from trout, with elongated and flattened jaws that resemble a duck's bill. They have extremely large, irregular teeth, and most are green with vertical rows of yellow-white spots on their sides.

Rainbow trout have black spots on a light background with red stripes on each side.
THE DENVER POST/CHARLIE MEYERS

Places to Hunt

Green Mountain Reservoir
30 miles north of Silverthorne off
Highway 9
The areas east of Green Mountain Reservoir, in the Arapaho National Forest, are good deer hunting spots, although they are remote and incredibly rugged. Access is by foot or horseback only. The areas recommended by David Rye in *Colorado's Guide to Hunting* (Marflow Publications, Arvada, Colorado) are Troublesome Creek and Muddy Creek, near Wolford Mountain and Calvin and Kenny Creek near Music Mountain.

OTHER RECREATION
Bicycling

The free *Summit County Mountain Bike Tail Guide*, available at all bike shops, the chambers of commerce, and visitor centers, is an excellent resource. It describes 23 rides around Copper Mountain, Breckenridge, Keystone, Frisco, Dillon, and the lower Blue River Valley. Summit County has hundreds of miles of backcountry roads and trails that will satisfy riders of all ages and abilities. There are smooth dirt roads and rugged single tracks. Many of the routes are more than a century old and follow the remnants of old mining roads, pack trails, wagon routes, and abandoned railroad grades. Stop at the Dillon Ranger District Office (U.S. Forest Service), 680 River Parkway, Silverthorne, (970) 468-6400. Another good resource is Laura Rossetter's *Mountain Bike Guide to Summit County*, available in sporting goods shops and bookstores.

Paved Bikeways
The 9-mile Blue River Bikeway connects Breckenridge and Frisco. The 6-mile Ten Mile Canyon Bikeway connects Frisco and Copper Mountain, and the 13½-mile Vail Pass Bikeway connects Copper Mountain and Vail (and traverses the 10,000-foot

pass). There's also a paved trail from Keystone to these other trails. A map of these trails is shown in the *Mountain Bike Guide to Summit County* (mentioned above). All are recommended for either fat or skinny tires. There are more than 40 miles of paved bike paths between Keystone, Breckenridge, and Copper Mountain ski resorts. There are numerous bike rentals, sales, and service shops in all these communities and resorts. For additional information, contact the Summit County Chamber of Commerce, 124 Main Street, Dillon, (970) 668-2051.

Keystone Resort
Keystone Activities and Dining Center
US 6, Keystone
(970) 468-2316
www.keystone.snow.com
Dirt Camp is the mountain bike instructional and guide experience offered at the Keystone Resort. There are two-hour, half-day, and weekend clinics. Keystone also offers an all-day gondola ride pass for mountain bikers to ride trails from the mountaintop.

BIKE SHOPS

Wilderness Sports
266 Summit Place, Silverthorne
(970) 468-5687

400 Main Street, Frisco
(970) 668-8804
www.wildsummit.com
This excellent shop rents all types of bikes and equipment, and the store in the Summit Place shopping center offers everything needed for outdoor recreation, including camping gear, hiking boots, and backpacks. It sells rental bikes at good prices as well.

Boating

The Dillon Marina
300 Marina Drive, Dillon
(970) 468-5100
Three rivers meet at Lake Dillon (the

Snake, Blue, and Ten Mile) and the human-made reservoir of Lake Dillon is the home of the Dillon Marina and North America's highest yacht club at 9,017 feet. All types of motorboats and sailboats are available for rent, plus single and double kayaks. The winds can be tricky, but that's one of the reasons that *Sailing* magazine routinely rates the marina one of the best places in the country to go sailing, believe it or not. Overnight and short-term slips are also available for weekly, monthly, and seasonal periods. To reach the marina take I–70 to exit 205, then drive 1 mile east of US 6 to Lake Dillon Drive.

The marina also offers the Lake Dillon Sailing School (group and semiprivate lessons), Sunset Dinner Cruises (sailboat or pontoon), and a public boat ramp set in a beautiful valley with spectacular mountain views.

Tennis/Racquetball

Silverthorne Recreation Center
430 Rainbow Drive, Silverthorne
(970) 262–7370
This local recreation center has two racquetball courts available for a small hourly charge. Call for rates, hours, and reservations. There are also weights, aerobics classes, a kids' section with indoor and outdoor play areas, a physical therapy center, and four swimming pools. In addition, the center offers walleyballs, basketballs, volleyballs, and soccer balls available for checkout.

SPAS AND HOT SPRINGS

Serenity Spa & Salon
23110 US 6, Keystone
(970) 513–9002, (800) 479–5131
www.serenitycolorado.c2
.ixwebhosting.com
This Aveda salon and spa is situated near the entrance to Keystone Resort, in the Gateway Center adjacent to River Run. It offers massage, body treatments, facials, waxing, makeup application, and services for men.

STEAMBOAT SPRINGS

Steamboat Springs is the northern-most of Colorado's ski resorts, but its ambiance is pure western. Long before it was a destination ski town, it was home to cattle ranchers and cow-boys. Much of that ambiance remains, although growth threatens to change all that.

Horses, cattle, buffalo, and cowboys still dominate that landscape, although ranch land is slowly being usurped by housing developments and business growth. Clark, an as yet untouched piece of the nostalgic West, is just 20 miles north, at the end of a very scenic ride along the sparkling Elk River. Clark is known for its guest ranches and the many trails that lead into the Mount Zirkel Wilderness Area.

Steamboat is home to 9,300, although almost 20,000 people live in Routt County. Long before they arrived, Native Americans used the Yampa Valley for hunting and fishing, and the mineral springs for medicinal and social purposes. Cattle drivers who passed through the area on long cattle drives from Texas dur-ing the late 1800s were the first settlers and gave the town its homespun com-plexion. A legendary Norse skier named Carl Howelsen added his imprint in the early 1900s, building a ski jump on a hill overlooking town and introducing locals to his sport of choice.

During the winter, skiing, snowboard-ing, snowshoeing, and other snowy pur-suits keep the economy healthy, but summer brings many tourists looking for an authentic western experience and friendly atmosphere not quite as preva-lent at many of Colorado's other ski resort towns.

HOTELS AND MOTELS

The Alpiner $
424 Lincoln Avenue
(970) 879-1430
A sister property of the Best Western Ptarmigan (see listing below), the Alpiner is a moderately priced Bavarian-style motel on the north edge of Steamboat's historic downtown. It has 32 basic rooms, some of which are adjoining. Don't expect anything fancy, but you'll be located near the town's namesake, the hot springs that used to chug like a steamboat, and also will be within walking distance of all downtown shopping and restaurants. Guests also have access to a free shuttle to and from the ski mountain.

Glen Eden Resort $$
Highway 129, Clark
(970) 879-3907, (800) 882-0854
www.glenedenresort.com
Across the road from the Home Ranch (see entry below), this pleasant resort has individual cottages and cabins nicely fur-nished with rustic decor (such as Indian blanket sofas), fireplaces, and complete kitchens. The cabins back right onto the pretty Elk River. There are tennis and vol-leyball courts, two outdoor hot tubs, and a pool. The resort serves dinner only and is popular with families and for corporate retreats and special events. The staff is friendly and helpful. Rub shoulders with local cowboys at the Elk River Tavern or enjoy a hearty, western-style meal at the Glen Eden Restaurant.

Holiday Inn $$
3190 South Lincoln Avenue
(970) 879-2250, (800) 654-3944
www.holidayinnsteamboat.com
Almost all Holiday Inns have the same, predictable features and furnishings, and the 82 rooms and two suites in this hotel

don't disappoint. The best parts are that it's only about a mile away from the ski area and it's served by the adjoining, 24-hour-a-day Village Inn restaurant and Fireside Lounge. Other amenities include a game room, ski shop, fitness center, spa, outdoor pool, room service, ski shuttle, and guest laundry.

Hotel Bristol $$
917 Lincoln Avenue
(970) 879-3083, (800) 851-0872
www.steamboathotelbristol.com

A cross between a European-style walk-up hotel and a bed-and-breakfast, the Hotel Bristol is one of a kind. It's centrally located in downtown Steamboat, has small but well-decorated rooms (done in a western/cowboy motif, with blanket print bedspreads and wall art that reflects nearby mountain scenery). Most have private baths, and all have access to the second-floor indoor hot tub.

Ptarmigan Best Western $$$
2304 Apres Ski Way
Steamboat Mountain Village
(970) 879-1730, (800) 538-7519

Among the more reasonable ski-out, ski-in properties in Steamboat, the Ptarmigan has 78 modest rooms decorated in pastels and earth tones. The motel's strong points are its slopeside location (right next to the Steamboat Gondola) and its comfortable Alpine design. It also offers a restaurant, lounge, outdoor heated pool, hot tub, sauna, and complimentary ski storage.

Rabbit Ears Motel $$
201 Lincoln Avenue
(970) 879-1150, (800) 828-7702
www.rabbitearsmotel.com

Like its namesake, the Rabbit Ears is a town landmark, named for the rock formation atop Rabbit Ears Pass. Its pink bunny neon sign was erected in 1952, marking what used to be the outskirts of town. Now that the town has grown up around it, the sign still serves as the informal gateway to Steamboat's historic

downtown area. The hotel itself is a modernized version of its former self, with standard but updated rooms that overlook the Yampa River to the west and the hot springs pool to the east.

Sheraton Steamboat Resort & Conference Center $$$
2200 Village Inn Court
Steamboat Mountain Village
(970) 879-2220

Steamboat's only luxury hotel, the Sheraton underwent an $18 million renovation in the summer of 1999. Guests in any of its 315 rooms or three suites can choose from golf at its championship 18-hole course, skiing from one of the few ski-in, ski-out facilities, or relaxing in the heated outdoor pool. Other amenities include private balconies in some rooms, two hot tubs, steam room, meeting rooms, and a ski shop.

Steamboat Central Reservations
(800) 922-2722

For questions about or reservations for Steamboat's hotels, motels, condos, bed-and-breakfast inns or guest ranches, you may call this central number or contact individual facilities yourself.

Steamboat Grand Hotel $$$
2300 Mount Werner Circle
(970) 871-5050
(877) 306-2628 toll-free
www.steamboatgrand.com

Steamboat's only AAA Four-Diamond resort is located at the base of the ski mountain, with 327 guest rooms and suites, a ballroom, a day-spa, and 17,000 square feet of meeting space. Built in 2000, the Steamboat Grand has a full fitness center, an outdoor heated pool, covered underground parking, and two restaurants (Chaps, a western-themed bar and grill that heats up during après-ski hours, and The Cabin, a fine dining establishment that serves beef and Colorado wild game). Eight private penthouse residences are located on the seventh floor.

CONDOS

Chateau Chamonix $$$
2340 Apres Ski Way
Steamboat Mountain Village
(970) 879-7511, (800) 833-9877
www.chateauchamonix.com
These two-, three-, and four-bedroom units come with Jacuzzis and a year-round outdoor heated pool with indoor entrance for the non-polar-bear types. They are considered ski-in, ski-out. They also have patios or balconies, ski lockers, fireplaces and kitchens, shuttle to town, and such business services as fax machines and high-speed Internet.

Torian Plum Condos $$$
1855 Ski Time Square Drive
Steamboat Mountain Village
(970) 879-8811, (800) 228-2458
www.steamboat.resortquest.com
Another of Steamboat Mountain's ski-in, ski-out facilities, this one has two indoor and two outdoor hot tubs, kitchen, washer and dryer, outdoor pool, town shuttle during the ski season, tennis courts, and air conditioning. It's highly rated in most travel guides.

BED-AND-BREAKFASTS

Alpine Rose $$
724 Grand Street
(970) 879-1528, (866) 638-4608
www.alpinerosesteamboat.com
The Alpine Rose, located near the historic downtown area, has just five rooms for rent. The King Room sleeps two; Queen Rooms 1 and 2 also sleep two and have a shared bath; the Family Suite is two adjoining rooms with a queen bed in one and bunk beds in the other; and the Efficiency Apartment can accommodate six people.

Dutch Creek Guest Ranch $$
61565 Rural County Road 62, Clark
(970) 879-8519, (800) 778-8519
www.dutchcreek.net

Within walking distance of Steamboat Lake, you can use this as your base for swimming, sailing, canoeing, riding in a pontoon boat, snowshoeing, cross-country skiing, or snowmobiling. Also fun for kids is a stocked fishing pond. The ranch's nine cabins include lofts, one-bedrooms and two-bedrooms, many with stone fireplaces and kitchens. It's located 25 miles northwest of Steamboat Springs. A two-night minimum stay is required year-round, with three nights required in summer months, three nights during Christmas week, and a full week during October's hunting season.

Steamboat Bed-and-Breakfast $$$
442 Pine Street
(970) 879-5724, (877) 335-4321
www.steamboatb-b.com
The former Euzoa Church, built in 1891, makes for a charming and unusual place to stay. It was struck by lightning several years ago and lost half of its roof in the fire. But the current owners have carefully restored the whole structure. The seven rooms are each decorated differently with antiques and collectibles. A music conservatory and parlor are pleasant social areas, and there's an outdoor hot tub. A full country breakfast is included in the price.

RESORTS

The Home Ranch $$$
Highway 129, Clark
(970) 879-1780
www.homeranch.com
This magnificent horse ranch 25 miles north of Steamboat Springs is top-of-the-line (as in cabins that rent for as much as $18,000, all inclusive, a week during peak summer months). The facilities, food, and prices are all five-star. Handmade furniture, wood stoves, and handsome log-cabin architecture create the perfect mountain get-away. There are eight cabins and six lodge rooms. Each cabin has its own private outdoor Jacuzzi on the porch and a refrigerator stocked with goodies—including a bottomless chocolate-chip

cookie jar. Bathrooms have hair dryers and terry-cloth robes.

The lodge has a cozy, rustic dining room in which gourmet meals are served, and the library's big windows frame the spectacular views in all directions. In winter the ranch offers 24 kilometers of groomed cross-country ski trails. In summer, horseback riding is offered, along with a heated outdoor pool and fly fishing at the on-site lake. The ranch is open during the summer and over the Christmas holidays. Picturesque barns, stables, and corrals of handsome horses (140 of them) are everywhere. In summer, a seven-night, Sunday-to-Sunday minimum stay is required. A three-night stay is required in winter during holiday seasons.

Vista Verde Guest Ranch $$$
Highway 129, Clark
(970) 879-3858, (800) 526-7433
www.vistaverde.com
This postcard-picturesque place is a 500-acre working cattle and horse ranch. That may be why it's one of the few that stays open year-round. Up to 20 guests can fit comfortably in the ranch's eight one-, two-, or three-bedroom log cabins or in two lodge rooms. All are decorated with antiques, down comforters, and snack bars; the cabins also have living rooms, full baths, and wood stoves. Guest prices (admittedly hefty at $2,700 to $3,100 per person per week) include three meals a day plus snacks in the lodge's gourmet dining room, transportation to and from Steamboat Springs, plus guides or instructors. Minimum weekly stays are required during the summer; three-, four-, and five-night stays are available in winter.

The ranch is adjacent to Routt National Forest and the Mount Zirkel Wilderness Area, which means the scenery is almost national-park quality. On the ranch itself, summer guests can choose from horseback riding, mountain biking, hiking, fishing, whitewater rafting, rock climbing, and even hot-air ballooning. In winter, it's a favorite place to cross-country ski on 30 kilometers of groomed trails. Guides also can lead guests on half- or full-day backcountry ski tours around Steamboat Lake, into Hahns Peak Village, or back into Clark. And if you're not a skier, the ranch also offers horseback riding, dog sledding, snowshoeing, sleigh rides, outdoor hot tubs, and a complete exercise facility.

RESTAURANTS

Antares $$$$
57½ Eighth Street
(970) 879-9939
Featuring new American cuisine, Antares has received several *Wine Spectator* Awards of Excellence. It was opened by Paul LeBrun, Ian Donovan, and Doug Enochs, all of whom learned the trade at L'Apogee and Harwig's (see below). The menu has such unusual items as roasted elephant garlic with almond pesto and goat cheese, Sichuan salmon cakes with spicy Bangkok sauce, and Thai chili sautéed prawns with snow peas and straw mushrooms over jasmine rice. Desserts include blueberries sautéed in Frangelico and served over homemade Mexican vanilla ice cream, and peach bread pudding served warm with a Grand Marnier sabayon. The Victorian building still retains its fieldstone walls, frosted windows, pressed tin ceilings, stained glass, and polished hardwood floors. Antares serves dinner only and is closed Sundays. Reservations are required.

The Cantina $$
818 Lincoln Avenue
(970) 879-0826
A downtown fixture, the Cantina has been a favorite of locals for years. It's not fancy—the low ceilings and dark-beamed decor are rustic—but the Tex-Mex food is good and the margaritas are plentiful. Kids are welcome here for lunch and dinner.

Cugino's $$
41 Eighth Street
(970) 879-5805
www.cuginosrestaurant.com
When locals want pizza, a lot of them

head to Cugino's. The place is known for its Philadelphia-style pizzas, strombolis, calzones, and Philly steak sandwiches, but it's also gaining attention for its entrees. The menu includes such Italian favorites as calamari salad (with calamari on mixed greens), tortellini genovese, baked penne rigati, and manicotti. The interior feels like an East Coast trattoria; patio seating is available outside.

Double Z Bar and Bar-B-Q $
1124 Yampa Street
(970) 879-0849

If Steamboat had an "other side of town," this would be it. The funky buildings and businesses along Yampa Street serve the river rats, the itinerant skiers, the mountain bikers, and the rodeo cowboys, which means the Double Z serves up a mass of good food without much fanfare and without a hefty price tag. The Zeasar Salad comes plain or with chicken, cajun seasonings, or shirmp. The shredded beef and sliced pork sirloin barbecue sandwiches are succulent, and the chicken lips are actually breaded and fried chicken tenders. A rustic bar is tucked around back of the restaurant tables.

Harwig's/L'Apogee $$$
911 Lincoln Avenue
(970) 879-1919
www.lapogee.com

Harwig's Grill and L'Apogee were sister restaurants, sharing kitchen space and wine cellar until the owner combined the dining spaces, retaining both the deep menus and wine lists. Entrees include New Orleans Jambalaya (a Harwig's holdover); Wildshire Tips, chunks of chicken or beef

(or both) sautéed with garlic, shallots, mushrooms, and wine in a mustard cream and served over fettuccine; Pistachio Chicken, a sautéed chicken breast with a pistachio peppered crust; and Shrimp Burano, tiger prawns sautéed in olive oil with garlic, tomatoes, grilled artichoke hearts, white wine, and fresh basil, served over pasta. The menu also includes a huge variety of authentic Thai dishes, some 25 offerings in all. Owner Jamie Jenny is a wine collector, with a cellar of more than 10,000 bottles that is cited annually by *The Wine Spectator.*

Hazie's $$$$
Mountainside atop Thunderhead Peak
Steamboat Mountain Village
(970) 871-5150

One of Steamboat's most elegant meals is served in Hazie's, a mountainside gem with a spectacular view. Diners take the Steamboat Gondola to the top of Thunderhead Peak and are greeted by china, crystal, sterling silver, live piano music, and (in the winter) a prix fixe four-course continental dinner. During the winter, it's open daily for lunch and Friday through Sunday for dinner. Summer guests can enjoy Sunday brunch, lunch daily, or a variety of Saturday evening three-course theme dinners.

Johnny B. Good's Diner $
738 Lincoln Avenue
(970) 870-8400
www.johnnybgoodsdiner.com

This 50s-style downtown diner serves up comfort food like meat loaf sandwiches, fried chicken, hot dogs, burgers, and chicken-fried steak. It's one of the best deals in town, with open-faced turkey dinners selling for $9.95, and more than 17 "sammies" (sandwiches) in the $7.00 range.

Off the Beaten Path $
56 Seventh Street
(970) 879-6830

The combination bookstore, coffeehouse, and bakery is fun to visit. You can just browse and enjoy the ambiance and good book selection, or you can sit down for a snack or whole meal (breakfast and lunch only). Freshly baked scones, muffins, cinnamon rolls, and coffee cakes are some of the specialties. Healthy, tasty sandwiches, salads, soups, quiche, and more are served for lunch, and it's an Internet wireless hot spot.

Old Town Pub & Restaurant $$
600 Lincoln Avenue
(970) 879-2101

Located in one of Steamboat's oldest historic buildings, the Old Town Pub is a great place to soak up local history along with Colorado microbrews and an interesting choice of margaritas. Built in 1904, the edifice was one of the area's finest hotels, then it became the town's first hospital. Next it was a general store, a post office under two different postmasters, and then a movie theater. The lower floor was once used as a library, a ceramic shop, a barber shop, and a radio/electric shop. The second floor housed the Odd Fellows lodge and was once used as a dance hall. The bar still welcomes thirsty cowboys, but the dining room is a cheerful calico-papered place, serving chicken, salads, steaks, prime rib, pasta, and seafood among the entrees. It's open for lunch and dinner.

Ore House at the Pine Grove $$$
1465 Pine Grove Road
(970) 879-1190, (800) 280-8310

The Ore House is a locals' favorite, for the food and the big warm barn it's served in. Families especially like the barn, which was built in 1889. The property was homesteaded by James Lewis in the 1880s and was a working ranch until 1971, when it was renovated into a restaurant. The silo still bears the ranch's brand, a quarter-circle "B" that actually is an upside down "P." Ranch memorabilia such as boots, saddles, wagon-wheel cores, and bison heads provide the decor. The menu features prime rib, steaks, baby back ribs, chicken, salmon, and red trout. Early bird specials are offered from 5:00 to 6:00 P.M. The Ore House is open seven days a week for dinner only, and reservations are recommended. It is nonsmoking and is located on the city's free bus route.

Ragnar's $$$$
(mountainside, in the Rendezvous Saddle on High Noon Ski Run)
Steamboat Ski Area
(970) 871-5150

During winter days, Ragnar's is a ski-in mountainside restaurant for lunch and cocktails. At night it is accessible only by snowcat-drawn sleighs. Diners interested in the elegant five-course meal must take a ride on the Steamboat Gondola; at the top they will be loaded into the sleighs for a brief ride to the awaiting Scandinavian feast. Because the restaurant is elegant, children under 5 are discouraged. Reservations are necessary for the evening, which includes dinner, entertainment, and transportation Friday through Sunday. Once the ski mountain closes for the year, so does Ragnar's.

Riggio's $$
1106 Lincoln Avenue
(970) 879-9010

A local favorite, Riggio's has unusual pizzas (goat cheese, grilled eggplant, black olives, roasted red peppers, garlic, and herbs, for example), a wide range of pasta specials, and such Italian favorites as chicken piccata and veal marsala. The atmosphere is sleek and understated, with black and white tile, exposed pipes, and plenty of art on the walls.

Steamboat Yacht Club $$
811 Yampa Avenue
(970) 879-4774
www.steamboatyachtclub.com

When lunch or dinner just has to be fish, the Yacht Club is the place to go. It stocks everything from salmon to snapper to trout to oysters on the half shell. Landlubbers can order prime rib, elk medallions, steak, or buffalo tenderloin, and all guests have access to the house binoculars, the better to see night skiing and ski jumping on adjacent Howelsen Hill. Get a table near the window so you can watch the show, or during the summer, eat on the riverside deck to catch the kayaking, rafting, and boating action on the Yampa River.

Winona's $
617 Lincoln Avenue
(970) 879-2483

If you can't find what you're looking for on this menu, you're not really hungry. Winona's menu takes up two pages, single-spaced. Locals and tourists alike love the breakfasts and lunches served from this downtown fixture, often lining up out the door to get a spot at the counter. Many of the breads and pastries (including scones, muffins, and cinnamon rolls) are homemade. Other breakfasts include Belgian waffles, eggs Benedict and huevos rancheros. At lunch, look for create-your-own deli sandwiches, burgers, homemade soups, and salads. Winona's is closed after breakfast on Sunday.

NIGHTLIFE

Dos Amigos
1910 Mount Werner
Steamboat Mountain Village
(970) 879-4270

Although Dos Amigos has a full menu of Mexican food, its prime location on Ski Time Square makes it a popular après-ski spot. Locals especially love the relaxed atmosphere and the great summer food and drink specials.

Mahogany Ridge
435 Lincoln Avenue
(970) 879-2233

The pub atmosphere is a little demure but the beer is good. It is known for its vast assortment of homemade ales, lagers, porters, and stouts, as well as excellent pub food. Locals come during happy hour in the winter for half-price beers and $1.00 tapas.

Old Town Pub
600 Lincoln Avenue
(970) 879-2101

This old western bar is so authentic it could actually double as a movie set. All it needs is a pair of swinging bar doors. At one time local cowboys did keep the pub in business, using it as a place to let off steam on Saturday nights. Now it's just another comfortable place to grab a few beers, watch the game on several strategically placed television sets, or satisfy your hamburger cravings (although locals filter back in between high seasons to reclaim the place, catch up on gossip, and while away a lazy afternoon or evening). The Old Town Pub has two bars, one on either end of the long, narrow room. It occasionally has live music, and has been known to snag a few nationally known acts.

Slopeside Grill
Torian Plum Plaza
Steamboat Mountain Village
(970) 879-2916
www.slopesidegrill.com

"Hang with the big dogs" at Slopeside Grill, or so the grill's motto reads. If you can find them, that is. The ski-in, ski-out bar and restaurant is a little off the beaten path in the Torian Plum Plaza across from the Sheraton. "Ski down the mountain and look to your right," the Slopeside advertises. "It's where the locals are." A year-round hangout, it is known for its inviting late night happy hours, during which it sells $6.00 pizzas and $2.00 pints from 10:00 P.M. to midnight during winter months and 8:00 to 11:00 P.M. during the summer. It also books live music to entertain its crowds, everything from reggae in the summer to jazz in the winter. Of course, the après-ski crowd loves it, partly because they can soak up the warm afternoon sun in the Slopeside's abundant outdoor seating.

Steamboat Smokehouse
912 Lincoln Avenue
(970) 879-7427
www.steamboatsmokehouse.com

With occasional loud music and a consistently raucous crowd, Steamboat Smokehouse is more than just a good place for barbecued brisket. Kids and families are welcome, but adults are the main audience here. The outside has the typical old-western false front and wooden sidewalk. The inside is wood and brick, a perfect place to hang your hat while you wash down a little dinner and kick up your heels.

The Tugboat Grill & Pub
1864 Mount Werner Road
Steamboat Mountain Village
(970) 879-7070

Both locals and tourists love the live bands that keep this popular place hopping on the weekends during summer months and Tuesday through Saturday during the winter ski season. The Tugboat has been around almost as long as the ski area, springing up on Ski Time Square as a casual sports bar and all-around comfortable place to spend a few hours. As it describes itself, the Tugboat is "fast times, hard laughs, grub, suds & liquor."

ATTRACTIONS

Bud Werner Memorial Library
1289 Lincoln Avenue
(970) 879-0240

Named for internationally known ski racer and Steamboat native Buddy Werner, who died in 1964 while trying to out-race an avalanche in the Swiss Alps, the library opened in 1967, built with money contributed in his memory. It has a large collection of the Olympic skier's memorabilia and boasts 45,000 volumes, audio tapes, video tapes, and free Internet service. It's open daily the following hours: 9:00 A.M. to 8:00 P.M. Monday through Thursday, 9:00 A.M. to 6:00 P.M. Friday, 9:00 A.M. to 5:00 P.M. Saturday, and noon to 5:00 P.M. Sunday.

Buffalo Pass

Buffalo Pass is an immense mountain area east of Steamboat Springs that reaches an elevation of 10,180 feet and provides one of the key gateways to the Mount Zirkel Wilderness Area. Check out the "Hiking" section of this chapter for more on this inspiring wilderness area.

Fish Creek Falls
4 miles northeast of Steamboat Springs
off Oak Street

Townspeople once gathered at this 283-foot waterfall to catch fish for the winter. Legend also has it that the waterfall is the one pictured on the original Coors beer can, although company officials say otherwise. Visitors get to a viewing spot at the bottom of the falls by walking about 200 yards from the parking lot. Hikers can continue another 7 miles up the trail to Long Lake, the origin of the water that rushes over the falls. Fish Creek Falls is free, but parking in the upper lot is $3.00 per car. (For more details, check out the "Hiking and Backpacking" section of this chapter.)

Flat Tops Wilderness Area

This magnificent area 20 miles south of Steamboat covers 235,230 acres filled with unique geological features, vistas, sheer volcanic cliffs, alpine lakes, and deep canyons. The 82-mile Flat Tops Scenic Byway runs between Yampa and Meeker and forms the northern border of the wilderness area. It was the road used by Utes, trappers, and settlers on their way across the mountains, and it makes for a pleasant mountain drive.

Lyons Soda Fountain
9th Street and Lincoln Avenue
(970) 879-1114

Among the reminders that Steamboat was once a small town, Lyons Corner Drug sits on the corner of 9th and Lincoln, in the heart of the old downtown. It still sells Hallmark cards and pharmaceuticals for whatever ails you. Even better, its old-fashioned soda fountain still stretches down one side of the shop, anchored by a neon jukebox. Imbibers crawl up on round, red vinyl and chrome stools and choose from ice cream concoctions or baked goods in the glass fronted display counter.

Mount Zirkel Wilderness Area
One of the state's most remote and spectacular wilderness areas, it's located in the 1.6 million acre Routt National Forest between Buffalo Pass and the Wyoming border. This area has 139,818 acres and is ideal for backpacking, fishing, and hunting.

Rabbit Ears Pass
Eleven miles southeast of downtown Steamboat on U.S. Highway 40, this scenic pass is named after a volcanic rock formation that resembles a pair of rabbit ears. Its summit is 10,654 feet. Camping, hunting, fishing, and hiking are available in the immediate vicinity.

Routt Divide Blowdown
Routt National Forest
(970) 879-1870
On October 25, 1997, winds blowing more than 120 miles per hour ripped over the Continental Divide, flattening a strip of trees in Routt National Forest almost 5 miles wide and 30 miles long. It was an unprecedented natural disturbance that locals have compared to the Mount Saint Helens volcano or Hurricane Hugo. With more than 4 million trees snapped off at the trunk or blown over, roots and all, spruce beetles have moved in with a vengeance and become an epidemic. The dead trees also are a fire hazard, and campgrounds and trails through the Blowdown have been closed for reconstruction. While nature will have things repaired in a few hundred years, those of us living in the 21st century may enjoy the opportunity to look at the eerie landscape and contemplate the strength of natural forces. The U.S. Forest Service office at 925 Weiss Drive, off U.S. Highway 40 near the mountain development, has maps and more information about the Blowdown.

Stagecoach State Park
Located 16 miles south of Steamboat off Routt County Road 14, this state park features fishing, swimming, boating, water skiing, mountain biking, and wildlife watching opportunities. It has a full-service marina and RV facilities.

Steamboat Lake State Park
Located 25 miles north of Steamboat on Routt County Road 129, Steamboat Lake offers camping, a marina with boat rentals, fishing, swimming, boating, water skiing, hiking, and wildlife watching. Pearl Lake offers camping and trophy fly fishing, and turn-of-the-century mining towns Hahns Peak and Columbine are also nearby.

Steamboat Springs Pro Rodeo
Brent Romick Rodeo Arena
Howelsen Park
www.steamboatprorodeo.com
Friday and Saturday throughout the summer, cowboys from throughout northern Colorado as well as professionals on the rodeo circuit, gather in Steamboat for a little down-home roping and riding. The action begins at 7:30 P.M. but the entertainment and barbecue dinner start at 6:30. Rodeo admission is $13.00 for adults, $7.00 for children 7 to 15, and free for 6 and under. Dinner is extra. Adults save $1.00 and children 50 cents pre-purchasing their tickets at F.M. Light & Sons or Soda Creek Mercantile stores (see our "Shopping" section for store details).

Tread of Pioneers Museum
800 Oak Street
(970) 879-2214
This refurbished home is a celebration of the Yampa Valley's rich and diverse heritage, from its Native American ancestors to Olympian skiers. A Ute Indian exhibit and a corresponding cowboy exhibit—complete with chuck wagon, bear traps, and guns—are on permanent display, as is a closet filled with early-day toys. Other exhibits change seasonally, including a ski collection from the 1800s through the 1940s and a mining exhibit. Volunteers also guide walking tours of downtown Steamboat in July and August at 9:30 A.M.

Wednesday mornings. The museum is open year-round but is open daily only during summer months, from 11:00 A.M. to 5:00 P.M. Monday through Saturday and noon to 4:00 P.M. on Sunday. During fall and spring low seasons, it's closed Sunday and Monday; from Thanksgiving to mid-April, it's closed Sunday. Admission is $5.00 for adults, $4.00 for seniors 62 and up, and $1.00 for children under 12.

Yampa River Trail
Various locations, downtown
Steamboat Springs

The full trail extends 4 miles and connects downtown Steamboat Springs with the ski mountain. Bikers, joggers, walkers, and in-line skaters use it for exercise, but visitors may want to concentrate on a 2-mile loop through downtown that is outlined in a Walking Tour brochure published by the Chamber Resort Association. It begins and ends at the Heart Springs (also known as the Steamboat Springs Health & Recreation Center) at 136 Lincoln Avenue, looping through town, passing seven hot springs. It takes an estimated two hours to visit the springs, the historic Depot Art Center, Lincoln Park, Yampa River Park, and the athletic complex at the base of Howelsen Hill. It's free.

KIDSTUFF

Amaze 'N Steamboat
1255 South Lincoln Avenue
(970) 870-8682

Colorado has a string of human-size mazes that are open during the summer. This one, like those in Breckenridge, Winter Park, and Grand Lake, has wooden walls high enough to get lost in. The object is to work your way through as best you can. If that loses its thrill, there's also an 18-hole minigolf course on site. They're open daily Memorial Day to Labor day from 10:00 A.M. to 9:00 P.M., weekends in September (hours vary). All-day passes are available for $22.

Howelsen Park and Howelsen Hill
Fifth Street Bridge
(970) 879-4300

The athletic complex best known as a ski-jumping facility has something to offer almost everyone year-round. During the winter months, visitors can watch Olympic ski jumpers training for their events (roughly 1:00 to 6:00 P.M. on weekdays), and on weekends ski competitions are held (call 970-879-0695 for details on competitions). An indoor ice-skating rink is open from mid-September through mid-May. (See the "Other Winter Activities" sections of this chapter for more details.)

From mid-June to mid-August the complex is home to mountain biking, horseback riding, hiking, tennis, in-line skating, and skateboarding. Activities are priced individually.

Steamboat Springs Health and
Recreation Association
136 Lincoln Avenue
(970) 879-1828
www.sshra.org

This complex includes three outdoor hot springs mineral pools, a 350-foot water slide, an Olympic-size lap pool, and a kiddie pool. The warm pool waters (80 degrees in the lap pool, 98 to 103 degrees in the mineral pools) actually come from the Heart Hot Springs, one of Steamboat's many geothermal water sources. The pools are open Monday through Friday from 5:45 A.M. to 8:45 P.M., Saturday and Sunday 7:00 A.M. to 8:45 P.M. year-round. Admission is $8.50 for adults 18 and older, $5.00 for young adults 13 to 17, and $3.50 for children 3 to 12 and seniors over 62. Water slide rides are extra.

Steamboat Springs Pro Rodeo
Brent Romick Rodeo Arena
Howelsen Park
(970) 879-4300

Kids love watching the authentic cowboys take a crack at riding and roping some of the West's wildest horses and cattle, and they also like seeing the rodeo clowns work their magic. The rodeo takes place every Friday and Saturday night during the summer; see the write-up above under "Attractions" for details on prices and times.

Teen Center
25 11th Street
(970) 879-6960
Teens 13 to 18 are welcome at the city-sponsored Teen Center, a drug- and alcohol-free club. The Center offers in-house activities as well as organized outings at affordable prices. Call to find out what's planned when you're in town.

Tread of Pioneers Museum
800 Oak Street
(970) 879-2214
A toy exhibit from the 1900s, turn-of-the-century furnishings, a ski collection from the 1800s through the 1940s, a Ute Indian exhibit, and cowboy and mining exhibits make this refurbished home a popular spot with imaginative youngsters. It's open year-round 11:00 A.M. to 5:00 P.M. From Labor Day to Thanksgiving and mid-April to June, it's closed Monday; from Thanksgiving to mid-April, it's closed Sunday. During summer months, it's open daily. Cost is $5.00 for adults, $4.00 for seniors 63 and up, $1.00 for children under 12.

Walking Tour of the Springs at Steamboat
Downtown Steamboat
(970) 879-0882
Walk your youngsters past the sites of seven mineral springs that flow into the

Yampa River as it makes its way through downtown Steamboat Springs. Among them are the springs that gave the town its name (called Steamboat Springs because water made a chugging noise as it escaped from the ground) and Black Sulphur Spring. Free. Pick up a self-guided tour map at the Chamber of Commerce, 1255 South Lincoln Avenue, across from Sundance Plaza.

SKIING LESSONS AND CHILD CARE

Steamboat Ski Area
2305 Mount Werner Circle
Steamboat Mountain Village
(970) 879-6111, (800) 922-2722
www.steamboat.com
Since 1982, children under 12 have been able to ski free the same number of days as their parents when a parent purchases a five-day (or more) lift ticket. Ski programs and child care are offered for children 2 to 15 years old, with the youngest eligible for all-day and half-day child care with a one-hour private ski clinic. Older children have access to either ski or snowboard lessons. Reservations are required.

SHOPPING

Since Steamboat Springs has two main areas—the old downtown area and the new village that has sprung up around the ski resort—it also has two distinct shopping districts. The downtown (bisected by Lincoln Avenue) has a few of the necessities plus dozens of tourist-oriented clothing, gift, and service-related shops. And since the area is bordered on the west side by the Yampa River, it also is home to a slew of kayaking, bicycling, outfitting, and boating shops. The ski area is home to pricier shops, but also is ringed by newer stores that provide the essentials—groceries at City Market, for example. Each March, the Downtown Business Association sponsors a spring

---

i *Steamboat Springs is in a class of its own among ski resorts. It was founded more than a century ago by cattlemen and has been home to real farmers and ranchers ever since. Boosters describe it as "real people who are real friendly."*

Sidewalk Sale of the old-fashioned variety. Merchants wheel out racks of discounted goods, and shoppers stroll from one end of town to the other ogling the merchandise.

Bohlmann Pine Designs
2730 Downhill Plaza, Unit 106
(970) 879-0985

Since 1989, the owners of Bohlmann Pine Designs have been building lodgepole pine furniture. The showroom and workshop are located in west Steamboat Springs. In addition to the classic and lodge collections, Bohlmann designs and builds custom pieces.

Christy Sports
1835 Central Park Plaza
(970) 879-1250

Clock Tower, 1724-A Mount Werner Circle, Steamboat Mountain Village
(970) 879-9011
www.christysports.com

Christy Sports is a well-known chain store throughout Colorado, renting, selling, and repairing sports gear of all kinds. In the winter, the two Steamboat stores are filled with skiing, snowboarding, and snowshoeing equipment. In summer months the inventory shifts toward camping, biking, and river gear.

8th Street West
817 Lincoln Avenue
(970) 879-7878

This cheerful downtown store carries a range of comfortable women's sportswear and shoes not unlike those you'd find in any big city. The special appeal is that they're suited for the kind of casual lifestyle people live in Steamboat and have a kind of whimsical, ageless quality.

Felix & Fido
Old Town Square
7th and Lincoln Avenue
(970) 870-6400
www.felixandfido.com

Animal lovers are welcome at this basement store in downtown Steamboat. Handmade collars, bowls, and treats for dogs and cats are joined by T-shirts, home accessories, jewelry, cards, and stuffed animals designed with their owners in mind.

F. M. Light & Sons
830 Lincoln Avenue
(970) 879-1822, (800) 530-8908
www.fmlight.com

You'll see their road signs miles outside of town, scattered Burma Shave-style along all roads that lead to Steamboat Springs. The store has been owned by the same family since 1905, when the Light family opened it to supply ranchers with the cowboy hats, boots, and work clothes they wore every day. You'll still find those western staples lining the walls (with name brands like Lucchese, Stetson, and Tony Lama), but the merchandise list has expanded to serve the valley's newer residents. The day we visited the windows were lined with plastic clogs in primary colors, cotton shortie overalls, and, for the men, Hawaiian shirts.

Into the West
807 Lincoln Avenue
(970) 879-8377

Owner Jace Romich shows his handcrafted furniture line here as well as items from artisans throughout the country. Original art, lamps, chandeliers, linens, and leather and upholstered furniture are among the things you'll find in the store.

Off The Beaten Path
56 7th Street
(970) 879-6830

Part bookstore, part breakfast nook, Off The Beaten Path is a downtown fixture. In addition to carrying a representative sample of bestsellers, Colorado guides, periodicals, and musical selections, it also sponsors special visiting author lectures and the annual Literary Sojourn, billed as a gathering of national authors and book lovers.

Soda Creek Western Outfitters
335 Lincoln Avenue
(970) 879-3146, (800) 824-8426
www.soda-creek.com
Located at the opposite end of Steamboat's downtown, Soda Creek is F. M. Light's newfangled sister store. In 10,000 square feet, it carries a deep inventory of western clothing, everyday farm implements, cowboy hats, and the more popular John Deere caps. Ads boast that Soda Creek can fit any foot in boots that range from AAA to EEEEE in width. Upstairs is an antique western wear and curio shop, part museum and part store.

Vario
5th and Lincoln Avenue
(970) 870-3099
For a taste of Italy (specifically, the Umbria region), visit Vario in its off-the-main-street shop. It carries hand-painted ceramic pottery, most of which is made in the town of Deruta, Italy, and some of it as much as 400 years old. From tableware to serving dishes and decorative pieces, the pottery is joined by Italian food products.

Yampatika
10th and Lincoln Avenue
(970) 871-9151
www.yampatika.org
Named after the Indian tribe that once called the Yampa Valley home, Yampatika bills itself as a nature store. Inside you'll find items handmade by Yampa Valley artisans, birdhouses, nature guides, and a range of goods that teach respect for the environment.

THE ARTS

Steamboat Springs Arts Council
1001 13th Street
(970) 879-9008
www.steamboatspringsarts.com
The council is Steamboat's pivotal cultural organization, the result of an NEA grant and matching city funds in the early 1990s that totaled $450,000. It now sponsors at least 30 arts organizations that program everything from dance performances to plays, art displays to classes, concerts to music camps. Members include Northwest Ballet, Columbine Singers, Perry-Mansfield Performing Arts School, Mountain Madrigal Singers, Rocky Mountain Dance, Steamboat Community Players, Steamboat Dance Theatre, Steamboat Springs Chamber Orchestra, Strings in The Mountains, Steamboat Writers Group, West Slope FM Radio, and the Yampa Valley Choral Society.

It's housed in the town's renovated train depot, built in 1908 alongside the railroad tracks on the west bank of the Yampa River and serving as a working terminal until 1968. Changing visual arts exhibits are displayed in the Depot galleries (open weekdays 9:00 A.M. to 5:00 P.M. and Saturday noon to 4:00 P.M. during the winter high season). Admission is free, but visitors are encouraged to make donations. The Depot is also a good place to stop for general information about arts and artists in the Yampa Valley.

The council also sponsors Kaleidoscope, a summer art workshop for children and an Art-In-The-Park show during Rainbow Weekend (usually mid-July) that features 150 artisans who exhibit and sell their works as well as entertainers. Call for details.

Theater

Perry-Mansfield Performing Arts School and Camp
4 miles northeast of Steamboat Springs
(970) 879-7125, (800) 430-ARTS
The oldest performing arts camp in America, Perry-Mansfield was started as an outdoor summer dance camp in 1913 by friends Portia Perry and Charlotte Mansfield. Over the years, it expanded to include education in theater, art, creative writing, and equestrian and environmental studies. Distinguished alumni include Dustin Hoffman, Julie Harris, and Lee

Remick. Several years ago, a local group called Friends of Perry-Mansfield bought the camp and has run it ever since as a private, nonprofit school. Students from fifth grade through college arrive from all over the country for its summer programs, and people of all ages come for the year-round theater workshops.

Visual Arts

Two Rivers Gallery
56 9th Street
(970) 879-0044
www.tworiversgallery.com
Specializing in fine art of the American West, Two Rivers carries an extensive collection of vintage photos, antique Native American art, 19th-century prints, drawings, paintings, and bronzes. Colorado landscapes join them, as do antique furniture and antler chandeliers.

Wild Horse Gallery of
Steamboat Springs
Sheraton on the Mountain
Steamboat Mountain Village
(970) 879-7660
www.wildhorsegallery.com
Located in the Sheraton Hotel, the Wild Horse is owned by Rich Galusha, a local high school teacher who now provides display space for fine local artists of all kinds. His stock includes original oils, pastels, watercolors, drawings, etchings, bronze sculptures, and limited-edition prints.

Music

Strings in the Mountains Music Festival
Various locations, Steamboat Springs
(970) 879-5056
www.stringsinthemountains.org
Throughout the year, visiting and resident musicians make their presence known in Steamboat, performing throughout the Yampa Valley. Formal concerts are performed in an intimate 500-seat tent at the Strings Music Festival Park featuring chamber music, jazz, bluegrass, and country music. In past years, visiting performers have included Maria Muldaur, Tracy Nelson, the Glenn Miller Orchestra, the Iguanas, Natalie MacMaster, William Hill, Jon Kimura Parker, Ukranian piano duo Valentina Lisitsa and Alexei Kuznetsoff, harpist Yolanda Kondonassis, and Andres Cardenes, concertmaster of the Pittsburgh Symphony.

EVENTS
January

Annual Cowboy Downhill
Steamboat Ski Area
(970) 879-6111
The National Western Stock Show in Denver is one of the country's largest and richest rodeos, so what do the cowboys do after they've had their fill of bucking broncs? For more than 30 years, they've been coming to Steamboat Ski Area for a unique kind of on-skis rodeo. More than 100 of the best professional rodeo cowboys negotiate a slalom course, then lasso a mountain host, and saddle a horse before crossing the finish line. It's hard to tell who has more fun—the contestants or the spectators.

February

Winter Carnival
Various locations, Steamboat Springs
(970) 879-0695
Begun in 1913 by the man who introduced skiing for fun to the area, Flying Norseman Carl Howelsen, this annual, early February event celebrates winter with ice sculpture competitions, a hockey tournament, and ski jumping through rings of fire. All proceeds fund the Steamboat Springs Winter Sports Club. There's a comical race in which competitors sitting

on snow shovels are pulled down the street by galloping horses. Everyone comes out on skis, including the high school band. There are fireworks at night, and the famous "lighted man" skis down Howelsen Hill.

June

**Steamboat Marathon/Half Marathon/
10K Run & Fun Run
Various locations, Steamboat Springs
(970) 879-0882**

Since 1982, runners have been attracted to the mild weather and scenic beauty of Steamboat's marathon. For the less-than-elite runners, organizers have also added a half marathon, a 10-kilometer run, and a fun run. All find themselves gathering in early June to travel the winding country roads near Steamboat. Call for race date and registration details.

**Yampa River Festival
Various locations, Steamboat Springs
(970) 879-0882**

For three days each June, people pause to celebrate the river that attracted founding fathers and that has since drawn world-class kayakers. The paddling is so good that some enthusiasts call Steamboat "the whitewater center of the universe," a reputation earned by the Yampa River's Class II status and the racecourse permanently staked out in its waters. Festival events include a kayak rodeo, slalom races, and the infamous "Crazy River Dog Contest," with proceeds going to the Friends of the Yampa Foundation.

July

**ProRodeo Series/
Cowboy Roundup Days
Brent Romick Rodeo Arena
Howelsen Park, Steamboat Springs
(970) 879-4300**

The series actually takes place from July

through late August, but the annual Cowboy Roundup Days—celebrating its 103rd year in 2006—take place during the Fourth of July weekend. Cowboys and cowgirls compete in bronc riding, steer wrestling, team roping, mixed-team roping, calf roping, barrel racing, and bull riding. The Strings in the Mountains Festival of Music coincides, with a chamber music concert and pre-rodeo performances.

There are special children's events such as the calf scramble, where kids from the audience attempt to recover a ribbon tied to the tail of a calf (or a ram for the younger kids). Other activities include an all-you-can-eat Flapjack Feed, the Steamboat Springs Sprint, and a parade down Lincoln Avenue complete with floats, clowns, horseback riders, bicycles, and synchronized precision bands. And, of course, there's the Fourth of July fireworks at night on Howelsen Hill.

**Rainbow Weekend
Various locations, Steamboat Springs
(970) 879-0882**

This mid-July festival of art and hot-air balloons is a colorful experience. There's a balloon rodeo with 50 hot-air balloons of all shapes, sizes, and colors rising in the morning light. Admission and parking are free for the balloon rodeo, and concessions sell coffee, pastries, breakfast burritos, and souvenirs. Art In the Park, after the balloon event, has a free shuttle from the balloon area. There are more than 100 local, regional, and national artisans and entertainers. Fine arts and crafts are on exhibit and for sale. The ongoing Strings in the Mountains Festival of Music presents special concerts and performances.

September

**Wild West Air Fest
Bob Adams Airport, North of Steamboat
Springs on Airport Circle
Romick Arena, Howelsen Park
(970) 879-0882**

The Wild West Air Fest is a Labor Day weekend celebration featuring a vintage- and war-aircraft flyby and display at the Bob Adams municipal airport. There's also hang gliding, remote-controlled aircraft displays, paragliders, a free concert, and the annual Art on The Mountain exhibit. F.M. Light & Sons sponsors the Great American Wild West Show for two per- formances Saturday night and Sunday afternoon.

SKIING

People like to ski in cowboy hats at Steamboat, perhaps in honor of the town's ranching heritage, but the largest collection of Stetsons can be seen during the annual Cowboy Downhill each January (see the "Events" section of this chapter for more details). Professional rodeo cow- boys in Denver for the National Western Stock Show are invited to the slopes of Steamboat Resort for a day of good- natured competition, and show up to lasso mountain hosts and saddle horses on skis before racing toward the finish line. The event was born in 1974, when rodeo pro Larry Mahan and Olympic skier Billy Kidd decided it might be fun. It was, and a tradition was born.

Steamboat Springs is both the site of Colorado's first ski slope (Howelsen Hill) and the site of two unrelated ski resorts. Howelsen is still owned by the city and used primarily for racers and jumpers in training, although locals with a lunch hour to kill often kill it on its slopes. (Nooner lift tickets—good from 11:00 A.M. to 1:00 P.M.— are available for around $5.00.) Steamboat Resort is privately owned by American Ski- ing Co., owners of seven other U.S. resorts, including Killington in Vermont. It is a large, full-service ski area spread out over six peaks. Over the years, 56 Olympians have called Steamboat Springs home, training at both Howelsen and Steamboat Ski Area.

Steamboat Ski Area
2305 Mount Werner Circle, Steamboat Mountain Village
(970) 879-6111, (800) 922-2722
www.steamboat.com
Resort elevation: *6,900 feet*
Top of highest lift: *10,568 feet*
Total vertical: *3,668 feet*
Longest run: *3 miles*
Average annual snowfall: *334 inches*
Ski season: late November to mid-April
Capacity: *32,000 skiers per hour*
Terrain: *2,939 acres, 164 trails (13 percent beginner, 56 percent intermediate, 31 per- cent advanced and expert)*
Lift tickets: *$72 all-day adult*
Snow report: *(970) 879-7300*
Getting there: *Steamboat Springs is 157 miles northwest of Denver via I-70 west to Silverthorne (exit 205), then north on High- way 9 to Kremmling and west on US 40 over Rabbit Ears Pass. The resort is 2 miles south of Steamboat Springs.*

Considered by ski writers to be among Colorado's top five ski resorts, Steamboat is famous for its tree skiing, its gigantic multi-peaked mountain, and the Cham- pagne Powder (a trademarked name) that turns the mountainside into a powder skiers' paradise. Because it comes from clouds that travel across the deserts of Utah and drop their load only when they're trapped by the northern Rockies, the snow is light, dry, and fluffy. Unlike the heavy powder at other resorts that seems to swallow skis whole, this powder is mostly air and billows up as high as your armpits as you ski through it. Whenever 6 or more inches of the stuff has fallen overnight, powder workshops are offered the next day to help novices learn to make the most of it.

Steamboat Ski Area is spread across six peaks that promise trails to please skiers and snowboarders of all experience levels. Three slow-skiing family zones and a few slow-skiing and snowboarding areas appeal to the beginner, while Rough Rider Basin is open only to those young enough to enjoy the teepees, log cabin playhouse, and Wild Western fort. Snowboarders are drawn to the Maverick's Superpipe, the longest snowboard superpipe on the continent. At 650-feet long, 50-feet wide, with 15-foot walls and a 17-foot radius, this is a snowboarder's dream. And right next to Maverick's is the SoBe terrain park featuring an outdoor sound system and a variety of rails: kinked, sliders, rainbows, "S's," mailboxes, double-barrels, and Mini-Mav, a scaled-down version of the superpipe, for novice riders. Adult skiers have their pick of dozens of steep, challenging runs on this massive mountain or can stay on broad, gentle trails that traverse between meadows and glades of pine and aspen trees. Trail names are themed to help visitors remember where they are and where they've been. The trails on Storm Peak, for example, are called Tornado, Hurricane, Twister, Sunset, and Rainbow.

Former Olympic silver medalist Billy Kidd, who grew up in Massachusetts, decided to hang his hat in Steamboat once his professional ski days were over. For the past 33 years he has been a mountain ambassador, and now serves as director of skiing. When he's in town, he meets all guests interested in skiing with him (intermediate level or above) atop Heavenly Daze trail at 1:00 P.M. for a free 45-minute ski clinic. When he's not in town, guests can still visit his bronze bust at the base of the Steamboat Gondola.

Other specialized programs offered at Steamboat include the Perfect Turn Learning Center for skiers who are physically and developmentally challenged, and an Over the Hill Gang program for skiers 45 and older who, as the resort describes them, "enjoy mellow cruising" on intermediate and advanced trails.

Howelsen Hill Ski Area
Fifth Street Bridge, Steamboat Springs
(970) 879-8499, (800) 525-2628
www.ci.steamboaat.co.us
Resort elevation: *6,696 feet*
Top of highest lift: *7,136 feet*
Total vertical: *440 feet*
Longest run: *1 mile*
Average annual snowfall: *150 inches*

Ski season: *late November to late March*
Terrain: 25 skiable acres, 15 trails (25 percent beginner, 25 percent intermediate, 50 percent advanced and expert)
Lift tickets: *$15 all-day adult*
Snow report: *(970) 879-8499*

The oldest continuously operating ski area in the nation (it opened in 1915), Howelsen is owned by the town of Steamboat Springs. The vertical drop is just 440 feet, but it's a renowned ski-jumping center (the largest in the United States) with six different jumps used for Olympic-level qualifying meets and training. The regular ski runs are open daily, and night skiing is available Tuesday through Friday until 9:00 P.M.

Over the years, 47 Olympic skiers have trained here, including 15 members of the Colorado Hall of Fame and six members of the National Ski Hall of Fame. In keeping with its hometown feel, Howelsen's hills are named after locals who were instrumental in developing the slopes: Wren's Run, Wither Chute, and Long John, for example.

For beginners, Howelsen offers a Learn to Ski Free program that teaches alpine skiing, snowboarding, and telemarking free! The jumping is only available for trained competitors.

CROSS-COUNTRY SKIING

Steamboat Ski Touring Center
Clubhouse Road
(970) 879-8180

Steamboat's touring center is one of the best in the state, with a variety of terrain ranging from flat open meadows to fun little rolling hills. There are more than 15 kilometers of groomed trails set among aspen groves and into meadows along Fish Creek, with beautiful views of the surrounding mountain scenery. The center is south from town and east on Mount Werner Road. Turn left on Steamboat Boulevard, then right onto Clubhouse Drive and follow the signs. Full- and half-day backcountry tours are also available. A trail pass costs about $14.

Howelsen Hill Ski Area
Fifth Street Bridge
(970) 879-8499

The Howelsen Ski Area has 20 kilometers of groomed cross-country trails, about a quarter of which are lighted for night skiing. Rental equipment is not available, and day passes cost $5.00.

Vista Verde Guest Ranch
(970) 879-3858, (800) 525-RIDE

Located 25 miles north of Steamboat Springs, Vista Verde is a private dude ranch, but it opens its 30 kilometers of groomed cross-country trails to the general public each winter. Guests get first chance at them, but non-guests can pay $20 a day to ski or $40 a day for skiing and lunch. Reservations are required, and gear should be rented in town before coming. Trails include double tracks and skating lanes, and some also provide access to the backcountry.

OTHER WINTER RECREATION

Hot-Air Ballooning

Wild West Balloon Adventures
Steamboat Springs
(970) 879-3298, (800) 748-2487
www.wildwestballooning.com

Owner/operator Ian Cox offers personalized champagne flights north and south over the Yampa Valley at altitudes of 2,000 and 3,000 feet. Transportation is provided from local hotels and condominiums to and from the launch site. Balloons hold four to six people and take off near the ski area about 9:00 A.M. daily during the winter. Adult prices are $125 for a half-hour ride, $185 for an hour. Kids 5 to 12 ride for $85 (half-hour) and $150 (hour). Children under 5 are not permitted. Reservations a day in advance are required.

Colorado skiers have been jumping at Howelsen Ski Area for nearly a century, which makes it the state's oldest continuously operated ski hill. It's one reason why Steamboat Springs has produced 56 winter Olympians, more than any other town in North America.

Ice Skating

Howelsen Ice Arena
next to Howelsen Hill Ski Area
Steamboat Springs
(970) 879-0341

Northwest Colorado's premier indoor ice facility is nestled into the base of Howelsen Hill ski area in the center of Steamboat Springs. The community facility has an Olympic-size rink that is used for ice hockey, figure skating, broomball, lessons, and open skating. Admission is $6.00, skate rental is $3.00. Call for hours.

Ice Climbing

Rocky Mountain Ventures
Steamboat Springs
(970) 870-8440
www.verticalgrip.com

Guides take guests to Fish Creek Falls, the famous 283-foot waterfall in northeast Steamboat Springs, where they are given an introduction to ice climbing and the chance to practice their skills. Novices start at the beginning, learning about gear, tools, and technique; more advanced climbers can brush up on their skills as they ascend the waterfall. Tours start in December, assuming the weather cooperates, and usually run through February. Price of $150 includes gear rental and transportation to and from Steamboat.

Snowcat Skiing

Steamboat Powdercats
Steamboat Springs
(970) 871-4260, (800) 288-0543
www.steamboatpowdercats.com
After nearly two decades of experience, owners of Steamboat Powdercats know how to give backcountry skiers a thrill. Buffalo Pass (2 miles north of Steamboat Springs) gets the state's heaviest snowload, most of it deep, untracked powder. Powerful (and heated) snowcats take as many as 12 skiers to those open snow fields near the Continental Divide, where skiers of at least advanced intermediate ability can ski to their hearts' content. The price of $259 to $359 (depending on the season) a day includes breakfast, lunch, après-ski cocktails and drinks, and hotel pickup and drop-off.

Sleigh Rides

Elk River Guest Ranch
29840 Routt County Road 64, Clark
(970) 879-6220, (800) 750-6220
www.elkriverguestranch.com
Located about 20 miles north of Steamboat Springs, Elk River Guest ranch has 70 acres of sleigh-pulling property. Guests can be picked up at their hotels and are deposited at an old-time western saloon for drinks and appetizers. Then they're loaded into sleighs pulled by Belgian draft horses for a 20 to 25- minute ride through aspen and pine groves to the teepees where dinner is served. After the meal, they ride back beneath heated wool blankets. Sometimes they catch a glimpse of the elk herds for which the ranch is named. Cost for the ride is $75 for adults, $60 for children. Dinner is included.

Ragnar's
(mountainside) Steamboat Ski Area
(970) 879-6111, (800) 922-2722
During the day, Ragnar's is a ski-in mountainside restaurant for lunch and cocktails. At night it is accessible only by snowcat-drawn sleighs. Diners interested in the elegant five-course meal must take a ride on the Steamboat Gondola; at the top they will be loaded into the sleighs for a brief ride to the awaiting Scandinavian meal. Because the restaurant is elegant, children are discouraged. Reservations are necessary for the evening, which includes dinner, entertainment, and transportation Thursday through Saturday. Prices are $93 for adults, $77 for teens 13 to 18 and, if you insist, $59 for children 6 to 12.

Wind Walker Tours
Gondola Square
Steamboat Mountain Village
(970) 879-8065, (800) 748-1642
Sleigh ride dinners leave Gondola Square at 4:30 and 7:30 P.M. daily during the ski season, and take guests to a nearby log cabin for a steak, beans, baked potato, and brownie dinner, and dancing to live country-and-western music. Cost is $65 for adults, $35 for children 6 to 12, and $10 for children under 6. Afternoon sleigh rides also are available.

Snowmobiling

High Mountain Snowmobile Tours
County Road 64, Clark
(970) 879-9073
www.stmbtsnowmobiletours.com
Half-day, full-day, and two-hour tours are offered that deliver breathtaking views of the Continental Divide and the Mount Zirkel Wilderness Area. Guides lead the way through the superb scenery of the Elk River Valley.

Steamboat Lake Outfitters
Hahns Peak
(970) 879-4404, (800) 342-1889
www.steamboatoutfitters.com
"SLO" is a full-service, year-round business that offers one- and two-bedroom cabins or bunkhouse lodging for the bring-your-own-snowmobile enthusiast. In fact, they provide everything you need except the snowmobile, including a restaurant, country

store, and 150 miles of groomed trails on thousands of acres in the Routt National Forest. Bunkhouse rooms run from $75 in the winter to $95 in the summer. One-bedroom cabins are $115 in the winter, $135 in the summer; two-bedroom cabins are $150 in the winter, $175 in the summer.

Steamboat Snowmobile Tours
Rabbit Ears Pass
south of Steamboat Springs
(970) 879-6500
www.stmbtsnowmobiletours.com
Steamboat Snowmobile maintains an extensive trail system on Rabbit Ears Pass that dips into protected meadows and leads to a secluded log cabin. Gourmet steak, chicken, and trout dinners are served there on dinner tours.

Snowshoeing

Howelsen Hill/Emerald Mountain
Fifth Street Bridge
(970) 879-8499, (800) 525-2628
Snowshoe trails ring downtown Steamboat's Howelsen Hill Ski Area, although it's important to be considerate. The area also is used by many of America's top Nordic skiers, and snowshoeing on their slopes can be annoying and dangerous. Daily passes are available for $5.00.

Tubing

Steamboat Springs Ski Area
(970) 879-6111, (800) 922-2722
After the skiers go home for the day, resort guests can hop into rubber sleds and tube down the lighted slopes of Preview, a beginner's hill at the base of the ski area. The price is $14 for everyone over 12, $12 for everyone under 12, and the fee includes tube rental as well as access to the tubing hill.

Winter Driving School

Bridgestone Winter Driving School
1850 Ski Time Square Drive
Steamboat Mountain Village
(970) 879-6104, (800) WHY-SKID
www.winterdrive.com
Tired of slipping and sliding on icy roads? The professionals at Bridgestone Winter Driving School teach the theory and practice of keeping your car on the road. Taught on a one-mile ice track with varied terrain, the classes teach everyone from the timid driver to the professional racer. Half-day, full-day, and two-day high performance programs are offered.

HIKING/BACKPACKING

The Mount Zirkel Wilderness Area extends for 50 miles along the Continental Divide and offers some great trails for hiking and backpacking. Many trailheads start at Buffalo Pass Road, which runs east from Steamboat Springs over the divide. Stop in the Ski Haus, 1457 Pine Grove Road, for maps, supplies, rental equipment, and local tips. The Clark General Store in Clark, (970) 879-3849, also has maps and information, as does the Hahns Peak Ranger District Office, 925 Weiss Drive, Steamboat Springs, (970) 879-1870.

Look for the free Steamboat Trails Map, published by and available at the Chamber Resort Association, 1255 South Lincoln Avenue, (970) 879-0880. It describes favorite day hikes and has a handy map showing all the hikes, plus trails for biking, horseback riding, four-wheeling, fishing, and camping. The map shows the locations of the three state parks, the Mount Zirkel Wilderness Area, and other points of interest.

Fish Creek Falls Trail to Long Lake
About three miles southeast of Steamboat Springs on Fish Creek Falls Road
Both day hikes and extended backpack trips begin at the base of Fish Creek Falls Trail. It may be Steamboat's most popular

tourist spot, a favorite because of the 283-foot waterfall that cascades down the canyon carved by glaciers during the Ice Age. The Crawford family homesteaded the falls area in 1901, named for the whitefish and brook trout that spawn in its waters each fall. About ¼ mile from the parking lot, a small footbridge crosses the creek to give strollers a good view of the falls. The upper portion of the trail leads to a view point above the falls, then continues to another falls. Long Lake is the end of the 6-mile trail that climbs 2,200 feet in elevation, which means only a select group of hikers make the entire trek. They're rewarded with campsites for overnighters or spurs for distance hikers that eventually reach Dumont Lake Campground on Rabbit Ears Pass. Plan to camp overnight at the lake or at Granite Campground (1 mile north) if you want to spend any time at the lake. Otherwise the 12-mile round-trip hike will be an all-day project. To reach the trailhead, take Lincoln Avenue (US 40) to 3rd Avenue, then turn north and drive one block to Fish Creek Falls Road. Turn right and travel another 4 miles. Fees are charged at the upper parking lot. Hikers may also arrange to be picked up by non-hikers at the Granite Campground, 1 mile north of Long Lake on the Lake Percy Trail.

Mad Creek Trail
About 7 miles northwest of Steamboat Springs along Elk River Road

If it's a relatively moderate, relatively low-elevation hike you're looking for, Mad Creek Trail may be just the thing. It begins at just under 7,000 feet and gains only 850 feet over the round-trip span of 5⁷⁄₁₀ miles. That also means it's accessible longer than higher trails—usually May through October. The hike is actually a loop that comprises three trails—Mad Creek until it intersects with Saddle Trail at 1³⁄₁₀ miles, which intersects with Red Dirt Trail at 2⁶⁄₁₀ miles. (If you shuttle two cars, leaving one at the Red Dirt trailhead and the other at Mad Creek trailhead, you can prevent a 1-mile walk along Routt County Road 129 back to the

Mad Creek trailhead.) Expect an early climb that takes you up a canyon wall that overlooks the angry waters of Mad Creek. At about 1 mile, the canyon will broaden into a wide valley carved by glaciers. Saddle Trail will take you to its namesake, a saddle that provides views and over the top of which is the intersection with Red Dirt Trail. To begin the hike, take Highway 40 west from Steamboat Springs to Elk River Road (Routt County Road 129) and turn right. Follow it north 5³⁄₁₀ miles to the trailhead, which will be on the right after you cross Mad Creek.

Rabbit Ears Peak Trail
About 23 miles southeast of Steamboat Springs near Rabbit Ears Pass

This easy hike is along a high-altitude trail that begins at about 9,600 feet and climbs 1,050 feet over the span of about 4 miles. (The round-trip hike is 8³⁄₁₀ miles.) Along the way you'll cross the Continental Divide Trail and pass through rolling meadows with one steep piece at about 2⁷⁄₁₀ miles that climbs to the base of one of the rabbit's "ears." It's best to limit your hikes on this trail to July through September because of altitude. Camping is available at Dumont Lake Campground near the trailhead. Take US 40 southeast from Steamboat Springs for about 20 miles up Rabbit Ears Pass to Dumont Lake Road (Forest Service Road 315) at the sign for Dumont Lake. Take the paved road for 1.5 miles and turn left on the dirt road past Dumont Lake Campground. Follow it ¹⁄₁₀ mile to the trailhead.

Sarvis Creek Trail
About 15 miles east of Yampa off Highway 131

This moderate trail extends 12 miles along Sarvis Creek, climbing from 7,000 to 9,400 feet in the process, although it's classified as moderate. Hikers will find themselves traveling through old logging territory, still visible through historic log homesteads and flumes built in 1913 by the Sarvis Timber Company. If you want to take the entire hike, plan to shuttle a car to the east end of the trail at Buffalo Park on Forest

Road 100, or camp before retracing your steps. Watch for bear, bighorn sheep, mountain lion, coyote, beaver, marmot, ptarmigan, and various raptors. Excellent brook trout fishing is available on the upper part of Sarvis Creek in Buffalo Park, an alpine meadow that once was a rangeland for buffalo. To reach the trailhead, take Highway 131 north from Yampa 8 miles to Routt County Road 14. Follow it to the east for 4 miles to Routt County Road 18A, and follow it past ⁶/₁₀ mile to Routt County Road 18. Follow it 3²/₁₀ miles past Stagecoach Reservoir and, below the dam, look for the STATE WILDLIFE AREA sign on the right and the trailhead across the Yampa River.

Three Island Lake Trail
About 30 miles northwest of Steamboat Springs in the Mount Zirkel Wilderness
At an elevation of just under 11,000 feet, this little lake is accessible only by foot, which means it's a nice, peaceful destination. Another reason for the tranquility: No camping is allowed around the lake, so only day hikers work their way in. The hike—the best months for which are July through September—is about 6⁴/₁₀ miles round trip, covering an elevation gain of 2,800 feet. The first half of the hike is moderate, with a brief climb via a series of switchbacks, during which you will enter the Mount Zirkel Wilderness. The last mile is almost flat, with the trail crossing a large meadow alongside the lake. Along the way, you'll pass through portions of the Blowdown, so called because winds estimated at more than 120 miles per hour raced through the forest in October 1997, leveling trees between Wyoming and Buffalo Pass (see the "Attractions" section for more information). Three Mile Creek gurgles alongside the trail in spots, offering some impressive cascades and some inviting fishing spots. To reach the trailhead, take Highway 40 west from Steamboat Springs for 2 miles, turn right on Elk River Road (also Routt County Road 129) and go north for 25 miles. Turn right on Seedhouse Road (Forest Service Road 400) and take it for 9³/₁₀ miles to North Lake Road (Forest Service Road 443). Turn right on North Lake Road and follow it for 3 miles to the trailhead.

CAMPING

Hahns Peak Lake
About 30 miles northwest of Steamboat Springs
(800) 280-2267
www.reserveamerica.com
Hikers, bikers, anglers, and horse lovers find this tiny campground an attractive choice. With only 26 campsites, it provides a great high-country lakeside base for quiet camping and outdoor activities. Campers have access to a boat ramp, water, picnic tables, and toilets. The trailhead for the Hahns Peak/Nipple Peak Mountain Bike Loop is less than a mile north on Forest Service Road 129. Sites are $10 a night. To reach it, take US 40 west from Steamboat Springs for 2 miles, then Routt County Road 129 for another 28 miles to Forest Service Road 486. Turn west, and the campground is on the northwest side of Hahns Peak Lake.

Pearl Lake State Park
27 miles north of Steamboat Springs
(970) 879-3922, (800) 678-2267
This gem of a park has 38 campsites for summer use only. Some of them are lakeside and all of them are good. The $12 site fee entitles campers to use the boat ramp, water, picnic tables, and toilets. (All campers must also pay a $4.00 park fee.) The most notable pastime here is fishing for grayling and cutthroat trout, with catch and release the policy for fish under 18 inches and a two-fish limit for those larger than 18. To reach the campground, take US 40 west for 2 miles to Routt County Road 129. Take it north for 23 miles to Pearl Lake Road, then continue 2 miles east to the campground. Reservations can be made up to 90 days early.

Stagecoach State Park
16 miles south of Steamboat Springs
(800) 678-2267

The nearest inexpensive campsites are available at Stagecoach State Park, south of Steamboat on US 40 to Highway 131, then on Routt County Road 14. Stagecoach is a hiker's paradise, with access to the nearby Sarvis Creek Trail (see the hiking section for more details), and an angler's and water lover's haven. Wetlands on the southwest end of the lake are a wildlife reserve and make for good wildlife viewing. The 92 sites are in the $12 range, plus $4.00 to enter the park. Amenities include boat ramps, water, dump station, fire rings, hiking/biking trails, marina, picnic tables, swim beach, toilets, and showers.

Steamboat Lake State Park
30 miles north of Steamboat Springs
(800) 678-2267

Just less than 200 campsites (some with electricity) ring this 1,100-acre lake, one of the state's best for rainbow and cutthroat trout fishing. And even with that many neighbors, there's more than enough solitude to go around. Reservations can be made by calling as much as 90 days in advance. Campsites are $12 a day, plus $4.00 to enter the park. That will buy you the opportunity to use the amphitheater (where rangers present daily activities and cowboy sing-alongs), boat ramp, water, dump station, fire rings, laundry, marina, picnic tables, public phone, snack bar, showers, swim beach, toilets, and visitor center. Another five cabins can be rented for $60 a night. If that's not enough for you, watercraft and horses are available for rental. During the winter, hiking trails become cross-country ski trails. The park is open year-round. To reach it, take US 40 west from Steamboat to Routt County Road 129. Follow it north for 26 miles.

GOLF

Haymaker
34855 US 40 East, Steamboat Springs
(970) 870-1846
www.haymakergolf.com

Haymaker is a Scottish links-style course 3 miles south of Steamboat Springs. Its rolling fairways and deep bunkers may be reminiscent of the old country, but you'll never forget you're in Colorado when playing it. With no housing on the 233-acre site and no trees to block the panoramic views, snowcapped mountains are visible on the horizon in any direction you care to look. The course is nestled into a broad valley at the eastern edge of town, an area still rural enough that red barns and barking farm dogs are the closest neighbors. Steamboat's western aura is captured in horseshoe tee box markers and holes named Westward Ho, Cattle Drive, Watering Hole, and Ten Gallon.

This 7,308-yard, par 72 course was designed by Keith Foster, opened in 1997, and by 1998 was nominated as one of *Golf Digest*'s "Best New Courses." One of the course's challenges is its unusually long holes—10 are more than 400 yards long, the longest a staggering 636 yards. The fairways are also mounded and uneven to increase the challenge, but the greens are large. Walk it if you dare (carts aren't required, but without trees the summer sun can feel as hot as the tropics). Greens fees are $83 (practice balls included).

Sheraton Steamboat Golf Club
2000 Clubhouse Drive
Steamboat Springs
(800) 276-6719

For more than two decades Sheraton Steamboat Golf Club was the Yampa Valley's only scenic resort course, wandering just a mile away and within full sight of the ski mountain, majestic Mount Werner, which frames downtown Steamboat. The 18-hole course makes the most of Fish Creek, which runs through seven of the holes, and the views of Fish Creek Canyon, Flat Tops Wilderness, and the Yampa Valley. Aspen and pine trees line most of the holes. The course is considered challenging, especially on the parts that are narrow enough to reward accuracy.

Robert Trent Jones Jr. designed the 6,902-yard, par 72 course in 1974. Pros give the following advice to newcomers: Putts break away from the ski mountain, regardless of how the greens may read. The course is open mid-April through October, with high season June 1 to September 19. Guests at the Sheraton Resort Hotels get a break on fees, depending on where you're staying. Non-resort guests should call for tee time availability and rates.

Steamboat Golf Club
West US 40, 6 miles northwest of Steamboat Springs
(970) 879-4295
www.steamboatgolfclub.com
This nine-hole course was designed by the Steamboat Men's Club and opened in 1964. Since then it has been known by locals as a pleasant and affordable place to play. Although it is still a private club, located 6 miles northwest of Steamboat Springs, the public is welcome. The 5,606-yard, par 72 course (if you play 18 holes) borders the Yampa River and is shaded by cottonwood trees and cooled by a small stream. Greens fees are $49 for 9 holes, $73 for 18 holes with cart. If you're willing to walk the course, you'll save $20 for 9 holes, and $34 for 18 holes.

FISHING/HUNTING

Outfitters and Tackle Shops

Bucking Rainbow Outfitters
729 Lincoln Avenue
(970) 879-8747, (888) 810-8747
www.buckingrainbow.com
Bucking Rainbow, located on Steamboat's busy main street, has a little bit of everything—a general store and deli, a full line of Orvis products, guide service that spe-

cializes in float trips on the Yampa and Colorado Rivers, and access to ponds, lakes, and rivers on private ranches.

Places to Fish

Steamboat Lake
Highway 129, about 40 miles north of Steamboat Springs
This 1,000-acre lake was designated Gold Medal water in 1996 for its spectacular rainbow trout. The Colorado Division of Wildlife reports rainbows that average 16 inches (some more than 20 inches) and Snake River cutthroats that average 16 to 18 inches. It's a favorite of locals and tourists alike, but beware of fickle weather, especially during mid-May thaw. Days can range from 70 degrees to late spring snows, so dress accordingly. The lake usually freezes between late November and early May.

To reach the lake, drive north from Steamboat Springs on County Road 129 for 26 miles to the Steamboat Lake State Park Office. You'll need to buy a state parks pass to get in. Camping and boat ramps also are available.

Yampa River
Downtown Steamboat Springs
Believe it or not, some of Steamboat's best fishing is available right in town, as the Yampa River splashes through on its way to Utah. The Colorado Division of Wildlife calls it a "best kept secret." The Yampa's ample waters carry rainbow trout, browns, Snake River cutthroats, brookies, and an occasional 36-inch pike. An especially nice 7-block stretch between Walton Creek and the James Brown Soul Center of the Universe Bridge (named after Mr. "I Feel Good" himself) has been the target of improvements to make it a more hospitable trout habitat.

Special regulations are in place—catch and release fishing only, with artificial flies and lures. Fishing season lasts all year, but licenses are required. Another unique aspect to fishing the Yampa River: It's one of the few in Colorado's high country considered to be free of whirling disease, a parasite that was first detected in the early 1980s and has reached epidemic levels in the state's rainbow trout population. Eleven of Colorado's 13 hatcheries have been infected with the parasite that causes fry to swim in a whirling fashion and usually die within the year.

Places to Hunt

Buffalo Pass
4 miles south of Steamboat Springs
(970) 879-1870
For hunters not interested in a long trek, Buffalo Pass is located just 4 miles south of town, bordering the Routt National Forest. For more details about access, license requirements, and good sites, inquire at the U.S. Forest Service Office in Steamboat Springs.

Mount Zirkel Wilderness
About 30 miles north of
Steamboat Springs
(970) 879-1870
Also known for its impressive elk herds, Mount Zirkel has better road access than Sarvis Creek. Hunters can drive into the national forest lands north of Clark and access the wilderness at several points along the way.

Sarvis Creek Wilderness
About 20 miles southeast of Steamboat
Springs off County Road 18
(970) 879-1870
Routt County has some of the state's best elk hunting, with the largest number of elk harvested there every year. For backpackers or horseback hunters, Sarvis Creek Wilderness is a favorite destination. (No motorized vehicles are allowed in, although camping is allowed around the edges.) Follow US 40 southeast of Steamboat to County Road 18 for about 20 miles and look for the SARVIS CREEK STATE WILDLIFE AREA sign at the trailhead.

OTHER RECREATION

Howelsen Park is the focus of many local activities. The park's Brent Romick Rodeo Arena hosts a Pro Rodeo Series during July and August (read more about that in the "Events" section). There's also a large ice rink, (970) 879-0341, with snack bar and skate rentals (for more details, see the "Other Winter Recreation" section). The Howelsen Skateboard Park features exciting half-pipes of several sizes. Two tennis courts are available at Howelsen on an hourly basis. Hikers can follow a number of different trails that start from the park and wind through aspen and fir forests with panoramic views of the city and surrounding mountains. Access Howelsen Park from downtown by crossing the river at Fifth Street or on one of the Yampa River Trail's pedestrian bridges. There is public parking on Yampa Avenue between 9th and 10th Streets.

Bicycling

As in the rest of the state, mountain biking is quite popular in the Steamboat area. Dirt roads and steep trails in the mountains provide endless possibilities. Contact the Hahns Peak Ranger District Office, 925 Weiss Drive, (970) 879-1870, for routes and maps, or talk to the folks at the Steamboat Springs Chamber Visitors Center, 1255 South Lincoln Avenue, (970) 879-0882.

Greenville-Reed Creek Loop
19 miles northeast of Steamboat
near Clark
A fairly easy, fairly level 11-mile route, the Greenville-Reed Creek Loop is popular with beginners with some mountain biking skills and intermediates out for a cruise. The trail gains only 600 feet of altitude and is 95 percent flat, but with mercifully short and extremely steep climbs (one at the start and another near the end). You'll be riding on four-wheel-drive and old log-

ging roads that are rutted and can be quite muddy when wet. The season is mid-June to late October, but because the area is popular during hunting season (mid-September through November), it's best to avoid it those months or wear blaze-orange clothing. Take US 40 north from Steamboat Springs to Highway 129. Turn right and continue another 15 miles to Clark. Turn right at Forest Service Road 440 (Greenville Road) and follow it 3 miles to a gate at the intersection of Forest Service Roads 440 and 471.

Mad Creek Loop
About 8.5 miles north of Steamboat on Highway 129

Mad Creek Loop is a 6-mile ride that starts along Mad Creek and ends with a 1-mile ride on tree-lined paved highway. It requires moderate technical skills, and some endurance, although it isn't a demanding route. It threads through forests and has only one steep climb about 2 miles along. The rest of the elevation gain is gradual. Because it also is a popular hiking trail (see the hiking section for more details), you'll have to share the trail with people on foot and on horseback. Follow the Mad Creek Trail 1½ miles to Saddle Trail. Follow it to the left, where you'll find a challenging climb that lasts only a half-mile to the saddle. The last short climb is to Red Dirt Trail, where you will turn left for a 2-mile descent to the Red Dirt trailhead and the final mile on pavement back to the Mad Creek trailhead. Ride it between late April and mid-October; it's especially pretty in fall when the leaves change color. Follow US 40 north of Steamboat to Highway 129. Turn right and travel 6½ miles to the Mad Creek trailhead alongside Mad Creek.

Rabbit Ears Pass to Fish Creek Falls
About 25 miles southeast of Steamboat Springs off US 40

The fist few miles are ridden on a four-wheel-drive road along easy terrain. After 4½ miles, a single-track trail will branch off to the right (Forest Service Road 1102, Base Camp Trail). Follow it due north 1 mile to Fish Hook Lake, another half-mile to Lost Lake, another mile more to Lake Elmo and Little Lost Lake, where you will see a four-way intersection of Lake Perry Trail, the Wyoming Trail, the Continental Divide Trail and Fish Creek Trail (Forest Service Road 1102). Follow the latter along the north side of Long Lake to a sign that points to Fish Creek Falls to the left. Unless you are an expert rider, consider retracing your path at the point for a pleasant 20-mile round-trip outing. The extreme athlete may prefer to continue on to Fish Creek Falls, traveling another 3½ miles to the Fish Creek Trail and nearly 3 miles down terrain so extreme authors Linda Gong and Gregg Bromka call it a monster trail, "the acid test to see what you're made of." In *Mountain Biking Colorado* (Falcon Publishing, 1994), the authors admit carrying their bikes down the final grueling miles. That option is a 16-mile ride requiring shuttle service from the base of Fish Creek Falls.

The Rabbit Ears Pass trail is best ridden between late May and mid-October because snow often lingers on the trail well into spring, and light snow may begin to fall as early as mid-September. The trailhead is at the Dumont Lake Campground, on the north side of US 40 about 2 miles west of Rabbit Ears Pass. The paved road leading to the site is Forest Service Road 311 (Base Camp Road).

Sore Saddle Cyclery
1136 Yampa Avenue
(970) 879-1675

Nestled up against the Yampa River and the original hot springs in the funky part of town, Sore Saddlery's building is an odd looking place. Owners bought the front half—a former wood chip incinerator from a logging operation—for $1.00 in 1981 and renovated it into a bike shop. It's now covered with adobe and attached to a long, low building by a distinctively New Mexican promenade. Owners have made a name for themselves selling, renting, and repairing bikes.

Steamboat Ski Area
2305 Mount Werner Circle
Steamboat Mountain Village
(970) 879-6111
The hiking and biking starts on 10,585-foot Mount Werner at the top of the Steamboat Gondola, then fans out into logging roads and singletrack. Trail maps are available at the Summer Activities Center at the base of the mountain. More than 50 miles of terrain on 15 different trails descend the mountain, but all are at least intermediate in difficulty. An easy trail circles the top of the mountain, however. Helmets are required on the mountain. Bikes can be rented from Steamboat Ski Corp. for a package rate starting at $40 an hour, which includes a full-day bike pass on the gondola. Cyclists who bring their own bikes must buy an $8.00 bicycle lift ticket plus pay the standard $18.00 to ride the gondola up the mountain.

Wyoming Trail
About 14 miles northeast of Steamboat Springs off Routt County Road 38
Starting at Buffalo Pass, the intermediate Wyoming Trail begins near the Summit Lake and Campground, loops 15 miles south along the Continental Divide Trail to join the northernmost portion of the Rabbit Ears Pass/Fish Creek Falls Trail, then returns north past Granite Campground on the shore of Fish Creek Reservoir, finally retracing the first few miles of the trail. No water is available along the trail. Because the trail hovers at timberline, the season is short—usually mid-June through mid-October, although riders should be prepared for rain and cold temperatures at any time. Wildflowers are at their peak in mid-July, but fir and spruce forests are always green. Turn north off Lincoln Avenue in downtown Steamboat onto Oak, then left on Amethyst Drive. Follows signs for Strawberry Park Hot Springs, then turn right on Routt County Road 38. Follow it 10 miles to the parking area at Buffalo Pass.

Cattle Drives

Saddleback Ranch
37350 County Road 179
Steamboat Springs
(970) 879-3711
www.saddlebackranch.net
This working 7,200-acre cattle ranch is owned by the Iacovetto family. You can become a cowboy or cowgirl for a half-day by helping the ranchers check, doctor, herd, and trail some of the 1,500 head of cattle. Horses, slickers, tack, snacks, and nonalcoholic beverages are provided. You'll learn the techniques for rounding up cattle and complete the daily tasks of an actual cowboy. Reservations are required.

Horseback Riding

Steamboat Springs is one of the most western of Colorado's ski resorts, so it stands to reason it would have some of the best horseback riding in the mountains. Area stables offer rides by the hour, half day, and full day, plus special rides such as breakfast, lunch, dinner, and hay rides.

Del's Triangle 3 Ranch
Two miles from Clark
(970) 879-3495
www.steamboathorses.com
Five generations of Heids have lived in the Yampa Valley, and owner Ray Heid isn't shy about saying so. They've been riding through the Mount Zirkel Wilderness area since 1962 and now have access to 114 square miles of wilderness that includes 40 lakes and miles of streams and trails. Rides are $65 for a two-hour ride, per person. You'll be saddled on horses that range from registered Arabians to registered Quarter Horses and even "a few old nags," according to the brochure. Summer Pack Trips start at $300 a day per person. Take US 40 west to Elk River Road (Routt County Road 129) and follow it north for 18 miles. Once you've reached Clark the

directions are simple—"Two miles left at the Clark Store."

Elk River Guest Ranch
29840 Routt County Road 64, Clark
(970) 879-6220, (800) 750-6220
www.elkriverguestranch.com
Located on the edge of the Mount Zirkel Wilderness, Elk River is a rural paradise. Riders can choose between one-hour rides, two-hour rides, half-day rides to the Beaver Ponds with a snack, full-day rides to Pearl Lake with lunch, or dinner rides near the Continental Divide with steak and potato in the open, dessert at the ranch's bonfire, and drinks at the Silhouette Saloon. Draft horses also pull a wagon to a clearing with Sioux Teepees for a candlelight dinner on couches and chairs.

High Meadows Ranch
20505 Routt County Road 16
(970) 736-8416, (800) 457-4453
www.hmranch.com
Actually located south of Steamboat Springs near Stagecoach Reservoir, High Meadows ranch offers two-hour, half-day, and full-day rides, with options for overnight and three-day extended rides. Price for the two-hour ride is $55 (regardless of age), $95 for a half-day, and $145 for full-day rides. The ranch is open year-round. Reach it by traveling south from Steamboat on US 40, turning right at Highway 131, then left at Routt County Road 14 (at the Stagecoach Reservoir sign). When Road 14 intersects with Routt County Road 16, turn left and follow it to the ranch.

Steamboat Lake Outfitters
Steamboat Lake, Highway 129, Clark
(970) 879-4404, (800) 342-1889
www.steamboatoutfitters.com
In addition to regular two-hour, half-day, and full-day rides, this outfitter offers extended trips into Routt National Forest and the Mount Zirkel Wilderness Area. They're the only outfitter licensed to operate on Steamboat Lake State Park. Breakfast, lunch, and dinner rides also are

available. One-hour rides are $35; two hours are $55; half-day is $105; full-day is $195 (half- and full-day rides include lunch, vegetarian on request). Rides depart daily at 9:00 and 11:30 A.M., and 2:00 and 4:30 P.M. Breakfast rides begin at 9:00 A.M. and cost $45. Dinner rides begin at 4:30 P.M. and cost $55.

Steamboat Stables/Sombrero Ranch
Howelsen Park
(970) 879-2306
www.sombrero.com
The stables, located at the end of Howelsen Park, offer horseback riding on trails around Emerald Mountain overlooking downtown. They offer hourly rides (about $25) and two-hour rides (for $40), as well as breakfast rides.

Gondola Rides

Steamboat Gondola
Base of Steamboat Ski Resort
Steamboat Mountain Village
(970) 879-2611
The enclosed gondola that transports skiers to the top of the mountain in winter also runs during the summer, but this time it serves guests interested in hiking or biking their way back down as well as those just along for the ride. Visitors will find a 1-mile nature trail with interpretative information about the trees and wildlife, as well as the 3-mile Thunderhead trail that takes about two hours to hike. Hours are 10:00 A.M. to 4:00 P.M. daily between mid-June and mid-September, with tickets priced at $18 each.

Hot Air Ballooning

Wild West Balloon Adventures
(970) 879-3298, (800) 748-2487
www.wildwestballooning.com
This mom-and-pop business is run by locals Ian and Lynne Cox, with Ian piloting each flight over the Yampa Valley. (He brags about flying more than 1,200 safe

flights since earning his license in 1982.) Lynne serves the continental breakfast and champagne celebration included in the price of each flight. Transportation is provided to and from local accommodations, and reservations are required. Adult prices are $125 for a half-hour ride, $185 for an hour. Children 12 and under are $85 (half-hour) and $150 (hour).

In-line Skating/ Skateboarding

Howelsen Skateboard/In-Line Skate Park
In Howelsen Park near the
9th Street bridge
(970) 879-4300

Skateboarders and in-line skaters enjoy the half- and quarter-pipes in this park, which opens as soon as spring weather allows and stays open as long as the sun is out. It has one vert ramp (half-pipe) and a street course for skaters to execute tricks on. Admission is free.

Steamboat Springs Core Trail
Between Lincoln Park and
Walton Creek Road

Voted Colorado's best in-line skating trail a few years back, it starts opposite Walton Creek Road, just south of the ski resort, and follows the Yampa River for 4½ miles of smooth pavement. Skaters on their way to West Lincoln Park or points in between share the path with runners, strollers, and dogs, and can entertain themselves by watching the rowdy kayakers and tubers floating past on the river, or by ogling the views of Mount Werner and the Yampa Valley.

Kayaking

Backdoor Sports Ltd.
9th Street and Yampa Avenue
(970) 879-6249
www.backdoorsports.com

The Steamboat Kayak School operates out of Backdoor Sports, with a location that can't be beat. It faces the Yampa River, is next door to the Steamboat Yacht Club restaurant, and has a footbridge on the other side that leads to Howelsen Hill. Classes are three to five hours, and cost $90 per person.

Mountain Sports Kayak School
Steamboat Resort
(877) 237-2628

Classes for all ages and skill levels are available at this school, which has offered top-quality kayak instruction since 1980. The beginner "never-ever" program is a three-hour experience for the whole family. Classes begin on shore, then move to a pond and, only after all are comfortable with the equipment, move to the Yampa River to paddle down a gentle stretch. Classes meet daily at 9:00 A.M. and 1:00 P.M. and cost $68, which includes equipment and instruction. Intermediate and Advanced classes take it from there, teaching specialized skills such as hole riding, eddy turns, rolling, and running slalom gates.

Swimming

Steamboat Health & Recreation
Association
136 Lincoln Avenue
(970) 879-1828
www.sshra.org

The town of Steamboat Springs began at the site of these hot springs, and it's only fitting that summertime fun still revolves around them. They're the best place to swim, with a large outdoor lap pool, a 350-foot water slide, and three heated pools of varying temperatures. They're fed by water from the original hot mineral springs and range from 82 to 102 degrees. That may sound hot for a warm summer day, but like most mountain towns, Steamboat can get chilly once the sun goes down. Swimsuits and towels can be rented on site, and a childcare center is there for kids who don't want to swim. Daily pool admission for adults 18 and older is $8.50. Younger teens are charged $5.00, and children 3 to 12 pay $3.50. If you also want access to the adjoining health club facilities, expect to pay about $7.00 more.

Tennis

Howelsen Tennis Courts
Howelsen Parkway
(970) 879-4300
Two courts are available on a first-come, first-served basis at the city's central park complex. Players are limited to an hour, but use is free.

Steamboat Health & Recreation Association
136 Lincoln Avenue
(970) 879-1828
The town's central swim and gym facility also has three tennis courts that are open for play from 8:00 in the morning to 8:00 in the evening. Visitors can reserve time on them for $7.00 an hour.

The Tennis Center at Steamboat
2500 Pine Grove Road
(970) 879-8400
The Tennis Center's 14 courts, both outdoor and indoor, are open to guests daily. Hourly rental price is $4.00 per person for the outdoor courts, $9.00 per person indoor.

White Water Rafting

High Adventures Whitewater Rafting
729 Lincoln Avenue
(970) 879-8747, (888) 810-8747
www.buckingrainbow.com
Located in Bucking Rainbow Outfitters, this white-water guide service offers everything from mild floats to wild rapids on the Arkansas, Colorado, Eagle, Elk, and Yampa Rivers. Trips range from half-day to multi-day.

HOT SPRINGS AND SPAS

Steamboat Springs was founded and grew up around the 150 hot springs that dot the Yampa River Valley; even before there was a town, there was a bathhouse. Homesteader James Crawford (the area's first white settler) found the spring that is now the Steamboat Springs Health & Recreation Association while he was hunting and named it Heart Spring (because of its shape). He built a bathhouse on that mesa 100 feet above the Yampa River and treated his family to warm baths.

Although most of the springs are either located on private land or are tiny seeps in hay fields, the town of Steamboat has preserved seven along what it calls The Springs Walk, a two-mile trail that cuts through town. The walk, free and open 24 hours a day, starts at Iron Springs Park at 13th Street and Lincoln Avenue, and travels to the Steamboat Springs Health & Recreation Center. Each spring along the way has its own claim to fame.

Iron Springs is the source of spring water that once was considered a tonic for "ailments of body and will" or, at the turn of the 20th century, everything from tuberculosis to depression, arthritis to schizophrenia. Although the water from Soda Spring has a higher iron content, generations of health seekers added lemon juice to the Iron Springs water and drank it as a cure. Sulphur Spring on the north bank is easy to smell (the Utes thought the odor was a sign of its powerful healing qualities). Steamboat Spring, for which the town was named in the 1820s, made the sound of a chugging steamboat when superheated water hit an underground rock chamber and escaped once the pressure built up enough to force the steam out. That bedrock was disturbed by construction workers building the railroad in 1908, and the chug has been silent ever since. Water does continue to spurt from the ground like a small geyser, however. Black Sulphur Spring on the river's south bank has dark black water that's high in sulphur; Narcisus and Terrace Springs are

clear; and Lithia Spring contains small amounts of the mood-elevating drug lithium. Its waters were bottled and sold in the 1930s, although it's no longer pure enough to be drinkable now. Cave Spring was formed when jets of hot water cut through rock walls to form a cavern that now is home to a bacteria-algae descended from myceum, a life form that dates back 4 billion years.

Steamboat Springs Health & Recreation Association
136 Lincoln Avenue
(970) 879-1828
www.sshra.org

The original hot springs used by James Crawford was sold to the town of Steamboat for $10 in 1935 and since has gained the reputation as a good place for a workout and a soak. The year-round hot springs and water slides are fed by hot mineral springs. Water from the original spring flows into a large outdoor lap pool and three heated pools that range in temperature from 82 to 102 degrees. The rec center features weights, fitness equipment, exercise classes, tennis courts, massage services, saunas, showers, a playground, and snack bar. Swimsuits and towels can be rented, and there's also a child care center. Daily pool admission for adults 18 and older is $8.50. Younger teens are charged $5.00, and children 3 to 12 pay $3.50. If you also want access to the health club facilities, expect to pay about $7.00 more.

Strawberry Park Hot Springs
Strawberry Park Road (44200 County Road 36), about 8 miles north of Steamboat Springs
(970) 879-0342

For a more natural soak or to spend some time in the woods, Strawberry Park Hot Springs is the place to go. It's located on private land 7,500 feet above sea level and 8 miles from downtown, the last three of which are on a rugged dirt road. Water from the 146-degree hot spring is captured in three rock-lined pools and diluted with enough river water to create hot pools at between 102 and 104 degrees, and a cool pool for the occasional refreshing plunge.

According to local lore, the Utes soothed their bodies and souls in its water after battling rival tribes. "The Utes believe now, as they did hundreds of years ago, that the vapors contained their creator's essence, and that soaking in them rejuvenated the soul," writes Deborah Frazier in *Colorado's Hot Springs* (Pruett Publishing Co.).

In the 1870s, Anglo settlers and miners took the land away from the Utes, and were known to cook fish, beef, eggs, tea, and vegetables in the 146-degree water, Frazier writes, but soon the owners found they had other enemies vying for the springs. Over the years such uninvited guests as drifters, biker gangs, and partiers kept county sheriffs busy responding to noise and trespassing reports.

Facilities are rustic, but include a changing room teepee and towel rental. Six rock and log cabins and a caboose are available for rent, but must be reserved in advance. Admission is $10.00 for adults; $5.00 for teens 13 to 17; and $3.00 for children 3 to 12. Because the springs are clothing optional after dark, no children are allowed.

BRECKENRIDGE, FRISCO, COPPER MOUNTAIN

BRECKENRIDGE

With its quaint Main Street lined with century-old Victorian buildings, the historic mining camp of Breckenridge has retained its charm while growing up into a major resort community. Breckenridge wears its colorful history on the sleeves of its ski parkas.

Located 98 miles west of Denver, Breckenridge sits in the upper end of the Blue River valley, lorded over by the craggy Ten-Mile Range and one of the state's tallest mountains, Quandary Peak. The most common route to Breckenridge is to take Interstate 70 west from Denver about 70 miles, then turn south on Highway 9 for 10 miles.

At an elevation of 9,603 feet, Breckenridge has a permanent population of about 2,000 people, but can accommodate some 23,000 visitors. What's more, surrounding Summit County, which also includes Keystone, Copper Mountain, Frisco, Silverthorne, and Dillon, can host nearly 100,000 people at once.

The town's long and brilliant history dates back to its incorporation in 1859—a week after gold was discovered—making it the oldest continually occupied community in Colorado's mountains. Even before the state's largest gold nugget, the 13-pound "Tom's Baby," was discovered in nearby French Gulch, sourdoughs were working the rich veins of ore that run throughout the valleys and turning the area into a boisterous mining camp. Wanting a post office, the miners chose to name the camp after Vice President John Cabell Breckinridge, who served under President James Buchanan. Breckinridge later became a

U.S. senator during Abraham Lincoln's tenure but soon resigned to join the Confederate Army. Since the Colorado Territory was allied with the Union forces, the town quietly changed its name to the current spelling, with an "e" in the middle.

Politics aside, mining defined Breckenridge. At one point, hundreds of working mines around the area generated untold riches. The legendary Tom's Baby nugget, discovered by Tom Lytton and Harry Groves in 1887, was kept in the assay office but mysteriously vanished, only to be recovered a century later from a Denver bank vault. Through World War II, Breckenridge rode booms and busts like many mining camps, and dredging—scouring the streambeds with giant earthmovers called dredgeboats—left huge piles of round river stone still visible on the banks of the Blue River.

With its mines dead in the 1960s, Breckenridge developed a ski area that quickly became the town's major attraction. Now expanded to cover 2,208 acres on four different peaks, the resort traditionally is one of the nation's busiest, offering tremendous bowl skiing above timberline and a variety of pleasant

Keep going south on Highway 9 after you leave Breckenridge and you'll cross the Continental Divide on Hoosier Pass, elevation 11,541, on your way to Fairplay. Veer southeast and you'll take a more rustic trip across the Continental Divide on Boreas Pass, elevation 11,482, to the old mining town of Como.

groomed runs. Naturally, some 200 bars and restaurants grew around the resort, as well as lodges and off-mountain activities. In 1997, the ski area was bought by Vail Resorts, which has committed to expansions of ski terrain as well as major real-estate development—the latest boom for this former mining camp.

In addition to a terrific local theater troupe and some of the best nightlife in a ski-resort town, major events include the top-notch Breckenridge Film Festival in September and Ullr Fest, a tribute to the Norse god of snow in January. Ullr Fest includes a zany parade, exquisite larger-than-life snow sculptures, and the Ullr-lympics, quasi-athletic competitions for all comers.

For all the changes, the town hasn't forgotten its past.

Breckenridge today includes one of the state's largest National Historic Districts, with 171 registered buildings. Among those is the Barney Ford House (still a private residence) at 111 East Washington Street, built for an emancipated slave who rose to prominence in mining and restaurants, then became a popular politician. Ford is one of only two people honored with a stained-glass depiction in the state Senate chambers.

And as a source of great amusement among locals, a mapmaker's error in the 1700s apparently omitted the entire region, turning Breckenridge into a "no-man's land." That led town officials jokingly to claim Breckenridge as a sovereign kingdom, a title still recognized in the royal crown insignia on the police department's Range Rovers.

FRISCO

On the shore of the Dillon Reservoir, Frisco is another former mining town enjoying a reincarnation as a resort area, a mix of antiques shops, trendy furniture boutiques, lodging, and good dining.

Frisco lies 9 miles north of Breckenridge on Highway 9, an easy drive—or, in the summer, a pleasant bike ride along the paved Peaks Trail bike path.

Incorporated in 1880, Frisco was named after San Francisco, but the peaks of the Ten-Mile Range towering over town make the hills of San Francisco look like, well, hills. Located just off I-70 about 70 miles west of Denver, Frisco is considered a gateway to Summit County and blends the old with the new.

With the pastoral Walter Byron Park attracting picnickers in the summertime and a slate of bars keeping the nightlife hopping in the winter, the town enjoys year-round activity. And located only a short drive—or a free shuttle bus ride—from Breckenridge, Copper Mountain, and Keystone, the town often plays host to skiers seeking variety during their vacations.

At one point in its 19th-century mining heyday, Frisco's 2,500 residents supported 19 dancehalls and 20 saloons, but following the silver bust of 1893, the population dwindled, reaching 18 lonely souls in 1930.

Main Street is where all the action is in Frisco; much of the rest of the community is located within walking distance of this strip of stores, restaurants, and lodges. But being adjacent to the interstate, the town also has its share of fast-food restaurants and even a Wal-Mart on the main route on the eastern edge of town.

Frisco's historic park on Main Street has 10 rough-hewn log buildings, including the town's original 1881 jail and a trapper's cabin. Ten-Mile Creek provides a greenbelt just off Main Street, and the county's wonderful bike path runs through town, turning into its own sort of pleasant highway as soon as the snow melts.

While the town hosts the nation's largest Corvette rally each summer and the Frisco Gold Rush snowshoe race every winter, perhaps the best event is the spectacular Fourth-of-July fireworks display over the reservoir.

Frisco shares Dillon Reservoir with Dillon and Silverthorne and has a respectably large marina and boatyard. THE DENVER POST/DAVE BURESH

COPPER MOUNTAIN

Heading west from Frisco along I-70, travelers destined for Copper Mountain are treated to Ten-Mile Canyon, a deep narrow gorge cut by a bubbling river and shadowed by craggy peaks. At the west end, the valley broadens to reveal Copper Mountain ski area. A product of the 1970s ski boom, Copper Mountain is known as the place "where the skiers ski," a mountain of such fortunate geography that terrain runs the gamut from mellow to steep as you traverse from east to west across the face. The U.S. Forest Service, in fact, considers it a model ski mountain in part because it segregates skiers by ability.

Owned by resort giant Intrawest, Copper Mountain has undergone more than $400 million in base-area development and mountain improvements that also made it where the "vacationers vacation." A pedestrian village lined by quaint shops, restaurants, and timber-and-stone condominiums, Copper is more of an all-around resort than solely is a place to ski.

In the summer, Copper's Pete Dye–designed championship golf course, horseback riding at the resort stables, and fly-fishing clinics offer pastoral activities. But in the winter, skiing dominates. In 1999 Copper opened the state's first six-person passenger chair, which theoretically would allow someone to ski 66,000 vertical feet—more than twice the height of Mount Everest—in one leg-numbing day. At night, don't miss the après-ski scene at JJ's Rocky Mountain Tavern.

Copper Mountain is considered a resort village and not a town in its own right. It has the same zip code as Frisco, grocery store, liquor store, and various shops and restaurants. All of Copper's accommodations are condo-style or hotel-type rooms in complexes, handled through a central reservation system. For more information call the Copper Mountain Resort at (800) 458-8386.

ACCOMMODATIONS
Breckenridge

**Beaver Run Resort and
Conference Center**   **$$$**
620 Village Road
(970) 453-6000, (800) 288-1282
www.beaverrun.com
Called a "Condotel," this newer resort is composed of privately owned condos rented out by the owners. It operates like a hotel with all the amenities of a resort hotel and the privileges of private ownership. Owners furnish the condos, which have nine different floor plans ranging from studios to four-bedroom, four-bath units. The units are attractive and com-

fortable, some with hot tubs in the middle of a room with great views. The resort is right at the base of Peak 9, placing guests just footsteps away from the Beaver Run SuperChair lift up the peak. There's an affordable family steak house, a full-service deli, and a sports bar. The resort offers complete ski and golf packages.

Breckenridge Mountain Lodge   **$$**
600 South Ridge Street
(970) 453-2333, (800) 800-7829
www.breckmountainlodge.com
An attractive log building with 71 rooms, this rustic picturesque lodge is close to both the slopes and town. Rooms are decorated in traditional western-style decor, and there's a free continental breakfast, hot tubs, a game room, and parking.

Great Divide Lodge   **$$$**
550 Village Road
(970) 453-4500, (800) 800-7829
www.greatdividelodge.com
Formerly the Hilton Hotel, the Great Divide was bought by Vail Resorts and fully refurbished, continuing its reputation for fine lodging and élan. Like Beaver Run, the Great Divide also is at the base of Peak 9 (albeit across the street). Each of the 208 spacious units comes with a refrigerator, wet bar, and coffeemaker. There's a 24-hour front desk, room service, valet parking, restaurant, lounge, swimming pool, hot tubs, saunas, an exercise room, and a ski shop. This lodge is very popular with British skiers.

The Lodge & Spa at Breckenridge   **$$$**
112 Overlook Drive
(970) 453-9300, (800) 736-1607
www.thelodgeatbreck.com
With a commanding view of the Ten-Mile Range, Hoosier Pass, and Mount Baldy, this luxurious spa resort sits atop a cliff overlooking Breckenridge on Boreas Pass. Most of the 45 rooms and suites have spectacular views—ask for one when booking. The decor is upscale western, and the rooms are spacious and comfortable. There's an indoor pool, Jacuzzi, two

indoor and outdoor hot tubs, saunas, a weight room, a full health spa, and racquetball center. The award-winning Top of the World restaurant serves breakfast at reduced rates for guests as well as dinner. Ask about package deals. The lodge is 2 miles up the pass at the end of town.

River Mountain Lodge $$
100 South Park Avenue
(970) 453-4711, (800) 627-3766
Across the street from Four O'Clock Run, the lodge offers easy walking access to town. There are 130 units ranging from studios to two bedrooms with full kitchens, terraces, and washer/dryers. The lodge has a health club, weight room, pool, steam room, sauna, indoor and outdoor hot tubs, and lounge.

Village at Breckenridge $$
535 South Park Avenue
(970) 453-2000, (800) 800-7829
www.villageatbreckenridge.com
This ski-in, ski-out complex run by Vail Resorts is right on the slopes at the base of Peak 9 and within walking distance of town. A large complex with over 250 rooms, it includes shops, restaurants, and lounges and offers ski packages for families and individuals and other bargains. Be sure to ask about packages. There's a health club, indoor/outdoor heated pool, hot tubs, ice skating, and a 24-hour front desk. The choices range from hotel rooms to studios and larger one- to three-bedroom apartments and chateaux.

Wildwood Suites $$
120 Sawmill Road
(970) 453-0232, (800) 866-0300
www.wildwood-suites.com
Next to a mountain stream and nestled in the woods only 2 blocks from the historic district on Main Street, this smaller condominium complex has 36 one- and two-bedroom units. It has a ski-in location, large outdoor hot tubs, a sauna, meeting rooms, and a massage service. The price includes a complimentary continental breakfast.

Frisco

Cross Creek Resort and Conference Center $$$
223 West Creekside Drive
(970) 668-5175, (800) 748-1849
www.crosscreekfrisco.com
Just outside Frisco, this modern condominium complex has pleasant two- and three-bedroom units with kitchens, whirlpool tubs, fireplaces, satellite TV, washers and dryers, and decks overlooking Mill Creek. Some units are bi-level. The clubhouse has an indoor/outdoor pool, spas, sauna, and a game room with a fireplace.

Mountain Side Condominiums $$
Bill's Ranch Road and Fifth Street
(970) 668-3174, (800) 766-1477
www.mtnmanagers.com
This popular, attractive condominium complex with seven buildings backs up to a national forest and is 4 blocks from Main Street. The property offers one-, two-, and two-bedroom-plus-loft condos. You can't bring your pets; but children are allowed. There's a large clubhouse with a pool, hot tub, and sauna, plus tennis courts. For reservations and information, call the number listed above, which is a management company called Mountain Managers.

Sky-Vue Motel $
305 Second Street
(970) 668-3311, (800) 672-3311
www.skyvuemotel.com
Only 2 blocks from Main Street, this motel offers a convenient and centeral location, plus it's quiet and economical. There's a free continental breakfast, an indoor pool, and hot tub. Some rooms have kitchenette units.

Snowshoe Motel $
521 Main Street
(970) 668-3444, (800) 445-8658
www.snowshoemotel.com
Also centrally located, this budget motel offers no frills but has serviceable, clean modern rooms. Some rooms with kitchenettes are available. There's a hot tub and sauna, and pets are allowed with a $20 deposit and $10 extra per pet.

i

The flashy Rocky Mountain Columbine is the state flower and reaches its peak in the mountains around July 4. Look for the purple and white petals surrounding a yellow center.

Copper Mountain

Carbonate Property Management
35 Wheeler Place
(970) 968-6854, (800) 526-7737
This company manages about 140 units and is strictly for lodging and real estate. There's a three-night-stay minimum at Christmas and a five-night minimum in March. The units range from studios to four-bedroom condominiums, and five-bedroom houses.

Copper Mountain Reservations $$$
209 Ten Mile Circle
(888) 219-2441
Copper Mountain Resort, owned by Intrawest, offers a wide variety of accommodations, from hotel rooms to five-bedroom mountain houses. In the East Village you can choose from Bronze (one-bedroom), Silver (two-bedroom and loft or four-bedroom), or Gold (three-bedroom) accommodations, or three-and four-bedroom townhouses or houses complete with garage. East Village is located at the base of the intermediate and expert ski terrain, with a complimentary shuttle available to take you to the beginner's areas. The Village at Copper is more centrally located, and you can choose from Bronze (two-bedroom, two-bedroom plus a loft), Silver (ranges from a hotel room to a four-bedroom unit) or Gold (also ranges from a hotel room to a four-bedroom unit). The difference in the various choices is in the size and quality of the units. Bronze are the least expensive, Gold the priciest. At the base of the beginner's terrain Union Creek offers Silver (ranges from a hotel room to a four-bedroom unit) or Platinum (one-bedroom

to three-bedroom units). Again, size and quality of the accommodations are the distinguishing factors. Amenities at these various lodging locations include bike and ski rentals, tennis courts, 24-hour front desk and security service, babysitting and day care (extra charges apply), bellman service, fitness rooms, golf, hot tubs, pools, sauna and spa services, and are within walking distance to the ski lifts or a free shuttle service to different terrain areas.

BED-AND-BREAKFASTS

Breckenridge

Allaire Timbers Inn $$$
9511 Highway 9
(970) 453-7530
www.allairetimbers.com
Lovingly built in 1991, this wood and stone structure offers 10 beautiful and unique rooms, each with its own theme. There are two deluxe suites with their own fireplaces and hot tubs. The inn occupies a pretty, forested site near the south end of town. A full breakfast is included and is served in the spacious common room. The outdoor Jacuzzi on the deck affords a great view of the Ten-Mile Range. The inn is listed among the *Distinctive Inns of Colorado: Romantic Hideaways in Colorado's Rocky Mountains*.

Fireside Inn $$
114 North French Street
(970) 453-6456
www.firesideinn.com
Housed in an 1879 home, this New England-style bed-and-breakfast was Breckenridge's first. There are five rooms with private baths and TVs and five dorm rooms. The Inn honors American Youth Hostel cards, providing some of Breckenridge's least expensive but attractive lodging. It's a historic building furnished with antiques, lace curtains, and nice woodwork. Private rooms have antiques, and if you want the best room ask for the Brandywine Suite, which used to come with a brandy

decanter (non-guest imbibing convinced the owners to remove it). There's a hot tub and pleasant parlor with a fireplace where guests can meet and make friends.

Frisco

Frisco Lodge $$
321 Main Street
(970) 668-0195, (800) 279-6000
www.friscolodge.com
Now a bed-and-breakfast, this former stagecoach stop and railroad depot dating back to 1885 has eight rooms with shared baths and three rooms with private baths in the motel annex. Stay here for a taste of the past with a low price tag. The log cabin decor will make you feel like a pioneer.

Galena Street Mountain Inn $$
106 Galena Street
(970) 668-3224, (800) 248-9138
www.galenastreet.com
A charming 13-room bed-and-breakfast right in the center of town, this inn offers a romantic atmosphere. One of the best views of the mountains is from the large windows of The King Tower room, which also has a lovely Victorian turret. All rooms have private baths and cable TV and are nicely furnished with mission-style furniture, natural-fiber bed linens, and down comforters. Four of the rooms have fireplaces, and three have private porches. Some rooms combine to form family suites. There's daily housekeeping, full breakfast, afternoon tea, a hot tub, sauna, and ski room. Smoking is not allowed.

RESTAURANTS
Breckenridge

The Blue Moose $
540 South Main Street
(970) 453-4859
Located at the south end of town, the Blue Moose is only open for breakfast, but offers

a full bar to go with their omelets and breakfast specials. Voted "The Best Breakfast in Summit County," the menu includes carbo-loading breakfasts for skiers, a variety of vegetarian dishes, and monster four-egg omelets. Try the Moose Sandwich, two eggs over hard with cheddar cheese and ham or bacon on wheat toast.

Breckenridge Brewery $
600 South Main Street
(970) 453-1550
www.breckbrew.com
The award-winning beers include Avalanche Ale, Trademark Pale Ale, and Oatmeal Stout. There are also plenty of appetizers, sandwiches, and light meals. The brewery is open for lunch and dinner. From the bar, patrons can watch the handcrafted brewing process. From the dining room, you can enjoy a nice view of the Ten-Mile Range.

Briar Rose $$
109 Lincoln Avenue
(970) 453-9948
Start off with a fine wine off the extensive wine list at the Briar Rose, housed in a historic turn-of-the-20th-century building located a half-block off Main Street. Then move on to delicious steaks, wild game, seafood, pasta, or a vegetarian entree.

Bubba Gump's Shrimp Co. $$
231 South Main Street
(970) 547-9000
www.bubbagump.com
Part of a resort-town chain inspired by the movie *Forrest Gump*—but having nothing to do with the mountain setting—this place is much more popular among tourists than

---

Locals like to tell the story of Sylvia, a young female ghost who some say haunts the Prospector Restaurant on Main Street. Several men say they have seen her "prospecting" for suitors, and a parapsychologist who visited the site in the 1990s confirmed Sylvia's presence.

locals but should not be overlooked. The shrimp plates come about as many ways as Forrest's friend Bubba mentioned in the movie, and all are excellent. Memorabilia from the movie, including Forrest's leg braces and his white suit, hangs on the walls, providing a fun trip down memory lane for both movie buffs and the baby boomers whose lives were portrayed by Tom Hanks and company.

Mi Casa Mexican Restaurant & Cantina $
600 South Park Avenue
(970) 453-2071
Mi Casa is jammed on Friday nights and loved by locals and tourists alike. There are two seating areas, one ground level and one a few steps down and overlooking the river. All the Mexican favorites are here (enchiladas, burritos, fajitas) plus some interesting specials such as poblano relleno, fresh roasted chilies filled with shredded chicken and spices encrusted in blue cornmeal on red chili sauce, or Baha fish tacos, Shrimp Diablo, and Tamales Con Puerco. Mi Casa features daily happy hour drink deals on beer and margaritas. The restaurant serves dinner only, but the Cantina opens at 3:00 P.M. for happy hour.

Rasta Pasta $
411 South Main Street
Four Seasons Plaza
(970) 453-7467
www.rastapasta.net
For a change of pace, try this wonderful restaurant, which specializes in recipes with a zippy Jamaican flavor. The "Rasta Pasta" namesake entree is pasta with jerk chicken, green onions, basil, and diced tomatoes sautéed and served with a garlic tomato sauce. Another novel item is Dreadlock Ravioli with ricotta cheese ravioli, spices, and a choice of fresh clams or spicy sausage, diced tomato, and green onion served with garlic tomato sauce. Reggae music plays constantly, but the volume is non-obtrusive. The loyal clientele includes families, seniors, local extreme jocks, lots of local workers, and tours. With a deck next to the Blue River and a bright,

cheerful interior, it's a good choice. Rasta Pasta serves lunch and dinner.

Frisco

Backcountry Brewery $
970 Main Street
(970) 668-BEER
www.backcountrybrewery.com
Backcountry Brewery features burgers, steaks, pastas, sandwiches, seafood, and chicken, plus seven different handcrafted Backcountry brews and a pizzeria conversation bar. This spacious, casual brewpub has two levels, two bars, sunny decks with mountain views, and a beer garden. It serves lunch and dinner.

The Blue Spruce Inn $$$
20 West Main Street
(970) 668-5900
www.thebluespruce.com
This rustic log cabin has lots of cozy ambiance along with good food. Try the Steak Diane or selection of fresh seafood or lamb. The cuisine is a combination of continental and Rocky Mountain with such exotic sauces as Grand Marnier lingonberry sauce or melted saga bleu cheese and dill lemon buerre served with boneless red trout. There's also a fine wine list. It's open for dinner only, and reservations are suggested.

Log Cabin Cafe $
121 Main Street
(970) 668-3947
A local's breakfast joint, the Log Cabin also serves good homemade chili, salads, and desserts. It's open for dinner Tuesday through Saturday and daily for breakfast and lunch.

Copper Mountain

Double Diamond Restaurant $$
Foxpine Inn
(970) 968-2880

Located just a few steps from the Super B lift, the Double Diamond offers reasonably priced, great pasta meals that are perfect for "carbo loading" after a hard day on the slopes. Fare includes spinach walnut fettucine, shrimp alfredo, and chicken marsala, as well as pizza and fish flown in fresh daily.

NIGHTLIFE

Breckenridge

Breckenridge Brewery
600 South Main Street
(970) 453-1550
www.breckbrew.com
With a daily happy hour from 3:00 to 6:00 P.M. and late-night menu until midnight, this is a favorite hangout for locals and tourists alike. Some of the brewery's award-winning beers are Avalanche Ale, Trademark Pale Ale, and Oatmeal Stout. There are also plenty of appetizers, sandwiches, and light meals. From the bar, patrons can watch the hand-crafted brewing process.

Sherpa and Yeti's
320 South Main Street (below Ole Moon Gallery)
(970) 547-9299
Live reggae music and hot deejays are some of the offerings of this blues and jazz lounge in Breckenridge, formerly known as the Alligator Lounge. There are also specials on well drinks and pints some nights.

Frisco

Moose Jaw Bar & Grill
208 Main Street
(970) 668-3931
This is a popular place for bargain beers, burgers, and pool. It's frequented by local skiers, athletes, construction workers, and the 30-something crowd.

Copper Mountain

JJ's Rocky Mountain Tavern
Copper Commons, base of ski area at lifts
(970) 968-2318
JJ's features Moe Dixon, a nationally recognized singer, songwriter, and guitarist and one of the locals' favorite artists. Live entertainment is from 3:00 to 6:00 P.M.

ATTRACTIONS

Breckenridge Town
From I-70, exit 203 to Highway 9
(970) 453-5579 (Breckenridge Resort County Chamber of Commerce)
The largest of Colorado's designated national historic districts, the Victorian town of Breckenridge is itself one of Summit County's main attractions—complementing Breckenridge Ski Resort, the largest of Summit County's four ski areas. Attractively restored Victorian buildings line Main Street and serve as shops, cafes, homes, and offices. During Christmas the town is especially pretty, twinkling with many lights and garlands entwining the old-fashioned lampposts. But in summer a dazzling array of flowers hang from those same lampposts and bloom in the plentiful Victorian gardens. Fall's slopes of golden aspen trees create another visual treat. The Breckenridge Gold Rush of 1859 established the first settlement there, and as other strikes in the area went boom and bust, many miners and their families settled in Breckenridge.

Breckenridge offers Summit County's largest array of restaurants, accommodations, shops, galleries, and activities, and visitors will never run out of interesting things to do and see.

Country Boy Mine
542 County Road 565, east of Breckenridge
(970) 453-4405
This intriguing 120-year-old mine tunnels 1,000 feet underground only 2 miles from

downtown Breckenridge. The tour offers an explanation of mining and an opportunity to do some gold panning on your own. Visitors receive hard hats to wear but should bring warm jackets for the underground tour. To get there, take Wellington Road east off Main Street. The pavement eventually turns to a groomed dirt road known as the "French Gulch" road, and the well marked mine is on the right. The tours run daily every hour on the hour from 10:00 A.M. to 5:00 P.M. from June through October 15.

Frisco Historical Park
120 Main Street, Frisco
(970) 668-3428
A collection of 10 buildings from the late 19th century give a good idea of early life in Frisco, which began as a logging and mining center. The old-fashioned schoolhouse in the park was originally built in the 1890s as a saloon. Inside are display cases of photographs, miners' equipment, and turn-of-the-20th-century clothing, along with some of the original school desks and blackboards. Also on the site is an old jail house (closed in winter), a log chapel, a trapper's cabin with animal pelts, a furnished Victorian-era home, and craft and gift shops. The park also hosts musical concerts, workshops on gold panning, and arts and crafts festivals. Call for the current schedule. Hours are 11:00 A.M. to 4:00 P.M. Tuesday through Saturday during winter and 11:00 A.M. to 4:00 P.M. Tuesday through Sunday during summer. Donations are requested.

Frisco Schoolhouse Museum
120 Main Street, Frisco
(970) 668-3428
The restored 19th-century schoolhouse is a work of art in itself and contains artifacts and information about mining, Dillon Reservoir, the Ute Indians, and life in old Frisco. The building was originally a saloon. Hours are 11:00 A.M. to 4:00 P.M. Tuesday through Sunday during summer and 11:00 A.M. to 4:00 P.M. Tuesday through Saturday during winter. Admission is free, but donations are requested.

Hoosier Pass and Quandary Peak (and on to Alma and Fairplay)
Highway 9
Only 10 miles from Breckenridge on Highway 9, the 11,541-foot summit of Hoosier Pass makes a spectacular outing just below 14,264-foot Quandary Peak. It provides great vistas of the surrounding mountains and the wildflower-filled land above the trees—along with an appreciation of the difficulties early settlers faced making this journey with only horses and wagons. Drive south on Highway 9 from Breckenridge, and you can't miss it. If time permits, continue south on to the rustic towns of Alma and Fairplay (about 15 miles from the pass). Alma is 7 miles northwest of Fairplay on Highway 9.

Fairplay is the larger of the two towns and has historic hotels, the Fairplay Hotel and Como Depot, both of which have good restaurants with lots of atmosphere. The South Park City Museum in Fairplay is a reconstructed 19th-century mining town with 30 buildings and 50,000 historic objects collected from all over Colorado. A picnic area called "The Beach" with a fishing lake and gold panning opportunities is also a good stop.

Summit Historical Society Tours
309 North Main Street, Breckenridge
(970) 453-9022
www.summithistorical.org
It has been said that Summit County is much richer in history than it is in museums, although the Summit Historical Society has been working to increase the public's exposure to this area's fascinating past. One way is through tours, offered by the society—both self-guided and with trained guides. Among the more interesting tours are the Washington Mine, where a guide leads visitors into the horizontal shaft with miners' candles. The mine includes displays of mining artifacts. Other historical society tour stops are at the 1880 Alice G. Milne House, built in 1880, and the circa 1875 Edwin Carter Museum. Call, or visit the Web site, for tour schedules and rates.

Washington Gold Mine Tour
Illinois Gulch Road, Breckenridge
Information Center, 309 North Main
Street, Breckenridge
(970) 453-9022
www.summithistorical.org
This year-round, guided underground
mine tour provides an in-depth look at the
area's historic mining life and industry. The
tour goes through two shafthouses and
the anteroom of this once-active mine.
Everyone gets a hard hat for the quick
trip into the mine, which comes complete
with recordings of booming dynamite
blasts. The tour lasts about 90 minutes
and is narrated by knowledgeable guides
from the Breckenridge Historical Society.
Tuesday through Saturday in July and
August, Friday and Saturday only in September. The mine is closed due to snow
conditions from October through May.
Admission is $3.00 for adults, $1.00 for
children under 12 and seniors over 65.

KIDSTUFF

Amaze 'N Breckenridge
Breckenridge Ski Area, at the base
of Peak 8, Breckenridge
(970) 453-7262
www.amazenmazes.com
Adults as well as kids will enjoy getting
lost in this human-size maze of wooden
walls. While those in the maze try to find
their way, spectators from a deck shout
directions. Talk about feeling like a rat.
People with the fastest times win prizes.
Save your pass for a discount the second
time you enter.

Breckenridge Recreation Center
880 Airport Road, Breckenridge
(970) 453-1734
This fine facility can provide a much-
needed break for kids (and adults)
cooped up in cars traveling. Indoors there
are two tennis courts, two racquetball/
wallyball courts, a gymnasium for basketball, two rock-climbing walls, a free-
weights room, a circuit weight area, cardio

equipment, a 25-yard, four-lane lap pool, a
pool with a water slide and kiddie area, a
steam room, hot tubs, a dry sauna, a running track, and locker rooms. Outside
you'll find four hard surface tennis courts,
four clay courts, a basketball court, skateboard park, another hot tub, tetherball,
volleyball courts, a soccer field, bike paths,
a playground, and a kayak park. Call
ahead for hours and schedules for the
various areas.

Breckenridge Ski School
Peak 8 and Peak 9 Children's Centers
Breckenridge Ski Resort, Highway 9
Breckenridge
(970) 453-5000, (800) 789-SNOW
Half- and full-day programs will get kids
on skis and loving it. Kids are sorted into
different camps based on age, and early
drop-off is available after tickets are purchased. Half-day lessons with a lift ticket
cost $90 for 3- and 4-year old skiers, $101
for 5- and 6-year olds, and $101 for 7- to
12-year olds. Full-day lessons with a lift
ticket, lunch, and snacks cost $105 for 3-
and 4-year olds, $116 for 5- and 6-year
olds, and $116 for 7- to 12-year olds. Pri-
vate lessons are also available, but are
about four times as expensive. Snowboarding lessons for kids ages 7 to 12 cost
the same as ski lessons and are offered in
half- and full-day programs. All children in
ski and snowboarding schools are strongly
encouraged to wear helmets, and rentals
are available.

Breckenridge Super Slide
Breckenridge Ski Resort, Highway 9
Breckenridge
(970) 453-5000
This alpine slide rides down from the top
of Peak 8 in a seat-gripping five minutes or
so. Sliders ride the lift up to the top of
Peak 8 and mount the sleds, which run in a
concrete track. The speed of descent can
be controlled by the rider with a center-
mounted lever. The sleds can hold an
adult and child; children ages 2 to 6 must
ride with an adult. Children younger than
2 are not permitted on the slide. Hours are

Nonskiers can enjoy the snow on Copper Mountain's tubing hill. THE DENVER POST/ERIC LUTZENS

9:00 A.M. to 5:00 P.M. daily from mid-June to early September and 9:00 A.M. to 5:00 P.M. on select days and times in early summer and late fall (call first).

Frisco Historical Park
120 Main Street, Frisco
(970) 668-3428

Children and adults alike can enjoy an old-fashioned schoolhouse topped by a school bell, as well as the rest of a fascinating glimpse at Summit County's early days. Originally built in the 1890s as a saloon, the old schoolhouse also houses display cases of photographs, miners' equipment, and turn-of-the-20th-century clothing, along with some of the original school desks and blackboards. Also on the site is an old jail house (closed in winter), a log chapel, a trapper's cabin with animal pelts, a furnished, Victorian-era home, and craft and gift shops. The park also hosts musical concerts, workshops on gold panning, and arts and crafts festivals. Call for the current schedule. Hours are 11:00 A.M. to 4:00 P.M. Tuesday through Saturday during winter and 11:00 A.M. to 4:00 P.M. Tuesday through Sunday during summer. Donations are requested.

Ice Skating on Maggie Pond
535 South Park Avenue, Breckenridge
(970) 547-5726

This small pond in the Village at Breckenridge duplicates the Christmas card image of ice skating outdoors and warming up with a cup of hot chocolate afterward. A small warming hut above the pond offers rental skates for toddlers to adults and a place to keep your things. There are sleds for babies and toddlers. Lounge and enjoy hot chocolate at one of the many cafes lining the lake. Hours are 10:00 A.M. to 10:00 P.M. daily, once the lake freezes (usually in November). Skate rentals are available from 10:00 A.M. until 9:00 P.M. Rentals and skating are reasonably priced.

Lomax Placer Gulch Tour
Ski Hill Road, Breckenridge
(970) 453-9022

Panning for gold, a thrill for adults and children alike, is the climax of this 90-minute guided tour sponsored by the Summit Historical Society. Older kids will find the information about hydraulic mining interesting, and all kids will enjoy the visit to a miner's cabin. There's a 45-minute talk, including a short slide show. Then everyone gets a pan of dirt that may contain some specks of gold and dips their pans into the water and swirls away looking for those sparkling specks. Most people find a few, which can then be placed in a small vial of water to magnify them and crate a great souvenir for a fee of 50 cents. The tour begins at 3:00 P.M. Tuesday through Saturday from July 1 through August 31, and Friday and Saturday in September weather permitting. Admission is $3.00 for adults and $1.00 for children ages 3 to 12. Tickets for the tour can be purchased at the Breckenridge Information Center, 309 North Main Street, across from the fire station, or at the mine site before the tour.

Washington Gold Mine Tour
Illinois Gulch Road, Breckenridge
(970) 453-9022

For those seeking an underground mine tour, this is the one. The tour goes through two shafthouses and the anteroom of this once-active mine. Everyone gets a hard hat for the quick trip into the mine, which comes complete with recordings of booming dynamite blasts. This long (90-minute) tour might be a bit long for some children, but kids can handle some of the artifacts of the miners and look for their own treasure outside the shafthouses. The Historical

Society guides are very knowledgeable and present in-depth looks at the mining life and industry of past times. Tuesday through Saturday in July and August, Friday and Saturday only in September. The mine is closed due to snow conditions from October through May. Admission is $3.00 for adults, $1.00 for children under 12 and seniors over 65. Purchase tickets at the Breckenridge Information Center, 309 North Main Street; at the Activity Center, 137 South Main Street; or at the mine site before the tour.

SHOPPING

Breckenridge is lined with shops along its historic main street—mostly souvenir shops, sporting goods outlets, art galleries, and cafes housed in brightly painted gingerbread Victorian buildings. Breckenridge caters to the ski crowd and supplies places to buy mementos, gifts, ski wear, and meals. There are lots of crafts and knick-knacks and a few shops with home furnishings. Frisco, too, has lots to offer along Main Street, and many utilitarian shops in a strip mall near the interstate, including a Wal-Mart.

Alpen Collections
211 South Main Street, Breckenridge
(970) 453-0107

Alpen specializes in ski and golf wear, offering a big selection of Bogner brand-name items. Men and women will find all types of casual and outdoor clothing, plus gifts. The store also specializes in personalized customer service.

Antlers Trading Post
908 North Summit Boulevard, Frisco
(970) 668-3152

This giant store has clothing and gear for every possible outdoor activity in its 15,000 square feet of space—sort of a sporting goods supermarket between the other supermarkets on either side. In addition to foot wear and camping and fishing gear, there's a great assortment of jewelry,

gifts, souvenirs, and T-shirts. Located between the Wal-Mart and the Safeway, this is a fun place to shop.

Breckenridge Toy Company
Lincoln West Mall, 326 South Main Street, Breckenridge
(970) 547-0445
Kids of all ages will love it here. (Parents may be overwhelmed with the big selection of Star Wars items from toys and T-shirts to various star-ship paraphernalia.) The shop has Ty Beanie Babies, Playmobile Brio and Thomas the Tank Trains, Legos, magic tricks, and many games. Plan on an hour, at least.

Designs for Time
324 South Main Street, Breckenridge
(970) 453-8800
Those who are taken by the picturesque Breckenridge storefronts can buy their own here and take them home. The shop specializes in "Main Street Breckenridge," with miniatures of the town's wooden storefront, measuring approximately 4 by 6 inches. The shop also has watches, jewelry, and other gifts.

Joy of Sox & Excessories
222 South Main Street, Breckenridge
(970) 453-4534
Looking for the socks of your dreams? Here's the place. Right next to the Rocky Mountain Chocolate Factory, there are socks here for all ages and inclinations. Socks make a great gift for everyone. In addition to socks, the shop also has practical and creatively designed gloves, hats, and other "excessories" and clothing

Lone Star Sports
Four O'Clock Road and Park Street
Breckenridge
(970) 453-2003, (800) 621-9733
www.skilonestar.com
Voted Breckenridge's No. 1 ski shop and operating since 1976, Lone Star provides ski rentals of major brand-name equipment, specializing in personalized service and perfect fit. The shop also provides

custom ski tuning, high-performance and demo rental equipment, and overnight repair services. This is where the locals get their skis tuned, too.

Main Street Outlet
324 South Main Street, Breckenridge
(970) 453-1300
Silverthorne isn't the only place with outlets. Shop here for name-brand skiwear, sportswear, boots, and shoes at factory outlet prices. There are also snowboards and children's equipment and clothing.

Pioneer Sports
842 North Summit Boulevard, Frisco
(970) 668-3668, (800) 888-3688
www.pioneer-sports.com
This shop rents and sells bikes, ski and snowboard gear, a full line of hockey gear, and in the summer rents camping and golf equipment. They're open 365 days a year, and their Web site offers links to summertime whitewater rafting opportunities.

Rocky Mountain Chocolate Factory
222 South Main Street, Breckenridge
(970) 453-2094
There's an overwhelming selection of luscious chocolate and even a selection of icy, refreshing sorbet with fruit and cappuccino flavors. Stop here for a snack or great gift assortment of locally made chocolate of the highest quality.

Sundance Hat Co.
411 South Main Street, Breckenridge
(970) 453-2737
Snowboarders and other young or young-at-heart folks will enjoy this shop filled with crazy and even practical hats for skiing, hiking, or just a fashion statement.

Two Feet Tall
137 South Main Street, Breckenridge
(970) 453-7917
This charming shop has children's toys, books, skiwear, and lots of irresistible kid-stuff, including stuffed animals and cuddly slippers for winter.

Weber's Books & Drawings
100 South Main Street, Breckenridge
(970) 453-4723
Weber's specializes in local and Colorado history and sports. But there's also a good selection of all types of books, including hardbacks and paperbacks. Greeting cards, posters, drawings, and topographical maps are also available. Authors give readings on a regular basis here, particularly authors of local history books.

Wilderness Sports
418 Main Street, Frisco
(970) 668-8804
www.wildsummit.com
A branch of a longtime Summit County favorite, the Main Street store offers everything for the backcountry enthusiast. Skis, backpacks, and outerwear are the specialties, but the shop also offers rental snowshoes and cross-country skis, guidebooks, and maps. Tom Jones Jr. and his staff know the backcountry around Summit County like the backs of their hands, too, so they're great for advice.

Winds of Change Books, Gifts & Healing Center
60 West Main Street, units A & B, Frisco
(970) 668-5399
Formerly Wolf Moon Books, this store has broadened its offerings. In addition to a wide variety of books, from local Colorado works to eastern religions, the store carries unique personal gifts such as soaps and bath salts, natural gemstone artwork, and indoor fountains. Next door, the Healing Center offers a wide choice of alternative healing programs.

Necessities

Black Diamond Video
824 North Summit Boulevard, Frisco
(970) 668-5531
Great customer service and a large selection set this video store apart. Located near the Safeway, Black Diamond also

offers video games for rent or sale and plenty of movie-watching snacks.

ARTS
Music

Breckenridge Music Festival
Riverwalk Center, 150 West Adams Street, Breckenridge
(970) 453-9142
www.breckenridgemusicfestival.com
An area institution, this annual music festival features a series of concerts ranging from classical to jazz. The festival is anchored by the acclaimed Breckenridge Music Festival Orchestra, under the direction of Maestro Gerhardt Zimmerman.

Genuine Jazz in July
Village at Breckenridge, Maggie Pond between Columbine Street and South Park Avenue, Breckenridge
(970) 453-5579
Free daytime outdoor concerts on Maggie Pond's floating stage are a special treat of this weekend festival. At night, pay for a performance in nearby clubs. Past performers have included Nelson Rangell, Dotsero, Wind Machine, Cat's Night Out, Laura Newman and A.O.A., Jennifer Hart, and many others. Ticket prices vary from $15 to $49 depending on the performance.

Theater

Backstage Theatre
355 Village Road, Breckenridge
(970) 453-0199
www.backstagetheatre.org
For more than 30 years this award-winning amateur acting company has entertained Breckenridge audiences year-round with musicals, dramas, comedies, one-actor shows, ensembles, and special performances. Past performances include brilliant versions of *Arsenic and Old Lace, Murder*

at the Howard Johnson's, and *Love Letters.* Reservations can be made online at the Web site listed above.

Film

Breckenridge Festival of Film
Riverwalk Center, 150 West Adams
Street, Breckenridge
(970) 453-6200
www.breckfilmfest.com
A fall special held in September, this annual festival features Hollywood stars, premieres, documentaries, many independent filmmakers, children's features, parties, film forums, special interest activities, and a really good time. Past attendees have included James Earl Jones, Sydney Pollack, Mary Steenburgen, Eva Marie Saint, Rod Steiger, Donald Sutherland, Ned Beatty, and the Toxic Avenger. Jeffrey Lyons of WNBC-TV is the master of ceremonies. Pick up a schedule at the festival headquarters and box office previously listed—prices vary according to performance choice. Since Breckenridge has no actual theater, the film festival is held at various locations around town, including Colorado Mountain College and Summit County High School.

Visual Arts

Breckenridge Gallery
124 South Main Street, Breckenridge
(970) 453-2592
www.breckenridge-gallery.com
A pleasant gallery featuring a wide variety of original art in all media, the shop's focus is on realistic landscapes by a number of nationally known artists. There's a good selection of watercolors, sculptures, and work in other media.

Hang Time & Buffalo Mountain Gallery
711 Granite Street, Frisco
(970) 668-0705
www.buffalomountaingallery.com

Look for the landmark, life-size, bronze buffalo out front. This buffalo is the second of an edition of five; the first graces the entry to the University of Colorado Buffaloes' football stadium. The gallery features original artwork, including watercolors, oils, and acrylics in addition to posters and prints, which are the focus at Hang Time. The theme of the work shown is western. There are also bronze wildlife sculptures.

Hibberd McGrath Gallery
101 North Main Street, Breckenridge
(970) 453-6391
www.hibberdmcgrath.com
This contemporary fine crafts gallery has a very high caliber of clay, fiber, and folk art. More sophisticated art lovers will enjoy the departure from western art here and the fine selection of work presented by local, regional, and national artists. The gallery's goal is to try to bring some of the best art of these media together from around the country.

Paint Horse Gallery
226 South Main Street, Breckenridge
(970) 453-6813
www.painthorsegallery.com
With a cozy, rustic living-room atmosphere, you'll want to move right into this gallery, which features paintings, sculpture, and all types of western paraphernalia including saddles, woven blankets, wall hangings, furniture, cowboy memorabilia, and antique Navajo weavings.

EVENTS
January

International Snow Sculpture
Championships
Main Street, Breckenridge
(970) 453-6018
In early January, amazing snow sculptures line the main street in town when more than a dozen teams from around the world try to outcarve each other. The cre-

ations are sculpted from 12-foot-tall 10-ton blocks of snow. The sculptors work during the week, and the judges make a decision over the weekend. Competitors come from as far away as Morocco, Belize, Japan, Canada, Scandinavia, Russia, Chile, and Wales. The giant sculptures usually last through the town's annual Ullr Fest (see listing below), which honors the Norse god of winter.

Ullr Fest
Various locations, Breckenridge
(970) 453-6018
In mid-January, Summit County holds this weeklong winter carnival throughout the town and on the slopes in Breckenridge in honor of Ullr, the Norse god of winter. It's a wacky celebration with lots of horned-helmeted Vikings brandishing swords and partying in the streets. Sometimes the festival coincides with the Freestyle World Cup Championship at the ski area, which features astounding aerial ski competitions, plus mogul skiing and ski ballet. Some of the highlights of the Ullr Fest are the parade, bonfire, and skating party on Maggie Pond. All the events are free.

February

Senior Games at the Summit
Breckenridge, Frisco, Keystone, and other locations
(970) 668-2940
Seniors compete in alpine and Nordic events, plus ice skating, snowshoeing, figure skating, and biathlon. The levels of physical fitness and skill at these games always amazes onlookers, who quickly lose any notion of doddering old folks. Any senior can compete; costs vary by event. Participants must call ahead to register.

Frisco Gold Rush
Frisco Nordic Center
Peninsula Recreation Area
(970) 668-5276
The citizen cross-country ski races com-

bine competition with fun. Different distances separate the serious athletes from the recreational strollers.

March

Special Olympics Colorado
Winter Games
Copper Mountain Resort
(970) 968-2318, (800) 458-8386
An inspiring story, developmentally disabled athletes from around the state compete in all of the downhill skiing disciplines. Their enthusiasm is infectious and their skill remarkably high, so Copper Mountain has gone to great lengths to keep the showcase event on its slopes.

Saint Patrick's Day Celebration
Copper Mountain Resort
Exit 195 off I-70, 75 miles west of Denver
(866) 841-2481, (888) 219-2441
A traditional St. Patrick's Day celebration takes place in the heart of Copper Mountain's main village on March 17. It's an Irish street fair with food and craft vendors, music, and the requisite green beer.

April

The Spring Massive
Town of Breckenridge, Breckenridge
(970) 453-5000
www.breckenridge.snow.com/info/ winter/ea.springmassive.asp
Billed as "a fusion of sport, music, family fun, and legendary spring (skiing) conditions," this festival is truly massive. It goes on through most of April with events scheduled every day from April 1 through 23. Events include the Bite of Breckenridge, where local restaurants offer three-course dinners at special prices; a snow volleyball tournament, barbecue, and April Fool's Day celebration, including the crowning of the official Town Fool; the Massive Slopestyle freestyle skiing competition; the Imperial Challenge, a kind of ski

resort triathlon combining a 6²⁄₁₀-mile mountain bike ride, a 2,500-foot climb to the top of the Imperial Bowl on equipment of the competitors' choice, and a descent on either skis or snowboard; and the annual Breckenridge Bump Buffet, where telemark skiers dressed in wacky costumes compete down a bump-filled ski run. Events are held in the town of Breckenridge or on the slopes of the Breckenridge ski area.

April Fool's Day Parade
Main Street, Breckenridge
(970) 453-6018

In Breckenridge, it's actually a high honor to be crowned the Town Fool. This irreverent event features some of the most respected community leaders trying to win votes by becoming pie-fight targets.

Breckenridge Bump Buffet
Breckenridge Ski Resort, Highway 9
Breckenridge
(970) 453-5000

Already handicapped in the bumps, amateur telemark skiers don wacky costumes and hit the slopes at Breckenridge in a visual spectacle. Teams and individuals compete in a contest that's more about style than ability.

Eenie Weenie Bikini Contest
Copper Mountain Resort
(970) 968-2318, (800) 458-8386

The best un-dressed wins this nutty contest. Participants must strip down and then ski down the slopes. On those sunny spring days, it's no problem, but as often as not, it snows. Goosebumps become the height of skiing fashion.

Imperial Challenge
Breckenridge Ski Resort, Highway 9
Breckenridge
(970) 453-5000

Here's a grueling race that really is a blast: Participants start off riding mountain bikes from the Breckenridge Recreation Center to the base of the ski mountain, then strap on snowshoes or cross-country skis to begin the ascent to the top of 13,000-foot Imperial Bowl on Peak 8. But the race isn't over yet—the finish line is down at the Bergenhof restaurant, meaning a harrowing descent on skis is in order for those tired legs.

June

Meet the Artists
Breckenridge Riverwalk Center, 150
West Adams Street, Breckenridge
(970) 453-0450
www.summitarts.org

Artists from all disciplines, including fine arts, literature, music, photography, and other areas, gather at the Riverwalk Center to lecture, meet with the public, and show and discuss art.

Breckenridge Music Festival
Riverwalk Center, 150 West Adams
Street, Breckenridge
(970) 453-9142
www.breckenridgemusicfestival.com

This annual music festival, which starts in late June and runs through September, features the acclaimed Breckenridge Music Festival Orchestra, under the direction of Gerhardt Zimmerman, and the National Repertory Orchestra. The festival runs all summer and features classical, chamber, and jazz performances. Elderhostels, workshops, and guest performers and conductors are also part of the program.

July

Independence Day
Dillon Reservoir, Frisco
(970) 668-5276

Perhaps the most spectacular fireworks display in the country takes place over the Dillon Reservoir, and it's free. The crowd gathers on the shores at the east end of Main Street. The festivities start about 7:00 P.M. with the fireworks commencing at dusk.

Genuine Jazz in July
Maggie Pond, Village at Breckenridge
535 South Park Avenue, Breckenridge
(970) 453-5579
www.genuinejazz.com
In mid-July free daytime outdoor concerts on Maggie Pond's floating stage are a special treat of this weekend festival. At night, pay for a performance in nearby clubs. Past performers have included Nelson Rangell, Dotsero, Wind Machine, Cat's Night Out, Laura Newman and A.O.A., Jennifer Hart, and many others. Ticket prices vary with performances.

August

'Vettes on the Rockies
Main Street, Frisco
(970) 668-5276
Classic Corvettes from more than 40 states converge on Main Street for a road rally, followed by a "show and shine" car show. The rally is held the first weekend in August every year.

September

Breckenridge Festival of Film
Riverwalk Center, 150 West Adams Street, Breckenridge
(970) 453-6200
www.breckfilmfest.com
A fall special, held in mid-September, this annual festival features Hollywood stars, premieres, documentaries, many independent filmmakers, children's features, parties, film forums, screenwriting seminars, and a really good time. Some of the most acclaimed films have debuted at the festival, including *Pleasantville* in 1998 and *L.A. Confidential* in 1997. Past attendees include James Earl Jones, Sydney Pollack, Mary Steenburgen, Eva Marie Saint, Rod Steiger, Donald Sutherland, Ned Beatty, and the Toxic Avenger. Jeffrey Lyons of WNBC-TV presides as master of ceremonies. Pick up a schedule at the festival headquarters and box office listed above—prices vary according to performance choice. Since Breckenridge has no actual theater, the film festival is held at various locations around town, including Colorado Mountain College and Summit County High School.

Oktoberfest
Various locations, Breckenridge
(970) 453-6018
Despite its name, this event is held in late September because King Ludwig of Germany held the first Oktoberfest in September of 1810 to honor his wife, Queen Theresia. The weekend event includes oompah bands, lots of food booths, kids activities, plenty of music—and of course, German beer.

October

Trick or Treat Street
Main Street, Frisco
(970) 668-5800
Perfect for those young ghosts and goblins who need to get to bed early, the merchants along Main Street offer a safe and fun opportunity for trick-or-treating. Entertainment and a pumpkin-decorating contest are part of the celebration.

December

Continental Divide Hot Air Balloon Challenge
Breckenridge
(970) 453-6018
A spectacular morning liftoff starts off dozens of balloonists heading over toward Vail. The goal each year is to snap the world record of 13 balloons crossing the Continental Divide simultaneously.

U.S. Snowboard Grand Prix
Peak 8, Breckenridge Resort
Breckenridge
(970) 453-5000
www.breckenridge.snow.com
Each December Breckenridge is the first
stop for this USSA-sanctioned snowboard
series. One of the most prestigious snowboard events in the world, the Grand Prix
includes a SuperPipe competition as well
as in-town events and entertainment at
night. World-class snowboarders put on
an incredible show, and the event is covered by national TV networks.

The Lighting of Breckenridge
Main Street, Breckenridge
(970) 453-6018
Held in mid-December, this annual cere-
mony provides the perfect old-fashioned
holiday celebration with choruses of
Christmas carolers wandering the street,
steaming cups of hot cocoa, and the lighting of the town tree.

DOWNHILL SKIING

Breckenridge

Breckenridge Ski Resort
Highway 9
(970) 453-5000, (800) 221-1091
www.breckenridge.snow.com
Base elevation: *9,600 feet*
Top of highest lift: *12,840 feet*
Total vertical: *3,398 feet*
Longest run: *3½ miles*
Average annual snowfall: *255 inches*
Ski season: *early November to late April*
Capacity: *37,280 skiers per hour*
Terrain: *2,208 acres, 147 trails (14 percent
beginner, 26 percent intermediate, 60 per-
cent advanced and expert)*
Lift tickets: *$75*
Snow reports: *(970) 453-6118*
Getting there: *Breckenridge Ski Resort is
101 miles west of Denver International Air-
port via I-70 to exit 203, then Highway 9
to Breckenridge.*

Breckenridge, the ski area, matches the
town's historic heritage with equally memorable terrain. This huge area has four distinct peaks that are the last four in the
aptly named Ten-Mile Range. Peak 7 was
opened for lift-served skiing in 2002, when
the resort installed its Independence Super-
Chair, which provides access to intermediate terrain. Peak 8 is the original mountain,
suited to skiers of various abilities and with
access to high, above-the-tree-line bowls
and chutes. In 2005 Breckenridge opened
the new Imperial Express SuperChair,
which ferries skiers and boarders to the
mountain's most difficult terrain, acreage
that previously was only accessed by hiking. The chair now drops them off at
12,840 feet, which makes it the highest lift
in North America. Beginners and novices
will enjoy the easier trails that are concentrated on Peak 9. And Peak 10's moguls are
renowned, along with its open glades. It is
possible to ski from mountain to mountain
by numerous different routes, each clearly
marked. In 2006 the resort also added a
skier's bridge called the Skyway Skiway
that allows them to ski or ride from Peak 8
to the free parking lots on Park Avenue.

With the additions and improvements
made since becoming a Vail Resorts property, Breckenridge expanded its already
generous offerings. This huge area boasts
four distinct peaks, four terrain parks, and
four pipes.

Copper Mountain

Copper Mountain Resort
I-70
(970) 968-2882, (800) 458-8386
www.coppercolorado.com
Base elevation: *9,712 feet*
Top of highest lift: *12,313 feet*
Total vertical: *2,601 feet*
Longest run: *2⁸⁄₁₀ miles*
Average annual snowfall: *280 inches*
Ski season: *mid-November to early May*
Capacity: *30,630 skiers per hour*
Terrain: *2,433 acres, 125 trails (21 percent*

Ski terrain at Copper Mountain is naturally separated into runs for beginner, intermediate, and advanced skiers. The resort also offers a strong learn-to-ski program. THE DENVER POST/CRAIG WALKER

beginner, 25 percent intermediate, 54 percent advanced)

Lift tickets: *$75*

Snow reports: *(970) 968-2100; (800) 789-7609*

Getting there: *Copper Mountain Resort is 75 miles west of Denver via I-70 to exit 195. From Colorado Springs, it's 120 miles northwest via U.S. Highway 24 and Highway 9.*

Copper Mountain, meanwhile, was destined for greatness when it opened with 2 feet of fresh powder in 1972. Copper is often preferred by locals since it frequently has fewer skiers than other areas of comparable size. Lots of great skiing, few lift lines, and an award-winning trail system make it a longtime Colorado favorite. With its beginner, intermediate, and advanced runs naturally separated by the terrain, skiers can follow their favorite terrain from

top to bottom. The steeper pitches are to the east, gentle slopes to the west, and cruising runs are in between. Facing the ski mountain with I-70 behind you, look to the right for the easy terrain, to the middle for intermediate runs, and to the left for the advanced. Copper has four bowls and 1,800-vertical-foot mogul runs under A-lift for the more adventurous skiers. All-around favorites are the long, groomed slopes under the American Eagle, American Flyer, and Timberline Express high-speed quad chairlifts. Union Creek offers excellent terrain for beginners or novices. Look for steep snow pockets of powder in Spaulding Bowl, Union Bowl, and Resolution Bowl.

Both resorts offer ski seminars dealing with such topics as skiing moguls, skiing powder, or generally improving one's technique. For snowboarders the terrain parks feature rails, jumps, and a half-pipe, and the slopes of both Breckenridge and Copper Mountain offer good all-around riding.

NORDIC/CROSS-COUNTRY

The Breckenridge Nordic Center
1200 Ski Hill Road
(970) 453-6855
www.breckenridgenordic.com
The Breckenridge Nordic Center boasts more than 32 kilometers of groomed track in the valleys below Peaks 7 and 8 plus about 16 kilometers of snowshoe trails. A trail pass is $14 and rental equipment is another $14. Rolling hills, flat meadows, and some steep hills provide terrain for all levels of skiers. Guided skiing is available for the blind.

Frisco Nordic Center
1 miles south of Frisco on Highway 9
(970) 668-0866
Frisco Nordic Center offers groomed trails for classical-style skiing and skating, plus snowshoeing with lovely views of Lake Dillon and a cozy day hut for break-time snacks. It is operated under the same management as The Breckenridge Nordic Center and shares trails and an interchangeable trail pass. They both offer free afternoon beginner lessons. A trail pass costs $14.

OTHER WINTER RECREATION

Sleigh Rides

Note: Dinner sleigh rides generally run about $70 to $75 per adult and $40 for kids. Because of the variety of choices all the different rates are not included here—call the numbers below for current prices. Most operate from November to early April.

Dinner in the Woods
Union Creek, Copper Mountain Resort
I-70
(970) 968-2232
Leaving right from Union Creek at the base of the ski area, the sleigh follows a torch-lit trail to a cozy heated tent in the woods for a hearty meal of chicken, ribs, or beef brisket—the menu changes daily. The ride is very romantic for couples or lots of fun with kids. The cost varies depending upon the menu but is around $73 for adults and $45 for children. Reservations are required.

Two Below Zero Dinner Sleigh Rides
Frisco Nordic Center, 1 mile south of
Frisco on Highway 9
(970) 453-1520, (800) 571-MULE
This small company owned by a husband-and-wife team has been operating since 1983 and focuses on quality in all aspects. It's the only company that uses mules to draw the sleighs. Mules are traditional to the area and are smarter and easier to care for than horses, says co-owner Cindy Lewis. Dinner rides include entertainment with singing guitarists and a delicious home-cooked meal of stir-fried shrimp appetizers, fresh veggies and dip, French bread, marinated and grilled top sirloin and chicken, baked potatoes, and delicious desserts with freshly ground coffee, teas, and other beverages. The sleigh rides run every night except Sunday, and advance reservations are required.

Dog Sledding

Good Times
6061 Tiger Road
(970) 453-7604, (800) 477-0144
www.snowmobilecolorado.com
Learn to be a musher as you drive your own team of purebred Siberian huskies. Usually six people go on the dog-sled tours, which can reach speeds of 35 mph and, alternately, head up such steep hills that the guests must do a little work. Rid-

Frisco Nordic Center offers groomed trails for cross-country skiing and snowshoeing, and hosts events such as the Colorado Governor's Cup 5K Snowshoe Race, shown here.
THE DENVER POST/JACK DEMPSEY

ing the sleigh offers great opportunities to photograph the dog sledders and enjoy the scenery. The cost is $60 for adults, $30 for children 8 and younger. Advance reservations are necessary.

Snowmobiling

Good Times
6061 Tiger Road
(970) 453-7604, (800) 477-0144
Good Times' special highlight is a two-hour trip to the Continental Divide with spectacular views all along the way. You will gain about 1,500 feet in elevation from the base facility to the Continental Divide and pass many historical sites, such as old mines and cabins. Cost is $85 for the driver and $40 for the passenger for the guided tour.

Tiger Run
Breckenridge
(970) 453-2231, (800) 318-1386
www.tigerruntours.com
A half-day, guided snowmobile tour takes riders from the restored old mining town of Dry Gulch (a 20-minute van ride) into the historic Golden Horseshoe mining district, reaching 12,000 feet. Children 8 and younger ride free, and boots, suits, and helmets are included in the cost. Lee and JoAnn Frost have been operating Tiger Run for 14 of its 37 years, making it one of the oldest snowmobile touring companies in the state. Call for more trip details.

Ice Skating

Copper Mountain Resort
I-70
(970) 968-2882
For ice-skating enthusiasts, there's free skating on the village pond, where the ice is machine-groomed and nearby shops offer skate rentals. Ice skating is available only during the colder months when the pond is frozen, from 11:00 A.M. to 9:00 P.M.

daily. Hot beverages, snacks, and meals are available at nearby cafes.

Maggie Pond
535 South Park Avenue, Breckenridge
(970) 453-2000
Behind the Bell Tower Mall in the Village at Breckenridge, this small pond becomes a center of fun and activity once it freezes. A small warming hut above the pond offers rental skates for toddlers to adults and a place to keep your things. There are sleds for babies and toddlers. Food and beverages are available at the many cafes around the lake. Hours are 10:00 A.M. to 10:00 P.M. daily. Skate rentals are available from 10:00 A.M. until 9:00 P.M.

Stephen C. West Ice Arena
0189 Boreas Pass Road, Breckenridge
(970) 547-9974
www.snowmobilecolorado.com
Built so it has a view of the mountains, this open-roof rink is operated by the town of Breckenridge and is so popular with recreational skaters, hockey players, and figure skaters that a second rink was built right next door. The rinks are located at the south end of town, across from the Conoco station and a block south of the Breckenridge Brewery, a good place to stop for a microbrew after skating. During the week, public session hours vary, so it's best to call ahead. Additional evening hours are on Monday, Wednesday, Friday, and Saturday. Admission and rental skates are a few bucks each.

HIKING

Stop at the Dillon Ranger District Office, 680 Blue River Parkway in Silverthorne, (970) 468-5400, for maps and detailed information about area trails and regulations. You might want to pick up a copy of the handy brochure *12 Short Hikes, Summit County* or *The New Summit Hiker* by Mary Ellen Gilliland, an excellent guide to 50 trails.

Ice skating is available on Copper Mountain's village pond during the colder months when the pond is frozen. THE DENVER POST/JERRY CLEVELAND

Black Powder Pass
West on Boreas Pass Road off Main Street just south of downtown Breckenridge

The hike is only 1⁷/₁₀ miles, but getting to the trailhead is half the fun. The route to the trail follows the old Denver, South Park & Pacific narrow-gauge rail route to the summit of Boreas Pass, where the ruins of an old railway section house still stand. This trail can be hard to follow since it peters out in places, so a USGS topographic map of Boreas Pass is helpful.

Drive south on Highway 9 from Breckenridge's Bell Tower Mall ²/₁₀ mile to the Boreas Pass Road (No. 10). Continue 9⁶/₁₀ miles to the summit. Those who wish to see the Washington Mine can take a detour at 1½ miles on Road No. 518 into Illinois Gulch. There you'll find a mine railway, dynamite shack, and old chart house along with other artifacts.

Without the detour, continue past various mines to Bakers Tank, a water tank at 6⁶/₁₀ miles. At 8⁴/₁₀ miles beyond open meadows, there are fine views of Lincoln, Silverheels, and Pacific Peaks. At the summit of the pass, look for stone ruins of an 1884 stone engine house that used to have a rail turntable.

And now, for the hike: Look for the trail near the stone house. Walk northeast from the building along a dirt track labeled "Boreas Ditch No. 2" on the topo map. The trail culminates at a 12,159-foot saddle between Boreas and Bald Mountains. The route follows a drainage ditch and affords fine wildflower viewing. On the saddle enjoy the views of South Park and historic French Pass, where stagecoaches brought visitors on tourist excursions.

Stronger hikers or backpackers spending the night may wish to scale the peaks of 13,082-foot Boreas Mountain or 13,684-foot Mount Baldy.

Loveland Pass/South Side Trail
Arapahoe National Forest

This less-difficult but highly rewarding hike of about 2 miles follows the spine of the Continental Divide at Loveland Pass. Fantastic views of Grays and Torreys Peaks, both 14,000-plus feet, join panoramas of the ski areas at Breckenridge, Keystone, and Copper Mountain. The ridge is usually very windy, so bring a windbreaker and be sure to go early to avoid the dangerous lightning of summer thunderstorms, which often strike around noon. To reach the trailhead, take U.S. Highway 6 east from the Dillon/Silverthorne exit of I-70. Pass the towns of Dillon and Keystone and the Keystone and Arapahoe Basin ski areas on the way to the summit of Loveland Pass and the trailhead, which begins as an asphalt path south from the summit of the pass.

Wheeler Lakes
Ten Mile Canyon bikeway parking area

A good hike for wildflowers in late summer, this 2⁸/₁₀-mile trail is steep but pretty. The two alpine lakes on top will reward the persevering hiker. Views of the Copper Mountain Ski area and the spectacular Ten-Mile Range of high peaks, snowfields, and cirques are also part of the view. To reach the trailhead, drive west on I-70 toward Vail and take exit 195 for Copper Mountain and Highway 91. As you approach a bridge (the I-70 overpass), look just north of it (before crossing it) for the trailhead. Park at the trailhead or past the bridge at the Tenmile Canyon bikeway parking area.

CAMPING

Tiger Run Resort
85 Tiger Run road, off Highway 9 between Frisco and Breckenridge
(970) 453-9690
www.tierrunresort.com

For RVs, Tiger Run Resort is the only

choice in Summit County, but it has everything: a hot tub, laundry, game room, indoor swimming pool, clubhouse, tennis courts, and RVs for rent—all of which have earned it a high national rating. But the place books up early, so for summer reservations call three to four months in advance.

GOLF

Breckenridge Golf Club
200 Clubhouse Drive, Breckenridge
(970) 453–9104
www.breckenridgegolfclub.com
Breckenridge Golf Club, elevation 9,324 feet, is the only 27-hole, Jack Nicklaus-designed municipal course in the world, and generally considered one of the most beautiful public courses in the state. The surrounding 14,000-foot mountain peaks are so beautiful they've inspired poetry. On the other hand the back tees of the Elk/Beaver rotation, playing at 7,145 yards with a course rating of 73.5 and a slope of 151, are so difficult they've probably inspired some colorful language. This set of tees has the second most difficult course rating in the state. *Golf Digest* describes the entire course as "tough, penal Nicklaus architecture" because each hole requires planning before it can be well played. But don't let this dampen the experience of playing this beautiful mountain course, and don't forget to look up and around every once in a while.

Copper Creek Golf Club
East Village, Copper Mountain
(970) 968–3333
www.coppercolorado.com
North America's highest championship golf course at 9,700 feet, the Copper Creek course is a challenging but scenic attraction. Designed by Pete and Perry Dye, the par 70 course runs 6,094 yards, but shots should fly farther in the thin air. Greens fees run about $80, including a cart.

FISHING AND HUNTING
Outfitters and Tackle Shops

Breckenridge Outfitters
100 North Main Street, Breckenridge
(970) 453–4135, (877) 898–6104
www.breckenridgeoutfitters.com
An Orvis-endorsed guide service, Breckenridge Outfitters offers lessons and guided fishing trips, including overnights and horse-pack trips. The guides here also have access to private fishing waters.

Mountain Angler
311 South Main Street, Breckenridge
(970) 453–4665, (800) 453–4669
www.mountainangler.com
The oldest fishing guide service in Summit County, this shop specializes in clothing, fly-tying materials, and all accessories for serious anglers. There's an experienced guide to take you to the best public and private fishing spots. There's an assortment of fine outdoor clothing and gear from Patagonia, Columbia, Abel, Simms, Sage, and other top manufacturers.

Places to Fish

Dillon Reservoir
I-70 between Dillon and Frisco exits
Dillon Reservoir is the focal point of Summit County, and many anglers are happy to stay along its 26-mile shoreline. Casting from the shore is not as effective as fishing from a boat, but it can be worthwhile. There are boat-launching ramps at Frisco Bay, Frisco Marina, Blue River Inlet, and Pine Cove Campground. Both the Frisco Marina and the Dillon Marina rent boats. Experts like fishing the lake just as the ice recedes and after it has been stocked with small kokanee salmon and cutthroat and brook trout. A few huge brown trout cruise the waters in the fall, but they're wise to humans and hard to catch. The lake has been known to hold all species of

Colorado trout and kokanee salmon. Dillon is also known for its night fishing, with anglers lining the shore as they pursue large brown trout.

Officer's Gulch Pond
Just off I-70, 4 miles west of Frisco and just before the turnoff to Copper Mountain

This pond is stocked with rainbow and brook trout. The ambiance isn't great, as the water is alongside the interstate, but it is readily accessible.

Upper Blue River
Along Colorado Highway 9

The Blue River begins its 45-mile run through Summit County (along Highway 9) from Hoosier Pass just south of Breckenridge. A number of small tributaries converge, and by the time the Upper Blue River reaches Breckenridge, the fishing can be pretty good. The town of Breckenridge spent millions of dollars to landscape the Blue River through town, and big brook trout have been known to lurk in the pools just below some of the dropoffs. Further downstream, the river runs through massive piles of round stones; these are relics of the mining days when giant dredge boats plowed up the river bottom in search of gold. The rock is clean, and the water cold. Downstream from Breckenridge, the river runs through an area that was dredged during the mining days, which left large piles of river rock along the banks. You may try early in the season for rainbows and in the fall for browns and brooks. This section (3 miles north of Breckenridge down to Dillon Reservoir) is closed to fishing from October 1 to January 31.

OTHER RECREATION
Bicycling

Summit County has hundreds of miles of backcountry roads and trails that will sat-isfy riders of all ages and abilities. For mountain bikers, there are smooth dirt roads and rugged single tracks. Many of the routes are more than a century old and follow the remnants of old mining roads, pack trails, wagon routes, and abandoned railroad grades. For information about current trail conditions, ideas on where to ride, trail access, closure situations, fat-tire events, and trail maintenance work days, go to www.summit activities.com.

Paved Bikeways

The 9-mile Blue River Bikeway connects Breckenridge and Frisco. The 6-mile Ten Mile Canyon bikeway connects Frisco and Copper Mountain, and the 13½ mile Vail Pass Bikeway connects Copper Mountain and Vail (and traverses the 10,000-foot pass). There's also a paved trail from Keystone to these other trails. A map of these trails is shown in the *Mountain Bike Guide to Summit County.* All are recommended for either fat or skinny tires. There are more than 40 miles of paved bike paths between Keystone, Breckenridge, and Copper Mountain ski resorts. There are numerous bike rentals, sales, and service shops in all these communities and resorts. For additional information, contact the Summit County Chamber of Commerce, 409 Main Street, Frisco, (907) 668-5800, or the Breckenridge Resort Chamber, 309 Main Street, Breckenridge, (970) 453-6018.

Breckenridge Ski Resort
Highway 9 at Breckenridge
(970) 453-5000, (800) 789-7669
www.breckenridge.snow.com

Breckenridge offers lift rides up Peak 8 for downhill runs, and the super-fit can try their lungs riding up to the top as well. There's a whole series of trails (eight different options), including wide service roads, single-track trails, creekside trails, and historic mining wagon roads. Call for rates and information.

Copper Mountain Resort
I-70 Copper Mountain
(970) 968-2882, ext. 7885
www.coppercolorado.com
The ski resort offers downhill mountain biking with $14 all-day chairlift passes for mountain bikers. Rentals are available at nearby Gravitee, (970) 968-0171. The lift rides begin around the third week in June, weather permitting, but call for dates and times.

BIKE SHOPS

A Racer's Edge
114 North Main Street, Breckenridge
(970) 453-0995
www.aracersedge.com
A ski shop in the winter time, a bike shop in the summer, the guys at A Racer's Edge really know their gear. They offer excellent high-end mountain bikes for rentals, and, if you really like your ride, they'll be glad to sell you one.

Christy Sports/SportStalker
849 Summit Boulevard, Frisco
(970) 668-5417
Christy Sports rents and sells all types of bikes and bike accessories and can perform repairs. It's also a great source for in-line skating gear.

Great Adventure Sports Center
400 North Park Street, Breckenridge
(970) 453-0333
www.greatadventuresports.com
Right on the bike path that runs along the Blue River in Breckenridge, this shop rents and sells a full line of bikes and biking gear. There's also a complete bicycle service center with overnight or same-day service.

Wilderness Sports
418 Main Street, Frisco
(970) 668-8804
www.wildsummit.com
Tom Jones runs a great outdoors shop right in the middle of Main Street in Frisco, where you can get everything from ice-climbing gear to stylish clothing. In the summers, though, mountain bike rentals and camping gear are the products of choice.

HORSEBACK RIDING

Copper Mountain Stables
355 Beeler Place, Copper Mountain
(970) 968-2232
www.coppermountainstables.com
At the end of the road past Cirque, this well-established company even offers rides through Routt and Arapaho national forests. All types of rides are available, including one- and two-hour rides; half-day and full-day rides; breakfast, lunch, and dinner rides; wilderness pack trips; and hunting trips.

Kingdom of Breckenridge Stables
(970) 453-4438
www.colorado-horses.com
Gentle horses for all levels and ages of riders are the rule at this stable right on the ski slope. There are hourly, breakfast, and dinner rides. There's a free cowboy breakfast on the two-hour 7:00 A.M. ride. Call for reservations and prices.

To get to the stables take South Park Avenue to Village Road, go past the Great Divide Lodge, and take the next left into the Beaver Run Resort parking lot. Continue to the far end of the parking lot and turn right onto the dirt road. Follow the signs for Ten Mile Station until you see the horses and corrals for Kingdom of Breckenridge Stables.

In-line Skating

The best places to skate are along the paved bike paths mentioned previously under bicycling.

Carvers Ski Board and Sport
203 North Main Street, Breckenridge
(970) 453-0132
www.breckenridgeskishop.com
Carvers rents and sells all sorts of skates and accessories as well as mountain bikes.

Check out the latest skating gear before you buy it here.

OTHER OUTDOOR ACTIVITIES

Jeep/Four-wheel Tours

Tiger Run
Breckenridge
(970) 453-2231, (800) 318-1386
www.tigerruntours.com
This company offers jeep tours, ATV and "mule" tours, mountain biking, gold mine and group dinner tours, plus gold panning. Call for more information on whatever activity appeals to you. In winter, Tiger Run has a whole range of different, snow-oriented activities.

Tennis/Racquetball

Breckenridge Recreation Center
880 Airport Road, Breckenridge
(970) 453-1734
Swim, lift weights, play racquetball, or climb a rock wall at this fine facility, which has many other offerings such as wine tastings and yoga. Times for the pool and swim vary seasonally so call for current times. The recreation center provides a

nice change from the resort and ski scene. Hours are 6:00 A.M. to 10:00 P.M. Monday through Friday; 7:00 A.M. to 10:00 P.M. Saturday; and 8:00 A.M. to 10:00 P.M. Sunday.

HOT SPRINGS AND SPAS

Sacred Tree Healing Center
201 South Ridge Street, Breckenridge
(970) 453-8578
www.sacredtree.com
Sacred Tree is a special kind of healing center, more full-body wellness center than spa. It's located in a renovated historic home near the town's Arts District and provides a wide range of natural healing services. Among them: acupuncture, naturopathic medicine, hypnotherapy, integrative kinesiology, massage therapy, yoga, and martial arts. Hours vary daily; closed Sunday. Director Ellen Brown also works with participants in Women's Week programs at Breckenridge Resort.

The Lodge and Spa at Breckenridge
112 Overlook Drive, Breckenridge
(970) 453-9300
With a full athletic club and fitness classes in addition to the usual array of pampering, this spa can beat you up and then repair you. The spa features aromatherapy; Swedish, Shiatsu, and neuromuscular massage; and body scrubs and facials.

LEADVILLE

Abe Lee struck gold in California Gulch in 1860, and through boom and bust from that day on, Leadville thrived as a prototype hard-rock mining town that set the standard by which all others were measured. It was no coincidence that Wallace Stegner drew a historical picture of colorful Leadville for his Pulitzer-winning masterpiece, *Angle of Repose*.

Leadville's last operating mine went out of business in 1999, ending a way of life that defined the historic town for more than a century. The decline had been steady since the end of World War II, bottoming out with the closure of the massive Climax molybdenum mine in the early 1980s that spun Leadville into a deep depression. The town has struggled in transition to a tourist community, but that just means the treasures of this wonderful town have not yet been fully discovered.

Start with the wondrous National Mining Hall of Fame and Museum, a Smithsonian-esque tribute to mining, where Leadville's amazing rough-and tumble history comes alive at the tip of a "widowmaker" drill. Then take the historic walking tour among the well-preserved Victorian brick buildings and bright "painted lady" houses, including the legendary Tabor Opera House and the Silver Dollar Saloon. A driving trip over reasonably groomed dirt roads takes visitors to the remnants of the actual mines where history was made.

The slopes at tiny Ski Cooper, where the Army's famed 10th Mountain Division trained, are secretly awesome, and the fishing at places such as Turquoise Lake has been a not-so-well-kept secret. In the shadow of the state's two tallest peaks, Mount Elbert and Mount Massive, the Leadville area also offers access to more backcountry for hiking and camping than almost anywhere in the state.

Home to many of the resort workers from Vail and Summit County, Leadville strives to maintain its unique identity and heritage through special events such as Boom Days, the grueling Leadville Trail 100-mile foot race, and the International Pack Burro Race. Additionally, its heavy Mexican influence provides the town with several of the best Mexican restaurants in the state.

Winters in Leadville can be harsh: cold, windy, and buried in snow. But summers in the state's highest incorporated town are divine. Temperatures rarely climb above 80, and watching a thunderstorm drench the mountains is as sublime a pastime as sipping coffee at a sidewalk café on the Champs Elysées.

Fabulous fortunes were chipped out of the thousands of mines in Leadville, including those of Meyer Guggenheim, Marshall Field, and the "Unsinkable" Molly Brown, a survivor of the Titanic. But perhaps no story mirrors Leadville better than the rags-to-riches-to-rags epic of Horace Tabor, a grocer who grubstaked two hard-luck miners in exchange for a one-third interest in the Little Pittsburgh mine. Striking a 30-foot vein of silver, the mine soon produced $50,000 a month. When Tabor later was duped into buying a tapped-out mine that had been "seeded" with ore, he blithely continued digging and soon hit the legendary Chrysolite lode, becoming an overnight millionaire. Tabor scandalously left his wife, Augusta, and married the much younger Baby Doe, and wielding his wealth, he established his famous opera house and barged into polite society. Tabor was elected to the U.S. Senate, but was helpless to prevent the 1893 silver crash, which left him destitute. In his deathbed advice to Baby Doe, he told her to "hold onto the Marchless" Mine, which she did until she was found in 1935, frozen to death in an unheated mine shack.

ACCOMMODATIONS

Delaware Hotel   **$$**
700 Harrison Avenue
(719) 486-1418, (800) 748-2004
www.delawarehotel.com
Doc Holliday, Butch Cassidy, and Billy the Kid all stayed at the Delaware. Listed among Historic Hotels of the Rockies, this delightful establishment was built in 1886 and was named by the first owner in honor of his home state. It has been beautifully restored right down to the plush, Victorian-style floral carpeting and gleaming oak woodwork. The long central staircase is guaranteed to cause heavy breathing with Leadville's rarified elevation of 10,152 feet. One of our personal favorites, the Delaware Hotel captures Leadville's historic aura, and you can almost see the ghosts of riches-to-rags couple Horace and Baby Doe Tabor, who topped the social register in the mining boom days but died penniless.

The Delaware's 36 rooms aren't big, but they're authentic and charming with brick walls, brass beds, lace curtains, and the original, wavy-glass windows. Some rooms have the old-fashioned wash basin out in the room and the shower and toilet in a separate bathroom. All the rooms have private baths except the two-room suites, which use a hallway bathroom and are a bargain for four people. There's a nice hot tub on the main floor. The room rate includes a continental breakfast.

Grand West Village Resort   **$$$**
99 Grand West Road (County Road 99)
(719) 486-0702, (800) 691-3999
www.grandwest.com
Grand West offers the only condominiums in the Leadville area. It's situated in the forest on 150 acres overlooking the Arkansas River Valley and lies halfway between Leadville and Ski Cooper, affording good access to hiking, bicycling, cross-country skiing, and fishing. No motorized vehicles are allowed in the surrounding forest. Units are two-level and have gas fireplaces, TVs with VCRs, jetted tubs, and shared laundry facilities. Behind the lodge is a nice picnic area, and there's a large front deck for enjoying the sunsets. The lodge is popular for family reunions.

Leadville Ski Country   **$$**
116 East 9th Street
(719) 486-3836, (800) 500-LEAD
www.leadville.com/skicountry
This company provides ski vacation packages in the area for church and family groups. The company offers package deals including lift tickets at Ski Cooper, and accommodations include hotels, motels, and private houses.

Mountain Peaks Motel   **$**
1 Harrison Avenue
(719) 468-3178, (877) 487-3178
With knotty-pine decor, this affordable and pleasant motel is just north of downtown and has ground-level units. It's a budget motel with no frills and a pleasant atmosphere. Daily housekeeping services keep the rooms tidy and comfortable.

Super 8   **$**
1128 South U.S. Highway 24
(719) 486-3637
Part of the national chain, this clean, bright hotel on the south end of town offers dependable accommodations and standard amenities. With a sauna, game room, and complimentary continental breakfast, the old standby offers comfort in an admittedly rather generic setting.

Timberline Motel   **$**
216 Harrison Avenue
(719) 486-1876, (800) 352-1876
www.timberlinemotel.net
Right downtown, the Timberline offers a suitable location for walking to Leadville's restaurants and bars. It has clean, modern, and economical rooms. Ice and daily housekeeping are available at this convenient economy motel.

**United Country Realty/
Alpine Realty** $$$
13th and Poplar Streets
(719) 486-1866, (800) 600-5663
www.mountainhideaway.com
This agency handles bookings for many
Victorian homes in Leadville and just out
of town. All of the private homes are fully
furnished, and a few allow pets. A three-
night minimum stay is required. In winter
the company offers discount tickets for
Ski Cooper. The owner of Alpine also
owns and operates Peri & Ed's Mountain
Hideaway, a bed-and-breakfast in an 1875
Leadville boarding house.

Bed-and-Breakfasts

The Apple Blossom Inn $$
120 West Fourth Street
(719) 486-2141, (800) 982-9279
www.theappleblossominn.com
Originally a banker's home dating from
1879, this charming Victorian inn has six
guest rooms furnished with beautiful
antiques. All rooms have private baths.
The price includes a full breakfast and
afternoon snacks. One large suite can
sleep up to nine people and has two bedrooms, a living room, kitchen, and bathroom. The inn is a half-block from
Leadville's main street and is booked solid
during summer, so be sure to call in
advance for reservations.

The Ice Palace Inn $$
813 Spruce Street
(719) 486-8272, (800) 754-2840
www.icepalaceinn.com
This history-steeped building was con-
structed from the original timbers used to
support Leadville's short-lived Ice Palace
in 1894—a huge and elaborate structure
made of ice, which melted after a few
months following an unusual warm spell.
All rooms include a gourmet breakfast
including home-baked breads, quiches,
omelets, juice, fruit, and hot beverages.

Leadville Country Inn $$
127 East Eighth Street
(719) 486-2354, (800) 748-2354
www.leadvillebednbreakfast.com
This picture-perfect bed-and-breakfast is
listed among the Distinctive Inns of Colorado and is well deserving of the honor.
Owners/innkeepers Maureen and
Gretchen Scanlon run this beautifully
restored 1893 Queen Anne Victorian
home, which has a carriage house and an
outdoor hot tub in a pretty garden
gazebo. The room price includes a deluxe
gourmet breakfast. Five rooms are available in the main house, with three more
rooms in the Carriage House. Prices at the
main inn vary according to weekday or
weekend. The deluxe suite at the inn
includes its own whirlpool tub.

Mount Elbert Lodge $$
10764 Highway 82, Twin Lakes
(719) 486-0594, (800) 381-4433
www.vtinet.com/mtelbert/lodge
With its original log structure dating from
around 1918, the lodge has five newly
remodeled rooms in the bed-and-breakfast
section, three with private baths. There are
eight different-size, log-exterior cabins,
dating from the '40s and '50s. Pets are
allowed in the cabins at an extra cost of
$12 each. Rates include a continental-plus
breakfast featuring such fresh breads as
currant scones and blueberry muffins,
along with juice, yogurt, milk, and coffee
or tea. Bed-and-breakfast rooms' break-
fasts include an egg dish.
   The lodge is at the base of Indepen-
dence Pass a few miles west of Twin Lakes
and is ideal for those who want to get into
the backcountry. Call well in advance for
summer reservations.

RESTAURANTS

Leadville isn't known for ritzy dining, but
there are lots of places to get good,
home-style meals and, especially, top-rate
Mexican food.

Casa Blanca Restaurant $
118 East Second Street
(719) 486-9969
Casa Blanca is located in a cute little white bungalow a few blocks east of Harrison Avenue. Come here for good Mexican cafe ambiance and food, including chile rellenos and stuffed sopapillas. There's a good selection of Mexican beers, and wines are also available. The decor is traditional Mexican with paintings on velvet and lots of color. It's a favorite of locals and is run by the Mascarenaz family. It's open daily, except Sunday, for lunch and dinner.

Golden Burro Cafe & Lounge $
710 Harrison Avenue
(719) 486-1239
www.goldenburro.com
Serving breakfast, lunch, dinner, and Sunday brunch, the Golden Burro specializes in friendly family dining in a western atmosphere. Booths, tables, and counter service are available, as is take-out. Homemade soups, pies, and other baked goods are some of the specialties of this very Leadville-flavored restaurant founded in 1938.

The Grill Bar and Cafe $
715 Elm Street
(719) 486-9930
Operated by the Martinez family since 1965, the Grill is a favorite Leadville stop for Mexican food lovers. The owners roast hundreds of bushels of green chili peppers each year that they personally buy in Hatch, New Mexico, an area known for its chilies. Mexican blankets, maracas, chili ristras, and bullfighting posters decorate the walls of the cafe, which is an 1878 bar that was moved from downtown Leadville to its current location. Some of the selections include tamales, chile rellenos, red and green chilies, and stuffed sopapillas—the owner's special sopapilla has chicken, mushrooms, cheese, avocados, olives, tomatoes, and green chili strips. The chile rellenos are some of the best around. The Grill is open at 4:00 P.M., seven days a week for dinner, and earlier on Saturday and Sunday for lunch.

Steph & Scott's Columbine Cafe $$
612 Harrison Avenue
(719) 486-3599
The young owners of this charming and eclectic cafe make sure everyone gets a belly full of delicious non-traditional food. Try their creole and vegetarian recipes for a refreshing change of pace. Open for breakfast, lunch, and dinner.

Wild Bill's Hamburgers and Ice Cream $
200 Harrison Avenue
(719) 486-0533
Fast-food restaurants rarely qualify as good dining, but this greasy spoon is one exception. The hamburgers and tacos are made to order and served hot and juicy, the ice cream concoctions are splendid, and the homemade soups and chili taste, well, homemade. Wild Bill's is a great spot for the kids.

NIGHTLIFE

Delaware Hotel
700 Harrison Avenue
(719) 486-1418, (800) 748-24
Early birds can enjoy a drink in the bar of the beautifully renovated historic Delaware Hotel, which first opened in 1886. The bar is in the hotel's lobby and open until 10:00 P.M. nightly. Enjoy a quiet drink while soaking up Leadville's rich heritage and thinking about Horace Tabor and Baby Doe.

Pastime Bar
120 West 2nd Street
(719) 486-9434
This restored saloon was founded in 1878. It has a full bar and drink specials. The Pastime serves buffalo burgers and chicken wings and is in competition with the Silver Dollar (see below): The Pastime claims to be the oldest original saloon on (old) State Street, while the Silver Dollar claims to be Leadville's oldest bar. We're not sure who's right, but they're both charming and definitely old. The Pastime, originally the Oro City Chinese bar, was Leadville's official

bordello and has a racy history. It specializes in—of all things—tropical drinks, here at 10,000 feet in the Rockies.

Silver Dollar Saloon
315 Harrison Avenue
(719) 486–9914
Opened in 1879, the Silver Dollar has a beautiful white oak bar with a diamond-dust mirror shipped by wagon from St. Louis. It's been a Leadville watering hole for more than 100 years and has weathered boom and bust. As if it didn't have enough history on its own, it currently promotes itself as an Irish pub and has a big St. Patrick's Day celebration and Irish atmosphere.

ATTRACTIONS

Leadville, Colorado & Southern Railroad
326 East Seventh Street
(719) 486–3936
www.leadville-train.com
This two-and-a-half-hour train ride goes from the Leadville depot up to treeline at the Climax Mine, following the Arkansas River Valley to the river's headwaters. Closed in 1986, the Climax Mine was the world's largest molybdenum mine and employed 3,000 workers at its peak. The train ride has a 15-minute break at the French Gulch water tower where passengers can get off, stretch, and look around. There are on-board restrooms and a concession/gift shop, and passengers can move about among the different open-air, semi-enclosed, and all-weather cars. The conductor explains the sites along the way. The train departs daily at 1:00 P.M. from May until mid-June; at 10:00 A.M. and 2:00 P.M. from mid-June to early September; at 1:00 P.M. on weekdays through September; and 10:00 A.M. and 2:00 P.M. Saturday and Sunday.

Leadville Heritage Museum and Gallery
102 East Ninth Street
(719) 486–1878
Old-time tools and other artifacts of early mining days pack this museum, along with dioramas of Leadville life. There's even a replica of Leadville's short-lived Ice Palace, skating rink, and dance hall, which were created completely from ice around the turn of the 20th century but melted soon after construction because of a warm spell. Hours are 10:00 A.M. to 6:00 P.M. May through October; winter visits may be scheduled by appointment only.

The Matchless Mine Cabin
1 mile east from Harrison Avenue on East Seventh Street
No visit to Leadville is complete without seeing the Matchless Mine—the heart and soul of Leadville lore. Stories abound, and even an opera was written about the sad Ballad of Baby Doe, who was found in this grim little cabin next to the mine of her husband Horace W. Tabor, whose dying words were "hold onto the Matchless." Horace and Baby Doe rose to the pinnacle of Denver society during the silver boom of the late 1800s only to lose it all in the silver panic of 1893. Baby Doe hung on alone here for 36 years after Horace died, and there are touching tales of her trudging many miles through the deep snow for supplies. She was found dead in 1935, frozen among the squalor she had been living in—and the story made national headlines. It's a very touching scene when you hear the story, which is well told at the cabin with old newspaper clips and photos. A visit to the Matchless also takes

Early-day fortunes were made and lost in Leadville by miners and the merchants who kept them supplied. Among those who eventually became household names were dry goods magnates Marshall Field and David May (whose empire became May Co.), miner Meyer Guggenheim and sons, the "Unsinkable Molly Brown," and local favorites, shopkeeper-turned-mine-owner Horace Tabor and his second wife, Baby Doe.

visitors into the mining heart of Leadville, an eerie no-man's-land of slag heaps topped with old wooden timbers that stand like crucifixes for the souls who sacrificed their lives here seeking mountain minerals.

The National Mining Hall of Fame
120 West Ninth Street
(719) 486-1229
www.mininghalloffame.org
The Smithsonian mineral exhibit will interest all rock hounds, and children will enjoy the colorful minerals illuminated by the black lights of the Fluorescent Room, along with a replica of an underground mine and a collection of beautiful minerals and precious metals. The hands-on exhibits are fun and educational, explaining the everyday use of the various minerals of the area, such as those found in toothpaste, showers, toasters, and alarm clocks. Twenty-two hand-carved dioramas depict the history of gold mining. The museum is housed in the four-story Victorian building that was formerly a junior high school. Colorful murals retell the history of mining in the United States. Upstairs, commemorative plaques of mining's most famous figures fill the rooms. Hours are 9:00 A.M. to 5:00 P.M. daily May through October; and from 10:00 A.M. to 4:00 P.M. Monday through Saturday, November through April.

Tabor Opera House
308 Harrison Avenue
(719) 486-8409
www.taboroperahouse.net
Horace Tabor built this lavish opera house and landmark in 1879 to enrich Leadville with culture and entertainment. He and his wife Baby Doe had a private box, and such celebrities as John Philip Sousa, Harry Houdini, Oscar Wilde, and Lillian Russell appeared here. In its heyday, the Tabor Opera House claimed to be the best theater west of the Mississippi. The original stage, dressing rooms, and red-velvet upholstered seats are still in place. During the summer, visitors can take a self-guided tour of the Tabor Opera House from 10:00 A.M. to 5:00 P.M. Monday through Saturday.

KIDSTUFF

Healy House and Dexter Cabin
912 Harrison Avenue
(719) 486-0487
These two turn-of-the-century landmarks offer a fine view of early Leadville life. The elaborate Victorian Healy House, built in 1878 as a single-family residence, became a boardinghouse in 1897. Visitors take a self-guided tour through the lovely house. Kids will enjoy seeing how the "old-timers" lived, with oil lamps and straight razors. The Dexter Cabin is only for looking through the windows; it's closed to the public. A primitive log cabin on the outside, it has a surprisingly luxurious interior because it functioned as an exclusive men's poker club. Volunteers provide a brief history of the site. Hours are 10:00 A.M. to 4:30 P.M. Monday through Saturday and 1:00 to 4:30 P.M. Sunday Memorial Day through Labor Day. Hours are abbreviated in September.

Leadville, Colorado & Southern Railroad
326 East Seventh Street
(719) 486-3936
www.leadville-train.com
Your youngsters will love this two-and-a-half-hour train ride that goes from the Leadville depot up to treeline to the Climax Mine, following the Arkansas River Valley to the river's headwaters. The train ride has a 15-minute break at the French Gulch water tower where kids can get off, stretch, and look around. Though this ride might be a little long for some children, it's very child-friendly with on-board restrooms and a concession and gift shop. Children can also move about freely from seat to seat and car to car. There are open-air, semi-enclosed, and all-weather cars. The conductor explains the sites along the way.

The train departs daily at 1:00 P.M. from May until mid-June; at 10:00 A.M. and 2:00 P.M. from mid-June to early September; and at 1:00 P.M. through September, weekdays, and 10:00 A.M. and 2:00 P.M. Saturday and Sunday.

The National Mining Hall of Fame
120 West Ninth Street
(719) 486-1229
www.mininghalloffame.org

Kids and adults alike will enjoy the colorful minerals illuminated by the black lights of the Fluorescent Room, along with a replica of an underground mine and a collection of beautiful minerals such as quartz, copper, amethysts, geodes, and foliated serpentine, and precious metals such as gold, silver, and platinum. The fun and educational hands-on exhibits tell children about the everyday use of the various minerals of the area, such as those found in toothpaste, toasters, and alarm clocks. Twenty-two hand-carved dioramas depict the history of gold mining. The museum is housed in the four-story Victorian building that was formerly the junior high school and truly is an excellent attraction. Colorful murals retell the history of mining in the United States. Upstairs, commemorative plaques of mining's most famous figures fill the rooms. Hours are 9:00 A.M. to 5:00 P.M. daily May through October; 10:00 A.M. to 4:00 P.M. Monday through Saturday, November through April.

SHOPPING

Like other small mountain towns, Leadville tends to concentrate on curio and souvenir shops and arts and crafts galleries, with some sporting goods available. There's a Safeway supermarket at the north end of town. Leadville's charming, historic main street (Harrison Avenue) is a pleasant place to spend an afternoon strolling and investigating the various shops housed in 19th-century buildings.

Book Mine
502 Harrison Avenue
(719) 486-2866

Look for all types of books in this small shop, one of many excellent independent booksellers in Colorado's mountains. Selling both the best new fiction and nonfiction, the shop also has a complete section on Leadville's amazing history as well as great selections on western American history. The Book Mine also stocks books for children, and authors make appearances and give readings occasionally.

Buckhorn Sporting Goods
616 Harrison Avenue
(719) 486-3944

Backpacks, boots, socks, shorts, and all types of camping and sporting gear fill this shop on Leadville's main street. Perhaps you need some long underwear or a light jacket for those chilly Leadville nights. Various brand-name sporting goods and clothing are available in this pleasant shop.

Colorado Mountain College
Timberline Campus Bookstore
901 Highway 21 South
(719) 486-2015

Although this is the bookstore for Colorado Mountain College, you may find a random book you're seeking, especially if it's on the topic of business and management or nature, the environment, or recreation. The bookstore also supplies computer software, T-shirts, college and office supplies, and some small gifts.

Melanzana Mountain Gear
609 Harrison Avenue
(719) 486-3245
www.melanzana.com

Outdoor clothing and activewear, designed and manufactured in Leadville, are available from this shop. Mail order is also available for most items.

The National Mining Hall of Fame
120 West 9th Street
(719) 486-1229

For unusual gifts from the Rocky Mountains, how about some rare gems, rock collections, or fool's gold? Look for these items in the museum's gift shop. Admission to the Hall of Fame is $6.00 for adults, $5.00 for seniors, $3.00 for children ages 6 through 11, and free for children younger than 6. Gift-shop browsers are admitted free, but the museum is well worth the price and time.

Sayer-McKee Drug Store
615 Harrison Avenue
(719) 486-1846
Gifts, T-shirts, and souvenirs are some of the items you'll find in this cute shop, which also features a bed and bath department.

Western Hardware Company
431 Harrison Avenue
(719) 486-2213
Perhaps the most interesting shop in town, this old hardware store—one of the town's oldest, most picturesque buildings—has antiques, knick-knacks, and just about everything you can imagine. It's almost more of a museum or gallery, but everything's for sale. Don't miss it, and plan on spending a couple of hours!

Miscellaneous and Necessities

Safeway
1900 US 24 (north)
(719) 486-0795
Stock up on groceries, snacks, and necessities and choose from a good selection of souvenir sweatshirts, T-shirts, and other locally labeled paraphernalia at the local Safeway.

At 10,152 feet, Leadville is the highest incorporated town in the United States. Nearby, Alma claims to be the highest unincorporated town, at 10,200 feet.

ARTS
Theater

Tale of Two Tabors and *Molly Brown: Unsinkable or Misunderstood*
Healy House, 912 Harrison Avenue
(719) 486-0487, (800) 933-3901
Performing in the historic Victorian Healy House, actors tell two stories that are based on the life of Leadville's most famous resident, Baby Doe Tabor. Baby Doe was married to millionaire miner Horace Tabor. The two were the toast of the town and high society during the silver boom, but when it all came crashing down with the drop in silver price, they lost everything and lived out their lives in poverty. Baby Doe survived Horace for 36 years, holding onto the worthless Matchless Mine, which he told her to do on his death bed. Advance ticket purchase is suggested.

EVENTS

Nearly every event in Leadville is sponsored by the Leadville Chamber of Commerce. For details on most events, call (719) 486-3900 or (800) 933-3901, or visit its Web site at www.leadville.com.

January

Annual Turquoise Lake 20-Mile Snowshoe Run
Sugar Loafin' Campground, off Turquoise Lake Road (near Leadville)
(719) 486-3900
This challenging early-January run around the lake on snowshoes is an annual favorite of locals and visitors alike. Like the Leadville Trail 100 (a 100-mile foot race through the mountains), it allows Leadville's tough locals and their equally tough competition from elsewhere to pit themselves against the terrain. The race's starting point varies each year for variety.

To reach Turquoise Lake, drive west on Sixth Street to the edge of town, turn right (northwest) on Turquoise Lake Road and continue 3 miles. Follow the signs for the campground.

February

Leadville Rod and Gun Club
Ice Fishing Derby
Turquoise Lake, off Turquoise Lake Road
(719) 486-3900
Anglers can test their mettle on the ice in this annual fishing derby sponsored by the Leadville Rod and Gun Club. Call for exact dates and times.

Snow Bike Race
(719) 486-3245
www.melanzana.com
Riding a bicycle on snow? Snowbike races? Why not? In 1997 Leadville's Chamber of Commerce sponsored the town's first snow-bike race and it has evolved into a series of successful and somewhat hair-raising events. Call for race dates or where to go snowbiking.

March

Crystal Carnival Ski Joring
(719) 486-3900, (800) 933-3901
This old Norwegian tradition involves a horse and rider pulling a skier down the street on a rope. The skier goes over jumps while simultaneously trying to catch rings with a handheld stick—kind of the same idea as catching the rings while riding an old-time merry-go-round. Then after a few rounds, the horseback riders and skiers switch places. Some say the Norwegians came up with this sport because they had nothing better to do with their time on those dark winter days. Leadville, one of the few places in North America where ski joring is held, closes the main street and diverts traffic for the event.

St. Patrick's Day Parade
Harrison Avenue
(719) 486-3900
The Leadville Hibernian Mining and Marching Society hosts this annual March 17 parade that ends—where else—at the Silver Dollar Saloon, the town's Irish pub. Show up and wear green to participate.

May

Children's Fishing Day
Leadville National Fish Hatchery
Highway 300
(719) 486-0189
The nation's second-oldest fish hatchery (established in 1889) offers tours and great opportunities for youngsters. Admission is free, and the hatchery also has nature trails and a picnic area.

July

Leadville USA
Independence Celebration
(719) 486-3900, (800) 933-3901
The world's highest fireworks display and the Firecracker 5K foot race starting from the town courthouse are the top draws for this small-town-USA Fourth-of-July celebration. Contact the Leadville Chamber of Commerce for details. Our favorite spot to view the fireworks is from the Mineral Belt Trail in the mining district west of town.

August

Boom Days Celebration Weekend
Various locations
(719) 486-3900, (800) 933-3901
In early August Leadville's oldest continual celebration, Boom Days, begins on Friday evening and continues through Sunday, featuring a large parade, street races, and mining events. The event celebrates Leadville's Victorian heritage and rough-and-tumble history with activities (mostly

centered on Harrison Avenue) that the whole family can enjoy.

International Pack Burro Race
Harrison Avenue
(719) 486-3900, (800) 933-3901
In early August this colorful Colorado tradition involves racers with burros who have to complete a course to win. Watching the interaction of human and animal competitors can be quite entertaining and interesting. The burro race is part of Leadville's Boom Days Celebration. Those who would like to enter (your own burro required) should write to Burro Race, P.O. Box 884, Leadville, CO 80561.

Leadville Trail 100 Bike Race
(719) 486-3502, (800) 933-3901
This grueling mid-August 100-mile, fat-tire bike race through the mountains starts at 6:30 A.M. and continues . . . and continues. Riders end up in Leadville for a big celebration. The best spot to watch the race is at the Twin Lakes aid station on the dam at the lakes.

Leadville Trail 100 Ultramarathon
(719) 486-3502, (800) 933-3901
Perhaps even more grueling than the mountain bike race, this mid-August 100-mile foot race through the mountains attracts about 500 courageous runners, only about half of whom finish—after some 20 to 30 hours of endurance. The race begins at 4:00 A.M. in Leadville and crosses 12,000-foot Hope Pass twice on its round-trip route to Winfield, a ghost

town at the 50-mile point. The race has a 30-hour cutoff (finishers after that time do not receive the coveted belt buckle given to the runners). Those interested in trying an ultramarathon should ask about the practice run held the weekend nearest July 4.

September

Annual Cowboy Poetry Gathering
County Courthouse Law
505 Harrison Avenue
(719) 486-3900
Get along, little doggerel: Leadville becomes a cowtown when the region's finest horseback bards let fly with their poetry. The festivities kick off with a Friday night performance at the Old Church at 8th Street and Harrison Avenue, then continue with a day of ropin' and rhymin' at the courthouse.

St. Patrick's Day Practice Parade
Harrison Avenue
(719) 486-3900
The town looks for any excuse to close off the main street and have a parade and party, so a practice parade is just the perfect reason. The parade leaves from one end of Harrison Avenue or the other—organizers never really know for sure very much in advance—but always ends at the Silver Dollar Saloon. Like for the real thing (above), show up and wear green.

October

Cemetery Tour/Murder Mayhem Tour
(they switch off annually)
Evergreen Cemetery
(719) 486-3900
On October 31, local historian Neil Reynolds, wearing a black coat and top hat, leads this spook tour through the Evergreen Cemetery at 7:00 P.M. Reynolds relates the stories of the deceased and some local history, providing lots of Hal-

---

Although Leadville is among the country's loftiest towns, residents brag about its "balmy" weather. On a typical summer day, the temperature can climb into the 70s yet fall into the 40s overnight. During the winter, however, more than 200 inches of snow fall, and a typical high temperature is in the 30s, with nights below 10 degrees F.

loween color. Reservations are required, and there's a small admission fee. Light refreshments are included in the prices. If the tour fills, a second one is scheduled at 8:30 P.M.

Trick or Treat Street
(719) 486-4282
A community-wide Halloween party, this annual event held at the town center offers games, contests, and lots of fun for kids. It's held from 6:30 to 8:30 P.M. on Halloween night, and there is an admission charge of a couple of dollars. Like similar events in many communities across the country, it was created as a safe way for kids to enjoy trick-or-treating.

November

Turkey and "Survival" Shoot
Leadville Rod and Gun Club
(719) 486-3900
Each year before Thanksgiving—and sometimes after Christmas—the Leadville Rod and Gun Club sponsors a turkey shoot. Dates vary; call for specifics.

December

Christmas at Ski Cooper
Ski Cooper, US 24, 10 miles north of Leadville
(719) 486-3684
Santa and his reindeer at Ski Cooper are a seasonal favorite in the area. Santa has real reindeer, and kids can pose for photos with him from 8:00 A.M. to 9:30 P.M., then spend the afternoon skiing at this family ski area. Breakfast is available at the lodge restaurant. Call for exact dates.

Annual Off-Track, Off-Beat 10K
Snowshoe Race
Ski Cooper, US 24, 10 miles
north of Leadville
(719) 486-3684
Ski Cooper's season begins in December

with an entertaining snowshoe race at the ski area—there's something essentially comical about people running on snowshoes. Join in the fun, or just watch. Snowshoes are available for rental.

Victorian Days Celebration
Various locations
(719) 486-3900, (800) 933-3901
The first Saturday in December boasts a tour of a half-dozen of the colorful, creaky Victorian homes in town. The event starts with a brunch in the morning, and participants snack on delightful treats at each stop during the afternoon tour. A nominal admission fee is charged.

DOWNHILL SKIING

Leadville

Ski Cooper
10 miles north of Leadville on US 24
(719) 486-3684
www.skicooper.com
Base elevation (Leadville): *10,500 feet*
Top of highest lift: *11,700 feet*
Total vertical: *1,200 feet*
Longest run: *1⁴/₁₀ miles*
Average annual snowfall: *260 inches*
Ski season: *Thanksgiving through the end of March or early April*
Capacity: *3,300 skiers per hour*
Terrain: *385 acres, 26 runs (30 percent beginner, 40 percent intermediate, 30 percent advanced and expert); Chicago Ridge Snowcat terrain, 2,400 acres (all intermediate, advanced and expert)*
Lift tickets: *$36*
Snow reports: *(719) 486-2277*
Getting there: *Ski Cooper is 120 miles west of Denver via I-70, Highway 91 and US 24.*

Ski Cooper is one of Colorado's oldest ski areas and boasts the state's lowest-priced lift ticket. It's a great place to go to escape from the glitz of the bigger areas and enjoy the simple pleasures of skiing. Ski Cooper is also full of history. The 10th Mountain Division troops chose this area for its variety of terrain and abundant snowfall to train for European mountain combat during World War II. There's even a museum of memorabilia dedicated to the 10th Mountain Division on the third floor of the base lodge. Some famous veterans of the 10th include former U.S. Senator Bob Dole and men who pioneered the Colorado ski industry after the war, including Vail founder Pete Seibert.

Although it's one of Colorado's smaller ski areas with only four lifts and 385 lift-served acres, its size is what draws many skiers who like a more homey and human-scaled resort. Ski Cooper offers a fine variety of terrain, from gladed tree skiing and challenging moguls to groomed open slopes. For experts eager for extreme skiing, Chicago Ridge has 2,400 acres of untracked powder on the Continental Divide with spectacular views of Mount Elbert, Colorado's highest peak, along with the Mount of the Holy Cross, another 14er—the nickname for Colorado's peaks higher than 14,000 feet. This upper area is not served by lifts; skiers reach it by snow-cat and take the challenge of 1,000-foot vertical runs for $250 each day. Ski Cooper has a pleasant lodge, bar, and restaurant with good homemade offerings. There are no overnight accommodations at the ski area (other than a backcountry yurt). The nearby town of Leadville offers plenty of accommodations plus lots of color and history from its silver-boom days.

NORDIC/CROSS-COUNTRY

Ski Cooper is a time-honored favorite for telemarkers to practice carving their graceful turns on the broad, open slopes. The unpretentious atmosphere and uncrowded slopes are a big draw, as is the low lift-ticket price.

Mineral Belt Trail
A 12-mile loop around town, the Mineral Belt Trail offers outstanding views and wonderful history, especially as it winds through the mining district on the west side of town. The trail is groomed by students at the Colorado Mountain College and can be completed in under four hours by fit skiers. Or try skiing only a portion—many trailheads exist for shuttles.

Tennessee Pass Nordic Center
Adjacent to Ski Cooper
(719) 486-1750
www.tennesseepass.com
Ski Cooper has Tennessee Pass Nordic Center with 24 kilometers of groomed trails, lessons, tours, and rentals. The system includes three short trails for novices and a greater number of intermediate and advanced routes. A trail pass costs $10.

OTHER WINTER RECREATION

Snowshoeing/ Yurt Meals

Ski Cooper
10 miles north of Leadville, on US 24
(719) 486-3684
www.tennesseepass.com/cookhouse
How about skiing or snowshoeing to a yurt (cylindrical tentlike dwelling) for lunch or dinner? From Ski Cooper's lodge, it's only 1¼ miles to a comfortable heated yurt for a gourmet meal. Ski by moonlight, or take a daytime trip. Either way, you'll enjoy a beautiful view of the Arkansas River Valley and Colorado's highest peak, Mount Elbert, along with many other high peaks. The yurt-meal package includes dinner or lunch, equipment, a guide, and headlamps for night skiing. A former gourmet cook from Ashcroft will prepare such dinner choices as elk streak, trout, lamb, or a vegetarian dish. The cost is $65 per person, which includes all equipment rental, trail pass, even a headlamp for traveling in the dark.

Snowmobiling

Alpine Snowmobiles & Dogsledding
Highway 24 West
(719) 486-9899
www.alpinesnowmobiles.com

For those who like their wintertime transportation motorized, and those who don't, Alpine offers both snowmobile rentals and dogsled tours. It's open seven days a week mid-November through mid-April, 8:00 A.M. to 6:00 P.M. Kids under 3 and pregnant women have to sit this one out. Cost for snowmobile rental is $100 to $125 for two hours, $150 to $175 for four hours. One-hour dogsled tours are $60 for guests over 9 years old, and $30 for those 3 to 8 years old.

Leadville Chamber of Commerce
809 Harrison Avenue
(719) 486-3900, (800) 933-3901
www.leadvilleusa.com

Pick up a free copy of the local cross-country ski and snowmobile map at the Leadville Chamber of Commerce. This large, easy-to-read map includes detailed trail descriptions, degree of difficulty, and clear directions. The chamber is in the north end of town right on the town's main avenue and provides visitor information for all the local activities as well as recommendations for different snowmobiling areas and rental companies that are near them. The chamber is open every day from 10:00 A.M. to 5:00 P.M. except Christmas, Thanksgiving, and New Year's days.

Leadville Ski Country
115 East Ninth Street
(719) 486-3836, (800) 500-LEAD

This shop rents snowmobiles and everything you need to go with them, such as snow boots, bibs, and jackets. Snowmobile rental is $90 for a two-hour minimum and $200 for all day (and includes boots and bibs). Extra riders cost $10, and the snowmobiles accommodate two people total. Rentals begin when the snow is good enough, usually around December,

and end about mid-April. The shop also rents downhill and cross-country skis and snowshoes. A one-day downhill rental package ranges from $15 to $25 (depending upon the type of equipment); cross-country packages cost $12, and snowshoes are $12. The shop also handles very affordable vacation packages in the area for church and family groups (please see our "Accommodations" section).

Ice Fishing

Turquoise Lake
West of Leadville, U.S. Forest Service
(719) 486-0749

Under the jurisdiction of the U.S. Forest Service, Turquoise Lake is an ice-fisherman's paradise. Auger through the thick ice that forms on the lake by late December and lasts through April and toss in your line for some huge, lethargic lake trout. The beautiful reservoir, set in the shadow of the state's highest peak, Mount Elbert, also makes for a wonderful summer fishing spot.

HIKING

For additional details on hiking and backpacking in the Leadville area, visit the Leadville Ranger District Office, 2015 Poplar Street, (719) 486-0749. Bill's Sport Shop, 225 Harrison Avenue, (719) 486-0739, sells topographical maps and outdoor equipment as does Buckhorn Sporting Goods, 616 Harrison Avenue, (719) 486-3944.

Colorado Trail
West of Leadville on Highway 82
www.coloradotrail.org

This 469-mile trail that stretches from Denver to Durango is a favorite for hikers and backpackers of all abilities. From Leadville there's a beautiful section between Tennessee Pass and Twin Lakes, ideal for backpackers who can leave a car at each end. From the Colorado Trail it's also possi-

Climbing a "14er"

They are, literally, the high points of the Rockies, Colorado's 54 peaks that rise 14,000 feet above sea level and offer the best of the mountain experience—incredible scenery, spectacular weather, sublime views, and physical challenges to those who attempt to climb them.

Ranging from simple uphill hikes to the technical 2,000-foot vertical wall known as the Diamond on Longs Peak, the 14ers beckon like sirens, and most actually are attainable to anyone with decent levels of fitness, energy, and time.

First, pick a peak. Novices are advised to try the easiest 14,000-footers although there's nothing easy about reaching their summits. Try Mount Sherman near Fairplay, Quandary Peak outside Breckenridge, or Mount Bierstadt near Georgetown.

Learn about the route through one of several excellent guide books readily available. Falcon Publishing, (800) 582–2665 or www.falcon.com, offers several books that cover hikes up Colorado's highest peaks.

Gather the "10 essentials" that every mountain traveler should carry in a backpack: extra warm clothing, high-energy food, plenty of water (at least two quarts), firestarter, survival blanket, first-aid kit, map and compass, rain gear, and a flashlight. Additionally, dress in several layers that can be added or removed, wear a comfortable pair of hiking boots, and avoid water-retaining cotton garments. Don't forget sunglasses and plenty of sunscreen.

Next, make sure to get a bracingly early start. The traditional rule of thumb is to be back down below timberline by 1:00 P.M., before the typical afternoon thunder-

ble to make a side trip and climb Mount Elbert, Colorado's highest mountain (14,433 feet), or Mount Massive (14,421), just a few feet lower and ranked number two in the state. To reach Twin Lakes, 22 miles southwest of Leadville, take US 24 south for 14 miles to Highway 82. Turn right, drive 8 miles west on Highway 82 and follow the signs for the Colorado Trail. You might want to pick up a copy of *The Colorado Trail: The Official Guidebook* by The Colorado Trail Foundation.

Galena Mountain
Turquoise Lake, 3 miles west of
Leadville on Highway 91

This rugged-looking 12,893-foot peak actually has an easy and interesting route to the summit despite its forbidding sheer cliffs on one side. The round trip is 7 miles. The summit lies on the Continental Divide. Look for the trailhead at Turquoise Lake, west of Leadville. Go to the far west end of the lake to a small parking area on the west side of the road where the road loops back to the east. Cross a creek and head west, bearing north through a meadow, and look for a trail leading north along the west side of the creek. The trail begins as an old road, then becomes quite scenic as it rises through forests, streams, and meadows. After an open area and

storms hit. That means hitting the trail by 6:00 A.M. in most cases, and even before sunrise for the longer trips.

Eager to get out, many hikers start up the trails too fast and wear themselves out before they reach their goals. It's important instead to pace yourself and save your energy for the difficult hiking near the summit, where the air is thin and the inclines steep. One tried-and-true method employed by many savvy mountaineers is the "rest step," which looks sort of like a wedding march. Take a step, lock the rear knee to "rest" on the bone rather than muscles, breathe deeply, then take the next step. The slow, steady pace actually covers ground faster than taking the typical 10 quick steps followed by a minute of gasping. Also, stop at least once an hour for food and water, making sure to avoid dehydration and maintain sufficient energy.

Make sure to stay on the trail, often marked by piles of rocks called cairns that have been left by other hikers. Short-cutting causes terrible erosion in the delicate tundra above timberline and can take centuries to repair.

Step by step, the goal gradually approaches. Tiny rodents called pikas squeak, and cat-sized marmots whistle as you pass. On some peaks, curious mountain goats watch bemusedly. Then, suddenly, the summit is within reach, and from there, the world is truly at your feet.

Enjoy the view, eat and drink again, and then start the trek down. Remember, however, that the summit is only the midpoint; take as much caution heading back down as you did on the way up.

For those without the time, the inclination, or the stamina necessary to climb a 14er, it's still possible to breathe the thin air and feel the chill of the high-altitude breeze on top. Two peaks, Mount Evans near Idaho Springs and Pikes Peak west of Colorado Springs, have roads that snake their way to the summits. Pikes Peak also has a wondrous cog railway that takes visitors to the top, where a gift shop and snack bar await.

switchbacks, the trail arrives at an 11,300-foot saddle on the south ridge of Galena Mountain. Here, leave the trail and head up this gentle ridge to the north all the way to the summit. Look for enormous Mount Massive to the south and Homestake Peak to the north.

Return via the same route or make a slight variation from the top of the mountain west of the ascent route to a small knoll at 11,920 feet. From there, the descent is easy heading south into the valley slightly west of the ascent route, and back to the trail.

Railroad Grade to Hagerman Tunnel
Turquoise Lake, 3 miles west of
Leadville on US 24

Another interesting and easy hike (6 miles round trip), this old railroad grade leads to two tunnels. The trailhead is on the Hagerman Pass road. From Leadville go west on the well-marked main road (Highway 91) to Turquoise Lake. Following the road west on the south side of the lake, take the left fork at the "Y" junction. This unpaved road (on which you'll drive for 4½ miles, though it may seem much longer) passes the Old Carlton Tunnel. It's dark and wet and worth a peek, but not safe to enter. Drive a mile past the tunnel and look for the trailhead and large parking area on the left after a curve around toward the northeast.

Walk up the railroad grade to the northwest through a narrow gully, which soon opens to a broader vista. Eventually, you'll reach an area where you can't continue on the railroad grade level because of a missing trestle. Climb to the grade above and continue along. As the trail curves to the northeast near Hagerman Lake, you'll notice another missing trestle. Before arriving at the portal of Hagerman Tunnel, notice the fallen timbers from an old collapsed snow shed. This was the original tunnel through the mountains for the train. It was later replaced by the Carlton Tunnel. Though interesting, such tunnels aren't safe to enter because of falling rocks.

The unpaved road to the trailhead for this hike is rocky, narrow, and muddy, with a steep dropoff on one side much of the way, but most passenger cars can handle it.

CAMPING

San Isabel National Forest
Leadville District Office
(719) 486-0749

The San Isabel National Forest offers many campsites in the Leadville area. Most popular is Turquoise Lake, 3 miles west of Leadville. At the lake eight campgrounds with 368 campsites hug the beautiful shore. There's plenty of fishing and boating and access to hiking trails. Reserve a site by calling (877) 444-6777, or online at www.reserveusa.com.

South of Leadville, several scenic campgrounds lie in the shadow of several spectacular 14,000-foot peaks, including Mount Elbert and Mount Massive. Halfmoon Campground offers 21 sites, and Elbert Creek Campground has 17. There are trailheads for climbing both Mount Elbert and Mount Massive near the campgrounds.

Drive south from Leadville on US 24 for 2 miles, then go west on Highway 300

as it turns south curving around a big bend. Go about a mile, and then look for Halfmoon Creek Road (Forest Road 110). Turn south on it, and continue 6 miles on a dirt road leading to both campgrounds. These campgrounds are nestled in groves of aspen and are beautiful in the early fall when the aspen turn golden.

Sugar Loafin' Campground
2665 County Road 4, west of Leadville
(719) 486-1031
www.leadville.com/sugarloafin

Near Turquoise Lake, tent campers and RV owners can find lovely spots at Sugar Loafin'. The private campground has hot showers, a grocery store, laundry, and even ice cream socials. Drive 3½ miles west of Leadville on County Road 4.

Twin Lakes
Highway 82, off Highway 24, south of Leadville

Also south of Leadville, the Twin Lakes area offers lots of great campsites with tremendous views of the mountains and lakes. Dexter Point Campground right on the lake has 22 sites. Two miles away, Lake View Campground offers 68 sites. Farther around the lake are White Star, with 64 sites, and Perry Peak with 26. Another choice is Twin Peaks Campground with 37 sites.

To reach Twin Lakes, drive south from Leadville on US 24 for 14 miles to Highway 82, which follows the north edge of Twin Lakes Reservoir. Drive 3 more miles, and you'll come to Dexter Point Campground. Continuing around the lake you'll arrive at the others mentioned above.

GOLF

Mount Massive Golf Club
259 County Road 5
(719) 486-2176

Mount Massive is best known as the highest golf course in the United States at 9,680 feet. That's the biggest plus, followed closely by the pristine views of Colorado's highest peak, 14,433-foot Mount Elbert, as well as a slew of lesser pinnacles. On the minus side, the Mount Massive course includes only nine holes, most of them flat, and snows limit the season to between mid-May and late October. Greens fees for the nine-holer are $16, and its $29 to make the loop twice. Walking is permitted anytime, and tee-time reservations are accepted five days in advance and recommended. Go west on West Sixth Street for 1¼ miles. Turn right at the end of the road, turn right onto County Road 4, 3 miles down the hill, cross the railroad tracks and the Arkansas, bear left and it's a quarter mile down County Road 5.

FISHING AND HUNTING

Turquoise Lake and Twin Lakes offer picturesque mountain reservoirs stocked with brook trout and cutthroats, and the Arkansas River south of town offers some fine fly fishing, especially when the May flies are hatching on the water. The Leadville area does offer some hunting, but all permits are issued in an annual draw by the state Division of Wildlife; no over-the-counter hunting licenses are available.

Outfitters and Tackle Shops

Buckhorn Sporting Goods
616 Harrison Avenue
(719) 486-3944
Buckhorn is the place in town to go for hunting and fishing equipment and information on conditions. The friendly staff really knows the area and the best "secret" spots.

Places to Fish

Turquoise Lake
County Road 4 U.S. Forest Service
District Ranger Station
(719) 486-0749
A popular spot for summer and winter recreation, the lake features U.S. Forest Service campgrounds, boat ramps, and a shoreline hiking trail. The ice fishing is excellent from January through mid-April, and private campsites with full hookups are nearby.

OTHER RECREATION

Lofty Leadville, at an elevation of 10,152 feet, will take your breath away even if you're just standing still. A flat, 6½-mile trail follows the pretty, tree-lined shore of Turquoise Lake, just outside of town and a good place for many activities such as bicycling, running, and walking for those not used to the high elevation. The lake is slightly lower than 10,000 feet. The nearby Arkansas River is Colorado's most popular rafting site, and dozens of outfitters line its shores near Buena Vista and Salida. Leadville is also an extremely popular hiking area and the starting point for a whole string of Colorado's 14,000-foot peaks called the Collegiate Range.

Biking

For those with strong legs and stronger lungs, Leadville offers terrific mountain biking, and the town hosts a big 100-mile mountain bike race each year. Old mining roads around town provide good mountain bike routes. Turquoise Lake makes for some nice, easy bicycling with beautiful views of the lake and surrounding mountains. The Chamber of Commerce, 809 Harrison Avenue, (719) 486-3900 or (800) 933-3901, distributes free maps of the area with descriptions of and direc-

tions to the area's many backcountry trails. In 2000, the town opened the acclaimed Mineral Belt Trail, a 12-mile paved loop around Leadville that offers spectacular views of the mountains and a wonderful journey through the ruins of the historic mining district on the west side of town. Numerous trailheads make riding the whole trail or a portion very easy.

Bill's Sport Shop
225 Harrison Avenue
(719) 486-0739
Stop here for mountain bike rentals, local maps, and advice from the helpful staff on the best places to ride.

Whitewater Rafting

The Arkansas Headwaters Recreation Area was created in 1990 as a partnership between state and federal agencies to foster recreation along the Arkansas River. This linear riverside park extends from Leadville to Pueblo for 148 miles and is dotted with river access points, camping and picnic areas, and changing rooms. Sixty percent of the land is privately owned, so boaters need to check with AHRA for regulations. The numerous outfitters along the river have maps of the river as do the chamber of commerce visitor centers in Buena Vista and Salida. Stop in at the AHRA office at 307 West Sackett Street, Salida, (719) 539-7289.

Acquired Tastes Whitewater Rafting
27410 County Road 319, Buena Vista
(719) 395-2992, (800) 888-8582
www.atraft.com
This company offers high-quality one- and two-day trips on the Arkansas. It has state-of-the-art, self-bailing rafts with foot cones, experienced guides, and great lunches. Call for a brochure and pricing information.

Bill Dvorak Kayak & Rafting Expeditions
17921-B U.S. Highway 285, Nathrop
(719) 539-6851, (800) 824-3795
www.dvorakexpeditions.com
Well-known in whitewater circles, Dvorak specializes in extended river trips on the Upper Arkansas and other major rivers in the state, country, and world. It also offers fishing expeditions and kayak lessons. Trips range from half-day to 12 days on 9 major U.S. rivers in the Southwest. Also available are combination trips, including river, mountain biking, horseback, four-wheeling, and fishing.

Wilderness Aware Rafting
28395 County Road 317, Buena Vista
(719) 395-2112, (800) 462-7238
www.inaraft.com
As the name implies, this company specializes in the natural history of the area. It won the Colorado Tourism Company of the Year award. Trips range from a half-day to 10 days on the Colorado, Arkansas, North Platte, and Dolores Rivers, plus the Gunnison Gorge on the Gunnison River. Inflatable kayaks are also available, as are wildwater, family whitewater, and guided float fishing trips. Call for a free brochure.

SPAS AND HOT SPRINGS

Cottonwood Hot Springs
18999 County Road 306, Buena Vista
(719) 395-6434
Delightfully funky, the adult-oriented au natural hot springs are a great place to soak and be pampered with a massage, but a little casual for the prim and proper. Five and a half miles west of the only spotlight in Buena Vista, a quaint Arkansas River town about a half-hour drive south of Leadville, the springs offer three private tubs and three open rock pools. Additionally, services such as tarot card readings and past-life regressions are

offered. The springs are open from 8:00 A.M. to midnight for "day" guests, and available round-the-clock for guests in the 12 motel rooms or four cabins on site. Admission is $10 a day. Clothing is optional after dark.

Mt. Princeton Hot Springs Resort
15870 County Road 162, Nathrop
(719) 395–2447
www.mtprinceton.com
Located at the base of one of the state's towering 14,000-foot peaks, the Mount Princeton Hot Springs is really more of a large, superheated swimming pool. The springs are open year-round, and bathing in the middle of a winter snowstorm is an amazing sensation. To get there, go south on US 24 from Leadville to the small town of Nathrop. Turn right and follow the signs for five miles to the springs. Hours are 9:00 A.M. to 9:00 P.M. on weekends, 9:00 A.M. to 11:00 P.M. on Friday and Saturday. Admission is $10.00, or $7.00 for those younger than 12 or older than 62.

VAIL VALLEY

VAIL

Posh, expensive, glamorous, crowded, cosmopolitan, and pretentious, Vail has come to represent both the best and—by some minority perspectives—the worst of Colorado resorts. Second only to Aspen in terms of glitz, Vail offers the nation's largest, most varied, and most expensive ski resort, but there's no arguing that a powder day in the Back Bowls ranks among the most spectacular experiences on skis. The award-winning ski school, wide-open groomed runs, and nouveau-Tyrolean village with $1,000-a-night condominiums and superior service consistently earn Vail a ranking in the top U.S. resorts by *Ski* magazine.

In the winter, Vail is the place where people arrive on the slopes late in the morning and leave early in the afternoon, eager to make their massage at the spa or conduct a little business—if they haven't already done that on the gondola with their cell phones. In the less-crowded summer, when most of the multimillion-dollar homes are vacant, the valley glows in amber light, allowing for idyllic days fly fishing, golfing, hiking, and enjoying a streamside meal on one of the numerous restaurant patios.

Although the town's permanent population is only about 4,600, the transient winter crowd can reach 20,000 in the narrow valley. The nation's largest free bus system eases traveling from one part of town to the next. A pleasant bike path also meanders through the 11-mile long town and even up to the top of 10,600-foot Vail Pass for the hardy cyclists in the summer.

Created in 1962 by Pete Seibert, a veteran of the famed 10th Mountain Division ski troops, who fought valiantly in World War II, Vail ski mountain dominates the valley, generating the area's economy and providing most of the recreation. But in town, a full complement of lodging, restaurants, shopping, and recreation fill out the picture of a world-class resort.

An interchangeable lift ticket allows skiers to choose between Vail, Beaver Creek, Breckenridge, Keystone, and Arapahoe Basin.

Beaver Creek is a second home to former President Gerald Ford, who, along with his wife, Betty, is considered the town's royalty. The Ford golf course, amphitheater, alpine gardens, and park clustered at the east end of Vail all are named after the couple and provide wonderful leisure experiences. Bad knees have sidelined Ford in recent years, but in the past it wasn't uncommon to see him zipping down Riva Ridge on his skis, Secret Service agents in anxious tow.

BEAVER CREEK/AVON

Just a few miles down the Eagle valley from Vail along Interstate 70, the former sheep-ranching community of Avon has grown in recent years into a thriving commercial center at the base of the exclusive upscale community and ski mountain of Beaver Creek. Vail's sister resort was born in 1972 from the vision of Vail founder Pete Seibert and would have been the host site of the 1976 Olympics if the state's voters hadn't nixed those plans out of environmental concerns. Now a gated community of $5 million stone-and-timber homes and some of the nicest hotels in the world, Beaver Creek has the feel of a private playground open to the public.

The skiing at Beaver Creek ranges from beginners slopes at the *top* of the mountain to the very challenging bump runs on the west side, as well as the ridiculously steep Birds of Prey downhill course. In the winter, one of the most charming cold-

Vail's clock tower is a central landmark, anchoring the downtown shopping district. VAIL
IMAGE/JACK AFFLECK

weather experiences is a sleigh ride up the slopes to Beano's Cabin for a fireside dinner. In the summer, a paddleboat ride on Nottingham Lake or hike into the backcountry pose the preferred pastimes.

Avon and nearby Edwards are rapidly adding nightlife, shopping, and restaurants, many of which are exceptional.

MINTURN

Nestled between Vail and Beaver Creek a couple of miles south of I-70, Minturn is a former mining town that now houses resort workers and some of the best secrets in the Vail valley.

Antiques stores and terrific casual restaurants as well as a great soda fountain give the town a hometown, Fourth-of-July feel all year round.

An essential crossroads for the mountain railroad system in the old days, now Minturn is best known for its world-class whitewater kayaking on the Eagle River.

True locals, by the way, pronounce it MINT-urn, with the "t" barely annunciated.

EDWARDS

Not so many years ago, there was no "there" in Edwards, other than an exit ramp off the interstate and a gas station. But as real-estate prices in Vail and Avon skyrocketed, the year-round residents started looking "down valley" for more affordable housing and found it in Edwards.

Now a bustling bedroom community of more than 8,000 residents—more than Vail and Avon combined—Edwards has come into its own as a commercial center with shops, a hotel, and a six-screen movie theater, the largest in the county. The Singletree, Lake Creek, and Homestead subdivisions offer much more affordable homes for resort workers, and the town also hosts numerous rental units for seasonal employees. Some 20 miles west of Vail, the weather down valley tends to be less severe in winter and warmer in summer.

EAGLE

The Eagle County seat has grown rapidly in recent years to about 3,700 people, and the county's only regional airport makes Eagle a hub for travelers heading to the slopes at Vail.

Located 30 miles west of Vail, Eagle is becoming another bedroom community for the expensive resort, although its history alone makes the town a worthwhile place to visit.

Eagle is home to the local offices of the U.S. Forest Service, the U.S. Department of Resource Conservation, and the Colorado Division of Wildlife, and access to the sparsely visited Brush Creek area south of town leads intrepid travelers into true wilderness.

ACCOMMODATIONS

Vail

Apollo Park Lodge $$$
442 South Frontage Road West
(970) 476-5881, (800) 872-8281
www.apolloparklodge.com
This lodge in the heart of Vail Village has 44 one- and two-bedroom condo units with kitchens, which may be why it's so popular with families. Other amenities include an outdoor pool.

Christiania Lodge $$$
356 Hanson Ranch Road
(970) 476-5641, (800) 530-3999
www.christiania.com
The Christiania is one of Vail's first lodges, open since 1963 and remodeled into six

Bavarian-style suites, lodge rooms, and condos. It's centrally located in Vail, within walking distance of the Vail Village lifts. Amenities include a complimentary breakfast, concierge, lounge, outdoor pool, and sauna.

Gasthof Gramshammer $$$
231 East Gore Creek Drive
(970) 476-5626, (800) 610-7374
www.pepis.com

Another original, Gasthof Gramshammer was opened by former Austrian Olympic ski racer Pepi Gramshammer, one of Vail's best-loved residents. The 28-room lodge is adjacent to the village center and has its owner's Austrian charm (beds come with down comforters, for example). Guests have access to a buffet breakfast, restaurant, bar, nightclub, and ski shop.

Lion Square Lodge $$$
660 West Lionshead Place
(970) 476-2281, (800) 525-5788
www.lionsquare.com

This lodge has 28 lodge rooms and 83 condos, most with fireplaces. It is within walking distance of the Lionshead gondola, an amenity as or more important than the valet service, outdoor pool, hot tubs, saunas, guest laundry, or restaurant. Guests also have access to the hotel's private shuttle van.

The Lodge at Vail $$$
174 East Gore Creek Drive
(970) 476-5011, (877) 528-7625
www.lodgeatvail.com

A Rock Resort hotel, the Lodge has earned numerous accolades. Guests choose between lodge room and two- and three-bedroom suites, all with Austrian/Swiss decor. The lodge is within steps of the Vail Village ski lifts, one of only a handful that are ski-in, ski-out. Hotel rooms come with humidifiers, marble baths, and mahogany and teak furnishings. The suites are individually owned and decorated. Amenities include a bell staff, valet, outdoor pool, sauna, exercise room, and two favorites with locals:

Cucina Rustica Italian restaurant and Mickey's piano bar, a popular après-ski spot.

Marriott's Vail Mountain Resort $$$
715 West Lionshead Circle
(970) 476-4444, (800) 648-0720
www.marriott.com

Just blocks from the Vail Cascade sits the Marriot Mountain Resort. It's smaller in terms of conference facilities but is no less lavish a retreat. Guests are housed in a 350-room high-rise tower that has been renovated in a mountain-lodge style. The Lionshead ski base area is about a block away and easily reachable by foot. Amenities include a concierge, a valet, restaurants, a lounge bar, indoor/outdoor pool, hot tubs, a sauna, a guest laundry, a small exercise room, and a spa facility.

Roost Lodge $
1783 North Frontage Road
(970) 476-5451, (800) 873-3065
www.roostlodge.com

Locals and those in the know keep this motel's name and phone number in a safe place. It's a poorly kept secret—a motel that is both friendly and so reasonably priced you'll think you are no longer in Vail. Its West Vail location keeps it out of the limelight, but it's accessible and close to supermarkets, liquor stores, and fast-food restaurants. There are 74 rooms and three suites. Room rates include a continental breakfast and a free shuttle to town and nearby ski areas. Amenities include a covered outdoor pool and hot tub.

Sonnenalp Resort $$$
82 East Meadow Drive
(970) 476-5656, (800) 654-8312
www.sonnenalp.com

The Sonnenalp has a prime location in the middle of Vail's central pedestrian area, with guesthouses in three connected buildings, each with distinct decor. The Bavaria Haus and the Austria Haus are more simple than the quaint Swiss Chalet. Guests can choose from two spas, guided skiing, and snowshoeing programs or golf

on one of the valley's best-designed courses a dozen miles away in the vicinity of Avon. Other amenities include a bell staff, a concierge, restaurants, heated underground parking, a lounge, an outdoor pool, a hot tub, and a fitness room.

Vail Cascade Hotel & Club $$$
1300 Westhaven Drive
(970) 476-7111, (800) 282-4183
www.vailcascade.com
From the moment you pull under the valet canopy until the moment you load your luggage back into the trunk, it's apparent that the Cascade is one top-notch facility. The 396-room resort hotel and conference center has an almost psychic bell staff (they're always there when you need them), valet parking, an outdoor pool, two whirlpools, shops that include the Vail classic Pepi's, restaurants, and a popular lobby bar. The Cascade chairlift, which delivers guests to the Lionshead slopes, stops just steps from the door, giving new meaning to the phase "ski-in, ski-out." Also adjacent are a movie theater and a fitness center/spa so well equipped that locals line up to join. The rooms are about as plush as you can get, short of encrusting the ceiling with diamonds and jewels.

Vail Mountain Lodge $$$
352 East Meadow Drive
(970) 476-0700
(866) 476-0700 ext. 233
www.vailmountainlodge.com
The Vail Mountain Lodge is a prestigious address with a central Vail Village location, one of the town's best fitness centers, and a full-service spa. The small hotel has individually furnished rooms and suites, valet service, fitness classes, beauty treatments, a restaurant that specializes in healthy cuisine, a racquetball court, an indoor climbing wall, an indoor pool, a hot tub, a sauna, and a guest laundry.

CONDOS

Antlers at Vail $$$
680 West Lionshead Place
(970) 476-2471, (800) 825-8445
www.antlersvail.com
A sort of condo/hotel, the Antlers features 92 units that range in size from studios to three-bedrooms, all of which have full kitchens and balconies. The complex is adjacent to the Lionshead gondola and has a front desk, outdoor pool, hot tub, two saunas, and a guest laundry.

Evergreen Lodge $$$
250 South Frontage Road, West Vail
(970) 476-7810, (800) 284-8245
www.evergreenvail.com
Another of the economical treasures kept close to the vest by locals, the Evergreen has 128 one- to three-bedroom condos centrally located between Vail Village and Lionshead base areas. Amenities include a restaurant, an outdoor pool, hot tub, and sauna.

Manor Vail Resort $$$
595 Vail Valley Drive
(970) 476-5651, (888) 774-3533
www.manorvail.com
One of Vail's earliest condo units, the Manor Vail Resort sits at the base of Golden Peak base area. It has 123 units of various sizes, all with kitchens, fireplaces, and either balconies or patios. Amenities include a restaurant, lounge, outdoor pool, hot tub, and sauna.

Marriott's Streamside at Vail $$$
2264 South Frontage Road
(970) 476-6000, (877) 824-5386
www.marriott.com
This timeshare resort west of Vail has moderately priced studio to two-bedroom units, all with kitchens and all designed to be family friendly. Amenities include a clubhouse with nightly movies, a complimentary shuttle van, a pool, hot tubs, racquetball courts, and a game room.

Montaneros Condominiums   **$$$**
641 West Lionshead Circle
(970) 476–2491, (800) 444–8245
www.montaneros.com
Montaneros is known for its luxury condos
close to the Lionshead gondola. Its 42
rental units range in size from one to four
bedrooms, some of which have lofts. Con-
dos are individually decorated. Amenities
include an outdoor pool, hot tub, sauna,
restaurant, and guest laundry.

Mountain Haus   **$$$**
292 East Meadow Drive
(970) 476–2434, (800) 237–0922
www.montainhaus.com
Centrally located in Vail Village next to the
covered bridge, this property offers 10
hotel units and 64 one- to four-bedroom
condos, all of which are large and luxuriously furnished. The two-bedroom condos
come equipped with sofa sleepers, two
bathrooms, and attached ski storage
rooms. Amenities include TV/VCR/DVD
systems, fireplaces, kitchens, concierge
service, a fitness center, outdoor pool,
indoor and outdoor Jacuzzis, steam
rooms, and saunas.

Sandstone Creek Club   **$$$**
1020 Vail View Drive
(970) 476–4405, (800) 421–1098
www.sandstonecreek.com
These reasonable units are across the
highway from town, but they can sleep up
to 10 people. Amenities include a private
shuttle van, an indoor/outdoor pool, hot
tubs, a sauna, an exercise room, a rac-
quetball court, a game room, a billiard
room, a guest laundry, and a lounge.

Simba Run   **$$$**
1100 North Frontage Road
(970) 476–0344
www.simbarun.com
Also across the highway from town,
Simba Run has 60 well-furnished one- and
two-bedroom units, all with fireplaces.
Each is individually owned, so decor
varies. The units are large, have boot
heaters in the dining rooms, and are well

soundproofed. A private shuttle runs into
town during the winter months; summer
guests can catch the bus nearby. Amenities include a front desk and lobby, a large
indoor pool, an exercise facility, a hot tub,
and a steam room.

Vail International   **$$$**
300 East Lionshead Circle
(970) 476–0111, (800) 622–3477
www.vailinternational.com
Centrally located between Vail Village and
Lionshead, Vail International has 38 taste-
ful one- to three-bedroom condos at
some of Vail's most affordable prices.
Guests can take a short walk to lifts at
either base area. All units have fireplaces,
kitchens, balconies, and ski storage.
Amenities include a front desk, outdoor
pool, hot tub, saunas, and guest laundry.

Vail Racquet Club   **$$$**
4690 Vail Racquet Club Drive
(970) 476–4840, (800) 428–4840
www.vailracquetclub.com
These one- to three-bedroom condos are
large and on the bus route, off exit 180 in
East Vail, 4 miles from the action. Amenities include free use of the health and racquet club, front desk, concierge,
restaurant, lounge, and sauna.

BED-AND-BREAKFASTS

Savory Inn   **$$$**
2405 Elliott Road
(970) 476–1304, (866) 728–6794
www.savoryinn.com
The Savory Inn is 1½ miles west of Vail on
the town's bus route. This cozy, log bed-
and-breakfast has 12 rooms, all with pri-
vate baths and most with bay windows
that overlook the mountains. Each of the
rooms, which come with queen or twin
beds and down comforters, also has a
sleeper sofa. The walls are decorated with
the work of local artists. The ample lodge
building has huge Englemann spruce tim-
bers across the ceiling, and most of the
furniture is made in Colorado from pine
trees. Guests can enjoy solitude or sunny

afternoons on the streamside deck. Room rates include a full breakfast and afternoon snack. Breakfast incorporates a daily special with homemade bread, granola, fruit, and beverages. Amenities include a concierge, staffed front desk, and ski storage room.

Beaver Creek/Avon

Beaver Creek Lodge   **$$$**
26 Avondale Lane, Beaver Creek
(970) 845-9800, (800) 525-7280
www.beavercreeklodge.net
In the heart of Beaver Creek, this lodge is an all-suite property. The 72 rooms range in size from one- to five-bedrooms, all with fireplaces, log beds, living rooms with sofa sleepers, and microwave ovens. Amenities include an indoor/outdoor pool, a spa, a sauna, a steam room, a workout room, restaurants, lounges, and a hair salon.

The Charter at Beaver Creek   **$$$**
120 Offerson Road, Beaver Creek
(970) 949-6660, (800) 525-6660
www.thecharter.com
This large 155-unit complex offers units with one to five bedrooms. Amenities include a concierge, private shuttle van, restaurants, lounge, indoor pool, indoor and outdoor hot tubs, health club, and sauna.

Christie Lodge   **$$**
47 East Beaver Creek Boulevard, Avon
(970) 949-7700, (888) 325-6343
www.christielodge.com
This dorm-like condo project offers suites that are small but functional. The lodge is moderately priced and well-situated in Avon, the stopping-off point for many Beaver Creek skiers whose budgets don't allow for the expensive mountainside hotels. Christie Lodge units have kitchenettes and fireplaces. Guests have access to an indoor/outdoor heated pool, hot tubs, and a sauna. Guests also have

access to an athletic club, a restaurant, a lounge, and guest laundry.

Comfort Inn   **$$**
161 West Beaver Creek Boulevard, Avon
(970) 949-5511, (800) 423-4374
This chain hotel (142 rooms, four suites) is functional, economical, and reliable. The heated pool in the center of the complex is filled with children until it closes at 9:00 P.M. when the weather is nice. A complimentary continental breakfast is served in the lobby, a free ski shuttle takes guests to Beaver Creek, and the nearest restaurants are a short drive away.

Inn at Beaver Creek   **$$$**
10 Elk Track Road, Beaver Creek
(970) 845-7800, (800) 859-8242
www.vbcrp.com
Just beyond the core of the pedestrian village and alongside a Beaver Creek base area chairlift, the Inn has 37 rooms and eight suites. The lobby has two mammoth parlors on either side of a stone fireplace, making it an inviting spot for après-ski drinks. Amenities include a free continental breakfast, shuttle service to Vail, an outdoor pool, whirlpool, and indoor parking.

The Lodge and Spa at Cordillera   **$$$**
2205 Cordillera Way, Edwards
(970) 926-2200, (866) 732-7271
www.cordillera.rockresorts.com
The Lodge at Cordillera sits on 6,500 mountaintop acres overlooking Vail Valley. As such, it is one of the valley's most exclusive hotels and spas. It has only 56 rooms that surround an outdoor pool, an indoor lap pool, a well-equipped fitness center, and one of the fanciest spas in the region, not to mention the four golf courses that ring the property. A gate-controlled community of resort homes supports the golf clubs, but hotel guests are welcome to play the three 18-hole courses and the 9-hole design. Many lodge rooms have fireplaces, lofts, and balconies. During the winter, guests have access to miles of cross-country ski trails or can catch shuttles to Vail or Beaver

Creek ski areas. In summer, they can hike, bike, fly fish, or go rafting. The spa offers a full range of massage, hydrotherapy, facials, skin polishes, and salon services.

Park Hyatt Beaver Creek $$$
136 Thomas Place, Beaver Creek
(970) 949-1234, (800) 778-7477
www.beavercreekhyatt.com
The Park Hyatt Beaver Creek sets the standards for other mountain resorts throughout the country and is the hub of the village. Its 286 rooms and nine suites are spacious and luxuriously furnished in rich forest greens, reds, and cornflower blues. Skiers on Beaver Creek's lower slopes head straight toward the Hyatt's outdoor pool and grounds when they work their way down the runs. Hotel guests can ski to the lift lines. The lobby piano bar is a popular place during the afternoons and evenings, perhaps because the Park Hyatt employs a full-time fire tender to keep the fireplaces lit. Amenities include concierge, valet parking, fitness center with classes, full-service spa, indoor/outdoor pool, six hot tubs, restaurants, and a ski valet for storing skis and boots overnight. The Camp Hyatt program provides extensive day care and camping for children of all ages.

Park Plaza $$$
46 Avondale Lane, Beaver Creek
(970) 845-7700, (800) 528-7275
www.parkplazaabc.com
Beaver Creek's base area was designed around several ski-in, ski-out resorts, and the Park Plaza is one. One side faces the pedestrian plaza in the heart of the town; the other is adjacent to the Centennial Express chairlift. It has 36 good-size condos, all with marble fireplaces, TV/VCR setups, kitchens, washers and dryers, and whirlpool tubs in the master suites. The three-bedroom units have two masters, one upstairs and another on the ground floor. Amenities include a free continental breakfast in the winter, an indoor pool, a sauna, heated underground parking, and a restaurant.

The Pines Lodge $$$
141 Scott Hill Road, Beaver Creek
(970) 845-7900, (888) 367-7625
www.pineslodge.rockresorts.com
The Pines is known for its opulent decor, a level of service usually reserved for royalty, and its exquisite mountain views. It is near Chair 12, which provides a cross-resort ride to the base area. Each of the lodge's 60 rooms has a refrigerator, humidifier, hair dryer, and TV with VCR. Amenities include housekeepers who visit three times a day, free ski waxing, overnight laundry service, ski valet, après-ski snacks, afternoon tea, the Grouse Mountain Grill, a lounge, an outdoor pool, a whirlpool, saunas, fitness equipment, a business service center, and a library.

Poste Montane $$$
76 Avondale Lane, Beaver Creek
(970) 845-7500, (800) 497-9238
www.postemontane.com
A Beaver Creek classic, the Poste Montane is in the center of the village. Guests in the 24 rooms and three suites have access to an athletic club and outdoor pool as well as a concierge, sauna, Jacuzzi, and free continental breakfast. The lobby has leather couches and dark wood paneling. The rooms are done in deep, flowery tones.

SaddleRidge at Beaver Creek $$$
44 Meadow Lane, Beaver Creek
(970) 845-5450
www.vbcrp.com
Originally built as a private corporate conference center, SaddleRidge is now a classic New West guest complex with 12 two- and three-bedroom villas (only two of which are for rent). It was designed by Naomi Leff, who also designed Ralph Lauren's New York Polo store. It's not surprising, then, to see Ralph Lauren furnishings, western art, and Native American pottery. Guests can ski in but must take a short walk or a shuttle to the slopes. Other amenities include multi-line telephones, fireplaces, balconies, deluxe kitchens, bathrooms with steam showers and whirlpool tubs, fitness facilities, an on-site

massage therapist, an indoor/outdoor pool, a hot tub, a restaurant, and a lounge.

St. James Place $$$
210 Offerson Road, Beaver Creek
(970) 845-9300, (800) 626-7100
www.condobeavercreek.com
Luxury one- to three-bedroom units are offered in this timeshare complex centrally located in the Beaver Creek Village. All units have kitchens, gas fireplaces, stereos, VCRs, and humidifiers. Other amenities include a concierge, an indoor pool, indoor and outdoor hot tubs, fitness facilities, a sauna, and a steam room.

Trapper's Cabin $$$
Mountainside, Beaver Creek
(970) 845-5788, (888) 485-4317
www.trapperscabincolorado.com
Some people want their privacy badly enough to ski away from the crowds. For them, Trapper's Cabin may be just the thing. It's a four-bedroom cabin inaccessible except by skis or snowcat. It sleeps 10 and has no TV or phones. Guests ski in during the late afternoon and out again in the morning. Owners bring the luggage in, provide a private chef and helper who prepare, serve, and clean up after dinner and cocktails. They return in the morning for breakfast. Aside from kid-glove service, free lift tickets in the winter, and horses in the summer, the only other amenity is an outdoor hot tub.

RESTAURANTS

Vail

Blu's $$
193 Gore Creek Drive
(970) 476-3113
www.blusrestaurant.com
Locals are attracted to Blu's by the inexpensive menu; tourists go at least once during their stay because it has been recommended by a local. The casual place serves American cuisine but borrows from many other styles. Its menu features

penne and grilled chicken, for example, alongside Jamaican shrimp, fantastic Thai curry beef, gypsy schnitzel, and mustard pepper steak. Reservations are not accepted, so go early enough to put your name on the waiting list. Blu's attracts a crowd, especially during high seasons.

Game Creek Club $$$$
Vail Resort, on Vail Mountain
(970) 479-4275
www.gamecreekclub.com
Vail homeowners may pay an initiation fee that rivals a new car sticker price plus annual dues to belong to this exclusive luncheon club, but tourists pony up for the chance to have dinner here. Those who do so make an evening of it. To reach the club, they must ride the Eagle Bahn gondola to Eagles Nest and then take a snowcat-drawn sleigh to the structure in the Game Creek Bowl. Once there, they're treated to spectacular Rocky Mountain views, live dinner music, and a multi-course gourmet meal. The menu is limited to nightly specials such as grilled venison loin or grilled vegetable ravioli, but a full bar and good wine list augment it. Reservations are required.

Kelly Liken $$$-$$$$
12 Vail Road, Suite 100
(970) 479-0175
www.kellyliken.com
Named for the chef/owner, this new star has made a name for itself by serving what it calls seasonal American cuisine. That translates into meals made from fresh, seasonal ingredients, often grown in Colorado. The intimate dining room seats 72, with a 15-seat wine bar. Extra touches include a free valet service, a welcome bonus in a town known for its lack of parking. Kelly Liken, the chef, graduated from the Culinary Institute of America and worked at Beaver Creek's delicious Splendido at the Chateau before opening her own place. Among the dishes that have brought her national press are the blue cheese tart with gooseberry conserve, the Colorado wildflower-honey glazed duck breast, and, for

Mountain chefs provide an amazingly sophisticated array of dishes, sometimes from restaurants that look like renovated miner cabins. VAIL IMAGE/JACK AFFLECK

dessert, sticky buns with vanilla-bean ice cream and spun sugar.

Lancelot $$
201 Gore Creek Drive
(970) 476-5828
www.lancelotinn.com
Although Lancelot made its name serving prime rib, after over 30 yeas it now offers a wider menu. Locals rub elbows with tourists in the popular dining room, eating steaks, rainbow trout, rack of lamb, and broiled chicken breast along with three different cuts of prime rib. The house salad is a delicious Caesar. Reservations are recommended.

The Left Bank $$$
Sitzmark Lodge, 183 Gore Creek Drive
(970) 476-3696
www.leftbankvail.com
Known for its French cuisine, this comfort-able bistro has been around long enough to become a Vail classic. It's centrally located in Vail Village, overlooks Gore Creek, and is known for the kid-glove treatment given to diners. Specialties are airy soufflés, veal, and elk steaks. Reservations are recommended as much as two weeks in advance during ski season. The Left Bank doesn't accept credit cards and is closed on Wednesdays.

Los Amigos $$
400 Bridge Street
(970) 476-5847
Vail's best Mexican restaurant is located conveniently at the top of Bridge Street in the Vail Village. From the grill you can get flavorful fajitas or pollo fiesta, while specials include chicken-stuffed tacos blancos and enchiladas especial del azul, made of blue-corn tortillas. Dinner is served until 10:00 P.M.

Pazzo's Pizzeria $
122 East Meadow Drive
(970) 476-9026

Tourists may be reluctant to enter this loud, funky little pizza place . . . unless their noses lead them. This local favorite has killer pizza and an up-to-date music collection. Look for the Grateful Dead-style skeleton patterns on the wall tiles. It's at the end of the Vail Village pedestrian mall, across the street from the parking garage.

Red Lion $$
304 Bridge Street
(970) 476-7676
www.theredlion.com

Stop for a burger, barbecue, or a plate of nachos big enough to feed four. The Red Lion is a fixture on Vail's busy Bridge Street and, even better, has both inside and outside seating. The bar may be a bigger attraction; read more about it in the "Nightlife" section.

Sweet Basil $$$
193 Gore Creek Drive
(970) 476-0125
www.sweetbasil-vail.com

In the heart of Vail Village on a pedestrian-only street, Sweet Basil is nondescript enough from the outside to walk right past. Don't let that fool you. Inside, the restaurant is larger than life. The bouquets and abstract art are a subtle backdrop to the star of the show—new American cuisine well known in restaurant circles from coast to coast. Expect such unusual pairings as chanterelle mashed potatoes and warm spinach salad, almond-crusted rack of lamb with shiitake potstickers, and mahogany sauce. Favorite dishes include a portobello mushroom and goat cheese tart appetizer, grilled quail salad with white beans, pears, and saga bleu cheese, and pistachio-crusted pork chops with spaetzle and apricot fig sauce. For dessert, try the Tahitian vanilla crème brulée in a phyllo shell. Reservations can be hot tickets during the ski season, so book them early.

Terra Bistro $$$
Vail Mountain Lodge and Spa
352 East Meadow Drive
(970) 476-6836
www.vailmountainlodge.com/terra

When the restaurant sits inside the Vail Mountain Lodge and Spa you can be fairly sure the food will be fresh and good for you. That's the case with Terra Bistro, a contemporary, elegant place that specializes in fresh, organic food. Locals go there when they're in the mood for something light that will make them feel good on the way out. Vegetarians love it, too, for its wide selection of meat-free dishes. Among the favorites are coriander-rubbed tuna; Greek penne with zucchini, garlic cloves, olives, feta cheese, basil, and sundried-tomato pesto; and sweet potato-poblano ravioli with Gorgonzola vinaigrette and toasted walnuts.

Vendetta's $$
291 Bridge Street
(970) 476-5070

There are two choices at Vendetta's—casual bar dinners upstairs in the Bridge Street pizza bar, and fine Northern Italian dining downstairs. Diners enter the latter through a mirrored tunnel that takes them to the casual but elegant dining room. There they can order fried calamari, bruschetta, pastas with any of seven different sauces, or house specialties such as veal piccata and boneless chicken breast stuffed with provolone, spinach, and herb-garlic butter served with roasted potatoes. The pizza upstairs is served late into the evening and can be delivered anywhere in Vail Village. Dinner reservations are recommended downstairs.

Beaver Creek/Avon

Beano's Cabin $$$
Mountainside, Beaver Creek
(970) 949-9090

This rustic log cabin in Beaver Creek Mountain's Larkspur Bowl can be reached one of two ways: in the winter in a sleigh drawn by snowcat, and in summer on horseback. So why would anyone endure such obstacles just for dinner? Because Beano's Cabin is exclusive (it's a private lunch club open only to members) and because it's a once-in-a-lifetime experience. The six-course dinner awaiting guests features steak, lamb, chicken, or fish; soup of the day; and exquisite desserts. Guests are ferried in, fed, entertained, and then ferried back home. There are two seatings at night, and reservations are required.

Grouse Mountain Grill $$$
141 Scott Hill Road, Beaver Creek
(970) 949-0600

The Grouse Mountain Grill describes its food as "Mountain Style American," heavy on the "mountain." That's because this posh dining room is perched above Beaver Creek Village, in The Pines luxury lodge. A fireplace, panoramic views, and live nightly dinner music complete the package. The food itself consists of creatively prepared steaks, seafood, pastas, and game. Specialties include a locally raised Limousin beef tenderloin steak and double-cut pork chop with tomato-apple chutney and pickled fig. Reservations are recommended.

Mirabelle $$$
55 Village Road, near Beaver
Creek entrance
(970) 949-7728
www.mirabelle1.com

In 1902 this homestead was billed as the biggest residence in Avon. Today it's home to some of the best French cuisine in the Vail Valley. Locals consider it a fancy place to take a date or celebrate an anniversary. Tourists enjoy the blend of flavors and textures created by Belgian chef Daniel Joly. Among their favorites are the lightly spiced crab egg roll with red ginger, rice vinegar, and baby green salad; free-range chicken breast with roasted Provençal eggplant "Charlotte" and jus de viande; and slow-roasted Mediterranean vegetables with quinoa seed and confit, garlic, and basil oil. No credit cards are

accepted, and Mirabelle is closed Mondays. Reservations are recommended.

Pazzo's Pizzeria $
82 East Beaver Creek Boulevard, Avon
(970) 949-9900

This funky pizza bar is a favorite of locals and young Beaver Creek employees who like their meals more casual than in that ritzy resort. At least four TV sets are tuned to ESPN, while the stereo blasts music geared to those in their 20s and 30s. A funky painting of snowy mountains covers one wall, with a Mexican desert seashore on the other. There are almost as many seats at the bar as at tables. Pizzas can be as simple as cheese and pepperoni or as interesting as feta with jalapeños. The menu also includes pasta, lasagna, and calzones.

Splendido $$$
17 Chateau Lane, Beaver Creek
(970) 845-8808
www.splendidobeavercreek.com

Splendido is the house restaurant at the Chateau, a private residence club that rides high on the hillside above Beaver Creek, so that should explain some things. The decor, for example, is early Roman Empire, with marble columns, statues, and tables covered with handmade linens. Guests will also pass an elegant piano bar on the way into the restaurant; some even arrive early so they can relax before dinner. Once inside, they're treated to the new American cuisine of executive chef David Walford. Among the nightly menu offerings are the jumbo lump blue crab cake with chervil-lemon butter sauce; wood-oven-roasted Colorado rack of lamb with rosemary olive sauce, ratatouille, and parsley-garlic potatoes; and warm gingerbread pudding with spice poached pear and eggnog ice cream.

traMonti $$$
120 Offerson Road, Beaver Creek
(970) 949-5552
www.thecharter.com

In the Charter lodge, traMonti is classic

Italian cuisine with a Colorado twist. All pasta and risotto dishes are offered in either appetizer or entree portions. Pizzas are presented with duck confit, red pepper, basil, and feta rather than just tomato sauce and cheese. Pasta dishes include linguine with shrimp, sun-dried peppers, and goat cheese. Meats to follow the pasta course include veal, pork tenderloin, and red snapper. During winter months the traMonti also hosts a piano bar that draws locals as well as tourists.

Minturn

Minturn Country Club $$
131 Main Street
(970) 827-4114
Minturn has gotten the reputation as a funky nook of off-the-beaten-path drinking and dining fun, and in that context, the Minturn Country Club may be one of the most unusual restaurants. Diners belly up to the meat market where they pick their own steak, kabob meat, fish, or chicken. Then they grill it to their own tastes over a charcoal grill. Some folks think it's fun; others wonder why they're out to dinner if they have to cook for themselves. During the ski season, diners are packed in elbow-to-elbow.

The Turntable $
160 Railroad Road
(970) 827-4164
An old Rio Grande engine turntable used to sit across the road from this diner, but it was removed after trains stopped traveling through Minturn. Now the artifacts displayed on the Turntable's walls are all that remain of those days. The diner is known for its hearty breakfasts, especially the Baby Boo Burrito, a mass of eggs, cheese, salsa, and beans. It also serves burgers and Mexican food after 11:00 A.M. A side room is decorated like an ice cream parlor and shake shop, with soda fountain, Betty Boop, and Wiggling Pelvis Elvis clocks.

The service can be slow, but kids love looking at the paraphernalia and watching the model train circle the restaurant.

Edwards

Fiesta's $
57 Edwards Access Road
(970) 926-2121
If you don't mind driving 30 minutes west of Vail, Fiesta's fixes up great Tex-Mex food at reasonable prices. Vail Valley locals often head this direction to escape the tourist crowds. Among the favorites are an award-winning green chile, white jalapeño sauce, cinnamon sopapillas, and hit-the-spot margaritas.

NIGHTLIFE
Vail

Altitude Billiards and Sports
250 South Frontage Road, West Vail
(970) 479-6137
Locals love the bar in the Evergreen Lodge because it has a satellite link that broadcasts to 14 televisions scattered through the room. They tend to congregate there to watch playoff games, hockey tournaments, boxing matches, and any other sporting events that capture their imagination. Between games they keep the pool tables busy. The crowd is mostly local, although an occasional tourist sometimes stumbles in.

Bully Ranch
20 Vail Road
(970) 476-5656
Although located in the Sonnenalp resort hotel, Bully Ranch is a favorite after-work hangout for local professionals who work in Vail Village. The bar is large, uncrowded, and has a nice rustic, old-time western motif with wooden barstools.

The Club
304 Bridge Street
(970) 479-0556

At the top of Bridge Street in Vail Village, The Club is one of the town's rowdiest nightspots. Stairs lead down from street level into an exposed-brick basement like those found on many college campuses. Local singers and guitar players entertain most nights; the crowds join in by dancing and singing along. It appeals to the young and active—the music is loud enough and the air smoky enough that older crowds go elsewhere.

Fireside Bar
1300 Westhaven Drive
(970) 476-7111

If you're staying in Cascade Village at the west end of Vail, the Fireside Bar at the Vail Cascade Hotel is a pleasant place to spend the evening. There's usually live music, and if that's not enough, the bar has a fireplace and picture windows that look out onto Gore Creek.

Garfinkel's
536 East Lionshead Circle
(970) 476-3789
www.garfsvail.com

Skiers who pack the Lionshead slopes gravitate at the end of the day to Garfinkel's, well located at the bottom of the lifts. It's a perfect place to meet people and sit on the deck when the sun is shining. Later in the evening a younger, grungier snowboard crowd takes over the bar and the pool tables.

The King's Club
20 Vail Road
(970) 476-5656

This genteel place in the Sonnenalp Resort serves high tea, cocktails, and the music of Don Watson. Locals view the King's Club as an intimate place to sit, relax, have a hot toddy, and chat with old friends.

Los Amigos
400 Bridge Street
(970) 476-5847

Right at the base of the Vista Bahn gondola on Vail mountain, Los Amigos is the logical first stop for après-ski action. Its outdoor deck faces up the slopes and is great for people-watching. It's a great place to have a margarita or two, nibble some chips and salsa, and maybe even stay for a Mexican dinner.

Mickey's
174 Gore Creek Drive
(970) 476-5011

The Lodge at Vail has been attracting guests to its civilized resort since the town of Vail was a newcomer. Mickey Poage has been entertaining those guests nearly as long. He plays piano in the bar that bears his name, attracting primarily older visitors who come year after year to hear his music.

The Red Lion
304 Bridge Street
(970) 476-7676

This is People Watching Central, elevated just enough to give the best view in town of Vail Village's pedestrian heart. The outdoor porch can be walled in during the winter or open in the summer. Guests who sit outside on the weekends can sing along to live music, eat burgers, watch the pedestrians, or go inside to watch sports on TV.

Sarah's
356 Hanson Ranch Road
(970) 476-5641

This room at the Christiania Lodge is a sentimental favorite, largely because of Helmut Fricker. For years he has played the pipes and the accordion, yodeled, and supplied the older tourists with lively oompah music. He's still a draw to "the older tourists who want to get the Vail experience," as one local describes it. Fricker only entertains during the winter months.

The Tap Room
333 Bridge Street
(970) 479-0500
www.taproomvail.com

The Tap Room has served diners since 2000, but its companion nightclub, Sanctuary, is a favorite place for locals to party. It has two cocktail bars, a fireside lounge, two VIP suites, a thumping sound system, and a penthouse dance floor.

Vendetta's
291 Bridge Street
(970) 476-5070

Well-situated across the street from the Red Lion, Vendetta's is a favorite late-night stop for partiers who need refueling. Downstairs is an elegant restaurant. The upstairs bar serves draft beer and pizza until 2:00 A.M. and often sweetens the pot with live music.

Beaver Creek/Avon

The Coyote Cafe
45 West Thomas Place, Beaver Creek
(970) 845-9030

If you ski at Beaver Creek, you can't miss this ski and sports bar as you walk down

The Town of Avon may have the nation's only bridge named Bob. City officials built it across the Eagle River in 1992 as part of roadway improvements that eased gridlock on the town's main thoroughfare, Avon Road. But once it was built, they couldn't agree what to call it. Merchants held a contest and chose the plainest name they could find. Residents embraced the name so much they staged a whimsical Bob festival. Over the years War, the Freddy Jones Band, Julian Lennon, and Soul Asylum entertained festival goers, but eventually the party ran out of steam. Bob the Bridge is still there, however, and tourists often take their pictures with it.

from the slopes. It's a favorite after-work spot for Beaver Creek employees as well as a lively après-ski spot for tourists. The specialty of the house is Mexican food, and it's part of the famous Santa Fe-based chain founded by legendary chef Mark Miller.

The Saloon
146 North Main Street, Minturn
(970) 827-5954

During the winter months, the Saloon, officially called the Saloon Across the Street from the Eagle River Motel, will always have at least 20 pairs of skis lined up outside. That's because it's best known as a warming stop for out-of-bounds skiers who have just completed the infamous Minturn Mile course. Maybe because these hardy skiers are game for anything, or maybe because they're just glad they made it down the mountain alive, the bar is the site of some serious, get-down partying. The rustic walls are covered with autographed photos of celebrities, skis, a kayak, and even a buffalo head. The huge fireplace makes a great focal point for eating nachos and drinking margaritas.

ATTRACTIONS

Beaver Creek Rodeo Series
Berry Creek Ranch
454 Edwards Access Road, Edwards
(970) 845-9090

Visitors can enjoy the bronc bustin', barrel racin', and steer tyin' the West is known for every Thursday evening from Memorial Day through September. Family-style barbecue dinners are served at 6:00 P.M. The rodeo starts at 7:00 P.M. Make sure to come early for some honest-to-goodness barbecue.

Betty Ford Alpine Gardens
183 Gore Creek Drive, next to the Gerald R. Ford Amphitheater, Vail
(970) 476-0103
www.bettyfordalpinegardens.org

The highest alpine garden in the world (at

Summers can be painfully short in Colorado's high country, but they are glorious while they last. VAIL IMAGE/JACK AFFLECK

an altitude of 8,200 feet), this is an oasis of forsythia, heather, wild roses, and shrubs planted among the 1,500 varieties in three small gardens. The Mountain Meditation Garden follows the Easter tradition of making water and rock the primary focal points of a peaceful, tranquil retreat for quiet contemplation. Several workshops and lectures about high-altitude plants are hosted during June when the gardens sponsor the Vail Valley Festival of Flowers. It's within walking distance of the Vail Nature Center and is open from snowmelt to snowfall, dawn to dusk. Admission is free. The gardens are named for former First Lady Betty Ford, a part-time resident of Vail, in honor of her contributions to the town.

Centennial Express Chairlift
Base of Beaver Creek Ski Resort (behind the Park Hyatt Beaver Creek)
(970) 845-5200
www.beavercreek.snow.com
An open-air ride to the top of the mountain takes 15 minutes each way. At the top you can stroll through a replica of a ghost town. From mid-June through summer, you can lunch at the Spruce Saddle Lodge between 10:00 A.M. and 3:00 P.M. or rent mountain bikes and ride down (12 and older). Many people enjoy the 4⁸⁄₁₀ mile walk down the mountain. Hours in the summer are 9:30 A.M. to 4:30 P.M. and in the winter from 8:30 A.M. to 3:45 P.M. It's closed mid-April to mid-June and Labor Day to about Thanksgiving.

Colorado Ski Museum
231 South Frontage Road East, in the Vail Village Transportation Center
(970) 476-1876
www.skimuseum.com
This little building holds 130 years of skiing history as well as the Ski Hall of Fame. You'll see old-fashioned ski gear and clothing, old chairlifts, and classic ski films that play in the background. An entire room is devoted to the 10th Mountain Division, soldiers who did snow training

nearby during World War II. It's a good way to spend a rainy summer afternoon or a lazy winter day. The museum is open 10:00 A.M. to 5:00 P.M. Tuesday through Sunday. It's closed May and October except by appointment. Admission is free.

4 Eagle Ranch
U.S. Highway 131, 4 miles north of I-70
Wolcott
(970) 926-3372
www.4eagleranch.com
During summer months, tourists can swarm all over this genuine, Old West working ranch. See the baby buffalo and other ranch animals, use the playground, play horseshoes, or watch the blacksmith for free. Parent-led pony rides are available for children 6 and younger, for a nominal fee. Hayrides, horseback riding, raft trips, cattle roundups, live entertainment, and western barbecue dinners charge fees. (Call for prices, as they vary by time and season.) Reservations are required for horseback riding. On winter Tuesdays and Thursdays, midday sleigh rides carry visitors around the property while hay is dropped for the horses.

Lionshead Gondola
The Village at Lionshead, Vail
(970) 476-9090
www.vail.snow.com
Ride inside heated cars to Adventure Ridge, an on-mountain activities center. During the winter it features tubing, ice skating, snowmobile tours, and dining. Some people just like to ride the gondola for the sake of riding. During the summer the area provides beautiful hiking and exploring areas, as well as casual restaurants. The gondola runs daily mid-June to mid-September from 10:00 A.M. to 4:30 P.M., weekends only for a few weeks before and after, then again during ski season.

Piney River Ranch
Forest Service Road 700, 15 miles north of Vail
(303) 707-1576
www.pineyriverranch.com

Summer months are spectacular at this secluded lakefront ranch. It includes a 60-acre lake, 100 miles of maintained hiking and biking trails, log cabins, teepees, tents, and a yurt for camping. The lake can be used for canoeing and is stocked for fishing. A Colorado fishing license is required. The Family Day package includes a horseback ride, canoeing on the lake, and lunch, and reservations are required. The ranch also offers guided ATV and horseback tours. On Tuesday and Wednesday evenings there is a classic Wild West Shootout and Barbecue dinner show, always a favorite with dudes and tenderfoots. During the winter the ranch is a hub for hunting outfitters (see our "Fishing and Hunting" section for details), offering exclusive access to private land elk hunting on 163,000 acres of wilderness. Also during the winter snowmobile tours are available, including lunch, dinner, and starlight trips of varying lengths. Round-trip transportation is free from properties in Vail, Avon, and Beaver Creek, but a 10 percent discount is offered if you drive yourself up to the ranch.

Vail Nature Center
831 Vail Valley Drive, Vail
(970) 479-2291
www.gorerange.org/vail_center
On Gore Creek near Ford Park, this center specializes in introducing mountain visitors to the many natural wonders of the valley. Daily wildflower tours led by expert guides are available. Hour-long tours focus on identifying indigenous plant life, flora, and fauna, with special attention to growth, medicinal values, and folklore. More ambitious hikers can take all-day hikes to the top of a different regional peak twice a week. Notch Mountain Hike is 9 miles through several microclimates to a 13,000-foot finish, past windflowers and edible berries. Other programs feature moonlight hikes, bird walks, and riverbed ecology tours. Naturalists take morning walks along the banks of Gore Creek and discuss aspects of a healthy river system, including talks on where and how trout

spend their time and the flies that hatch in this alpine river climate. The afternoon is then spent fly fishing on the river with an experienced guide. The nature center is open from 9:00 A.M. to 5:00 P.M. daily Memorial Day through September. Admission is free, except for special programs.

Vail Wildlife Center
At the top of the Lionshead Gondola
Vail
(970) 476-9090
A small hut hosts a wildlife center directly in front of the gondola exit. It features several interactive displays on wildlife and local flowers. In conjunction with the U.S. Forest Service, the Colorado Division of Wildlife and Vail Associates, it offers guided tours twice a day, usually from 11:00 A.M. to noon and from 1:00 to 2:00 P.M. Hikes are easy, and guides talk about local history. This is not recommended for children younger than 6.

Vista Bahn Chairlift
At the base of Vail Village, Vail
(970) 476-9090
Enjoy this high-speed ride halfway up Vail Mountain. Ride your bike, hike the trail down, or take a round-trip scenic ride. Details about the trails and difficulty, etc., are available in brochures at any information booth. Cook Shack restaurant serves lunch, although it's expensive. The lift operates from the first weekend in July through the first week of September daily from 10:00 A.M. to 4:30 P.M. and then again during the ski season.

KIDSTUFF

Avon Recreation Center
325 Benchmark Road, Avon
(970) 748-4060
www.avon.org/reccenter.cfm
A great bad-weather destination as well as a cool way to beat the midsummer heat, this center has four different kinds of indoor swimming pools (laps, kids, diving, and leisure) and a slide that towers 142

feet above the water. If the kids are old enough, parents can park them by the water while they're using the workout facilities. It's open 6:00 A.M. to 9:00 P.M. weekdays, 8:00 A.M. to 9:00 P.M. weekends.

Beaver Creek Children's Theatre
Pedestrian Plaza, Beaver Creek
(970) 845-9090
A troupe of professional performers roams the plaza performing children's poems, fairy tales, and folk tales. Parents and children can join in if they want. Performances take place from mid-June to mid-September Wednesday through Saturday. Hours vary; check once you're in town. There is no admission fee.

Centennial Express Chairlift
Base of Beaver Creek Ski Resort
Beaver Creek
(970) 845-5200
An scenic, open-air ride to the top of the mountain takes 15 minutes each way. At the top you can stroll through a replica of a ghost town. From mid-June through summer, you can lunch at the Spruce Saddle Lodge between 10:00 A.M. and 3:00 P.M. or rent mountain bikes for those 12 and older who want to ride back down. Many people enjoy the 4.8-mile walk down the mountain. The chairlift operates in the summer from 9:30 A.M. to 4:30 P.M. and in the winter from 8:30 A.M. to 3:45 P.M. It's closed mid-April to mid-June and Labor Day to about Thanksgiving.

Colorado Ski Museum
231 South Frontage Road East, in the
Vail Village Transportation Center
(970) 476-1876
www.skimuseum.com
This little building holds 130 years of skiing history as well as the Ski Hall of Fame. You'll see old-fashioned ski gear and clothing, old chairlifts, and classic ski films that play in the background. An entire room is devoted to the 10th Mountain Division, soldiers who did snow training nearby during World War II. It's a good way to spend a rainy summer afternoon

or a lazy winter day. The museum is open 10:00 A.M. to 5:00 P.M. Tuesday through Sunday. It's closed in May and October except by appointment. Admission is free.

Dobson Ice Arena
321 West Lionshead Circle, Vail
(970) 479-2270
When the kids get too hot in the summer or too cold in the winter, take them indoors for an ice-skating reprieve. Public hours vary because they're built around hockey games, lessons, and special events, so call ahead for times. The arena is closed in May

Ford Park and Gore Creek School
¼ mile east of Vail's main village, near
the Gerald R. Ford Amphitheater, Vail
Sometimes a kid just has to swing. When the urge hits in East Vail, head to the playground in this park for a ride in the tire swing, an imaginary battle in the fort, and a stroll through the one-room school built in 1922 that served all kids in the valley. Vail officials brought a gaggle of kids on a tour of local parks and used their input to revamp the entire Ford Park play area, making it a "showcase" park.

4 Eagle Ranch
US 131, 4 miles north of I-70, Wolcott
(970) 926-3372
www.4eagleranch.com
During summer months, tourists can swarm all over this genuine, Old West working ranch. Guests can see the baby buffalo and other ranch animals, use the playground, play horseshoes, or watch the blacksmith for free. Parent-led pony rides are available for children 6 and younger for a nominal fee. Hayrides, horseback riding, raft trips, cattle roundups, live entertainment, and western barbecue dinners cost money. (Call for prices, as they vary by time and season.) Reservations are required for horseback riding. Tuesday and Thursday, midday sleigh rides carry visitors around the property while hay is dropped for the horses.

Lionshead Gondola
The Village at Lionshead, Vail
(970) 476-9090
www.vail.snow.com

Ride inside heated cars to Adventure Ridge, an on-mountain activities center. During the winter it features tubing, ice skating, snowmobile tours, and dining (see our "Other Winter Recreation" section), although some people just like to ride for the sake of riding. During summer, the area provides beautiful hiking and exploring and casual restaurants. It's open daily mid-June to mid-September from 10:00 A.M. to 4:30 P.M., weekends only for a few weeks before and after, then again during ski season.

Nottingham Park
I-70 west to Avon/Beaver Creek exit
Avon
(970) 748-4000

Nottingham Lake is the center of this 48-acre enclave, so activities are heavy on kayaking and fishing in the summer, ice skating in the winter. Landlubbers can skate, bike, and play everything from horseshoes to soccer. You can rent all the gear you need at the Log Cabin: paddleboats, canoes, kayaks, and in-line skates. All incidentals, including croquet sets, footballs, basketballs, flying disks, horseshoes, soccer balls, tennis racquets, are $1.00. Mountain bikes and helmets also are available, and fishing in the stocked lake is allowed from shore during boating hours or from the dock before 10:00 A.M. and after 8:00 P.M. Licensees are required. Open Memorial Day to Labor Day, 10:00 A.M. to 8:00 P.M. daily.

Piney River Ranch
Forest Road 700, 15 miles north of Vail
(970) 477-1171
www.pineyriverranch.com

Summer months are spectacular at this secluded lakefront ranch. It includes a 60-acre lake, 100 miles of maintained hiking and biking trails, log cabins, teepees, tents, and a yurt for camping. The lake can be used for canoeing and is stocked for fishing. A Colorado fishing license is required. The Family Day package includes a horseback ride, canoeing on the lake, and lunch, and reservations are required. The ranch also offers guided ATV and horseback tours. On Tuesday and Wednesday evenings there is a classic Wild West Shootout and Barbecue dinner show, always a favorite with dudes and tenderfoots. During the winter the ranch is a hub for hunting outfitters (see our "Fishing and Hunting" section for details), offering exclusive access to private land elk hunting on 163,000 acres of wilderness. Also during the winter snowmobile tours are available, including lunch, dinner, and starlight trips of varying lengths. Round-trip transportation is free from properties in Vail, Avon, and Beaver Creek, but a 10 percent discount is offered if you drive yourself up to the ranch.

Pirate Ship Park
At the base of the Vista Bahn ski lift
Vail

While the adults shop in Vail Village, kids can play their hearts out in this park, named for the ship that anchors it. Best of all, it's free—a rarity in pricey Vail.

Vail Nature Center
601 Vail Valley Drive, Vail
(970) 479-2291
www.gorerange.org/vail_center

Although primarily an adult attraction, this center is adjacent to the Betty Ford Alpine Gardens and has a small museum and easy hiking trails alongside the river that may be of interest to children. Museum exhibits include animal pelts, bird nests, stuffed birds, and butterfly displays. Kids also like the beaver pond walk, which takes them to see real beaver habitats. The center's hours are from 9:00 A.M. to 5:00 P.M. daily, from Memorial Day through September. Admission is free, although fees are charged for special programs. (Also see the listing in our "Attractions" section.)

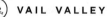

Vail Public Library
292 West Meadow Drive, Vail
(970) 479-2185
Another rainy-day location kids may not think of, this library has a self-contained playroom with train sets, play equipment, and a cozy reading room. Younger kids can show up for biweekly story hours; their computer-savvy older siblings have access to computers with games galore. You can't check out books unless you're a resident, but you can do everything else. Hours are Monday to Thursday, 10:00 A.M. to 8:00 P.M.; Friday through Sunday 11:00 A.M. to 6:00 P.M. Toddler story hours are 10:00 A.M. Tuesday and Wednesday; pre-school story hours are 11:00 A.M. Tuesday and Wednesday. Admission is free.

Vista Bahn Chairlift
At the base of Vail Village, Vail
(970) 476-9090
Take a high-speed ride halfway up Vail Mountain. Bring your bike, hike the trail down, or take a round-trip scenic ride. Details about the trails and difficulty, etc., are available in brochures at any information booth. Cook Shack restaurant serves lunch, although it's expensive. The lift operates from the first weekend in July through the first week of September daily from 10:00 A.M. to 4:30 P.M. and then again during the ski season.

Summer Camps

Camp Vail and Pre-camp Vail for Kids
Gold Peak Children's Center, at the base of Gold Peak, Vail
(970) 479-2290
www.vailrec.com/camp_day_vail.htm
Run by the Vail Recreation District, this camp serves kids ages 2½ to 12 years. It features outdoor games, hikes, arts and crafts, and field trips to local sites. Hours are 7:30 A.M. to 5:30 P.M. weekends. Prices are about on par for typical day care, with five-day packages available. Occasional night hikes, backpacking trips, and overnights are scheduled throughout the summer. Call for details. The Center also offers Friday night fun, including movies and activities from 5:30 to 11:00 P.M.

Park Hyatt Regency
136 Thomas Place, Beaver Creek
(970) 949-1234
A special Camp Hyatt is available for kids year-round, in groups for ages 3 to 12. Younger campers fish, hike, explore, sled, cook, swim, ice skate, do arts and crafts, and go to the park. Hours are 9:00 A.M. to 10:00 P.M. in the winter; 9:00 A.M. to 4:00 P.M. Monday through Wednesday and 9:00 A.M. to 10:00 P.M. Thursday through Sunday in the summer.

SHOPPING

Many of Vail's wealthier visitors come here just to shop and be seen, then move on to Aspen for more of the same. You'll find dozens of exclusive boutiques that cater to them, carrying exclusive items with price tags too hefty for locals or the average tourist. Shopping in late September and October can help. Vail holds an annual sidewalk sale in October to help stores clear out old merchandise and make room for the new. Spring sales in March and April also clear out leftover ski things, but the biggest price cuts come in the fall, just before store owners take a month off to recuperate before the ski season begins again. Interesting stores dot the entire town of Vail, but the best are congregated along the central pedestrian mall, the Crossroads Shopping Center, and in Beaver Creek along the Promenade. Some retailers maintain two shops, one in Vail and the other in Beaver Creek. Stores in West Vail are less glamorous and more geared toward locals, as are the stores in Avon, which provide your last stop before entering the rarefied air of Beaver Creek.

American Ski Exchange and Rentals
225 Wall Street, Vail
(970) 476-1477
www.vailskishop.com

You can rent everything from skis to clothing at this handy rental store just steps from the Vail Village ticket window. You can also buy hats, gloves, goggles, or any other ski necessity you've forgotten to pack. Reserve your rentals ahead of time by calling (800) 327–1137.

Annie's
100 East Meadow Drive, Vail
(970) 476–4197
A local institution, this store is a home-grown kind of Williams-Sonoma, with kitchen accessories and treats for the person who loves to cook.

Cogswell Gallery
223 Gore Creek Drive, Vail
(970) 476–1769
www.cogswellgallery.com
With a distinctive collection of western art, this place offers the ambiance of Santa Fe. Check out the paintings, furniture, pottery, sculpture, and weavings.

The Englishman
143 East Meadow Drive, Vail
(970) 476–3570
Specializing in 18th- and 19th-century European art and antiquities, this shop is like going into some of the world's finest museums, and priced to match. Also has access to an impressive amount of antique European furnishings.

Fly Fishing Outfitters
1060 West Beaver Creek Boulevard
Avon
(970) 845–8090
www.flyfishingoutfitters.net
A tackle shop and guide service rolled into one, Fly Fishing Outfitters is the valley's only Orvis supplier. It also carries clothing, gifts, artwork, books, and luggage geared toward anglers. It's open year-round and offers weekend fly-casting clinics.

The Golden Bear
Bridge Street, Vail
(970) 476–4082
www.thegoldenbear.com

At this store in the pedestrian hub of Vail, clothing and jewelry are treated as art forms. The golden bear charm originally designed here has become a signature of Vail, a sleek, rounded creature with a chain threaded invisibly through his back. Inside the store, expect to see it in all sizes and a variety of materials tucked into the tasteful glass-covered displays.

Gorsuch, Ltd.
263 Gore Creek Drive, Vail
(970) 476–2294

70 Promenade, Beaver Creek
(970) 949–7115
The Vail institution offers everything from alpaca sweaters to buffalo coats and pottery to potpourri. It's such a trendsetter in the world of ski shops that, at markets, smaller retailers follow the Gorsuch buyer for hints on what to order.

Pepi Sports
231 Bridge Street, Vail
(970) 476–5202

1300 Westhaven Drive, Vail
(970) 479–7053
www.pepisports.com
One of the town's toniest ski shops, Pepi's is known among the international crowd as the place to go for glamorous designer goods, many with a western flair. Shoppers don't bat an eyelash over such things as $1,000 ski outfits and $200 gold-sequined cowboy hats, for example.

Roxy
172 Gore Creek Drive, Vail
(970) 476–7774

50 Promenade, Beaver Creek
(970) 845–7774
Even people who shop in Vail need real clothes occasionally too. Those with the cash to do so shop here. Roxy stocks such things as slacks and sweaters, bathrobes, and lingerie.

A Secret Garden
100 East Meadow Dive, Vail
(970) 476–2241

Fresh flowers and gifts for garden lovers fill these walls. You'll also find ironwork, antiques, and architectural pieces for the garden.

Surefoot
**278 Hanson Ranch Road, Vail
(970) 476-8890**

**15 West Thomas Place, Beaver Creek
(970) 949-4545**
Owners Russ Shay and his brother, Bob, lay claim to the title of custom boot fitting pioneers, opening a store in Park City, Utah, in 1982 that did nothing but customize people's stiff or uncomfortable ski boots. Now there are 20 stores worldwide that promise skiers a fit they won't forget.

Verbatim Booksellers
**450 East Lionshead Circle, Vail
(970) 476-3032**
The largest full-service bookstore along the I-70 corridor, Verbatim stocks a full range of books with everything from current best sellers to older specialty books.

Necessities

Bouquets
**15 West Thomas Place, Beaver Creek
(970) 949-5900
www.bouquets.org**
This store near the Covered Bridge carries a wide range of fresh flowers and arrangements, but also sells an interesting collection of gifts and home accessories. Items include picture frames, vases, baskets, wicker baskets, Mexican pottery, stationery, and soaps. Two other Bouquets stores are located in Denver, one in Lower Downtown and the other in Capitol Hill.

West Vail Mall
2131 North Frontage Road, West Vail
The West Vail Mall is a godsend for tourists tired of eating in restaurants and paying $5.00 a cocktail. You'll find a large Safeway store squared off against a good-size City Market, its local competitor. On

either side are dry cleaners, gas stations, and all the other services needed by locals. The West Vail Liquor Mart, (970) 476-2420, is large enough to carry many of your favorite brands at prices that aren't much higher than you would pay at home. Ace Hardware, (970) 476-8282, carries 60,000 of those items, like hand tools and other gadgets, you never think about until you need them.

ARTS
Music

Bravo! Vail Valley Music Festival
**(970) 827-5700
www.vailmusicfestival.org**
For the past 15 years, world-class musicians have been gathering each summer in Vail to cross-pollinate, enjoy the mountain air, and stage jazz, classical music, and chamber music concerts throughout the Vail Valley. The concerts are held in the open-air Gerald R. Ford Amphitheater, with others scheduled in the Vilar Center for the Arts in Beaver Creek. The Rochester Philharmonic, the New York Philharmonic, and the Dallas Symphony are the resident orchestras, joined throughout the summer season by renowned soloists from around the world. Tickets are available throughout town, and locations vary with performances.

Hot Summer Nights
**Gerald R. Ford Amphitheater, Vail
(970) 949-1999
www.vvf.org**
This free concert series, sponsored by the Vail Valley Foundation, is held every Tuesday night from mid-June through July at the Gerald R. Ford Amphitheater. Musical acts range from Scottish rock to salsa, from Cajun and zydeco to Texas country.

Vilar Center for the Arts
**68 Avondale Lane, Avon
(970) 845-8497
www.vilarcenter.org**

Opened in February 1998, the Vilar Center has brought world-class performances to the Vail Valley and has been a smash success among locals and visitors alike. The Broadway-caliber venue seats 530 people, including 24 in box seats, and hosts chamber orchestras, jazz ensembles, live theater, film premieres, dance, and lectures.

Theater

Beaver Creek Children's Theater
Pedestrian Promenade, Beaver Creek
(970) 845-9090
This lively theater group performs children's plays, brings to life children's poetry and fairy tales, and even performs folk tales from around the world. During the summer, actors perform free in various locations along Beaver Creek's pedestrian mall from Wednesday through Sunday. Actors do occasional special appearances during the winter too.

Dance

Vail International Dance Festival
Various locations, Vail
(970) 949-1999
www.vvf.org
This summer-long series of dance events, sponsored by the Vail Valley Foundation and the Giordano Family Foundation, includes a dance festival with Ensemble and Evenings of Dance performances as well as performances by dance and ballet companies from around the world. The International Evenings of Dance performances feature principal couples dancing popular pas de deux from classical ballets.

Visual Arts

Bader/Melnick Gallery
141 East Meadow Drive, Vail
(970) 476-0600

Original paintings and sculpture from artists throughout the country are represented in this gallery in the Crossroads Shopping Center. It features everything from still-lifes by painter David Riedel to modern interpretations of primitive Native American sculpture by Bill Worrell.

Claggett-Rey Gallery
100 East Meadow Drive, Vail
(970) 476-9350
www.claggettrey.com
Traditional and western paintings and sculpture fill this warm gallery in the Village Inn Plaza. Staff members feel strongly about educating, enlightening, and helping patrons enjoy their purchases, so don't expect to view the works in silence. The gallery carries bronze sculpture, paintings of western landscapes, and Native American scenes.

Cogswell Gallery
223 Gore Creek Drive, Vail
(970) 476-1769
www.cogswellgallery.com
The Cogswell Gallery has assembled a distinctive collection of western and southwestern art that encompasses traditional artworks as well as more contemporary takes on the same subject matter. Walt Wooten's paintings, for example, range from a traditional Native-American-paddling-his-canoe scene to a brave showing off his 1938 Indian motorcycle. The gallery also features painted gourd sculpture, turn-of-the-century Indian photography by Edward S. Curtis, weavings, furniture, and steel sculpture.

DeMott Gallery
183 Gore Creek Drive, Vail
(970) 476-8948
www.demottgallery.com
The DeMott Gallery has been in business for over 20 years. It specializes in forming strong bonds with more than 30 artists and represents artists to clients. Works are described as "traditional American art" and include mountain landscapes, Old West scenes, and bronze eagle sculptures.

Gateway Gallery
141 East Meadow Drive, Vail
(970) 477-1112
www.avonpage.com/gateway

An imaginative array of paintings and graphics cover the walls of this gallery in Vail Gateway Plaza. The owners have a broad selection of bright whimsical contemporary paintings by Alvar, Boulanger, and Thomas Pradzynki; classical sculpture by Frederick Hart; and an extensive collection of Southwestern paintings by such artists as Frank Howell and Earl Bliss.

J. Cotter Gallery
234 East Wall Street, Vail
(970) 476-3131

This internationally recognized gallery was founded in 1970. It features contemporary jewelry designed by artists from throughout the United States and Europe. Owner Jim Cotter is a jewelry designer and sculptor, which may be why he has devoted his gallery to treating jewelry as art.

Karats
122 East Meadow Drive, Vail
(970) 476-4760
www.karatsvail.com

Local jewelry designer Dan Telleen owns the gallery and features his imaginative gold and silver pieces that are embedded with meteorites, fossils, antique seals, semiprecious jewels, diamonds, and even snake vertebrae. If that's not enough for you, he also represents a few painters and sculptors.

The Squash Blossom
198 Gore Creek Drive, Vail
(970) 476-3129

Cross-cultural pieces are the forte of this gallery, which has been in business since 1972. Selected historical Native American jewelry and artifacts are carried, as well as contemporary jewelry, Hopi-inspired paintings and dolls, historic weavings, baskets,

pottery, and beadwork. Designers include Alex Sepkus, Gurhan, Sarah Graham, Doug Moore, Gaia Pelikan, and Carol Ackerman.

Vail Fine Art Gallery
141 East Meadow Drive, Vail
(970) 476-2900
www.vailfineart.com

This is the place to turn for old masters, impressionist masters, and some regional artists. Visitors will find real Dalis, Picassos, and Pissarros. Monthly openings are held for regional artists, and the galleries also work as brokers for more expensive old masters. The Vail gallery is located in Vail Village's Crossroads Center. The Beaver Creek gallery is in the St. James Place building on the Pedestrian Promenade.

Vail Promenade Gallery
166 Gore Creek Drive #140, Vail
(970) 476-0600

Original paintings and sculpture from artists throughout the country are represented in this gallery in the Vail Promenade shopping district. It features works of artists such as Thomas DeDecker and William Kennedy.

EVENTS

January

U.S. Freeskiing Open Championship
Golden Peak, Vail Mountain
(970) 476-1000
www.usfreeskiingopen.com

The U.S. Freeskiing Open Championship is this sport's most prestigious event. Started in 1997, it is the longest-running competition of its kind. Athletes from around the world compete in the Slopestyle, Superpipe, and Big Air events, in what is billed as the showcase for freeskiing's top stars.

February

**Beaver Creek Snowshoe
Adventure Series
Beaver Creek Resort
(970) 476-6797
www.bcsnowshoe.com**
This is a series of fun and competitive races starting at the Beaver Creek Nordic Center. Varying distances allow everyone to participate.

March

**American Ski Classic
Vail and Beaver Creek Mountains
(970) 949-1999**
A weekend of ski racing for celebrities and ski legends, this fun spectator event reveals the lifestyles of the rich and famous. It's a good chance to get a gondola ride with someone you've seen in the movies.

**Thursday Night Lights
Beaver Creek Resort
(970) 845-9090**
Actually running all winter, this weekly visual spectacle features a string of volunteer skiers carrying lighted torches down the face of Beaver Creek Mountain. Intermediate skiing ability is required to participate but not to watch.

April

**Taste of Vail
Various locations, Vail
(970) 926-5665
www.tasteofvail.com**
For five days in early April, chefs and vintners set up camp in Vail, cooking and pouring in locations that stretch from après-ski bars to the top of Vail Mountain. The event culminates with a Saturday night dinner, wine tasting, and auction. The event also features cooking demonstrations and seminars. Event packages

(including admission to all events except the Winemaker Dinners) were $375 recently, with proceeds going to various charities in the Vail Valley.

May

**Beaver Creek Rodeo Series
Berry Creek Ranch, 454 Edwards Access Road, Edwards
(970) 845-9090**
From Memorial Day through September, visitors can enjoy the bronc-bustin', barrel racin', and steer-tyin' the West is known for every Thursday evening from Memorial Day through September. Family style barbecue dinners are served at 6:00 P.M.; the rodeo starts at 7:00 P.M.

June

**Beaver Creek Rodeo Series
Berry Creek Ranch, 454 Edwards Access Road, Edwards
(970) 845-9090**
Through September every Thursday at 7:00 P.M., Vail Valley Cowboys compete at Berry Creek Ranch. Check the May listing for details.

**Bravo! Vail Valley Music Festival
Gerald R. Ford Amphitheater, Vail**

**Vilar Center for the Arts, Beaver Creek
(970) 827-5700
www.vailmusicfestival.org**
From June through August world-class musicians gather in Vail and Beaver Creek and stage jazz, classical, and chamber music concerts. See our listing under "Arts/Music" for more details.

Christmas season in Vail has to rival that of New York City, only with the guarantee of snow on the ground. The lighted shops, the warm fires, the cold air, and the palpable excitement of the season are a delight.

Colorado's country heritage is still revered, with summer rodeos and rodeo queens a staple in many mountain towns. VAIL IMAGE/JACK AFFLECK

July

Beaver Creek Rodeo Series
Berry Creek Ranch, 454 Edwards Access Road, Edwards
(970) 845-9090
Every Thursday through September, Vail Valley Cowboys compete at Berry Creek Ranch. Check the May listing for details.

Vail America Days Fourth of July Parade
Various Vail locations
(970) 476-1000
The Vail Valley Chamber and Tourism Bureau outdoes itself on the holiday weekend, coordinating events in all the surrounding towns. Vail starts things off with a parade that takes hours to finish and includes floats, patriotic perform-ances, and even an appearance by the Pavement Skiing Superstars (they're locals who are towed by a Chevy truck). Avon kicks in with a 30-minutes fireworks dis-play over Nottingham Lake. Other events include the Vail Hill Climb, an all-star lacrosse tournament, a free concert at the Gerald R. Ford Amphitheater, and kayak races in Minturn. Most of the events are free.

Bravo! Vail Valley Music Festival
Gerald R. Ford Amphitheater, Vail

Vilar Center for the Arts, Beaver Creek
(970) 827-5700
www.vailmusicfestival.org
From June through August world-class musicians gather in Vail and Beaver Creek and stage jazz, classical, and chamber music concerts. See our listing under "Arts/Music" for more details.

August

Beaver Creek Rodeo Series
Berry Creek Ranch, 454 Edwards Access
Road, Edwards
(970) 845-9090
Every Thursday at 7:00 P.M. Vail Valley
Cowboys compete at Berry Creek Ranch.
Check the May listing for details.

Beaver Creek Arts Festival
Various locations, Beaver Creek
(970) 845-9090
In early August, more than 100 artists
from around the country make appearances, demonstrate techniques, and sell
their works. Admission to the weekend
event is free.

Eagle County Fair and Rodeo
Eagle County Fairgrounds
0426 Fairgrounds Road, Eagle
(970) 328-8600
A traditional county fair draws the best of
the county's livestock, pie bakers, and hog
callers, including some of the nicest, most
wholesome teens you'll ever meet, showing off their 4-H projects. The rodeo is a
dandy, too.

September

Beaver Creek Rodeo Series
Berry Creek Ranch, 454 Edwards Access
Road, Edwards
(970) 845-9090
Every Thursday in September at 7:00 P.M.
Vail Valley Cowboys compete at Berry
Creek Ranch. Check the May listing for
details.

Oktoberfest
Various locations, Vail
(970) 476-6797
www.vailoktoberfest.com
In late September, Vail takes advantage of
the colorful fall foliage and warm autumn
weather to stage a full-scale German festival. Since much of the town's architecture

is derived from Bavaria, and many of the
original restaurants specialize in German
cuisine, the theme fits well here. Expect live
oompah, rhythm and blues, and pop music,
traditional food, German beers, sidewalk
sales, a street fair, and Oktoberfest-4-Kids
activities on Lionshead Mall. Most events
are free; food is purchased separately.

November

Ski Season Kick-off
Vail Mountain
(877) 204-7881
www.vail.snow.com
Depending on snow conditions, sometime
before Thanksgiving the ski season gets
underway at Vail Mountain, and it's cause
for celebration. Many locals take the day
off to get a jump on the season.

December

New Year's Eve
The Village at Vail
For the wildest celebration outside of
Times Square, head to the Vail Village,
where the revelry gets going about 10:00
P.M. In the past, even the cops have gotten
in on the action (perhaps unwillingly):
Chief Greg Morrison once lost his hat to a
reveler.

DOWNHILL SKIING
Vail

Vail
I-70
(970) 476-5601, (800) 525-2257
www.vail.snow.com
Resort elevation: *8,120 feet*
Top of highest lift: *11,570 feet*
Total vertical: *3,450 feet*
Longest run: *4½ miles*
Average annual snowfall: *346 inches*
Ski season: *mid-November to late April*

Capacity: *53,381 skiers per hour*
Terrain: *5,295 acres, 193 trails (frontside: 21 percent beginner, 31 percent intermediate, 48 percent advanced and expert); backside 13 percent intermediate, 87 percent advanced and expert)*
Lift tickets: *$81 all-day adult*
Snow reports: *(970) 476-4888*
Getting there: *Vail is 100 miles west of Denver on I-70. You may fly nonstop from many major cities into Vail/Eagle County Airport.*

Vail is the giant of Rocky Mountain ski resorts, the most popular snow destination in Colorado, and the home of such celebrities as former U.S. President Gerald Ford. It hasn't always been so famous. Until it was "discovered" by World War II ski troops training in Leadville, the narrow mountain valley was a sheep meadow. Now it's a Bavarian-style resort town that strings together three major base areas.

Vail was opened in 1962 by Pete Seibert, who had scouted the site while enlisted in the famed 10th Mountain Division of the Army that fought in Italy during World War II. Today it consists of seven back bowls, three base areas, and terrain for skiers of all levels, and a massive terrain expansion called Blue Sky Basin that's as big as the entire Aspen ski mountain. The faux Alpine village below attracts a monied crowd, 90 percent of which is drawn from outside the state. Tourists from New York and Texas are the biggest U.S. fans, and nearly 13 percent of its visitors

come from Great Britain, Mexico, South America, Canada, Europe, and Australia/New Zealand. Be prepared to put on the dog while in Vail. Expect to see fur coats and hear people speaking many languages; you're likely to see some celebrities too. Just don't gawk or ask for autographs. Locals take celebrities in stride, maybe because they see so many!

Vail and Beaver Creek, its sister resort 10 miles to the west, attract nearly 2 million skiers a year, or about 20 percent of those who schuss down Colorado slopes. Both have been host to World Alpine Ski Championship races, including the 1999 version, which was a critical and popular smash, introducing Americans to the frenzied world of ski racing.

Skiing magazine consistently includes Vail among its Top 10 resorts, citing its terrain, amenities, and village. Actually, that should be "villages." Vail Village, Lionshead, and Cascade Village are mini-resorts built up around the base areas. One of their strengths: All are pedestrian villages designed for walking, shopping, dining, and socializing without the interference of cars. Vail's public bus system, Colorado's second-largest, makes it all possible. Rides are free and frequent within Vail and low-cost when connecting Vail with nearby Avon, Beaver Creek, and Arrowhead. Large hotels supplement the service with their own complimentary shuttle vans (see our Getting Here, Getting Around chapter for more information).

First-time visitors may want to learn more about the area through free Mountain Welcome ski tours, which leave Vail Village daily at 9:00 A.M. and are for skiers of intermediate level or above. The ski school offers special gentle-technique weeks for female beginners, Mountain Skills workshops that teach survival skills, and Integrated Skiing Seminars led by instructors who stress re-educating nerves and muscles to boost coordination on the slopes; call (800) 475-4543. The Disabled Ski Program offers lessons and adaptive equipment; call (970) 479-3264.

i

Until sheep and cattle ranchers settled the Gore Creek Valley in the early 1800s, it was home only to Indian hunters and their prey. When Earl Eaton happened upon it in 1959, six families owned the entire valley. Eaton and friend Pete Seibert asked investors that included George H. W. Bush for about $5,000 each and, on 550 acres, built a town, some ski lifts, and a few paths down Vail Mountain.

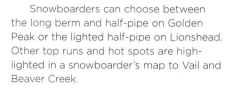

Snowboarders can choose between the long berm and half-pipe on Golden Peak or the lighted half-pipe on Lionshead. Other top runs and hot spots are highlighted in a snowboarder's map to Vail and Beaver Creek.

Beaver Creek

Beaver Creek
Off I-70, 6 miles southeast of Avon
(970) 496-4500, (800) 830-SNOW
www.beavercreek.snow.com
Resort elevation: *8,100 feet*
Top of highest lift: *11,440 feet*
Total vertical: *3,340 feet*
Longest run: *2¼ miles*
Average annual snowfall: *310 inches*
Ski season: *mid-November to mid-April*
Capacity: *25,939 skiers per hour*
Terrain: *1,625 acres, 146 trails (34 percent beginner, 39 percent intermediate, 27 percent advanced and expert)*
Lift tickets: *$81 all-day adult*
Snow reports: *(970) 476-4888*
Getting there: *Beaver Creek is 110 miles from Denver via I-70. Take the Avon exit south and follow it to the guard station.*

Spectacular Beaver Creek was developed by Vail Associates in 1980 as a more intimate, more exclusive, and less crowded resort than Vail. It's also more highbrow than Vail, if that's possible, tucked behind a gated entryway and serviced by luxury lodges and hotels that provide guests with everything from on-demand Dial-A-Ride van service to heated towel racks. The ski area is open to visitors who stay in cheaper hotels in Avon or Eagle, but beware: Unless you're registered in a Beaver Creek hotel, you'll have to pay to park your car at the base area.

Once inside the entryway gates, you'll drive on a winding road that passes exclusive houses built alongside the golf course and leads to posh resort hotels that look more like Alpine castles. If that's not enough to remind you you're in big-bucks country, there's Beano's Club, a private mountainside club open only to members during the day. The general public is invited in at night, but only if they buy tickets for a sleighride dinner (see our "Restaurants" section).

Beaver Creek Mountain is relatively unforgiving, designed for skiers who already know what they're doing. The beginners' area is perched high atop the mountain, and the trail back down to the base meanders back and forth across steep, bumpy mountainsides populated by excellent skiers and boarders racing their way to the bottom. It's easy to see why the slopes are the training ground for World Cup skiers. One run in particular, the Birds of Prey designed by Swiss Olympic gold medalist Bernhard Russi, offers frightening 45-degree pitches and is ranked as one of the best downhill courses in the world. A better place for beginners is the newer Bachelor Gulch area to the south of Beaver Creek Mountain.

In 1990 a ski lift was installed to link Beaver Creek with Arrowhead, a golf and ski resort in the nearby Eagle River Valley. Although small, it's even more secluded. A performing arts complex and year-round ice skating rink are the finishing touches, completed in the early 1998. Two pedestrian shopping and residential projects, Market Square and One Beaver Creek, face the ice arena and provide covered escalators—yet another luxury for skiers who would rather save their energy for the slopes.

NORDIC/CROSS-COUNTRY

Beaver Creek Nordic Centers
McCoy Park Center, Avon
(970) 845-5313
Beaver Creek's Cross-Country Center has 37 kilometers of double-tracked trails plus skating lanes high atop the mountain, accessible by riding the Strawberry Park Express lift. Lessons and tours are available.

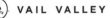

Vail Nordic Centers
Vail Golf Club, 1778 Vail Valley
Drive, Vail
(970) 476-8366
Vail maintains 18 kilometers of groomed trails and has two centers for cross-country skiing. The Nordic centers provide lessons, clinics, rentals, and guided tours during the regular ski season, roughly Thanksgiving through April.

OTHER WINTER RECREATION
Chairlift Rides

Centennial Express Chairlift
Beaver Creek Resort, 6 miles southeast
of Avon
(970) 496-4500
This scenic, open-air ride to the top of the mountain takes 15 minutes each way. At the top you can stroll through replica of a ghost town or lunch at the Spruce Saddle Lodge. Winter hours are 8:30 A.M. to 3:45 P.M. The ride is free with a lift ticket or $17 for nonskiers.

Lionshead Gondola
I-70 to the Village at Lionshead, Vail
(970) 476-9090
Ride inside heated cars to Eagles Nest to reach Vail's on-mountain activities center, Adventure Ridge. During the winter it features tubing, ice skating, ski bikes, laser tag, snowmobile tours, and dining (see other listings in this chapter), although some people just like to ride for the sake of riding. Winter hours are about 8:30 A.M. to 3:45 P.M. Rides are free with lift tickets of $17 for nonskiing adults, $10 for nonskiing children.

Dog Sledding

Mountain Musher
0004 Lady Street, Eagle
(970) 328-7877
www.mountainmusher.com

Vail's original dog-sled company takes guests on a half-day ride through open meadows and aspen and pine forests in the Vail Valley. Teams of 12 dogs pull two-person sleds. Guests are picked up at hotels or private homes throughout the Vail Valley at 8:30 A.M. and 1:00 P.M. Rides are scheduled daily between Thanksgiving and early April.

Ice Skating

Adventure Ridge
Vail Mountain at Eagles Nest, atop the
Lionshead Gondola
(970) 476-9090
For an outdoor skating experience at 10,000 feet, try this rink at the top of the Lionshead Gondola. It's open 2:30 to 8:00 P.M., with rentals available. Admission is free, and skate rental is $8.00.

Dobson Ice Arena
321 West Lionshead Circle, Vail
(970) 479-2270
When the kids are tired of skiing or the weather turns icy, take them indoors for an ice-skating reprieve. Public hours vary because they're built around hockey games, lessons, and special events, so call ahead for times.

Sleigh Rides

Beano's Cabin
Beaver Creek Resort, I-70, Beaver Creek
(970) 949-9090
If fine dining is more your style, take a moonlit, snowcat-drawn sleigh ride to Beano's Cabin for dinner. Located mid-mountain in Beaver Creek, the former log home of lettuce farmer Frank Bienkowski is a private club by day, highly acclaimed restaurant by night. The ride is so popular that Beano's starts taking winter reservations in the beginning of September. Prices and times vary based on menu and availability. Call ahead for specifics.

4 Eagle Ranch
US 131, 4 miles north of I-70, Wolcott
(970) 926-3372
www.4eagleranch.com
The Starry Night horse-drawn sleighride dinner on this western ranch takes you to the historic Nelson Cabin for dinner and an evening cowboy serenade. Transportation is provided from your hotel. Sleighrides are offered nightly Wednesday through Saturday. Call for times and prices.

Snowcat Tours

Nova Guides
7088 U.S. Highway 24, Avon
(719) 486-2656, (888) 949-6682
www.novaguides.com
Some people hire Nova Guides to transport them into the wilderness for backcountry skiing. If you'd rather just stay in the snowcat, that's OK too. The guides will drive you through the White River National Forest in a fully enclosed, heated two-track vehicle that maneuvers easily over snow. Along the way, they'll tell you stories about Vail's Back Bowls and the ghost town of Gilman and warm you with hot chocolate.

Snowmobiles

Nova Guides
(719) 486-2656, (888) 949-6682
www.novaguides.com
Snowmobilers can start at 8,000 feet and clibe to 10,500 feet, where a rustic cabin built in the 1930s awaits with a roaring fire. Drive yourself down groomed trails, take an hourly tour or catch half- or full-day tours or Camp Hale, the Army training camp that prepared skiing troops to fight in World War II. Cost is $70. for one hour, $100 for two.

Snowshoes

Adventure Ridge
Vail Mountain at Eagles Nest, atop the
Lionshead Gondola
(970) 949-9090
Snowshoeing is available from 2:30 P.M. to 9:00 P.M. You can watch the sun set, see the stars come out, and enjoy the outdoors, even after the ski trails close for the evening. A suggested $10 donation benefits the Gore Range Natural Science School, and includes your snowshoe rental.

Vail Nordic Center
Vail Golf Club
1778 Vail Valley Drive, Vail
(970) 476-8366
Rent your own snowshoes from the Vail Nordic Center, and follow the map provided with your shoes. Or join naturalists from the Vail Recreation District on a guided snowshoe tour of marked and maintained trails. Trails are open only daylight hours. Call for specific rates and times.

Tubing

Adventure Ridge
Vail Mountain at Eagles Nest, atop the
Lionshead Gondola
(970) 949-9090
Groomed tubing hills are open to the public during ski season starting daily at 2:30 P.M.

HIKING

Only 20 miles from Vail, the Holy Cross and Eagles Nest wilderness areas offer 100 miles of trails for hikers and backpackers. The Holy Cross Ranger District Office serves these wilderness areas and provides information. The office is located at Dowd Junction just after turning onto US 24 off I-70 and can be reached at (970) 827-5715. *The Vail Hiker* by Mary

Ellen Gilliland is considered the definitive guide for hiking and cross-country skiing in this area.

Booth Falls Trail
Eagles Nest Wilderness, off I-70

This rushing 60-foot cascade is a treat for hot, weary hikers. This trail begins with a steep section then levels out to meadows of wildflowers and rises gradually 2 miles through thick aspen, fir, and pine groves. The last quarter-mile gets steep again, but it's not a difficult hike overall for those used to walking. The falls make a lovely lunch spot. To reach the trailhead, follow I-70 east 3⁶/₁₀ miles to the East Vail exit (exit 180). Turn left under the freeway, then left again onto the north frontage road. Head west for ⁹/₁₀ mile to Booth Falls Road. Turn right on Booth Falls Road and drive ²/₁₀ mile to the trailhead.

Gore Creek Trail
Eagles Nest Wilderness

The spectacular Gore Range is the backdrop for this popular hike up the Gore Creek drainage. Glades of aspen, fir, and spruce shade the trail as it ascends an easy 600 feet in 1½ miles. The whole hike is a 3-mile round trip. To reach the trailhead, take I-70 east 3⁶/₁₀ miles to the East Vail exit (exit 180). Follow the south frontage road east for 2³/₁₀ miles to a marked trailhead. There's parking at the Vail Pass bike route there; the Gore Creek campground is here too.

Hardier hikers and backpackers planning on a several-day outing can continue on this trail to Gore Lake (6⁴/₁₀ miles) or Red Buffalo Pass. At the fork for these two trails, two 19th-century miners are buried with marked graves. Be sure to get detailed maps of this area if you're planning a backpacking trip.

Two Elk Trail
South of Gore Creek Campground on old U.S. Highway 6

With a National Scenic Trail designation, this 11-mile trail can be done in a day, but it's best as a backpacking trip with two cars. It leads to the summit of Two Elk Pass, which offers unrivaled views of the Gore and Sawatch ranges along with the back bowls of the Vail ski area. Farther along, there are views of the Mount of the Holy Cross. But a good chance of spotting elk is why many people choose this trail. August and September are the best times to see the elk and hear their eerie bugling (mating call).

To reach the trailhead, take I-70 east 3⁶/₁₀ miles to the East Vail exit (exit 180). Follow the south frontage road east 2³/₁₀ miles to a marked trailhead. Look for Vail Pass bike route and parking area. The Gore Creek campground is here too. The trailhead is just south of the Gore Creek Campground on old US 6 at the closed gate. Since the trail ends in Minturn, drive the second car to the bridge over Eagle River in Minturn. Cross the bridge and continue past the cemetery. Turn right at the first fork and left at the second to the mouth of Two Elk Canyon, near the foot of Battle Mountain. The trail comes out at Two Elk Creek.

CAMPING

Sylvan Lake State Park
West Brush Creek Road, south of Eagle
(970) 328-2021

This beautiful state park offers two campgrounds with sites for tents, trailers, campers, and some larger units. Elk Run Campground has 34 sites, and Fisherman's Paradise Campground has 12 sites. Reach the state park by traveling 16 miles south of Eagle on West Brush Creek Road. Call the number above for reservations and more information. Camp sites cost around $14 per night.

White River National Forest
Various sites, Vail area
(877) 444-6777

Numerous sites in this national forest range from the Vail area to Minturn. Closest to Vail, and the most popular, is the Gore Creek Campground with 25 sites.

The campground is 5 miles east of Vail Village close to the Eagles Nest Wilderness boundary. From I-70 take exit 180 from East Vail to US 6. Continue east for 2 miles.

Tigiwon Campground is south of Minturn and is the site of a stone lodge built for pilgrims visiting the Mount of the Holy Cross. It's available for rent to groups on a free reservation basis through the Holy Cross Ranger District Office, (970) 827-5715. To reach Tigiwon follow US 24 2⁸/₁₀ miles south of Minturn, then 6 miles up Tigiwon Road. Half Moon Campground, with seven sites, is 2½ miles farther along Tigiwon Road. Look for two trailheads for the Holy Cross Wilderness.

Camp Hale Memorial Campground sites are $12 per night. To reach Camp Hale Memorial Campground, take I-70 west from Denver for 105 miles to exit 171 and US 24. Camp Hale was a former training site for the 10th Mountain Division. From Leadville, Camp Hale is 15 miles south.

Other campgrounds in the area include Hornsilver Campground, 1.5 miles south of Redcliff with 12 sites, right of US 24. Blodgett Campground, also on US 24, is 12 miles south of Minturn on Homestake Road (Forest Road 703). It has six sites.

Formerly a gold mining camp, Gold Park Campground, with 11 sites, is 10 miles farther on Homestake Road. It's the departure point for various hiking trails and Jeep roads to Holy Cross City ghost town and the Holy Cross Wilderness. Sites cost from $10 to $12 per night.

GOLF

Beaver Creek Golf Club
100 Offerson Road, Beaver Creek
(970) 845-5775
The namesake Beaver Creek is the subtle focus of the golf course, which starts at an elevation of 8,100 feet, just below the ski mountain. Hole 1 starts high, jumps Beaver Creek, and hopscotches from one mowed landing area to the next. The first

house appears just before No. 3: it's a 32,000-square-foot, four-story affair owned by the Mexican oil minister until it was sold to a Colorado family. They still fly Colorado, U.S., and Mexican flags along the driveway. Other interesting buildings along the course are the smokehouse, barn, and bunkhouse that once belonged to the Holden family, dairy farmers until the 1930s. Watch for signs along the 16th hole that describe the buildings.

The course itself is one of Colorado's narrowest, plus some holes hop the creek twice between tee box and green. Holes 7 to 9 are shoehorned in at the bottom of the ravine, but at 10 the course begins to climb back up to the top. The view is dominated by the green, treelined slopes of Beaver Creek ski mountain. Robert Trent Jones Jr. designed this 6,400-yard, par 70 course. It is considered average in difficulty for people who hit the ball straight but extremely challenging for those who don't. The course is open to the public, but resort guests and club members enjoy exclusive access from June 16 to September 14. Expect to pay more than $150 for greens fees and a cart.

Cordillera Mountain Golf Club
0650 Clubhouse Drive, Edwards
(970) 926-5100
At an elevation of 8,250 feet, Cordillera's Mountain golf course is the jewel in the crown of this exclusive resort and housing development perched above Edwards in the Vail Valley. The resort opened with a 28-room inn, then developed neighborhoods of exclusive second homes. In 1995 the 200-acre, 7,396 yard, par 72 Mountain course opened in a high alpine meadow to rave reviews. *Golf Digest* calls it "Sherpa golf, with precipitous drops and climbs." We call it formidable and definitely not for the novice.

The fairways undulate erratically, with many of the slopes breaking toward the rough. The greens are small but without a lot of tricks or undulations. The course was designed to meet Hale Irwin's personal tastes, which means it rewards

Mountain Golf Etiquette

Although mountain resorts are so casual that guests can feel comfortable wearing almost anything they want to any place they go, mountain golf courses tend to be more formal. Maybe that's because the sport is so old and traditional, or maybe it's because golfers who pay between $100 and $200 a round expect a little class·in exchange for the greens fees.

Whatever the case, golfers are expected to pay attention to etiquette. All clubs announce that "proper golf attire is required." That means all golfers—and spectators—are expected to wear shirts with collars (no tank tops or T-shirts), fabric shorts or trousers (no cutoffs or jeans), and golf shoes. No bathing suits or short shorts are allowed. Clubs also require that guests keep up the pace of play, sometimes going so far as to suggest that each hole should take 12 to 15 minutes. Anyone who has ever spent five or more hours playing 18 holes can sympathize.

With rough as thick as the forests that sometimes line these mountain fairways, golfers could (but shouldn't) spend hours hunting for each lost ball. Many of the courses are also narrow and crisscrossed by rivers, which means players who hit straight are rewarded, and those who don't can take as many as 10 or 12 strokes hopping back and forth between landing pads or digging out of river banks. Course rangers are vigilant about speeding up slow players. That's also why carts are often required at mountain courses.

On many holes, carts are confined to the cart paths. Some courses require that because of fragile environmental conditions (the grass on rain-soaked fairways can be destroyed by golf carts in less than a day). Others border environmentally protected areas such as bald eagle

golfers who play a strategic game. Golfers are treated to a 360-degree panorama of New York Mountain, the Sawatch Range, and the Gore Range just beyond. Deer and elk often watch from the forests. At Hole 16, paw prints of a mama and baby bear were left in the wet cement on the golf cart path. The semi-private course is open only to resort guests and members' guests. Greens fees with cart, caddy, and range balls are upwards of $225. Walking is not permitted.

Cordillera Short Course
Hawks Leap Road, Edwards
(970) 926-5550
Cordillera's 14-acre Short Course was designed for resort golfers of all types. The 10-hole course, designed by Dave Pelz, is good for anyone interested in practicing their chipping, putting, pitching, and bump-and-run game. It also is advertised for beginners, families, or anyone who doesn't have the time to play 18 holes. Guests can play nine of the 100- to 175-yard holes and use the 10th to prac-

In addition to breathtaking views, mountian golfers benefit from the high altitude at Colorado's resort courses. Balls really travel farther here than at sea level. VAIL IMAGE/JACK AFFLECK

nesting areas or beaver habitat. Cart drivers must also be at least 18 years old and have a driver's license. Course managers also strongly urge players to replace their divots and reseed any grass that has been disturbed. That's because growing grass at 9,000 feet can be tricky under even the best of circumstances. Harsh winter weather can kill tender greens and fairways, not because of the below-zero temperatures but because the snow thaws, then refreezes into icy crusts that suffocate the grass.

Veteran mountain players offer some packing tips for golfers: Make sure to bring bug spray because Rocky Mountain flies bite as if they're starving and can descend in swarms when the afternoon breeze dies down; sunscreen with an SPF of at least 15 because the strong, unforgiving mountain sun can cause serious burns; and lots of extra balls. Many of the courses are narrow and have rough so dense it's nearly impossible to find a stray ball. If you're in a pinch, local kids sometimes set up stands on the back nine and sell balls they've recovered from the woods, four for $1.00.

tice the shots or skills they'd like to improve. The Short Course is near Cordillera's Lodge in the center of the resort.

Cordillera Valley Golf Club
0101 Legends Drive, Edwards
(970) 926-5900
Nearly 2,000 feet lower than its sister Mountain course—but only 6 miles and 20 minutes away by car—the Cordillera Valley course opened in 1997. It is a perfect companion to the challenging Mountain course, providing a friendly 18-hole tour of the mountain desertscape near Edwards. The holes are more forgiving than those on the Mountain course, with roughs that often slope back into the fairways and greens that pitch slightly toward the pins.

Because of its lowland setting, the Valley course is open nearly a month longer each year than the Mountain course, usually mid-April to early November. The 7,001 yard, par 72 course was designed by Tom Fazio and wraps around a lavish clubhouse. Guests of members and of

Cordillera Lodge pay about $225 a round, which includes cart, caddy, and free range balls. Walking is not permitted.

Cotton Ranch Golf Club
0520 Cotton Ranch Drive, Gypsum
(970) 524-6200
Located in the "banana belt" 37 miles down valley from Vail and only at 6,300 feet, the Cotton Ranch Club traditionally is the fist golf course in the county to open, sometimes as early as February. That makes this course, designed by Pete and Perry Dye, perfect for the optional ski-golf vacation. The course also is among the most affordable in the Eagle Valley, costing about $100 a round, including cart.

Eagle-Vail Golf Club
0431 Eagle Drive, Avon
(970) 949-5267
At an elevation of 7,500 feet, Eagle-Vail is at the end of Colorado's rugged Rockies. In 1975 this bedroom community built a municipal course between I-70 and the Eagle River. It has since developed a reputation as the relatively inexpensive alternative to more exclusive courses in the vicinity. The challenging course is known as a ball-eater. Two holes are cut by the swift river, eight are bordered by the dense White River National Forest, and several more drive off ledges or over aspen groves. The design is a cross between country club and traditional mountain courses, with half the holes playing through a housing development and the other half climbing a valley to the south that holds Stone Creek. This 6,819-yard, par 72 course was designed by Bruce Devlin and Bob Von Hagge. Look for bargains during the early season, when some holes are closed due to snow. Also available is a friendlier par 3 course just a bit west of the main course.

Red Sky Golf Club
Red Sky Road, near Wolcott
(970) 477-8404
www.redskygolfclub.com
Designed as a private membership club,

this facility is also accessible to guests staying at Vail Resorts properties. The property includes two courses, one designed by Greg Norman and the other by Tom Fazio. Both have gotten national attention. The Norman course is 7,500 yards, par 72, offering players stunning views of Castle Peak. The Fazio course is 7,113 yards, par 72, and provides views of Vail's Back Bowls. Both are open May through October, weather permitting, with tee times accepted one month in advance. Guests must adhere to the dress code, but have access to their own clubhouse, which includes a bar and restaurant. Greens fees are $175 to $200 for 18 holes, depending on the season.

Sonnenalp Golf Club
1265 Berry Creek Road, Edwards
(970) 477-5370
Built on the scrubby north side of I-70, Sonnenalp is situated on a high mountain desert. The course winds its way through Singletree, an exclusive community, and was called Singletree until purchased by the Sonnenalp Resort in Vail. The semi-private course, designed by Jack Nicklaus, is imaginative and includes long fairways and fast greens. The houses that line the course have gorgeous landscaping, and course planters are filled with mountain wildflowers. This 7,059-yard, par 71 course is perennially rated among the top resort courses in the world by *Golf Digest.* Resort guests get first priority at Sonnenalp, but the public is welcome. Greens fees with cart run as high as $200 during peak days.

Vail Golf Club
1778 Vail Valley Drive, Vail
(970) 479-2260
The oldest club in the valley, Vail Golf Club was designed in 1966 by resident Ben Krueger, who also ran the club for 25 years. It is best known as a longtime favorite of valley resident and former President Gerald Ford. The course is narrow, wedged into the Gore Creek Valley and contained on the north edge by I-70. Eight holes cross the creek as the course

meanders up and back along the valley floor. Golfers are treated to views of the Gore Range and the Gold Medal fishing waters of Gore Creek.

The 18-hole, par 71, 7,048-yard course has an elevation of 8,200 feet and follows a traditional links format. Greens fees with cart are about $115 throughout the season, but rates drop for non-peak times. The course also offers a driving range clearly seen from I-70 through the 50-foot mesh fence.

FISHING AND HUNTING

Outfitters and Tackle Shops

Fly Fishing Outfitters
1060 West Beaver Creek
Boulevard, Avon
(970) 476-3474
www.flyfishingoutfitters.net
This tackle shop and guide service is the Vail Valley's only year-round Orvis dealership and endorsed guide service. It stocks more than 50,000 flies and carries a complete line of Patagonia products. Guests can be guided to alpine lakes, headwaters, or Gold Medal waters on the Colorado, Eagle, and Roaring Fork Rivers. Full- and half-day trips are offered in waders, floats, and belly boats. Overnight and horseback trips also are available, as are trips to fishing streams that cross private ranches. These guides also present two-day, Orvis-endorsed fly-fishing schools. The shop is across from the west entrance to Beaver Creek Ski Area.

Gore Creek Fly Fisherman
(Vail Fishing Guides)
183 East Gore Creek Drive #7, Vail
(970) 476-3296
www.gorecreekflyfisherman.com
Gear and guided tours are this shop's specialties. Free daily casting clinics are offered at 10:30 A.M. during the summer on Gore Creek behind the shop. Guides

also lead overnight trips, horseback trips, and shorter fishing trips on private land along the Eagle River.

Gorsuch Outfitters
263 Gore Creek Drive, Vail
(970) 926-0900
www.gorsuch-outfitters.com
Started as a partnership with the legendary Gorsuch Ltd. clothing stores, now owned by John and Marianne Cochran, guides arrange wade, float, and overnight trips for visiting anglers. The guides also teach fly-fishing classes and popular women-only clinics. The company has access to 17 miles of private water, including remote canyon stretches of the Piney River and the meadows of Sweetwater Creek. Gorsuch also maintains full-service fly shops at its downtown Vail Village and Park Hyatt in Beaver Creek locations.

Nova Guides
7088 US 24, Avon
(719) 486-2656, (888) 949-6682
www.novaguides.com
These guides lead both float and shore fishing expeditions along local lakes and rivers within the White River National Forest. They promote catch and release but will clean any fish you wish to keep, up to your limit. All fly or spin rods are provided as well as transportation and a snack or lunch. Licenses are extra, but will be provided by Nova Guides. Half-day trips run from 8:00 A.M. to 1:00 P.M., or 2:00 to 7:00 P.M. Full-day trips are 8:00 A.M. to 4:00 P.M.

Places to Fish

Beaver Lake
Beaver Creek Resort
Brook and cutthroat trout thrive in Beaver Lake, on the upper edges of Beaver Creek in the Holy Cross Wilderness. Access it by driving through the Beaver Creek Resort guard station and getting directions to the Beaver Creek Nature Center. From there, it's an easy hike alongside the creek to Beaver Lake.

Black Lakes
Near the summit of Vail Pass

Because these two lakes are so easy to reach from I-70, they are fairly crowded during the summer. They are usually well stocked though, and worth the effort. Park at the Vail Pass rest area and head west on the dirt road toward Shrine Pass.

Eagle River
Alongside I-70

The river flows north along the mountain pass from Leadville to Minturn then joins Gore Creek before flowing west down Vail Valley ranchlands and pastures between US 6 and I-70. Stretches of it have classic trout fishing, with 10- to 14-inch rainbow and brown trout swimming in the portion of the river between Wolcott and Gypsum. Much of the land alongside the Eagle River is private, but there are still some excellent public waters. Just before it joins the Colorado River, the Eagle has pools of deep flat water that harbor giant fish. Locals recommend fly fishing for them with 12- to 16-elk hair caddis imitations or prince nymphs. For great wade fishing, try just below the I-70 bridges and the Wolcott trestles.

Gore Creek

Gore Creek begins in the Eagles Nest Wilderness near Red Buffalo Pass and runs right through Vail before joining the Eagle River 2 miles northwest of Minturn. In spite of the throng of humanity in Vail, the creek is filled with rainbow, brown, cutthroat, and brook trout. The fish population is so high between Red Sandstone Creek and the Eagle, in fact, that it is designated Gold Medal water. Locals suggest throwing your line into the beaver ponds just east of the Vail Golf Club (avoid the course itself, however). If you prefer fishing in pristine surroundings, you may enjoy the creek's origins in the Eagles Nest Wilderness. Hike to it from the Gore Creek Campground in East Vail.

Homestake Reservoir
South of Redcliff off US 24

This 300-acre reservoir adjacent to the Holy Cross Wilderness has steep, rocky banks, but local anglers don't seem to mind. They enjoy the easy-to-catch 10- to 14-inch brook and brown trout that inhabit the reservoir and Homestake Creek just below. The creek is stocked and not very crowded. Wade out into the knee-deep waters and do a little dry fly fishing. To reach the reservoir, take US 24 3 miles south of Redcliff, turn right onto Homestake Road (Forest Road 703) at Blodgett Campground and drive 11 miles.

Lost Lake
North of Vail

This lake on the headwaters of Red Sandstone Creek is on the edge of the Eagles Nest Wilderness. To reach it, follow Red Sandstone Road north from Vail for 6 miles toward Piney Lake. The marked trailhead is on your right.

Missouri Lakes
South of Vail

Brook and cutthroat trout call the three Missouri Lakes home. They're located in the Holy Cross Wilderness, but to reach them you'll have to drive 3 miles south on US 24, then turn right on Homestake Road to Gold Park Campground. Follow the road up Missouri Creek until it ends, then hike about 3 more miles.

Nottingham Park
Avon
(970) 748-4000

This recreational lake belonging to the town of Avon is stocked with trout and can be fished from the shore or the dock between 10:00 A.M. and 8:00 P.M. Head south from the Avon exit off I-70 and take a right on West Beaver Creek Boulevard to the park just east of Benchmark Road. Licenses are required.

Piney Lake
15 miles north of Vail off
Red Sandstone Road

This 60-acre lake is surrounded by public and private land—Piney River Ranch is on the southwestern side—but the entire shoreline is open to the public. Anglers can fish for brook, native, and cutthroat trout. Piney River Ranch rents canoes, float fishing boats, rods, and waders and also conducts day and overnight fishing trips. To reach the lake, follow Red Sandstone Road (Forest Road 700) until it ends.

Sylvan Lake State Park
West Brush Creek Road
16 miles south of Eagle
The brook and rainbow trout in this 40-acre lake bite all year, but locals rave more about the scenery. You'll need a boat if you want to chase the big fish. It's located on West Brush Creek Road south of Eagle.

Places to Hunt

Piney Lake
15 miles north of Vail
Deer and elk hunting is good on the public land that surrounds this 60-acre lake. The access from Red Sandstone Road (Forest Road 700) is fair until it ends, but the side roads that lead into the forest are dicey. Four-wheel-drive vehicles are recommended.

OTHER RECREATION

Climbing

Timberline Tours
3931 Bighorn Road, Vail
(970) 476-1414, (800) 831-1414
www.timberlinetours.com
Through the Rock 'n Raft program, this company actually combines both experiences. Tours take rafters down Class II-III rapids on the upper Colorado River, then stop for rock climbing along the way. With an instructor/student ration of 1-to-4, experienced rock-climbing instructors present top-roping techniques (the safest belay method for rock climbing) and foot-

work for beginners and intermediates. All necessary equipment and lunch are included in the full-day tours, which are limited to 8 people. Reservations must be made in advance.

Whitewater Rafting/ Kayaking

Timberline Tours
3931 Bighorn Road, Vail
(970) 476-1414, (800) 831-1414
www.timberlinetours.com
This company offers a variety of activities, including Jeep tours. With tours that depart twice daily, the company has gourmet coffee brunch and sunset trips and sightseeing trips that go into the rugged Castle Peak backcountry about 30 minutes northwest of Vail, bordering the Flattops Wilderness area. Some of the trips explore old mining sites, and all have a spectacular view of the Sawatch and Gore ranges with vistas of Vail and Beaver Creek ski mountains.

Bicycling

Both the Vail and Beaver Creek ski areas offer lift ride passes up the mountain for downhill and trail riding on the mountains. Various lifts at both resorts ferry the cyclists up the mountains for scenic rides. The Vail Pass Bikeway runs from Vail to Frisco, peaking out at the 10,666-foot summit of Vail Pass—not for the casual rider. From the Vail side, the elevation gain is 2,206 feet—a lot more strenuous than from the Copper Mountain side, where cyclists climb only 1,400 feet. But it's a great ride if you're in shape. Some folks start in Copper Mountain, spend the night in Vail, then return the following day—a good option, and you can soak your aching muscles in your hotel's hot tub. Vail's a tough place for cycling because it's at the bottom of a steep valley. The

10th Mountain Trail Association Hut System opened up its cabins to mountain bikers, so that's another option.

Christy Sports
293 Bridge Street, Vail
(970) 476-2244

182 Avon Road, Avon
(970) 949-0241
www.christysports.com
Rent all types of bikes here as well as service and repairs and all types of accessories. Helmets are included with the bike rental. The shops also have detailed maps of the areas, and the friendly staff will tell you the best places to ride depending on your ability and desires.

Venture Sports
51 Beaver Creek Place, Avon
(970) 949-1318
www.avonventuresports.com
This shop guarantees satisfaction with a 100 percent money-back guarantee on all rentals and repairs if you're not happy. Rent all kinds of bikes, in-line skates, and camping equipment, including children's bikes and kiddie carriers. The helpful staff will provide all the information you need about where to ride.

In-line Skating

Vail's pretty, flower-lined pedestrian village is a great place for in-line skating. Rent in-line skates at the bike shops previously mentioned or the many other shops all over town. Look for the *Vail Walking Map*, which is free at shops all over town.

Jeep and Hummer Tours

Timberline Tours
3931 Bighorn Road, Vail
(970) 476-1414, (800) 831-1414
www.timberlinetours.com
This company offers a variety of activities, including Jeep and Hummer tours. With

tours that depart twice daily, the company has gourmet coffee brunch and sunset trips, sightseeing trips that go into the rugged Castle Peak backcountry about 30 minutes northwest of Vail, bordering the Flattops Wilderness area. Some of the trips explore old mining sites and have spectacular views of the Sawatch and Gore ranges with vistas of Vail and Beaver Creek ski mountains.

Rafting

Timberline Tours
3931 Bighorn Road, Vail
(970) 476-1414, (800) 831-1414
www.timberlinetours.com
This company combines rock-climbing and whitewater rafting experiences. Tours lead rafters down Class II-III rapids on the upper Colorado River, then stop for rock climbing along the way. With an instructor/student ration of 1:4, experienced rock-climbing instructors present top-roping techniques (the safest belay method for rock climbing) and footwork for beginners and intermediates. All necessary equipment and lunch are included in the full-day tours, which are limited to 8 people. Reservations must be made in advance.

Swimming

Avon Recreation Center
325 Benchmark Road, Avon
(970) 748-4060
This splendid facility has an array of indoor pools for children, lap swimming, diving, and plenty of room to just float around. The kids are sure to enjoy the 142-foot slide. Open year-round, the publicly owned center also offers typical health-club amenities.

Tennis

Vail Tennis Center
700 South Frontage Road East, Vail
(970) 479-2294

The Vail Recreation District runs this center for all types of activities for youth and adults, including leagues, tournaments, camps, running races, and other special events. Program information is available at the Vail Tennis Center on weekdays from 8:00 A.M. to 5:00 P.M. or by calling. The professional staff offers a pro shop, tennis camps, private lessons, and clinics, plus league and tournament play. There are eight clay courts at Ford Park and nine hard courts between Lionshead, Golden Peak, and Booth Falls.

Walking/Running

Vail Walking Map

This free map, distributed by local shops and advertisers, is handy for both walking and running (and shopping—or finding your way back to your hotel). It also includes information on dining, lodging, recreation, and other services. Pick it up all over town.

SPAS

Aria Spa and Club
1300 Westhaven Drive, Vail
(970) 479-5942, (888) 824-5772

The 78,000-square-foot Aria Spa and Club has its share of local members, many of them tennis pros, golfers, and champion ski racers, but visitors are also welcome to the full-service health club and spa. Exercise facilities include indoor and outdoor tennis courts, an outdoor swimming pool, racquetball and squash courts, a basketball gym, a weight-training area, and a aerobics room. The spa offers body polishes, wraps, skin-care treatments, and massage. Therapists also visit guests at the Vail Cascade Hotel and the Lion Square Lodge.

Allegria Spa
Park Hyatt Beaver Creek, 100 East Thomas Road, Beaver Creek
(970) 748-7500

Located at the unimaginably posh Park Hyatt Beaver Creek, the total body center takes care of everything from sore muscles to skin that has been dehydrated by the high altitude air. The full-service spa offers exfoliation, herbal wraps, and facials but its most popular package for her is "The Classics," a five-hour extravaganza that combines a 50-minute Swedish, sports, or Shiatsu massage; a 60-minute holistic facial; a Signature Spa manicure; and a honey ginger spa pedicure for the princessly sum of $340, not including 18 percent tip and 5 percent resort service fee. For him, try the "What Men Want package," an 80-minute barefoot or 75-minute hot stone massage, followed by a 60-minute gentlemen's facial, and 25-minute Asian foot and scalp massage. The 3½-hour treatment runs $350, plus tip and service fee.

The Charter at Beaver Creek
120 Offerson Road, Beaver Creek
(970) 949-6660, (800) 525-6660
www.thecharter.com

After a hard day of skiing, therapists employed by Spa Struck, a wellness company that contracts to both The Charter and to Marriott's Mountain Resort, are on hand to work out the kinks with Swedish, sports, prenatal, or Shiatsu massage, foot reflexology, deep-pressure and hydrating massages, seaweed mud baths, hydrotherapy baths, acupuncture, and Boot Off treatments to sooth tired feet. Personal training and aerobics classes are offered in the adjoining health club. The Charter also has indoor and outdoor pools and hot tubs.

Cordillera Spa
2205 Cordillera Way, Edwards
(970) 926-2200, (800) 548-2721
www.cordillera.rockresorts.com

This highly acclaimed spa was named ninth among spas worldwide by *Condé Nast Traveler,* as well it should. The spa is an integral part of the elite Cordillera Lodge, located on a mountaintop overlooking the Vail Valley. Spa staff approach wellness as a holistic process, designing personalized fitness programs that integrate physical and mental well-being and that are meant to be continued long after guests return home. Spa visitors are treated to a glass of white wine or mineral water, then turned over to personal trainers who design custom programs that balance flexibility, strength, and cardio-respiratory fitness.

Exercise and weight machines are lined up in front of floor-to-ceiling windows that overlook the mountain ranges that surround Cordillera. Those who would rather not contemplate nature can use treadmills with individual televisions attached, choosing between movies and cable television stations. Spa services include cleansing, detoxifying wraps and therapies (from hydrotherapy baths to seaweed wraps), and a vast menu of massages: Swedish, neuromuscular, Shiatsu, reflexology, acupressure, sports, prenatal, cranio-sacral, deep-tissue, trigger-point, Reiki, lymphatic drainage, and combinations of all. Spa meals are provided by the gourmet Picasso restaurant. Wellness packages range from half-day to seven-day programs, and all services are available on an a la carte basis.

Sonnenalp Resort
82 East Meadow Drive, Vail
(970) 476-5656
www.sonnenalp.com
Guests at this tranquil alpine resort have their choice of two spas; the general public can visit only one. Sonnenalp has three distinct but connected buildings, each with its own decor. The Bavaria Haus has a smaller spa just for guests that comes with an indoor/outdoor pool. The quaint Swiss Chalet has a full spa open to anyone. It offers everything from beauty treatments to massages, body wraps, and an especially nice total body exfoliation. A nearby fitness room also has steam rooms, saunas, a Jacuzzi, and a heated outdoor pool. Massage therapists take their tables to guests' rooms, if requested. Resort guests also have access to guided skiing and snowshoeing programs in the winter and golf at one of the valley's best courses in the summer and fall.

Vail Athletic Club and Spa
352 East Meadow Drive, Vail
(970) 476-7960, (800) 822-4754
www.vailmountainlodge.com
One of the biggest fitness centers and spas in the Vail Valley is affiliated with the Vail Mountain Lodge in Vail Village. The spa offers a full range of beauty treatments as well as massage, body treatments, and hydrotherapy treatments using two botanically based product lines from Germany and Austria and Moor mud imported from Austria. The 18,000-square-foot health club has cardio-based classes as well as alternative classes such as yoga, Pilates, Feldenkrais, and the Alexander Technique. The club also has an indoor climbing wall, racquetball courts, an indoor pool in which water aerobics classes are held, hot tubs, saunas, a physical therapy clinic, a complete Cybex weight room, and state-of-the-art cardio machines. The club and spa are open to hotel guests, local members, and the general public. The attached restaurant, Terra Bistro, serves "haute health cuisine." For more details, refer to the "Restaurant" section.

GLENWOOD SPRINGS

Once thought of as just a wide spot in the road, Glenwood Springs is coming into its own. It is now known among locals as one of the last bastions of affordable fun. During the summer months it's a comfortable home base for those in search of good hiking and biking, great fishing, and an incredible, family-friendly swimming pool. During the winter, its draw is Sunlight Mountain Resort, a down-home local ski area, and its proximity to big-league slopes at Aspen and Vail.

The hot springs first brought life to Glenwood Springs in the 1800s. The Ute Indians had always known about the springs' curative powers, but once silver miners in Leadville got wind of them, they started trudging across the pass to soak their weary limbs in the 100-degree pools. Before long, a small town had been settled there. In the early days it provided the rough and rowdy a place to party but, like most other places in the West, it was tamed by settlers who brought religion, education, farming, and ranching to the area.

About 8,475 people live in Glenwood Springs, and more are arriving every year. Land prices are still reasonable, compared to those in nearby Aspen, and property that used to be a comfortable buffer between neighbors Basalt and Carbondale is now sprouting housing developments. Even so, the stunning red cliffs of Glenwood Canyon and the Gold Medal fishing waters of the Roaring Fork River provide visitors with the kind of one-on-one nature experience that keeps them coming back year after year.

ACCOMMODATIONS

Hotels and Motels

GLENWOOD SPRINGS

Affordable Inns $
51823 U.S. Highways 6 and 24
(970) 945-8888, (800) 292-5050
www.affordableinns.com
If it's economy you're after, this is the place. Affordable Inns has 60 comfortable rooms, some with kitchenettes. Part of the savings come from its location—in West Glenwood Springs alongside the highway. But the less popular translates into lighter crowds during the hectic high seasons. The Bavarian-style inn offers free continental breakfasts, a hot tub, and a pet-friendly policy. Those interested in ski/hotel packages during the winter or swim/hotel packages during the summer should ask for details. Good Mexican and American restaurants are located a few doors down.

America's Best Value Inn $
51871 US 6 and 24
(970) 945-6279, (888) 315-2378
www.bestvalueglenwood.com
This extremely clean motel has 23 rooms, all furnished traditionally with king and queen beds, and a few with microwaves and refrigerators. Although downtown and Hot Springs Pool are a car ride away, guests are within walking distance of restaurants and the indoor shopping mall on the west end of town. A free train shuttle is provided for Amtrak guests, but it must be reserved ahead of time.

Best Western Antlers Motel $$
171 West Sixth Street
(970) 945-8535
One of the town's pricier motels, the Antlers has rooms in four different buildings. On days when you don't want to pay

Residents of Glenwood Springs vividly remember the Storm King Mountain Fire that raged through town in 1994. Visitors can now hike the mountain and find 14 crosses that serve as memorials to the 14 firefighters killed in the blaze. THE DENVER POST/HELEN H. RICHARDSON

the $12 admission to the nearby Hot Springs Pool (see our "Hot Springs and Spas" section below), the kids are almost satisfied with the Antlers' indoor and outdoor pools. Other amenities include a guest laundry, indoor hot tub, and stone fireplace in the lobby. Restaurants are a short walk away.

Best Western Caravan Inn $$
1826 Grand Avenue
(970) 945-7451, (800) 945-5495
www.caravaninn.com

The Caravan Inn is the town's other Best Western, located several miles from downtown and the Hot Springs Pool on the south side of town. Most of the 70 rooms circle a heated pool that is covered during the winter. Other amenities include a free continental breakfast, a hot tub, and ski packages at nearby Sunlight ski area. Pets are welcome. Some rooms come with kitchenettes, but we prefer to hoof it to the 19th Street Diner (one block away, see entry below) for one of the best breakfasts in town.

First Choice Inn of Glenwood Springs $$
51359 US 6 and 24
(970) 945-8551, (877) 740-2822
www.1stchoiceinns.com

This used to be a Holiday Inn and still has the predictable chain motel layout and design. There are 123 rooms in wings that form a U around the courtyard pool, hot tub, and sauna. A steakhouse restaurant and bar are located in front. First Choice is one of the largest inns in town. Guests also have access to a free continental breakfast, room service, a game room, a guest laundry, and a striking view of Red Mountain to the south.

Glenwood Motor Inn $
141 West Sixth Street
(970) 945-5438, (800) 543-5906
www.glenwoodmotorinn.com

Just two blocks from the Hot Springs Pool, this 45-room motel has a hot tub, a sauna, and a guest laundry. Some rooms have refrigerators and microwaves. Next door is Rosie's Bavarian restaurant, popular for breakfast and lunch. A half-dozen other restaurants are within walking distance.

Glenwood Springs Hostel $
1021 Grand Avenue
(970) 945-8545, (800) 9-HOSTEL
www.hostelcolorado.com

This is a typical hostel fare, frequented by young skiers and anyone else with limited funds. (Prices are as low as $14 a night for a dorm room, $21 a night for a private room.) It's got a great main street location as well as both dorm-style and private rooms. Guests can often be found sitting on the broad front porch. Glenwood and Aspen buses stop across the street. Guests have kitchen privileges.

Hampton Inn $$
401 West 1st Street
(970) 947-9400, (800) HAMPTON

Each of the Hampton's 70 mini-suites has a refrigerator, microwave, coffeemaker, and separate sitting area. A few also come with a whirlpool in the middle of the suite. Other amenities at this centrally located hotel, built in 1999, are a swimming pool and fitness center, free continental breakfast, and guest laundry. It's located next door to the Holiday Inn Express and within walking distance of the Hot Springs Pool.

Hideout Cabins $$
1293 County Road 117
(303) 652-6114, (866) 611-6114
www.hideoutcabins.com

It is possible to lose oneself amid the hustle and bustle of Glenwood's mountain resort town. Nestled in the woods 9 miles from Sunlight ski area, the Hideout has six modern cabins of various sizes that range from studios to three-bedroom units; cabins sleep from 2 to 12 people. Many have kitchens, some have fireplaces, all have access to the guest laundry.

Holiday Inn Express $$
501 West 1st Street
(970) 928-7800, (888) HOLIDAY
New in 1998, the Holiday Inn Express has that standard look patrons of the chain have gotten familiar with. This one has 69 rooms, an outdoor heated swimming pool and hot tub, a guest laundry, and free continental breakfasts. It's halfway between the historic downtown Glenwood and the more reasonable West Glenwood corridor, within walking distance of the Hot Spring Pool.

Hot Springs Lodge $$$
415 Sixth Street
(970) 945-6571, (800) 537-SWIM
www.hotspringspool.com
If you're planning a weekend around the Hot Springs Pool, this is the most convenient place to stay between soaks. The lodge has 107 rooms, some with minifridges and either a patio or balcony. Room rental includes free unlimited access to the pools, athletic club discount, shuttle to the train station, guest laundry, outdoor hot tub, sauna, and game room. The nearest bar and restaurant are poolside, downstairs from the lodge.

Hotel Colorado $$$
526 Pine Street
(970) 945-6511, (800) 544-3998
www.hotelcolorado.com
Perhaps Glenwood's most famous landmark, the 130-room Hotel Colorado opened in 1893 near the famous Hot Springs Pool. It was modeled after the Villa de Medici in Italy and soon became fashionable among socialites and such politicians as Teddy Roosevelt. The former president made it his unofficial "Little White House" in 1905 when he used it as a base for a hunting trip. The outside still has a glorious appearance, as does the sumptuous lobby, although the interior has been through its share of ups and downs. In 1999 $850,000 was spent on room renovations, with another $2 million in 2005–2006 to remodel the first floor. The best rooms in the house are the suites and sixth-floor tower rooms tucked into the bottom of the U-shape courtyard. From them, you'll have dramatic views of old-town Glenwood, Red Mountain, and the Roaring Fork Valley. Ask about the ghost tour, during which guides will introduce you to the genial spirits that haunt "the Wallpaper Room" (ghosts reportedly chose their own paper and hung it themselves), the basement (which served as a speakeasy for Al Capone during the '20s and military hospital, morgue, and brig during the '40s), among others. Amenities include a bell staff, room service, indoor and courtyard restaurants, a lounge, a basement health club, a sauna and Jacuzzi, massage and chiropractic services, and a bike rental shop. Room prices run the gamut from $118 for basic doubles to $400 for the President Suite on the second floor, which Teddy Roosevelt used and from which he delivered a balcony address to the citizens of Glenwood. An extensive $2 million renovation planned for 2006 was undertaken to restore some areas of the hotel to their 19th-century splendor. The Lobby Cafe will be moved into the hotel's interior, making room for two grand fireplaces in the lobby. The dining room will get a new rendition of the historic 25-foot waterfall that once was a focal point of the hotel, and a cocktail and cigar bar will be opened next to the restaurant.

Hotel Denver $$
402 Seventh Street
(970) 945-6565, (800) 826-8820
www.thehoteldenver.com
When this hotel was built in 1906, no one had any idea how plush it would become. A dramatic remodel in the 1990s left it the most luxurious place in town, with maroon and teal art-deco decor, morning newspaper delivered to the room, and a three-story New Orleans-style atrium. The 73 rooms are soundproof, so don't worry that the Amtrak station is directly across the street. The Hot Springs Pool is a short walk across the bridge. Downtown begins a block away. Amenities include

microwaves and refrigerators in a few rooms, an exercise room, a lounge, and the Glenwood Canyon Brewing Company, an on-site restaurant. If you want to bring along the family dog or cat, you're in luck; pets are welcome.

Ramada Inn of Glenwood Springs $$
124 West Sixth Street
(970) 945-2500, (800) 332-1472
www.ramadaglenwood.com

With 120 rooms, Ramada is the largest chain hotel in town, just a block from the Hot Springs Pool and next door to the always-crowded Village Inn Pancake House. This full-service hotel had a full $1.5 million facelift in 1998, leaving guest rooms heavy on exposed bricks but tastefully decorated with mission-style furniture. The lobby, for example, is light wood with orangish lamps and a fireplace adorned with deer and elk heads. The hotel has all the big-city amenities: room service, a restaurant, a lounge, an indoor pool and Jacuzzi, guest laundry, and a large exercise facility. Some of the rooms are suites with kitchens, fireplaces, and Jacuzzi baths. Pets are welcome for a $10 per pet, per day charge, and free shuttle service is provided to the railroad station.

Red Mountain Inn $
51637 US 6 and 24
(970) 945-6353, (800) 748-2565
www.redmountaininn.com

On the commercial corridor in West Glenwood, this little 40-room hotel has an outdoor pool and hot tub, and some rooms have kitchenettes and fireplaces. Pets are accepted with a $10 charge. A restaurant and miniature golf are nearby; more restaurants and the indoor shopping mall are just a little farther west.

Silver Spruce Motel $
162 West Sixth Street
(970) 945-5458, (800) 523-4742
www.silversprucemotel.com

This faux-Swiss mountain inn has 90 rooms, all the typical motel style except for four large units located in the street-side turrets. The innkeepers call them the bridal suites. We call them good buys if you want to sleep four and still have room to spread out. Amenities include a guest laundry, some rooms with fireplaces, a two-bedroom unit with kitchen, and an outdoor hot tub that's good for après-ski soaking. Pets are OK for $10 a night; the Hot Springs Pool is about four blocks away.

CARBONDALE

Comfort Inn & Suites $$
920 Cowen Drive
(970) 963-8880, (800) 473-5980

Centrally located at the intersection of Highway 133 (which goes to Redstone) and Highway 82 (which links Glenwood Springs to Aspen), this chain hotel has an indoor heated pool and Jacuzzi, a guest laundry, and a free continental breakfast. Of the 76 rooms, 16 are suites with two rooms, a king bed, and queen sofa sleeper. Children under 18 stay free with their parents and pets are welcome at $10 per day.

Days Inn $$
950 Cowen Drive
(970) 963-9111, (800) 944-3297

Also centrally located, Days Inn has 69 rooms, including some specially designed for guests with disabilities and suites with king bed, queen futon, and parlor room with refrigerator and wet bar. On-site, guests have access to a large continental breakfast, guest laundry, and an indoor pool, hot tub, and dry sauna.

REDSTONE

Avalanche Ranch $$
12863 Highway 133
(970) 963-2846, (877) 963-9339
www.avalancheranch.com

If you've always wanted to own a little spread in the mountains, you can dream about it while spending the night at this 36-acre ranch, 7 acres of which border the Crystal River. Choose from 13 small cabins or a 2,000-square-foot ranch house, all of which have kitchens but none of which are fully wheelchair accessible. When

you're not sleeping, you have access to a petting zoo, volleyball and horseshoe pits, hiking trails, a pond for fishing, an antiques store, and a community room with games and television. Pets are permitted but cost $12 extra. Smoking is not allowed in any of the accommodations.

The Redstone Inn $$
0082 Redstone Boulevard
(970) 963-2526, (800) 748-2524
www.redstoneinn.com
Steel baron J.C. Osgood's married employees were given their own bungalows; the single men were housed in the Redstone Inn, a Tudor-style building with a striking clock tower that is an exact replica of one attached to a Dutch inn in Rotterdam. The 35-room inn also is listed in the National Register of Historic Places and its Victorian furnishings are striking, as is the relatively new health spa that faces the creek. The rooms vary greatly in size, from the large bridal suite to inexpensive dormer rooms with half-baths and showers down the hall. Rooms clustered on the top floor open onto a private veranda. Amenities include an outdoor lap pool, a hot tub, and tennis courts. The restaurant serves elegant meals, including Sunday brunch, and the bar is comfortable. The inn is not wheelchair accessible. Pets are allowed in the rooms; guests with pets are charged $15 extra.

Condos

Brettelberg Condominiums $
11101 County Road 117
(970) 945-7421, (800) 634-0481
www.brettelberg.com
The Brettelberg offers one of the best ski-in, ski-out deals in the Colorado mountains. The only lodge of that kind at Sunlight, it's also one of the most reasonable properties in Glenwood (only about $20 per person during the summer months, and during the winter months, guests get a break on lift tickets). Don't

expect luxury. These 43 studio and one-bedroom units are pure function, with microwaves, full kitchens, satellite TV (in most units), porches, and fireplaces. Small units sleep up to four, larger ones up to six. Amenities include a large outdoor hot tub, a rec room with pool table and video games, barbecue pits, and in-room movies. During the winter, you can walk to the base lodge for breakfast, lunch, and après-ski libations. In the evening and during the summer months, you'll have to drive to town for any meals you don't want to cook yourself. The adjacent Sunlight Mountain Inn sometimes serves meals to nonguests with reservations.

Bed-and-Breakfasts

The Bed-and-Breakfast on
Mitchell Creek $$
1686 Mitchell Creek Road
(970) 945-4002
www.mitchellcreekbb.com
Just two rooms are rented nightly at this bed-and-breakfast, but they offer incredible privacy. They're in the 80-year-old log hideaway of innkeepers Carole and Stan Rachesky, five minutes northwest of downtown Glenwood. It's located on private land so secluded that if you open the window on one side and spit, you'll hit the mountainside. And from the vantage point of the deck, all sounds will mingle with the din of rushing Mitchell Creek. The private entry opens out onto a patio with campfire pit and the trailheads to two nature trails. Snowmobile trails are another five minutes away. Just down the road is the state fish hatchery, which means you can look at the gilled beauties or hike 2 miles farther to the Colorado River for a chance to hook one with your rod. When the weather permits, breakfast can be served al fresco on an elevated patio. The suite is not wheelchair accessible. Pets and smoking are not allowed.

Sunlight Mountain Inn $$
10252 County Road 117
(970) 945-5225, (800) 733-4757
www.sunlightinn.com

This traditional ski lodge has had its ups
and downs, but new owners in 1997
replaced the Bavarian theme with western
ambiance. Its 20 cedar-paneled rooms are
rustic, but they can sleep up to six people;
half the rooms overlook the ski slopes.
Guests walk a few hundred feet to the
base of Sunlight Mountain Resort and,
during the coldest winter months, can ice
skate on the lighted rink. The inn's restau-
rant is open to guests and the public for
breakfast and dinner during the ski sea-
son. The rest of the year guests are served
a hot breakfast and make do the rest of
the day with snacks from the adjoining
Trail's End bar. It has a big-screen TV,
carved fireplace, and all the necessary
beverages to warm a cold evening. Other
amenities include an outdoor hot tub, a
game room, and a romance suite with a
king-size bed, Jacuzzi, and fireplace.
Wheelchair access is limited, and pets are
not allowed.

RESTAURANTS

The Bayou $$
52103 US 6 and 24
(970) 945-1047

The *Aspen Times* champions the Bayou as
"the best place to go down valley," high
praise coming from a city well-known for
its haute cuisine. Some of the credit goes
to the fine Louisiana food, billed on the
menu as "food so good you'll slap yo'
mama." The rest is earned by the joint's
party-time atmosphere. A green frog
awning over the door marks the spot, and
a huge deck lets early evening drinkers
and diners savor the last rays of each day.
(Live musicians entertain on the deck during summer weekends.) Choose from
gumbo, étouffée, and freshwater fish.
Then wash it down with a Cajun martini or
a jalapeño beer.

Dos Hombres $$
51738 US 6
(970) 928-0490

The building that now houses Dos Hom-
bres has been a dozen other things over
the years, but Tex-Mex lovers are glad it's
now the home of Southwestern food.
Located on West Glenwood's motel row
(a short drive away from the more popu-
lar downtown tourist area), the restaurant
is large enough to seat 100 people at any
given time. That's unusual in this town of
tiny converted storefronts, but it's not the
only reason people come here. The food is
reasonably priced and varied, including
the standard smothered burritos as well
as more creative daily specials. The staff is
friendly and the service quick, both god-
sends after a long day of skiing or swim-
ming at the Hot Springs Pool.

Florindo's $$
721 Grand Avenue
(970) 925-1245

Although Glenwood's main street is
known for its honky-tonk tourist action,
Florindo's is a welcome breath of fresh
sophisticated air. Its dining room decor is
spare but crisp, with linen tablecloths and
contemporary art on the walls. The food is
just as genteel—northern and southern
Italian dishes, elegantly served, with gnoc-
chi so well prepared it earns A's even from
connoisseurs. The menu also includes veal,
seafood, and chicken, but the pastas pre-
dominate. Visitors often compare the
atmosphere to an upscale favorite in any
urban neighborhood. This nonsmoking
restaurant has another unusual feature in
Glenwood—it takes reservations, important during summer months and for all
parties of more than six.

Glenwood Canyon Brewing Company $$
402 Seventh Street
(970) 945-1276
www.glenwoodcanyon.com

Glenwood's first brewpub, this bar/restau-
rant in the Hotel Denver has quickly
caught on as the place for local profes-
sionals to gather on Friday afternoons.

Exposed brick and light wood decor complement the hotel's new art-deco facelift. Its Hanging Lake Honey Ale and Red Mountain ESB are standouts among the brewed beers kept in on-site kettles. The kitchen serves both light and trendy meals, including grilled ribs, fulfilling pot-pies, and one of the region's best bread puddings. Like everywhere else in downtown Glenwood, the booths and tables fill up fast around lunch time and after 5:00, but even locals like it enough to wait their turn.

19th Street Diner $
1908 Grand Avenue
(970) 945-9133

Breakfast time in Glenwood can get kind of dicey, with more tourists prowling for grub than there are booths in the city. Locals and those with cars make the short drive south from downtown Glenwood to a real Insiders' treat. The 19th Street Diner is as close to the real thing as we get in the West: a black-and-white checkerboard floor, vinyl booths, soda fountain, jukebox music, and pictures of Marilyn Monroe and James Dean staring down from the walls. The food is just what you would expect—pancakes shaped like Mickey Mouse for kids, sausage and eggs for the grown-ups. Lunches are pure Americana, with blue-plate specials and chicken-fried steak. A full bar in the back serves cocktails all day.

Carbondale/El Jebel

Bella Mia $$$
19105-A Highway 82, El Jebel
(970) 963-2600

This little jewel of an urbane bar and restaurant is a well-kept secret, and locals would like to see it stay that way. When the touristy hubbub of Glenwood gets to be too much, they gladly drive 20 minutes south for a quiet, delicious feast. Bella Mia is located in a strip mall at the El Jebel traffic signal, but don't let that fool you. Inside, it's a slice of Manhattan elegance,

with modern art, soft jazz, and shiny black decor. The menu varies, but chefs make the most of seafood, veal, chicken, and pasta. The bartender complements them with a wide wine selection and well-made cocktails.

Redstone

The Redstone Inn $$$
0082 Redstone Boulevard
(970) 963-2526, (800) 748-2524
www.redstoneinn.com

Steel baron J. C. Osgood's married employees were given their own bunga-lows; the single men were housed in the Redstone Inn, now a hotel and National Historic Place (see the "Accommodations" listing for more details). The restaurant serves elegant meals, including a Sunday brunch that draws visitors from the entire Roaring Fork Valley. A grand piano beck-ons the musically inclined from one end of the restaurant, but tables wrap far beyond it and into what must have been banquet halls at one time. Specialties of the house include grilled duck breast, elk in phyllo dough, chicken breast and thigh roasted with sun-dried cherries, prime rib, and regional favorites. A comfortable pub-type bar is tucked into a nook in the back of the Inn and offers more reason-ably priced meals served an hour later than the restaurant. Its specialty is stone-baked pizzas.

NIGHTLIFE

The Bayou
US 6 and 24
(970) 945-1047

This joint has a party-time atmosphere that is broadcast even before you go inside by the jaunty green frog awning over the front door. Live musicians entertain on the deck during summer weekends. The rest of the year revelers stay inside to sip their Cajun martinis and jalapeño beers.

Glenwood Canyon Brewing Company
402 Seventh Street
(970) 945-1276
www.glenwoodcanyon.com
When there's elbow-bending to be done, locals often head to the Hotel Denver, where the town's only brewpub is located. The spot is especially popular with local professionals who celebrate the end of a long work week with Friday Afternoon Club, but tourists join in too. Enjoy a fantastic selection of freshly brewed beers. It's the perfect place to shoot pool.

Hot Springs Lodge and Pool
401 North River Street
(970) 945-6571, (800) 537-SWIM
www.hotspringspool.com
Believe it or not, much of Glenwood's nightlife revolves around the pool, advertised as the world's largest outdoor hot springs pool. Townsfolk and visitors alike gather year-round in the two-block pool to soak sore muscles, do a few laps, and lounge in the therapeutic water. (See our "Hot Springs and Spas" section of this chapter for more details.)

ATTRACTIONS

Doc Holliday's Grave
Trailhead at 12th Street and
Bennett Avenue
Old West gunfighter Doc Holliday was allegedly put to rest in this cemetery located at the top of a hill overlooking Glenwood Springs. A sign at the trailhead explains his life. The half-mile climb is steep, but the view from the top is superb. Holliday's gravestone is the star of the show and often is decorated with flowers, coins, and other memorabilia. Many other stones date back to the 1800s and teach

Gunslinger and card shark Doc Holliday died of tuberculosis in 1887 in Glenwood Springs. His body was buried in Glenwood's Pioneer Cemetery. THE DENVER POST/JERRY CLEVELAND

Glenwood Springs is known among tourists for its giant hot springs pool, its gentle ski hill, and its wide variety of kid-friendly hotels and motels. The town now makes the most of that reputation, offering a popular "Ski Swim Stay" package. Visit www.skiswimstay.com for the latest promotions, most of which allow kids 12 and under to ski free.

more about the hardships of frontier life than any history book. There is no admission fee.

Frontier Historical Museum
1001 Colorado Avenue
(970) 945-4448
www.glenwoodhistory.com
This Glenwood home was built in 1905, the same year U.S. President Teddy Roosevelt came to the area for a hunting expedition. It was donated to the historical society in 1971. Among its treasured possessions are the saddle Roosevelt used on his hunting trip; an elaborate bed and dresser used by silver baron Horace Tabor and his second wife Baby Doe; a silent movie starring Tom Mix (*The Great K & A Train Robbery*) that was filmed in Glenwood Canyon in 1929; and hundreds of arrowheads collected over the years on the property of local rancher Raymond Hopkins. History of the region's settlers, miners, and Native Americans is brought to life with dioramas, photos, and turn-of-the-century furnishings. It's open May to September, Monday to Saturday 11:00 A.M. to 4:00 P.M.; October to April, Monday and Thursday to Saturday from 1:00 to 4:00 P.M. Admission is $3.00 for adults and children older than 12, $2.00 for seniors 60 and older, free under 12.

Hanging Lake
Interstate 70, 10 miles east of Glenwood Springs (at exit 121 if heading west, exit 125 if heading east)
Hanging Lake is a jewel of a destination, an isolated body of water tucked into one wall of stunning Glenwood Canyon. It was formed when a fault along the mountainside shifted and dropped, forming a basin that collects snowmelt. That explains the ice-cold water that floods into Hanging Lake, forming a waterfall on one side and depositing water that's clear enough to see the fish swim through. Getting there requires a strenuous 1²⁄₁₀ mile hike, and ²⁄₁₀ mile farther is Spouting Rock, a cliffside out of which a waterfall "miraculously" spouts. Younger children will not be strong enough for the climb, and there are no facilities at the top so use the porta-potty at the parking lot before you start. Because of heavy use and the fragile ecosystem, tread lightly, stay on the trail, and pack out all your trash. It's open during daylight hours, and admission is free.

Hot Springs Pool
401 North River Street
(970) 945-6571, (800) 537-SWIM
www.hotspringspool.com
The biggest outdoor hot springs pool in the United States is in Glenwood Springs, and boy, is it big. One of several natural hot springs that flow up into the Colorado River, the Yampah Hot Springs (Ute for "Big Medicine") feed the 2-block-long, million-gallon pool and have enough capacity left over to heat the nearby lodge.

The resort at the pool is open year-round. Admission is $12.00 for adults and teens, $8.00 for children 3 to 12. Children 2 and younger are admitted free. (For much more information on this attraction, see our "Hot Springs and Spas" section.)

Marble
Highway 133, 17 miles west of Carbondale
Mountains near the Yule River are pumped full of marble that rivals that quarried in Italy. It was discovered by miners in the late 1800s, and in 1905 the Yule Marble Quarry was opened. The town of Marble sprung up to house employees, and once was home to 1,500 people. The fine white stone with pale brown veins was used for the Tomb of the Unknown Soldier and the Lincoln Memorial in Washington, D.C.

Local sculptors still come to the site and carve remnants that are strewn around the almost-ghost town. Visitors can walk to the quarry entrance and look into the mine pit. Because it is a working mine, however, they can't go in.

Redstone
Highway 133, 12 miles west of Carbondale

Once home to a coal company town, Redstone now is a pleasant artist's colony and popular tourist spot in the Crystal River Valley. About equidistant from Glenwood Springs and Aspen, it's a secluded but colorful place to spend a few days. The town takes its name from the sandstone cliffs that ring it, although the rushing Crystal River is just as appealing. Visitors can't overlook its history because so many of the turn-of-the-century relics are still standing.

The village was built by John Osgood, founder of Pueblo's Colorado Fuel & Iron Company and owner of several coal mines in the area. He envisioned it as a model town, with his baronial residence on one end of the valley and his workers' homes on the other. His Cleveholm Manor, also called Redstone Castle, is the jewel of the valley. In that home, he entertained such notables as Teddy Roosevelt, J.P. Morgan, and John D. Rockefeller. By 1903 Osgood was forced out of business by an unstable economy, and he left the valley. Embellished with Tiffany lamps, velvet walls, and gold-leaf ceilings, the castle is a hotel listed in the National Register of Historic Places and was for many years a hotel. It was auctioned off by the IRS in 2005 for $4 million. The nearby Redstone Inn, 82 Redstone Boulevard, (970) 963–2526, was the Tudor rooming house built for single miners who lived in Osgood's company town. Also designated a National Historic Place, it serves as a less fancy hotel, complete with a Tudor bell town and antique furnishings. Early reservations are recommended (see our "Accommodations" section for more details). The remaining cabins were built for married employees and are now used as homes, galleries, and shops. Ovens in which the coal was baked into coke, which resemble huge beehives, are overgrown with weeds but still visible alongside the road.

Yampah Spa and Vapor Caves
709 East Sixth Street
(970) 945–0667

Two blocks down the street from the Hot Springs Pool is a series of three natural underground steam baths. The same 124-degree springs that supply the Glenwood Springs pool flow under the cave floors. Each chamber is successively hotter than the next. You can move between rooms as you purify your body (and soul, according to Ute legend), splash yourself with cool water, or visit the upstairs spa for a wide range of treatments—everything from massages to body wraps to herbal loofa rubs to manicures and pedicures. Admission for cave alone is $12. It's open daily from 9:00 A.M. to 9:00 P.M.

KIDSTUFF

Doc Holliday's Grave
Trailhead at 12th Street and
Bennett Avenue

Old West gunfighter Doc Holliday was allegedly put to rest in this cemetery located at the top of a hill overlooking Glenwood Springs. A sign at the trailhead explains his life. The half-mile climb is steep, but the view from the top is superb. Although Holliday's gravestone is the star of the show, and often is decorated with flowers, coins, and other memorabilia, children will enjoy browsing through the other gravestones. Many date back to the 1800s and teach more about the hardships of frontier life than any history book. There is no admission fee.

Frontier Historical Museum
1001 Colorado Avenue
(970) 945–4448
www.glenwoodhistory.com

This Glenwood home was built in 1905, the same year U.S. President Teddy Roosevelt came to the area for a hunting expedition. It was donated to the historical society in 1971. Among its treasured possessions are the saddle Roosevelt used on his hunting trip; an elaborate bed and dresser used by silver baron Horace Tabor and his second wife Baby Doe; a silent movie starring Tom Mix (*The Great K & A Train Robbery*) that was filmed in Glenwood Canyon in 1929; and hundreds of arrowheads collected over the years on the property of local rancher Raymond Hopkins. History of the region's settlers, miners, and Native Americans is brought to life with dioramas, photos, and turn-of-the-century furnishings. It's open May to September, Monday to Saturday 11:00 A.M. to 4:00 P.M.; October to April, Monday and Thursday to Saturday from 1:00 to 4:00 P.M. Admission is $3.00 for adults and children older than 12, $2.00 for seniors 60 and older, free under 12.

Glenwood Springs Fish Hatchery
1342 132nd Road
(970) 945-5293
Many of those five- and six-pound cutthroats, rainbow trout, and brookies that grownups love to pursue in local fishing waters get their start in state hatcheries like this one. During daylight hours, kids (and their adults) can learn about the life cycle of the trout, get a close-up look at the fish, and learn about breeding and

feeding habits. Those who bring quarters can also feed the inhabitants with kibble purchased form feed dispensers.

Hot Springs Pool
401 North River Street
(970) 945-6571, (800) 537-SWIM
www.hotspringspool.com
Billed as the world's largest outdoor hot springs pool, this 405-foot-long mass of water is a comfy 90 degrees. In the summer that feels almost cool. In the winter it's warm enough to make up for the ice and snow collecting nearby. A smaller therapy pool is 104 degrees, best visited in spells no longer than 15 minutes at a time. Glenwood's star attraction attracted its first inhabitants, Ute Indians who though the hot water was "Big Medicine" for all kinds of ills. It has been a tourist magnet ever since. (Read more about it in our "Hot Springs and Spas" section.) Kids love the gently sloping bottom—most can stand up in the water for nearly half its length. They also love the twisting water slide that dives from several stories up down to a shallow receiving pool. It's open daily in the summer from 7:30 A.M. to 10:00 P.M. and during the winter from 9:00 A.M. to 10:00 P.M. and during the winter from 9:00 A.M. to 10:00 P.M. Admission is $12.00 adults and teens, $8.00 for children 3 to 12. Children 2 and younger are admitted free. Water slide rides are extra. You can also rent swimsuits and towels.

Hot Springs Pool Miniature Golf Course
401 North River Street
(970) 945-6571, ext. 668
Almost a landmark in Glenwood Springs, this minigolf course is about as centrally located as it could be. It's at the crossroads of the town's two busiest streets—Grand Avenue and 6th Street—which means kids traveling anywhere are bound to see it and beg for the chance to play. It has gone through several incarnations over the years, but the 18-hole course is a refreshing change of pace after a long, hot day at the pool. Hours are 11:00 A.M. to 10:00 P.M. Sunday through Thursday, 11:00

A.M. to 10:30 P.M. Friday and Saturday. Cost for 18 holes is $5.25 for adults, $4.25 for children 12 and under.

Johnson Park Miniature Golf
51579 US 6 and 24
West Glenwood Springs
(970) 945-9608

The town's newer minigolf course is known for its waterfalls, barrels of flowers, and challenging water obstacles. Choose from two 18-hole courses, one more challenging than the other. Johnson Park is open daily Memorial Day to Labor Day 9:00 A.M. to 10:00 P.M. and spring and fall months from noon to 9:00 P.M. For each 18 holes, expect to pay about $5.50 for adults, and $4.50 for under 12 and over 60.

Skiing Lessons and Child Care

Sunlight Mountain Resort
10901 County Road 117
(970) 945-7491, (800) 445-7931

Non-skiing children 18 months to 6 years old can get day care at Cricket Corner. The second child in the same family gets a discount. Super Tots lessons are for children 4 to 6, with half- or full-day programs available.

SHOPPING
Glenwood Springs

Glenwood's main street, Grand Avenue, maintains the air of a honky-tonk mining town, complete with historical wooden buildings that now house bars, restaurants, and a wide range of gift stores. If you're doing more than buying souvenirs, however, you'll probably want to drive west to Glenwood Springs Mall or south to the strip malls that line South Grand Avenue. The newest entry along the corridor is the Roaring Fork Marketplace.

The Book Train
723 Grand Avenue
(970) 945-7045

Glenwood's largest bookstore stocks 12,000 titles, including hardback, paperback, and children's books. It specializes in books about Colorado and natural history but also sells newspapers, 2,000 magazines, maps, and greeting cards from this central downtown location.

Glenwood Springs Mall
51027 US 6 and 24
(970) 945-1200
www.gwsmall.com

This mall is anchored by JCPenney, Kmart, and Staples Office Supplies, but also has a Bath & Body Works, Famous Footwear, GNC, Radio Shack, and a three-screen movie theater.

Red Mountain Books
51027 US 6 and 24
(970) 928-0588

Located in Glenwood Springs Mall, this chain store stocks 2,000 titles in hardback, paperback, and trade paperback. It also sells art supplies, gifts, games, maps, and software.

Roaring Fork Marketplace
South Highway 82

Wal-Mart and American Furniture Warehouse are the anchors of this mall. In between are stores that specialize in stereo equipment, video rentals, secondhand children's clothing, exercise and sports gear, books, magazines, and music.

Sioux Villa Curio
114 6th Avenue
(970) 945-6134

The lifelike Indian sitting in front of this store should be you first clue. Sioux Villa is as kitschy as it gets, but longtime visitors look forward to their next browse around the display cases. The store just across the road from the Hot Springs Pool is stuffed with such gag gifts as exploding cigarettes, plastic doo-doo piles, ice cubes with ants in them, and inflatable pillows that make rude noises when sat upon. The store also carries a good selection of respectable and affordable gifts—Indian beaded belts, aspen leaf earrings, and postcards of Colorado, to name just a few—but the politically incorrect gag gifts have kept people coming back for decades.

Summit Canyon Mountaineering
732 Grand Avenue
(970) 945-6994
www.summitcanyon.com
Summit Canyon is a top-notch adventure store that stocks everything from kayaking gear to climbing essentials. You can't miss it in the busiest block of historic downtown Glenwood.

Sunlight Ski and Bike Shop
309 9th Street
(970) 945-9425
www.sunlightmtn.com
Sunlight Mountain Resort is the local ski area, just 10 miles south of town, but its owners know that may be too far to drive for a shopping trip. They maintain a helpful sporting goods store on the town's main drag, stocking items that are appropriate for the season. Break your ski goggles on your way up to the mountain? Forget your skates? Want to go biking? Chances are good they have what you need.

Through the Looking Glass
816 Grand Avenue
(9700 945-5931
Children's books of all kinds—mingled with bestsellers and other adult books—make this downtown Glenwood store unique. It also stocks greeting cards and stationery.

The Watersweeper and the Dwarf
717 Grand Avenue
(970) 945-2000
This downtown landmark sells handicrafts and functional art made by Colorado artisans. The merchandise includes everything from silver and gold to clay, candles, glass, and wood.

Necessities

Hot Springs Lodge & Pool
401 North River Drive
(970) 945-6571
www.hotspringspool.com
If you've come up to swim in the blocks-long hot springs pool but forget something important, chances are you can purchase it in the pool's gift shop. It stocks everything from sunscreen to bathing suits, trashy novels to beach towels. It's also responsible for the pool-toy-of-the-year fad. Your kids will arrive contented, then see other kids swimming with Orca the Whale or throwing a cool new kind of beach ball. Prepare to trudge down to the gift store for whatever the "item of the month" may be.

Carbondale/El Jebel/ Redstone

Four towns on the road between Glenwood Springs and Aspen—El Jebel, Carbondale, Basalt, and Redstone—were little more than building clusters just over a decade ago. In the 1990s, they grew into towns that serve both as affordable suburbs and artists' enclaves. A few unique shops draw visitors from both ends of the valley.

Artists' Collective
647 Main Street, Carbondale
(970) 963-9194
More than 50 local artists are represented in this store, with works that range from pottery to paintings, birdhouses, stamps, and handmade doll clothes.

Crystal Farm
18 Antelope Road, Redstone
(970) 963-2350
www.crystalfarm.com
This place specializes in chandeliers and furniture made from antlers. You've probably seen this uniquely western kind of decor in area resorts and guest lodges: mirrors rimmed with hundreds of two-point antlers, tables supported by large

moose racks, and chandeliers that stack lights in among concentric circles of deer, elk, and antelope antlers.

Crystal Glass Studio
50 Weant Boulevard, Carbondale
(970) 963-3227
www.crystalglassstudio.com
This working studio/gallery in downtown Carbondale is home to lamps, chandeliers, tables, and sculptures of such things as fish and tree branches. Artisans also take commissions to do stained, beveled, and etched glass pieces.

The Great Camp Collection
358 Main Street, Carbondale
(970) 963-0786
www.thegreatcampcollection.com
Interior designer Bonnie Sherwood has an original line of custom lodge furniture (think overstuffed leather cushions with pine logs forming the frames) that she sells from this store. She also carries rustic American and European antiques, fine art, chandeliers, and vintage Navaho rugs.

THE ARTS
Theater

Colorado Mountain College Theatre
215 Ninth Street
(970) 947-8252
www.coloradomtn.edu/theatre
Students from the local two-year college perform three major productions a year during the school year, including a drama and a musical. Schedules vary each year, so call ahead for times and titles. Summer workshops also are taught by CMC's drama department.

Defiance Community Players
(970) 945-3074
In 2006 the local troupe celebrates its 35th year of productions. The group normally performs only during the fall and winter months, sometimes with only one show a year. In past years a cast and crew

of more than 100 have presented *Bye Bye Birdie, Guys and Dolls, The Sound of Music,* and *The Wizard of Oz.*

Thunder River Theatre Company
Town Center, Carbondale
(970) 963-8200
www.thunderrivertheatre.com
This professional theater company puts on four shows a year, most of which are new works. Past productions have included *Talley's Folley, True West, The Little Foxes,* and *Oleanna.* Until it gets its own performance space, the company uses the auditorium at Carbondale Community School.

Visual Art

Carbondale Council on the Arts and Humanities
645 Main Street, Carbondale
www.carbondalearts.com
This loose-knit council on the arts is working to promote the emerging arts scene in growing Carbondale, located between Glenwood Springs and Aspen. It sponsors regular performances at the Bohemian Coffee House during the fall, winter, and spring months as well as organizing and acting as a clearinghouse for local artists. During summer months, it sponsors free performances in the town's Sopris Park on Thursday evening, and organizes Carbondale Mountain Fair in late July.

Glenwood Springs Center for the Arts
601 East Sixth Street
(970) 945-2414
www.glenwoodspringscenter forthearts.com
Located in what used to be the electric building behind the Hot Springs Pool, the center serves as a hub for the Glenwood Springs arts scene. It maintains a gallery that features a different artist every month; a pottery studio; a sculpture studio that features sculptors carving stone from the nearby mines in Marble; and a performance space that seats 150 people.

It also rents studio space to local artists. Past art shows have included Native American portraits, watercolor land-scapes, Russian art, and quilts. The center also sponsors a wide variety of concerts, festivals, and art shows throughout the year, ranging from cabaret shows and jazz to dance and culinary art festivals.

Oneirica Ranch
4618 Cattle Creek Road, Carbondale
(970) 945-7929
www.wewerart.com
Artist Wewer Keohane maintains a studio and gallery at her home and also uses the space to teach adults drawing, painting, mixed media, book art, and collage tech-niques. Her works include watercolors, mixed media canvasses, collages, wood-cuts, and photograms.

Redstone Art Center
0173 Redstone Boulevard, Redstone
(970) 963-3790
www.redstoneart.com
Marble was the first artistic medium to be used in the Crystal River Valley, especially the white rock mined in the town of Mar-ble, upstream from Redstone. Today the Art Center also features pottery, jewelry, woodwork, and watercolor art.

EVENTS
January

Robert Burns Dinner
Hotel Colorado, 526 Pine Street
Glenwood Springs
(970) 945-6511, (800) 544-3998
www.hotelcolorado.com
Celebrate Scotland's National poet, Robert Burns (1759-1796), in late January with Celtic songs, dancing, dinner and, of course, poetry, including Burns's famous "Ode to the Haggis." Guests will dine on lamb, sausage, and mushroom pie, root vegetables, bread pudding, and haggis, the Scottish dish best known as a pau-per's meal because it uses parts of the

sheep that otherwise would have been wasted. Special overnight packages are available from the hotel. Reservations are required.

June

Strawberry Days
Various locations, Glenwood Springs
(970) 945-6589
www.strawberrydaysfestival.com
Celebrated since 1898, Strawberry Days is Colorado's oldest civic festival. A carnival with midway games sets up in Sayre Park, as do tents filled with arts and crafts for sale and booths hawking food. Partici-pants in the week-long, mid-June event are treated to strawberries and ice cream one day, and sports lovers can choose between the 5K and 10K Strawberry Shortcut foot race and a softball tourna-ment. Admission is free, except for carni-val rides, race entrance fees, and food.

Summer of Jazz
Two Rivers Park, Centennial Street at
the confluence of the Colorado and
Roaring Fork Rivers, Glenwood Springs
(970) 945-6589
www.summerofjazz.com
If it's a summer Wednesday night in Glen-wood, you can expect to hear jazz floating upstream from the Two Rivers Park. Musi-cians gather there to perform free con-certs at 7:00 P.M. from mid-June through August, with their selections ranging from progressive and traditional jazz to Dix-ieland.

August

Doc Hollidays
Various locations, Glenwood Springs
(970) 945-6589
In mid-August, the town of Glenwood Springs celebrates its most famous past resident, gunfighter Doc Holliday, who died from tuberculosis less than a year

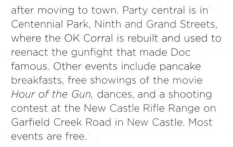

after moving to town. Party central is in Centennial Park, Ninth and Grand Streets, where the OK Corral is rebuilt and used to reenact the gunfight that made Doc famous. Other events include pancake breakfasts, free showings of the movie *Hour of the Gun,* dances, and a shooting contest at the New Castle Rifle Range on Garfield Creek Road in New Castle. Most events are free.

SKIING

Glenwood Springs

Sunlight Mountain Resort
10901 County Road 117
(970) 945–7491, (800) 445–7931
www.sunlightmtn.com
Base elevation: *7,885 feet*
Top of highest lift: *9,895 feet*
Total vertical: *2,010 feet*
Longest run: *2½ miles*
Average annual snowfall: *250 inches*
Ski season: Thanksgiving through mid-April
Capacity: *4,600 skiers per hour*
Terrain: *470 acres, 68 trails (20 percent beginner, 55 percent intermediate, 25 percent advanced and expert)*
Lift tickets: *$39 all-day adult*
Snow reports: *(970) 945-7491*
Getting there: *Sunlight Mountain Resort is about 167 miles west of Denver International Airport via I-70 through scenic Glenwood Canyon. Turn south on U.S. Highway 82 to County Road 117. Glenwood Springs is a daily Amtrak stop if you don't want to fly or drive in.*

Like many of Colorado's hometown ski areas, Sunlight was developed by locals who were determined to make themselves a winter playground. They found the best snow 10 miles southeast of and 2,000 feet above Glenwood Springs in a valley that, until the turn of the 20th century, was home to a coal mine. There they carved out a slope they called Holiday Hill. When they got tired of tramping their way to the top, they installed a 1929 Buick engine at the summit and connected it to a rope

tow. On ski days the president of a local bank hiked up to the engine and sat with his foot on the gas pedal as long as there were skiers to tow.

More than fifty years later, Sunlight Mountain Resort still has that down-home feel. Since it opened as a formal ski area in 1966, its primary market has come from surrounding areas. Most of the 100,000 skiers who visit each year come from nearby Rifle, Basalt, Carbondale, and Glenwood Springs and ski on season passes they buy for a song. The others on the slopes are Colorado residents who would rather ski than rub shoulders with celebrities, and church or social groups from Kansas, Oklahoma, and Nebraska.

Locally, Sunlight is known as a forgiving place to learn the sport and an economical place to warm up before moving on to glamorous Aspen (about 40 miles south) or glitzy Vail (about the same distance east). Local business professionals promote the idea, advertising Glenwood Springs as a perfect home base for a Colorado ski vacation, with affordable lodging and skiing and good roads on which to take day trips to the pricier places.

In the mid-1990s, Sunlight was bought by national investors who came with plans for expansion. In 1996 it added five new extreme trails; in 1997 it spent money on snowmaking equipment to frost the base area on warm spring days. In 1998 they built a new day lodge at the base.

About three dozen trails are arranged in an arc above the simple base lodge. Real beginners start on a super-gentle area to one side of the parking lot, then move up to the west face of the mountain. The easiest slopes are wide and gentle and are split down the middle with an aspen glade called The Enchanted Forest that's riddled with child-size trails. Better beginners ride the chairlift to the top of Compass Mountain, a 10,000-foot peak skirted by a scenic trail they sometimes share with cross-country skiers who climb it for aerobic exercise. The eastern trails are harder, with steep moguled runs and, to the far east, Sunlight Extreme. It provides Colorado's steepest inbounds skiing, with one ledge that is twice as steep as the average U.S. expert slope.

Snowboarders have access to all Sunlight slopes, but a snowboard park east of the base lodge has quarter-turns, camel bumps, rail slides, and other obstacles.

Cross-country

The cross-country center maintains 29 kilometers of free trails, 10 of which are groomed, and telemarkers can buy single-ride tickets on lifts so they can ski down the Alpine slopes. The center has two warming huts, rentals, and instruction services. Trails are exceptionally wide, with a skating lane in the middle. A rustic backcountry cabin is available for overnight use. It hosts the annual 10K Coal Dust Classic, one of the state's oldest cross-country citizens' races.

OTHER WINTER RECREATION
Snowmobiles

Sunlight Snowmobile Tours
10901 County Road 117
Glenwood Springs
(970) 945-7491, (800) 445-7931
Sunlight Mountain offers snowmobile rentals and tours through the White River National Forest. From there you have 360-degree views of Mount Sopris, the West Elk Mountains, and the Flattops Wilderness area. For the more adventuresome the Wild Ride Performance tour takes off into untouched powder fields on high-powered machines for an extreme experience. Tours are usually half-day affairs, and cost $130 for a single rider, $185 for double riders. The Wild Ride tour is two hours long and costs $175, single riders only.

Snowshoeing

Sunlight Mountain Resort
10901 County Road 117
(970) 945-7491, (800) 445-7931
More than 29 kilometers of snowshoe terrain is located adjacent to the ski resort, most of it in the White River National Forest. Access is free to the trails that serve as hiking and biking favorites during summer months. Ask at the ticket booth for help finding the trailhead.

HIKING/BACKPACKING

The White River National Forest Headquarters in Glenwood Springs has excellent details on dozens of hikes, suggested backpacking destinations, and campgrounds. It offers one of the most comprehensive displays of information of any National Forest Headquarters, including a *Hiking & Bike Trails* brochure. The office is located at 900 Grand Avenue in the Old Federal Building, (970) 945-2521. The Glenwood Springs Chamber Visitors Center at 1102 Grand Avenue, (970) 945-6589, also has information about hiking and camping.

In Carbondale, the Sopris Ranger District at 620 Main Street, (970) 963-2266, has information on the White River National Forest and the wilderness area.

Doc Holliday's Trail
13th Street and Bennett Avenue
The trailhead is just off the town's main street, Grand Avenue, and leads ½ mile to the pioneer cemetery that holds the remains of Glenwood's most famous gunslinger, Doc Holliday. A mudslide mixed up the graves years ago, so his exact burial plot is not known. An honorary spot has been chosen and sports a large engraved headstone and fenced-in plot.

Grizzly Creek
About 6 miles east of Glenwood Springs off I-70
Much less crowded than Hanging Lake, this 6-mile trail is still fairly well traveled

because it is so accessible. The trailhead is at the east end of the Grizzly Creek Rest Area on the north side of I-70. The trail starts wide at an elevation of 6,000 feet, then narrows into a single-track trail that climbs to 8,000 feet, all the while following the creek that begins on the White River Plateau as snowmelt and cuts through a limestone canyon on its way to joining the Colorado River. It's very rocky (watch your step) and offers good fishing for brook trout and whitefish, but the fishing is difficult because big boulders and the narrow canyon make it hard to cast. You can camp in the upper reaches of the canyon or return the way you came for a 12-mile round-trip hike. It's best hiked in the summer and fall.

Hanging Lake
Off I-70, 10 miles east of Glenwood Springs

Easily accessible from I-70, this popular hike is short, steep, and spectacular. The lake formed from a geologic fault that "hung" the lake down from the valley floor above, where cascading waterfalls keep it filled. The 1²⁄₁₀-mile trail climbs 1,000 feet from Glenwood Canyon, and reasonably fit folks can make it in about an hour with some huffing and puffing. Deadhorse Canyon, seen from the top, offers some pretty views. Those with enough energy left to climb another 200 feet above the lake can view Spouting Rock, a hole in the cliffside where an entire creek spouts with fury. Be sure to stay on the trails since this area is heavily used and vulnerable to damage with the large number of visitors. To find the trailhead, drive east from Glenwood Springs 10 miles up Glenwood Canyon on I-70. There's a well-marked exit for Hanging Lake and a parking area.

CAMPING

Ami's Acres
502355 US 6 and 24
(970) 945-5340

If you're looking for easy access, Ami's is

the place. It's located on the frontage road that parallels I-70 and works its way through West Glenwood. The campground has 70 sites, 44 of which have full hookups, and also offers laundry, picnic tables, grills, and showers. You'll hear highway noise, but you'll also be within a mile or so of all Glenwood's attractions, including the nearby golf course. Sites are $20 to $28 a night. Reach it from exit 114 on I-70, then go 1 mile west on the frontage road.

Aspen-Basalt Campground
20640 Highway 82, Basalt
(970) 927-3405, (800) 567-2773

The only full-service RV park near Aspen, this commercial campground has 75 sites, 57 with full hookups, some of which are on the Roaring Fork River. It's open year-round, but during the summer months it offers on-site fishing, hiking, and easy access to both Aspen and Glenwood Springs. Amenities include a laundry, dump station, grills, fire rings, store, swimming pool, and hot tub. Cost is $33 to $36 a night. The campground is 2 miles northwest of Basalt on Highway 82.

Bogan Flats
About 20 miles south of Carbondale on Highway 133
(970) 963-2266
(877) 444-6777 for reservations

Located just off Highway 133 on the road to Marble, Bogan Flats is about as remote as a car camper can get. It's just south of Redstone, a company town founded by a steel baron in the 1900s, and just up the road from the historic marble quarry that supplied the stone for the Lincoln Memorial and the Tomb of the Unknown Soldier (see "Attractions" section for details). The public campground has 37 sites and has water, fire rings, and toilets. Campers can fish, hike, ride horses, or search through the marble discards that line the banks of the Crystal River. Good sightseeing is within driving distance, as are Glenwood Springs and Aspen. As the quarry is still being mined, remember it is private prop-

Hanging Lake is a well-known jewel at the top of a 1½ mile hike east of Glenwood Springs. It's particularly beautiful in winter, when ice crystals form along the cascading waterfalls.
THE DENVER POST/JERRY CLEVELAND

erty, but surrounding land is designated a national historical site. Camping fee is $15 per night. To reach the campground, take Highway 133 south from Carbondale to Forest Service Road 314. Turn left and follow it southeast for 1½ miles.

Chapman Campground
About 25 miles east of Basalt off Highway 82
(970) 963-2266,
(877) 444-6777 for reservations

The ultimate angler's campground, Chapman has 84 sites along Chapman Reservoir, fed by the world famous Fryingpan River. Because it's upriver from the more popular fishing waters of Ruedi Reservoir, it's also less populated and has dramatic high-altitude scenery. Only non-motorized boats are allowed on the reservoir, but those in need of a mechanical fix can make use of a network of four-wheel-drive roads that lead, among other places, across Hagerman Pass to Leadville and Turquoise Lake. Amenities include water, fire rings, a few wheelchair-accessible sites, and toilets. Fee is $15 per night.

Glenwood Canyon Resort
1308 Garfield County Road 129
(970) 945-6737, (800) 958-6737
www.glenwoodcanyonresort.com

Formerly known as Rock Gardens Camping and Rafting, this campground has developed into a full-scale camping resort, complete with RV and tent sites, unfurnished camper cabins, and fully furnished resort cabins. It's still affiliated with the rafting part of the business and still has its spectacular location alongside the Colorado River. New amenities include a bathhouse, laundry room, game room, convenience store, shuttle service to local area attractions, and private access to the river. You can book yourself a raft trip from here, take a Jeep tour, rent a kayak or mountain bike, or just toss a line in the river for some fine fishing (a license is required). Take exit 119, then follow the frontage road along the river.

Hideout Cabins & Campground
1293 Garfield County Road 117
(970) 945-5621

A little pocket of old Glenwood, the Hideout is nestled into the wooded banks of the Roaring Fork River. Campers in any of the 53 sites (38 have full hookups) have access to a playground, laundry, showers, and all the fishing they can stand (state fishing licenses are required). The town's bike path passes nearby, as does the road to Sunlight Mountain Resort. The campground is open year-round. Reach it by taking exit 114 on I-70, then traveling south on Midland Avenue for 3¾ miles and another mile south on 27th Street/Midland Avenue.

Meadow Lake
About 32 miles northwest of New Castle
(970) 625-2371

If you're looking for something remote, Meadow Lake may be just the thing. At an elevation of 9,600 feet and at the end of a rough and winding road, Meadow Lake's 10 campsites provide solitude, high-altitude scenery, fishing, and Jeep trails in every direction. Other amenities include a boat dock, water, fire rings, picnic tables, and toilets. Don't attempt the drive unless you've called the ranger station to ask about road conditions or without detailed maps of the area. Sites cost $13 a night. To reach it, take exit 105 on I-70 at New Castle, then go northwest on Garfield County Road 245 for 9 miles until it turns into Forest Service Road 245. Keep traveling north for 20 miles to Forest Service Road 601, then turn east. Continue another 4 miles to Forest Service Road 823, and the campground is another 3 miles south.

Redstone Campground
About 13 miles southwest of Carbondale off Highway 133
(970) 963-2266
(877) 444-6777 for reservations

With 20 modernized sites on the banks of the Crystal River, Redstone Campground is about as picturesque as you'll find

Many courses and clubs see a rush of activity on certain days of the week. To avoid the hassles of a busy day, call ahead and reserve a tee time.

within a 20-mile radius of I-70. Campers have access to water, fire rings, showers, toilets, electricity, horseshoe pits, and a playground. They're also within walking distance of the historic town of Redstone (read more about it in the "Attractions" portion of this chapter), and a short drive away from the glitter of Aspen and the tranquil beauty of the Maroon Bells-Snowmass Wilderness Area. Sites are also some of the most expensive in the national forest service's chain at between $19 and $26 a night.

Ruedi Reservoir
**About 16 miles east of Basalt
off Highway 82
(970) 963-2266
(877) 444-6777 for reservations**
Near Basalt, the beautiful Fryingpan River offers some pretty sites that might be less crowded than areas around Aspen. There are four campgrounds at Ruedi Reservoir that charge a fee of $14 to $16 per night: Mollie B with 26 sites, Little Maud with 22 sites, Little Mattie with 20 sites, and Deerhamer with 13 sites. All have water, fire rings, and toilets, but their primary claim to fame is the fishing at Ruedi and along the Gold Medal streams of the Fryingpan River. A few of the sites at Mollie B, Little Maud, and Little Mattie offer shade. Those at Deerhamer, on the eastern edge of the reservoir, may be quieter than the others. It has its own boat ramp. In addition to fishing, campers may also hike, sailboard, and sail. To reach these campgrounds, take the Basalt exit off Highway 82 and travel east through the business district on Midland Road. It becomes Fryingpan Road (Eagle County Road 105). Follow it another 16 miles.

GOLF

Glenwood Springs Golf Club
**193 Sunny Acres Road
(970) 945-7086**
Located on a bluff above West Glenwood, this nine-hole course (nicknamed "The Hill") opened in 1952 and has since served the town as an accessible and inexpensive venue. The course is narrow and surrounded by trees, but the view south onto the Colorado River and Red Mountain is still spectacular. An Insiders' tip from the pros: The greens generally break toward the Colorado River.

Reservations are taken up to seven days in advance. Carts are not required, although they are available. Green fees from May through the club's closing are $32 for 18 holes, $19 for 9 holes.

Rifle Creek Golf Course
**3004 Highway 325, Rifle
(970) 625-1093
www.riflecreekgolf.com**
Opened in 1960, the Rifle Creek course was designed by Richard M. Phelps and named for the creek that winds through the front nine. Because it's off the beaten path and not surrounded by a posh housing project, it's a favorite of locals interested in challenging and scenic golf at a bargain price. As growth spills west from Glenwood Springs, however, it may not stay that way long. Rifle is about 27 miles west of Glenwood off I-70, and Rifle Creek is another six miles off the interstate.

The 6,234-yard, par 72 course incorporates two distinct types of terrain: the front nine is fairly flat and dissected by the meandering Riffle Creek; the back nine is hilly, with holes more like those traditionally found on mountain courses. Because much of the surrounding countryside is still used for agricultural purposes, the mood is bucolic and the scenery spectacular. As with Glenwood Springs Golf Club, putts usually break south toward the Colorado River. Carts are not required, but are available. Greens fees for 18 holes are $51 with cart, $37 without.

River Valley Ranch
303 River Valley Ranch Road, Carbondale
(970) 963-3625
www.rvrgolf.com
River Valley Ranch elbowed its way into a valley more known for its skiing and scenery than its golf when it opened in April 1998. The course sits on pastureland at the confluence of the Crystal and Roaring Fork Rivers, just 12 miles south of Glenwood Springs and 30 miles north of Aspen. The public course is being ringed by upscale houses.

The Crystal River rushes through the valley, making it the focal point for seven of the 18 holes. The first shot off the first tee box sets the pace, flying across the river (if all goes well) to the fairway on the other side. Another breathtaking tee box is on hole 16, perched yards above the green and providing a panoramic view of the course, the valley, and Mount Sopris beyond. The river also is home to bald eagle nesting sites, so it is off limits between December 1 and March 15. That doesn't interfere with the golfing season, even though it's long at this gentle mountain meadow, elevation 6,200 feet. Depending on the weather, the course is open April 1 through Thanksgiving. It was designed by Jay Morrish as a blend of Scottish and American golfing designs. The bunkers are intimidatingly steep, a Morris trademark, and a few are dropped into unusual spots that are out of play and shouldn't see much action. The 7,348-yard par 72 course is owned by Crown Golf Properties, owner of the Snowmass Club.

Green fees are $85 a person (cart included).

FISHING/HUNTING
Outfitters and Tackle Shops

Black Elk Guides & Outfitters
1085 Highway 133, Carbondale
(970) 963-9666

Hunting trips for elk, mule deer, and black bear are this company's specialty. It's about 30 miles north of Aspen at the confluence of the Crystal and Roaring Fork Rivers. Prices vary, depending on whether guides drop hunters at a camp or guide them throughout the hunt.

Capitol Peak Outfitters
552 County Road 110
(970) 923-4420
www.capitolpeak.com
Another guide service for fall hunting trips and summer pack trips, fishing trips, and trail rides, Capitol Peak is also a good source for information about herd sizes and locations. Call for details and prices.

Roaring Fork Outfitters
2022 Grand Avenue
(970) 945-5800, (877) 945-5800
www.rfoutfitters.com
For more than 20 years, owners of Roaring Fork Outfitters have been floating down the Colorado, Fryingpan, and Roaring Fork Rivers. They're good sources of information about where the fish are biting, plus they lead guided wade and float trips all around the region. Call for information on prices.

Places to Fish

Beaver Lake
Marble, off Highway 133
The Crystal River keeps this lake filled, although it also is occasionally stocked with rainbow and brook trout. It's located on the east end of Marble, but that doesn't mean it's urban. Marble's year-round population is in the single digits. Locals enjoy paddling past the weed-choked shoreline in canoes or rowboats. Boats with motors aren't allowed on the lake.

Crystal River
Between Marble and Carbondale, off Highway 133
The Crystal River starts in the ghost town of Crystal but winds up joining the Roar-

ing Fork River 35 miles down valley. In the meantime, it plays host to brook trout. It's easily accessible from Highway 133, so it does get crowded. The higher you go, the fewer people you'll rub shoulders with.

Dinkle Lake
Northeast of Redstone, off Highway 133
Two lakes near the edge of White River National Forest—Dinkle and Thomas—are wonderful places to fish for rainbow, cutthroat, and brook trout. Hiking between the two involves covering 3½ miles and 1,600 feet in elevation gain. You may also stay overnight in campsites near the lakes. Find them by driving a mile south of Carbondale to Prince Creek Road across from the fish hatchery on Highway 133. You'll see a Dinkle Lake turnoff sign there.

Rifle Gap Reservoir State Park
10 miles northeast of Rifle
Brown and rainbow trout, walleyes, and bass populate Rifle Gap Reservoir, about 35 miles northwest of Glenwood Springs. Rifle Gap is 26 miles west of Glenwood on I-70, then 5 miles north of Highway 13 to the junction with Highway 325. Take the right fork and travel 5 more miles.

Roaring Fork River
Highway 82 between Glenwood Springs and Aspen
Fishing is possible the entire span of the Roaring Fork River, from its origin atop Independence Pass to its confluence with the Colorado River in Glenwood Springs. The Gold Medal waters are between Woody Creek and Glenwood Springs. Between Carbondale and Glenwood Springs you'll find rainbow and brown trout, and the best mountain whitefish waters in the state, but you'll have to fight through crowds to get them. Keep a careful eye on posted public and private lands along the river, though, because public and private lands are heavily mixed throughout the valley. In waters that aren't Gold Medal, anglers have a two-fish limit, and only artificial lures and flies are permitted between April and October.

Yule Creek
Near Marble, off Highway 133
Small cutthroat trout thrive in Yule Creek, a fast, narrow stream that flows north into the town of Marble. The town is named for its principal wealth, the high-grade marble mined nearby. The creek rushes over cast off chunks of the stuff as it follows the dirt road to the marble quarry. To reach Yule Creek, drive through Marble to Third Street, then turn right and follow it past the mill's parking area and across the one-lane bridge.

Places to Hunt

Dinkle Lake
Northeast of Redstone
For excellent high-country elk hunting, Dinkle Lake is a well-known destination. One of two lakes near the edge of White River National Forest (the other is Thomas), Dinkle has overnight campsites. The terrain is rugged and subject to early snows. Find it by driving a mile south of Carbondale to Prince Creek Road across from the fish hatchery on Highway 133. You'll see a Dinkle Lake turnoff sign here. Ask for information about Game Unit 43.

Flat Tops Wilderness Area
North of Glenwood Springs to Steamboat Springs
Part of the White River National Forest, the Flat Tops Wilderness Area is world-renowned for its deer and elk hunting. It can be accessed by following I-70 to the Dotsero exit (between Glenwood Springs and Gypsum), then continuing north along Deep Creek to the Deep Lake area. Hunters may also access the Flat Tops by exiting I-70 at New Castle (east of Glenwood Springs), then following the Forest Road to Buford. Ask for information about Game Units 33 and 34.

OTHER RECREATION

The Glenwood Springs Chamber Resort Association
1102 Grand Avenue
(970) 945-6589, (888) 4-GLENWOOD
www.glenwoodchamber.com
With a 24-hour visitor center open daily, you'll find out anything you need here. Glenwood is known for its hot springs (please refer to the section on "Hot Springs and Spas"). There's also fine rafting on the nearby Colorado River, which cuts through scenic Glenwood Canyon. A beautiful paved bike path runs alongside the river, providing smooth riding with breathtaking scenery of the river and red canyon walls. Stop at the chamber for information about all types of activities and hundreds of local outfitters that provide everything from river rafting to rock climbing.

Bicycling

Canyon Bikes
319 6th Street, in the Hotel Colorado
(970) 945-8904
www.canyonbikes.com
The Glenwood Canyon Recreational Trail opened in 1993, and offers bicyclists miles of broad, smooth concrete alongside the Colorado River. Canyon Bikes is located less than a block from the trailhead. Rental bikes, tandems, and trailers are available in hourly, half-, and full-day blocks, with special twilight rates after 4:00 P.M. Included in the rental are gel seats, helmets, locks, packs, and trail information. For those who would rather pedal downhill, Canyon's shuttle will drive bikes to the east end of the trail for an extra $13.00. Rental prices range from $5.00 to $12.00 an hour, $18.00 to $36.00 for half-day, and $23.00 to $46.00 for full-day, depending on what kind of bike is rented.

White River National Forest
900 Grand Avenue
(970) 945-2521

Ask for the *Hiking & Bike Trails* brochure, which details 19 trails. This map is also available at local bike and outdoor shops and the resort chamber listed above.

Cave Tours

Glenwood Caverns/Historic Fairy Caves
508 Pine Street
(800) 530-1635
www.glenwoodcaverns.com
Around the turn of the century, the Fairy Caves in the limestone cliffs above Glenwood were as big a tourist attraction as the hot springs pool. Unfortunately, many of the Victorian visitors carried away the stalagmite and stalactites that made this cave so unique. World War I put an end to the visits. In 1999, petroleum geologist and avid caver Steve Beckley re-opened them, as well as another 2 miles of more pristine caves. The Fairy Caves are thought to have been named for a series of fragile winglike formations near the mouth (all but a few that aren't on the tour became souvenirs). The Glenwood Caverns have two of the state's largest underground rooms—The Barn, with a ceiling five-stories tall, and King's Row, which has striking gypsum flowers and needles, aragonite crystals, colorful coral formations, long tendrils called soda straws, and a multi-colored ribbon-candy style formation called cave bacon for its brown and beige stripes. See this chapter's close-up for more information.

Horseback Riding

Chair Mountain Stables
County Road 3, Redstone
(970) 963-1232
www.chairmountainstables.com
Chair Mountain Stables are the oldest full-service facility in the Crystal Valley, located just across the street from the town of Redstone, behind the beehive-shaped coke ovens that once turned ore

Underground Glenwood

Between 1886 and 1917, these spectacular caverns outside of Glenwood Springs were called the "Fairy Caves." They were named for the fragile fish-tail helictites that sprouted from the walls and looked like fairy wings. Early visitors pocketed them as souvenirs, so by the time engineer Steve Beckley reopened the caves to 21st-century visitors, the wings were long gone. He now calls them the Glenwood Caverns and operates tours April through November for casual observers (the family tour) as well as spelunkers interested in a crawl through as yet unexplored regions of the underground caverns he estimates to be 8 miles long (the wild tour).

Beckley first got interested in the caves over 20 years ago after reading about them in a book about Colorado caves. They had been closed to the public for 65 years by that time, and were owned by an unsociable fellow who was known to shoot at trespassers. Beckley spent nearly a decade developing a friendship with the man before suggesting that he lease them in exchange for developing, restoring, and exploring them. In 1999, his dream became a reality when the caves opened to the public.

Now visitors can catch a shuttle van at the Caverns office, located next door to the Hotel Colorado, and travel to the entrance on Iron Mountain north of Glenwood Springs. Once there, they'll get a look at the power of the geothermal hot springs that bubble up below in Glenwood's hot springs pool. Starting 9 million years ago, the hot waters began to eat away at the Earth's interior, dissolving the weak layers of stone and leaving behind the strongest. Over time external rivers carved 1,300 feet into the Earth's crust to form Glenwood Canyon. Geologists believe the cavern-forming springs flowed out to join them and left the caves behind.

Even so, mineral deposits continue to form in the caves, a result of trapped moisture that drip, drip, drips until the minerals it is carrying are left behind. Cave bacon is perhaps the most spectacular of the formations. It curves around on the walls and ceiling like ribbon candy, but in shades of brown instead of pastel greens and pinks. It represents a lazy flow of moisture down the cavern walls, depositing its mineral load at the rate of one foot of cave bacon every 1,000 years.

Of course, you'll also find your share of stalactites and stalagmites in Glenwood Caverns, plus the state's largest cave room, The Barn, which is 250 feet long and 60 feet high, and a shorter but longer (300 feet) room called King's Row.

Tours leave daily between 9:00 a.m. and 6:00 p.m. from April 15 through November 1 from the Glenwood Caverns office, 508 Pine Street, Glenwood Springs. Tickets for the family tour are $12.00 for adults, $7.00 for children 6 to 15, and free for children 5 and under when accompanied by a parent. Tickets for the wild tour are $50 per person. For more information, call (970) 945-4CAV.

to coke. Guests of all abilities can ride on 200 to 300 acres of private property, most of which is undeveloped and some of which is high enough to be called high-altitude. Children 5 and under ride with adults. Chair Mountain offers one-hour rides for $35 per person or a full-day ride through beautiful Coal Basin, including a picnic lunch, for $150 per person. The Overnighter takes riders deep into high country for an overnight stay. The $275-per-person charge includes lunch and dinner, a night under the stars, and breakfast the next morning. From Glenwood Springs, take Highway 82 to Highway 133 in Carbondale. Turn right and drive 18 miles, past the first entrance to Redstone to the second. Turn right (left will take you into town).

Rafting/Kayaking

Blue Sky Adventures
319 6th Street, in the Hotel Colorado
Glenwood Springs
(970) 945–6605
www.blueskyadventure.com
Boasting its 30th season, this company offers full- and half-day raft trips on the Colorado River in nearby Glenwood Canyon and on the Roaring Fork River to the south. River trips range from exciting whitewater rafting to casual float trips through Glenwood Canyon. Raft trips range in price from $32 to $69 for adults, depending on length of the trip, and $27 to $53 for children 15 and under. Guided trips in inflatable kayaks are also available for people at least 15 years old who have prior rafting experience. At least four paddlers are required. A third option for those who have trouble making choices is the Peddles & Paddles combo, with half day spent biking and half day spent floating. Expect to spend at least $50 for adults, $40 for children 15 and under.

Rock Gardens Rafting
1308 County Road 129
Glenwood Springs
(970) 945–6737
www.rockgardens.com
Rock Gardens has been in business since 1974, guiding thrill-seekers of all experience levels through full-day, half-day, and short trips along the Roaring Fork or Colorado Rivers. The rafting business is located at the Glenwood Canyon Resort, 1.5 miles east of Glenwood Springs at the No Name exit (exit 119) off I-70. The campground on the premises has tent and RV sites with electric hookups and full-furnished camper cabins (see our listing under "Camping"). Expect to spend between $45 and $75 for rafting, depending on the length of the trip, with children 12 and under $30 to $60.

Whitewater Rafting, L.L.C.
2000 Devereux Road
West Glenwood Springs
(970) 945–8477
www.coloradowhitewaterrafting.com
Trips up to 90 minutes, a half-day, or a full day on the Colorado are available here. Or try a Yahoo, the revolutionary new kayak. The price range is from $21 for a short trip for children younger than 12 to $69 for a full-day adult trip. Yahoos cost $35 a day. To reach Whitewater Rafting, take exit 114 of I-70.

Running/Walking/ In-line Skating

Glenwood Canyon Recreation Trail
I-70 between Glenwood Springs and Dotsero
A multi-use path that parallels I-70 and the Colorado River opened to the public in 1994. It's perfect for joggers, strollers, and in-line skaters because most is broad, smooth, and, unfortunately, crowded on weekends. To reach the trailhead, go east from the Yampah Vapor Caves on Sixth Avenue. The trail continues for 20 miles

through the stunning steep red-walled Glenwood Canyon. The smoothest and gentlest skating portion is the 6-mile stretch between the Bair Ranch Rest Area and Hanging Lake Trailhead. Walkers interested in a more strenuous outing can walk to the trailhead for Hanging Lake, then take the steep 1-mile hike up to the jewel of a lake perched on a shelf above the canyon (see the "Hiking/Backpacking" section for more details).

HOT SPRINGS AND SPAS

Hot Springs Lodge & Pool
401 North River Street
(970) 945-6571, (800) 537-SWIM
www.hotspringspool.com
The biggest outdoor hot springs pool in the United States is in Glenwood Springs, and boy, is it big. One of several natural hot springs that flow up into the Colorado River, the Yampah Hot Springs (Ute for "Big Medicine") feed the 2-block-long, 1-million-gallon pool and have enough capacity left over to heat the nearby lodge. Guests can take a peek at the original spring, which is protected behind a chain-link fence at the east end of the pool. It produces 3.5 million gallons of 124-degree water each day, all of which is diluted with cooler water and piped away. The pool actually consists of three pools: a small, shallow rectangle for children, a 100-foot-long soaking pool kept at 104 degrees, and the granddaddy of all hot springs pools, which is 405 feet long and is kept at 90 degrees.

Civil War veteran and ex-miner Isaac Cooper bought the pool after the Utes were exiled from the region in 1881. He built the original sandstone and terra-cotta lodge in 1890, which still serves as offices, with one bathhouse and a casino for gentlemen only. Diamond Jim Brady, Doc Holliday, and Buffalo Bill Cody were known to have gambled at the casino. Gunslinger and cardshark Holliday actually came to Glenwood in 1887 hoping the curative waters would heal his tuberculosis, but he

died of the disease six month later. The pool and hotel were drafted by the Navy and became a hospital and rehabilitation center during World War II. In 1956 22 local businesspeople bought the property and still own it today. The resort is open year-round. Admission is $14.25 for adults and teens, $9.00 for children 3 to 12. Children 2 and younger are admitted free.

Penny Hot Springs
Highway 133, between Carbondale and Aspen
www.marblecolorado.net/ pennyhotsprings
Another of the Utes' favorite springs, Penny is a free and undeveloped springs that changes in size and shape from day to day. It flows from beneath the Crystal River, so defining it is a bit difficult. Locals try to carve out pools for themselves in the river, using large rocks for borders. Because the spring flows at 130 degrees, they attempt to trap enough of the hot water to keep it warm while also diverting enough cool river water to make it bearable. In the 1980s skinny-dippers and a nearby rancher went to court over their right to bathe and his right to be shielded from naked bodies. The skinny-dippers won the right to continue their free soaks, although many bathers now wear suits.

The real trick is finding the springs, which are along Highway 133 but 15 feet down a dirt trail. A sign that says C.R. 11 at the turnoff is your only clue, unless the weather is so cold you can see the steam coming off the river.

Yampah Hot Springs Vapor Caves and Spa
709 East 6th Avenue
(970) 945-0667
www.yampahspa.com
Just down the street and east of the Hot Springs Pool are three natural underground vapor caves, each kept about 110 degrees. They're fed by the Yampah hot springs as it flows beneath the vapor cave floors, leaving behind water, steam, and heat in these naturally formed caverns.

Glenwood's Hot Springs Pool is the country's largest outdoor hot springs pool. Fed by the Yampah Hot Springs, it's over 3 blocks long and the water is kept at 90 degrees. *THE DENVER POST/STEVE DYKES*

The Utes used them for ceremonies and healing and return every Memorial Day for a conference and spiritual purification ritual. Guests can use mud from the walls for facials, or can relax on the marble benches. The 125-degree spring water is piped along the sides of each cave. There is no pool here, only cold showers in the caves and warm showers upstairs in the locker room area. A solarium, massage rooms, and private hot tubs also are located on ground level. Spa services range from massages to facials and body wraps. The caves are open year-round. Admission is $12 for the caves along with extra charges for spa treatments.

ASPEN

Named for the lush aspen forests that surround the valley, Aspen was first settled in the 1880s when miners spilled over the hill from Leadville and found a rich cache of silver buried beneath Aspen Mountain. For nearly a decade times were good, as fast fortunes were made—and spent. After the bust in 1893, the crowds deserted Aspen. Half a century later they were lured back, first by a makeshift ski area, and then by an institute that promised to challenge their intellects while bathing them in beautiful surroundings.

Today Aspen is a mecca for people with good taste and lots of money. Movie stars and barons of business arrive in personal Learjets to visit their second homes or party with their pals. Musicians, dancers, artists, actors, and thinkers spend the summer in residence at creative festivals and retreats. Glam gals come for the shopping, and for the services of discreet plastic surgeons who promise quick and professional touch-ups in the privacy of Aspen's well-equipped hospital.

During the winter, life revolves around skiing and après skiing. Four ski areas provide slopes for skiers and boarders of all experience levels. Restaurants and nightclubs fulfill the same range of appetites, although they're more heavily weighted on the expensive end of the scale. Any time of the year, Aspen and the surrounding valleys are as beautiful as Colorado gets. Those patient enough to drive into the narrow never-never land almost always feel privileged to be there.

ACCOMMODATIONS

Hotels and Motels

Hotel Durant $$$
122 East Durant Avenue
(970) 925-8500, (877) 438-7268
www.durantaspen.com
With French country decor and central location (only 3 to 5 blocks from Aspen Mountain ski lifts), the Hotel Durant is a locals' favorite. Its 19 rooms are large and pleasantly decorated, each one unique. They share a central Jacuzzi and fireplace.

Hotel Jerome $$$
330 East Main Street
(970) 920-1000, (800) 331-7213
www.hoteljerome.com
Considered a national treasure, this glorious restored historic hotel is named for Jerome B. Wheeler, the one-time president of Macy's department store in New York City. He took over the completion of the hotel after the original owners skipped town. The hotel's grand opening on Thanksgiving Eve in 1889 was perhaps Aspen's most glamorous event ever with guests attending from Europe. The Jerome's original building houses 25 luxu-

Aspen may seem like a little town, with fewer than 6,000 year-round residents, but it has lots of room for visitors. Aspen/Snowmass has an overnight bed base of 14,000, with 8,000 of those rooms in Aspen and another 6,000 in Snowmass.

rious rooms including seven guest suites, and a new wing has 67 rooms. After decades of decline, the Jerome went through a major restoration in 1989. The original iron door fixtures, tile, sandstone, and wood were all refurbished, and furniture was restored to its original grandeur. The central lobby is a masterpiece of Victorian splendor and worth a visit even if you're not staying at the hotel.

Don't miss the J Bar on the building's west side with the original bar still in place. Be sure to stop in and admire the Jerome's restoration, which is well documented with before and during photos lining the hallway. The Jerome has a restaurant, the original ballroom—well worth a look—and a swimming pool. Make reservations far in advance for holidays and high-season periods.

Hotel Lenado $$$
200 South Aspen Street
(970) 925-6246, (800) 321-3457
www.hotellenado.com
Another elegant choice, this boutique hotel with 19 rooms provides an intimate atmosphere. The rooms are all beautifully unique, and guests enjoy a rooftop hot tub, a library and lounge, and a complimentary full breakfast. All luxury-class amenities are included, such as a concierge, room service, and courtesy airport transfers.

The Limelite Lodge $-$$$
228 East Cooper Avenue
(970) 925-3025, (800) 433-0832
www.limelite-lodge.com
The Limelite is an Aspen institution and, in some ways, an anachronism. It's one of the few remaining affordable hotels as others have been condominimized or converted to low-cost housing projects. The Limelite survived by absorbing its neighbors, the Snowflake Inn and Deep Powder Lodge, in 2005 and remodeling them into a centralized group that now has 63 hotel rooms and nine furnished apartments. The location is prime, just across the park from Aspen's bustling downtown core and a few blocks from the ski mountain. Rooms come with a complimentary breakfast and rates vary with the season. Pets are $10 per night.

The Little Nell $$$
675 East Durant Avenue
(970) 920-4600, (888) 843-6355
www.thelittlenell.com
Little Nell offers Aspen's lushest rooms and only ski-in, ski-out hotel. Absolutely top of the line, The Little Nell's hotel and restaurant are highly rated. A contemporary-style hotel, The Little Nell has 92 rooms, including eight suites and five executive suites. The rooms are spacious and decorated in rich but subdued colors. Each has a gas fireplace and huge marble bathroom with two vanities, a glass-enclosed shower, and a separate bathtub in a mirrored alcove. Each room has a mini-bar, gas-burning fireplace, and high-speed Internet. Amenities include twice-daily housekeeping, room service, ski valet, overnight ski tuning, valet/laundry services, valet parking, a concierge, massage, a sauna, business services, guest privileges at the Snowmass Club & Lodges' fitness and tennis center, and courtesy airport transfers. There's also a good bookstore in the lobby.

Outside by the heated swimming pool and hot tub, a covered alcove lets you enjoy the snowflakes in steamy comfort. Best of all is the ski concierge connected to the building. You can pad down the hallway in your socks from your room and walk right into the ski concierge room, where your boots and skis await you. Call ahead, and they'll set them out. Then it's a grueling 50-foot walk to the Silver Queen gondola at the base of Aspen Mountain, which will whisk you to the top of the mountain for a day of skiing—the ultimate in skiing luxury and convenience. The end of the day is even better. For the final run of the day, you can ski right to the deck of the ski concierge, slip off your equipment, and they'll put it away for you. Ah, luxury. If you didn't get enough exercise skiing, The Little Nell also has an excellent state-of-the-art exercise facility. The restaurant is sublime (see "Restaurants" in this chapter). You certainly get what you pay for at The Little Nell, and reservations are necessary well in advance.

Little Red Ski Haus   **$$**
118 East Cooper Avenue
(970) 925-3333, (866) 630-6119
www.littleredskihaus.net
One of Aspen's last bargain accommodations, this Ski Haus has a great location for low-priced lodging. The cute, cozy rooms have shared baths and are popular with younger skiers. The best deals are for the triple and quad rooms.

Molly Gibson Lodge   **$$**
101 West Main Street
(970) 925-3434, (800) 356-6559
www.mollygibson.com
An elegant small inn with 50 rooms and some suites, this lodge is 3 blocks from town. Some of the suites have jetted tubs, woodburning fireplaces, and kitchens. Amenities include a courtesy airport van, après-ski bar, two pools, and two hot tubs. A continental breakfast is included in the room price.

St. Moritz Lodge   **$$**
334 West Hyman Avenue
(970) 925-3220, (800) 817-2069
www.stmoritzlodge.com
Only 5 blocks from downtown, this European-style lodge offers private rooms, dorms, and some of the best bargain rooms in town. It's dubbed by some as Apen's unofficial youth hostel. There's a small heated pool and a comfortable common room looking out onto a deck. Weekly and monthly rentals are also available.

St. Regis Aspen   **$$$**
315 Dean Street
(970) 920-3300, (888) 454-9005
www.stregisaspen.com
Now under new ownership by Starwood Hotels, this hotel was formerly the Ritz Carlton. Every amenity is available at this luxury 257-room mountain-style hotel, 1 block from the Silver Queen gondola at the base of Aspen Mountain. The St. Regis has a bit more formal atmosphere and decor than its luxury counterpart, The Little Nell, and is more than three times the size. There are 26 suites and a Club Level, keyed off and with an even higher level of service than the top quality. The rooms have three phones, a safe, bathroom scales, fresh flowers, and round-the-clock service.

Opened in 1991 the hotel features four restaurants, two lounges, an outdoor pool, two hot tubs, a fitness center, steam room, saunas, a beauty salon, and shops. Of course, there are all the amenities such as twice-daily housekeeping, concierge, bell staff, valet parking, business services, a sports concierge, dry-cleaning, laundry, and massage. Ten rooms are designed specifically for guests with disabilities.

SNOWMASS

Mountain Chalet   **$$**
15 Daly Lane
(970) 923-3900, (800) 843-1579
www.mountainchalet.com
Complimentary full breakfasts are included in the room price at this well-maintained hotel right by the ski slopes. There's also a fitness center, pool, hot tub, sauna, restaurant, and lounge. Courtesy airport transfers are provided too. Book early at this popular hotel.

Pokolodi Lodge   **$$**
25 Daly Lane
(970) 923-4310, (800) 666-4556
www.pokolodi.com
Pokolodi Lodge and its sister property, the Snowmass Inn (see subsequent entry), both provide more modestly priced but very nicely appointed accommodations right at the foot of the ski slopes. Rooms have refrigerators and coffeemakers along with daily housekeeping and a 24-hour front desk. Enjoy a swimming pool and courtesy airport transfers.

The Silvertree $$$
100 Elbert Lane
(970) 923-3520, (800) 525-9402
www.silvertreehotel.com
This luxury slopeside hotel has 262 rooms and suites, most of which have private patios or balconies. Decorated in attractive contemporary decor, the rooms have refrigerators, coffeemakers, hair dryers, and Nintendo on TV. The hotel is just steps away from the ski slopes, Snowmass Mall, and the Snowmass Conference Center. All amenities are available including a 24-hour front desk, bell staff, room service, concierge, and massage. There are four restaurants, a piano bar, two heated pools, hot tubs, a fitness center, a steam room, a sauna, and a ski rental shop.

Snowmass Inn $$
25 Daly Lane
(970) 923-4202
www.snowmassinn.com
The economy-priced sister property to the Pokolodi Lodge (see previous listing), the inn is a chalet-style multilevel building with no elevators, but very nice, affordable accommodations. The rooms are hotel-style, and guests share amenities with the Pokolodi Lodge, including a complimentary continental breakfast, heated pool and hot tub, free transportation to and from the airport, and a great central location.

Wildwood Lodge $$-$$$
40 Elbert Lane
(970) 923-3520, (800) 525-9402
www.silvertreehotel.com
This friendly, midsize and mid-priced hotel has remodeled guest rooms and suites in a rustic style with hunter greens and burgundies. Each unit has a minifridge, coffeemaker with coffee, a hair dryer, and daily housekeeping. The plentiful amenities include an outdoor heated pool, hot tub, sauna, guest laundry, restaurant, and lounge. The lodge provides courtesy airport transfers, and a complimentary continental breakfast comes with the rooms.

Condos and Vacation Rentals

Aspen Central Reservations and Travel
(970) 925-9000, (888) 649-5982
www.stayaspensnowmass.com
Call this office for a wide variety of options in the area, including private homes, condos, hotels, bed-and-breakfasts, and cabins. Ask about other services, such as airport transfers, flights into Aspen, and discount lift tickets.

ASPEN

Aspen Alps $$$
700 East Ute Avenue
(970) 925-7820, (800) 228-7820
www.aspenalps.com
Luxury two-, three-, and four-bedroom units each have fireplaces and balconies and are adjacent to the Silver Queen Gondola right on the slopes of Aspen Mountain—the location couldn't be better. Amenities include daily housekeeping, courtesy airport transfers, and a pool, hot tub, and sauna.

Chalet Lisl $$
100 East Hyman Avenue
(970) 925-3520, (877) 925-3520
www.chaletlisl.com
The modestly priced condominium complex may be a lot more affordable for some folks. Pleasant and comfortable, it offers nicely decorated studio and one-bedroom units. Amenities include a game room, hot tub, ski-tuning bench, and library.

Lift One Condominiums $$$
131 East Durant Street
(970) 925-1670, (800) 543-8001
www.liftone.com
These moderately priced condos come in one- to three-bedroom units. Also well located at the base of Aspen Mountain, the condos have daily housekeeping, a heated pool, hot tub, saunas, and living

rooms with fireplaces. A guest laundry room is available.

The Residence $$$
305 South Galena Street
(970) 925-6532
www.aspenresidence.com

If your taste runs to first-edition volumes of English classics flanking an antique fireplace from the old Brown Palace Hotel in Denver, Mario Buatta fabric-covered walls, marble appointments, and hand-painted sinks with gold fixtures, the Residence is for you. With a $200 deposit, you can even bring your pet.

The bedrooms have Ralph Lauren linens over European down-filled duvets and feather beds. In the Raj Suite, which captures the feeling of Colonial India, there's a crystal chandelier collected from Aspen's old Hotel Jerome. Also featured are the Country Suite, with a beautiful Mexican ceramic-tiled kitchen; the English Victorian; the French Studio; and the Penthouse, with spectacular views of area mountains. Suites range from $249 to $3,295 per night depending upon the suite and the season. A minimum stay is required during the holiday season, and cancellation policies are very strict; call for specific details, or visit the Web site listed above.

This amazing small hotel right in the heart of Aspen contains six European-flavored suites and apartments, each with its own theme and furnished with Persian rugs, museum-quality art work, and designer fabrics. Most suites have wood-burning fireplaces, and all have such modern conveniences as TVs, VCRs, stereos, and alarm-clock radios. The Residence is on the second level of an historic building, so is not very wheelchair-accessible. Each apartment has a fully equipped gourmet kitchen and fine dining service, including china, crystal, and silver.

Owner Terry Butler loves to chat about Mexico, where she spent much of her childhood. She can also tell you about her frequent encounters and friendships with various movie stars and celebrities who frequented a health club she used to operate in Aspen. Look around for photos of Ms. Butler with Sylvester Stallone and other celebrities. Call in advance for reservations.

SNOWMASS

Alpine Property Management
16 Kearns Road, Suite 206
(970) 923-5860, (800) 984-9488
www.alpineproperty.com

For private homes in the area, this company and the one listed below have the largest inventory of properties in the area. Alpine handles about 60 to 70 properties, most of which require a one-week stay. Look for bargains in January and before Christmas, and ask for discounted lift ticket coupons.

Aspen/Snowmass Central Reservations
(970) 925-9000, (888) 649-5982
www.stayaspensnowmass.com

Call this office for a wide variety of options in the area, including private homes, condos, hotels, bed-and-breakfasts, and cabins. Ask about other services, such as airport transfers, flights into the area, and discount lift tickets.

The Crestwood $$
400 Wood Road
(970) 923-2450, (800) 356-5949
www.thecrestwood.com

These slopeside condos have balconies with gas barbecues, fireplaces, full kitchens, washers/dryers, and a bathroom for each bedroom. There are 124 units ranging from studios to three-bedroom apartments. You'll also enjoy a courtesy airport transfer, a pool, two whirlpools, a sauna, an exercise room, and easy access to grocery and liquor stores.

The Laurelwood $$
640 Carriage Way
(970) 923-3110, (800) 356-7893
www.laurelwoodcondominiums.com

Two levels up from Snowmass Mall, these modestly priced studio units are very close to the ski slopes and the shops of Snowmass Mall. All 52 units have kitchens, balconies, and fireplaces, and some have upgraded furnishings. There's a front desk, a pool, a hot tub, and daily housekeeping except on Sunday. It's possible to stay a minimum of one or two nights.

Parmelee and Company
25 Lower Woodbridge Road
(970) 923-3636, (800) 999-0816
www.snowmasshomes.net
Parmelee has one of the largest inventories of private homes in the area, and it handles one condominium complex. There's usually a seven-night minimum stay for properties, depending upon the time of year. Low season for house rentals in the Snowmass-Aspen area is spring through fall, including summer months.

Bed-and-Breakfasts

Sardy House $$$
128 East Main Street, Aspen
(970) 920-2525, (800) 321-3457
www.sardyhouse.com
Once a 19-room bed-and-breakfast housed in a Queen Anne Victorian mansion, the recently remodeled Sardy House has elevated the concept to new heights. The main residence is now rented as a single unit consisting of six bedrooms, nine-and-a-half baths, two kitchens and dining rooms, two media rooms, and a spacious executive office—over 9,000 square feet of space, with a full staff of 10 employees. Each of the six bedroom suites offers privacy, romantic and dramatic views of Aspen, and up-to-date amenities such as steam showers and whirlpool tubs. The decor and luxurious furnishings in each room are so soothing and restful you may never want to venture outside, and you may catch only a glimpse of the guests you bring with you to share this quintessentially Aspen bed-and-breakfast.

For smaller parties—say, just you and your spouse on a romantic getaway—the Sardy House offers a more traditional bed-and-breakfast experience in one of the eight Carriage House rooms, tucked neatly behind the main house. Here you can enjoy the same amenities and luxury of the main house, without actually having to rent the entire building. Plush bedding, heated towel racks, terry robes, and private whirlpool tubs will ease the pain after a day on the slopes. In the morning, a gourmet breakfast is served in the West End Room.

Without question this is the pinnacle of the bed-and-breakfast experience, and it's priced to match. For one of the Carriage House rooms expect to pay from $575 to $1,075 per night during the winter, from $325 to $695 during the summer. For the magnificent Sardy House itself, rates are available only upon request.

Resorts

Snowmass Lodge & Club $$$
0239 Snowmass Club Circle
Snowmass Village
(970) 923-5600, (800) 525-0710
www.snowmassclub.com
With 76 hotel rooms and 60 one- to three-bedroom villa units (condos), this country-club-style resort hotel is situated on 567 acres at the base of Snowmass's ski slopes. There's a first-class spa, year-round racquetball, the adjoining Snowmass Golf Club, and the Snowmass cross-country ski center. Complete hotel services include daily housekeeping, a 24-hour front desk, a bell staff, a slopeside ski concierge, a courtesy shuttle to Aspen, and first-rate restaurants and bar. Take advantage of a health and fitness center; hot tubs; steam rooms; indoor tennis, squash, and racquetball courts; and ski rentals. A children's nursery is on-site. Ask about special golf and ski packages.

RESTAURANTS

Aspen

Ajax Tavern $$$
The Little Nell, 685 Durant Avenue
(970) 920-9333
www.ajaxtavern.com

This well-placed landmark at the base of the gondola on Aspen Mountain fills up fast, often as early as 5:00 P.M., which makes it a real coup to snag a seat. (Reservations are a must.) The patio has one of the best views in town—straight up the imposing mountain—and also is one of the best people-watching spots. Inside, it's a cozy, jazzy nook filled with the aroma of Cal-Mediterranean cuisine; the sleek mahogany room feels like a swank ship's tavern. The menu features Northern Italian cuisine following the traditional antipasti (appetizers), pasta, secondi ("second" or main course), and contorni (side dishes) presentation. If you're with a group, go for the Antipasto alla Famiglia, a classic offering of meats, olives, cheese, and peppers. For a smaller plate try the Whole Roasted Artichoke alla Romana with garlic, chili flakes, pinot grigio, and mint. Pasta dishes range from the traditional lasagna, served either vegetarian or with sausage, to the cutting-edge ravioloni of sweet pepper polenta, roasted rabbit, sage, and garlic. If your appetite pushes you onward to the "Secondi," you can choose between an assortment of seafood or pesce di giorno (fish of the day), or go with one of the meat selections such as a grilled center cut veal loin chop served with smashed red potatoes and cippolini onions. The wine selection features vintages from all the major wine areas including the Napa Valley, Tuscany, France, and New Zealand, and are available by the glass.

Boogies Diner $
534 East Cooper Street
(970) 925-6610
www.boogiesaspen.com

This is a fun place with '50s decor that will especially delight baby boomers. There's a jukebox, photos of the kids who were televised on *American Bandstand,* and lots of '50s memorabilia. You can get all types of sandwiches and salads, including a good ol' grilled cheese (the Aspen touch includes sprouts), BLTs, and burgers, such as the 1-pound "Boogie Burger (Rolaids on request)." There are also heart-healthy and veggie specialties. Take advantage of a full bar plus special drinks such as coffee amaretto, cherry Pepsi, milk shakes, malts, and a full soda fountain. Sit in one of the salmon-pink vinyl booths, and relive the past with a modern twist. A big greenhouse-type roof lets in lots of that mountain light, and neon fans twirl overhead. It's a great place for dining with the kids, too.

Cache Cache $$$
205 South Mill Street
(970) 925-3835
www.cachecache.com

The hot spot with the fancy name is a French bistro that serves light food in Provençal tradition. Its specialty is a non-piercing rotisserie that grills duck, chicken, game, and other meats. Among the items on its menu are black mussels, pernod, and tomatoes in a lobster broth; Tasmanian salmon with jasmine rice and citrus vinaigrette; and Colorado rack of lamb with potatoes au gratin. There are also daily menu specials across the board. Dinner is served nightly starting at 5:30 P.M.

Campo di Fiori $$
205 South Mill Street
(970) 920-7717

This relative newcomer serves northern Italian food in a rustic trattoria setting. Tables are close, and servers are friendly. Locals consider it a nice mid-range restaurant known for its risotto with porcini mushrooms, pasta, lamb chops, and quail. It serves dinner only.

Century Room at Hotel Jerome $$$$
330 East Main Street
(970) 920-1000
www.hoteljerome.com
Select from lamb, Rocky Mountain trout, and beef amid the Victorian splendor of this historic hotel. The lush, elegant decor and the first-class service combine to make this a special occasion kind of place. The food is Contemporary American, and includes such items as rack of lamb, prime sirloin, and striped bass. Dinner is served nightly from 6:00 to 10:00 P.M.

Explore Booksellers and Bistro $$$
221 Main Street
(970) 925-5338
www.explorebooksellers.com
Pick your favorite subject matter and relax among shelves of books while seated at antique library tables and chairs. Oriental-type carpets help make the atmosphere charming and cozy with the tables distributed here and there in the many rooms of the rambling house. Explore advertises itself as Aspen's only totally vegetarian restaurant, but even non-vegetarians will enjoy the ambiance and food. The entire kitchen is meat-free, and even the coffees and teas are organically grown. The eggs are from free-range chickens, the water is filtered and deionized, the butter is organic, and whole-organic-grain breads are baked on the premises. Diners can choose from an extensive menu of vegetarian and vegan dishes including Mediterranean pizza, the house tempeh burger, and chef specialties like the vegetable tamales or buckwheat crepes stuffed with grilled portobello mushrooms. There's a full cappuccino bar and lots of great desserts—both regular and dairy-free. While you're dining, you can also read a copy of the *London Sunday Times*, the *Jerusalem Post*, the *Japan Times*, the *New York Times*, and the main German and French newspapers.

Gusto Ristorante $$
415 East Main
(970) 925-8222
www.gustoristorante.com
Another good place to pull up to the bar and eat—at a discount—the same entree that's served in the dining room, Gusto is known for its Italian food served in a casual setting. Among its favorites are Rigatoni di Bosco, pasta tubes stuffed with assorted wild mushrooms and shallots; Agnello in Crosta, roasted rack of lamb with an herb-bread crumb crust; and an assortment of baked foccacia and thin crust pizzas. It serves lunch and dinner daily.

ink! Coffee $
520 East Durant Avenue
(970) 544-0588
Attached to a snowboard shop (D&E Snowboards), ink! Coffee is a great coffeehouse favored by locals. Some call it the place to go for espresso and a bagel before hitting the slopes. It's furnished with couches and game machines, and includes on its menu bagels, scones, smoothies, and of course, coffees of all kinds.

Kenichi $$$
533 East Hopkins
(970) 920-2212
www.kenichiaspen.com
One of two top-flight sushi bars and Japanese restaurants in Aspen, locals and visitors rally around Kenichi. Its motto is "creating edible art"; its food is modern Japanese with diverse Asian influences. Kenichi boasts that it has Aspen's only private Tatami Room. The appetizer menu alone is huge, and includes everything from an assortment of fresh lettuce wraps, dumplings, and fried calamari strips to lobster and shitake mushroom spring rolls and blackened tuna. The sushi menu is also extensive and includes traditional sushi in two-piece orders or rolls in six-piece orders. Try the Kenichi Special Roll with snow crab, tuna, cucumber and avocado, inside out and topped with masago.

And don't forget the sake; Kenichi offers a sake menu with over 20 selections. Kenichi is open nightly at 5:30 P.M. for dinner.

La Cocina $
308 East Hopkins Avenue
(970) 925-9714

A good mid-range Mexican restaurant recommended by locals, La Cocina is especially popular with families and those in search of a nice patio during warm weather. The food and surroundings are no frills, but the food is the Real McCoy.

Little Annie's Eating House $
517 East Hyman Avenue
(970) 925-1098

If there is such a thing as a neighborhood restaurant in this tiny town, Little Annie's is it. The interior looks like a mining claim, with rough wood planks and gear hanging from the ceiling. The food is down-home good, ranging from barbecue brisket on a bun, beef stew, chili, and chicken-fried steak. It's open for lunch and dinner.

Main Street Bakery & Cafe $
201 East Main Street
(970) 925-6446

Have a treat or make a whole meal of it. This cute, casual cafe in an old Victorian house on the corner has antique furniture and a patio view of Aspen Mountain. It also has a glorious assortment of home-baked goods, including raspberry truffle brownies, breads, pastries, and all kinds of mountainous pies. In addition to baked goods, there are stir-fried dishes, potpies, espresso drinks, beers, and wines. It's open for breakfast, lunch, and dinner.

Mezzaluna $$$
600 East Cooper Street
(970) 925-5882
www.mezzalunaaspen.com

This is the kind of light, urban bistro you'd expect to find in Manhattan's upper west side, with long window-walls that can be opened onto an outdoor patio when the weather permits. The bright yellow chairs are the loudest thing in the place, so loud they look almost like happy faces. For locals or tourists on budgets, Mezzaluna offers a bar menu from 3:00 to 6:30 P.M. that includes pizzas at less than half price, soups, salads, and appetizers. The regular menu includes wood-burning oven pizzas and big portions of northern Italian dishes. Après-ski, it's a noisy, energetic place for a beer and a pizza.

Montagna $$$$
675 East Durant Street
(970) 920-6330
www.thelittlenell.com

The recipient of *Wine Spectator's* Grand Award, Montagna remains the centerpiece of the dining experience at The Little Nell, and chef Ryan Hardy and master sommelier Richard Betts combine their talents to continue the long tradition of excellence here. Dinner entrees feature Milagro Ranch organic grass-fed beef, grown locally in nearby Carbondale, and prepared as a chef's selection nightly. There is also the Riesling Braised Rabbit with creamy polenta and melted Taleggio, and the Whole Grilled Branzino with lemon roasted potatoes. Montagna is open daily for breakfast, lunch, and dinner.

Pine Creek Cookhouse $$$
11399 Castle Creek Road, Ashcroft
(970) 925-1044
www.pinecreekcookhouse.com

Located at the Ashcroft Touring Center in the ghost town of Ashcroft, this old cookhouse offers a unique dining experience. In winter, diners must ski or ride a sleigh to their dinner. The cookhouse is 1½ miles from the end of the plowed road. In summer you can drive to it. The gourmet meals include Cornish game hen, herbed Rocky Mountain trout, roast leg of lamb, and other changing choices. There's a set dinner price, which includes a cross-country ski rental and a miner's lamp. The sleigh ride is extra. The cookhouse serves lunch and dinner. Reservations are required for dinner.

Piñons $$$
105 South Mill
(970) 920-2021
www.pinons.net
Innovative American cuisine with a Col-
orado touch is featured in the elegant
atmosphere of one of the mostly highly
recommended award-winning Aspen
restaurants (and there are quite a few in
that category). Wild game, meat, and
seafood, plus exceptional desserts have
earned this restaurant high ratings. Sub-
dued Southwestern decor makes for a
very pleasant dining experience. Dishes
sound simple—New Zealand elk loin with
country potatoes, baby carrots, and huck
leberry jam, for example, or the herb-
crusted Ruby Red trout with a spinach,
crab, pancetta, and potato hash and
sweet corn puree—but the simple combi-
nations make for outstanding dining.

Range Restaurant $$$$
304 East Hopkins
(970) 925-2402
www.rangerestaurant.com
This widely acclaimed and award-winning
restaurant prides itself on being truly
regional. It features regional products
spanning from Colorado to the Pacific,
Baja, and Alaska. There are two ways to
enjoy this elegant restaurant—in the R Bar
or in the main dining room. The R Bar
menu is smaller, more casual, and less
expensive. Diners can choose from not-so-
typical bar munchies such as yam fries
with chipotle dipping sauce, native elk chili,
or lamb quesadillas. R Bar entrees include
Pan Roasted Tenderloin Tips with sweet
onions and poblano chiles, and a Moroccan
Spiced Free Range Chicken Breast with
black lentil and basmati rice pilaf and vin-
daloo sauce. Offerings are decidedly more
upscale in the dining room. The appetizer
menu starts out with a butternut squash
and Tillamook cheddar soup, moves on to
a beefsteak tomato tower with Ancho
bacon and balsamic vinegar, and finishes
with American Bison carpaccio. For shar-
ing, try The Three Ceviches with tequila
shrimp, halibut, and smoked tomato gua-

camole. Entrees include the California Veg-
etable Lasagna with portobello mush-
rooms, buffalo mozzarella, and yellow
tomato sauce; Honey and Orange Lac-
quered Organic Salmon fillet, served with
Napa cabbage, wood ear mushrooms, and
glass noodles; and the magnificent Reyes
Blue and Hazelnut Crusted Elk Rack, with
wild mushroom strudel. But wait, there's
more! Dessert offerings include the Choco-
late Lava cake, with a warm gooey center
or, for something lighter to finish with,
there is the daily sorbet. Reservations are
highly recommended.

Syzygy $$$$
520 East Hyman Street
(970) 925-3700
www.syzygyrestaurant.com
Syzygy means yoked together, and this
restaurant is intimately stashed on the
second floor above a rug store. Here you
will find a quiet, understated elegance
with soft piano music and dribbling,
translucent glass-panel "waterfalls" in the
dining room. If you've been seeking that
1989 bottle of Le Montrachet ($1,200),
search no more. The wine list features
more than 600 choices. You've never
tasted Parmesan until you've had Rechi-
anno Parmesan, aged two years and
served in razor-thin wafers in the salad.
The tomatoes, marinated in a 30-year-old
sherry, pack quite a punch. The black
chairs resemble an exotic musical instru-
ment based on a cello. Tall windows open
onto the quiet street. The menu includes
such items as Lime Stone Salad with
pumpkin oil vinaigrette, tomatoes, apple
cider, and buffalo ricotta; Ginger Wrapped
Yellow fin Ahi, accompanied by Forbidden
Black Rice, tempura vegetables, wasabi,
and yuzo sauce; and Pistachio Veal
Schnitzel with truffled potato gnocchi. A
bar menu is served nightly until midnight,
and jazz starts every night at 10:00 P.M.

Takah Sushi $$$
420 East Hyman Avaenue
(970) 925-8588
www.takahsushi.com

Locals have made this sushi bar and restaurant a hit for more than 20 years, but tourists are welcome, too. The Japanese and Pacific Rim dishes are served in an intimate, packed-with-locals atmosphere, although it's not such a well-kept secret. The decor has been described as sleek subterranean, and the fish has been praised as ultrafresh, made possible by daily nonstop flights into the Aspen airport. Another plus: Takah Sushi has been praised as one of the few that hasn't gotten uppity in too-trendy Aspen.

Snowmass

Krabloonik $$$$
4250 Divide Road
(970) 923-3953
www.krabloonik.com
Few fine restaurants can also boast Iditarod sled-dog teams. In this rustic log-cabin restaurant, you feel more like you're in Alaska with the 300 yelping huskies at a kennel near the restaurant (don't worry, you'll have a quiet meal inside). Though rustic, the atmosphere is elegant Alaskan with white tablecloths, fine crystal, and gourmet cuisine. Choose from such wild game offerings as moose, caribou, quail, fallow deer, elk, and wild boar. A wine list includes more than 200 selections, and there's a substantial imported beer list, too. Lunch and dinner dog-sled rides are available (please see our "Other Winter Recreation" section). The restaurant has spectacular views of the nearby 14,000-foot mountains. It's open for lunch and dinner daily. Skiers can reach the restaurant via the Dawdler Trail. Reservations are a must and should be made months in advance for the holidays.

The Sage Bistro $$$
0239 Snowmass Club Circle
(970) 923-0923
www.snowmassclub.com
With a definite European flavor, the Sage at the Snowmass Lodge & Club offers three meals a day with indoor or outdoor seating. The patio can get nippy even on summer nights, so there are huge gas heaters they can fire up as well as smaller heaters in the ceiling that do fire if it's just slightly breezy. The patio overlooks the pool and the 18th hole of the golf course. Spacious and trendy, there's creative cuisine, traditional dishes, a "health and fitness menu," and children's menu. The food is as fancy as you want it. Penne pastas, Caesar salad, trout with herb and crushed-nut batter are delicious, as is the fabulous peach strudel for dessert. Dress is casual "Colorado," as it is everywhere in the mountains. The management says, "Come as causal and as comfortable as you want to be." Reservations are strongly suggested.

The Stew Pot $
Snowmass Village Mall
(970) 923-2263
Try this local favorite with moderately priced stews, sandwiches, soups, and salads and a children's menu. Enjoy wine and beer with the meal, too. The atmosphere is warm, cozy, and casual, and The Stew Pot is open for lunch and dinner.

Wildcat Cafe
Snowmass Center, 0065 Hearns Road
(970) 923-5990
Here's the bargain meal you've been looking for in this area. Tucked in a shopping complex along with the area's biggest supermarket, the Wildcat serves breakfast, lunch, light snacks, and early dinner in a coffee shop atmosphere. There are also microbrews, highly recommended bloody

For a fairly remote mountain town, Aspen has a surprisingly broad range of food offerings. Within a 1-mile radius, visitors can find more than 80 restaurants that serve everything from Japanese/South American fusion to fresh Colorado cuisine.

Marys, and a children's menu. Among the offerings are breakfast burritos, Philly steaks, homemade soups, and special events, such as Prime Rib Sundays and Fiesta Fridays.

NIGHTLIFE

The Bar at Little Nell
865 East Durant Avenue
(970) 920-4600
www.thelittlenell.com
This five-star hotel's bar is dark and cozy with a more sedate, older clientele—the 35-and-older crowd and among them many out-of-state (and country) professionals.

The Cigar Bar
315 East Hyman Street
(970) 920-4244
This very cool New York–style cigar bar offers the finest liquors, ports, cognacs, Armagnacs, wines, and a large selection of cigars. It's an exception in a town with a no-smoking ordinance, but that may be what makes it so popular. The club is a dark "living room" in downtown Aspen that seems to attract clients of all ages. It's open until 1:00 A.M. and has wheelchair access, despite being down a long flight of stairs.

Club Chelsea
415 East Hyman Avenue
(970) 920-0066
This rocking place includes a small disco room, a cigar bar, and a giant main bar with local live music and djs. It's at least as popular as the toney private Caribou Club (we don't list it because only members are allowed inside) a few blocks over. The entrance is down a flight of stairs, and window-shoppers can see as far as the maitre'd and the expansive dark wood bar.

Cooper St. Pier
508 East Cooper Avenue
(970) 925-7758
Locals love this dive, a dark bar with

cheap beer, game room upstairs, and softball trophies galore. It's wheelchair accessible and has televisions strategically mounted so patrons can drink and carouse without missing even a minute of the game.

The Crystal Palace
300 East Hyman Avenue
(970) 925-1455
www.cpalace.net
The "palace" is really an old mining assay office built in 1890, but in 1960 owner Mead Metcalf turned it into an intimate venue for cabaret dinner revues. The balcony and stained glass windows help with the ambiance. The talented waitstaff serve everything from escargot to roast duckling before slipping into costumes for the song, dance, and satirical revue. Tickets are in the $75 range, with children getting a break to $40 during low seasons.

Explore Booksellers and Bistro
221 Main Street
(970) 925-5336
www.explorebooksellers.com
Explore is a great place to while away the evening over books and a cappuccino. The clientele ranges from the New Agers to body Nazis (those who persecute their own bodies by overzealous exercise) and other types—all, of course, with a bit of a literary bent. It's open till midnight. Pick you favorite subject matter and sit among shelves of books at antique library tables. Oriental-type carpets make it all quite charming and cozy with the tables distributed here and there in the many rooms of the rambling house. There's a full cappuccino bar and lots of great desserts, both regular and dairy free. While you're dining, you can also read a copy of the *London Sunday Times,* the *Jerusalem Post,* the *Japan Times,* the *New York Times* and the main German and French newspapers.

Flying Dog Brew Pub & Grill
424 East Cooper Street
(970) 925-7464
www.flyingdogales.com

Aspen's only microbrewery is open for lunch and dinner and is a great choice for dog and beer lovers—it's filled with dogs in every art media, over the bar are many amusing dog photos, and the pub's signature brew is Doggie Style Amber Ale. But even more than a restaurant, it's a comfortable bar where tourists and locals can drink in harmony. All types of salads, sandwiches, plus trout, pastas, baby-back ribs, and Limousin beef fill the menu. The outdoor patio, located below street level on the pedestrian mall, is great for people watching, and on Sunday live bluegrass bands entertain.

The J-Bar (Hotel Jerome)
330 East Main Street
(970) 920-1000
www.hoteljerome.com
The Jerome Bar has been Aspen's favorite watering hole since 1889 and is on the National Register of Historic Places. Miners used to belly up to the beautiful cherrywood bar to celebrate their silver strikes. John Wayne slung down a few here, and Thornton Wilder upheld his legendary drinking capacity here. The original bar is still in place and serves the après-ski crowd and gets quite lively as the evening progresses with the 20- to 30-something crowd. It's one of the best places to people watch, since the Jerome attracts world travelers and superstars alike.

The Red Onion
420 East Cooper Street
(970) 925-9043
For more than a century this bar has been wetting whistles, which qualifies it as Aspen's oldest watering hole. If you have any doubts, look for the genuine tin ceiling, dark wood trim, and wainscoting. It's a fun place to have a beer or margarita, and from 4:00 to 6:00 P.M. there's a happy hour with half-priced drinks. It also serves lunch and dinner, with such menu items as Mexican food, burgers, sandwiches, and soups.

ATTRACTIONS

Ashcroft Ghost Town
12 miles south of Aspen, East Highway
82 to Castle Creek Road
(970) 925-3721
www.aspenhistory.org
In 1880, silver attracted two prospectors to this site, at 9,500 feet elevation at the base of Express Creek and Pearl Mountain passes. They camped near the future town of Ashcroft and watched 21 more flow into town and pitch their tents. Seven stayed through the winter, enduring 18 feet of snow and bone-chilling frost. The town peaked in 1883 when 2,500 miners called it home. They were served by a dozen saloons, two newspapers, a school, two sawmills, and an assay office, among other things. Eventually the richer mines in Aspen lured them away, leaving only two hermits in town to ring in the new century. Nine buildings now stand, making it one of Colorado's best preserved ghost towns. Each year about 30,000 visitors pass through, but the Aspen Historical Society has protected it since 1975. Visitors may tour this National Historic Site at any time for free or take a tour. Tours are offered during the summer and winter, but it's best to call first and confirm times. Admission is $3.00 for adults, and free for children 10 and under.

Aspen Art Museum
590 North Mill Street
(970) 925-8050
www.aspenartmuseum.org
Housed in a historic brick building on the Roaring Fork River, this museum has been open since 1979 and features rotating exhibitions including contemporary art and other historic periods. (It has no collection of its own.) According to a poll by the *Aspen Times* newspaper, the museum is second only to the Music Festival as a cultural draw for summer visitors and hosts more than 15,000 guests annually. Throughout the year, the Aspen Art Museum offers lectures and educational classes in the visual arts. Museum hours

are 10:00 A.M. to 6:00 P.M. Tuesday through Saturday and noon to 6:00 P.M. Sunday (closed Monday). Admission is $5.00 for adults, $3.00 for students and seniors, and free for children younger than 12.

Aspen Center for Environmental Studies
100 Puppy Smith Street
(970) 925-5756
www.aspennature.org
Local benefactor Elizabeth Paepcke founded this nonprofit foundation to protect Hallam Lake on Aspen's north end, alongside the Roaring Fork River. This little gem is a great place to learn about the flora and fauna of the area and even do some wildlife spotting. After stopping at the small building and viewing exhibits about what's to come, visitors can take a 30- to 45-minute walk along the self-guided nature trail, watch the resident birds of prey (a golden eagle and great horned owls), and talk to on-site naturalists. There's a "touch table" with lots of feathers, bones, and other interesting nature items. Microscopes give youngsters a close look at insects and other nifty things. The "Scavenger Hunt" sheet for kids makes a game out of nature identification. The center offers programs throughout the year, including seminars, hikes, and snowshoe tours on top of Aspen Mountain geared for all ages. The center is open Monday through Saturday from 9:00 A.M. to 5:00 P.M. during June, July, and August, and on Monday through Friday from 9:00 A.M. to 5:00 P.M. other months. Admission is free, but donations are strongly recommended.

Aspen Institute
1000 North 3rd Street
(970) 925-7010
www.aspeninstitute.com
One of Aspen's founding fathers, Walter Paepcke, arrived in the mid-'40s intent on making Aspen a beautiful think tank. The owner of Chicago's Container Corporation of America built the Institute on 40 acres in Aspen's historic West End and invited thinkers and businessmen to study the

Great Books and discuss ways they could change the world. The auditorium, seminar building, health center, lodge, restaurant, pool, and tennis courts still attract international guests.

Hotel Jerome
330 East Main Street
(970) 920-1000
www.hoteljerome.com
Drop by for coffee in the elegant Victorian lobby or a drink at the beautiful historic bar, complete with an ornate pressed-tin ceiling, and soak up the atmosphere of this landmark. A Spanish coffee on a velvet settee by the fireplace beneath a twinkling Christmas tree is especially memorable. Undergoing a major renovation in 1989, the Jerome now sparkles with its original glory, after falling into decline for many decades. Photos in a hallway off the lobby show the painstaking process of restoration, layer upon layer. Jerome Wheeler was the president of Macy's department store in New York City and Aspen's major benefactor. He financed the completion of the hotel after its original developers left town and opened it on Thanksgiving Eve 1889 in a gala still unrivaled in Aspen. Check out the ballroom, the three-story-high glass ceiling in the center of the building, and the pool on the west side of the building. One needn't be a guest to enjoy the Jerome, and just looking costs nothing. Among the glitterati to check in: John Wayne, Gary Cooper, Lana Turner, Hedy Lamarr, and Thornton Wilder. Actor Don Johnson also threw a party there to announce his second engagement to ex-wife Melanie Griffith. (See our "Accommodations" listing for more information about the hotel.)

Independence Pass
17 miles south of Aspen on Highway 82
One of the most thrilling mountain passes, Independence is so high (elevation 12,500 feet) and so narrow (12 feet wide in spots) that it closes about October 1 and stays closed until Memorial Day weekend. Tortuous turns and sheer drop-offs make it

challenging even in dry weather, so those with acrophobia may want to skip it. But the road is paved and safe as long as drivers observe the speed limit and road signs. The golden aspen trees in fall make for a very special experience. The name Independence Pass comes supposedly from a July 4 gold strike in 1879, 4 miles west of the summit. The town of Independence quickly sprung up with its own daily stage service to Leadville in the 1880s. The population soared to 2,000 and supported 10 saloons. Look for the ruins of the town about 15 miles from Aspen to the right of the road before reaching the summit. There's a parking area on the summit and a short trail. About 8 miles from Aspen is an area called the Grottos, a series of granite canyons along the Roaring Fork River and a pretty picnic area. The caves were carved by the river. Look for a dirt road about a half-mile past mile-marker 50. A small foot bridge crosses the river. To reach Independence Pass, drive south from Aspen on Highway 82 (the main street through Aspen).

Maroon Bells Scenic Area
Aspen Ranger District Office
806 West Hallam
(970) 925-3445

This twin set of 14,000-foot peaks—named for their shape (bell) and color (deep red)—are the most photographed mountains in Colorado, and it's easy to see why. The interesting horizontal rock striations make them unusually stunning, especially when reflected in the lake below. These rugged peaks are part of the Elk Range and the Maroon Bells-Snowmass Wilderness. In close proximity are six of Colorado's highest peaks: Castle, Maroon, North Maroon, Pyramid, and Capitol peaks, plus Snowmass Mountain—all higher than 14,000 feet. The Maroon Bells are some of the most treacherous of Colorado's 14ers for climbers, and their steep and unreliable, rotten rock has claimed many lives.

They're also ecologically endangered, due to heavy tourist traffic. Ute Indians used their valley for summer hunting and fishing, and still think the peaks are sacred. During summer days (8:30 A.M. to 5:00 P.M.), the road is closed to car travel, but visitors can take buses from the Ruby Park Transit Center. The road stops at Maroon Lake, where visitors can picnic, hike, fish, or soak in the looming peaks. At the lake, a guide from the Aspen Center for Environmental Studies is available every hour on the hour from 10:00 A.M. until 2:00 P.M. to lead a 45-minute tour around Maroon Lake. There's also a powerful telescope at the lake to spot resident elk, bighorn sheep, and eagles. Trails are well marked, so if you miss the tour, it's easy to find your own way. There are restrooms, water, and picnic tables but no food concessions, so bring your own lunch. Buses leave from Ruby Park Transit Center on Durant Avenue between Galena and Mill Streets in Aspen daily in summer between 9:00 A.M. and 4:30 P.M. The half-hour ride to Maroon Lake is narrated by the driver. Bus tickets are $6.00 for adults and $3.00 for seniors 65 and older and children ages 6 to 16; children younger than 6 ride free. During winter and other times of the year, the Maroon Lake Road is not plowed above the T-Lazy-7 Ranch due to extreme avalanche danger.

Pedestrian Mall
Cooper and Hyman Avenues between South Galena and South Mill Streets, and South Mill Street between Cooper and Hyman

Three of Aspen's core downtown blocks are closed to traffic, which means pedestrians can stroll, shop, dine, play in a street fountain, or tour the historic buildings. As a result, they serve as the town's hub and the logical place to start any visit to Aspen.

Wheeler Opera House
320 East Hyman Avenue
(970) 920-5770
www.wheeleroperahouse.com

Jerome B. Wheeler, early-day president of Macy's Department stores, built this Victorian theater in 1889 during the height of the silver boom, and opened a bank in front. He went bankrupt in the Silver Crash of 1893, and the 500-seat theater closed. The town of Aspen bought it in 1984, renovated the tarnished jewel, and now fills it with musicals, a comedy festival, operas, movies, and Aspen Ballet Company's annual Nutcracker performance. When not being used for performances or rehearsals, the Wheeler is open for tours. Call for the schedule when you're in town.

Wheeler/Stallard House Museum
620 West Bleeker Street
(970) 925-3721
www.aspenhistory.org
The third of Jerome Wheeler's projects (in addition to the opera house and the Hotel Jerome), this Queen Anne house was built in 1888 for his wife, but she was too happy in Denver even to set eyes on it. Instead, Mary Ella and Edgar Stallard moved in in 1905 and spent the next 40 years in the house. Now it is home to Aspen's Historical Society and, in the summer, opens as a historical museum. Take a self-guided tour, and enjoy the beautiful period furniture and decor. Upstairs are rooms with photos and children's toys and clothing ca. 1900. The museum gift shop sells books and other interesting items. The museum is open from 1:00 to 5:00 P.M. Tuesday through Friday from mid-June through September and from early January to Easter. Admission is $6.00 for adults, $5.00 for seniors, $3.00 for children 12 and under, and includes admission to the Holden/Marolt Mining and Ranching Museum.

Snowmass

Anderson Ranch
5263 Owl Creek Road
(970) 923-3181
www.andersonranch.org
Before the Snowmass Resort was devel-

oped, this was one of the valley's working ranches. It was preserved as an enclave for artists in residence—local, national, and international—who teach 100 summer workshops and spend the winter creating their own pieces. Free visits are possible daily during summer months or weekdays during the winter. It is closed in September.

KIDSTUFF

Aspen

Ashcroft Ghost Town
11 miles south of Aspen, take Highway
82 to Castle Creek Road
(970) 925-3721
www.aspenhistory.org
Once larger than Aspen, this ghost town was booming in 1883 with silver mining, two newspapers, a school, two sawmills, 2,500 residents, and 20 saloons. All that's left now is a cluster of nine ramshackle buildings in the meadow. The Aspen Historical Society is working to save them, and has installed a wooden sidewalk for visitors who would like to stroll down the dirt road that once was Main Street. An on-your-honor box at the parking area requests that visitors deposit an admission fee of $3.00 for adults. It's free for children 10 and under. During summer months, the Historical Society leads historical walking tours of the site. Call for details.

Aspen Center for Environmental Studies
100 Puppy Smith Street
(970) 925-5756
www.aspennature.org
Located in the Hallam Lake Wildlife Sanctuary alongside the Roaring Fork River, this little gem is a great place to learn about the flora and fauna of the area and even do some wildlife spotting. After stopping at the small building and viewing exhibits about what's to come, visitors can take a 30- to 45-minute walk along the

The ESPN Winter X Games are the biggest game in town during January. Competitions are broadcast live, giving Aspen international exposure. THE DENVER POST/CYRUS MCCRIMMON

self-guided nature trail, watch the resident birds of prey (a golden eagle and great horned owls), and talk to on-site naturalists. There's a "touch table" with lots of feathers, bones, and other interesting nature items. Microscopes give youngsters a close look at insects and other nifty things. The "Scavenger Hunt" sheet for kids makes a game out of nature identification. The center offers programs throughout the year, including seminars, hikes, and snowshoe tours on top of Aspen Mountain geared for all ages. The center is open Monday through Saturday from 9:00 A.M. to 5:00 P.M. during June, July, and August, and on Monday through Friday from 9:00 A.M. to 5:00 P.M. other months. Admission is free, but donations are strongly recommended.

Aspen Ice Garden
233 West Hyman Avenue
(970) 920-5141

Here's an almost year-round skating rink for those diehard ice skaters. Operated by the Aspen Recreation Department, this indoor rink offers a nice option for normally non-skating months and rainy days. The Ice Garden is closed for three weeks at the end of May, but otherwise opens daily in the afternoon and some evenings. Hours vary seasonally; call ahead. Admission is $4.00 for adults, $3.00 for kids ages 6 to 17 and $2.00 for children 5 and younger. Skate rental is $2.00.

Aspen Mountain Silver Queen Gondola
At the base of Aspen Mountain
(970) 925-1227, (877) 282-7736
www.aspensnowmass.com

Once the snow melts, the heavy ski traffic on Aspen Mountain is replaced by the gentle foot traffic of sightseers and nature lovers. The enclosed six-person Silver Queen gondola cars make the transformation as well, carrying visitors to the mountain's 11,212-foot summit, where they can take a 45-minute guided hike with naturalists from the Aspen Center for Environmental Studies or just look around. The hike is recommended and easy, and takes hikers past an old cabin site as well as stunning mountain flora and fauna. A restaurant and restrooms are at the summit. The gondola operates daily between 10:00 A.M. and 4:00 P.M. from mid-June through Labor Day. Guided nature walks from the summit are daily from 10:00 A.M. to 2:00 P.M. every hour on the hour, from mid-June to Labor Day. The ride and nature walk cost $18 for adults on weekdays, $20 on weekends; $15 for children 13 to 17 on weekdays, $17 on weekends; $10 for kids 4 to 12, and seniors over 70 on weekdays, $12 on weekends. Children under 3 ride for free.

Boogies Diner
534 East Cooper Avenue
(970) 925-6610
www.boogiesaspen.com
One of the few Aspen eateries catering to kids, this family favorite has crayons for the children and champagne and '50s decor for their parents. It's a healthful menu with everything from burgers to gourmet specialties. Though Boogies is kid-comfortable, nothing comes cheaply in Aspen, so don't expect any bargains— but portions are quite large and kids can easily split an order.

Hyman Avenue Mall Fountain
At the east end of the
Hyman Avenue Mall
This whimsical fountain is sort of like a fireworks of water, and kids love to play in it. Water shoots out randomly, challenging kids to make a run for it, but they generally get blasted anyway. It's just a little free summertime diversion in pricey Aspen.

Independence Ghost Town
Highway 32, 13.5 miles east of Aspen
(970) 925-3721 (Aspen Historical
Society)
www.aspenhistory.org
A couple of log cabins mark the spot of this early mining settlement on Independence Pass. Look for the remains of a general store, boarding house, stables, and a few other ruins. Independence was settled in the 1880s by miners in search of gold, but they were soon distracted by nearby Aspen and its silver bonanzas. Although there's not much left of the town, it makes a beautiful drive and interesting excursion. The Aspen Historical Society maintains the site and sponsors self-guided tours daily until Independence Pass closes for the winter. There is no fee, but donations are suggested.

Maroon Bells Nature Tour
Maroon Lake, Maroon Lake Road
(970) 925-5756
www.aspennature.org
The Maroon Bells are probably the most photographed spot in Colorado, and it's easy to see why. The interesting red, horizontal rock striations of these mountains make them quite visually stunning, especially as they are reflected in the lovely lake below. This area has become so popular—threatening the fragile environment— that the road is closed, and visitors must take a special bus to the lake. At the lake, a guide from the Aspen Center for Environmental Studies leads a tour around Maroon Lake. Trails are well-marked, and, if you miss the tour, it's easy to find your own way. There are restrooms, water, and picnic tables but no food concessions, so bring your own lunch. Maroon Bells is closed to car traffic most of the day. Buses leave from Ruby Park Transit Center, Durant Avenue and Mill Street in Aspen, (970) 925-8484. Buses cost $6.00 for adults, $4.00 for seniors and children 6 to 16, and are free for children 5 and younger.

Paradise Bakery
320 South Galena Street
(970) 925-7585

74 Snowmass Village Mall
(970) 923-4712
If it's a treat your kids are craving, this is the place to find it. There are cookies warm from the oven, homemade muffins, and ice cream and all kinds of goodies that make you feel like you've truly arrived

in paradise. The bakeries are open daily from 6:30 A.M. to 10:00 P.M.

Wagner Park Playground
West end of Hyman Avenue Mall
The swings, slides, and a jungle gym appeal to kids 10 and younger at this centrally located playground. So if you and the kids need a little break, stop here. Mom and Dad can watch the sometimes wacky world of Aspen go by while the kids cavort.

Snowmass

Anderson Ranch Arts Center
5263 Owl Creek Road
(970) 923-3181
www.andersonranch.org
Children who are interested in art might enjoy a visit to this four-acre mountain enclave of artists, some famous, who work and often chat with strolling visitors. Artists from around the country and world participate here in visiting artist programs, workshops, residency programs, and lectures. Their specialties include photography, sculpture, painting, woodworking, and lots of other media. For those staying in the area for an extended period, the center offers numerous children's workshops in various arts including weaving, photography, and Native American art, plus summer lectures and a nearby playground for blowing off steam. Ask for a catalog of classes. To see the artists in action, visit from June to August or October to May when the formal artist programs are going on. In September, the studios are empty. Anderson Ranch is open to the public from 9:00 A.M. to 5:00 P.M. Monday through Friday in winter, 9:00 A.M. to 5:00 P.M. Monday to Saturday, and noon to 5:00 P.M. Sunday in the summer. Hours are subject to change, so it's best to call beforehand. Admission is free, and guided tours are available with a reservation.

Snowmass Rodeo
Snowmass Stables, Brush Creek Road
(970) 925-9000, (888) 649-5982
www.stayaspensnowmass.com
On Wednesdays between mid-June and the end of August, local cowboys and cowgirls kick up dust doing what's always been done in this valley—riding horses and chasing cattle. The formal fun begins at 7:00 P.M. although a barbecue dinner is served at 5:00 P.M. During the rodeo there is a wonderful opportunity for kids to experience the real thing by becoming rodeo participants themselves. The Calf Scramble sets the young 'uns to chasing calves around the arena while they try to pull ribbons from their tails. Mutton Bustin' is always the crowd favorite though, as aspiring young cowpokes climb onto wooly sheep and hang on for as long as they can. Call for details on signing up for these events. Admission to the rodeo is $16 for adults, $10 for children 11 to 15, and free for kids 10 and younger. The barbecue buffet is $18.00 for adults, $8.00 for kids 6 to 11, and $4.00 for kids under 5.

SHOPPING

Aspen probably has the most interesting shopping possibilities of any mountain town, ranging from gourmet kitchen shops and haute couture to used clothing and ski equipment. There are many art galleries, clothing shops, antiques and furniture stores, and all types of whimsical shops that defy categories. In recent years, the high-end chain stores have appeared as well. Nestled between the home-owned stores are Gap, Banana Republic, Chanel, Christian Dior, FENDI, DKNY, Bulgari, and Eddie Bauer, among others. Locals aren't quite sure how they feel about the additions, but some join the tourists standing in line at the cash registers.

Aspen Book Store
665 East Durant (at the Little Nell Hotel)
(970) 925-7427
Tucked into the award-winning Little Nell, one of Aspen's finest hotels, this store offers bestsellers in hard and soft cover, new releases, travel and cookbooks, art and gift books, plus cards, newspapers and magazines, and video rentals. The shop also does gift wrapping and shipping.

Aspen Domain Inc.
400 East Main Street
(970) 925-1211
Look for gifts and home accessories, home furnishings, and other decorative items for the distinctive interior here.

Aspen Luggage Co.
529 East Cooper Avenue
(970) 925-9368
www.aspenluggage.com
This shop carries top-of-the-line luggage, totes, and duffels, as well as a variety of personal travel items and gifts. The shop makes its own luggage and also carries lines from top quality manufacturers such as Mulholland Brothers and Briggs & Riley. They also specialize in TSA (Transit Security Authority) approved travel locks for luggage.

Aspen Sports
408 East Cooper Avenue
(970) 925-6331

16 Kearns Road, Snowmass Village
(970) 923-3566

70 Snowmass Village Mall
Snowmass Village
(970) 923-6111
www.aspensports.com
Aspen's oldest and most complete skiing and camping center (with eight locations; we've listed a representative sample) sells boots, packs, tents, clothing, cooking equipment, and camping food, and rents various equipment.

Explore Booksellers and Bistro
221 East Main Street
(970) 925-5336
www.explorebooksellers.com
Explore claims to have the largest book selection on Colorado's Western Slope. It has a charming location in a brown and white Victorian house and is also a great place for a meal or a quick snack (look for details under the "Restaurants" heading). Also for sale are all types of CDs, magazines, notecards, and espresso.

Goldies & the Kids
205 Mill Street
(970) 925-6802
"Beautiful infant and funky baby" are a couple of the styles sold at this children's boutique with clothing from around the world. The shop carries infant to size 8 clothing.

Gorsuch Ltd.
611 East Durant Avenue
(970) 920-9388
Located near the base of the Silver Queen Gondola, this established Aspen boutique carries exquisite ski lines, imported sweaters, home decor, books, and gifts with a mountain theme for men and women. It's best known for the kind of European luxuries worn by the well-to-do for skiing and après-ski partying.

Gracy's
517 East Hopkins Street
(970) 925-5131
Surprisingly, Aspen has some of the best secondhand shops in the state, because all those rich folks and movie stars tire quickly of their designer duds and sports gear and sell them off for a song to us bargain hunters via stores like Gracy's, First-Class, Second-Hand, and the other stores listed. There are extraordinary finds in men's, women's, and children's clothing, sportswear, skiwear, outerwear, skis, and accessories at Gracy's, plus antiques, furniture, gifts, and housewares.

Kemo Sabe
434 East Cooper Avenue
(970) 925-7878
www.kemosabe.com
You'll know you've arrived at Kemo Sabe when you see the new cowboy hats that have been battered and stained to look broken in. They're displayed along with all the other cowboy-themed memorabilia, clothing, and decor.

Les Chefs D'Aspen
405 South Hunter Street
(970) 925-6217
Stop here for an amazing array of amusing pet accessories—all types of dog and cat bowls—plus such whimsical gourmet kitchen items as kitty-shaped tea kettles, martini glasses decorated with pink elephants, and decorative wooden pig troughs from the Philippines. All these share shelf space with such practical items as garlic presses and placemats.

Replay Sports
465 North Mill Street
(970) 925-2483
Like Gracy's and Susie's, Replay Sports handles high-quality used items, but only in the sporting goods arena. Skis, boots, poles, snowboards, and all kinds of sporting goods are sold for a fraction of the original retail price. The sports gear arrives daily and comes in all shapes and sizes, but the predominant category is ski equipment.

Stefan Kaelin Ski & Sporting Equipment
516 East Durant Avenue
(970) 925-7266
www.stefankaelin.com
A favorite of locals, Stefan Kaelin sells and rents all the kinds of things active people need in Aspen. Its downtown location makes it convenient for tourists, too.

Susie's Consignment
623 East Hopkins
(970) 920-2376
This high-end consignment store offers all kinds of men's and women's designer and sports clothing, some worn only once by the rich and famous. It also has furniture, housewares, gifts, and jewelry.

THE ARTS

Snowmass

MUSIC

Jazz Aspen Snowmass
110 East Hallam, Suite 104
(970) 920-4996
www.jazzaspen.org
This annual festival, founded in 1991, has grown into five events: a three-day festival in mid-June; a three-day festival over Labor Day weekend; the Winter Series, featuring performances sponsored by Belly Up, a local venue; the Snowmass Free Series of concerts held every Thursday during the summer at the base of Snowmass Mountain; and the JAS Education Performances, held in conjunction with the JAS Education Program for young musicians. Formerly known as the Thelonious Monk Institute Jazz Colony, the education program attracts many of the most gifted young musicians in the country to study under the auspices of JAS Distinguished Artist in Residence Herbie Hancock, and JAS Academy Artistic Director Christian McBride. The festivals have featured jazz, gospel, soul, R&B, and blues legends such as B.B. King, the Neville Brothers, Ray Charles, Tony Bennett, George Benson, the Manhattan Transfer, Branford and Ellis Marsalis, The Count Basie Orchestra, and Willie Nelson. (See our "Annual Events" heading for more information.)

VISUAL ARTS

Anderson Ranch Arts Center
5263 Owl Creek Road
Snowmass Village
(970) 923-3181
www.andersonranch.org
A four-acre mountain enclave of artists—some famous—Anderson Ranch is a treat for serious art lovers. Working artists will

often chat with strolling visitors. Artists from around the country and world participate here in visiting artist programs, workshops, residency programs, and lectures. They work in every medium from photography to sculpture, painting to woodworking. For those staying in the area for an extended period, there are workshops in various arts including weaving, photography, and Native American art, plus summer slide lectures. Ask for the catalog of classes. To see the artists in action, visit from June to August, or October to May when the formal artist programs are going on. In September, the studios are empty. There's also a gallery and gift shop. Anderson Ranch is open to the public from 9:00 A.M. to 5:00 P.M. Monday through Friday in winter, 9:00 A.M. to 5:00 P.M. Monday to Saturday and noon to 5:00 P.M. Sunday in the summer. Hours are subject to change, so it's best to call beforehand. Admission is free, and guided tours are available with a reservation.

J. Fenton Gallery/Quilts Unlimited
Snowmass Village Mall
Snowmass Village
(970) 923-5467
This crafts gallery is actually two. One part features fine contemporary handcrafts, including jewelry, wooden games and boxes, kaleidoscopes, wearable art, and toys. The other part features beautiful traditional and unusual handmade quilts.

Aspen

MUSIC

Aspen Music Festival
Aspen Music Festival and School
2 Music School Road
(970) 925-3254
www.aspenmusicfestival.com
The Aspen Music Festival's parent organization is Music Associates of Aspen, which also operates the Aspen Music School. Both the school and festival are strictly summer only, with the main festi-

val artists teaching in the school, but the music festival is Aspen's most well-known annual event and has become an institution over the last 50 years. Classical symphonic music is the main focus, but the festival also features jazz, avant-garde, and some pop concerts. Performances are all top-notch and include operas, special children's concerts, special programs, chamber symphonies, the Aspen Festival Orchestra, and benefit concerts. Performers are internationally renowned and have included such musical giants as flutist James Galway; violinists Itzhak Perlman, Nadja Salerno-Sonnenberg, and Gil Shaham; the American Brass Quintet; the Auerbach American String Quartet; and even actor John Lithgow, who read works by Shakespeare, Yeats, and Emily Brontë to the cello music of Lynn Harrell. Ticket prices and performances vary widely throughout the season depending on the performer and type of concert. For complete ticket and schedule information, visit the Web site listed above, or call the Festival's main number.

THEATER

Aspen Theatre in the Park
Rio Grande Park
(970) 925-9313
www.theatreaspen.org
Every summer professional actors perform intimate live theater in a charming open-air tent by the Roaring Fork River. Past performances have included *Private Lives, Educating Rita, The Heidi Chronicles,* and *The Compleat Works of Wllm Shkspr* (abridged). Tickets range from $20 to $35 and can be purchased at the Wheeler Box Office, (970) 920-5770, on Mill Street and Hyman Avenue. Shows run from late June through August.

Wheeler Opera House
Mill Street and Hyman Avenue
(970) 520-5770
www.wheeleroperahouse.com
With a gala opening in 1889, this elegant opera house has played a central role in

Aspen's cultural life. Jerome B. Wheeler, of of Aspen's founding fathers and financiers, called it a "perfect bijou of a theatre." The theater has been restored to its original grandeur, and it attracts performers from around the world on a regular basis, as well as showing films. Call for a current schedule of performances. The box office is open 10:00 A.M. to 6:00 P.M. Monday through Saturday, 10:00 A.M. to 5:00 P.M. Sunday, and 30 minutes prior to curtain time on performance days.

DANCE

Aspen Santa Fe Ballet
110 East Hallam
(970) 925-7175
www.aspensantafeballet.com
Formerly the Aspen Ballet Company, this local ballet company provides lessons and performances, and sponsors a celebration of dance each summer from late July to early August. During that time, local dancers have the chance to work with visiting performers from companies in Miami, New York City, and Chicago.

VISUAL ARTS

Aspen Art Museum
590 North Mill Street
(970) 925-8050
www.aspenartmuseum.org
Housed in a historic brick building on the Roaring Fork River, this museum has been open since 1979 and features rotating exhibitions including contemporary art and other historic periods. (It has no collection of its own.) According to a poll by the *Aspen Times* newspaper, the museum is second only to the Music Festival as a cultural draw for summer visitors and hosts more than 15,000 guests annually. Throughout the year, the Aspen Art Museum offers lectures and educational classes in the visual arts. Museum hours are 10:00 A.M. to 6:00 P.M. Tuesday through Saturday and noon to 6:00 P.M. Sunday (closed Monday). Admission is $5.00 for adults, $3.00 for students and seniors, and free for children younger than 12.

LITERARY ARTS

Aspen Writers' Foundation
(970) 925-3122
www.aspenwriters.org
The Aspen Writers' Foundation serves and promotes the literary art through the annual Aspen Summer Words Literary Festival and other writing venues. Award-winning writers and authors speak at annual events. National Book Award winner Andrea Barrett and Rudolfo Anaya, the Pen-West award-winning author of *Albuquerque* were keynote speakers at one past summer Writers' Conference.

EVENTS

January

Annual Winterskol Carnival
Various locations
(970) 925-1940
www.stayaspensnowmass.com
All kinds of fun ski races, art shows, strudel and schnapps parties, a snow-sculpting competition, and a torchlight descent and fireworks display are some of the highlights of this weeklong celebration of winter in Aspen in mid-January. Watch or compete in the locked-arm downhill race or freestyle competition at Aspen Highlands, wear a costume to the Madhatter's Ball, and enjoy a parade and various dance and music performances throughout the festival. Costs for events vary, but many are free. Call for more specific schedule information.

Gay Ski Week
Various locations
(970) 925-9249
www.gayskiweek.com
Aspen was one of the first cities in the country to have a gay rights ordinance. Gay Ski Week was one of the celebrations that followed and became an annual mid-January event. It started small and got bigger, and it's now a huge event that attracts thousands of people from all over the

country and world. The focus is on skiing, but there's a lot of partying, outrageous costume parties, and town-wide events, including music and other entertainment. Gay Ski Week has been held for more than a decade and even attracts non-skiers. Nationally, it was one of the first highly publicized gay-oriented events, predating today's gay travel guides and gay cruises.

June

Food & Wine Magazine Classic at Aspen
(970) 925-9000
www.foodandwine.com
Sponsored by *Food & Wine Magazine*, this three-day affair attracts chefs, vintners, and lovers of fine wine in mid-June. Industry leaders lead wine-tasting seminars and cooking demonstrations, and those in attendance get ample opportunities to eat and drink to their hearts' content. Tickets and hotel rooms sell out early, so this event requires ample pre-planning.

Jazz Festival at Snowmass
Snowmass Village
(970) 920-4996
www.jazzaspen.org
This annual festival now in its second decade has featured such jazz, gospel, south, R&B, and blues legends as B.B. King, the Neville Brothers, Ray Charles, Tony Bennett, George Benson, the Manhattan Transfer, Branford and Ellis Marsalis, The Count Basie Orchestra, and Al Green. It's so popular, in fact, that two festivals are held each summer, one in mid-June and a second over the Labor Day weekend. Call for schedules and ticket prices.

Aspen Music Festival
Aspen Music Festival and School
2 Music School Road, Aspen
(970) 925-3254
www.aspenmusicfestival.com
An institution for the last 50 years, classical symphonic music is the main focus, but the festival also features jazz, avantgarde, and some pop concerts. Perfor-

mances from late June through August are all top-notch and include operas, special children's concerts, special programs, chamber symphonies, the Aspen Festival Orchestra, and benefit concerts. Performers are internationally renowned and have included such musical giants as flutist James Galway; violinists Itzhak Perlman, Nadja Salerno-Sonnenberg, and Gil Shaham; the American Brass Quintet; the Auerbach American String Quartet; and even actor John Lithgow, who read works by Shakespeare, Yeats, and Emily Brontë to the cello music of Lynn Harrell. Ticket prices and performances vary widely throughout the season depending on the performer and type of concert. For complete ticket and schedule information, visit the Web site listed above, or call the Festival's main number. Tickets may be purchased by mail, phone, fax, Internet, or in person. The main box office is located in the Gondola Building at the base of Aspen Mountain at East Durant Avenue and South Hunter Street.

Aspen Summer Words
110 East Hallam Street #116, Aspen
(970) 925-3122
www.aspenwriters.org
This weeklong writers' conference, sponsored by the Aspen Writers' Foundation in mid-June, attracts writers from far and wide. National Book Award winner Andrea Barrett and Rudolfo Anaya, the Pen-West award-winning author of *Albuquerque,* have been keynote speakers in past years. Writers come to rub elbows with one another and hone their skills. It is followed by a literary festival.

Snowmass Rodeo
Brush Creek Road, Snowmass Village
(970) 925-9000, (888) 649-5982
www.stayaspensnowmass.com
This local rodeo is full of fun with clowns, cowboys, cowgirls, and bullriding. It runs each week in the summer for 10 weeks starting the end of June. The rodeo begins at 7:30 P.M. on Wednesday, and a barbecue dinner starts at 5:00 P.M.

July

Snowmass Rodeo
Brush Creek Road, Snowmass Village
(970) 925-9000, (888) 649-5982
www.stayaspensnowmass.com
This local rodeo is full of fun with clowns,
cowboys, cowgirls, and bullriding. It runs
each week in the summer for 10 weeks
starting the end of June. See our June
entry for more information.

Aspen Dance Festival
Aspen Dance Theatre, Aspen
(970) 925-7175
www.aspenballet.com
After 30 years of summer festivals,
DanceAspen closed up shop in 1998. It
was replaced by a smaller celebration of
dance sponsored by the Aspen Ballet
Company. The three-week festival runs
from late July to early August, with rotating performances that feature local
dancers as well as visiting performers
from companies in Miami, New York City,
and Chicago. Tickets are available at the
Gondola Box Office and by phone.

August

Snowmass Rodeo
Brush Creek Road, Snowmass Village
(970) 925-9000, (888) 649-5982
www.stayaspensnowmass.com
This local rodeo is full of fun with clowns,
cowboys, cowgirls, and bullriding. It runs
each week in the summer for 10 weeks
starting the end of June. See our June
entry for more information.

September

Jazz Festival at Snowmass
Snowmass Village
(970) 920-4996
The second of two festivals is held over
the Labor Day weekend, and usually features a wide range of new and established

performers. See the June entry for more
details.

Snowmass Balloon Festival
Snowmass Village
(970) 925-9000
www.stayaspensnowmass.com
In mid-September, Snowmass claims to
have the largest high-altitude balloon festival in the world. Started in 1975, the
event has gotten bigger each year. More
than 50 balloonists compete in various
races and maneuvers. Spectators can
enjoy live classical music along with a big
champagne breakfast served at the launch
site (a field across from the rodeo
grounds on Brush Creek Road) as the balloonists prepare to take off. The event is
free, but balloonists must call to register,
and prices for the champagne breakfast
change every year.

December

Aspen Filmfest Academy Screenings
Harris Concert Hall, Aspen
(970) 920-5770
www.aspenfilm.org
Each year as the Oscar races heat up, the
Aspen Filmfest offers movie buffs the
opportunity to see the year's hottest
movies and award contenders. From first-
run films to more obscure documentaries,
the festival offers screenings almost every
night from mid-December to early January. The screenings are open to everyone
and are shown at the Harris Concert Hall.
Tickets are in the $11 range (subject to
change each season), and are available at
the Wheeler Opera House, by phone, or
online at www.wheeleroperahouse.com.

SKIING

The four ski areas near Aspen—Aspen
Highlands, Aspen Mountain, Buttermilk,
and Snowmass—are a skier's and snowboarder's dream; the town of Aspen is an
aesthetic and historic treasure. This skiers'

In early December young women converge on Aspen for the Alpine World Cup competition. Skiers often use the event as a qualifying race for the Olympics. THE DENVER POST/HELEN H. RICHARDSON

paradise doesn't come cheaply, though. You'll ride the lifts with movie stars and the international set and hear conversations about how the skiing was last week in Switzerland or Sweden. Here's where the other half go to ski, and the multilingual ski pros give instructions in Spanish, Portuguese, German, French, Italian, Swedish, and other languages.

You get what you pay for, and at Aspen it's service, skiing, and scenery—all with a capital S. The Ambassador program is a great free service offering multilingual ski and snowboard guides. This is a wonderful and easy way to learn the lay of the land and find the best slopes for your ability. All four areas offer this service. There are free cookies at the shuttle stops and

friendly staff offering you tissues, sunscreen, trail maps, grooming reports, tools, refreshments, and free courtesy phones at the Guest Service Centers. Another morning perk at the far mountains: free Cafe de Columbia is served at the base to any skier in need of a caffeine jumpstart.

Getting There: Aspen is 220 miles from Denver via Interstate 70 and Highway 82. Before reaching Aspen from Glenwood Springs, there's a turnoff to Snowmass Village, the resort built at the base of the ski slope, which is the largest of Aspen's foursome. Continuing toward Aspen, there's the airport, Buttermilk, the access road to Aspen Highlands, the northwest end of town, and finally, Aspen Mountain right up the mountainside from the heart of town.

Aspen Highlands
Highway 82
(970) 925-1220
www.aspensnowmass.com
Base elevation: *8,040 feet*
Top of highest lift: *11,675 feet*
Total vertical: *3,635 feet*
Longest run: *3½ miles*
Average annual snowfall: *300 inches*
Ski season: *mid-December through early April*
Capacity: *6,500 skiers per hour*
Terrain: *970 acres, 131 trails (18 percent beginner, 30 percent intermediate, 52 percent advanced and expert)*
Lift tickets: *$78*
Snow reports: *(970) 925-1221 or (888) ASPENSNOW*

With a ridge-top setting, Aspen Highlands' runs and scenery provide some of Colorado's best adventure skiing and riding. The area is tucked into a long, narrow mountainside just south of the town of Aspen, and has long been a favorite of locals. Though known for its expert terrain, almost half of Aspen Highlands' acres are rated beginner or intermediate. In 1994 two new lifts were added for the first time in 20 years, cutting in half the lift time to the 11,675-foot summit to 20 minutes. Expert skiers and boarders will enjoy such runs as Temerity, the Twilight Zone, Sherwood Forest, Moment Chutes, the P-chutes, Boomerang Woods, and Golden Horn Woods. These areas feature steep, gladed terrain and offer a backcountry-like experience.

A new base village replaced the funky '60s-style area in 1999, and in 2000 was joined by a new bar, restaurant, and Ritz-Carlton private residence club. Freestyle Fridays are a favorite tradition, with spectators lounging at the base to watch the area's best freestyle skiers compete.

Aspen Mountain
Highway 82
(970) 925-1220
www.aspensnowmass.com
Base elevation: *7,945 feet*
Top of highest lift: *11,212 feet*

Total vertical: *3,267 feet*
Longest run: *3 miles*
Average annual snowfall: *300 inches*
Ski season: *Thanksgiving to mid-April*
Capacity: *10,755 skiers per hour*
Terrain: *675 acres, 76 trails (48 percent intermediate, 52 percent advanced and expert)*
Lift tickets: *$78*
Snow reports: *(970) 925-1221 or (888) ASPENSNOW*

Aspen will celebrate its 60th anniversary in 2007, and though it's not Colorado's oldest ski area, it's probably the most renowned and glamorous—and Aspen Mountain is its centerpiece. Aspen Mountain opened in 1947, and three years later established notoriety for hosting the first Federation Internationale de Ski (FIS) World Alpine Championship held in the United States. The mountain continued to attract such international ski legends as Emile Alais, Zeno Colo, Jean-Claude Killy, Phil and Steve Mahre, Anderl Molterer, Tommy Moe, Spider Sabich, and Alberto Tomba, all who competed there in Junior Olympics, World Cups, and World Professional Championships.

Aspen Mountain is not for beginners or even nervous intermediates. There are no green runs, and the blue ones require solid skills. But strong and confident intermediates need not be intimidated. The mountain's runs are challenging but very pleasant with stupendous summit views of the town below and endless mountains beyond.

Locals call Aspen Mountain "Ajax," a nickname coined by the 19th-century silver miners after the old Ajax mine there. Aspen Mountain's eight lifts include the high-speed, six-passenger *Silver Queen* gondola, which zips skiers to the summit in 13 minutes. This and seven other lifts carry up to 10,755 skiers per hour up the mountain, giving it a more exclusive feel than larger resorts that accommodate more than twice that number. Aspen Mountain's topography consists of three ridges: Ruthie's, Bell Mountain, and Gentleman's Ridge. From these a series of trails and glades work their way down with gullies in between. The best skiing and snow are near the summit, where a maze of lifts runs skiers back up. But to avoid the congestion, some smart skiers prefer to ski all the way down the mountain and catch the speedy *Silver Queen* gondola back to the top. Tired skiers should avoid Spar Gulch at the end of the day when the knees have turned rubbery. It's a somewhat narrow chute crowded with lots of fast skiers on their last run of the day—and orange net fences to slow them down—but earlier in the day it's great fun, zigging and zagging. From Spar Gulch, the final run down to the *Silver Queen* gondola is usually skied off and a bit unnerving as well.

Two mountain restaurants offer a variety of cuisines and service, from cafeteria-style to sit-down tables. Expect a lovely presentation with exotic field greens and arugula even with your hot dog. You'll enjoy fantastic service, even in the cafeteria-style restaurant.

Buttermilk Mountain
Highway 82
(970) 925-1220
www.aspensnowmass.com
Base elevation: *7,870 feet*
Top of highest lift: *9,900 feet*
Total vertical: *2,030 feet*
Longest run: *3 miles*
Average annual snowfall: *200 inches*
Ski season: early December to early April
Capacity: *7,500 skiers per hour*
Terrain: *420 acres, 43 trails (35 percent beginner, 39 percent intermediate, 26 percent advanced and expert)*
Lift tickets: *$78*
Snow reports: *(970) 925-1221 or (888) ASPENSNOW*

Originally developed as an easier alternative to Aspen Mountain's steep runs, Buttermilk is renowned as one of the nation's finest teaching and learning mountains. Beginners on this broad, gentle peak can choose from Panda Peak for first-timers, Homestead Road for a new skiers' first top-to-bottom run, and the smooth,

meandering runs of West Buttermilk. But hotshot family members or friends can enjoy the day here, too. Sterner and Savio runs will entertain intermediate or advanced skiers and boarders with steeper slopes and bumps.

With 2,030 feet of vertical gain and two summits, Buttermilk divides into three sections: Tiehack, Main Buttermilk, and West Buttermilk. Look for the easiest and most difficult terrain and features on Main Buttermilk, plus a NASTAR and self-timed racecourse. At the base of Main Buttermilk is a snowboard park for experienced riders, and Spruce Face is a popular advanced or "black diamond" run that funnels out of the park. Tiehack is more advanced and offers great powder after a snowstorm. Compared to the other Aspen areas, Tiehack's most difficult runs are less difficult, and strong intermediates might enjoy them. West Buttermilk is the gentlest section. Buttermilk hosts an annual snowboard festival called BoarderFest, during which more than 3,000 boarders descend on the ski area, and no skiers are allowed.

The best view is from the Cliffhouse restaurant atop Buttermilk, which serves Mongolian barbecue.

Snowmass Ski Area
Take Snowmass Village Turnoff from Highway 82, Snowmass Village
(970) 925-1220
www.aspensnowmass.com
Base elevation: *8,104 feet*
Top of highest lift: *12,510 feet*
Total vertical: *4,406 feet*
Longest run: *5³/₁₀ miles*
Average annual snowfall: *300 inches*
Ski season: *Thanksgiving to mid-April*
Capacity: *27,181 skiers per hour*
Terrain: *3,128 acres, 88 trails (7 percent beginner, 55 percent intermediate, 38 percent advanced and expert)*
Lift tickets: *$78*
Snow reports: *(970) 925-1221 or (888) ASPENSNOW*

Twelve miles from Aspen Mountain, the wide-open terrain of Snowmass contrasts markedly with Aspen's steeper and nar-

The ESPN Winter X Games are held at Buttermilk Mountain in Aspen, attracting a colorful group of skiers, snowboarders, and young fans. They provide a sharp contrast to the monied visitors who line Aspen's streets over the Christmas holidays. *THE DENVER POST*/HELEN H. RICHARDSON

rower runs. This huge area is actually four distinct ones, each with its own lifts and restaurants; skiers and snowboarders can enjoy all four or pick one. Each area can be reached from any point on the mountain. Snowmass Village was built around this broad ski mountain, which may explain why 95 percent of the lodging offers ski-in, ski-out convenience.

The ski area was built more than 25 years ago with ultra-wide runs spread out over fanshaped terrain to inspire skiers who might be intimidated by the challenges of Aspen Mountain or Aspen Highlands' steep, narrow trails. The Big Burn trail (named after a fire in the 1880s) is a good example of their successes; it's an open, mile-wide cruising run, but don't let that fool you. Snowmass also has more black-diamond and double-diamond terrain than any of Aspen's other areas—due in large part to backcountry areas such as Hanging Valley and The Cirque, with chutes, glades, and gulches. Another plus for expert skiers: Because Snowmass is known primarily as an intermediate skiers' haven, they may have advanced runs like Bear Claw, Wildcat, and Zugspitze all to themselves.

Snowmass may also have the best-named trails in the state. Naked Lady got its name from the Playboy centerfolds that were once plastered on a tree midway down the rollercoaster-like run. Rocky Mountain High, an intermediate run with stunning views from atop its 12,510 foot summit, was named in tribute to singer John Denver. Spider Sabich Picnic Palace, a picturesque spot for picnics and group

functions, is named for the fabled Olympic skier who was shot during an argument by Claudine Longet, the estranged wife of singer Andy Williams. And Fanny Hill got its name because . . . well, you guess.

In 1998–1999 resort owners set out to make Snowmass a snowboarders' paradise, building (for air junkies) Coney Glade, and have since expanded the effort to include three terrain parks—Pipeline, Makaha, and Scooper—a superpipe, and a minipipe.

CROSS-COUNTRY SKIING

Aspen sometimes refers to its cross-country ski trails as its "Fifth Mountain." Said to be the largest system of free maintained tracks in North America, some 60 kilometers of groomed trails connect Aspen and Snowmass. Though the trails are groomed by the Aspen/ Snowmass Nordic Council, they are not otherwise patrolled. Access them at one of the centers listed below. For more details go to www.aspennordic.com.

Aspen Cross Country Center
39551 West Highway 82
(970) 925–2145
The Aspen Cross-Country Center offers easy skiing on a golf course, plus rentals and instructions on 4 kilometers. Skiing is free, but there's a charge for equipment and lessons.

Ashcroft Ski Touring Unlimited
11399 Castle Creek Road, Ashcroft
(970) 925–1971
www.pinecreekcookhouse.com
This is Aspen's best-known Nordic facility and is in the old mining ghost town of Ashcroft, located 12 miles southeast of Aspen. There are 35 kilometers of beautifully groomed trails. Lessons and rentals are available. A favorite package is the ski-to-lunch or dinner at the Pine Creek Cookhouse, 2 kilometers from the Ashcroft trailhead; it's known for its gourmet cuisine. The trail fee is about $15.

Spring arrives in different ways at ski resorts. Although the calendar heralds the first day of spring as March 21, it's celebrated each year at Snowmass with a "Chicken Legs Contest" dedicated to the appreciation of pale, scrawny legs that have been hidden beneath ski pants during the long, cold winter months.

OTHER WINTER RECREATION

Carriage Rides

Aspen Carriage Co.
Galena Street Mall
(970) 925-3394
For a romantic after-dinner, in-town excursion, try a horse-drawn carriage ride through historic Aspen. Carriages run only during high seasons (Thanksgiving through the close of the ski season, then late June through Labor Day) and offer 20-minute town tours or 30-minute taxi service. Expect to pay a minimum of $30 for the town tour, or $20 for each adult and $10 for kids..Reservations are accepted, but when tourist season is in full swing, regularly scheduled rides leave from the Galena Street Mall.

Dog Sledding

Krabloonik
4250 Divide Road, Snowmass Village
(970) 923-4342
www.krabloonik.com
Every day of the winter, teams of 10 Husky hybrids from the Krabloonik kennel (their ancestors were Malamute, Eskimo, and Siberian) pull hand-crafted Eskimo bone and rawhide sleds. Each sled can carry two adults, a child, and a musher through the breathtaking Snowmass-Maroon Bells Wilderness area. Half-day trips (two hours each) leave the adjoining Krabloonik Restaurant at 8:30 A.M. and 1:45 P.M. and include a complimentary lunch. Owner Dan MacEachen has been operating the rides since 1974 and named his business after the first lead dog he raised. (Krabloonik means "big eyebrows," and is the Eskimo term for "white man.") Some of his dogs have competed in the Iditarod, the challenging Alaskan race over hundreds of miles—so hold on. The half-day rides cost $225 for adults and $170

Cross-country skiers can travel between Aspen and Snowmass along 48 miles of trails in the White River National Forest. The Snowmass Cross-Country Center has a shooting range, which makes it the Roaring Fork Valley's only biathlon course.

for children ages 3 to 8. Children younger than 3 are not allowed in the sleds. Reservations are required.

Ice Skating

Aspen Ice Garden
233 West Hyman Avenue
(970) 920-5141
Although the town's serious skaters often reserve the indoor rink for lessons or hockey games, casual skaters can share the ice at prescribed times. It's operated by the Aspen Recreation Department and is open nearly year-round. It closes for seasonal maintenance from mid-April through early June. Public skates vary seasonally, but usually include some afternoon and evening hours daily. Admission is $4.00 for adults, $3.00 for kids ages 6 to 17, and $2.00 for children 5 and younger. Skate rental is $2.00.

Sleigh Rides

Burlingame Cabin Dinner Rides
Snowmass Village
(970) 923-0460
www.aspenchamber.org
Not quite a romantic as horses, a 32-passenger snowcat pulls a sleigh to the rustic Burlingame Cabin for fine food and entertainment by a bluegrass duo. If the weather is bad, it's especially nice to ride inside the snowcat. Cost is $55 for adults, $30 for kids 4 to 12, and free for kids

under 4. Reservations are required, and the dinner ride leaves from the ticket pavilion at the base of the ski mountain in Snowmass Village.

Pine Creek Cookhouse
11399 Castle Creek Road, Ashcroft
(970) 925-1044
www.pinecreekcookhouse.com
Cross-country ski in or ride in a horse-drawn sleigh to this classic cabin in the Castle Creek Valley, 12 miles from Aspen. For your effort, you'll be rewarded with a romantic, candle-lit dinner in the forest. The 1.5-mile ride starts at the ghost town of Ashcroft and goes through the woods to a historic mining camp cookhouse, where you're served a gourmet meal that might feature Rocky Mountain trout, Cornish game hen, or lamb. After dinner, those who skied in get headlamps to help them ski back out again. Reservations are required.

Snowmobiling

T-Lazy-7 Ranch
3129 Maroon Creek Road
(970) 925-4614
www.tlazy7.com
Since 1938, the Deane family has been hosting guests at its working horse ranch 5 minutes from Aspen and 15 minutes from Snowmass. The ranch extends over 400 acres of privately owned land and is surrounded by National Forest. Snowmobilers can sign up for guided tours of the ghost town Independence, the Klondike cabin in the White River National Forest, or the lake at the base of Maroon Bells, the most photographed mountains in the United States. Prices range from $160 to $200 for a single rider (depending on the tour), and from $240 to $300 for two persons. Either lunch or hot cocoa is included in the price. Tours run between 9:00 A.M. and 2:30 P.M. and reservations are required.

Snowshoe Tours

Fresh Track Nature Tours
Aspen Mountain
(970) 925-5756
www.aspennature.org
Snowshoe tours led by naturalists from the Aspen Center for Environmental Studies introduce visitors to the unique geology and ecology of the area, including winter animals and birds, trees, and weather. The tours are offered daily at 10:00 A.M. and 1:00 P.M. atop Aspen Mountain and Snowmass Mountain; a half-day tour, starting at 10:30 A.M., leaves from the King Cabin at the Ashcroft Ski Touring Center and winds through the pristine Castle Creek Valley. The Aspen and Snowmass Mountain tours cost $45 for adults, $29 for children 7 to 17 and seniors. The price includes the lift ride to the top of the mountains, where the tours begin; a snack and a warm drink; snowshoes; a guide; and beginner's instructions. Reservations are not required. The Castle Creek Valley tour costs $85 per person; add another $20 per person, with a two-person minimum, for a shuttle ride up to Ashcroft. The price includes the tour, a gourmet lunch at the Pine Creek Cookhouse, snowshoe rental, and an Ashcroft trail pass. Reservations are required. For meeting times and places, go to the Web site or call the number listed above.

HIKING/BACKPACKING

Because Aspen is ringed by some of Colorado's highest mountains, five of which are at elevations over 14,000 feet, the hiking is unparalleled. Lists of trails that range from easy to difficult are available from the Aspen Chamber Resort Association, 425 Rio Grande Place, (970) 925-1940, or the Aspen Ranger District, (970) 925-3445. The Maroon Bells-Snowmass Wilderness Area is another stupendous choice for hiking and backpacking near Aspen and Snowmass. It's managed by two different ranger districts.

The Aspen Ranger district of the White River National Forest, 806 West Hallam Street, in Aspen, (970) 925-3445, manages the eastern portion of the wilderness and the Taylor River Ranger District of the Gunnison National Forest, (719) 641-0471, manages the western portion (which will not be covered in this book). Ute Mountaineer in Aspen at 308 South Mill Street, (970) 925-2849, has a knowledgeable staff plus a good selection of maps and equipment.

American Lake Trail
About 10 miles southwest of Aspen off Highway 82
At 6⁴⁄₁₀ miles round-trip, the American Lake Trail doesn't sound too strenuous for a day hike, but don't be fooled. You'll gain 1,975 feet in the relatively short span of 3 miles, rising from just under 9,500 feet to nearly 11,500. The climb is relentlessly uphill as you enter the Maroon Bells-Snowmass Wilderness, but you'll be rewarded for the effort with old-growth aspen, columbines, wildflowers, a meadow, and views of the peaks above American Lake. Camping is permissible on a small bench about half a mile from the alpine lake, or you may return the way you came. The season runs from July through September but is particularly nice during the fall. To reach the trailhead, drive west on Highway 82 to Maroon Creek Road, turn left at the stone church, and make an immediate left onto Castle Creek Road (Forest Road 102). Drive 10 miles to the Elk Mountain Lodge; the trailhead is on the right.

Braille Trail
Highway 82, 10 miles east of Aspen
Created especially for blind hikers, this quarter-mile-long trail explains the flora, fauna, and other natural history of the area in both Braille and regular print with more than 20 signs. Blind hikers are guided by a nylon cord. Stop first at the Aspen Ranger District, 806 West Hallam Street in Aspen, to borrow a free miniature tape player and cassette designed especially for this hike. The trail is 10 miles

east of Aspen up Independence Pass on Highway 82. The turnoff is on the right side of the road.

Buckskin Pass
About 10 miles southwest of Aspen off Maroon Creek Road
For a strenuous 9⁶⁄₁₀ mile round-trip hike, take the Buckskin Pass Trail through the Maroon Bells-Snowmass Wilderness Area, working your way up the Minnehaha Gulch to the passageway between two 12,000 peaks (the Buckskin Pass). Along the way you'll have beautiful views of the Elk Mountain Range and the well-photographed Maroon Bells (see the "Attractions" section for more about them). You'll also see a beaver dam, glacial moraine, mountain rabbits, wildflowers, and tundra, and once you've reached the pass, enjoy views of Snowmass Lake, Snowmass Peak, Snowmass Mountain, and Hagerman Peak. You may also use this as a staging spot to climb Buckskin Mountain (13,370 feet) to the north or take a longer backpack trip up and over the pass into the Snowmass Creek Campground above Snowmass Village. Camping is available at Crater Lake (about halfway along the Buckskin Pass Trail) or in the basin just before the final pitch to Buckskin Pass. The trail climbs 2,900 feet from about 9,600 to 12,500 feet and is best done between July and September. To reach the trailhead, drive west of Aspen on Highway 82 for ½ mile and bear south at the Maroon Creek Road turnoff. Turn right and continue 9½ miles to the Maroon Lake parking area (day parking only). From mid-June through August and on weekends in September, Maroon Creek Road is closed to traffic 8:30 A.M. to 5:00 P.M. During those times, the trailhead is accessible only by shuttle bus from Aspen's Ruby Park transit area.

Cathedral Lake and Electric Pass
Castle Creek Road, off Highway 82 west of Aspen
For the hardier hiker this can be a 5-mile round trip to 11,866-foot Cathedral Lake or

8⁸/₁₀ miles round trip to 13,500-foot Electric Pass. From the trailhead, there's an elevation gain of 1,970 feet to the lake and 3,610 feet to the pass—a substantial difference. Either hike is gorgeous and well worth the effort. The trail begins through aspen woodlands then parallels Pine Creek as the trail gets steeper. But beautiful blue gentians and harebells blooming along the way make it easier. About an hour into the hike, look for an old mine carved into the red rock wall across the creek.

Around treeline the trail opens to a beautiful willow- and flower-filled meadow and marshy area. A series of switchbacks ends with a wooden sign at a fork in the trail. To the left is a short, ³/₁₀-mile walk to Cathedral Lake. To the right await 2 miles of strenuous climbing to Electric Pass. The pass affords a wonderful view of Electric Pass Peak and to the south, Cathedral Peak. To the west are Pyramid Peak and the Maroon Bells, all higher than 14,000 feet and awe-inspiring. Those headed for the pass should start early to avoid afternoon thunderstorms. Try to reach the pass by noon. Cathedral Lake is a shimmering mirror reflecting mountains, clouds, and wildflowers—a great spot for lunch.

To reach the trailhead, which is 13⁹/₁₀ miles from Mill and Main Streets in downtown Aspen, head west on Highway 82. At 1³/₁₀ miles from Mill and Main turn left at the light and chapel onto Maroon Creek Road. Turn left immediately onto Castle Creek Road. Drive up this dirt road for 12 miles past the Elk Mountain Lodge and the ghost town of Ashcroft. Past Ashcroft look for a dirt road on the right. Follow that road for ⁷/₁₀ mile to a parking area where the trail begins.

Midway Pass to Hunter Creek (backpack trip)
Across from Lost Creek Campground on Highway 82

This 20-mile trek takes about three days. Traversing the Hunter-Fryingpan Wilderness, it's less popular than many of the Maroon Bells-Snowmass Wilderness trails, but equally beautiful and a good place to see elk and deer. The trail begins at around 10,000 feet, affording views of Independence Pass. About a half-mile up the trail, follow the left fork up Midway Creek Trail, which crosses Midway Pass, then drops down and winds through marshes until it crosses Hunter Creek Trail. At this intersection, go left and you'll wind up back in Aspen. Two cars or a pickup arrangement are necessary. Be sure to get detailed maps and directions for this area from the Forest Service offices or sporting goods shop listed above.

To find the trailhead, drive east of Aspen on Highway 82 and look for Lost Creek Campground. The trail is on the left side of the road across from the campground.

West Snowmass Trail
About 3 miles west of Snowmass Village (as the crow flies)

A difficult 11-mile round-trip trail, West Snowmass is the classic Colorado hike. It climbs 3,500 feet, from 8,500 feet elevation to 12,000 feet, where visitors can overlook the Maroon Bells-Snowmass Wilderness and high peaks that include several 14ers (Capitol Peak at 14,130 feet, Maroon Bells at 14,014 and 14,1156, Snowmass Mountain at 14,092, and Mount Sopris near Carbondale at 12,953). Even better—it's a lightly used trail, which means you may find solitude in the midst of a heavily traveled region. Along the challenging trail, you'll encounter switchbacks, cross the chilly Snowmass Creek, pass through a poorly signed area crisscrossed by non-forest system trails, pass through several meadows and climb to a saddle between Mount Daly (the landmark visible from Snowmass Village) and Haystack Mountain. You can retrace your steps or continue another 2½ miles to Capitol Creek, which leads to the Crystal River north of Redstone. Numerous campsites line the trail, and fishing is fair to good for small brook trout along Snowmass Creek. To reach the trailhead, which is just over the mountain from Snowmass

Village as the crow flies, follow Highway 82 north to Old Snowmass and turn south at the FOREST ACCESS sign there. After 2 miles, turn left at the sign for Snowmass Campground and follow this road 10 miles to the campground. Bear right and follow the road to a parking area ½ mile beyond. Hike along the main Maroon-Snowmass Trail for about a mile to a sign that points to the West Snowmass Trail.

CAMPING

Independence Pass Area
Highway 82
(970) 925-3445, (877) 444-6777
or www.reserveamerica.com for
reservations

Five campgrounds along Highway 82 into (or out of) Aspen via Independence Pass offer numerous sites. All are strung along the road open only seasonally between July and September, and many are at elevations higher than some mountains. Most serve as staging areas for fishing, hiking, four-wheel driving, horseback riding, and mountain biking. Because the terrain is so beautiful, they tend to fill up fast, so reservations are almost a must.

Difficult Campground has 47 sites and is only 5 miles from Aspen. Next along the pass, Lincoln Gulch has seven sites, 10 miles from Aspen; 11 miles from Aspen is Weller with 11 sites; and finally Lost Man Campground with 10 sites, 14 miles from Aspen. Campsites cost between $13 and $16 per night. All have fire rings, water, picnic tables, and toilets. Weller has some wheelchair-accessible sites.

Another choice 11 miles from Aspen is Portal Campground, accessible only by four-wheel-drive vehicles. The dirt road is very rough and unmaintained, but it leads to seven sites perched just below the Continental Divide in the Collegiate Peaks Wilderness. Fishing is available in nearby Grizzly Reservoir and in two creeks. Hiking Trail 1478 will take only the most serious hikers over the Continental Divide. To reach it from Aspen, travel 10 miles south-

east on Highway 82, then turn south onto Forest Service Road 106 for another 6½ miles. Site fee is $18 per night.

Maroon Bells Area
About 8 miles west of Aspen off
Highway 82
(970) 925-3445, (877) 444-6777
or www.reserveamerica.com for
reservations

Three campgrounds provide only 14 campsites within the scenic Maroon Bells area: Silver Bar with four tent sites at 8,300 feet; Silver Bell at 8,400 feet, with four sites large enough to hold small trailers; and Silver Queen at 9,100 feet, with six sites the highest place to car camp in the Wilderness area. All are about six miles from the entrance to Maroon Bells. All require at least three- and no more than five-night stays. They all have fire rings and toilets; Silver Bell has no water. Remember that no vehicle traffic is allowed during the day, so campers must hike out or take the shuttle into Aspen. Sites are $15 a night. To reach them from Aspen, take Highway 82 north about 1.5 miles, then turn southwest onto Forest Service Road 125 (Pitkin County Road 13) and travel another 6 miles.

White River National Forest
Aspen Ranger District Office
806 West Hallam
(970) 925-3445

Fifteen forest service campgrounds in the Aspen area offer everything from primitive camping to RV hookups. Most of the campsites are first-come, first-served, but phone reservations may be made for a fee. Complete area maps and information about camping and campsites are available at this office.

GOLF

Aspen Golf Course
39551 Highway 82
(970) 925-2145
www.aspenrecreation.com

The only municipal golf course in the Aspen area, this golf club is known for relatively flat holes and meticulous conditions. Groundskeepers keep the fairways lush and emerald in color and the greens healthy and evenly mowed; that may explain why irrigation ditches and lakes form the biggest hazards on the course. All totaled, 14 of the holes have some type of water hazard.

The course design is rather flat and very long, with undulating and sloping greens that are difficult to play. The design is not as interesting as some courses, veteran golfers say, but the conditions and the views more than make up for it. Golfers say that regardless of where they are on the course, they can always see a beautiful valley. Because the course is low and sunny, it often opens for the season before the skiers have left the mountains. Its typical season runs from April through October, with occasional closures for late fall snow. Only foursomes are allowed. Greens fees with cart are $110 during the high season, with walkers saving $18. In October, prices drop to $63 with cart.

The Snowmass Club
239 Snowmass Club Circle
Snowmass Village
(970) 923-3148
www.snowmassclub.com
The golf course at Snowmass, elevation 8,000 feet, is shaped like the state of South Carolina. Holes 1 through 6 work up into and back out of the point at the top of the state; the clubhouse is buried in the heart; and the remainder of the holes snake across the state's broad base. To the southwest, Mount Daly and the slopes of Snowmass Ski Resort are visible. To the northeast is the valley's rodeo ring and equestrian complex. The Snowmass Lodge is a focal point of the club, with the 18th hole playing past the pool terrace and restaurant patio.

Played from the championship tees, the par 3 holes are monstrously long, and the greens are almost impossible to read because of the optical illusion created by the sloping mountainsides. (Hint: Putt all greens downhill from Mount Daly, even if they appear to run uphill.) The 18-hole 7,008-yard, par 72 course was designed by renowned golf architect Jim Engh.

FISHING/HUNTING

Outfitters and Tackle Shops

Aspen Outfitting Co.
315 East Dean Street
(970) 925-3406
This fly-fishing guide service, located in the St. Regis Aspen hotel, leads fishing trips on local waterways and big-game and waterfowl hunting trips through surrounding forest lands. Call for details and information on prices.

Frying Pan Anglers
132 Basalt Center Circle, Basalt
(970) 927-3441
www.fryingpananglers.com
Basalt straddles some of the best fishing waters in the state, especially the Gold Medal waters on the Fryingpan River. Guides from this company lead wade trips along the Fryingpan and float fishing trips in McKenzie-style boats on Ruedi Reservoir.

Oxbow Outfitters
196 Riverdown Road
(970) 925-1505
www.oxbowoutfitters.com

Oxbow organizes wade fishing on the Fryingpan and Roaring Fork Rivers, and float trips on the Roaring Fork and Colorado Rivers. Anglers can rent all equipment and need not have fishing experience. Prices range from $200 for one person on the half-day trip to $375 for a full-day trip for one.

Taylor Creek Fly Shop
183 Basalt Center Circle, Basalt
(970) 927–4374
www.taylorcreek.com
Taylor Creek tries to be more than just another fly shop. In addition to leading wade and float fishing in McKenzie-style boats, it teaches fly fishing, dispenses information about current fishing conditions, sells sports clothing and equipment, and offers books about fly-fishing travel around the world.

Places to Fish

Fryingpan River
From Ruedi Reservoir to Basalt
Every real angler has heard about the Fryingpan, one of Colorado's best stretches of Gold Medal water. It flows from Ruedi Reservoir above Basalt down into the town before joining the Roaring Fork River 24 miles southwest of Glenwood Springs. This river's legendary 20-inch brown and rainbow trout can be fished only with artificial flies and lures, and all catches must be released on the stretch of river that runs from Ruedi Dam to 4 miles downstream. (Anything caught from there to Basalt can be kept, assuming it's at least 16 inches and you keep only two.) During summer weekends, anglers line up shoulder to shoulder in the precious waters. You'll have less company if you come again during winter on the upper Fryingpan.

Hunter Creek
Northeast Aspen
Small brook, brown, and cutthroat trout

can be pulled from this little creek, which flows on the northeast side of Aspen into the Roaring Fork River. Hunter Creek Road, a dirt track, roughly traces the creek as it flows 6 miles to the boundary of the Hunter-Fryingpan Wilderness Area.

Ivanhoe Lake
Near Basalt
This mountain lake is stocked with rainbow trout, so don't expect to catch anything else there. It's located 5 miles from Ruedi Reservoir near Basalt, up Forest Roads 105 and 527 alongside Ivanhoe Creek.

Willow Lake
Maroon Bells-Snowmass Wilderness
Area, 8 miles from Old Snowmass
Large brook and cutthroat trout live in this 11,705-feet high lake, but you'll have to hike 5 miles from Maroon Bells Lake to reach it. Both are in the Maroon Bells-Snowmass Wilderness Area.

Places to Hunt

Maroon Bells-Snowmass
Wilderness Area
Between Aspen and Redstone in the
White River National Forest
Because the elevation reaches as high as 14,000 feet in this wilderness area, the snows are earlier and deeper than in other parts of the state. That makes Maroon Bells-Snowmass exceptional for hunting elk driven by the snow to lower feeding grounds. Accessing it is difficult because of the craggy terrain. Hunters should be expert backpackers or ride horses into the backcountry. Ask for information about Game Unit 43.

OTHER RECREATION

Aspen Chamber Resort Association
425 Rio Grande Place
(970) 925–1940
www.aspenchamber.org

Aspen has one of the state's most inform-
ative visitor centers, filled with brochures
and information sheets about everything
from historical tours to day care options.
Chamber members list their services,
including the range of summer hiking, biking, fishing, four-wheeling, and even
paragliding guides. This was our first stop
when visiting Aspen, which streamlined
the rest of our trip.

Biking

Aspen Ranger District Office
806 West Hallam Street
(970) 925-3445
Visit the ranger office for maps and information about backcountry trails of all
kinds.

Blazing Pedals
105 Village Square, Snowmass Village
(970) 923-4544, (800) 282-7238
www.blazingadventures.com
Guides from this service, an offshoot of
Blazing Adventures, lead mountain bike
tours to Maroon Lake, Ashcroft ghost
town, the Continental Divide, and other
scenic areas. All are downhill tours and
include a meal and a tour at the destination. Rides can be geared toward children,
adults, or families.

Smuggler Loop
Off Park Circle
This 7²⁄₁₀ mile loop on the north side of the
river is an Aspen favorite for workouts. It's
a steep climb on a four-wheel-drive road.
Once on top, you can retrace your tracks
or loop around on Red Mountain Road.
The full loop takes between 45 and 90
minutes to complete. Access it by following Mill Street north past the Art Museum,
then bearing right on Gibson Avenue. Take
a left on Park Circle, and the trailhead will
be on your right.

Climbing

Aspen Alpine Guides
(970) 925-6618
Guides lead a wide variety of hikes, backpacking excursions, and rock climbing
adventures, as well as providing expert
instruction, either privately or in small
groups. Day hikes can last from two hours
up to a full day of seven hours, and cost
from $175 to $270 for a group of three,
$50 to $65 for each extra hiker. Rock
climbing trips are half- or full-day, and
cost $260 or $345, respectively, for one or
two people. For the adventurous there are
two-day backpacking excursions, or the
Colorado Classic, a six-day trip over four
passes through the Elk Mountains and the
Maroon Bells. Bring your sleeping bag,
personal gear, snacks, and trail lunches,
plus $1,140 per person; everything else is
provided.

Gondola/Lift Rides

Burlingame Lift
Snowmass Village Mall
Snowmass ski area
(970) 925-1220
The double-seat scenic Burlingame chairlift takes passengers midway up the
slopes of Snowmass during warm-weather
months. Between mid-June and early September, the lift ferries hikers, bikers, and
sightseers to the midway point on the ski
mountain. The best part is the price is
right—FREE!

Silver Queen Gondola
Aspen Mountain
(970) 925-1220
Between Memorial Day and mid-September,
the Silver Queen gondola provides scenic
rides to the top of Aspen Mountain. Board
at the base of Aspen Mountain, roughly
located at the corner of East Durant

Skiing on the Cheap

So lift-ticket prices have climbed over $75. Throw in ski rentals, transportation, and meals, and you're in for nearly $200 a day per person—before you've even doled out the money for lodging and après-ski entertainment. Feeling priced out of the market? No need. There are ways to ski on the cheap, without taking out a second mortgage.

For starters, don't buy lift tickets at the ski-area ticket window if you're skiing only one day. When coming through the Denver metro area, as most Colorado skiers do, stop at any major grocery store or even a gas station and save up to $15 off the going rate. If you're on a longer vacation, it pays to buy a multi-day ticket at the resort for greater savings. And for even cheaper tickets, hit the slopes before Thanksgiving or in April, avoiding the peak season and its premium prices. Finally, if you're skiing more than a week, it might pay to buy a season pass. The "Front Range" resorts—Breckenridge, Keystone, Copper Mountain, Arapahoe Basin, and Winter Park—have engaged in a price war that dropped a full season lift ticket as low as $200, less than most vacationers paid in a week. But you have to be alert because those typically are available only during limited times. Four-packs are the latest gimmick, with ski areas bundling four separate days on the mountain into one package deal that can

be priced as low as $60, or $15 a day. They're usually available from the resorts during summer months before the ski season begins. Watch their Web sites for details.

There are a number of cost-cutters you can use at the slopes as well. For one, bring your lunch and avoid paying $7.50 for a hamburger. Most resort cafeterias have areas where brown-baggers can eat, although they don't publicize it. Also, don't buy ski gear on the mountain; rather, wait until you go into town to snag a replacement pair of goggles or a hat when the sunny spring day unexpectedly turns cold. And on the subject of clothing, most peoples' wardrobes already have suitable ski gear, so you don't have to go out and buy a new $400 parka and pants. Several layers of clothing provide the warmth, and waterproof windbreakers and nylon warm-up pants work fine for keeping dry.

For a cheaper overall vacation, consider joining a ski club or tagging along on an organized group outing. Package deals for larger groups, including discounted airfare, lift tickets, lessons, and lodging can save you a bundle. Also, the resorts all offer special deals if you can travel on short notice—when the rooms don't fill, even during that crowded holiday season, it's not unusual to pay less than half the going rate.

Avenue and South Hunter Street (the gondola is at the end of a pedestrian plaza). Enclosed cars travel between 10:00 A.M. and 6:00 P.M. with passengers free to get off and wander at the top before continuing their trip back down. Rides are $18.00 for adults, $15.00 for youths 13 to 17, and $10.00 for children 4 to 12 on weekdays; weekends are $2.00 more for everybody.

Horseback Riding

H2J Riding School
Cozy Point
(970) 923-9297
www.h2j.com
Children 7 to 16 are students at this comprehensive summer equestrian camp, held at Cozy Point Ranch. Children learn to groom their horses; do the daily feeding and cleaning chores; learn about breeds, anatomy, tack, and veterinary skills; and take daily group riding lessons in the English riding style. The summer session runs from early June through August, and campers pay roughly $90 a day. Discounts are available for weekly enrollments of 5 to 10 days.

Snowmass Stables
1020 Brush Creek Road
Snowmass Village
(888) 649-5982
www.stayaspensnowmass.com
This valley used to be a cattle ranch, but all that remains is Snowmass Stables and the Snowmass Village Rodeo Grounds (they are no longer affiliated). The Stables offer hourly trail rides, two-hour rides to the top of the ski mountain, breakfast and lunch rides, half- and full-day rides, lessons, pony rides, and cattle drives. Prices range from $43 for a one-hour ride to $120 for half-day ride. Reservations must be made a day in advance.

Jeep Tours

Blazing Trails
105 Village Square, Snowmass Village
(970) 923-4544, (800) 282-7238
www.blazingadventures.com
An offshoot of Blazing Adventures, this four-wheel-drive service provides guided tours of gold-mining towns, an elk camp wilderness area, the historic town of Lenado, and the summit of Larkspur Mountain. Participants meet as Aspen Sports stores in Snowmass Village or Aspen and are returned there after the tour.

Mine Tours

Compromise Mine
Atop Aspen Mountain, Aspen
(970) 925-3699
The entrance to the Compromise, one of the Aspen Mining District's largest and richest silver mines, is atop the Little Nell ski run on Aspen Mountain. The tour takes visitors through caves that extend from 1,400 above Aspen to 700 feet below the city streets. Local miners conduct two-hour tours of the working mine during summer months only. The tour begins with a four-wheel-drive ride to the entrance, where visitors board a mine train for a 2,000-foot tour of the old and new workings. One highlight is a 1,200-foot-deep stope (an underground chamber left behind after the ore is removed). Tours are offered Saturday at 9:00 and 11:00 A.M. and 1:00 and 3:00 P.M. or by appointment for groups of six or more. This tour is seasonal, so call ahead for times and prices.

Smuggler Mine
Atop Smuggler Mountain
(970) 925-2049
One of Aspen's longest operating mines, Smuggler is on the National Register of Historic Places even though it still produces silver ore. The mine opened in 1880, and in 1894, the world's largest silver nugget was removed, weighing 1,840 pounds. Local miners take visitors on a one- to two-hour walking tour, depending on crowd size, that delves 1,200 foot into the mine. Tours are offered year-round with advance reservations. During the winter tours are for a minimum of four people. Because mine temperatures stay about 50 degrees F. year-round, jackets are recommended.

Paragliding

Aspen Paragliding
426 South Spring Street
(970) 925-7625
www.aspenparagliding.com
The USHGA-certified pilots at Aspen Paragliding ease their clients into paragliding starting with a tandem flight on which the client rides passenger with the pilot in a specially designed tandem paraglider. Over the course of five such flights, clients begin taking over the steering and landing responsibilities and can then graduate to single flights. All paragliders are launched mornings and late afternoons off Aspen Mountain. Flights include ground handling, classroom and video work, and radio-assisted flight instructions. Plan to spend at least a week on the first level training, two weeks for the second level training. Reservations are required.

Tennis

The Aspen Meadows Tennis Center
845 Meadows Road
(970) 544-7111
Privately owned but open to the public, Aspen Meadows has four cushioned concrete courts and two clay courts that are rentable by the hour. During summer months, they're open 7:30 A.M. to 7:00 P.M. Other services include a pro shop and lessons. Reservations are suggested.

City of Aspen
Aspen Golf & Tennis Club
39551 Highway 82
(970) 920-2575

Iselin Park
0450 Maroon Creek Road
www.aspenrecreation.com
The City of Aspen maintains six clay tennis courts at the Aspen Golf & Tennis Club on Highway 82, and two hard courts at Iselin Park, located on Maroon Creek Road

at the Aspen Recreation Center. Both facilities are open 8:00 A.M. to 7:00 P.M. The Golf & Tennis Club courts require reservations; the Iselin Park courts are first-come, first-served.

Snowmass Lodge & Club
239 Snowmass Club Circle
Snowmass Village
(970) 923-0818
www.snowmassclub.com
The private Snowmass Club has 11 outdoor and two indoor courts that it also rents to hotel guests and the public. In addition to the courts, the club has a pro shop, ball machines, weekly mixed doubles programs, weekly adult and junior clinics, and lessons.

Swimming

City of Aspen
James E. Moore Pool
Maroon Creek Road
(970) 544-4100
www.aspenrecreation.com
Aspen's municipal swimming pool is located next to its tennis courts at Iselin Park, south on Maroon Creek Road to the High School Campus. Check before you go to find out what programs are scheduled for the day, because the pool is sometimes reserved for lessons, adult lap swims, water aerobics, family swims, kayak lessons, masters swim club, scuba lessons, and other organized activities.

Whitewater Rafting

Blazing Paddles
105 Village Square, Snowmass Village
(970) 923-4544, (800) 282-7238
www.blazingadventures.com
Guided river rafting trips on the Colorado, Roaring Fork, Arkansas, Gunnison, and Dolores Rivers are offered by this company, an offshoot of Blazing Adventures. Guests are welcome at any experience

Legendary Woody Creek Tavern

When it's time for a hamburger, Aspen locals hop in the car and drive to a rustic hole in the wall called Woody Creek Tavern, No. 2 Woody Creek Plaza, (970) 923–4585. But don't be fooled by its appearance. The comfy dive was home away from home to the late gonzo journalist Hunter S. Thompson and has seen its share of celebrities, too (including Don Johnson, whose second home is in Woody Creek).

It's located in a town by the same name, but to most visitors' standards, Woody Creek isn't much of a town. The beauty of Woody Creek, 7 miles down the road from ritzy Aspen, is its down-home nature. Before movie stars found it, Woody Creek was merely home of outlaws, renegade authors, and about 600 people who liked things a bit scrungy. The town proper includes an art gallery, a post office, a laundromat, and the Woody Creek Tavern, several of which are in one log building. (The post office moved into its own digs across the street in 2000.) That log building is surrounded by a trailer park that dates to the 1940s and a handful of trophy homes that are smallish by Aspen standards.

The valley carved by Woody Creek, the river that loaned its name to the town, was founded by cattle ranchers and northern Italians who felt at home in the Alp-like mountains. Hunter S. Thompson brought national attention to the lazy place, as have homeowners Don Johnson and Don Henley. During tourist season they stay away from the tavern, but when sightseers clear out they wander down for burgers and locally brewed Flying Dog ales at the souvenir-festooned bar, and smokes in the Smoking Lounge (a lean-to with lawn chairs on the side of the building).

The Tavern is a favorite in the *Denver Post*'s "Best Burger" category, with its sandwich described as "something you can chow down on." We can attest to its merits, but the tavern also offers soups, salads, sandwiches, great Mexican dishes, and special children's dishes. (Although tourists might think it's nothing but a biker bar, the Tavern is considered a neighborhood restaurant to locals whose kids have grown up playing with toys from any of several toy boxes strewn around the joint.)

level, as trips can be arranged that range from beginning to intermediate level. The season runs May through September. Participants should meet at the Aspen Sports stores in Snowmass Village or Aspen and will return there after the raft trip.

Colorado Riff-Raft Inc.
555 East Durant Street
(970) 925-5405, (800) 759-3939
www.riffraft.com
Guides conduct three types of raft trips—from "mild" to "outrageous"—on Aspen-area waterways. Mild trips, suitable for

first-timers and families, follow the Class II waters on the Lower Roaring Fork, Grizzly Creek, and the Colorado River as it meanders through Glenwood Canyon. Wild trips, for more adventurous beginners or intermediates, move up to Class III rapids in the Upper Roaring Fork and the Shosone portion of the Colorado River. Outrageous excursions tackle Class IV/V rapids on Slaughterhouse Falls and Gore Canyon, and are restricted to people with previous boating experience. Average prices are $85 per person for half-day trips, $110 per person for full-day trips.

HOT SPRINGS AND SPAS

Aspen Club and Spa
1450 Crystal Lake Road
(970) 925–8900
www.aspenclub.com

The most prestigious of Aspen's private athletic clubs, with a membership that includes tennis pro Martina Navratilova, underwent a renovation and addition that now makes it 77,000 square feet of wellness and fitness. Completed in late 1997, the new building includes a 6,000-square-foot, multilevel health and fitness center, a wellness center, a European spa with 34 treatment rooms, and a Spectrum store. The fitness center has cardio equipment on the upper level, a weight room on the bottom level, and fitness classrooms and simulated ski training rooms. The wellness center is used for acupuncture, stress management, sports performance, women's health services, and energy and balancing treatments.

The spa offers a menu of different treatments, done in rooms that can accommodate the entire process rather than shuttling clients from one room to the next. The store sells fitness equipment and activewear. In addition to members, the general public may use the entire club by purchasing any one treatment at the spa. The spa also offers a variety of day and multi-day packages. Call for information and prices.

Conundrum Hot Springs
Maroon Bells-Snowmass Wilderness Area, between Snowmass and Aspen

Free to anyone hardy enough to find them, Conundrum Hot Springs are open to hikers in the summer. They're at the top of a 9-mile hike that rises 2,700 feet as you climb—to a whopping 11,200-foot elevation. Due to the length and steepness of the hike, most visitors prefer to camp over before hiking back out the next day. And because they're tucked into ranges so high, snow remains into July and can start falling again in mid-September.

As a payback for the effort it takes to get there, Conundrum offers three pools fed by a 122-degree spring and connected by rocks and plastic pipe. The largest is about 15 feet across and 4 feet deep, room for a dozen people to soak as they enjoy views of cliffs, mountaintops, and meadows. The lower two are a few degrees cooler and slightly smaller.

The creek was named by prospectors in the late 1800s who found gold in the water and followed the stream upward looking for the mother lode. They found hot water instead and called it "a conundrum." The springs are over-used and abused, with camping, fires, and defecation prohibited within 100 feet of the spring but happening anyway. Each year rangers threaten to close it to the public to protect it. To reach the trailhead, drive from Aspen about 5 miles up Castle Creek Road. Turn right at Forest Road 128, and drive another mile to the parking lot. They're a popular destination; it's not uncommon to find 75 to 100 cars parked at the trailhead on warm summer days.

St. Regis Aspen
315 East Dean Street
(970) 920–3300, (888) 454–9005

This luxury hotel in downtown Aspen embraced the necessity of providing guests with access to a sophisticated spa with the opening of the Remede Spa in 2004. A spin-off of Laboratoire Remede, makers of high-end skincare products, the spa offers a menu of facial, massage, and body treatments, as well as manicure and waxing services. They also add a special touch that includes chilled champagne, truffles, and Kashwere throws. Customized massages are available in 30-minute increments, up to 90 minutes, and run $80 to $230. A variety of specialty massages are also available, costing from $130 to $190 depending on length and technique. Mani-cure and pedicure services are in the $50 to $75 range; waxing is a bit less. The spa packages, combining different massages, facials, and treatments start around $240 and work their way up to $555 for the five-hour long Remede Spa Indulgence. Prices do not include tip, and reservations are required.

OTHER DESTINATIONS

With possibilities that include climbing over the incongruous 700-foot dunes at the Great Sand Dunes National Monument, riding mountain bikes through the canyon country near Grand Junction, attending a county fair on the pastel-colored Eastern Plains, or hiking along a mountain stream out of the resort areas, the state has plenty of vacation options. For those readers interested in other mountain escapes, however, we offer the following towns as exceptional destinations.

In this chapter, we'll introduce four more Colorado mountain getaways. For two of these—Crested Butte and Estes Park—our introduction will be brief. For much more on Estes Park and the Rocky Mountain National Park area, we encourage you to pick up a copy of *The Insiders' Guide to Boulder and Rocky Mountain National Park*. Our sister publication includes much more information on Estes Park and the Front Range than we could here.

The other destinations in this chapter—Durango and Telluride—we'll examine in greater detail. These two towns, in the Southwestern quadrant of the state, provide unparalleled scenery, as well as a strong sense of early American history. Mesa Verde National Park is home to some of the finest Native American architecture remaining in the country. We'll take a close look at Mesa Verde below.

Mountains surround remote highland reaches such as this one near Telluride. LINDA CASTRONE

CRESTED BUTTE

Located in south-central Colorado, Crested Butte is many things. A picturesque former mining town that has been designated a National Historic District. A modern ski resort offering some of the best powder and wildest terrain in the country. The wildflower capital of Colorado. A hangout at the end of a dead-end road for both the rich and famous and the out-of-work ski bum.

Crested Butte is far enough away from everything—a five-hour drive from Denver—that it should be considered its own destination with a wide array of things to do. Skiing, obviously, is the big attraction in the winter. Summers allow all sorts of outdoor activities, especially mountain biking. Any time of year, make sure to take a walking tour through the historic downtown area, check out the quaint shops, and enjoy the rustic ambience of Kochever's bar, a nightlife hotspot. Butch Cassidy once left his pistol there in his haste to leave town with partner, the Sundance Kid, one step ahead of a sheriff's pose.

Accommodations

Crested Butte offers everything from a Club Med to charming bed-and-breakfasts for lodging, but book early because the town fills up quickly winter or summer. Conveniently, the Gunnison Crested Butte Tourism Association offers a central reservation service at (800) 814-8893 or www.gunnisoncrestedbutte.com that can handle all the details of your stay.

The Elizabeth Anne Bed & Breakfast $$$
703 Maroon Avenue
(970) 349-0147, (888) 745-4620
www.crested-butte-inn.com
One of a number of bed-and-breakfasts in Crested Butte, the Elizabeth Anne is in a five-bedroom Victorian home. Private baths, antique Queen Ann furnishings, and a full gourmet breakfast make the stay seem more like a visit to a relative's home rather than a commercial enterprise. Most dogs are welcome.

The Elk Mountain Lodge
Bed-and-Breakfast $$
129 Gothic Avenue
(970) 349-7533, (800) 374-6521
www.elkmountainlodge.net
The Elk Mountain Lodge was built in 1919 as a miner's hotel with 19 rooms and private baths. The third-floor rooms have balconies overlooking the Elk Mountains, and a lobby bar provides a friendly welcome.

The Forest Queen Hotel
129 Elk Avenue
(970) 349-5336
A historic hotel dating to 1881 in old town Crested Butte, the false-fronted Forest Queen also offers a restaurant and bar popular as an après-ski spot. Five of the rooms have shared baths.

Grand Lodge Crested Butte $$$
6 Emmons Loop
(970) 349-8000, (888) 823-4446
www.grandlodgecrestedbutte.com
Located just 200 yards from the lifts, the Grand Lodge offers 246 rooms renovated in 2004, including 104 suites with kitchenettes. An outdoor swimming pool tempts those who dare, and the full-service Wildflower Spa is open daily 9:00 A.M. to 9:00 P.M.

Water Wheel Inn $$
Highway 50, 2 miles west of Gunnison
(970) 641-1650, (800) 642-1650
www.waterwheelinnatgunnison.com
With 52 rooms and 2 suites with full kitchens, the Water Wheel Inn provides AAA-approved accommodations that border the public Dos Rios Golf Course. Amenities include an exercise room, hot tub, picnic grills, and landscaping that features mature trees and ponds. Meals are available at The Trough, the next-door restaurant that specializes in steaks, prime rib, and wild game. Pets and horses are welcome.

Restaurants

Bacchanale $$
208 Elk Avenue
(970) 349-5257
Bacchanale features delicious Northern
Italian food such as mouth-watering veal
dishes, shrimp fra Diavalo, cannelloni, Italian fried zucchini, and spaghetti for the
kids. Check out the dessert menu before
ordering dinner, however, and make sure
to save room.

Donita's Cantina $$
330 Elk Avenue
(970) 349-6674
The restaurant most often recommended
by locals, Donita's offers typical Mexican
food such as enchiladas, burritos,
chimichangas, quesadillas, fajitas, and
more. Lots of vegetarian dishes dot the
menu, as well.

Garlic Mikes $$
2674 North Highway 135, Gunnison
(970) 641-2493
Locals love Garlic Mikes' steaks, seafood,
pasta, veal, and nightly specials. Outdoor
tables on the heated patio overlook the
Gunnison River. Open daily for dinner
and on Sunday for a champagne brunch
buffet.

Downhill Skiing

Crested Butte Mountain Resort
2 Snowmass Road
(970) 349-2323, (800) 810-SNOW
Base elevation: *9,375 feet*
Top of highest lift: *12,162 feet*
Total vertical: *3,062 feet*
Longest run: *2⁶/₁₀ miles*
Average annual snowfall: *240 inches*
Ski season: *mid-November to early April*
Terrain: *1,125 acres, 121 trails (23 percent
beginner, 57 percent intermediate, 20 per-
cent advanced)*
Lift tickets: *$69*
Snow reports: *(970) 349-2323*

Getting there: *Crested Butte is 230 miles
southwest of Denver via U.S. Highway 285,
U.S. Highway 50, and Highway 135. The
Gunnison Airport, 31 miles away, is served
by American, United Express, and United
Airlines.*

Crested Butte was once considered an
expert's resort, home of the Jeep King of
the Mountain racing series and the U.S.
Extreme Skiing Championships, but the
scenery and gentle runs—not to mention a
great ski school—welcome even the rank
of beginners. The Extreme Limits, 550
acres of un-groomed double black diamond runs are enough to challenge any
skier, however. Crested Butte has grown
and expanded greatly in recent years but
has retained its hard-core skiing appeal. An
18-foot high superpipe, the 2,600-foot
Canaan Terrain Park, an all-ages Kid's Park
with slopes and jumps for beginners, a 2-
mile snowshoe loop, moonlight snowshoe
tours, and a lit tubing hill round out the
experience at Crested Butte Mountain.

Other Activities

Adventures to the Edge
P.O. Box 91, 81224
(970) 209-3980
www.atedge.com
This professional guide service leads
overnight backcountry skiing trips to several different huts in the area, offers lessons in alpine and telemark skiing and
snowboarding, and in the summer leads
climbing, hiking, and trekking outings. It
also offers treks all around the world.

Alpine Outside
635 Sixth Avenue
(970) 349-5011, (800) 833-8052
www.3riversresort.com
A complete adventure activity center,
Alpine Outside has a full fly-fishing shop
and books activities such as whitewater
rafting, kayak lessons, horse rides and
pack trips, big-game hunting, mountain-
bike rentals, balloon rides, and four-wheel-

drive tours. In the winter, check out the snowmobile rides, sleigh rides, and ice fishing.

Crested Butte Nordic Center
620 2nd Street
(970) 349-1707
www.cbnordic.org
Organized in 1987, the Nordic center is known for its well-groomed ski and snow-shoe trails, ice skating rink, and sledding hill. Guided trips, lessons, and rentals are available. The center is located on the town's free bus route. It sponsors Crested Butte's winter carnival, leads tours to the Forest Queen backcountry hut, and holds clinics and races. Adult trail passes are $14, although seniors 70 and older and dogs of any age are free. Sledding and ice skating also are free; skates and sleds can be rented for a fee.

Lazy F Bar Ranch
2991 County Road 738
(970) 349-1755
www.lazyfbarranch.com
Family owned and operated since 1953, the Lazy F Bar Ranch & Outfitters provides summer horseback and wagon rides, winter sleigh ride dinners, and fall hunting trips. The ranch kitchen can cater events for up to 150 people, providing barbecue and prime rib dinners as well as wedding cakes.

Shopping

Circus Train
125 North Main Street, Gunnison
(970) 641-0635
Circus Train boasts the largest selection of children's toys in the Gunnison area, stocking such things as Radio Flyer wagons, cowboy stuff, Bryer horses, Ertl tractors, kites, dolls, art supplies, children's books, and clothing, swimwear, and dancewear for tots through teens.

Creekside Pottery
126 Elk Avenue
(970) 349-6459
Fine handcrafted pottery, stunning lamps, accent pieces, and dinnerware sets are the specialities of this niche store. It also has window coverings, imported rugs, and functional pieces to complement South-western, country, and contemporary decor.

Zacchariah Zypp and Co.
317 Elk Avenue
(970) 349-5913
A jewelry store and more, Zypp's carries handcrafted gold and sterling pieces, fine gem stones, mineral specimens, and works by local artists. It also has an extensive collection of Indian jewelry and artifacts, leatherwork, coats, backpacks, and luggage.

Real Estate

Prudential Becky Hamlin Realty
211 Elk Avenue
(970) 349-6691, (866) 604-7565 toll free
www.cbproperty.com
The largest real-estate firm in Gunnison County, this company has 20 agents who can find the slopeside condo, downtown commercial property, or remote ranch that fits the bill.

ESTES PARK/ROCKY MOUNTAIN NATIONAL PARK

On the eastern flanks of Rocky Mountain National Park, Estes Park has long defined the tourist town in Colorado. A charming downtown filled with boutiques, restaurants, and T-shirt shops, nestled in a valley surrounded by snowcapped peaks, Estes has introduced millions to Colorado. Mild weather, incredible scenery, abundant wildlife—even in the middle of town—and the world's best candy shops all add to the allure of Estes.

Inventor F.O. Stanley, who created the first steam-powered car to reach the mountain valley, settled here and established his famous Stanley Hotel, a white-washed wood manse that has a commanding view of the surrounding area and has become popular among honeymooners despite being the setting for Stephen King's book *The Shining*. Elk and deer spill out from the national park, which is Colorado's number-one attraction with more than 3 million visitors annually. Entire books are written about the park, in fact, with its high peaks, babbling brooks, scenic overlooks, and hundreds of miles of hiking trails and camping opportunities. Trail Ridge Road, which winds across the peaks and over the Continental Divide to Grand Lake, is the highest continuous paved road in North America and absolutely a required trip while in the area.

Accommodations

Numerous cabins and cottages are scattered throughout Estes Park and the surrounding canyons leading down to the towns of Lyons and Fort Collins, and 120 hotels and lodges are available in town. For lodging referrals, contact the Estes Park central reservation line at (800) 44-ESTES, or try the following highlights.

The Aspen Lodge $$$
6120 Highway 7, seven miles south of Estes Park
(970) 586-8133, (800) 332-MTNS
A full dude ranch that offers 36 lodge rooms, 23 one- to three-bedroom cabins, and a weeklong horseback riding program in the summer, the Aspen Lodge brags that it's 7 miles and 100 years from Estes Park. Set in the shadow of Long's Peak, the ranch is open year-round and offers a full resort experience with sleigh rides, ice skat-

ing, cross-country skiing, hiking, and snow-shoeing, guide service, overnight camps, and summer hay rides on its 82 acres. Rates are cheaper during the off-season.

The Baldpate Inn $$$
4900 South Highway 7, Estes Park
(970) 586-6151
www.baldpateinn.com
Spectacular views, friendly hospitality, and scrumptious food are the hallmark of this bed-and-breakfast inn located at 9,000 feet elevation 7 miles south of town. It also has the largest key collection in the world, a bit of whimsy that provides much of the decor.

The Stanley Hotel $$$
333 Wonderview Avenue, Estes Park
(970) 586-3371, (800) 976-1377
www.stanleyhotel.com
The famous hotel on the hill, the Stanley was opened in 1909 and completely remodeled in 1997, restoring its elegance and charm to 138 guest rooms. On the National Register of Historic Places, the Stanley's creaky wood floors and world-class views make it a terrific retreat. Cascades Restaurant and Lounge is terrific. Two- and three-bedroom villas provide deluxe options just feet from the main hotel.

Wild Basin Lodge $$$
1130 County Road 84, Allenspark
(970) 747-2274
www.wildbasinlodge.com
This reasonably priced six-room lodge is near the entrance to Rocky Mountain National Park at 8,300 feet elevation. It offers a relaxing setting for vacations and weddings. Pets are not allowed.

Restaurants

Ed's Cantina & Grill $
362 East Elkhorn Avenue, Estes Park
(970) 586-2919
The best Mexican food in town, Ed's

serves spicy breakfasts, lunches, and dinners and offers a bar featuring local microbrewery beers. On the east end of town, Ed's offers take-out food, but it's best to sit down and sip one of the tasty giant margaritas right at the source.

Penelope's World Famous Burgers and Fries $
229 West Elkhorn Avenue, Estes Park
(970) 586-2277

A fast-food joint, but a darn good one. The hamburgers are fresh—never frozen— and the special menu items such as chili-cheese fries, stuffed baked potatoes, and flavored Cokes make this place a hit with kids as well as adults.

Twin Owls Steakhouse $$
800 MacGregor Avenue, Estes Park
(970) 586-9344
www.blackcanyoninn.com

The highly rated Twin Owls Steakhouse at the Black Canyon Inn specializes in fresh seafood, beef, wild game, and pasta. Entertainment in the 1927 log cabin a half-mile from town usually consists of elk wandering past the windows.

Activities

Colorado Bicycling Adventures
184 East Elkhorn Avenue, Estes Park
(970) 586-4241

Offering a huge rental fleet of bicycles for the whole family, Colorado Bicycling Adventures can send you on your way along forest service dirt roads and town streets. Or, if you prefer, the company offers guided tours through Rocky Mountain National Park, including an incredible downhill trip that requires virtually no pedaling.

Jackson Stables/Y.M.C.A. of the Rockies Livery
2515 Tunnel Road
(Colorado Spur Highway 66), Estes Park
(970) 586-3341 ext. 1140 or 1149
www.jacksonstables.com

Longtime wrangler Allen Jackson and his wife, Julie, run this top-notch livery operation, a clean, friendly livery that stands out from the crowd of public riding stables throughout Estes Park. Putting guests on well-matched horses, the most popular hour-long rides take cowpokes into Rocky Mountain National Park, but some of the best experiences are the all-day rides. The stables also offer hayrides on wagons pulled by matched blonde Belgian draft horses.

Ride-A-Kart
2250 Big Thompson Avenue
(U.S. Highway 34), Estes Park
(970) 586-6495

The best amusement park in a town that seems straight out of an amusement park, Ride-A-Kart is just east of Lake Estes and offers surprisingly fast go-karts for adults and kids, bumper boats, two 18-hole miniature golf courses, and a miniature train arcade.

Attractions

Rocky Mountain National Park
1000 Big Moraine Avenue (US 34)
Estes Park
(970) 586-1206
www.nps.gov/romo

The attraction in Estes Park, Rocky Mountain National Park is a breathtaking collection of craggy peaks that offer world-class views at every turn. Its 415 square miles make it about one-ninth the size of Yellowstone National Park, but it hosts just as many visitors, most of whom stick to the 48-mile Trail Ridge Road that courses through the park and over the Continental Divide to Grand Lake, cresting at 12,183 feet above sea level. And while the journey over the highest continuously paved road in the continent is a must-do trip (summertime only; it is closed in the winter), some of the best treasures of the park are just a short distance off the beaten path. Try hiking out of the popular

Bear Lake area or even climbing one of the park's 60 peaks that are higher than 12,000 feet, such as 14,255-foot Long's Peak, an all-day endeavor that begins before dawn. Numerous riding stables in the area offer horseback trips into the park, a wonderful way to experience the area, and twilight ventures allow the best opportunities for wildlife viewing. It's not unusual to see herds of several hundred elk in the valleys. While summer is the peak time to visit the park, it is open year-round and offers something special in every season. In autumn, for example, the aspens are turning gorgeous shades of gold and the elk start bugling, a weird, whistling mating call. In the winter, snow-shoe and cross-country ski trips from Bear Lake are popular.

Rocky Mountain National Park has five established campgrounds and allows camping in the backcountry with a special permit from park headquarters. In the summer, park rangers lead free evening shows on the flora and fauna. Hiking trails wind throughout the park, ranging from short, wheelchair-accessible loops around roadside lakes to serious cross-country treks that should only be attempted by those in good shape and equipped with necessary camping gear. Small stores operated at the visitor centers and at the Trial Ridge Store offer guidebooks, posters, kids materials, and souvenirs and support a nonprofit organization that helps maintain and enhance the park.

Shopping

Eagle Plume's
9853 Highway 7, Allenspark
(303) 747-2861
www.eagleplume.com
A few miles south of Estes Park sits one of the most stunning collections of Indian artifacts, jewelry, clothing, and decor in the Rocky Mountains. Established in 1917 as The Whatnot Inn, and run by Charles

Park rangers lead popular Sunday snow-shoe tours from the Grand Lake side of Rocky Mountain National Park between mid-December and mid-March. Intermediate two-hour tours leave at 9:00 A.M., and beginner tours leave at 1:00 P.M. They're restricted to participants 8 and older. They're also free, although park passes and snowshoes are required. For reservations and information, call (970) 627-3471.

Eagle Plume since the 1930s, the trading post is packed with kachina dolls and headdresses, authentic bows and arrows, and artwork. Eagle Plume's 1,000-piece collection of Indian art is on display here.

Trail Ridge Store
Trail Ridge Road, Rocky Mountain National Park
(970) 586-3097
www.trailridgestone.com
One of the world's highest souvenir shops, the Trail Ridge Store sits off Trail Ridge Road near the 12,000-foot high point and offers upscale curios, Native American jewelry and crafts, and handmade regional items. The store, in conjunction with a snack shop, is run by concessionaires to the park service and is the perfect place for finding—and mailing—postcards as well as gifts.

The Twisted Pine Fur & Leather
450 Moraine Avenue, Estes Park
(970) 586-4539, (800) 896-8086
www.thetwistedpine.com
In a town where every shop seems to sell curios and T-shirts, the Twisted Pine stands out for its fine collection of outer-wear such as leather and fleece coats. It also offers fur and woven rugs and hides, pelts, taxidermy, and Native American home decor and jewelry.

Real Estate

Range Realty
300 Elkhorn Avenue, Estes Park
(970) 586-2345, (888) 319-2345
www.rangerealty.com
The oldest real estate company in Estes Park, Range Realty has since 1969 specialized in cabins, homes, condominium, and commercial properties. It also has a full rental management department.

DURANGO

Although it was home to the mysterious Ancestral Puebloan Indians until about A.D. 1300, southwestern Colorado and its largest town, Durango, are now better known as a playground for skiers, railroad buffs, kayakers, mountain bikers, and history hunters.

Today Durango's full-time residents number more than 15,000, with more coming every year. During the summer they're joined by tourists who use the town as a stopping-off point for touring southwestern Colorado. The Durango & Silverton Narrow Gauge Railroad is the town's biggest warm-weather attraction. It's the last remaining spur of the cross-country railroad that tied together a state full of isolated mining claims. It now chugs back and forth between Durango and Silverton, giving riders a slow, up-close look at the rocky canyons that once bore gold and silver.

Visitors also come for the Iron Horse Bicycle Classic, a 52-mile road race against the narrow gauge train that's held on Memorial Day weekend; and for the Durango Pro Rodeo, a place where neighboring cowboys have their chance to perform and compete from mid-June through July. Also during the warm months, visitors flock to Mesa Verde National Park, where they view all that remains of the region's earliest settlers.

Golfers have been attracted by the 18-hole Scottish links course at Dalton Ranch and Golf Club. Mountain bikers have been drawn to Durango by the challenging hill courses near town, and by the rugged, individualistic culture that has been preserved in this Wild West town. Billy Crystal and co-stars came to film *City Slickers*, a film about men in mid-life crises who found themselves while herding cattle through Colorado's rugged ranchlands. And during the winter, powder hounds line up to snake their way down ski mountains geologically formed into natural stair steps.

All who come find themselves surrounded by natural beauty nearly incomparable in Colorado. If there's any doubt about that, a drive on the Million Dollar Highway should erase that. It stretches from Durango to Ouray, following U.S. Highway 550 through the mining town of Silverton, across 11,008-foot Red Mountain Pass and into the historical mining town of Ouray (nicknamed "the Switzerland of America") before sweeping down into Telluride, another well-preserved survivor from the glory days of the Old West (see below for much more on Telluride).

Getting There, Getting Around

Durango Regional Airport welcomes daily flights from Dallas, Denver, and Phoenix. It is served by United Express, America West Express, and Southwest Charter. From Denver, take US 285 southwest to Monte Vista, then go west on U.S. Highway 160 until it intersects with US 550 in Durango (about 379 miles). If you prefer driving interstate highways, you may also go south on Interstate 25 to Walsenburg, then west on US 160. Once in Durango, Durango Transportation provides taxi/van service to town and Durango Mountain Resort. During winter months, Mountain TranSport provides daily bus service between the early morning and late night hours from town to the resort. Many lodging properties also provide ski shuttles for their guests.

History

Ancestral Puebloan Indian sites that pepper the region—the biggest concentration of which are huddled together at Mesa Verde National Park 37 miles west—date as far back as the first millennium A.D. No one is sure why, but the early Native Americans disappeared from the area about 1300, leaving their intricate cliff dwellings behind. They were replaced by the Utes who, in 1868, were swapped land here in return for property in central Colorado that was heavily settled by pioneers. After gold and silver were found in nearby mountains, however, the Utes in 1873 were shuffled farther south to land they still inhabit in Ignacio, just south of Durango, and near Towaoc to the west.

Durango was settled in 1880, the brainchild of cavalry Gen. William Jackson Palmer, who envisioned the town as a railroad center that would serve such mining towns as nearby Silverton. The town was platted in the wide lush valley of El Rio de Las Animas Perdidas (the River of Lost Souls), a brief transition zone between the arid canyonlands to the south and the San Juan Mountains, some of the state's steepest, to the north. In addition to housing the railroads, Durango opened smelters to process the incoming ore and thriving saloons and brothels to keep the miners entertained during their leisure hours.

The town wavered after the mines were shut in the early 1900s and didn't begin to pick up again until Fort Lewis College was founded there in 1956. It now attracts students as well as young adventurers who come to kayak the Animas River, mountain bike through the surrounding hills, work as cowboys at nearby ranches and dude ranches, and ski the heavy snows at tiny Wolf Creek ski area to the west and Durango Mountain Resort to the north.

The town's honky-tonk flavor has been preserved, especially in Durango's historic downtown area. For information about Durango, call or visit the Durango Chamber Resort Association, 111 South Camino

Until the mid-1990s, Colorado cliff dwellers were known as the Anasazi Indians. After translations of the word were discussed by neighboring tribes— Anasazi means Ancient Invaders or Outsiders in some languages—they came up with a more gentle name, the Ancestral Puebloans.

del Rio, (970) 247-0312, (888) 414-0835, www.durangobusiness.org.

Accommodations

Best Western Rio Grande   **$-$$**
400 East 2nd Avenue
(970) 385-4980, (800) 245-4466
www.bwriograndeinn.com
Located in the heart of Durango's historic downtown, the Rio Grande is 2 blocks from the railroad station. It also has an indoor pool, a Jacuzzi, an exercise room, a sauna, a poolside lounge that serves complimentary cocktails during happy hour, shuttle service, and a free continental breakfast.

Doubletree Hotel   **$-$$**
501 Camino Del Rio
(970) 259-6580, (800) 222-8733
www.doubletreehilton.com
This 159-room chain hotel has standard, comfortable rooms as well as a restaurant and lounge, indoor pool, sauna, spa, exercise room, gift shop, guest laundry, beauty salon, massage therapist, and free airport shuttle. It's 1 block from downtown, 2 blocks from the railway station, and it backs up to the Animas River and the riverside walking/bike path.

General Palmer Hotel   **$$**
567 Main Avenue
(970) 247-4747, (800) 523-3358
www.generalpalmer.com
This 39-room historical hotel has been reviewed favorably by travel writers from

throughout the country. Built in 1898 and
named for Durango's founder, the hotel is
known for its Victorian flourishes (four-
poster beds with crocheted canopies and
fringed lamp shades, for example) as well
as its modern solarium, where guests are
served complimentary muffins and orange
juice. Queen Murphy suites are available
with queen-size Murphy beds hidden
away to make room for living areas with
wet bars and refrigerators.

Hampton Inn $
3777 North Main Avenue
(970) 247-2600, (800) 247-6885
www.hamptoninn.com
One of Durango's newest hotels, this chain
property has 76 rooms, an indoor heated
swimming pool, Jacuzzi, deluxe continental breakfast, ski shuttle service, and guest
laundry. Several restaurants and the City
Market grocery store are within walking
distance.

Iron Horse Inn $$
5800 North Main Avenue
(970) 259-1010, (800) 748-2990
www.ironhorseinndurango.com
All 142 units at this modern motel are
bilevel suites, with a queen bedroom
upstairs and a couch or a queen bed
below. The downstairs also includes a fire-
place, television, dining table, and bath-
room. Deluxe suites with two beds are
also available. The adjoining restaurant
serves breakfast and dinner; the sports
bar has a big-screen television. Other
amenities include an indoor pool, hot tub,
sauna, general store, sports shop, and
guest laundry.

The Lodge at Tamarron $$-$$$
40292 US 550 North
(970) 259-2000, (800) 982-6103
www.durangomountainresort.com
With 300 rental units, this development
on 750 acres of land surrounded by San
Juan National Forest is a luxurious place
to rough it. The main lodge has South-
western decor and sits on a sandstone
cliff that overlooks the private Glacier

Club golf courses. Townhouses may have
kitchens and terraces. Tamarron offers
two tennis courts, a health spa,
indoor/outdoor pool, and a gourmet
restaurant called The Hamilton Chop
House. Tamarron is about 10 miles south
of Durango mountain ski resort and pro-
vides guests with a ski shuttle.

Purgatory Village
Condominium Hotel $$-$$$
5 Skier Place
(970) 385-2100, (800) 982-6103
www.durangomountainresort.com
At the base of the ski mountain, this ski-in,
ski-out hotel is surrounded by shops, bars,
restaurants, and beautiful scenery. The
hotel's 133 units are decorated in South-
western style with Indian rugs and prints.
King rooms have kitchens, fireplaces, and
private decks as well as snow rooms with
ski lockers. Purgatory Village also has one-
to three-bedroom condominiums with pri-
vate balconies, whirlpool baths and/or
saunas, fireplaces, and kitchens. Efficiency
units have Murphy beds that double as
dining tables.

Strater Hotel $$-$$$
699 Main Avenue
(970) 247-4431, (800) 247-4431
www.strater.com
The most famous of Durango's hotels, this
four-story red brick building was built in
1887 by prominent druggist Henry H.
Strater. It has preserved the elegance of
that era with original ornamental brick-
work and white-stone cornices, the
world's largest collection of Victorian wal-
nut antiques, flocked wallpaper, velour
curtains, and chandeliers.
    One of the most popular of the hotel's
93 rooms is Room 222, at the corner of
Seventh Street and Main Avenue just above
the Diamond Belle Saloon. Author Louis
L'Amour lived in it while writing several of
his best-selling western novels, reportedly
inspired by the honky-tonk music that fil-
tered up through the floorboards. Among
the other celebrities who have spent the
night at the Strater are Butch Cassidy, Ger-

ald Ford, Francis Ford Coppola, John F. Kennedy, and Marilyn Monroe. The Diamond Belle has live piano music; The Office Spiritorium serves cocktails and coffee; The Mahogany Grille serves dinner; and the Diamond Circle Theatre features summer melodramas. Other amenities include evening room service, valet laundry, a Victorian-style Jacuzzi tub, and complimentary breakfast. No smoking is allowed.

Restaurants and Nightlife

Although Durango supports a variety of chain restaurants around town, most visitors confine themselves to the historic downtown region for dining and nightlife. Restaurants and saloons line Main Avenue, much as they did when 19th-century miners drove into town for rest and recreation. Tourists staying at nearby Durango Mountain ski area will also find themselves with plenty of après-ski venues and restaurants mountainside or at nearby Tamarron.

Ariano's
160 East College Drive
(970) 247-8146
Northern Italian specialties made to order have earned this restaurant the status of "favorite pasta place" among locals. The decor is that of a 65-seat Italian country inn; the food relies heavily on homemade pastas and fresh ingredients. Menu favorites include shrimp sautéed with garlic and herbs on a bed of linguine, veal sautéed with fresh sage and garlic, and beef tenderloin medallions sautéed with shallots, parsley, white wine, and bleu cheese. Ariano's is open only for dinner.

Carver's Restaurant & Brew Pub
1022 Main Avenue
(970) 259-2545
In the morning, this is the place to go in Durango for breakfast. The bakery churns out bread, giant pastries, or bagels as well as hefty egg dishes and breakfast burritos.

Although Durango is rated one of America's top ski towns, its busiest season is summer. That means in-town lodging prices are 30 to 60 percent lower during the ski season.

In the evening, it becomes a spirited microbrew pub. Guests crowd around the wood tables and sample the pub's homebrewed beers. The restaurant's motto is "Fresh food, fresh brewed," as it specializes in light and healthy dishes for the meat eater as well as the vegetarian. Carver's also is known for lunch and dinner bread bowls filled with soup or stew.

Diamond Belle Saloon
699 Main Avenue
(970) 247-4431
Located in the lobby of the Strater Hotel, this nightspot has swinging doors, Victorian ambiance hostesses dressed ca. 1880, and a bartender complete with gartered sleeve. Honky-tonk piano is the music of choice six nights a week, with bluegrass on Sunday. During the summer months, a nightly melodrama is performed in the adjacent theater at 8:00 P.M. for $17 a seat, $12 for children under 12.

Farquahrts
725 Main Avenue
(970) 247-5440
www.farquahrts.com
Located on prime property in downtown Durango, Farquahrts is a favorite for casual lunches and dinners as well as a nightlife standby. The menu includes pizza, Italian, and Mexican food. On weekend evenings, the atmosphere turns funky as patrons pack the place to toast a great day of skiing, biking, or rafting.

Francisco's Restaurante
619 Main Avenue
(970) 247-4098
www.franciscosrestaurant.com
Francisco's has made a name for itself by serving some of the best New Mexico-

style lunch and dinner dishes in Colorado. This large and busy restaurant is decorated Santa Fe style, with tables strewn throughout a labyrinth of adobe walls. Among the house specialties are enchiladas Durango and beef wrapped in blue-corn tortillas and smothered in green chili. For the gringo who would rather keep things simple, the menu also includes steak, chicken, and trout.

Lady Falconburgh's Barley Exchange
640 Main Avenue
(970) 382-9664
www.ladyfalconburgh.com
Good for lunch, dinner, and nightlife, Lady Falconburgh's has a ground floor bar that stocks more than 130 different kinds of beer, with 38 on tap. Downstairs is a restaurant that feels like an English pub but features upscale bar food favorites such as Philly steaks, fish and chips, and hamburgers.

Ore House
147 East College Drive
(970) 247-5707
www.orehouserestaurant.com
If you're in the mood for steak, the Ore House is Durango's most popular place to go. The Angus beef is aged on the premises and served in monster slabs. The menu also includes seafood, Australian lobster, and an impressive wine selection. It's open for dinner only; senior citizens and children's menus are available.

The Palace Restaurant
505 Main Avenue
(970) 247-2018
www.palacedurango.com
Located in the former Palace Hotel, a warm red-brick Victorian next to the train depot, the Palace Restaurant is a locals' favorite for high-end occasions. It's known for elegantly prepared meats, game, and fresh fish. A bar menu is available all day at the Quiet Lady Tavern, adjacent to the restaurant.

Skiing

Purgatory at Durango Mountain Resort
1 Skier Place
(970) 247-9000, (800) 982-6103
www.durangomountainresort.com
Resort elevation: *8,793 feet*
Top of highest lift: *10,822 feet*
Total vertical: *2,029 feet*
Longest run: *2 miles*
Average annual snowfall: *260 inches*
Ski season: *December through March*
Capacity: *15,050 skiers per hour*
Terrain: *1,200 acres, 85 trails (23 percent beginner, 51 percent intermediate, 26 percent advanced and expert)*
Lift tickets: *$59 all-day adult*

Twenty-five miles north of Durango, Purgatory is tucked up into the San Juan Mountains. It's the state's southernmost ski area with peaks on three sides and high desert on the fourth. It is known as an intermediate mountain with varied terrain, which means that half its 1,200 groomed acres are rated intermediate, with the other half split evenly between beginner and advanced slopes.

The main slopes are built into glacier-carved benches that work their way down the mountainside like stair steps. Translated into a skiing experience, the ride is a little like being on a rollercoaster, with a few minutes of 20-degree drop that levels to a 10-degree drop before falling into another 30-degree plunge. Beginners have an area to themselves away from the main slope. Kids 5 and under ski free. Expert runs on the mountain's backside take advantage of the average 260 inches of snow that fall each year to provide an excellent challenge.

Snowboarders are served at parks called Pitchfork Terrain Garden and Paradise Freestyle Arena, where even the patrollers are on boards, and visitors navigate log slides, banked turns, and snow ramps. In 1998–99, Purgatory introduced snowcat skiing and snowboarding services in conjunction with the San Juan Ski Company. The independent guiding company takes skiers to thousands of skiable acres in the San Juan National Forest between Durango and Silverton. Terrain is gladed meadows, tight trees, and slopes that require upper intermediate or extreme ability to negotiate. Rates are $200 to $220 per day per person, which includes lunch, ski and avalanche beacon rental.

The resort also offers cross-country skiing on 16 kilometers of trails, snowmobile rides, sleighride dinners, snowshoe rentals, and soaking at nearby Trimble Hot Springs. During summer it attracts visitors with an alpine slide, chairlift rides, a mountain bike lift, and miniature golf. Fishing, carriage rides, and horseback and pony rides are other summer favorites. Mountain bikers love it for the 50 miles of trails carved in 1990 when Purgatory hosted the first unified World Mountain Bike Championships. They're now open to mountain bikers of all ability levels.

Purgatory offers day care for children 2 months to 5 years old, day care with skiing for children 3 to 5, and ski or snowboard school for children 6 to 12. Hours are 9:00 A.M. to 4:00 P.M. On Friday and Saturday 2:00 to 7:00 P.M., Purgatory offers snowtubing on a lighted hill. A specially designed surface lift called the Alpine SnowCoaster pulls you uphill; special tubes carry you down the 600-foot hill. And every Sunday morning, U.S. Forest Service rangers lead a free nature tour of the mountain for guests interested in learning about the winter ecology and wildlife. They leave at 9:45 A.M. from the base of the Twilight Lift.

Cross-country Skiing

Nordic Center at Purgatory
Across Highway 550 from Purgatory Village
(970) 259-2114, (970) 385-2114
Purgatory also maintains 16 kilometers of groomed trails for classic- and skating-style Nordic skiing. The trails are rated for beginners through experts. Rental equipment is available at the Nordic center, as are lessons.

Ice Skating

Chapman Hill Ice Rink
500 Florida Road at Riverview Drive
(970) 375-7395
www.durangogov.org
Durango's winter playground opened in December 1998, with 15,000 square feet of maintained ice. The rink is covered, but has open sides to mimic the appeal of an outdoor rink. Rentals and supervision are available at the facility, operated by Durango's Parks & Recreation Department. Normal admission fees are charged. During summer months the rink is used for in-line skating.

Sleigh Rides

Buck's Livery
Durango Mountain Resort
(970) 385-2110
www.buckslivery.com
Horse-drawn sleigh rides take guests through the woods at the base of Purgatory ski mountain nightly during the ski season. Guests arrive at a mountain cabin, where they are served hot chocolate and a rib-eye steak or chicken dinner, and return to their starting point two hours later. During summer months, Buck's guides lead trail rides and dinner rides.

Other Recreational Options

BICYCLING

Purgatory Resort
1 Skier Place
(970) 247-9000
Ever since Purgatory hosted the 1990 World Biking Championships, the region has been known as a fat-tire mecca, and was one of the first to allow bikes on its chairlift. With 50 miles of trails on resort property and another 150 miles on national forest land, Purgatory could be the center

of a mountain biking experience. The 4-mile Harris Park Loop is for intermediate riders, with a downhill finish across the ski mountain. "The Worlds," a 6-mile loop of singletrack and access roads, climbs to 9,900 feet and is only for serious cyclists. The loop was created for the first unified World Championships in 1990.

CLIMBING

Animas City Rock
1111 Camino del Rio
(970) 259-5700
(877) 496-4ACR toll free
www.animascityrock.com
Animas City Rock gym ha about 6,500 square feet of vertical surface, including a series of strategically placed rocks that can hold up to 40 climbers at a time. Also found at the gym are a 1,000-square-foot bouldering cave, circuit training, cardio machines, weights, massage therapy, aerobics, yoga, and martial arts classes. Instructors and guides also can teach climbing skills at the gym or in outdoor climbing areas. The gym is open daily. Admission fee is $12.00 with gear, $9.00 without, $6.00 for fitness facility only.

Southwest Adventure Guides
12th Street and Camino del Rio
(970) 259-0370, (800) 642-5389
www.mtnguide.net
Ice climbing instructors and guides teach students at Cascade Canyon, a few minutes from Durango Mountain Resort. Guides also take experienced climbers to Ouray ice park, Silverton, and areas closer to Durango. Full-day rate is $285 for private lessons.

Golf

Dalton Ranch and Golf Club
589 County Road 252
(970) 247-8774
The second of Durango's resort courses,

Dalton Ranch is an American links course on the outskirts of town that opened in July 1993. The fairways are fairly flat and provide views of the Animas River Valley. The course is rated semi-private, which means members have priority, but non-members can reserve tee times 48 hours in advance. Greens fees are $59–$89; with carts, add an extra $10 per person. The course is open April through October.

Tamarron Golf Course
40292 Highway 550 North
(970) 259-2000 ext. 422
Tamarron is one of the state's finest with a 6,885-yard, par 72, 18-hole golf course. It is tucked beneath the 10,000-foot Hermosa Cliffs and carved into a plateau filled with ponderosa pines. It opened in 1975, and was designed by Arthur Hills. Tamarron has been called one of Colorado's most beautiful mountain courses because of its elevated trees, the narrow and rolling fairways, and the sheer rock clings. This private club can be played by guests staying at Durango Mountain Resort properties. Call (800) 982–6102 for Stay and Play Package rates.

Kayaking and Rafting

From near Silverton 28 miles north of Durango, through town and 20 miles south, the Animas River is a whitewater wonderland (even though acids from old mines tint its waters green). Durango is a paddler's dream, with 10 professional river guiding companies and a top-notch kayak school. Serious kayakers and rafters dare each other to navigate the Upper Animas, which drops an average 85 feet per mile as it moves down the mountainside from Silverton to Rockwood before entering a 3-mile stretch that churns through a boxed-in chasm. A more languid 10-mile stretch is closer to town, near Trimble Hot Springs, and a kayak course called Whitewater Park is laid out

Hiking trails are often shared by mountain bikers during summer months. VAIL IMAGE/JACK AFFLECK

on the waterway as it flows through Durango. On the Lower Animas, from Durango's city limits 20 miles south on the Southern Ute Indian Reservation, the rapids are calmer but still popular. Book a guide to show you the ropes, or try them on your own. Here are some suggestions to help get you started.

Four Corners Riversports
360 South Camino del Rio
(970) 259-3893, (800) 426-7637
www.riversports.com
Two-time world champion Olympic paddler Kent Ford is co-owner of Riversports, a store that specializes in boats, gear, equipment rental, and lessons, as well as a partner in the paddling school, which offers group lessons and one-on-one instruction. Classes range from flatwater to freestyle rodeo kayaking, rafting, and canoe clinics. Call for details and prices.

Mountain Waters Rafting
108 West 6th Street
(970) 259-4191
www.durangorafting.com
Mountain Waters is one of the oldest and largest of Durango's rafting companies and offers trips to suit all ability levels. Families or beginners might enjoy half- or full-day trips down the Lower Animas River (led daily between Memorial Day weekend and Labor Day weekend). Prices range from $27 for adults, $21 for children to $65 for adults, $55 for children. On the other end of the spectrum, two-day trips along the Upper Animas cover 28 miles of Class IV/V water with an average drop of 85 feet per mile. A physical fitness test and pretrip swim are required before rafting. Shuttle service on the way home is provided by the narrow gauge railroad. One-day price is $225 per person; two-day trips are $375, which includes the train fare. Wetsuits, sleeping bags, pads, and tents may also be rented.

Peregrine River Outfitters
64 Ptarmigan Lane
(970) 385-7600, (800) 598-7600
www.peregrineriver.com
In business for over 30 years, Peregrine River Outfitters guide everything from 2-hour to 10-day wilderness river trips on the finest rivers in the Southwest. Guests can choose between the whitewater of the Dolores River, Gold Medal trout waters of the Gunnison Gorge, Class IV and V waters of the Upper Animas and Piedra Rivers, intermediate rapids of the Upper San Juan River, lazy Animas River rides through historic Durango, and the fast moving Class III waters of the San Miguel River. Prices range from $24 adults, $18 children 12 and under (for two-hour trips) to $300–$440 for two- and three-day trips.

Attractions

Bar D Chuckwagon Suppers
8080 County Road 250, 9 miles
north of Durango
(970) 247-5753, (888) 800-5753
www.bardchuckwagon.com
For barbecue beef and cowboy singers, a miniature railroad, and gift shops, Bar D is the place to go. This ranch just north of Durango is open daily for dinner shows from Memorial Day through mid-September, although reservations are required. The ranch opens at 5:30 P.M. so guests can walk through the amusement park-style western village and shop the stores. When supper is served, crowds line up as the wranglers load tin plates with a meal of barbecue biscuits, baked potatoes, and baked beans. Bar D is more than just an outdoor meal, though. Once the wranglers start to sing, it's a chance to spend several hours listening to the sounds of the Old West. Admission is $17.00 for adults, $8.00 for children 3 to 8, and it includes dinner and the show.

Durango & Silverton Narrow Gauge Railroad
479 Main Street
(970) 247-2733, (877) 872-4607
www.durangotrain.com

Durango's most popular tourist attraction is the last remaining spur of the interstate railroad. Until the 1960s, the Denver & Rio Grande Western Railroad continued on to Antonito and then into the New Mexico town of Chama. After most of that route was disbanded, Durango continued its 3¼-hour, 45-mile route to the mining town of Silverton. (The Antonito to Chama train still runs as a tourist attraction, too.) The train now makes two round trips from Durango to Silverton every day between May and late October, and less-frequent trips during other months. (Its winter schedule begins the day before Thanksgiving and runs daily through April from Durango to Cascade Canyon.) Passengers must be prepared for the long trip up, a two-hour layover in Silverton, and an equally long trip back to the downtown Durango Station. Round-trip fares are steep—$62 for adults and teens and $31 for children 11 and younger, $109 for parlor car seating—but that doesn't seem to deter tourists. The train is booked four to six weeks in advance during the summer months; eight to 12 weeks early for rides in July and August. Some people, however, prefer to ride the bus back to Durango or catch a ride with friends, cutting the travel time in half without missing any of the scenery.

Sky Ute Casino
14826 Highway 172 North, Ignacio
(970) 563-3000, (888) 842-4180
www.skyutecasino.com

Just 25 miles southeast of Durango, the climate changes dramatically. The Southern Ute Indian Reservation is a sovereign nation, which means casino gambling is legal. Casino owners offer electronic and live poker and keno, bingo, blackjack, and slot machines 24 hours a day, 7 days a week. The adjacent lodge rents motel rooms; food is served in the Rolling Thunder Cafe and the Pino Nuche restaurant, and information about the local Native American tribe is available at the nearby Southern Ute Museum and Cultural Center. Complimentary shuttles run between Durango and the Casino.

Trimble Hot Springs
6475 County Road 203
(970) 247-0111
www.trimblehotsprings.com

Another of Colorado's geothermally heated springs emerges beneath the La Plata Mountains, about halfway between Durango and Purgatory. When the water leaves the ground, it's 128 degrees, then it is mixed with cooler water to fill an Olympic-size outdoor pool, kept at 83 degrees, and two smaller therapy pools, kept at 102 to 110 degrees. The Hot Springs were founded by Frank Trimble in 1874, but Native Americans had been using the water for centuries before. In fact, the cliffs above the pool are sprinkled with Ancestral Puebloan ruins that are now inaccessible. In the "wild west" years after Trimble opened the place to European visitors, the springs were owned by a cattle baron, served as a "social house" with exotic dancers, and finally collapsed under mud and debris. They were reopened in 1979 by former ski racer Reudi Bear.

The resort now complements the thermal pools with massage therapists who offer a full range of body and skin care treatments, a landscaped park, outdoor grills, and a volleyball court. It is open summers from 8:00 A.M. to 11:00 P.M. daily. Winter hours are 9:00 A.M. to 11:00 P.M. Admission is $11.00 for adults and teens, and $7.50 for children 12 and younger.

Ute Mountain Casino
3 Weeminuchi Drive, Towaoc
(970) 565-8800, (800) 258-8007
www.utemountaincasino.com

Come On and Take a Free Ride That's Beyond Extreme

Josh Hoyer of Durango started skiing with his parents when he was 2. That may be why, at 24, the only way he could find challenging terrain was by tromping to the tops of backcountry mountain ranges and then flinging himself down the bowls and cliff faces that stand between him and the ground. He calls the sport "free riding"—one step removed from what used to be called "extreme skiing."

Hoyer defines free riding as fast, steep skiing (or snowboarding) that's done off cliffs and in deep, fresh powder. In other words, it's not done on traditional groomed resort slopes, which makes it free and also potentially dangerous. Because the snow isn't groomed, it also is susceptible to the avalanches that routinely claim the lives of unlucky free skiers.

Most free skiing is done on national forest or Bureau of Land Management property previously considered to jagged or craggy to be anything but beautiful scenery. (A few ski resorts allow skiers to ride their lifts and then hike into backcountry bowls or cirques for what they call "out-of-bounds" skiing. Most free skiers know where to find extreme terrain near the groomed resorts at such places as Snowmass, Aspen Mountain, Aspen

Highlands, Crested Butte, Vail, Arapahoe Basin, and Loveland Ski Area, although a lot of it isn't advertised.) Free skiers who want to live to ski another day carefully research the hazards and snow history of any slopes they want to ski, then set out for a day of exhilarating fun.

When they're lucky, they set up snowmobile shuttles with one person driving two others to the top, then driving back to the bottom to retrieve them after their run. As long as the drivers keep rotating, everyone gets to ski. Free skiers also can hire guides to drive them by snowcat or snowmobile to skiable acreage.

Without transportation, free skiers must hike through deep snow up the mountains they want to ski down, a grueling process than can take as long as three or four hours. Hoyer wears hiking boots or snowshoes as he hikes, carrying his ski boots in a backpack to which he also straps his skis.

"Not just any Joe Schmoe can do that," Hoyer admitted. Hiking at 10,000 to 12,000 feet above sea level requires tremendous physical conditioning in itself, but then choosing a path down and navigating the challenges it presents—including such obstacles as trees, rocks, drop-offs, and sometimes chest-deep snow—requires skiing expertise that took

Located 11 miles south of Cortez, Ute Mountain is the first live casino to open in Colorado. It's owned by the Ute Mountain Indian tribe, owners of an extensive reser-

vation in the four-corners area that includes excellent examples of Ancestral Puebloan cliff dwellings, abandoned pueblos, and historic rock art. The casino

Hoyer 22 years to acquire. He suspects that only about 15 to 20 percent of all skiers ever get the chance to do free skiing. And every year skiers who overestimate their ability die after slamming into trees, landing badly after a jump, or misjudging avalanche danger.

Avalanches scare even the daredevils who ski the uncharted wilderness. Unpacked, ungroomed snow faces are notoriously unstable. If the snow on a mountainside melts slightly during the day, refreezes, and is covered by new snow the next day, the entire face is unstable. Anyone caught in an avalanche is quickly buried with snow that packs as tightly as cement and can crush and/or suffocate anyone beneath. Skiers who value their lives carry avalanche beacons that broadcast locator signals to rescue crews. Those who don't usually die while the crews probe each inch of the mountainside looking for signs of life.

Hoyer spent seven years arranging the rest of his life around his skiing before settling into a job as regional rep for Oakley, Inc. He started jumping off cliffs and skiing in deep powder at age 14, but didn't start competing until he turned 18. That year he entered mogul competitions (moguls are the snowy bumps on ski slopes that are created by skis as they turn back and forth across a steep mountain face), and at 20 he made the American Mogul Select Team.

During those same years he was enrolled at Fort Lewis College in Durango so he could be close to good skiing at Purgatory and some of the state's steepest backcountry terrain in the San Juan and La Plata mountains. He interrupted his education with long visits to Aspen, where he slept on couches and shared $2,000-a-month apartments with four buddies while competing with the mogul team. To finance his skiing, Hoyer did what most hard-core skiers do: He worked a host of service jobs that included waiting tables, doing construction, and, in winter, running the snowmaking machines at local ski resorts.

After graduating from Fort Lewis, Hoyer started skiing as much as possible, competing in International Free Skiing Association events whenever he could. He spent winters in Park City, Utah, and summers in Chile and Argentina (during their winter months) and paid for his passion by picking up endorsements whenever he could. Each time he was photographed wearing Sessions clothing, Nordica skis and boots, Bula headware, Smith optics, or Little Bear snowshoes, it was money in his bank. And in 1998, he was featured in the ski film *Clay Pigeons* kicking up snow in Utah's backcountry.

Free skiing is definitely a sport that scares mothers, Hoyer admits, but he did it for a host of reasons. "It's exhilarating, challenging, fast, serene, and calm when you're all alone on the mountain," he said. "Plus there's the beautiful view, and when you're hiking in, it's rewarding. You feel like you've earned your run."

Hoyer's advice for anyone interested in free skiing? Ask instructors or ski patrollers at any ski resort for help plugging into the local network or contact the International Free Skiers Association in Park City, Utah, (435) 647-9114.

has slot machines, blackjack, poker, keno, and bingo with hotel rooms and an 80-site RV park nearby. Southwestern and American food is served at Kuchu's Restaurant and Patio. Free shuttles run daily to Cortez. The casino is open daily from 8:00 A.M. to 4:00 A.M.

Events

FEBRUARY

Snowdown
Various locations
www.snowdown.org

In early February Durango gets ready to party as the town holds its annual Snowdown celebration. More than 60 events are planned over the space of four nights and five days for adults and kids, athletes and artists, comedians and canines. Among them are a downtown light parade, cream pie hit squads, bar golfing, skijouring (being pulled on skies behind a horse), snow softball, and dog and cat fashion shows.

MAY

Iron Horse Bicycle Classic
Memorial Day weekend
(970) 259-4621
www.ironhorsebicycleclassic.com

Cyclists race against the Durango & Silverton Narrow Gauge Railroad in one of the top mountain bike races in the Rockies. The course is 52 miles; also scheduled for the weekend are cross-country, relay, and kids' bicycling events. Non-racers can ride the train, and racers can hop aboard for the return trip.

JUNE

Durango Pro Rodeo
La Plata County Fairgrounds
25th Street and Main Avenue
(602) 237-3000
www.durangoprorodeo.com

Cowhands and traveling pros join together every Tuesday and Wednesday at 7:30 P.M. from mid-June to late July to show off their skills in bull riding, steer wrestling, and barrel racing competitions. Tourists and locals alike show up to cheer them on. Admission is $12.00 for adults and teens and $5.00 for children 12 and younger.

Animas River Days
Whitewater Park
(970) 247-3893, (800) 426-7637
www.riversports.com

Colorado's premier whitewater festival runs three days in late June and includes kayak, canoe, and river races, as well as a slalom and whitewater rodeo. Event organizers took the year off in 2005, so check about its status before you make plans.

SEPTEMBER

Four Corners Iron Horse
Motorcycle Rally
Labor Day weekend, Ignacio
(888) 284-9212
www.fourcornersrally.com

For four days, some 30,000 motorcyclists sweep into town for a parade, field competitions, music, a custom bike show, self-guided rides, and a performance by Durango's all women motorcycle drill team, the Hardly Angels. The rally raises money for local nonprofit organizations. One celebrity rider who often shows up is former Colorado congressman Ben Nighthorse Campbell, who lives in Ignacio, makes jewelry, and rides a Harley.

MESA VERDE NATIONAL PARK

US 160, 36 miles west of Durango and
10 miles east of Cortez
(970) 529-4465, (800) 449-2288
(reservations)
http://nps.gov/meve/ or
www.visitmesaverde.com

An hour's drive west of Durango, Mesa Verde is the site of the world's largest Native American cliff dwellings. Until 1997 those inhabitants were called Anasazis, but in deference to Native American consultants, they are now called Ancestral Puebloans. The 100- to 200-room houses were built between 1200 and 1300 by enigmatic settlers who had thrived in the canyons since about A.D. 500. Scholars are still trying to determine what caused their exodus less than 100 years after they moved from the mesa into their cliff dwellings.

Ute tribes moved into the Mesa Verde area after the Ancestral Puebloans left but avoided the ancient cities because they thought they were haunted. In 1888 ranchers Richard Wetherill and Charlie Mason came upon the cliff dwellings while searching for lost cattle during a snowstorm, and by the 1890s tourists were streaming in to collect souvenirs. In 1906 the land became a national park and was protected from further looting. Visitors may now visit the 80-square-mile park year-round (although many sites are open only Memorial Day to Labor Day) and see as much or as little as they're interested in seeing.

Major dwellings are concentrated on two mesas: Chapin Mesa, which is south of Park Headquarters, and Wetherill Mesa, which follows the northwest rim of the park. All cliff dwellings on them require guided tours, but there are two options. The National Park rangers offer daily tours from the Far View Visitor Center, starting at 8:00 A.M. Tickets are $2.75 and are sold on a first-come, first-served basis. Aramark also offers half-day and full-day guided tours to the cliff dwellings for $39 to $65 a person.

Chapin Mesa has the most popular sites—Cliff Palace, Spruce Tree House, and Balcony House. Wetherill Mesa is harder to reach and therefore is less crowded; it's a 12-mile drive from the visitor center. Once there, a small tram drives to trailheads where rangers lecture about the dwellings, the most spectacular of which is Long House.

Getting There, Getting Around

The entrance to Mesa Verde is 36 miles east of Durango on US 160. From Cortez, travel 10 miles west to the entrance. The first building in the park, Far View Visitor Center, is another 15 miles from the entrance, and Spruce Tree House and

Chapin Mesa are another 5 miles beyond. Be aware that July and August are the park's busiest months, and as many as 3,000 visitors a day pass through the entrance in mid-August. That's another reason that campground and lodge reservations should be made at least four to six weeks in advance.

The park's entry fee is $10.00 a carload. Tickets for the major sites are $2.75 each and are handed out daily after 8:00 A.M. between late spring and early autumn at Far View Visitor Center (970–529–4543); they are often gone for the day by 11:00 A.M. Overnight accommodations are limited to summer months only. Guests can choose from Morefield Campground's 435 sites ($20 each, $25 for a site with RV hookups), or 150 rooms at the Far View Lodge ($110 to $175 each). Reservations to either can be made at (800) 449–2288. Food is served at Spruce Tree Terrace, Far View Terrace, and Far View Lodge. Of these, Spruce Tree is the only restaurant open year-round.

History

For centuries the People, as they were called before being named the Ancestral Puebloans, roamed the Southwest. By A.D. 600 the first of these hunter-gatherers had planted corn, beans, and squash with a stick. While waiting for their crops to grow, the People used the rocky landscape to make stone rooms, held together with mortar. Their homes got progressively fancier as they tunneled into rocky cliffs and built elaborate stone and mud cities on rock outcroppings and in caves. By A.D. 1300 they were gone, posing archaeologists with one of their most intriguing puzzles. Why did the People leave?

The most common theories are that a lengthy drought caused crops to fail, that game was hunted to near extinction, that most available firewood was burned, and that erosion had deepened the arroyos and lowered the water table. Scholars believe their descendants can be found living in similar regions of northern New Mexico and Arizona, having migrated from the sterile Mesa Verde to more promising lands.

The dwellings were hidden from all but the region's native populations until 1888, when cowhands in search of wandering "doggies" ventured into a canyon that held the sleeping cities. Congress designated the region a national park in 1906 to protect its cultural resources. It also was designated a World Heritage Site in 1978. Until 1990, when the Native American Grave Protection and Repatriation Act was passed, human remains and burial goods had been unearthed and, in earlier days, displayed at Mesa Verde. Now they have been stored and in some cases, returned to tribal elders. In 1996, a fire roared through the park, burning 4,750 acres and both destroying some features (including petroglyphs on Battleship Rock) and exposing new dwellings previously covered with foliage. Since the summer of 2000 four fires have raged through the park, burning over 20,000 acres inside the park itself, destroying four structures and damaging five others.

Twenty-four tribes now claim cultural affiliation with the park, including Hopi, Ute, and Navajo tribes, and 21 pueblos of New Mexico who are affirmed to have descended from Mesa Verde settlers. Tribal elders have shared their stories of the Ancestral Puebloans, as passed down from one generation to the next, and their oral history has been integrated with the scientific data collected by American researchers.

Major Attractions

Balcony House
Often considered the highlight of a Mesa Verde visit, this site requires visitors to climb ladders and crawl through a tunnel. It's tucked beneath a sandstone overhang 600 feet above the floor of Soda Canyon.

It has 35 to 40 rooms and once housed 75 to 100 people. Unlike other dwellings, Balcony House had two springs, which means residents didn't have to carry water from springs on the canyon floor. No self-guided tours are possible here. Ranger-guided tours are conducted every half hour between 9:00 A.M. and 5:00 P.M. from mid-May through early September, then every hour through early October.

Chapin Mesa Museum
This facility includes exhibits that help explain the everyday life of the Ancestral Puebloans. A display of rocks shows how geology influenced every aspect of life at Mesa Verde. A weaving exhibit showcases looms and weavers' tools. The pottery exhibit has samples of vessels from throughout the Southwest. Among the museum's other features are original 1930s paintings and a children's area. It's open 8:00 A.M. to 6:30 P.M. daily during the summer; until 5:00 P.M. daily the rest of the year.

Cliff Palace
The largest cliff dwelling in North America, Cliff Palace has 217 rooms and 23 kivas (or ceremonial rooms), and once housed 200 to 250 people. It's the dwelling Wetherill and Mason found while they were cowboying, spotting something in the blowing snow that looked like "a magnificent city," as they described it. In places, the sandstone and mud structure is four stories tall. It's open 9:00 A.M. to 4:00 P.M. daily, later most days. Guests may take self-guided tours, get tickets for a ranger-guided tour between April and October (details are above), or take a full-day Aramark tour during those months. Tickets for those tours are $65 for adults, $48 for children 5 to 12, and free for children under 5.

Long House
Long House is the most spectacular dwelling on Wetherill Mesa, housing 150 people in its heyday. A ranger-guided tour is available for the site during the summer

only. The Wetherill Mesa road is open from 8:00 A.M. to 4:30 P.M. All-day tours of Wetherill Mesa are offered by Aramark from Memorial Day through Labor Day, and leave the Far View Terrace daily at 9:00 A.M. and return at 4:30 P.M. Tickets are $65 for adults, $48 for children 5 to 12, and free for children under 5.

Spruce Tree House

The park's third largest cliff dwelling is adjacent to the Chapin Mesa Museum. To reach it, walk up the paved but steep sidewalk. From that walk you can access Petroglyph Point Trail, a little-used 2⁸/₁₀ mile loop that shows hikers how the People took care of food, clothing, and shelter needs. You'll notice that a spring bubbles near the entrance to Spruce Tree House, generating enough water to support 100 people in the site's 114 rooms and eight kivas. The building is etched into a natural cave and was named for the large Douglas spruce that ranchers found growing from the front of the dwelling to the top of the mesa. They first entered the dwelling by climbing down the tree, although it was later cut down. Guests may take self-guided tours between 8:30 A.M. and 6:30 P.M. Aramark also offers half-day tours mid-April through October. Adults pay $39, children 5 to 12 pay $28, and children under 5 are free.

Other Sites of Interest

Anasazi Heritage Center

Located in Dolores, this federal museum and research center holds artifacts, photos, and displays. Adjacent to the center are the Dominguez and Escalante ruins, named after the Franciscan friars who were the first to excavate these prehistoric sites.

Chimney Rock Archaeological Area

Located 45 miles east of Durango, just south of US 160 on U.S. Highway 151, more than 3,000 acres of land hold a wealth of pre-Puebloan treasures. The two most prominent features are sandstone spires atop beds of dark-gray shale. The taller, Chimney Rock, is 7,900 feet above sea level. Its shorter sibling is Companion Rock. It's open daily for tours, $8.00 adults, $2.00 children 5 to 11.

Crow Canyon Archaeological Center
www.crowcanyon.org

The center is a not-for-profit research and education center near Cortez, about 50 miles from Durango. It excavates archaeological sites and offers weeklong volunteer excavation programs and hands-on tours Wednesday and Thursday June through August.

Hovenweep National Monument
www.nps.gov/hove

The ruins at this remote national monument contain six stunning Ancestral Puebloan sites noted for square, oval, circular, and D-shaped designs. A $6.00 entrance fee is charged for every car that enters the monument.

TELLURIDE

The Southern Ute tribe once inhabited nearby regions, but even they didn't live in the remote box canyon that now holds Telluride, for a number of reasons. Altitude and accessibility are the most practical—at 8,750 feet above sea level, Telluride gets snow nine months of the year and has a 20-day growing season (days when the temperatures drop no lower than 32 degrees). There also is only one way into and out of the canyon—west along the San Miguel River. Perhaps more important to the Indian tribe: They considered the valley sacred and believed their gods lived on the high peaks that form the canyon rim. Braves visited the current site of Telluride only to hunt elk and for three days of summer ceremonies.

The miners who descended on Colorado in the 1800s were the first to settle the area, "discovering" it in 1872 after exhausting claimable land in Silverton, 20 miles to the southeast. Enterprising prospectors found a way across Ophir Pass, spotted the San Miguel River and followed it until they found silver deposits at the mouth of the valley. During the next 32 years, more than $360 million of silver and gold was extracted from Telluride's mines, not to mention the zinc, lead, and copper pulled from mines with names like Tomboy, Sheridan, Silverbell, Union, and Smuggler.

The town of Columbia was incorporated in 1879, but changed its name to Telluride in 1883 after being asked by the U.S. Postal Service. Another California boomtown was named Columbia, and mail errors were annoyingly frequent. No one really knows where the name came from, although there are two theories. Tellurium is a gold-bearing ore found in many of Colorado's mines, although none was mined near Telluride.

Another, more colorful explanation comes from the warning issued to travelers as they undertook the rugged overland route by mule and horseback through Indian country and up treacherous mountain roads, or from the wild, hard-partying life miners sought while in town. In 1891, 4,000 residents supported 26 saloons and 12 bordellos, causing the more God-fearing to warn, "It's to hell you ride." By the 1890s, gold and silver strikes in the mountains above town were so lucrative that Telluride supported a whopping 5,200 residents, and mining towns scattered throughout the hills supported thousands more. About 2,000 people lived at the site of the Tomboy Mine alone, high above Telluride at an altitude of 11,500 feet.

Telluride's remote, high mountain location also attracted outlaws, who found it an excellent place to keep a low profile. After the mines went bust in the 1930s, the town was kept alive by a stubborn group of old-timers and a new group of recluses and drop-outs. It was reborn in the 1970s, when California developer Joseph Zoline envisioned a ski area on the 11,000-foot mountain face that hovered over town. He opened the first few runs in 1973.

The opening of a commercial airport in 1985 and the 1995 incorporation of Mountain Village above town have led to rapid growth—from a population of 300 during the leanest times to nearly 2,500 year-round residents and another 20,000 visitors during the town's busiest weekends—and this has stirred considerable local debate. The town itself has been preserved since 1964 as a National Historic District and, as such, is filled with tiny Victorian buildings strung along unpaved back streets. The nearest stoplight is 65 miles away in Montrose, and Colorado Avenue, the town's main street, still frames a heart-stopping view of jagged peaks punctuated by Ingram and Bridal Veil falls, the latter Colorado's longest free-falling waterfall.

The new Mountain Village is as glitzy as the old town is funky, with plush homes and condos, capped by resort spa, the Peaks at Telluride, and an 18-hole golf course. Retired U.S. General Norman Schwartzkopf and actress Susan St. James own second homes in the village. At the turn of the century, when the mines were producing gold, silver, lead, and zinc, Telluride had more millionaires per capita than New York City. That honor may now be claimed by Mountain Village, with a median home price of at least $2.8 million.

During summer, Telluride becomes festival central, hosting a nationally known Bluegrass Festival in late June, a Mushroom Festival in August, and an internationally known film festival over Labor Day weekend (see our "Events and Festivals" listing for more details). The mushroom extravaganza is the smallest event, with only 200 participants, but it's the most bizarre. For two days mushroom lovers comb the woods around town hunting for and picking the few dozen edible species that grow alongside some 500 other species. After days of conferences and classes, they turn their finds over to local cooks, who use them in a gourmet meal served before the mushroom dance and after the parade of mushroom-costumed marchers down the main street of town. And just so that locals can catch their breath, one week in mid-July is designated the "Nothing Festival," described as "Nothing, nothing . . . and more nothing."

Tourists tenacious enough to drive in love Telluride for its hiking and mountain climbing, horseback riding, fishing, mountain biking, river rafting, and four-wheel-drive roads. The peaks around town are filled with old mining towns that are preserved at least nine months of the year by impassible snow. Imogene Pass, built over the mountain from Ouray to Telluride, for example, passes the Tomboy Mine site, once the home of thousands of miners who enjoyed tennis courts, a bowling alley, and a YMCA. At Imogene's 13,509-foot summit, you'll find the remains of Fort Peabody, built in the early 1900s so national guardsmen could watch union miners who struck in 1903–04 for better working conditions.

For information about the Telluride area, call or visit the Telluride Visitors Center, 630 West Colorado Avenue, (970) 728-3041, (888) 355-8743 toll free, www.visittelluride.com.

Getting There, Getting Around

Getting to Telluride isn't quite as hard as it was at the turn of the century, but it's close. Its airport is America's highest—and the world's second highest—commercial airport, perched on a 9,085-foot plateau. (The world's highest is in Peru.) The airport often closes due to bad weather, diverting travelers to Montrose Regional Airport, 67 miles northeast of town, or Cortez Airport, 71 miles to the southwest. Great Lakes Airlines and America West Express have flights into Telluride. American, Continental, and United fly to Montrose. For flight information, call (970) 728-5313 for Telluride, (970) 249-3203 for Montrose. Shuttles, taxis, and Telluride Transit buses provide service to and from the airports. Try Alpine Luxury Limo at (970) 728-8750 or (877) 728-8750;

Mountain Limo at (970) 228-9606; or Telluride Express at (970) 728-6000 or (888) 212-TAXI.

By car, Telluride is 330 miles (or about 7 hours) southwest of Denver, located midway between Durango and Grand Junction (roughly 125 miles from each). The nearest major highway (US 550) is an hour away, connected to Telluride's dead-end canyon by twisty mountain roads, Highway 62 and Highway 145, that pick their way through the surrounding 13,000- and 14,000-foot peaks.

Once in town, getting around without a car is easy. A free shuttle circulates through Telluride about every 12 minutes (information at 970-728-5700), and a free gondola transports riders between the historic town of Mountain Village.

Montrose Regional Airport
Montrose
Located 69 miles northeast of Telluride, Montrose Airport is bigger than and hosts 10 times as many flights as Telluride's, and often serves as the default landing strip when weather closes the Telluride Airport. Shuttles take travelers the rest of the way, a 60-minute trip. United, Continental, American, and America West fly nonstop to Montrose from Houston, Dallas/Ft. Worth, Los Angeles, Chicago, Newark, Phoenix, and Denver.

Telluride Airport
5 miles west of Telluride
(970) 728-5313
Flying into Telluride is an awe-inspiring experience, for several reasons. Because the commuter planes are so small (19 and 37 seats) and fly so low, views of the countryside below are unmatchable. As you approach Telluride, the peaks grow in size and number until they're everywhere. Pilots fly past the box canyon that shelters Telluride, circle over the flat, green Wilson Mesa, and then line up with an as yet invisible clearing in the mountains. Passengers must go on faith that the pilots know what they're doing and have found the secret passageway. Locals call

the airport "The Aircraft Carrier" because it's built on a short shelf that sticks out from the side of a cliff and somewhat resembles the deck of a carrier. Landing on it requires the same set of skills: accuracy of approach and good brakes! The ledge on which the landing strip has been carved slopes up to decrease speed, but planes traveling too fast to stop have the potential to fall off into the canyon below. Both are good reasons why takeoffs and landings are allowed only during daylight hours. America West schedules daily flights from Phoenix; Great Lakes Airlines schedules daily flights from Denver.

History

Butch Cassidy practiced his horseback getaways in Telluride and then made his first unauthorized withdrawal at the San Miguel Valley Bank on June 24, 1889. He got away with $24,580, literally walking as far as the courthouse before firing his guns to celebrate. Until then, no one had noticed, but the gunfire drew attention—and a posse that unsuccessfully chased Cassidy and his pals miles from town. Legend has it that the area's first skiers were Swedish and Finnish miners who beat other miners to the bordellos on payday by schussing down the mountains on skis.

The mines played out in the 1930s, and the population hovered at 500 or less until 1968, when Zoline, a Beverly Hills developer, came to Telluride and found a soon-to-be ghost town populated by hippies and diehards. He envisioned a ski area on the 11,000-foot mountain face and opened the first few runs in 1973. They were quickly described as some of the toughest and bumpiest in the country, runs *Skiing* magazine describes as akin to an egg carton tacked on a wall.

The opening of the airport and the development of the opulent Mountain Village opened the way for rapid growth. Telluride and neighboring towns now serve as second-home to such celebrities as Ralph

Lauren (his ranch is sprawled along the road from Montrose to Telluride) and Oliver Stone. Tom Cruise and Nicole Kidman were married there, and the slopes have attracted the likes of Darryl Hannah, Sting, James Taylor, Dustin Hoffman, and Clint Eastwood. Model Christie Brinkley made perhaps the biggest news by crashing while helicopter skiing in the area, then falling in love with fellow crash victim and real estate developer Richard Taubman. Their short marriage was formalized with a mountaintop wedding. She left a little more than a year later, claiming she had been misled about the size of Taubman's fortune, although many locals still remember her as a booster of the arts and friend of actor Keith Carradine and his ex-wife.

Accommodations

Between the historic downtown area and the brand-spanking-new Mountain Village, visitors can choose from a wide range of lodging options. Prices are higher during the winter ski season (roughly Thanksgiving through spring vacation), slightly lower during the summer months, and dramatically lower during the "shoulder seasons" in May and October.

**Telluride Central Reservations
(970) 728-3041, (800) 450-0735
www.visittelluride.com**
Maintained by the Telluride Visitor Information Center, this central reservations service can provide information and reservations for all area accommodations, book air and ground transportation, sell lift and festival tickets, and plan conventions and reunions and even organize weddings. It provides one-stop shopping for a Telluride vacation.

Hotel Columbia $$$
**300 West San Juan Avenue
(970) 728-0660, (800) 204-9505
www.columbiatelluride.com**
Twenty-one luxurious rooms, each with

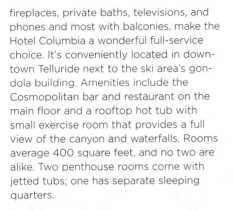

fireplaces, private baths, televisions, and phones and most with balconies, make the Hotel Columbia a wonderful full-service choice. It's conveniently located in downtown Telluride next to the ski area's gondola building. Amenities include the Cosmopolitan bar and restaurant on the main floor and a rooftop hot tub with small exercise room that provides a full view of the canyon and waterfalls. Rooms average 400 square feet, and no two are alike. Two penthouse rooms come with jetted tubs; one has separate sleeping quarters.

The Ice House Lodge and Condos $$$
310 South Fir Street
(970) 728-6300, (800) 544-3436
www.icehouselodge.com

One of Telluride's lesser known treasures, the Ice House is tucked against the San Miguel River 100 yards form the Oak Street ski lift and adjacent to the River Trail's cross-country ski trails. On the outside, it looks every bit the ski condo, although it actually is a renovated four-story elevator building. That explains the sky-lit atrium in the center of the building. Continental breakfast is served in the mezzanine. The lodge has 42 hotel rooms; 16 two- and three-bedroom condos are adjacent. Amenities include a pool, hot tub and steam room, fireplaces, Navajo rugs, and European comforters.

The Inn at Lost Creek $$$
119 Lost Creek Lane, Mountain Village
(970) 728-5678, (888) 601-5678
www.innatlostcreek.com

Designed in an "old world tradition," the Inn is a small boutique hotel with ski-in, ski-out facilities. Its 32 rooms (some owned by the Inn and others rented from private owners) range in size from a studio to a two-bedroom suite. Each is individually decorated with hand-crafted items, many of them made by local artists. Their living rooms have stone-faced fireplaces; each has a balcony, a fully equipped kitchenette, a washer/dryer, a steam shower, and a jetted tub. Ask about

the beds, reportedly the most comfortable money can buy because the owner has a "thing" about hard hotel beds.

Amenities include two roof-top hot tubs, heated underground parking, ski lockers with boot warmers, a specialty sporting goods and clothing store, and a gourmet restaurant (9545, so named because that's its elevation) and its companion bar. The restaurant is overseen by Chef Daniel Rosa. The concierge calls guests before their arrival to ask what they would like to do while visiting, then arranges the activities before the guests arrive. The lobby is worth lingering in, even if you don't stay at the hotel. The double-sided fireplace allows guests inside and out to enjoy the blaze, many of the couches are chaises with soft throws draped over them to cuddle up in on cold days; kilim rugs soften the stone floors; the furnishings are haute rustic—a glass coffee table perched on wrought-iron spurs, for example, and rich honey brown couches with leather seats and velour sides and backs.

Dogs are pampered when they stay with their humans at The Peaks at Telluride and Hotel Columbia.

Mountain Lodge at Telluride $$-$$$
457 Mountain Village Boulevard
Mountain Village
(970) 728-4549, (866) 368-6867
www.mountainlodgetelluride.com

This ski-in, ski-out log and stone project on a six-acre parcel is one of Mountain Village's newest, with 10 cottages and 90 lodge rooms and condominiums that are individually owned but rented to nightly guests. The lodge has a grand scale main lodge that houses a floor-to-ceiling, two-sided fireplace and an adjoining bar. The decor is luxuriously rustic, predominantly stone and metals. The cottages and condos are just across the drive, pleasantly decorated with contemporary furnishings and earth-tone interiors. Amenities include an outdoor heated pool, exercise room, spa and steam room, bar, hot tub, and laundry. Guests also have access to a general store and the Tavern Lobby Bar.

New Sheridan Hotel $$-$$$
231 West Colorado Avenue
(970) 728-4351, (800) 200-1891
www.newsheridan.com

The hotel was built in 1894 by two Swedish immigrants who came to search for gold but soon realized they weren't cut out for that life. They named their hotel after Yankee General Philip P. Sheridan—no one really knows why. It burned in 1898 and was rebuilt as the "new" Sheri-

First visited by American Indians and then settled by miners and ranchers, Colorado's high country is filled with relics from those times. LINDA CASTRONE

dan, as it has been called ever since. In 1913 they built the adjoining Sheridan Opera House (read more about it under the "Attractions" listing) as an entertainment venue for their high society guests.

The Four Sisters Inns took over the management in 1994 and did a thorough renovation. The 26 rooms all have baths, phones, ceiling fans, cable TV, and tasteful period furnishings; all but eight have private baths. Another six suites are in a separate building nearby. Breakfast and afternoon tea are complimentary. Food and beverages are available at the New Sheridan Chop House and the New Sheridan Bar. Amenities include a historic Victorian bar, a restaurant, a fitness room, ski lockers, and two roof-top hot tubs. Guests may want to visit the "Ladies Waiting Room" behind the lobby, where ladies were left to sip tea while their husbands frequented the bar next door. After appetites had been heightened, the couples then reunited for dinner in what is now the pool room. The New Sheridan has hosted such celebrities as Sarah Bernhardt, Lillian Gish, and William Jennings Bryan, a presidential candidate from Colorado who delivered a famous campaign speech on the street outside. (Look for pictures of him delivering that speech in the hotel.)

Peaks Resort & Golden Door Spa
136 Country Club Drive
Mountain Village
(970) 728-6800, (866) 282-4557

Formerly the Doral at Telluride, this 174-room deluxe resort spa in Mountain Village opened in 1993 and promptly went into receivership. It emerged as the Peaks (now owned by Wyndham Resorts) and has done everything in its power to lure big-spenders through its ample doors. Oprah Winfrey met her favorite trainer here, the one who helped her get the weight off. But the well-heeled unknown guest is the Peaks's bread and butter. Locals complain about the stark architecture on the otherwise log and stone mountaintop, calling it "The Penitentiary," but inside the Peaks is a subtle Southwestern retreat.

The common rooms are big on windows, great for gazing at the mountain peak that graces the Coors beer can (Mount Wilson). The 42,000-square-foot spa, owned by the Golden Door, is one of the nicest and most complete in the state, with beauty and wellness treatments as well as a large fitness center with personal trainers, indoor and outdoor pools, a two-story indoor water slide, whirlpool tubs, saunas, and steam rooms. Amenities include three restaurants, a comfortable bar, five tennis courts, and a nearby golf course.

San Sophia Inn $$-$$$
330 West Pacific Avenue
(970) 728-3001, (800) 537-4781
www.sansophia.com
This downtown inn's 16 unique rooms have handmade quilts and brass beds, and the building itself is decorated with stained-glass windows and original artwork. The sunken hot tub under an outdoor gazebo provides views to the ski slopes. A rooftop observatory offers 360-degree views of the St. Sophia Ridge, Ingram Falls, and surrounding peaks. Other amenities include boot dryers, in-hotel massage therapy, and a full gourmet breakfast. It's located just around the corner from the Gondola and the Oak Street ski lift.

Victorian Inn $-$$
401 West Pacific Avenue
(970) 728-6601, (800) 611-9893
www.tellurideinn.com
Although this hotel looks like it was built at the turn of the century, it is just over 25 years old. It was built in keeping with the covenants that protect Telluride's National Historic District feel. The inn has 33 rooms with both private and shared baths. Each room has a queen-size bed, phone, cable TV, and a refrigerator. The hotel, a half-block from the ski gondola, also has a sauna and a hot tub. Guests are served a free continental breakfast.

Restaurants and Nightlife

Once a party town, always a party town. There are some great spots in Telluride to enjoy a terrific meal and a beer or cocktail in a Wild West atmosphere.

Baked in Telluride
127 South Fir Street
(970) 728-4705
Locals who want a quiet breakfast often get their coffee and baked goods here. The patio catches morning light; the pizzas and microbrews attract a strong afternoon and evening following. Also look for daily specials and light dinners.

Cosmopolitan Restaurant
300 West San Juan Avenue
(970) 728-1292
Located in the Hotel Columbia, the Cosmopolitan is known for its creative meals and breathtaking views of the ski mountain outside. When viewed from the Gondola, it looks like a diamond, with light glittering out through the ample windows of the greenhouse-style dining room. From inside, the dining room is just as elegant, although guests may also eat in the cherry-wood bar or, in the summer, on the deck. Entrees include mussels in red curry and chile relleno with house-smoked salmon, goat cheese and spinach; roast chicken with butternut squash risotto with truffle oil; peppered tuna with jasmine rice, barbecued eggplant, calamari, and chive-lime vinaigrette. Downstairs, guests can be seated in the wine cellar, called Tasting Cellar. It seats 30 and offers a six-course meal paired with wines. The restaurant is open for dinner only.

Eagle's Bar & Grill
100 West Colorado Avenue
(970) 728-0886
Another local's favorite, Eagle's is centrally located on Telluride's main street in an elegantly restored turn-of-the-century storefront. Patrons enter on the side and

can choose to turn right into the large, warm bar, or turn left into the dining room. Both are equally comfortable, and both have views of the stunning carved wood sculptures that dominate the room. Entrees include such cosmopolitan combinations as barbecued duck, green chile, pesto, and papaya quesadillas; ginger teriyaki beef skewers served over Thai meekrob noodle salad; tagliatelli tossed with lobster, Roma tomatoes in asparagus; spinach and goat cheese gnocci; fennel and green apple risotto; black pepper and dark rum painted Chilean sea bass; roasted pepper, spinach, and artichoke calzone; and Thai shrimp, cilantro, carrot, crushed red chile, daikon radish sprout, and bean sprout pizza.

Fat Alley BBQ
122 South Oak Street
(970) 728-3985
You can't get too much more centrally located than Fat Alley BBQ, although it's easy to wander past this laid-back place without looking twice. Unless the 'Q is cooking, that is. From its historic house off Colorado Avenue, Fat Alley cooks up batches of beef or pork ribs, burgers, sandwiches, and even vegetarian specials for a very reasonable price. Southern-style side dishes complete the feast.

Fly Me to the Moon Saloon
136 East Colorado Avenue
(970) 728-6666
www.flymetothemoonsaloon.com
The best live bands in town are booked to play in this nightclub's underground room. The spring-loaded dance floor absorbs shocks when partiers get busy dancing to the rock, jazz, funk, disco, and bluegrass music. Live bands perform daily during high seasons. Go early if you want to get a seat during the ski season or when a festival is in town. Tickets are sold on nights when there is entertainment.

La Marmotte
150 West San Juan Avenue
(970) 728-6232
www.lamarmotte.com
Perhaps the fanciest special-occasion restaurant in town, La Marmotte is in a former icehouse in what used to be the warehouse district. The building has been transformed by lace curtains and weathered wood decor. It's been called the best French restaurant in the region, for good reason. Representative entrees range from sauté of Muscovy duck to medallions of pork; expect to pay at least $20 per entree. Reservations are recommended.

Last Dollar Saloon
100 East Colorado Avenue
(970) 728-4800
This local western bar is a good place for a cold beer and a game of pool, darts, and foosball. The stone fireplace keeps things warm in the winter. It isn't chic, and it's proud of that fact. Bartenders swear there's "no cover, ever, ever" and no need for live music. "We are the entertainment," they boast.

New Sheridan Bar
231 West Colorado Avenue
(970) 728-3911, (800) 200-1891
www.newsheridan.com
Since the late 1800s, gentlemen have been imbibing at the New Sheridan Bar. For the latter half of the century, they've been joined by women. The bar retains many of its historical characteristics—a long-carved bar behind which bartenders make their magic; small tables along the opposite side of the long, narrow room; period antiques and replicas dominating the decor. After work, it's a favorite rest stop for professionals on their way home from work. Later in the evening, it's a mellow place to kick back, play a little pool in the back room, or pretend you're surrounded by gunslingers and miners.

Rustico Ristorante
114 East Colorado Avenue
(970) 728-4046

Rustico is known as an Italian trattoria that specializes in mixed grills, fresh homemade pastas, and pizza made in a wood-fired oven, but that's not all the chefs can do. The night we visited, they prepared a family-style feast in four courses. The antipasto was a platter of Tuscan cannellini beans, assorted cold cuts, roasted bell peppers, dry marinated black olives, bruschetta, marinated vegetables, fresh mozzarella, tomatoes, and fresh basil. The pasta dish was ravioli filled with ricotta and spinach in a light cream sauce. The meat dish was a selection of grilled lamb, steak, sausage, shrimp, and salmon served with polenta and fontina, mashed potatoes, green beans, and carrots. Dessert was tiramisu with coffee. Those with smaller stomachs can order any portion of that, of course, or dozens of other entrees. Owners renovated the historic downtown building to create the feeling of a friendly rustic setting. Stone walls were blasted clean and left exposed, paintings are held up by chains and ribbons, faux-marble finishes have been applied on the plaster, and a pressed-tin ceiling was restored to its 18th-century elegance. Diners may sit outside in an enclosed brick porch or inside in the main building, the front of which holds a refurbished 18th-century bar from Ouray.

The Steaming Bean
221 West Colorado Avenue
(970) 728-0793

When we were in Telluride, the strangest mix of locals and tourists filled the benches in front of the Steaming Bean. Some were the so-called Dread Heads, young white kids with dreadlocks and, as the story goes, big trust funds (hence the alternate nickname, Trustafarians). Some were sightseers cooling their heels, and on one afternoon, the dogs rested on the benches while their young owners sat on the ground nearby. During ski season, the Steaming Bean is the central "morning coffee" station for skiers and boarders on their way to the slopes, and when Darryl Hannah is in town, she's likely to plop herself on the benches and try to blend in with the townies. The coffee itself may take a backseat to the atmosphere, but the Steaming Bean offers a menu of choice that include organics, all-day blends, after dinners, and brews from medium through dark, darker, even darker, and darkest.

221 South Oak
221 South Oak Street
(970) 728-9507

An upscale bistro in a historic home, 221 South Oak gets its name from its address. Owners have filled the home with homey touches—a couch in the entryway next to the bar, gold-framed paintings, and elegant dining tables. The food weaves together myriad influences. Chef Robert Scherner prepares everything from a tasting menu to a five-course meal, with entrees such as seared tuna with warm spinach salad served with shrimp dumplings in a citrus soy vinaigrette; smoked salmon with pickled baby beets and a mustard vinaigrette; and goat cheese strudel wrapped in filo and served with a citrus vinaigrette and diced Asian pear.

Wildflour Cooking Co.
250 West San Juan
(970) 728-8887

If it's a light breakfast or lunch you're after, Wildflour may be just the place to find it during summer months. It's located at the base of the ski mountain just steps from the Gondola and around the corner from the Oak Street lift. Patrons order from a broad range of breads and pastries, soups, sandwiches, and salads, then serve themselves beverages and wait for the orders to be delivered. The interior is clean and modern. The outside porch faces west and is a fine place to catch the afternoon sun.

Skiing

Telluride Ski Area
562 Mountain Village Boulevard
(970) 728-6900, (800) 525-3455
www.tellurideskiresort.com
Resort elevation: *8,725 feet*
Top of highest lift: *12,260 feet*
Total vertical: *3,530 feet*
Longest run: *4⁶/₁₀ miles, Galloping Goose*
Average annual snowfall: *309 inches*
Ski season: *Thanksgiving to mid-April*
Capacity: *21,186 skiers per hour*
Terrain: *1,050 acres, 84 trails (24 percent beginner, 38 percent intermediate, 38 percent advanced)*
Lift tickets: *$76 all-day adult*
Snow reports: *(970) 728-7425*

The Telluride Ski Area is reputed to have the longest, steepest, bumpiest runs in the country, and those who have been seduced into skiing beyond their skills can attest to that. The expert runs are so scary here that they've broken the expert category into two phases: black diamonds and double-black diamonds. The most advanced are even scarier because once you're on them, you're committed. There are no reassuring blue slopes to exit onto midway through the run.

The Spiral Stairs run may be the best-known, with a 40-degree slope and a dramatic view from the 11,000-foot mountain summit. And The Plunge has been called the state's "best ski run" because of its combination of pitch (a vertical drop of 3,100 feet), terrain variety, and scenic splendor (historic Telluride is just below). It's actually the least steep of the mountain's black diamond runs, but the bumps

---

The scariest hill on Telluride's ski mountain is the "Locals' Lap," an impromptu amalgam that begins at Kant-Mak-M, then shifts to Spiral Stairs to Lower Plunge and finally to Mine Shaft. It's a killer ride or run that drops 3,000 vertical feet on hills filled with large bumps.

---

and the panoramic view of the valley below make it live up to its name.

But that's just the shady north side of the mountain that faces town. The back side is sunnier, more gentle, and much more enjoyable for the novice. In keeping with the something-for-everyone philosophy, Telluride also thrills adventure skiers who want more than the double-blacks can offer with Mountain Quail, the new guided hike-to terrain within the ski area boundary.

Snowboarders congregate on East Drain and West Drain, both of which have natural half-pipes, and Gold Hill, which has steep chutes and knolls from which to catch air. In the winter of 1997–98, Telluride opened the Surge Terrain Park, the biggest snowboard park in the Southwest with 16 acres of obstacles, solid hits, and a half-pipe built to Olympic specifications. Telluride also offers 50 kilometers of groomed cross-country trails that cover Town Park, the valley floor, the golf course at Mountain Village, and several mountain basins.

Telluride's women's program is one of the country's oldest. In 1981 it began as a way to give women a supportive place to learn at their own rate, and it has grown each year since. Three three- or five-day programs are scheduled each year that include six hours a day of on-snow instruction, usually between January and March. Cost is in the $460 to $750 range.

Telluride Ski Corp. also offers ski and snowboard lessons for children 3 to 12. Reservations are required; information is available at (970) 728-7507.

Telluride Helitrax
Telluride
(970) 728-8377, (866) 435-4754
www.helitrax.net
Colorado's last helicopter-based ski expeditions leave from Telluride during the winter's snowiest months, usually mid-December through March. They're for adventurers who want to ski through virgin powder in basins that haven't been tamed into lift-served runs. Ecologists

protest the practice, and liability insurance is astronomically expensive, which may be one reason helicopter skiing patrons must have very deep pockets. Day rates start at $795 per person. Call for details.

Cross-country Skiing

San Juan Hut System
117 North Willow Street
(970) 626-3033
www.sanjuanhuts.com
Five huts are sprinkled along a system of backcountry cross-country ski trails that link Telluride, Ridgway, and Ouray. Skiers of all levels can use the hut system, although the route through U.S. Forest Service roads and hiking trails around the Mount Sneffels Wilderness Area is designed for intermediate skiers, and the terrain above each hut is for advanced and expert skiers only. For $26 a night, skiers have access to one of the hut's eight padded bunks (if there aren't eight in your party, you may be bunked with strangers), propane cook stoves, propane lamps, wood stoves, firewood, and kitchen facilities. Rentals are available, as are guide and shuttle service.

Telluride Nordic Center
Town Park
(970) 728-1144
www.telluridenordic.com
Telluride has 100 kilometers of Nordic terrain, more than half of which is accessed from the Telluride Nordic Center in Town Park. Practice trails stretch along the park and the valley floor. Lessons begin daily at 11:00 A.M. Another 20 to 30 kilometers of intermediate and advanced trails are accessed from the top of Sunshine Peak (take the Sunshine Express chairlift to reach it). One winding trail leads to Alta Lakes and the ghost town of Alta. The other reaches Prospect Bowl, site of future ski mountain expansion.

Call for lesson rates and lift ticket prices.

Snowshoeing

Snowshoe Naturalist Tours
Atop the Telluride Ski Resort
Mountain Village
(970) 728-6900
www.tellurideskiresort.com
Free tours conducted by U.S. Forest Service employees are offered at Telluride Ski Resort. Participants meet the rangers at the top of the Gondola and explore the local forest and breathtaking on-mountain scenery.

Other Recreational Options

Telluride's Town Park, (970) 728-2173, is the center of most town recreation. It has tennis courts that are free and open on a first-come, first-served basis, a kid's fishing pond, an Imagination Station playground, softball and soccer fields, volleyball courts, a basketball court, a skateboard ramp (open to skateboarders from 9:00 A.M. to 10:00 P.M.), and a swimming pool (open late May through early September 1:00 to 5:30 P.M. Tuesday through Saturday, 10:00 A.M. to 6:00 P.M. weekends; $4.00 admission). The park is bordered by a pavilion, a picnic area, beaver ponds, and a riverside walking trail.

BICYCLING

San Juan Hut System
117 North Willow Street
(970) 626-3033
www.sanjuanhuts.com
A series of six backcountry huts line this 206-mile mountain bike trail to Moab, Utah. Huts sleep eight, are spread about 35 miles apart, and are equipped with padded bunks, propane cook stoves, propane lamps, wood stoves, firewood, food, drinking water, sleeping bags, and kitchen facilities. Riders follow dirt roads from the high alpine tundra near Telluride to the desert slickrock and canyonlands of

If it's the extreme you're looking for, these mountains have it. GUNNISON-CRESTED BUTTE TOURISM ASSOCIATION/GCBTA.COM

Utah. Cyclists must be in good physical condition, but the riding isn't technically difficult. The trip package costs about $533 a person and includes three meals a day and hut facilities. Rental bikes are available, as are guide and shuttle services.

FOUR-WHEELING

Dave's Mountain Tours
(970) 728-9747
www.telluridetours.com
Dave's Jeeps are the heavy-duty, open-air type often driven by actors like Humphrey Bogart in African safari movies. Dave drives them slowly up bumpy mountain roads no wider than the Jeep, on his way to the historic mining towns of Alta, Tomboy, and Dunton, and across Imogene, Ophir, and Black Bear passes. Guests bump along with him, learning

about the geology, the history, the politics, and the gossip that flow through Telluride's past and present. Bring a sweater or a coat even on the warmest days, because high elevation breezes and potential rainstorms can chill things considerably. In the event of a downpour, Dave also packs blankets. If you're at all squeamish, sit on the side closest to the mountain (and farthest from the shoulder of the road and the deep canyons below).

Golf

Telluride Golf Club
565 Mountain Village Boulevard
Mountain Village
(9700 728-6157
www.tellurideskiresort.com

The playing season is necessarily short on this 6,739-yard, par 71 course that winds through Telluride's Mountain Village. That's because winter comes early at nearly 10,000 feet and stays long into the spring. While playing the course, you'll have excellent views of the surrounding mountains and expensive homes, plus you're likely to see elk and deer crossing the fairways. You also are likely to encounter an afternoon thunderstorm, although don't fret about it. Squalls blow through most afternoons and are gone before you know it. Watching the clouds build and swirl above the box canyon can be worth the price of a few raindrops.

The links-style course is enclosed in places by a thick forest of aspen and pines and is criss-crossed by mountain streams, but nothing blocks the panoramic view of mountain ranges. The rough is indeed rough, well-vegetated forest floor decorated by the occasional fallen tree. This isn't really the forest primeval, though; a British phonebooth on No. 5 connects you with the clubhouse so you can order a meal to be ready by the time you reach the 6th hole. The middle nine meander along the valley floor and are ringed by expensive log and stone vacation homes (watch for the giant one on 15 that has a Gatsby-esque feel to it). At 16, you'll begin to climb back through the forest. And if the setting seems familiar to those who have played Beaver Creek, that's because it was designed and built by the same people who designed Beaver Creek Resort and its golf course.

Telluride Golf Club is open to the public most days, and even though it is housed on the lower level of The Peaks, the two are not connected.

Hiking

Bridal Veil Falls

The easy to moderate 1⁸/₁₀ mile trail leads up to Bridal Veil Falls (read more about them in the "Attractions" section), then continues on to Blue and Silver Lakes. The initial hike takes 1 hour to climb, another 45 minutes to descend and gains about 1,200 feet in altitude. If you have trouble breathing as you go, it may be because the falls are at 10,000 feet. The trailhead is at Pandora Mill at the end of the U.S. Highway 145 spur. Follow the Jeep road to the top of the falls. Please respect the privacy of the person who lives in the Power Plant building atop the falls. It once housed a hydroelectric plant for the Smuggler Union Mine, then served as the summer home for mining boss Bulkley Wells and his mistress, Denver's socialite Mrs. Crawford Hill.

Jud Weibe Trail

A moderate 2⁷/₁₀ mile loop, this trail stretches from the north end of Aspen Street past Coronet Creek Falls. From the top you'll see the upper ski mountain, Bridal Veil Falls, and Ingram Falls. At the trailhead, cross the Coronet Creek bridge, then continue to Tomboy Road and back to town. You'll wind up on Oak Street.

River Trail

One of Telluride's easiest hikes, this 6-mile trail gains only about 170 feet in altitude and takes one to two hours, depending on your pace. The trail begins in Town Park (or anywhere in town along the San Miguel River), and is a loop that runs from the east end of town to the cutoff to Mountain Village (Boomerang Road) and back. Follow the trail west until it intersects with Boomerang Road, take a right to the Texaco, turn around and follow it back where you came from.

Tomboy Trail

Tomboy Road begins at the south end of Oak Street and climbs 5 miles to the Tomboy Mine ruins. The moderate to difficult 10-mile hike takes about two hours each way, climbs 2,300 feet in altitude, and takes you to a final elevation of 13,385 feet. Along the way, you'll see waterfalls, reach a breathtaking overhang from which you have a birds-eye view of Telluride, and pass through the Social Tunnel, so-called because prostitutes from the bordellos below sometimes set up camp here and moved their business into the tunnel when the weather turned rainy or snowy.

Horseback Riding

Ride with Roudy
Telluride
(970) 728-9611 (the barn)
www.ridewithroudy.com
Roudy Roudebush is a familiar figure in Telluride, known as a hard-living cowboy who used to ride his mare down the main street and into the New Sheridan Bar when he wanted a cold one. His chiseled face is just what tourists think of when they conjure up the image of a trail boss, and Roudy tries hard not to let them down. He leads them on one-hour, two-hour, all-day, and breakfast or dinner rides through U.S. Forest Service lands near Telluride.

The ride we chose took us on a long and looping trail through aspen groves, including the infamous "Art Gallery." Trees in that section served as canvasses for lonely sheepherders in the '20s and '30s, many of whom carved images of the women they dreamed of or the men they wish they were. It's strictly X-rated, but provides a fine conversation starter for adult riders. At the end of the trail, a chuckwagon is set up to serve steaks and beans, salad and pies, with wine or soft drinks to wash it all down with. Horses are mainly tame, but Roudy boasts he has "gentle horses for gentle people, fast horses for fast people, and for people who don't like to ride, horses that don't like to be rode."

Whitewater Rafting

Telluride Outside
121 West Colorado Avenue
(970) 728-3895, (800) 831-6230
www.tellurideoutside.com

River guides in waterproof shorts and Teva sandals will meet you at the Telluride Outside store, load you into a shuttle bus, and drive you to put-in spots along the San Miguel or Dolores Rivers, depending on what kind of adventure you're after and how the water is running. The best beginner's trips are along the San Miguel River, about an hour's drive from Telluride. Six rafters and a guide will then make their way down river for several hours, making their way through Class II–III rapids and soaking in the scenery, the rock canyons, and the cobalt sky. After reaching the pull-out sites, rafters can snack on Gatorade and cookies while the guides pack up the rafts for the drive back to Telluride. Single- and multi-day guided fly-fishing float trips also are available along the Dolores River. Call for details.

Arts

Telluride boasts two indoor theaters, an outdoor stage, and a conference center with a 550-seat performing arts center. Films are shown at the Sheridan Opera house, Nugget Theater, and the Masons Hall, all in downtown Telluride. Live theater and concerts are performed at the Sheridan Opera House, Nugget Theater, the Town Park Stage, the Art Factory (all in downtown Telluride), and the Telluride Conference Center in Mountain Village.

Attractions

Bachelor-Syracuse Mine Tour
County Road 14 off US 550
1 mile north of Ouray
(970) 325-0220
www.bachelorsyracuse.com
If you're curious about what life in the mines was like, you'll get a good idea on this mine tour. Bachelor-Syracuse was founded by three single men (hence the

name) in 1884 and produced 15 million ounces of silver valued at $90 million, 250,000 ounces of gold valued at $8 million, and $5 million worth of lead, zinc, and copper before it closed. The Syracuse part of the name comes from a group of men from Syracuse, New York, who pooled the money to tunnel down to a rich ore deposit at the bottom of the mine.

To get a close-up look at its interior, you'll slip into a yellow slicker and a hard hat before taking a 3,350-foot train ride into the dark, 50-degree caverns. An outdoor cafe at the mouth sells breakfast and lunch foods. The tours leave daily on the hour 9:00 A.M. to 4:00 P.M. between late May and mid-September (a 5:00 P.M. tour is added during the height of summer). Reservations are recommended. Drive 1 mile north of Ouray on US 550, then take County Road 14 for 1.5 miles to the site.

Box Canyon Falls
Off US 550, southwest corner of Ouray

The turbulent waters of Clear Creek pound their way 285 feet down to a narrow gorge at the bottom of the falls. A swinging suspension bridge takes visitors across the canyon, or you can take the stairs beneath the falls and trails leading to the top of the canyon. The park is open daily mid-May to mid-October.

Bridal Veil Falls
End of the box canyon that contains Telluride

Colorado' longest free-falling waterfall, Bridal Veil Falls flows 425 feet down a mountainside west of town to form the headwaters of the San Miguel River. Visitors can make the steep 1-mile hike to the falls by catching the trailhead at the end of Colorado Avenue. Once there, they'll be rewarded with a view of Ingram Falls on the left and a peek at a restored hydro-electric plant that was built in 1905. It is a designated National Historic Landmark and now serves as a private residence. In the winter, Bridal Veil is transformed into a public ice climbing park.

The Galloping Goose
Colorado Avenue

In 1922, a Russian immigrant named Otto Mears solved one of Telluride's transportation problems. At a time when coal and wood were too expensive as train fuels, he invented an unusual vehicle that was driven on train tracks but was powered by gasoline. The amalgam of a Pierce Arrow bus chassis mounted on railroad wheels and powered by a 1927 Buick engine was nicknamed the Galloping Goose because it looked so silly swaying down the tracks. His fleet traveled between Telluride, Mancos, Cortez, and Durango. Engine No. 4 is on display next to the San Miguel Courthouse on Colorado Avenue; there is no charge to view it. Two more "geese" also survived, one in Dolores and one in a railroad museum in Golden.

Ouray Hot Springs Pool and Park
Main Street, Ouray
(970) 325-7073
www.ouraycolorado.com

Yet another in Colorado's series of hot springs pools, the Ouray spa has a giant outdoor pool with water temperatures that range from 88 to 105 degrees, depending on what part of it you swim in. It was built in 1925 as the recreational anchor of this early-day mining town. Its location takes full advantage of the stunning red-rock canyons and rugged cliffs of the San Juan Mountains just beyond. Also included in the complex are a fitness and aerobics center with weights, a bathhouse, and a swim shop. It's open daily during the summer and Monday through Wednesday from October to May. The pool and park are at the north end of Main Street. Admission is $8.00 a person.

Sheridan Opera House
110 North Oak Street
(970) 728-6363
www.sheridanoperahouse.com

This 214-seat opera house was built in 1898 as a complement to the New Sheridan Hotel, designed by the same architect who built the Wheeler Opera House in

Aspen. Both have the same vaulted ceilings and the same flawless acoustics—so good that bands can perform unplugged. In the early days, masquerade balls were held here, for which the social elite sent to Denver for costumes. The opera house is still used as a venue for chamber music, jazz, bluegrass, and popular music concerts, theater performances, classes, and performances and film viewing. In addition to comfortably padded seats on the main floor, the opera house has a balcony and boxes. Luminaries who have been on stage include Lillian Gish, Sarah Bernhardt, Mel Gibson, Keith and Bobby Carradine, James Taylor, and Shawn Colvin.

Telluride Gondola
From downtown Telluride to Mountain Village
(970) 728-2710

The only free public gondola of its kind in North America, this 13-minute, 2½-mile lift transports visitors and residents alike between the historic town and the ski village. During the winter, skiers use it to access both faces of the ski mountain. During the summer, locals use it to commute back and forth to work, and visitors ride it for its scenic value (you can't match the bird's-eye view of Telluride in its craggy box canyon) or to travel between lodging, restaurants, and activities. Bikers and hikers can also ride it to the top of Coonskin Ridge, where they can pick up mountain trails to ride or walk. It's open daily from 7:00 A.M. to midnight during summer and winter seasons.

Telluride National Historic District
Downtown Telluride

In 1964 the entire turn-of-the-century

Fort Peabody was built in 1904 at an elevation of 13,400 feet, making it the nation's highest military fort. Soldiers manned it to keep union sympathizers from coming into Telluride across Imogene Pass.

---

town was designated a national Historic District, but an 8-block area in the town's core forms a good walking or sightseeing loop. The area is defined by Aspen Street on the east, Columbia Street on the north, Spruce Street on the west, and Pacific Avenue on the south. Within that quadrant, visitors will find the bank Butch Cassidy robbed (now occupied by Jagged Edge Mountain Gear at 131 Colorado Avenue); the Galloping Goose; the historic Sheridan Opera House; the old jail, which is now used as a children's reading room; and Popcorn Alley, the red light district that, at its peak, employed 176 "soiled doves" and got its name from the sound of doors swinging shut as men came and went.

Events and Festivals

MAY
Mountain Film Festival
Memorial Day Weekend
(970) 728-4123

Four days of films and presentations that celebrate mountain life and the environment are booked for filmmakers, artists, and outdoor enthusiasts.

JUNE
Telluride Bluegrass Festival
(303) 823-0848, (800) 624-2422
www.bluegrass.com

Telluride's Bluegrass Festival was started in 1973 and has since become one of the town's most popular events. For three days in June, Telluride's Town Park is overrun by as many as 18,000 bluegrass fans. Since Telluride's overnight bed base can only accommodate about 5,000 at any one time, most ticket-holders camp in either of the town's two designated campgrounds. But many have been known to crawl into any enclosure that will hold them—front porch swings, cars, lawn chairs, garage—and locals know enough to lock their doors when the Woodstockstyle festival is in progress. Some who haven't locked up have come home to find strangers helping themselves to a free shower or an indoor nap.

Among the artists who have graced the outdoor stage are Willie Nelson, guitarist Leo Kottke, folkie Shawn Colvin, crossover singer Lyle Lovett, banjo great Bela Fleck, and legends Johnny Cash and James Taylor. Their tunes can be heard for free from surrounding box-canyon walls, but locals say the fun is on the field, mingling with the masses and shopping the booths.

Wine Festival
(970) 369-5336

Top chefs, winemakers, and sommeliers do tastings, seminars, and dinners for participants interested in exploring the topic of wine. In past years, they have included Joshua Wesson, John Ash, Steve Olson, and Even Goldstein.

JULY

Fireman's Picnic and Parade
July 4
(888) 605-2578

Telluride's firemen are the spark behind this legendary Independence Day celebration. The day includes games, a barbecue, and fireworks in Town Park, but the wackiest part is the morning parade through town. Residents plan their costumes for months and have been known to dress as everything from cowgirl-style cheerleaders to Valley Cows (it's an inside joke, but locals know it's spring when the valley's pasturelands fill with Grazing cattle they call "the valley cows"). Retired General Norman Schwartzkopf, a part-year resident, sometimes reviews the troops during the parade, and the Rauncherettes, a drill team of wild women over 40, lead the way. Most events are free.

AUGUST

Jazz Celebration
early August
(970) 728-7009
www.telluridejazz.com

> *Telluride's permanent population is about 1,500, only 8 percent of whom have lived here longer than 8 years. The population swells to 20,000 during the Bluegrass Festival, an interesting challenge since there are only 5,000 hotel beds to serve them. Forty-eight bars and restaurant serve that population, as do 158 real estate agents.*

Since 1976 Telluride has hosted such talents as Stanley Turrentine, Les McCann, and Regina Carter for three days of jazz performances. Daytime concerts are staged in Town Park, but when the sun goes down, festivalgoers move indoors for more intimate evening shows.

Chamber Music Festival
mid-August
(970) 728-8686
www.telluridechambermusic.com

For two weeks, nationally acclaimed musicians take up residency in Telluride. Their performances begin with a free sunset concert in Town Park and end with a dessert concert.

Mushroom Festival
late August
(303) 296-9359
www.shroomfestival.com

Lectures, forays into the mountains in search of mushrooms, identification of "found" species, dining, and a mushroom parade fill this unique weekend.

SEPTEMBER

Telluride Film Festival
Labor Day weekend
(603) 433-9202
www.telluridefilmfestival.com

Since 1973 the Telluride Film Festival has been screening flicks that have had, until then, limited audiences. It offers half a dozen screening sites that are continuously booked with premieres, classics, seminars, and discussions with the world's leading filmmakers. Tickets are limited as is lodging, so make your plans early if this one appeals to you. In past years, honored guests have included Meryl Streep, Tracy Chapman, Rosanna Arquette, Peter Bogdanovich, Clint Eastwood, John Ford, and cinematographer Vittorio Storaro.

Imogene Pass Run
mid-September
(970) 728-0251
www.imogenerun.com
Here's a race that will test what you're made of. Runners climb the 13,000-foot Imogene Pass from Ouray, then descend into Telluride, feet and knees flaming from the 18-mile effort. Locals in training can be spotted throughout the summer. Flat-landers would be smart to acclimate to the altitude before they even think of attempting it. See our "Mountain Safety and Environment" chapter for tips.

RELOCATION

REAL ESTATE

When Aspen's priciest home sold for $19.7 million in the spring of 1997, Pitkin County Assessor Tom Isaac quipped, "The problem here in Aspen is that the billionaires are driving out the millionaires." Nine years later, a survey of homes for sale in the Aspen area included three homes listed for prices ranging from $24.5 million up to $35 million. It seems the billionaires are still pushing.

That's good news for Realtors and tax collectors but bad news for almost everyone else. The people who keep Aspen running—the lift-line attendants, waitresses, and bus drivers—were forced to look elsewhere for housing years ago, but now the "merely rich" are moving down valley, too. As they move, so move the property values. Bedroom communities such as Basalt, Carbondale, El Jebel, and even Glenwood Springs look pretty darned attractive to people shocked by million-dollar price tags, but they too can seem expensive for the common person.

Basalt, just 20 minutes northwest of Aspen, used to be known as an affordable working-class town. Now the average sale price for a single-family home is well over $400,000, and that buys a standard 2,000- to 2,500-square-foot home. In Carbondale, 12 miles farther down the Roaring Fork Valley, the average sale price is now $237,000. In Glenwood Springs, another 10 miles down valley, it's $235,000, and those who can't pay that kind of money keep traveling west. A new home in Rifle, about 70 miles northwest of Aspen, can be had for $134,000.

This age-old story is familiar in mountains that have endured mining booms and busts for more than a century. Until Colorado's ski industry blossomed in the 1960s, property owners couldn't give their land away. Too remote. Too barren. Now

that Hollywood actors and New York tycoons have second homes there, the land is too hot to handle.

That's not to say affordable real estate can't be had in Colorado's mountains, but you won't find it in such posh places as Vail or Aspen. Bargains in those towns dried up in the 1970s. Expect to pay top dollar for location and very little else. Or prepare to look in towns with more obscure names. Take Dillon, for example. Once a frontier stage stop, it now sits at an opportune crossroads. Just east are Keystone and Arapahoe Basin ski areas; to the west are Breckenridge and Copper Mountain. In the late 1990s, the average sale price for a single-family home was $210,000, the average condo a mere $85,000. That may be expensive by most standards, but it's a steal compared to current prices that range from $300,000 to well over $1 million just for condos and townhomes in Summit County.

Colorado's mountain real estate has been brisk since 1992, when sales picked up after a two-year slump. Tom Malmgren, broker at Carbonate Real Estate in Copper Mountain, credited the boom to "a combination of baby boomers who now have the money and a major consolidation of ski areas that has the momentum building." Boomers have made their fortunes or, in some cases, inherited them from parents who pinched their pennies, Malmgren says. They now want second homes that have hot tubs, heated parking, and proximity to the ski mountains. Homes close enough to ski to the slopes draw top dollar. Those farther away, but with mountain views, also are desirable.

Since Canadian ski resort giant Intrawest and Colorado mega-resort Vail Resorts purchased the lion's share of Colorado resorts during the 1996–1997 season, interest in real estate—and property values—has picked up. "It has become an

The Price of a Piece of Paradise

SUMMIT AND GRAND COUNTIES

Summit and Grand Counties offer some of the best deals of any mountain resort areas, although they may not always sound like deals.

Home buyers can still find a single-family home in Grand County in the low $200,000s, but it won't be anything lavish. In 2005 the average buyer paid around $205,000 in Grand County and got about 2,000 square feet of living space on a quarter-acre lot. Condominiums and townhomes typically sold for less.

In Summit County the average home price climbs to $317,500 because of the proximity to several major ski resorts. Breckenridge prices skew the figure, however, with homes that average close to $600,000. Breckenridge is a tourists' delight, a Victorian town filled with quaint shops and restaurants nestled beneath the ski mountain. Silverthorne prices average around $265,000, Frisco nudges the $300,000 mark, and Keystone and Dillon are just over $350,000.

VAIL AND ENVIRONS

Real estate in the Vail Valley runs the gamut, depending on which part of the valley you choose. Mid-Vail—in the town's central core—is among the most expensive real estate in the valley. A recent survey of properties listed for sale there showed an average price of $4 million. Some of that money buys luxuries such as cathedral ceilings and marble floors, but most pays for the walk-to-the-slopes location. Property on the east and west fringes of town is a real steal, comparatively speaking. The same size single-family home can be had there for a mere $600,000 to $700,000.

Farther west are Avon and Eagle/Vail, bedroom communities that serve the working class. They still have homes in the upper $300,000s and lower $400,000s. Still farther west is Edwards, a former ranching community that Vail wannabes have converged upon. The average home price in Edwards has shot up to $488,000 in the past 10 years, an increase of almost 250 percent. Exclusive Beaver Creek is removed from the valley floor and protected by a guard station. A survey of single family homes listed for sale there showed an average price of slightly more than $6.6 million.

ASPEN AND ENVIRONS

Glenwood Springs is the bargain of the Roaring Fork Valley, but even this resort town on the valley's northern edge is feeling the effects of growth. Its average home price is $235,800, but undeveloped land is at a premium. Home sites in the Victorian downtown section are downright small. Those in the hills above town cost a far sight more. The farther south the land, the dearer it gets.

Aspen, at the valley's southern edge, is the priciest, with an average home selling in the neighborhood of $4 million. If you're a good shopper, that $4 million will buy four bedrooms and 3,500 square feet of living space. If you prefer to live in central Aspen, that $4 million might buy a two-room refurbished miner's cabin.

Snowmass is a newer development 14 miles northwest of Aspen. Buyers can save a few hundred thousand dollars by buying a home there and commuting into Aspen. If you're willing to drive another 9 miles north to Basalt, you can get a home for just over $400,000. Even farther north is Carbondale, where homes are $50,000 more than they would be in Glenwood Springs, just because they're 12 miles closer to Aspen.

extremely desirable place to vacation, and once they're here, people want to own a piece of the rock," says Malmgren. Ninety percent of the property sold in Breckenridge goes to people with primary homes elsewhere, says Dennis Johnson, member broker at Paffrath and Thomas Real Estate in Breckenridge. "These are people who have done well in the stock market or in the sale of a business, or have taken early retirement after the sale of a California property. Or, thanks to computer technology, they don't have to be in the office anymore. If they work from home, it can just as easily be from their second home in the mountains."

Like most millionaires, Aspen's record-setting buyer uses his $19.7 million property as a vacation property. So what kind of vacation home does $35 million buy in Aspen these days? How about 14,300 square feet, 11 bedrooms, 12 baths, and 200 acres, with top-of-the-world views?

Renting

Affordable long-term rentals are difficult to find in Colorado's most glamorous destination resorts, especially during the ski season. Summit County reported a 1.3 percent vacancy rate in early 2005, and Glenwood Springs registered 2.3 percent. During the same months, median monthly rent in the mountain resorts ranged from $624 in Glenwood Springs to $913 in Summit County and $1,082 in Aspen. By fall 2005 Aspen reported a 1.6 percent apartment vacancy rate, the state's lowest.

The good news? Because skiing is such a seasonal business, vacancy rates ease some during summer and fall. The local papers are a good source of information about sublets and short-term leases during those times. Especially good times to rent are during mud seasons, in May and early June before the summer tourists arrive in force, and again in late September and October, before resorts begin hiring their winter crews. Look for more details in give-

away real estate and rental guides, available in each mountain community at supermarkets and visitor centers. Or check with the local chamber of commerce for housing referrals.

Investment Property

Many buyers try to have their cake and eat it too by buying a rental unit to use whenever they're in town and then to rent out the rest of the year. It's a popular solution but not without risk. "Anyone who tells you he's making money is probably exaggerating," say James Horkovich, a 25-year condo owner with property in Breckenridge and Durango. "My wife and I have been renting ski condos for over 20 years and have yet to achieve a positive cash flow because repairs, upgrades, and management costs eat up all of your 'profits.'"

Horkovich's statement is backed up by veteran Realtor Johnson, who agrees that investors buy rental condos for the tax breaks and the convenience of having a place to stay on ski weekends, not for their income potential. Horkovich, a retired U.S. Air Force colonel who lives in Tucson, Arizona, likes it because he and wife Betsy love to ski. They spend most of their vacation time in Breckenridge, but visit the state more frequently because they always have a place to stay. On the down side: The expenses of hiring a management company to rent and clean the properties eat up nearly half of their rental income, and homeowners association fees, mortgage payments, repairs, and seasonal vacancies are steep enough to consume much of the other half.

Depending on what tax bracket you're in, rental properties can come with substantial tax benefits, adds Johnson. If that's what you have in mind, remember that the vast majority of your rentals will come during the winter. Colorado's resorts average 180 ski days a year, give or take, and the normal condo will be rented 100 of those nights. Summer months have become very busy rental times in some resorts, but don't plan on having too many rental days during April, May, October, and November.

Still interested? We've listed some places to start looking. You can find affiliates of most of the major national real estate companies in each mountain community, plus some notable independents and full-fledged resort sales divisions maintained by each major resort. We've listed the Realtors and resort sales offices that have established themselves over the years.

Winter Park

Grand County has been discovered by second homeowners and investors, and luxury homes are sprouting like wildflowers. Still, despite a significant countywide growth over the past decade, the real estate prices are considered a good bargain for a resort area.

Median home prices in Grand County—which includes Winter Park, Fraser, Tabernash, Granby, Kremmling, Hot Sulphur Springs, Parshall, and Grand Lake—have more than doubled in the past decade. The 2000 U.S. Census listed the median value for single-family, owner-occupied homes as $205,500, but a stroll through real estate listings is all you need to realize that prices have continued to rise. Luxury-home projects are underway at Granby Ranch, Grand Elk Ranch, and Pole Creek Meadows. And by 2014, owner Intrawest plans to have turned Winter Park ski area's base into a thriving live/vacation/play ground, anchored by upscale riverside cabins and condo projects. When its first project was launched there in the early 2000s, units "presold" before a single shovel of dirt was turned at more than $400 a square foot, or twice the amount of any other project in Grand County.

Century 21 Winter Park Real Estate
78967 U.S. Highway 40
(970) 722-2121, (866) 726-2121 toll-free
www.c21winterpark.com

Owned by broker Michael Ray, this office employs 22 agents who specialize in everything from commercial and investment property to residential sales. The agency has been open since the mid-1970s and has a second office at Kings Crossing, a town home project between Winter Park and Fraser.

Coldwell Banker Mountain Properties
78902 US 40
(970) 726-6988, (800) 728-0585
www.cbwinterpark.com
Since 1982, this agency has served the Winter Park area. It now has more than 30 agents, a second full-service office in Grand Lake, and satellite offices at Grand Elk Ranch in Granby and at the Winter Park ski area. In 2004 the agency owned by brokers Paul Lewis and Dennis Saffell was involved in Grand County real estate sales worth more than $100 million.

Ryan Real Estate
411 Zerex Street, Fraser
(970) 726-8316, (800) 562-8316
www.ryanrealestateinc.com
This agency opened in 1968, and was recently purchased by broker Theresa Ryan. It specializes in homes, ski condos, vacant land, and businesses in the Winter Park/Fraser area.

Georgetown

Building land in Georgetown is geographically limited—the narrow river valley is bounded on both sides by unyielding mountains—but the existing downtown properties are primarily historic and pretty. They'll also cost you a pretty penny, first because of their limited quantity (town population is only about 1,100), and second because most are in need of extensive upgrading. That doesn't mean there aren't bargains to be had, but don't expect to find the kind of modern subdivisions and tract homes that are available farther west on Interstate 70. The median home in Georgetown is valued at $174,700.

Peak One Realty
600 Rose Street, Georgetown
(303) 569-3215
Owner/broker Bob Pagano has lived in Georgetown for more than 25 years and has more than 20 years of experience as a Realtor. He specializes in properties in Georgetown, Silver Plume, and Idaho Springs.

Steamboat Springs

Proximity to a ski resort can do all kinds of strange things to land prices, and the land near Steamboat Springs is no exception. Ranch packages that once were priced for agriculture (read: cheap) are now on the market for as much as $11 million, soon to be the homes of gentleman farmers or the sites of resort home communities. It's not uncommon to see listings for ski-in, ski-out townhomes valued at $5 million alongside those for 3,000-acre ranches priced at $7 million.

The median value of homes in this town of 9,300 is $308,100.

Coldwell Banker Silver Oak Ltd.
200 Lincoln Avenue
(970) 879-8814, (800) 282-8814
www.coldwellbanker.com
Owner/broker Kay Beauvais has been selling real estate in Steamboat Springs since 1970, and has been at Silver Oak Ltd. since 1983. The agency now has 21 agents who handle everything from condos and luxury homes to farms and ranches.

Prudential Steamboat Realty
610 Marketplace Plaza
(970) 879-8100, (800) 430-4121
www.prudentialsteamboatrealty.com
Brokers Pam Rager-Vanatta and Cam Boyde own the agency and are joined by 30 agents in this office. They handle properties of all types, but specialize in homes and large land parcels for development.

Leadville

Leadville continues to offer some of the most affordable mountain-resort real estate in Colorado, with quaint turn-of-the-century Victorians, hidden log cabins, and a smattering of new development available at less than $200,000. One reason is that since the early 1980s, the entire town of Leadville has been a U.S. Environmental Protection Agency Superfund site, an unflattering designation that stems from its legacy of hard-rock mining. The chief health concern has been elevated levels of lead in the soil and water, but the EPA has been monitoring the situation and, to date, not a single ill effect has been revealed. The town expects to be "delisted" soon.

Some development is creeping into the upper Arkansas Valley, but it has been late in coming compared with the more upscale areas of Summit and Eagle Counties. The town's economy slowly is swinging around from its devastating days of the mid-1980s, when the region's last big mine, the Climax Molybdenum Mine, closed. Unemployment then exploded to more than 30 percent.

Centennial Enterprises & Real Estate
1020 Poplar Street
(719) 486-1409
The office has been open since 1976, and two of its four agents have been with the company from the beginning. They specialize in vacant land sales. The other two do residential sales and long-term property management in Lake County.

Lake County Realty
401 Harrison Avenue
(719) 486-0576
Five agents are located in this agency, which opened in 1969. They specialize in vacant land and mountain property throughout Lake County.

Keystone, Dillon, and Silverthorne

When Keystone Resort launched a cooperative effort with resort giant Intrawest Corp. in 1995 to build a stylish new village at the base of the ski area, it opened the way for decades of dramatic real estate growth around the resort. Called River Run, the $400 million development included a pedestrian village, lively restaurants and taverns, condos, and a terrific slope-side location. It was so successful that it became the model for similar projects at Winter Park, Steamboat Springs, Copper Mountain, and Breckenridge. Intrawest rival Vail Resorts now owns both Keystone resort and its River Run Village.

Vail's Keystone Resort spans 7 miles along the Snake River, on which an estimated $700 million in real estate will be developed by about 2010. Prices vary dramatically, from about $145,000 for starter condos to $3 million for a home abutting Keystone's Ranch or River golf courses. Buyers interested in owning property near the ski mountain can pay as much as $1 million for a 1,600-square-foot ski-in, ski-out condo, or as little as $109,000 for 420 square feet in outlying condo buildings. Want to build your own? Lots are available for between $175,000 and $1.2 million.

Property in Dillon (population of about 800) and Silverthorne (population 3,600) is much more affordable, relatively speaking. The median home value in Dillon is $364,300 and in Silverthorne is $264,300.

Keystone Resort Real Estate
0140 Ida Belle Drive, F-5A, Keystone
(970) 496-4522, (800) 548-3307
www.summitcountyrealestate.com
A joint venture between Vail Resorts and local superstar Realtors Slifer Smith & Frampton, this is the official sales office for all types of Keystone Resort property. It also manages sales for new developments planned by the resort.

Prudential O'Brien and Associates
325 Lake Dillon Drive #103, Dillon
(970) 468-1210, (800) 449-5613
www.coloradoml.com
Located in the Dillon Commons, this nationally affiliated agency is owned by broker Eddie O'Brien. It specializes in ski condos, land, homes, and property throughout Summit County.

Breckenridge, Copper Mountain, and Frisco

Breckenridge is by far Summit County's most expensive town, with median real estate prices of $580,100, as measured by the most recent U.S. Census. A tight housing market exacerbated by the proximity to a ski area have driven prices upwards artificially, although there are no signs that the boom is going to abate. In fact, Vail Resorts, which owns Breckenridge ski area, has built a series of affordable apartments to house around 235 employees on short-term and long-term leases. The high-rise projects located at the base of Breckenridge ski resort and the Victorians in the historic downtown district are protected by strict design guidelines. Expect to pay $700,000+ for the rare "Classic Victorian" that comes on the market.

By comparison, Frisco seems to be a bargain, although median home prices of $298,800 aren't necessarily cheap. While in real estate terms Frisco is not as nice an area as Breckenridge, it is hardly "the wrong side of the tracks." Residents say the neighborhoods in many ways are much more tight-knit than bustling Breckenridge.

Nearby Copper Mountain is slow in comparison and doesn't even qualify as a full-time city. It has no schools and no real-town services, and nearly all its real estate is owned by vacation homeowners. Intrawest Corp., which owns the resort, just finished a massive base-area redesign, which created a pleasant pedestrian village at the bottom of the ski mountain. During an initial buying spree, the resort sold 140 homes—$53 million worth—in less than seven hours before construction even began. Sales slowed considerably as the project continued and excess inventory diluted the market. As of early 2006 home prices were sluggish and hadn't yet begun to match those in Breckenridge.

Carbonate Real Estate
0035 Wheeler Place, Copper Mountain
(970) 945-9762
www.carbonate-real-estate.com
Tom Malmgren is the owner/broker of this one-man office. He specializes in property at Copper Mountain resort and has amassed a wealth of knowledge about the area in the 30 years his company has been open. He also runs a property management company that keeps investment condos rented and maintained.

Copper Real Estate
Copper One Lodge, Copper Mountain
(970) 968-2018, (888) 426-9524
www.copperliving.com
This office handles all the real estate developed by Intrawest Corp., in the resort's base village and beyond.

Executive Resorts Real Estate
203 North Main Street, Breckenridge
(970) 453-5600, (800) 545-2484
www.executiveresortsrealestate.com
Karyn Contino has been selling real estate in Breckenridge since the early 1980s. She lists both land and homes, and also manages rental property.

Paffrath & Thomas Real Estate
311 South Main Street, Breckenridge
(800) 709-0909
www.ptbreck.com
This firm's main downtown office houses seven brokers who specialize in investments and resort properties.

Vail Valley

More than 23,000 people live in the Vail Valley, only 4,600 of them in Vail proper. Another 2,900 live 9 miles west in Eagle-Vail, and 6,300 in Avon, 1 mile past Eagle-Vail. Exclusive Beaver Creek is removed from the valley floor above Avon, and although just 250 people consider it their primary home, thousands more own second homes within the gated community. Edwards is 16 miles west, with a year-round populations of about 8,250.

Real estate prices in the valley run the gamut from some of the state's most expensive (behind Aspen and Telluride's Mountain Village) to relatively reasonable. Buildings located in mid-Vail—in the town's central core—have historically been the most expensive, but new high-rise developments to the west in Lionshead may soon top them. Median home values were $575,000 in 2004. Prices fall in Eagle-Vail (median $377,500) and Avon ($373,000), but begin to soar as you reach Edwards ($487,900). Some of that money buys amenities such as cathedral ceilings, marble floors, and panoramic views, but much of it pays for convenience. Like many other ski towns, Vail's most expensive square footage is within walking distance to the slopes.

Of increasing concern to community leaders, business owners, and residents alike is the lack of affordable housing for the resorts' workers. In Vail, for example, nearly 80 percent of the homes are "dark" most of the year, owned by people who use them as vacation homes. As a result, the workers who keep the ski area, lodges, and restaurants operating have been forced farther and farther away, robbing the town of a real community.

Prudential Colorado Properties
511 Lionshead Mall
(970) 476-2482, (800) 283-2480
www.prudentialgorerange.com
This company has been in business since 1973, and now has 65 brokers and 7 offices in Vail, Beaver Creek, Edwards,

Eagle, and Gypsum. In addition to residential property and land sales, it offers property management services.

Slifer Smith & Frampton/Vail Associates
230 Bridge Street
(970) 476-2421, (800) 544-2421
www.slifer.net
With 18 offices in Vail, Avon, Beaver Creek, Cordillera, Edwards, Eagle, and Wolcott, this is the biggest, most established giant in the Vail Valley. It also has the prime client, Vail Associates. In 2005 Slifer Smith & Frampton achieved $1 billion in sales from its Vail Valley offices, a new record for the company. Call for information about resort properties as well as residential sales throughout the valley.

Vail Board of Realtors
0275 Main Street, Edwards
(970) 766-1028
www.vbr.net
This office is the first place to start for basic information about local markets and a list of member Realtors.

Glenwood Springs

Glenwood Springs is one of the best bargains of the Roaring Fork Valley, but even this town on the valley's northern edge is feeling the effects of growth. Its median home price is still $235,800, but unbuilt land is at a premium. Home sites in the Victorian downtown section are small. Those in the hills above town cost more than the median home price. The farther south the land, the dearer it gets. Carbondale is 12 miles closer to Aspen, for example, but for that privilege, residents pay a median price of $237,700. In Basalt, another 18 miles closer to Aspen, the median price is $417,400.

Bray & Company
1429 Grand Avenue
(970) 945-8626, (800) 285-0409
www.brayglenwood.com

With 14 agents who have called Glenwood Springs home for dozens of years, Bray & Company is a hometown favorite. The agency handles residential, commercial, and land purchases, and does property management.

Glenwood Springs Association of Realtors
2520 South Grand Avenue
(970) 945-9762
Call here for a list of member Realtors and basic information about the local markets, such as the number of properties for sale and average prices.

Mason & Morse Real Estate
801 Colorado Avenue
(970) 928-9000, (888) 840-0836
www.masonmorse.com
Opened in 1970, Mason & Morse is a spin-off of the Aspen agency by the same name. This office is home to 14 agents who specialize in residential, commercial, land, and ranch sales. They also provide property management.

Aspen

Land in Aspen, at the southwestern edge of the Roaring Fork Valley, is the priciest, with a median home sales price of more than $3 million. If you're a good shopper, that $3 million will buy four bedrooms and 3,500 square feet of living space. If you insist on living in central Aspen, that might buy a two-room refurbished miner's cabin. Snowmass Village is a newer development 14 miles north of Aspen. Buyers can save $500,000 by buying there and commuting to Aspen. Many younger buyers and working families have gone 19 miles down valley to Basalt for their homes, where the median sales price was still $510,000. Still expensive, that figure sounds downright reasonable compared with the 650-acre Mandalay Ranch between Snowmass and Aspen, which sold in 2004 for $46 million, one of nation's top home sales ever.

Aspen Board of Realtors
23400 Two Rivers Road, Suite 44
Basalt
(970) 927-0235
www.aspenrealtors.com
Call here for a list of member Realtors and basic information about the local markets, such as the number of properties that are for sale and average prices.

Aspen/Pitkin County Housing Office
503 East Main Street
(970) 920-5050
Call this local agency if you think you qualify for subsidized and rent-restricted housing. It's available to full-time residents or workers who meet maximum income requirements. Expect to get in line behind hundreds of others even if you do qualify.

Houston & O'Leary
620 East Hyman Avenue, Suite 102
(970) 925-8664
Broker Heidi Houston opened this office in 1990, and in 1997 made Aspen's biggest residential sale, a $19.7 million house. She and the other agents in her office continue to specialize in high-end residential sales.

Mason & Morse Real Estate
514 East Hyman Avenue
(970) 925-7000, (888) 354-7500
www.masonmorse.com
The agency opened in 1961 with this office, then expanded down the Roaring Fork Valley to Basalt, 144 Midland Avenue, (888) 354-7500; Carbondale, 0290 Highway 133, (800) 748-2831; Redstone, 385 Redstone Boulevard, toll-free (866) 520-4880; and Glenwood Springs (see separate listing).The Aspen office houses 21 agents who specialize in commercial and residential sales.

HEALTH CARE

Colorado's "hills" are alive with the sound of sports physicians, who keep themselves busy repairing broken bones and liga-

ments torn by overzealous skiers, cyclists, hikers, or runners. Because so many of the people attracted to the state's dazzling mountain playgrounds are sports enthusiasts, local doctors see more than their fair share of injured weekend warriors. Each year they also come face to face with hundreds of tourists who come from sea level and find themselves suffering from altitude sickness, a potentially fatal illness that requires time and sometimes oxygen to overcome. (See our Mountain Safety and Environment chapter for more on altitude sickness.)

That doesn't mean they don't also treat the normal range of people with colds, eye infections, rashes, and heart palpitations. Mountain medical facilities are ready to handle people with all but the most urgent problems, and those with emergencies are airlifted via helicopter to Level I trauma centers in Denver or St. Mary's Regional Medical Center's Level II trauma center in Grand Junction.

Most visitors never need the help of a physician, but it may calm those who do to learn that mountain medical care is more sophisticated than one might expect in such remote areas. All ski areas maintain ski patrols as their first line of treatment. These medical posses are trained to retrieve skiers who have (literally) become one with the mountain, stabilize them, and carry them to a medical clinic at the mountain's base. In many cases, those clinics are a combination family practice/emergency room, with staff that can stabilize patients with serious injuries as well as perform well-baby checks for local families.

Hospitals in Vail, Leadville, Glenwood Springs, and Aspen care for visitors who need overnight supervision. All other communities use medical and emergency clinics as their first line of defense. For dental care, holistic care, acupuncture, or chiropractors, refer to the Yellow Pages .

As with most care providers nationwide, payment normally will be expected at the time of service. Check to see if the clinic accepts your type of insurance, or simply pay with cash or a credit card.

Winter Park

St. Anthony Granby Medical Center
480 East Agate Avenue, Granby
(970) 887-7400
www.stanthonyhosp.org
Grand County locals and visitors alike come to this facility for family medicine and routine services, as well as for 24-hour-a-day treatment in its Level IV trauma center. Nurses are trained in trauma, pediatric, and cardiac care. Severely ill or injured patients can be air-lifted to hospitals in Denver or Kremmling for additional care aboard St. Anthony Hospitals' Flight for Life helicopter, which is based in Frisco. Roughly 10,000 local residents visit the clinic each year, and about 5,000 patients are treated each year in the emergency department.

Seven Mile Medical Clinic
144 Parsenn Road
(970) 887-7470
www.stanthonyhosp.org
Seven Mile Medical Clinic is a full-service family practice and emergency center located at the base of Winter Park ski area. During the winter and summer, it is open seven days a week; during spring and fall it closes on Friday. Hours are generally 9:00 A.M. to 5:00 P.M. In addition to providing family medical care, this clinic specializes in ski injuries, altitude sickness, broken bones, and cardiopulmonary problems. With a Level IV trauma center and 10 to 14 medical professionals, it also can treat medical emergencies. Patients in need of immediate transport to Denver hospitals can be airlifted by the St. Anthony Hospitals' Flight for Life helicopter.

Timberline Medical Clinic
62801 US 40, Granby
(970) 887-1216
Owned by Kremmling Memorial Hospital, this family practice clinic provides medical treatment and walk-in care weekdays from 9:00 A.M. to 5:00 P.M.

Important Numbers to Know:
Alcoholics Anonymous: Winter Park/Fraser (970) 725-3388
Mental Health Crisis Line: Winter Park/Fraser (970) 887-2179.

Georgetown

Georgetown has no hospital of its own, and medical care is spotty, but that shouldn't matter if you're injured on the slopes of Loveland Ski Area. Ski patrol will stabilize or treat you in their station at the hill's base. For anything more serious, you'll be transported by ambulance or air-lifted to nearby Denver hospitals.

Steamboat Springs

If you are injured while skiing at Steam-boat or Howelsen ski areas, you will be treated on-site by certified ski patrollers and, if necessary, transported to Yampa Valley Medical Center for further care.

Northwest Colorado Visiting Nurse Association
940 Central Park Drive
(970) 879-1632
www.nwcovna.info
This nursing group has been around since 1964, providing such things as family planning, well-child care, immunizations, health and dental care for uninsured children, home health care, hospice care, and clinics for special needs children. It is a United Way agency.

Steamboat Mental Health Center
407 South Lincoln Avenue
(970) 879-2141
(970) 870-1244 24-hour mental health crisis line
Outpatient and 24-hour emergency mental health services are available through this agency, which charges on a sliding scale based on ability to pay. DUI education, substance abuse counseling, and

mental health counseling are available. The agency also works with employee assistance programs.

Yampa Valley Medical Center
1024 Central Park Drive
(970) 879-1322
www.yvmc.org

This not-for-profit facility serves the entire county from its central Steamboat Springs location. The hospital provides such services as 24-hour emergency care, laboratory, cancer services, cardiac care, obstetrics, respiratory therapy, pediatrics, and SportsMed, its sports medicine and rehabilitation clinic. Its attached Doak Walker Care center is a 59-bed skilled and intermediate care nursing home and also home to the GrandKids Child Care Center, which provides day care to grandchildren from birth through preschool age.

Keystone, Dillon, and Silverthorne

Keystone Medical Center
1252 County Road 8, Keystone
(970) 468-6677
www.vvmc.com

This medical center, located at the base of the Keystone ski area, is owned and operated by the Vail Valley Medical Center. It is a Level V trauma center staffed by emergency medicine physicians, but also provides occupational health and physical therapy services.

Breckenridge, Copper Mountain, and Frisco

Breckenridge Medical Center
555 South Park Plaza II, Breckenridge
(970) 453-1010

Open seven days a week, this medical center fields many of the ski injuries from Breckenridge mountain because of its proximity. It is a combination family practice/emergency room. Patients who need hospitalization must transfer to hospitals in the area.

Sacred Tree Healing Center
201 South Ridge Street, Breckenridge
(970) 453-8578
www.sacredtree.com

Sacred Tree is part healing center, part spa, but everything offered at this center is focused on wellness. Natural healing services such as acupuncture, naturopathic medicine, hypnotherapy, integrative kinesiology, martial arts, and massage therapy are provided by experts in their fields.

St. Anthony Copper Mountain Clinic
860 Copper Road, Copper Mountain
(970) 968-2330
www.stanthonyhosp.org

Open November through April, this ski resort clinic treats ski-related accidents, altitude sickness, and employees' illnesses and injuries. It is affiliated with St. Anthony Hospitals in Denver, and has access to the system's Flight for Life air ambulances, should patients need more medical care than is available on-site.

The Summit Medical Center
U.S. Highway 9 at School Road, Frisco
(970) 668-3300
www.stanthonyhosp.org

A new 95,000-square-foot, 25-bed Summit Medical Center opened in December 2005 to serve Summit County residents and visitors alike. In addition to maintaining a 24-hour emergency room for injuries and trauma of all kinds, it has medical, surgical, radiology, lab, cardiology, and maternity services. St. Anthony Hospital's Flight for Life air ambulances also have their mountain base here. Patients in need of more care than can be provided at the Medical Center can be airlifted to Denver.

Leadville

Leadville Medical Center
825 West Sixth Street
(719) 486-1264
Family practitioners in this small clinic are available between 8:00 A.M. to 5:00 P.M. Appointments are required.

St. Vincent General Hospital
822 West Fourth Street
(719) 486-0230
St. Vincent General Hospital handles emergencies from Ski Cooper, Leadville, and surrounding towns. Its 24-hour emergency room can handle most emergencies, including altitude sickness, and babies are delivered in the maternity ward. People with run-of-the-mill illnesses are seen next door at the Leadville Medical Center during the normal workweek and on Saturday mornings. The hospital provides an evening clinic from 5:00 to 8:00 P.M. Walk-ins are welcome, but appointments are preferred.

Vail Valley

Doctors on Call
142 Beaver Creek Place, Avon
(970) 949-5434
Walk-ins are welcome at Doctors on Call. Two physicians staff this small clinic weekdays 8:00 A.M. to 6:00 P.M. and Saturday 8:00 A.M. to 4:00 P.M. to treat the full range of illnesses as well as ski, sports, and work injuries.

Steadman Hawkins Clinic
181 West Meadow Drive, Suite 400
(970) 476-1100
www.steadman-hawkins.com
Steadman Hawkins is a world leader in orthopedic care and injuries, serving both weekend warriors and professional athletes. It provides diagnosis, treatment, and surgical services. Among those who have come for treatment are members of the

U.S. Ski Team, the Denver Broncos football team, and international athletes who regularly fly in for specialized care. Nine physicians staff the facility, including whose name is on the door, Dr. Richard Steadman.

Vail Valley Medical Center
181 West Meadow Drive
(970) 476-2451 or
(970) 476-8065 emergencies
www.vvmc.com
This is the only major mountain hospital between Denver and Glenwood Springs. As such, it provides care to residents of six counties with 58 beds, more than 190 physicians and more than 700 staff. The private, nonprofit hospital was founded in 1962 and now offers all the regular services plus a Level III trauma center and a 24-hour emergency room. The medical center also operates satellite clinics in nearby Breckenridge, Keystone, Frisco, Avon (urgent and emergency care daily 8:00 A.M. to 8:00 P.M., 230 Chapel Place, 970-949-6100), Beaver Creek (urgent and emergency care on the ski mountain's base daily 8:00 A.M. to 5:30 P.M., 1280 Village Road, Beaver Creek, 970-949-0800), and Edwards (Eagle Care for indigent patients, bilingual, weekdays 8:00 A.M. to 5:00 P.M., 320 Beard Creek Road, 970-569-7520). In addition, it sponsors the 60,000-square-foot Shaw Regional Cancer Center at 322 Beard Creek Road in Edwards, (970) 569-7429; the Vail Valley Home Health and Mountain Hospice program, the Women & Children's Center, and Howard Head Sports Medicine Centers at the hospital and at clinics in Breckenridge, Beaver Creek, Keystone, Edwards, and Silverthorne.

Glenwood Springs

Glenwood Medical Associates
1830 Blake Avenue
(970) 945-8503
www.glenwoodmedical.org
Six family physicians, five general

internists, two gastroenterologists, three nurse practitioners, and a registered dietician are based in this facility. The majority of its patients are treated during daytime office hours (Monday through Thursday 8:00 A.M. to 6:00 P.M., Friday 8:00 A.M. to 5:00 P.M., and Saturday 9:00 A.M. to noon), but doctors are on call 24 hours a day. Appointments are recommended. Glenwood Medical also maintains a clinic in Silt at 2001 Horseshoe Trail, (970) 876-5700.

Valley View Hospital
1906 Blake Avenue
(970) 945-6535
www.vvh.org
Valley View Hospital is community owned, but in addition to serving the residents of Glenwood Springs, it treats those from many of the other small communities nearby. It has 80 beds, a 24-hour emergency room, and acute care, intensive care, surgical, and maternity care facilities. A Pediatric Rehab program is maintained on-site for young substance abusers. Also in the building is the Mountain Family Health Center, (970) 945-2840, which treats underserved and uninsured families. Operators also can refer callers to local physicians and mental health practitioners. Valley View maintains satellite clinics in Eagle, Rifle, and Silt.

Aspen

Aspen Clinic Internal Medicine Associates
100 East Main Street, Suite 201
(970) 544-1131
If you feel ill while staying in Aspen, but not ill enough for a hospital visit, you can visit some of the same physicians in a more relaxed setting. This clinic specializes in internal medicine and is open weekdays from 9:00 A.M. to 5:00 P.M. For after-hours care, a message machine will refer you to the doctor on call.

Aspen Valley Hospital
0401 Castle Creek Road
(970) 925-1120
www.avhaspen.org
This 25-bed hospital provides residents of Aspen and surrounding communities with a 24-hour emergency room, a Level III trauma center, intensive care, maternity care, and the normal range of non-critical services. Those requiring more critical care are flown to hospitals in Denver or Grand Junction. The Aspen hospital has strong orthopedics and sports medicine specialties, and is home base for orthopedics specialists who perform and teach others how to perform joint replacements, (970) 925-4141. It also has a plastic surgery department that attracts patients from around the country, (970) 544-1296, and an outpatient pain management center that is well thought of in the area, (970) 544-1146.

COMMUNITY RESOURCES
Winter Park

Grand County contains Winter Park, Fraser, Tabernash, Granby, Grand Lake, Parshall, Hot Sulphur Springs, and Kremmling. For information about Grand Lake, consult the Other Destinations chapter under Rocky Mountain National Park. For more information about any of the listings in this chapter, contact the Winter Park/Fraser Valley Chamber of Commerce, 78841 US 40, (970) 726-4118, (800) 903-7275 or http://winterpark-info.com, or the Town of Winter Park, 50 Vasquez Road, (970) 725-8081.

Steamboat Springs

The Steamboat Springs Chamber Resort Association, 1255 South Lincoln Avenue, (970) 879-0880, www.steamboatchamber.com, and the Yampa Valley & Steamboat Springs Community Informa-

tion Center, 1289 Lincoln Avenue, (970) 870-0240, ext. 350, are the clearing-houses for information about Steamboat Springs and the towns of Hayden, Oak Creek, Yampa, and Clark. The latter maintains a Web site at http://yampavalley.info that purports to be "an electronic gathering place for citizens." It's as good as its word, with listings that range from "Agriculture" to "What's WZ?" (Hint: WZ was the prefix used in the early days on Routt County license plates. It now refers to all things distinctly Steamboat, such as the town's lore, songs, ski legends, and celebrations.)

Keystone, Dillon, and Silverthorne

Keystone is primarily a resort town that empties during spring and fall months, although the adjacent communities of Dillon and Silverthorne are year-round towns. Both are burgeoning centers for housing and amenities. A City Market grocery store anchors a suburban-style strip mall in Dillon, and Silverthorne has an excellent tax-supported recreation center. An organization called Shaping Our Summit has produced a video, *So You Want to Be a Local,* for those interested in moving to the area. It also publishes helpful lists of phone numbers and local information. All are available from the Meridian Institute at 105 Village Place, Dillon, (970) 513-8340, ext. 213, or at www.summitnet.com/shapingoursummit.

Breckenridge, Copper Mountain, and Frisco

Breckenridge and Frisco are real towns filled with year-round residents who stay through the "mud seasons" between winter's snow and summer's sunshine. They have parks, dry cleaners, and a fabulous recreation center in Breckenridge. City Market, Food Kingdom, and Amazing Grace Natural Foods keep residents stocked up on groceries.

Leadville

With a permanent population of about 2,700, Leadville has a fascinating mining history and a rough-and-tumble attitude. These days, the town plays home to many of the resort workers from Vail and Summit County. Leadville's social services community holds its own, serving its small but hardy community. Detailed information is available from the Leadville-Twin Lakes Chamber of Commerce, 809 Harrison Street, (719) 486-3900 or (800) 933-3901.

Vail Valley

Vail, Beaver Creek, and Avon are contained within Eagle County, and the combined population of these towns, plus the nearby towns of Minturn, Eagle-Vail, and Edwards, is nearly 23,400. The Vail Valley, as it is called, is still primarily a resort area whose main economy is tourism and skiing. The communities of Eagle-Vail, Edwards, and Avon house more than 50 percent of the population. Vail has a permanent population of about 4,600, while Edwards is home to more than 8,200.

The Vail Chamber of Commerce, 241 South Frontage Road, Suite 2, (970) 477-0075, is a business consortium that serves the town of Vail. The much larger Vail Valley Chamber & Tourism Bureau, 100 East Meadow Drive, Suite 34, (970) 476-1000, has a larger mission. It promotes the town's summer tourist season, schedules business events, distributes visitor information, and maintains a toll-free reservations number, (800) 653-4523.

Glenwood Springs

Glenwood Springs is part of Garfield County, with 43,800 residents spread among Silt, New Castle, Rifle, Glenwood Springs, Parachute, and Carbondale. Glenwood has about 8,475 residents; Rifle has 7,683; and Carbondale has 5,700. Most are year-round residents, although as many as half commute outside the county for work. County population has grown at least 10 percent in the past decade.

The City of Glenwood Springs provides general information on its Web site, www.ci.glenwood-springs.co.us. For visitors' information and published visitors' guides, contact the Glenwood Chamber of Commerce, 1102 Grand Avenue, (970) 945-6589. The chamber also maintains a centralized toll-free reservations line at (888) 4-GLENWOOD. Visit Carbondale's Web site at www.carbondalegov.org for facts about the town. The Carbondale Community Chamber of Commerce, 981 Cowen Drive, Suite C, (970) 963-1890, publishes an annual *Answer Book,* with information about the town and the Roaring Fork Valley.

Aspen

Aspen and Snowmass Village, in Pitkin County, are star-studded, internationally renowned winter and summer resorts. Aspen's year-round population is 5,717; Snowmass Village totals 1,822. As world-class resorts, they support a population mostly involved with one of the four ski areas operated by Aspen Skiing Co. Housing local employees is a severe problem in the Aspen area, since most can't afford the superstar prices. Some workers live as far away as Rifle and commute into Aspen each day.

The Aspen Chamber Resort Association, 425 Rio Grande Place, (970) 925-1920, www.aspenchamber.org, has a wealth of information for both the visitor and the potential resident. The *Valley Jour-*

nal also publishes an annual guide called *The Answer Book* that is filled with phone numbers for community services of all types. Get it at 768 Highway 133, Carbondale, (970) 963-3211.

EDUCATION

Winter Park

Public education is provided by East Grand School District No. 2, which serves Winter Park, Fraser, Granby, Grand Lake, Hot Sulphur Springs, and unincorporated areas of eastern Grand County. West Grand School District No. 1 serves Kremmling and the rest of western Grand County. The districts include five elementary schools, one a charter (Fraser, Granby, Grand Lake, and Kremmling); two middle schools (Granby and Kremmling); and two high schools (Granby and Kremmling). Total enrollment in the two districts during the 2004–2005 school year was 1,824. The average pupil-teacher ratio in East Grand School District is 14 to 1; in West Grand School District it is 13 to 1. For information, contact West Grand District No. 1, 304 12th Street, Kremmling, (970) 724-3217, or East Grand District No. 2, 299 County Road 611, Granby, (970) 887-2581.

Steamboat Springs

Students in Steamboat Springs are served by Steamboat Springs School District (RE-2) in five public schools: two elementary schools, one charter school that serves grades K through 7, one middle school, and one high school. Total enrollment in the district was 1,930 during the 2004-2005 school year. The average pupil-teacher ratio is 15 to 1. For information, contact Steamboat Springs School District RE-2 at 325 7th Street, (970) 879-1530. Steamboat is also home to the private Lowell Whiteman Primary School, 818 Oak Street, (970) 879-8081, www.lwps.org, which serves about 50 children in grades K through 8; and the Lowell Whiteman School, 42605 Routt County Road, (970) 879-1350, www.whiteman.edu, a classic boarding school that enrolls children from throughout the country in grades 9 through 12. The latter is known for combining both academics and adventure in a rustic environment, with special programs for competitive skiers. Also private, the Christian Heritage School at 27285 Brandon Circle, (970) 879-1760, has an interdenominational, Bible-based curriculum for grades K through 12.

Colorado Mountain College has a residential campus in Steamboat Springs, at 1330 Bob Adams Drive, (970) 870-4444. It is one of Colorado Mountain College's 12 campuses sprinkled throughout the central mountains, and provides two-year associate of arts degrees in a variety of subjects. This campus specializes in programs based on the ski industry and resort management and is headquarters for the college's ski team.

Dillon, Silverthorne, Breckenridge, and Frisco

The Summit (RE-1) School District, (970) 668-3011, operates six elementary, one middle, and one high school that serve residents in Dillon, Silverthorne, Frisco, and Breckenridge. Total enrollment in the district was 2,900 during the 2004-2005 school year. The average pupil-teacher ratio is 14 to 1, and all schools rank well above the national norm on standardized achievement tests. For information, contact Summit RE-1 District, 0150 School Road, Frisco, (970) 668-3011.

The Breckenridge Outdoor Education Center, (970) 453-6422 or www.boec.org, offers outdoor experiences for all ages. Keystone Science School, (970) 513-5800 or www.keystone.org, is a residential field science facility for students and teachers

that offers science programs throughout the year, including workshops for educators and workshops at local schools, plus summer programs to bring environmental questions to the classrooms.

Colorado Mountain College has two branches that serve Summit County and a culinary institute at Keystone Resort. Academic and occupational post-secondary courses, seminars, and workshops are offered on a year-round basis in Breckenridge and Dillon. Information is available at www.coloradomtn.edu or at (970) 468-5989 in Dillon and (970) 453-6757 in Breckenridge.

Leadville

Leadville is served by the Lake County (R-1) School District. Its students are served by four schools: two elementary, an intermediate, and a high school. Total enrollment during the 2004-2005 school year was about 1,100. The average student-teacher ratio was 14 to 1, and students scored low on standardized tests. For information, contact the district at 107 Spruce Street, (719) 486-6800.

Colorado Mountain College also maintains a residential campus at 901 South Highway 24 in Leadville that specializes in ski operations management and natural resources management. Information is available at www.coloradomtn.edu or at (719) 486-2015.

Vail Valley

The Eagle County (RE 50J) School District, 575 West 3rd Street, Eagle, (970) 328-6321, serves 5,000 students in 17 schools throughout the district. It includes eight elementary, four middle schools, three high schools, one alternative high school, and one charter school. More information about each is available at www.eagleschools.net. Three private schools also serve Vail Valley children: the

Vail Mountain School, 3000 Booth Falls Road, Vail, (970) 476-3850, serves more than 260 students K through 12; Vail Christian High in Edwards, (970) 926-3015, serves 56 students in grades 9 through 12; Eagle Valley Christian Academy in Avon, (970) 845-0783, teaches about 100 pre-kindergarten through 8th grade students. The schools are well supported by the residents with bond issues and community involvement. Not surprisingly, the school curriculum includes Learn to Ski programs for students and families, and a Discovery Ski program, in which middle ski students get ski/job partnerships with nearby ski areas. Student-teacher ratio is 14 to 1. An Early Childhood Connections program is available in Eagle for children with special needs from birth through age 3, (970) 471-4879.

Colorado Mountain College, a two-year comprehensive community college operating on seven campuses, has one full-service campus as well as annexes that serve the Vail Valley. The main campus at 1139 Broadway, Eagle, serves 4,600 students. Annexes serve students in Edwards, Gypsum, and Avon. Information is available at www.coloradomtn.edu or at (970) 328-6304 in Eagle.

Glenwood Springs

The Roaring Fork (RE-1) School District, 1405 Grand Avenue, (970) 945-6558, serves nearly 5,000 students in 13 schools spread among the towns of Glenwood Springs, Carbondale, and Basalt. Glenwood Springs has two elementary, one middle school, two high schools, one combination middle and high school, and one day treatment center for grades 5 through 12. Carbondale has one elementary, one middle school, one high school, and a charter school for grades K through 8. Basalt has one elementary, one middle school, and one high school. Glenwood is also home to two private schools: St. Stephen's Catholic School, 414 South

Hyland Park Drive, (970) 945-7746, for grades K through 7; and Columbine Christian School, 2314 Blake Avenue, (970) 945-7630, for grades 1 through 8.

The extensive Colorado Mountain College system is based in Glenwood Springs, at 215 Ninth Street, (970) 945-8691. It also has two campuses in Glenwood—1402 Blake Avenue, (970) 945-7486, and 3000 County Road 114, (970) 945-7481—and one in Carbondale, 690 Colorado Avenue, (970) 963-2172. Students major in a wide range of fields, including wilderness studies, professional photography, theater, and criminal justice. CMC's program results in associates of arts or sciences degrees.

Aspen

Public schools are operated by the Aspen 1 School District, 0235 High School Road, (970) 925-3760. It maintains four schools that enroll 1,604 students, including one elementary, one middle school, one high school, and one charter school that accepts children pre-kindergarten through eighth grade. Student-teacher ratios are well below the state's average at 13 to 1, compared with the state's 18 to 1. Aspen also has a number of private schools, including Aspen Country Day, 3 Music School Road, Aspen, (970) 925-1909, a co-ed day school that serves children pre-kindergarten through eighth grade. The Waldorf School of the Roaring Fork, 16543 Old Highway 82, Carbondale, (970) 963-1960, www.waldorfschoolrf.com, sits on a 14-acre campus and teaches children pre-kindergarten through eighth grade in solar buildings made of straw bales.

Colorado Mountain College has a branch in Aspen at 221 High School Road, (970) 925-7740. It offers associate of arts or sciences degrees, creative arts certificates, and microcomputer specialist certificates.

Another important part of Aspen's educational and intellectual community is The Aspen Institute, 1000 North Third

Street, (970) 925-7010, www.aspeninstitute
.org. Founded in 1949, the institute has
established Aspen's identity around the
world. It was founded on the principle of
fostering communication and understand-
ing among world leaders, spawned the
Aspen Music Festival and the International
Design Conference, and hosted some of
the greatest thinkers of our time. Among
those who have spoken at the institute are
Margaret Thatcher, Adlai Stevenson, Mor-
timer Adler, Arnold Toynbee, Thurgood
Marshall, R. Buckminster Fuller, Saul Bellow,
Chief Justice Warren Burger, and Robert S.
McNamara.

CHILD CARE

Most ski areas provide child care and ski
instruction for children of all ages. That
information has been included in the "Kid-
stuff" and "Skiing and Snowboarding" sections of each chapter. The following
information pertains to long-term child
care for residents of the Colorado mountain towns covered by this guide.

Winter Park

Local child care is provided by the Fraser
Creative Learning Center, 120 Easton
Avenue, Fraser, (970) 726-5681. Winter
Park Resort operates an Early Education
Center for locals and employees (970)
726-5514, ext. 1908, and a day-care serv-
ice for guests (970) 726-5514, ext. 1710.
For more child care referrals, contact
Grand Beginnings, Grand County's child
care resource and referral service, week-
days at (970) 726-7272.

Steamboat Springs

The Child Care Network, (970) 879-7330,
maintains a list of child care providers.
The network exists as a referral service to
those interested in finding licensed family
child care homes as well as preschools.
Contact the following numbers for specific literature and information: Northwest
Early Childhood Connections, (970)
871-1962; First Impressions of Routt
County, (970) 870-5270.

Dillon, Silverthorne, Breckenridge, and Frisco

Comprehensive programs for children,
youth, and families exist in Summit
County. Contact the following number for
specific literature and information: Early
Childhood Options, (970) 513-1170, ext.
312 or www.earlychildhoodoptions.org for
child care referrals; Summit County Social
Services, (970) 668-4100, for child care
and foster care licensing; Summit County
Family and Intercultural Resource Center,
(970) 513-1170, for assistance to families,
immigrants, and refugees; and Youth and
Family Services, (970) 668-4167. For
recreation opportunities for children of all
ages, contact the various town government recreation programs: Silverthorne,
(970) 262-7370; Breckenridge, (970)
453-2251, or Frisco, (970) 668-5276.

Leadville

The Lake County School District operates
a nationally recognized family learning
program called The Center at 315 West
Sixth Street, (719) 486-6920 that serves
infants and preschoolers. It also offers
Head Start programs and before- and
after-school care for school-age children.
The Lake County Health Department, 505
Harrison Avenue, (719) 486-0118, maintains a list of licensed, private day-care
centers.

Vail Valley

Babysitting and child care are available in Vail from Mountain Sitters, (970) 477-0024; Small World Nursery, (970) 479-3285; and Child's Garden of Learning, (970) 476-1420.

Glenwood Springs and Aspen

Kids First Referral Service, 0405 Castle Creek Road, Aspen, (970) 920-5363, maintains a list of child care providers and services for Garfield and Pitkin Counties. Early Childhood Connections provides services for children with special needs. In Garfield County, contact (970) 984-0220; in Pitkin County, contact toll-free (888) 777-4041.

MEDIA

The Denver Post and the *Rocky Mountain News,* Denver's two daily newspapers, and national newspapers such as the *New York Times,* the *Wall Street Journal,* and *USA Today* are widely available throughout the state, and Denver-based television channels are the ones most likely to be carried on mountain cable television systems. KWGN (channel 2), KCNC (channel 4), KMGH (channel 7), KUSA (channel 9), KDVR (channel 31) and PBS (KRMA channel 6 and KBDI channel 12). In addition individual towns often have their own local radio and television stations as well as daily, weekly, or free-circulations newspapers. Here's where you're likely to find local news when you're visiting Colorado ski resort towns.

Winter Park

Several local publications cover the area's news and events. Print media include two weeklies, the *Winter Park Manifest,* 78622

Winter Park Drive, (970) 726-5721; and *Ski-Hi News,* 424 East Agate Avenue, Granby, (970) 887-3334. The *Daily Tribune* is a free paper that is widely distributed, 111 Central Avenue, Kremmling, (970) 724-3350. Cable television, wireless Internet, and DSL Internet service are available throughout Grand County. Guest Guide Publications prints free visitors' guides to the county. Request copies of *Guest Guide, The Official Guide Book to Winter Park and Grand Lake; The Official Grand County Relocation Guide; The Grand Lake Vacation Planner;* and *The Official Mountain Bike and Trail Guide to Winter Park and the Fraser Valley* at www.guestguide publications.com.

Leadville

Leadville offers two weekly newspapers, the *Herald Democrat,* (719) 486-0641, and the *Leadville Chronicle,* (719) 486-3666. There are no local radio or television stations. Limited radio reception of stations in surrounding communities is possible, and both of the major Denver newspapers are widely available.

Silverthorne, Dillon, Breckenridge, and Frisco

Everyone in Summit County reads the free *Summit Daily News,* (970) 668-3998, which does a great job of covering local issues and runs state, national, and international wire stories to give a cup-of-coffee glimpse at the world. *Great Divide Magazine,* (970) 668-3998, is published a few times a year by owners of the *Summit Daily News.* Local radio stations are KRKY country at 930 AM, KHTH oldies at 1130 AM, KRKM country at 106.3 FM, KSMT (The Mountain) modern rock at 102.3 FM, and KYSL (Krystal) adult contemporary at 93.9 FM. Local television network, the

Resort Sports Network, is locally produced, (970) 262-6388.

Steamboat Springs

Three radio stations are based in Steamboat Springs, and several others from Craig, Denver, and Grand Junction are available by repeater. KBCR plays classic oldies at 1230 AM and country on its sister station at 96.9 FM. KIDN plays alternative music at 95.5 FM, and KFMU is at 1104.1 FM. Craig provides KRAI, which plays country at 550 AM and top 40 at 93.7 FM.

Local television programming is available on cable TV. K03CL (channel 3), K06CF (channel 6), K09GX (channel 9), and K13ES (channel 13) are owned by Yampa Valley TV Association. Channel 10 and two newspapers disseminate the news from throughout the Yampa Valley. K07GK (channel 7), K11FW (channel 11), K58AQ (channel 58), and K64AR (channel 64) are owned by Moffat County. Telemundo of Steamboat Springs owns KMAS-TV (channel 24).

The Steamboat Pilot has been publishing since 1885. It now publishes only on Sunday, but its sister publication, *Steamboat Today,* covers the other six days of the week. For information about them, call (970) 879-1505.

Vail

Eagle County has numerous daily and weekly newspapers, three local television stations, and three local radio stations. All serve the entire Vail Valley.

Local print publications include the *Vail Daily,* (970) 949-0555; and the weekly *Vail Trail,* (970) 748-0049. Local television programming is available 18 hours a day on KVBA-TV8 and its sister station TV17, (970) 479-0800, as well as Vail Valley Community TV, channel 5, (970) 494-5657.

On the radio, KTUN plays classic rock at 101.5 FM, KYZR plays modern rock at 103.1 FM, and KSKE plays country music at 99.3 FM and 104.7 FM.

Glenwood Springs

Glenwood Springs is served by two newspapers, both owned by Reno, Nevada-based Swift Newspapers Inc.—the *Glenwood Springs Post Independent,* 2014 Grand Avenue, (970) 945-8515, and the *Valley Journal,* 467 Main Street, Carbondale, (970) 963-3211.

Glenwood also has one local CBS television affiliate, KREG (channel 3). Four local radio stations provide service: KGLN at 980 AM plays oldies; KDRH at 91.9 FM is a Christian station; KKCH at 92.7 FM plays adult contemporary music; and KMTS at 99.1 FM plays country music. Carbondale's KDNK at 90.5 FM is a public radio station, and Rifle's KZKS at 105.3 FM is a country music station.

Aspen

Three newspapers serve residents of Aspen and Snowmass. Two are owned by Swift Newspapers Inc.: *The Aspen Times,* 310 East Main Street, (970) 925-3414, www.aspentimes.com; and *The Snowmass Village Sun,* 16 Kearns Road, Suite 211, Snowmass Village, (970) 923-5829, www.snowmassvillagesun.com. The *Aspen Daily News,* 517 East Hopkins Avenue, (970) 925-2220, is the oldest daily and carries local news, real estate, and entertainment listings.

Four radio stations serve the area. KAJX at 91.5 FM is a public radio station that plays jazz and classical music. KSPN at 97.7 FM and KSNO at 103.9 FM play adult rock. And KFNO at 106.1 FM is a news and talk radio station.

RETIREMENT

Winter Park

The active, younger retiree might come here to ski, but senior bus tours don't even come through this area. Like other Colorado resort areas, the Winter Park/Fraser area is not known as a prime retirement area because of the climate, remoteness, and expense. Senior Citizens' services are available through the Grand County Council on Aging, 129 Third Street, Granby, (970) 887-3222. These seniors are active and meeting once a week at the Fraser Community Center for a potluck.

Leadville

Not many people retire in 10,000-foot-high Leadville because of the severity of the climate, but it's not unheard of. The median age is 33.7.

Silverthorne, Dillon, Breckenridge, and Frisco

With median ages of 25.5 in Keystone, 29.4 in Breckenridge, 30.3 in Silverthorne, and 33.4 in Frisco, Summit County's residents are decidedly young. Those who chose the county for their retirement home do so for the outdoor recreational opportunities. Seniors found here are busy hiking, skiing, and participating in other activities. Summit County, because it includes a number of towns and four ski areas, has a Senior Services office at 110 South Third Street, Frisco, (970) 668-5486, and a Senior/Community Center that has less than 1,000 names on its mailing list. A good percentage of them are year-round residents, but many are just part-timers who come for skiing in the winter and vacationing in the summer. The Senior Center serves them lunch several days a week and schedules occasional programs and events.

Steamboat Springs

The median age of a Steamboat Springs resident is 32.4 years old, but that doesn't mean there are no older citizens in the valley. Most of those who qualify as seniors arrived at younger ages and never left. The weather can seem harsh to people looking for a comfortable place to retire, with average temperatures ranging from about 14 degrees in January to about 60 in July. The lowest winter temperature in recent history was -37 degrees F., recorded on December 23, 1990, and the annual snowfall ranges from 170 to 450 inches, depending on location. Those needing assisted living usually find their way to the Doak Walker Care Center, listed above in the "Health Care" section. For those still living on their own, the Routt County Council on Aging, (970) 879-0633, organizes group meal sites, Meals on Wheels deliveries, transportation, information and referral services, and a foot-care clinic, as well as serving as an ombudsman for seniors.

Vail Valley

As a world-class resort, Vail and the surrounding area is a prime second-home location for well-heeled skiers who fall in love with the scenery and decide to buy a piece of it. Most don't live there year round, however, since the climate can be rigorous. Prime times for second-homeowners are summer months and the holidays, when extended families often converge for ski vacations. Median age of residents is 31.9.

Glenwood Springs

Glenwood may be more attractive to the retired set than other Colorado mountain towns because of its natural assets. The Hot Springs Pool has been used for centuries by aging warriors whose joints needed a soak (see the "Hot Springs and Spas" section of our Glenwood Springs chapter for more information). And 40 miles west on I-70 is Battlement Mesa, a former oil company town that has been transformed into a retirement community, complete with golf course and planned seniors activities. With a median age of 36.2, Glenwood gets its own share of retirees who are attracted to the bold red valley walls and its proximity to the more expensive resort towns of Aspen and Snowmass. Many choose the northeast corner of the Roaring Fork Valley for their second homes, then drive southwest when they feel like rubbing elbows with jet setters. When more supervised care is required, the Colorado Veterans Nursing Home is located in Rifle, 15 miles west on I-70, (970) 625-0842, and Glenwood has three nursing homes and assisted living centers of its own.

Aspen

Not all Aspen residents moved here after the real estate boom, which means that many of the old-timers are "just plain folks." They may be overshadowed by the celebrities and barons of business who have made affordable housing nearly impossible to find, but they provide the core around which Aspen operates. Although the town's median age is 36.7, many senior citizens came while they were young for reasons other than hobnobbing elbows with Hollywood stars, and many stay well into their golden years for the things that attracted them in the first place. The intellectual and artistic often came for the rich cultural amenities, for example, and adventurers came for the valley's outstanding summer and winter recreation. It is not unusual to find residents who ski well into their golden years and hike as long as their legs will carry them.

INDEX

ABOUT THE AUTHORS

LINDA CASTRONE

Linda Castrone has been telling stories for as long as she can remember, but only since graduating from the University of Colorado's journalism school has she been encouraged to do so—and gotten paid in the process. Her first newspaper job (at age 4) was selling display ads door-to-door for her father's four-page southwestern Colorado weekly, *The Dove Creek Press*. She has worked as a reporter and editor at the *Boulder Daily Camera*, *Charlotte Observer*, and *Rocky Mountain News*, and now is an assistant business editor at *The Denver Post*.

JIM CASTRONE

Jim came to Colorado with his family in 1965 when he was 14 years old. He spent his first three years here swearing that when he turned 18 he was going back east, going "home." Forty-one years later Colorado is an irremovable part of his life and spirit. He has explored all four corners of the state—from traveling the backstreets and cosmopolitan nightlife of Denver, to driving over the wide open eastern plains; from the one-horse, one-stoplight towns of the central western slope, to elk hunting in the majestic and humbling San Juan Mountains. One of his greatest pleasures is telling strangers in other states that he is from Colorado and watching their eyes light up.

After selling the last of his businesses two years ago, Jim has waved good-bye to the corporate rush-about world and begun a new journey on paths he has dreamed of for years. After studying with a renowned Denver-area jazz musician, Jim now devotes his time to the art of jazz drumming, playing with small local groups in the Denver area. He is also an annual participant at the Iowa Summer Writing Festival where he risks everything—or so it seems—by showing his works in progress to other aspiring authors and asking for their insights. He remains an avid sports enthusiast, enjoying the year-round opportunities for golfing, fishing, hunting, and just sitting in the Colorado sun.

He has been married to the coauthor of this book, Linda, since 1973, the year after he met her in a mixed-doubles bowling league. They share a home just north of Denver, two extraordinary daughters, a manic miniature schnauzer, a life-long love of the state, and back-to-back desks in the office where this book was put together.